D0509763

The Rhetoric of Western Thought

Third Edition

James L. Golden
Goodwin F. Berquist
The Ohio State University

William E. Coleman
Mount Union College

**KENDALL/HUNT
PUBLISHING COMPANY**
Dubuque, Iowa

C   402916   01

To Ruth, Nancy, and Ruth
our best listeners

Contents

Preface

The first edition of *The Rhetoric of Western Thought* was published in 1976, with the second edition following two years later.

Since then the entire book has been reexamined. Many portions have been rewritten, and several essays have been replaced by other, newer writings. We would like to call your special attention to these major changes: (1) three essays—those by William R. Brown and Ernest Bormann and the co-authored piece by Susan Mura and Elizabeth Waggenspack—were written specifically for this edition; (2) the ideas of Isocrates and Plato have been expanded; (3) the essay "Rhetoric in Transition" has been revised and become a separate chapter; (4) the chapter on the "Rhetoric of Conversion" has been extensively modified, now containing an important addendum on the conversion rhetoric of Jim Jones; and (5) the total number of chapters has been increased from twenty to twenty-four. Three of these additions occur in unit IV, Contemporary Rhetorical Theory; the discussion of Rhetoric as Meaning has been increased from two to four chapters, and an additional chapter is included in the discussion of "Rhetoric as a Way of Knowing." The length of this unit stems from our belief that rhetorical theory follows an evolutionary course in which the influence of theories from earlier periods is still evident today.

However, the two most significant changes in this edition, we feel, are the inclusion of explanatory introductions which hopefully will serve as a preview of the essays written by other authors, and the reprinting for the first time of original works from I. A. Richards, Marshall McLuhan, and Stephen Toulmin. The essay by Toulmin appears in print only in this edition. We owe a special thanks to him for his willingness to let us have this manuscript when he presented it at the University of Michigan in October, 1982.

In sum, we have made revisions when we thought that by doing so, we would enhance the organizational structure, readability, and content.

The rhetoric of Western thought is a subject both broad and challenging, for its roots extend back in time some twenty-five hundred years and its contributors are many. This book represents an attempt to survey major rhetorical theories from Plato to Perelman. Of specialized studies of the rhetoric of a particular period, we have a goodly number. But of attempts to trace the dynamic evolution of rhetorical theory from the Greeks to the present, there are almost none.

Such an undertaking would be enormous were it to include treatment of every rhetorical theorist and practitioner, every concept and change known to man. Instead, we chose to focus upon the principal rhetorical developments which occurred during three great periods of Western thought. We are indebted to Douglas Ehninger of the University of Iowa for suggesting the preeminent importance of the classical world of Greece and Rome; the British period of the seventeenth to the nineteenth century, roughly corresponding to the Age of Reason; and the contemporary era of twentieth-century theorists in Western Europe and America.

Because the word "rhetoric" means different things to different people, it seems appropriate to begin this volume by identifying how contemporary Americans define and describe the term. The authors' use of the word is made clear at this point.

In order to orient the reader to the study of Western rhetoric, we have included three essays by our peers which have influenced the emphasis and structure of this work. The first of these is Everett Lee Hunt's seminal convention speech entitled "Rhetoric as a Humane Study." The second is Lloyd Bitzer's *Philosophy and Rhetoric* lead essay, "The Rhetorical Situation." The third is Douglas Ehninger's suggestive piece, "On Systems of Rhetoric," alluded to earlier. These three studies viewed in their entirety combine traditional as well as contemporary perspectives in rhetorical theory. Hunt is concerned with the role rhetoric plays when men persuade other men to make free choices. Bitzer calls our attention to the dynamic interaction of exigence, audience, and constraints in a rhetorical setting. Ehninger delineates the primary characteristics of each of the three major systems which comprise the rhetoric of Western thought.

Since the Greeks were the first to devise a written rhetoric, our survey begins with them. "The World of Greece and Rome" is designed to provide a bridge between the classical world and our own. Plato's moral-philosophical view of rhetoric and Aristotle's scientific approach to the subject together constitute a unique teacher-pupil contribution; in essence the work of the latter emanates from that of the former. To educate an orator in ancient times meant to train a civic leader. Consequently instruction in rhetoric dominated Isocrates' political school of Athens, heavily influenced Cicero's program for personal excellence, and formed the core of Quintilian's comprehensive educational system. Plato, Aristotle, Isocrates, Cicero, and Quintilian—these five men, we maintain, were the most important early contributors to the field.

Half a century before the birth of Christ, Roman rhetoric underwent a marked shift in emphasis. Prior to this time the Romans systematized Greek theory, translated it into Latin, and imitated Attic oratory. But the replacement of the Republic with the reign of the Caesars resulted in the demise of free speech. Invention gave way to style, content to form. Aesthetic discourse replaced practical oratory as the focus of rhetorical training. This period has since become known as the Second Sophistic for it reminded men of an earlier time when a truncated, artificial rhetoric dominated their thinking. Toward the close of the empire, St. Augustine directed the attention of his fellow Christians to Ciceronian rhetoric and in the process provided the Western world with its first manual on preaching. Religious discourse was thereby added to legal, political, and ceremonial forms of speaking. Although rhetoric formed part of the trivium in the medieval curriculum, logic and grammar received primary stress. An account of these and related developments appears in the chapter entitled "Rhetoric in Transition."

Four schools of thought dominated British rhetorical theory. The first two are treated in a chapter entitled "Neoclassicism and Belles Lettres." Among the early British rhetoricians were a group of scholars who saw their primary function as the transmission of classical rhetoric into British culture. These "neoclassicists" maintained that Roman standards of excellence should dominate English literature. Consequently they came to be described as "Augustan" after their Roman models. Chief among the rhetorical thinkers of the belletristic school was the Reverend Hugh Blair of Edinburgh, Scotland. One of the most popular preachers of his day, Blair lectured to students at the University of Edinburgh on taste, style, criticism, and the sublime. His lecture on rhetoric and belles lettres wedded oral and written prose besides conveying much of the substance of classical rhetoric in popular terms.

A quite different point of view was that of the epistemologists, a group of British, French, and Italian thinkers who sought to cope with rhetoric as part of their effort to understand human nature. While most of the precursors of this school of thought were not themselves professional rhetoricians, their teachings and writings profoundly influenced George Campbell and Richard Whately who were. Campbell was the most original thinker among the British theorists, combining as he did classical humanism, modern science, rationalism, Christianity, and educational psychology. Richard Whately, a churchman like Campbell and Blair, laid the groundwork for modern debate through his study of argumentation, presumption, and burden of proof.

A final chapter in this section deals with the elocutionary movement, the last of the four schools. Here the special emphasis was upon style and delivery, and upon the interpretation and appreciation of literature.

Contemporary rhetorical theory at once calls to mind the names of Richards, McLuhan, Weaver, Burke, Toulmin, and Perelman. Our purpose here is to convey the thrust of these thinkers meaningfully rather than to catalogue their concepts and contributions. Consequently we chose to divide the period into four subsections: rhetoric as meaning, rhetoric as value, rhetoric as motive, and rhetoric as a way of knowing.

James L. Golden
Goodwin F. Berquist
William E. Coleman

Acknowledgments

Among those to whom we are especially indebted for their helpful suggestions in the preparation of this work are Russ Corley, Douglas Ehninger, Wilbur S. Howell, Melvin H. Miller, Robert L. Scott, Donal Stanton, and Richard Stovall. We wish also to express our appreciation to those whose writings have influenced our thinking: Carroll Arnold, Lloyd Bitzer, Ernest Bormann, Wayne Brockriede, William R. Brown, Kenneth Burke, Douglas Ehninger, Ralph T. Eubanks, Frederick W. Haberman, Forbes Hill, Everett Lee Hunt, Marshall McLuhan, Marie Nichols, Chaim Perelman, I. A. Richards, Robert L. Scott, Donald K. Smith, Stephen Toulmin, Karl Wallace, and Richard Weaver. To this list we should add the names of such classical translators as Jebb, Norlin, and Watson, and various of the leading rhetoricians themselves: Blair, Campbell, Hume, Smith, Vico, and Whately.

Part One
The Field of
Rhetoric

A characteristic way of coping with information overload in our society is to reduce the unknown to familiar categories. We like to think that we are in control of our lives if we can but find the proper label for the phenomena which take place around us. If we are introduced to a professional historian, for example, we immediately conclude that this person is a careful student of the past. A professor of literature is an expert on the written word—novels, short stories, biographies, plays, and the like. But what is a rhetorician? Countless shifts of emphasis and usage in the past twenty-five hundred years have made the term ambiguous almost everywhere. Consequently it seems fitting to begin this work on the rhetoric of Western thought by establishing what the authors intend by their use of the term. The four essays which follow should provide us all with a common frame of reference.

1

Nature and Relevance

One of the most commonly used words in contemporary society is the term "rhetoric." It is employed almost daily by politicians, educators, and lawyers, as well as by members of countless other groups. Regrettably, however, when one alludes to the notion of rhetoric the intended meaning often has no resemblance to the art first developed by Corax in the fifth century, B.C., and later amplified by Socrates, Plato, and Aristotle.

As we begin our survey of Western thought, it will be our purpose in this first chapter to provide an overview of what we believe to be the general nature and relevance of rhetoric as taught by major theoreticians during the past twenty-five hundred years. Before doing so, however, we would like to pause briefly to discuss four myths which have contributed significantly to the contemporary practice of relegating the idea of rhetoric to the level of a pejorative concept.

Myth One. Rhetoric, it is argued, deals with ornamental language rather than with substantive ideas. Such a perspective prompted the German scholar Ernst Robert Curtius, after tracing the historical thrust of rhetoric in the Middle Ages, to express the view that the subject has little more than a "waste of paper" appeal for the contemporary student of literature.[1] Those who, like Curtius, continue to perpetuate the myth that rhetoric is associated with flowery figures of speech and empty verbalism and bombast are not inclined to give this traditional art a central place in modern education.

Myth Two. Concurrent with the association of rhetoric with ornamentation is a present attempt, like that employed by Plato in his dialogue *Gorgias,* to ally it with appearance rather than reality. But whereas Plato then proceeded to construct a true rhetoric in the *Phaedrus,* numerous modern critics, treating all rhetoric as a monolithic form, have portrayed its permanent nature as a hollow discipline without substance or utility. Several years ago a group of two hundred professors at Ohio State University signed their names to a petition as a gesture of opposition to the War in Vietnam. Above their signature was the caption: "Rhetoric or Reality?" This damaging dichotomy, so widely accepted by activists throughout the United States, has contributed further to the deterioration of the meaning of rhetoric. What is perhaps most alarming is the image of rhetoric held by student leaders on university campuses. In the transcript of former Vice President Agnew's confrontation with five representative college students in October, 1970, the term rhetoric appears eleven times, and in each instance as a devil word. Observe, for example, how one of the students named Silverman spoke with a cutting edge when he said to the other panelists: "It strikes me as macabre that we are sitting here pondering the wisdom of one's rhetoric . . . when we really have some very real questions before us."[2]

A careful review of extant literature will show clearly that these are not isolated examples selected for the purpose of making a convenient generalization. Among other representative illustrations that might be cited are the following:

1. A. Lalande's refusal to include the word rhetoric in his lexicon.
2. Eric Hoffer's description of rhetoric or persuasion as propaganda whose influence is over-rated.
3. Eugene McCarthy's use of the following title for Chapter 5 in his book *The Limits of Power:* "Rhetoric or Reality in Latin America."
4. The *Wall Street Journal's* expressed hope that Anwar Sadat's proposed visit to Isreal in November, 1977 would soon be transformed "from rhetoric to reality."
5. The occasional troubling reminders by our last six presidents that what is needed is action, not rhetoric.
6. NBC Tom Brokaw's suggestion on the eve of the televised presidential debate between Carter and Reagan that at long last we would hear the "real views" of the candidates, ". . . something other than rhetoric."

Myth Three. Rhetoric, it is suggested by others, is a truncated art primarily concerned with style and/or delivery; or with limited aspects of invention. In the sixteenth century Richard Sherry and Henry Peacham felt justified in limiting rhetoric to the single canon of style. In the same century Peter Ramus generously awarded the canons of invention and disposition to logic, thereby reducing rhetoric to style and delivery. A century later other separatists, including Thomas Sheridan and John Walker, further truncated rhetoric by identifying it with voice control and bodily activity.[3] Nor has this debilitating truncation process been limited to a separation of the canons. Equally deleterious is the practice of corrupting a canon by removing from its sphere some essential parts. When the Romans following the death of the Republic in 43 B.C. instituted a monarchial system of government under Caesar Augustus, meaningful controversial ideas no longer fell under the province of rhetoric. The central canon of invention or message forthwith was reduced to the ceremonial genre. As a result there was "a decay of eloquence."[4]

But if the Romans in the period of the emperors amputated vital segments of rhetoric, so too have many modernists. Some businessmen and advertisers, for example, have removed hard core logos from their inventional theory. Not a few historians and literary figures, moreover, have excluded the spoken word in their discussion of the flow of ideas. In doing so, these groups and others holding similar views have become what the late Bower Aly called "the natural enemies of rhetoric."[5] For together they have adhered to a policy of truncation by cutting off important elements, then picking and choosing only those aspects of rhetoric that may serve their immediate purposes or promote their long range biases.

Myth Four. The separatists are not alone in their adherence to a myth regarding the meaning of rhetoric. They are joined by their counterparts, the expansionists, who have enlarged the scope of rhetoric to such a point that all types of communication fall within its range. The following list of appendages is typical:

1. Literary or dramatic productions without an identifiable purpose
2. Painting, art, and architecture
3. Color and form
4. Confrontation with its metaphor, the closed fist
5. Subliminal nonverbal patterns
6. Reflective thought

That all of these activities are communication forms that may in varying degrees lead to a persuasive effect there can be little doubt. But when appended to rhetoric they give to this field of study a scope so broad and general that it lacks the utility to be relevant.

If the myths surrounding rhetoric are due largely to persistent attempts to define it too narrowly or too broadly, let us seek to examine its true nature and scope, and then apply to it the test of relevance for the 1980s. At the outset several basic principles seem in order. *Rhetoric is, first of all, a humane discipline grounded in choice and designed primarily to persuade.*[6] The communicator's function is to influence choice by developing meaningful probabilities in support of a proposition that is being contested. By associating rhetoric with probability, the major classical scholars devised comprehensive, yet flexible definitions to describe their art. Consider, for example, the infinite possibilities inherent in Aristotle's celebrated definition that rhetoric "is the faculty of discovering all of the available means of persuasion in any given case." Such a definition embraces the concept of choice and the use of symbols—both verbal and non-verbal—that have as their principal intent to change a listener's attitudes, modify his behavior, or stimulate him to follow a particular course of action.

Consistent with the emphasis of Aristotle, the Roman authors Cicero and Quintilian caught the essence of rhetoric when they described it as one great art comprised of five lesser arts. This five-fold division included *inventio* (the investigative function); *dispositio* (the disposing and adapting of materials); *elocutio* (the use of language control); *memoria* (recalling the discovered materials); and *pronunciatio* (delivering the message). Only he who could excel in each of the five arts could be called the ideal orator portrayed in Cicero's *de Oratore.*

But it is not enough to say that the purpose of rhetoric is to influence choice on subjects where contention exists, or that rhetoric is the combination of five canons interacting with each other in a particular situation. Not to be overlooked in our quest for a satisfactory definition of rhetoric is the equally compelling fact that a rhetoric grounded in choice carries with it a strong ethical dimension. Observe the emphasis on ethics and values in the classical discussion of rhetoric. The purpose of rhetoric, said Plato, was to make the will of God known. Aristotle not only listed ethics as one of the major subject areas for rhetoric but suggested that one of the functions of rhetoric was to make truth and justice prevail. In 95 A.D. Quintilian, who is regarded as the definitive

summarizer of classical theory, developed the thesis that an orator is a good man skilled in speaking. It is not surprising, therefore, that these writers condemned the practices of the sophistical speakers because of their lack of moral purpose, their claim to be able to speak on any subject, and their tendency to use an artificial, showy style as a substitute for substance.

In the eighteenth and early nineteenth-century period the major rhetoricians such as Hugh Blair, George Campbell, and Richard Whately criticized sophistical evasion and the deliberate use of obscurity to conceal thoughts. Moreover, they condemned all trickery in speechmaking, and gave primacy to a speaker's character.

Today we have similar standards of ethics of rhetoric. We severely indict a speaker if we think he is a demagogue, or if he has what we believe to be a credibility gap. Richard Weaver, in his insightful book, *The Ethics of Rhetoric,* goes so far as to examine the intrinsic worth of a speaker's premises. He criticized Edmund Burke's speech "On Conciliation with America" on the grounds that it derived its strength from an argument based on circumstance. He praised Lincoln's presentation in the Douglas debates, on the other hand, because the principal argument used was based on definition or the essential nature of things.[7] Consistent with Weaver's high standards is the policy of the Speaker of the Year Board of the national forensic society Delta Sigma Rho-Tau Kappa Alpha. This organization holds that a speaker must not only be articulate and effective; he must also be responsible.

In addition to emphasizing persuasion that permits choice and derives its strength from ethics, *rhetoric is, secondly, a dynamic, developing process which is culture bound and multidisciplinary in nature.* As Douglas Ehninger has correctly observed, there are three great periods in the rhetoric of Western thought—each of which has distinguishing characteristics reflecting the peculiar dynamics of the age. The classical period—extending from the 5th century B.C. to the first century A.D.—gave a unique stamp to the rhetorical theory by focusing on its oral characteristics and grammatical structure. The British period, covering the era from the sixteenth century to 1830, borrowed many ideas from the ancients, but nevertheless altered the scope of rhetoric. For these thinkers the listener, rather than the occasion, became the starting point; and psychology was the key to construct not only an oral but a written rhetoric that would conform to the basic nature of man. The contemporary period which began in the 1920s, Ehninger further argues, is sociological in its thrust because of its concern with meaning, communication breakdown, and interpersonal relations.[8]

Although rhetoric, as we have seen, is an ongoing, dynamic process geared to a particular culture, there has remained through the years a consistent body of knowledge, unity, and emphasis to warrant a renewed attempt to conceive its true nature and limits. Each of the three rhetorics outlined above contains the constituent elements of communicator, message, and audience. Similarly, they view as outside the scope of rhetoric all verbal and non-verbal written and oral messages that only incidentally produce a persuasive effect; and situations of force which eliminate genuine choice. Finally, they hold, as Lloyd Bitzer has pointed out, that rhetoric does not exist when the intended receiver lacks the power to act in accordance with the message intent.[9] Out of this framework we would like to present the following perspective: *Genuine rhetoric occurs when a communicator presents an informative or suasory ethical verbal (written or oral) or non-verbal message specifically designed to create a persuasive effect in an audience comprised of readers or listeners who have a choice or perceived choice and the power to modify the exigencies upon which the discourse is constructed.*

It is against the background of this definition that reheteric may claim an enormous contemporary relevance for the 1980s. First, we might observe as a self-evident premise that all disciplines and fields of study must rely upon rhetoric to communicate their content. Consider, for instance, the subject of philosophy. Plato set for himself the task of constructing a rhetorical system in the *Phaedrus* that would enable man to express his thoughts and sentiments to the gods. In subsequent years philosophy was disassociated with rhetoric. As a response to this trend in 1953, Chaim Perelman and his colleague L. Olbrechts-Tyteca, concerned with the neglect of rhetoric on the part of the epistemologists and logicians for three hundred years, developed a "new rhetoric" based on the analysis of the methods utilized to gain adherence.[10] In this volume they assail the typical philosopher's devotion to the Cartesian principle that self-evidence is the prime characteristic of reason. They further argue, as the Italian author Giambattista Vico noted early in the eighteenth century, that the use of rhetorical topics and commonplaces drawn from the realm of probability and verisimilitude, leads to the generation of hypotheses which, in turn, may be put to empirical tests. It is for this reason Perelman and Olbrechts-Tyteca conclude that "logicians owe it to themselves to complete the theory of demonstration" by adding to self-evident truths a theory of argumentation. *The New Rhetoric,* in short, is a masterful treatise designed to show philosophers how they may use rhetoric to convey the content and methodology of their subject and to gain adherents for an epistemological view.

Anthropology constitutes a second area where rhetoric performs a vital function. Since it deals with man's physical and mental characteristics, customs, and social relationships, it seeks to describe the cohesive nature of race and culture and to lift primitive man to a higher plane. Since man is a "transcending animal" capable of responding to intellectual and emotional appeals, Kenneth Burke observes: "We can place in terms of rhetoric all those statements by anthropologists, ethnologists, individual and social psychologists, and the like, that bear upon the *persuasive* aspects of language, the function of language as *addressed.* . . ."[11]

In still another field, political science, the role of rhetoric seems clear. As early as the fourth century, B.C., Greek thinkers associated politics with rhetoric. That this close relationship has persisted to the present day is observable in the writings and speeches of theorists and practitioners. Adlai Stevenson, who sought mightily to "talk sense to the American people" and "to tell them the truth," saw in rhetoric a "great opportunity to educate and elevate a people whose destiny is leadership. . . ."[12] It is illuminating to note that Stevenson, who put his own high ideals into practice, later had the privilege of praising Churchill and Kennedy for their successful attempts to marshall the elements of rhetoric in order to achieve their goal of educating and elevating their countrymen in moments of crisis.

Perhaps the strongest case for the social scientist's need to rely upon rhetoric may be found in the works of Richard Weaver. He argues that insofar as the social sciences seek to modify attitude, appeal to authority, and order facts in accordance with values, they are engaged in a "rhetorical expression," not an "analytical one. . . ."[13]

The demand for rhetoric as a means of communicating the findings of social and behavioral science research is even more compelling when we turn to the physical and biological sciences and to engineering. In 1963, John Osmundsen of the *New York Times* attended the 130th convention of the American Association for the Advancement of Science. In the summary analysis of the proceedings which followed, he reported a growing hostility toward scientists because of their inability to communicate adequately with the Federal Government, general public, and themselves. Three years later a brief article appeared on the editorial page of the *New York Times,* entitled "Incomprehensible Science." Again the author focused on the communication gap that exists between science and its publics. Pointing out that the communications problem tends to get worse as the volume of scientific data increases rapidly, he said:

. . . **the need has probably never been greater than now for adequate public understanding of what scientists are up to. One reason is the tremendous impact of science and technology upon modern civilization. A second reason is the heavy dependence**

scientific research now must place upon financial support from Government agencies, which in turn must look to the layman and to Congress for their budgets. The poorer the communication between scientists the greater the danger that wrong decisions may be made in a period when the competition among scientists and scientific fields for limited research funds is becoming unprecedentedly intense.[14]

Thus far we have seen the relevance of rhetoric for a wide variety of disciplines and fields of study. This in no way implies that these same subject areas do not have a similar impact on rhetoric.[15] What we have, in effect, is a reciprocal influence in which communication theory contributes to and benefits from all disciplines.[16]

Not only may rhetoric function as a means of communicating an understanding of and an appreciation for the content of a discipline, it also, as noted earlier, has an ethical dimension and is instrumental in producing an action goal. The best rhetorical thought of the modern era, as well as the classical tradition, tends to support Chaim Perelman's claim that the purpose of rhetoric "is to intensify an adherence to values, to create a disposition to act, and finally to bring people to act."[17] Since it is the essential nature of man to have a scheme of values, any communicator, regardless of his orientation or specific aim in a particular rhetorical situation, must function as a minister who urges his listeners to make a choice concerning values. For this reason Richard Weaver is corrrct in describing language as sermonic, and in observing that "society cannot live without rhetoric. . . ."[18] So, too, is Karl Wallace on target when he argues that "the substance of rhetoric" is "good reasons," and "the basic materials of discourse are ethical and moral values and information relevant to these."[19] Seen in this light, rhetoric cannot avoid relevance whether one is engaged in interpersonal communication or formal public address.

The challenge facing the communicator is to know how he may convey a message of values that will ultimately lead to a desired action. To put the question more clearly, let us turn to actual examples in the field of science. In 1966, a group of 124 delegates from various universities attended the seventy-fifth anniversary of the California Institute of Technology. The major recommendation emanating from the conference was the need for science and technology to place greater stress on human values.[20] Five years later in 1971, twenty-one scholars meeting in Washington, D.C. ended a similar session with a plea for scientists to initiate a campaign to stress ethics as a factor in scientific gains.[21] What occurred in both of these incidents was a call for a response to a genuine rhetorical situation. Unfortunately, however, these participants listed no guidelines for carrying out the campaign.

It is to this type of problem that contemporary rhetoricians are able to provide relevant suggestions for communicating values. As the speaker begins his message, Kenneth Burke reminds us, he can assume that a division exists between himself and the audience. That division takes the form of "social estrangement"—a human condition which may be eliminated through identification based on courtship. The speaker, in effect, woos his listeners by using a common language and by expressing shared values early in his remarks. In this process understanding becomes important; for it becomes the key to the reinforcement of old values and the institution of new ones. Observe how Burke pinpoints the relationship between understanding and persuasion in the following excerpt drawn from his *Rhetoric of Motives:* "Wherever there is persuasion, there is rhetoric. . . . And wherever there is 'meaning,' there is 'persuasion'. . . . And so, out of persuasion, we can . . . derive *pure information.* . . ."[22] Burke is here proclaiming that meaning is always accompanied by persuasion or rhetoric. Moreover, he is implying that understanding and meaning are synonymous terms. Richard Weaver, who doubtless was strongly influenced by Burke, similarly strove to highlight the importance of a rhetoric that is grounded in understanding. The model of communication which he cre-

ated has as its base *dialectic* in the tradition of Plato. And dialectic to Weaver is rooted in scientific occurrence and designed to ascertain truth that may be verifiable. What he wants, in sum, is a universe of discourse that begins with understanding.[23]

If Burke and Weaver constructed a theory of rhetoric that starts with understanding, the semanticist I. A. Richards produced a philosophy of communication that begins and ends with a rhetoric of meaning. In one of his most celebrated phrases, he said: "Rhetoric, I shall urge, should be a study of misunderstanding and its remedies."[24] Burke, Weaver, and Richards, it would appear, developed an action-centered rhetoric that uses identification and an understanding and ordering of values for generating an improvement of man and his environment.

When we accept the view that a rhetorical transaction, if properly conceived and executed, culminates in an intended action, we have little difficulty seeing the strong bond between rhetoric and reality. That this is a cardinal tenet of communication dating back to the classical period seems clear in the example of Cicero. Throughout his writings Cicero, who perhaps more than anyone else, personified the Roman Republic, preached action. His rhetorical treatises are reinforced with practical personal illustrations showing rhetors on the Rostrum or in the Curia. His great essay "On Moral Duties," written in the year of his death, placed action above philosophical speculation.[25] How difficult it was for the medieval scholars to recognize this need for action. They idolized Cicero for his thoughtful essays and treatises, and for his eminent position as a Stoic sage. Moreover they perhaps would have agreed with the modern classical historian Chester Starr who said that Cicero was the most important man of letters in a thousand years.[26] Yet they denigrated his orations because they were part of action. Why, they asked, did he challenge the monarchy that Caesar was to initiate? Petrarch, writing in 1345, bemoaned the fact that his fallen idol Cicero refused to accept the clemency offered by Caesar.

Why did you choose to involve yourself in so many vain contentions and unprofitable quarrels? Why did you abandon the retirement proper to your age, profession and fortune? What false dazzle of glory led you, an old man, to implicate yourself in the wars of the young? What tempted you to dealings that brought you to a death unworthy of a philosopher? . . . How much better it would have been for you, the philosopher, to have grown old in country peace, meditating, as you yourself write somewhere, on eternal life, not on this transitory existence! How much better if you had never held the fasces of power, never longed for triumphs, never corrupted your spirit with any Catilines![27]

Several years ago we stood in the Roman Forum and relived the public life of Cicero. We stood near the Rostrum and the Curia where he had made so many of his famous speeches on behalf of the Roman Republic. Then we remembered how he left public life and enjoyed a few years in contemplation as an essayist and historian of Roman culture—a scholar who placed the original stamp of his genius on the Latin language. With Petrarch we found ourselves asking why Cicero left the life of an author to come back into the Forum following the assassination of Caesar. But had Petrarch and we paused to reflect on the unmistakable connecting links that bind rhetoric and action, we would perhaps not have raised the question. It simply was unthinkable that Cicero would place contemplation on a higher plane than action. For the action-centered quality inherent in its nature gave to rhetoric, according to Cicero, the power of relevance.

In the preceding discussion it has been our purpose to demonstrate that the field of study called rhetoric has an honorable tradition spanning twenty-five centuries. It has frequently fallen into disrepute because of faulty definition and use. But at his highest, rhetoric represents an attempt to speak to the whole man—his cognitive and affective nature—by stimulating his understanding as a means of intensifying his values, thereby causing action. Such a perspective rejects the popular notion of the phrase "rhetoric or reality" and substitutes in its place the phrase "rhetoric and reality." And therein lies its relevance as a theoretical discipline.

The relevance of rhetoric as depicted here has come into sharp focus with the publication of the 1981 Carnegie Foundation essay entitled, "A Quest for Common Learning: The Aims of General Education."[28] The authors of this challenging report emphasize the cultural role that rhetorical communication can play in removing potential and real barriers that tend to exist among members in similar and in different cultures, in creating meaning and understanding so that our knowledge is enlarged, in promoting an appreciation of and commitment to important personal and societal values, and in causing action designed to enhance our quality of life. After noting that all students must be taught "to read with understanding, write with clarity, and listen and speak effectively"—both verbally and nonverbally—they make these representative claims, each of which strongly buttresses the goals of a timely and vital rhetoric:

(1) Language gives individuals their identities, makes transactions among people possible, and provides the connecting tissue that binds society together. . . . Learning about the significance of our shared use of symbols is . . . a central goal of common learning. (p. 36)
(2) More than at any time in our memory, researchers feel the need to communicate with colleagues in other fields. (p. 51)
(3) The aim of general education should be to help students think clearly about how values are shaped, and how each one of us must build and periodically review an authentic, satisfying value structure of our own. (p. 45)

As implied in the Carnegie Foundation essay, rhetoric is more than a process or a body of theory that may be described from the armchair or the ivory tower. It has a set of principles which, if followed, can enable a communicator either to achieve his purpose or to do all that is possible within a given situation. The application of rhetorical precepts constitutes what we call public address. In the remaining part of this presentation we would like to examine briefly several case studies involving major issues of the past two decades: Vietnam, Civil Rights, and Watergate. These three themes, we maintain, are almost as salient now as they proved to be at the time of their dramatic occurrence in the 1960s and 1970s. The issue of human rights, for example, conforms to Lloyd Bitzer's notion of a recurring rhetorical situation that repeatedly demands an informed response. Of equal significance for our purposes is the fact that when current "undergraduates are asked what events most influenced their thinking, they answer most frequently 'Watergate' and 'Vietnam.'"[29] The question which now concerns us is this: To what extent did a particular speaker on each of these problems achieve relevance? Let us consider first the Vietnam War rhetoric of President Lyndon B. Johnson from 1964 through 1968.

The most pressing issue facing Johnson during his last four years in office was the war in Vietnam. Repeatedly this troublesome theme provided him with opportunities to gain an adherence by establishing identification and understanding as it related to the past, present, and future implications of the war. Yet he consistently failed to take advantage of such opportunities. There is no evidence to suggest, for example, that he was willing to follow Adlai Stevenson's advice "to talk sense to the American people" and "to tell them the truth." In refusing to fulfill these noble aims that are so essential for a relevant rhetoric, he promoted a credibility gap which doubtless played a major part in his surprise decision to withdraw from the 1968 campaign.

On February 21, 1964, reiterating the sentiments of his predecessor John F. Kennedy, Johnson declared: "The contest in which South Vietnam is now engaged is first and foremost a contest to be won by the Government and the people of that country for themselves."[30] Later, during the presidential campaign, he attempted to blunt the aggressive arguments of his rival Senator Barry Goldwater with these

words: "We don't want our American boys to do the fighting for Asian boys. We don't want to get involved with a nation of 700 million people and get tied down to a land war in Asia. . . ."[31] Despite these claims the President in July of the following year, then convinced that circumstances had changed, observed: "If we are to be driven from the field in Vietnam, then no nation can ever again have the same confidence in American promise, or in American protection."[32] Even if we grant the principle that changing circumstances require alterations in policy, it is difficult to support a rhetorical practice which changed so drastically in such a short period of time—especially when commitment remained stable.[33] Thus these statements, along with comparable ones by Secretary of State Dean Rusk, prompted Tom Wicker of the *New York Times* to say: "Never look ahead. Something may be gaining on you."[34] That critics were correct in implying that Johnson "fuzzed" his policies in his addresses on Vietnam may be seen from the following excerpt taken from the Pentagon Papers, September, 1964: "White House Strategy meeting. Analyst finds 'general consensus' on necessity for early 1965 air strikes but says 'tactical considerations' require delay. Cites President's 'presenting himself as the candidate of reason and restraint,' need for 'maximum public and congressional support,' fear of 'premature negotiations,' Saigon weakness."[35] In retrospect, Johnson, notwithstanding his tendency to employ a rhetoric of justification, faulted himself for his failure to communicate the truth as he knew it. On February 6, 1970, he told Walter Cronkite on a C.B.S. interview that he "did a poor job in pointing up to the American people our attempts to have peace."[36] And in his memoirs, he conceded he failed to "brace the American people for the Tet offensive by informing them that he was anticipating it." He further noted that he had made a mistake in "not saying more about Vietnam in his State of the Union address on January 17, 1968." Most of all, he confessed: "If I had forecast the possibilities the American people would have been better prepared for what was soon to come."[37]

Not content to withhold vital data from the American electorate in his own addresses, Johnson also used the power of the executive office in an attempt to stifle free discussion on the Vietnam issue in Congress. Partly because of pressures which began to build in the summer and fall of 1967, and partly because of President Johnson's declining popularity and influence, some legislators, after years of relative silence, suddenly decided to initiate meaningful discussions on Vietnam. On October 2, 1967, John Sherman Cooper, Republican Senator from Kentucky, urged "the unconditional cessation of the bombing of North Vietnam." These remarks prompted extended rejoinders from twelve other senators from both parties. In all, the arguments covered thirty-one pages in the *Congressional Record*.[38] What was the response to this animated confrontation? President Johnson who, according to his own Vice President, preferred action to advocacy,[39] viewed the debate not as helpful dialogue but as a vehicle to convey comfort to Ho Chi Minh. Within hours he gained the support of one of his closest confidants—Republican Senator Everett Dirksen. On the following day the sympathetic Illinois senator, armed with documents defending the Administration position, scolded his colleagues for demeaning the Office of the Presidency. Dirksen's principal thesis was that excessive freedom in debate—however conscientious—would endanger the lives of American fighting men in Vietnam.[40] Shortly afterwards, what had promised to be a productive debate ended.

By January, 1968, these rhetorical tactics had tarnished the image of the president, prompting Max Frankel of the *New York Times* to write a column, entitled: "Why the Gap between Lyndon B. Johnson and the Nation?" In his analysis, Frankel argued that "the measure of Mr. Johnson's trouble is not only Vietnam. . . . It is his failure to persuade much of the country that his war policy is right. . . ."[41]

The foregoing analysis suggests that an evaluation of Johnson's rhetorical transactions on Vietnam, along with the testimony of critics and of the former president himself, reveals a remarkable failure to create a relevant rhetoric. By contrast, however, one of Johnson's contemporaries, Martin Luther King, Jr., spoke feelingly and effectively on the other great issue of the 1960's—civil and human rights. In 1954 the Brown v. Topeka Board of Education ruling brought consternation to many Southern whites, but heralded good tidings for blacks throughout the country. Now convinced that a united campaign could change personal attitudes on racial prejudice and influence the federal government to take positive action, black leaders organized other civil rights groups with similar goals but different strategies. One of these was the Southern Christian Leadership Conference, the only organization on race relations begun in the South. The inspiration for the movement came from King, as he led a bus boycott in Montgomery, Alabama in 1955. Catapulted into national fame following his role in the incident, King began a distinguished career as an advocate of human rights. It was clear from the outset that King, a disciple of Mahatma Gandhi, felt non-violence was the key to social change. What he saw in the remarkable successes of the N.A.A.C.P. legal cases and the Montgomery bus boycott simply reinforced his faith in the philosophy. With renewed spirit, therefore, he expressed the hopes and aspirations of his race, using language that symbolized the black American's quest for freedom and justice.

We saw Martin Luther King and 200,000 of his followers as they came to the nation's capital on August 28, 1963. One of the authors watched them pass on Constitution Avenue waving their banners in the warm summer breeze. They stopped on the Washington Monument Grounds and chanted the word "freedom," then marched in unison toward the Lincoln Memorial. It was, in short, a revolution of non-violent resistance that dramatized the Negro's serious intent to assimilate as an equal into the American society. What King said on this occasion in his "I Have a Dream Speech" already has gained a permanent place in literature. This address and his "Letter from Birmingham Jail" demonstrate King's ability to speak to man's nobler nature. Through such messages and the thrust of his forceful personality and graphic style, he identified with the masses of his race and won the respect of the enlightened members of the white community. Later, as he was attacked by more militant leaders in the civil rights movement, he modified his attitudes on "black power" but refused to alter his basic strategy of non-violence. Shortly after his tragic death the *New York Times,* in capsuling his career, spoke the sentiments of the majority of Americans:

Martin Luther King was a preacher, a man from Georgia and a Negro who became a golden-tongued orator, a spokesman for the Deep South and the Ghetto North, a symbol above color of undying yearnings and imperishable rights. He was an American in the truest sense: for he had a dream. . . . He was a Negro who made Americans aware that the better angels of our nature could dominate the struggle of the United States and its people. The dream of true equality of rights and opportunities without regard to race is nearer because in our lifetime there lived an American named Martin Luther King.[42]

One of the writers went to Washington, D.C. during the days following King's death for the purpose of presenting a Delta Sigma Rho-Tau Kappa Alpha Award to Eric Sevareid as Speaker of the Year. During the course of our dinner conversation Mr. Sevareid was asked to name the greatest speaker he had known. Without hesitation he ranked Martin Luther King first. His choice was a good one, for until the end, King's faith in the power of rhetoric to alter attitudes and exalt mankind never diminished.

The challenging issue of the 1970s, that of Watergate, also is instructive in revealing the major differences between a relevant and an irrelevant rhetoric. As in the case of Johnson on Vietnam, President Nixon and his men opted for a false rhetoric based on appearances. Recall the following overt acts which,

according to the Senate Select Committee Hearings and several Grand Juries, were undertaken by members of the Nixon Administration: (1) the gathering of secret intelligence data on political opponents; (2) the breaking-in of a psychiatrist's office in California where the confidential records of Daniel Ellsberg were stored; (3) the deliberate destruction of tape-recorded evidence; (4) the promise of "hush money" to defendants who took part in a plan to steal documents from the Democratic National Headquarters; and (5) the construction and implementation of a cover-up plan.

Before these acts occurred, the President and his co-agents apparently chose national security as the rationale for their argument of justification. Once they had concluded that national security provided adequate justification to engage in extra-legal or unethical acts, the Administration—especially John Mitchell, John Ehrlichman, H. R. Haldeman, and the President himself—saw no need to submit their arguments to others for analysis and possible refutation. Instead they sought refuge behind silence and, in some cases, either encouraged or condoned acts of perjury.

In evaluating the rhetorical implications of the type of communication strategy noted here, we cannot help but see the theoretical and practical shortcomings of the premise and its application. For when Nixon and his principal aides did discuss the question of national security, they presented an unconvincing rationale and often refused to begin dialogue on the level of a shared frame of reference.[43] They did not demonstrate that precedents on national security supported their ethical and legal claims.[44] What they did offer as their perceived rationale was in direct conflict with the notion of justice as fairness. In fact, the overt acts constituted "an obstruction of justice." The end result was a total disregard of consequences pertaining to the common good.

In retrospect, it seems clear why the American people in general and rhetorical critics in particular could fault the reasoning that made up the rhetorical stance of President Nixon. Longing for an articulation of good reasons to support the acts of the Administration, we repeatedly heard inconsistent statements on "ends" and "means," misleading claims suggesting the full story of Watergate had already been told, false allusions to national security, and begrudging references to post-Watergate morality.

Fortunately, not all of the rhetoric triggered by the Watergate affair was irrelevant. As the congressional impeachment proceedings engrossed millions of television viewers around the world, a relatively unknown rhetor from Houston, Texas, Barbara Jordan, presented a memorable plea. Armed with the tenets of the Declaration of Independence and the Constitution, she eloquently upheld the principles of democracy and expressed an abiding faith in the stability of our government, even in time of dire emergency. By constructing arguments grounded in traditional American beliefs, clothing them in language that stimulated the imagination, and delivering them in a stately and compelling manner, she taught us anew the nature of a genuine and relevant rhetoric based on understanding, values, and action.

Let us restate a quotation from Chaim Perelman used earlier in this chapter. The goal of rhetoric, he said, "is to intensify an adherence to values, to create a disposition to act, and finally to bring people to act." "Seen in such a perspective," Perelman adds, "rhetoric becomes a subject of great philosophic interest. . . ."[45] Instead of being separated from reality, rhetoric is joined with it. Instead of being divorced from action, it embraces it. Out of these dynamic relationships the relevance of rhetoric is derived.

Notes

1. Ernst Robert Curtius, *European Literature and the Latin Middle Ages,* Willard R. Trask, tr. (New York: Harper & Row, Publishers, 1953), p. 78.
2. "Agnew's Talk with Five Students," *U.S. News & World Report,* October 12, 1970, p. 94.
3. Those who had a special concern with language constituted leaders in "The Rhetoric of Style," while those who focused primarily on delivery became disciples of "The Elocutionary Movement." For an analysis of these two trends in British theory, see Douglas Ehninger, "Dominant Trends in English Rhetorical Thought, 1750–1800," *The Southern Speech Journal,* XVII (September 1952), 3–12.
4. Harry Caplan, "The Decay of Eloquence at Rome in the First Century," *Studies in Speech and Drama in Honor of Alexander M. Drummond* (Ithaca, N.Y.: Cornell University Press, 1944), pp. 295–325.
5. Bower Aly, "Rhetoric: Its Natural Enemies," *The Speech Teacher,* XVII (January 1968), 1–10.
6. Everett L. Hunt, "Rhetoric as a Humane Study," *Quarterly Journal of Speech,* XLI (April 1965), 30–33.
7. Richard Weaver, *The Ethics of Rhetoric* (Chicago: Henry Regnery Co., 1953), pp. 85–114.
8. Douglas Ehninger, "On Systems of Rhetoric," *Philosophy & Rhetoric,* I (Summer 1968), 131–144.
9. Lloyd Bitzer, "The Rhetorical Situation," *Philosophy & Rhetoric,* I (January 1968), 1–15.
10. Chaim Perelman and L. Olbrechts-Tyteca, *The New Rhetoric: A Treatise on Argumentation* (Notre Dame: University of Notre Dame Press, 1969), pp. 1–10.
11. Kenneth Burke, *A Grammar of Motives and a Rhetoric of Motives* (Cleveland: The World Publishing Company, 1962), pp. 567–68.
12. Adlai E. Stevenson, "Acceptance of Nomination, July 26, 1952," in John Graham, *Great American Speeches* (New York: Appleton-Century-Crofts, 1970), p. 99.
13. Richard L. Johannesen, Rennard Strickland, and Ralph T. Eubanks, eds., *Language is Sermonic: Richard Weaver on the Nature of Rhetoric* (Baton Rouge: Louisiana State University Press, 1970), p. 144.
14. *New York Times,* November 6, 1966.
15. For an illustration of this point, see the following source: James L. Golden, "The Influence of Rhetoric on the Social Science Theories of Giambattista Vico and David Hume," *Western Speech,* XXXIV (Summer 1970), 170–180.
16. This is demonstrated in Henry W. Johnstone's essay, "The Relevance of Rhetoric to Philosophy and of Philosophy to Rhetoric," *Quarterly Journal of Speech,* 52 (February 1966), 41–46.
17. Perelman, "The New Rhetoric: A Theory of Practical Reasoning," p. 279.
18. *Language is Sermonic,* p. 174.
19. Karl Wallace, "The Substance of Rhetoric: Good Reasons," *Quarterly Journal of Speech,* 49 (October 1963), 239–49.
20. Peter Bart, "Scientists Define Technology's Aim," *New York Times,* October 30, 1966, p. 52.
21. "Ethics as a Factor in Scientific Gains Urged by Scholars," *New York Times,* October 24, 1971, p. 51.
22. Burke, p. 696.
23. *Language is Sermonic,* pp. 181–84; *Ethics of Rhetoric,* p. 17.
24. I. A. Richards, *The Philosophy of Rhetoric* (New York: Oxford University Press, 1965), p. 3.
25. Moses Hadas, ed., *The Basic Works of Cicero* (New York: The Modern Library, 1951), p. 57.
26. Chester G. Starr, *A History of the Ancient World* (New York: Oxford University Press, 1965), p. 526.

27. To Marcus Tullius Cicero; from Verona, 16 June 1345. Cited in Morris Bishop, ed., *Letters from Petrarch* (Bloomington: Indiana University Press, 1966), pp. 206–207.
28. Ernest L. Boyer and Arthur Levine, *A Quest for Common Learning: The Aims of General Education* (Washington, D.C.: Carnegie Foundation, 1981), pp. 1–77.
29. *Ibid*, p. 20.
30. Tom Wicker, "Into the Quicksand," *New York Times,* November 27, 1966, p. E 13.
31. *Ibid.*
32. *Ibid.*
33. For some of the most authoritative published statements on the history of the Vietnamese War, see the late Bernard Fall's works: *Vietnam Witness* (New York: Frederick A. Praeger, 1966) and *Last Reflections on a War* (New York: Doubleday and Company, Inc., 1967).
34. Wicker, "Into the Quicksand."
35. *The Pentagon Papers* (New York: The New York Times Company, 1971), p. 308.
36. Interview on Columbia Broadcasting System Television, February 6, 1970.
37. See frequent references to Johnson's admitted inability to remove division regarding the controversy over the war in Vietnam in Lyndon B. Johnson, *The Vantage Point* (New York: Holt, Rinehart and Winston, 1971).
38. *U.S. Congressional Record,* 90th Cong., 1st Sess., 1967, S 13991–14021.
39. Emmet Hughes, "The Stammering Advocate," *Newsweek,* October 30, 1967, p. 19.
40. *U.S. Congressional Record,* 90th Cong., 1st Sess., 1967, S 14055–14063.
41. Max Frankel, "Why the Gap between L. B. J. and the Nation?" *New York Times Magazine,* January 7, 1968.
42. *New York Times,* April 7, 1968, p. E 12.
43. We are indebted to Wayne Brockriede for the use of these criteria to evaluate argument. See his essay on "Where Is Argument?" *Journal of American Forensic Association* (Spring 1975), 179–182.
44. Interview with Stephen Toulmin, Columbus, Ohio, November 22, 1974.
45. *The New Rhetoric: A Theory of Practical Reasoning,* p. 279.

In this opening chapter on the nature and relevance of rhetoric, the ensuing essay by Everett Lee Hunt is of central importance. Despite its brevity, the study catches the significance of the role the humane tradition has performed in shaping the rhetoric of Western thought. With conciseness and clarity, Hunt focuses on learning, understanding, and values as forming the core of enlightened decision-making emanating from the freedom of choice. A humane rhetoric, he argues, is a responsible and persuasive rhetoric consistent with the teachings of Plato and the communication practices of Lincoln. This strong commitment to a belief in the salutary influence of the humanities on discourse also leads Hunt to warn us of the "dehumanizing effects of technology." Many of the leading theorists of each of the three major chronological periods featured in this volume, as we shall later observe, share the insights and concerns articulated in this essay.

Rhetoric as a Humane Study

The case for rhetoric as a humane study may be stated with deceptive simplicity. Rhetoric is the study of men persuading men to make free choices. It may well be regarded as the oldest and most central of humane studies. Man's first great free choice was to sin by eating the apple. The first persuader was the devil, and there are many who feel that there always has been and always will be something devil-ish about persuasion. That first decision has often been referred to as the victory of passion over reason, or as the result of an over-ambitious refusal to be content with the estate wherein man found himself. The long history

Reprinted from the *Quarterly Journal of Speech,* "Rhetoric as a Humane Study," by Everett Lee Hunt, Vol. 41,2 (April 1955), 114–117, by permission of the author and editor of Quarterly Journal of Speech.

of the arguments about the nature and effects of this first decision shows how many human qualities are involved in the discussion of any choice.

In fact, the definition of a humanistic study that I present as basic to this discussion is that the "humanities" embrace whatever contributes to freedom in making enlightened choices. An enlightened choice is a choice based upon a wide knowledge of all the alternatives, but knowledge about the alternatives is not enough. There must be imagination to envisage all the possibilities, and sympathy to make some of the options appeal to the emotions and powers of the will. Such dignity as man may have is achieved by the exercise of free choice through the qualities of learning, imagination, and sympathy; and we should add to these qualities as a fitting accompaniment, what may be called civility.

These qualities are sometimes recognized more readily by considering their opposites. The man who lacks learning is often narrow-minded, ignorant, and dogmatic; the man who lacks imagination is literal-minded and pedantic; the man who lacks sympathy is self-centered, opportunistic, and insensitive; if he lacks dignity and civility he may be base, boorish, brutal, or merely trivial and snobbish. The exercise of free choices through an imaginative and sympathetic learning and a dignified civility, then, is the mark of the liberally educated, humane man.

Applying this to a study of rhetoric, we go back to the old debate between Plato and Isocrates. Plato believed that a man should search for a reality above and beyond the vain shows of his world; and he thought that he could be found through mathematics and philosophy. Conformity to the ways of the world was mere sophistry. Isocrates, on the other hand, defined the liberally educated man as one who, in an uncertain situation, could make the best guess as to what he ought to do next. Making these guesses upon the basis of whatever learning, imagination, and sympathy he could command, and strengthening all these qualifications by attempting to make himself

and his conclusions acceptable to others, he might well acquire dignity and civility and become a persuasive man, a rhetorician, in the best ancient sense of that now debased word. He would become acquainted in a general way with those persistent questions about which generations of men continually debate, he would know the characteristics of different types of audiences, what kind of ends, aims, and values would appeal to them, and without necessarily attempting to be all things to all men, would both consciously and unconsciously attempt to commend himself as a personally trustworthy agent of the policy he was supporting.

Now there is a large measure of identity between this ideal of Isocrates, and the modern ideal of the humane man, which I have taken largely from a contemporary philosopher, Ralph Barton Perry of Harvard.[1]

But what happens when this integrated and understandable ideal is presented for recognition amidst the curricular and administrative machinery of departments and divisions—of deans and presidents?

In an age of specialization this conception of rhetoric seems almost primitively simple-minded. It is as if one went up to a psychiatrist and said, "Sir, do you believe that he that controlleth his spirit is mightier than he that taketh a city?" The reply would probably be, "Man, do you realize all the implications of what you are saying?"

Or if you went to a philosopher in agony of spirit and said, "Tell me what I ought to do," you would hear him reply, "First let us decide what it means to ask, What ought I to do? Who are you, and how did you get your concept of self? What do you mean by it and where did you get your sense of duty?"

This academic necessity of dealing analytically and semantically with all questions makes it difficult to talk to the lay mind, to the man in the street, without seeming hopelessly naive and superficial. One answer, of course, has been to think with the learned and talk with the vulgar, but the success of academic specialists in writing and talking to the general public suggests that talking with the vulgar may be a more difficult achievement than thinking with the learned.

If academic men could talk with the vulgar, under the terms of the definition of the humanities that I have offered, it ought to be possible for all subjects in the curriculum to contribute to the making of free and enlightened choices.

Natural science can reveal the world around us as the source and environment of human life, and enable us to make our choices of the ends of action with a recognition of our qualities as children of nature, and with admiration for the human qualities displayed in the disinterested pursuit of truth. But science is perpetually being dehumanized by its quite necessary concern with technology.

The social sciences were once concerned with the good life, with the appraisal of purposes for which social institutions exist, but now they identify themselves more and more with the development of scientific technique. A colleague of mine, Professor J. M. Moore, recently spent a semester traveling among colleges and discussing concern with values; and he found that many social scientists in talking of this, repudiated any responsibility for value, although in arguments he did occasionally convict them of having a social conscience.

History and philosophy, which now appear at times as social sciences and not as humanities, often seem definitely to repudiate the humanistic ideal. Where history might humanize a man by leading him to participate imaginatively in the life of the past, it often becomes absorbed in the techniques of factfinding, with statistics and cycles, Philosophy, which can fertilize thought and strengthen the will by criticizing the ultimate principles of thought and action, seems more and more to abandon the classical problems as insoluble and to devote itself to semantics.

Literature is most commonly allowed to deserve the title of "the humanities," because, as Professor Perry has remarked, literature and the arts seem to be the studies which inhumane teachers are least able to dehumanize.

In courses on Sophocles, Dante, and Shakespeare, it is difficult to counteract wholly the influence of Sophocles, Dante, and Shakespeare. Literature presents experience concretely and simply, not as abstracted by scientists and philosophers. But the critics of literature, writing for each other, seem to relegate literature to the simple-minded. Only the other day I heard a scholar state that the criticism of Hamlet had progressed beyond the point where it could be treated in any essay for the general reader.

Rhetoric has certainly not been immune from the dehumanizing influences of technology, and some of the most eloquent passages of Longinus were written in protest against the absorption of rhetoric with technique. Now we are faced with a scientific development of rhetoric under the heading of communication. It seems a little paradoxical, but typical of our age, that the most vigorous claims for the fundamental importance of communication should come from those concerned with development of communicating machines. Norbert Wiener, in *The Human Use of Human Beings,* makes clear the central place of communication in the history of science, and writes that communication and control belong to the essence of man's inner life even as they are of the essence of his life in society. Wiener is fully aware of the human possibilities and human dangers of the new technology. But in many of the books on communication the development of techniques seems all out of proportion to the results—as, for instance, an elaborate series of experiments to show that obsessional neuroses make persuasion more difficult, or that persons who have established a high degree of credibility are more persuasive than those with a low degree of credibility.

I am sure all these technical studies in the psychology of persuasion are going to expand enormously, and they will eventually prove useful in statistical estimates of the effectiveness of mass media of communication; but they seem to me to contribute little to individual understanding. It is difficult for me to believe that a person receiving a specialized training in these procedures would ever be much more than a statistical calculator of tests and measurements. I am reminded of George Kennan's recent Princeton address on training for statesmanship, when he said that graduate departments of political science had replaced human significance with technicalities, but that it was really more important to read the Bible and Plutarch than to learn all the tricks. The study of Lincoln's First Inaugural as published in *American Speeches* by Parrish and Hochmuth seems to me to typify the very best tradition of rhetoric as humane letters. It presents concretely, with literary skill, the historical background of tension and excitement in which a noble character appeals to people to make a choice which will elevate them as a nation. It is difficult to read such a chapter without being moved and inspired, and without having one's own style improved by unconscious emulation. This kind of study seems to me what we most need in the field of rhetoric to make clear our significance as one of the humanities.

This paper may sound a little like the petulant complaint of one who fears that he is defending a lost cause, but I have no desire to scold all intellectual workers into conformity with the conception of humanism here set forth. We can no more all be "humanists" than we could all agree to contemplate timeless beauty together without eternal boredom. The quantitative, the technical, the utilitarian, are the raw stuff of life, from which the human must be extracted by processes of interpretation. Their ever-expanding development leads to a continuous demand, even from the technologists, for human reinterpretation, and more insights may come from the studies of new examples of men persuading men to make free choices, than from too rigid a concentration on the examples whose human values have been long established.

We are met here to honor Max Parrish, whose work rightfully belongs to the central humanistic traditions of liberal education, and we honor ourselves, I think, in expressing our gratitude and admiration for his devotion and achievement, and for his understanding of rhetoric as a humane study.

Everett Hunt

Everett Lee Hunt is a former dean and professor emeritus at Swarthmore College and past editor (1927–1929) of the QJS. This paper was presented during the Convention of the Speech Association of America at a luncheon on December 28, 1954, in honor of Professor Wayland M. Parrish.

Notes

1. Ralph Barton Perry, "A Definition of the Humanities," in *The Meaning of the Humanities*, ed. Theodore M. Greene (Princeton: Princeton University Press, 1938).

In establishing the parameters for a relevant rhetoric, Lloyd Bitzer, in the following essay on "The Rhetorical Situation," expresses ideas that are a natural extension of the views set forth by Hunt. Rhetoric, Bitzer convincingly argues, cannot take place in a vacuum or, indeed, in an unstructured or haphazard environment. Rather it is the product of a simple or complex situation or setting consisting of three elements: (1) an exigence or urgent needs that must be addressed; (2) an audience containing the potential power to act; and (3) a series of societal constraints that function as a deterrent to action. According to this notion, the starting point of rhetoric is the situation. Once the dimensions of the situation become clear, the rhetor, of necessity, is challenged to construct a timely and appropriate response which speaks to the problem of the exigencies and the constraints. What makes Bitzer's essay so valuable to the contemporary student of rhetoric are its far-reaching implications not only for communication theory but for public address and criticism as well.

The Rhetorical Situation

If someone says, That is a dangerous situation, his words suggest the presence of events, persons, or objects which threaten him, someone else, or something of value. If someone remarks, I find myself in an embarrassing situation, again the statement implies certain situational characteristics. If someone remarks that he found himself in an ethical situation, we understand that he probably either contemplated or made some choice of action from a sense of duty or obligation or with a view to the Good. In other words, there are circumstances of this or that kind of structure which are recognized as ethical, dangerous, or embarrassing. What characteristics, then, are implied when one refers to "the rhetorical situation"—the context in which speakers or writers create rhetorical discourse? Perhaps this question is puzzling because "situation" is not a standard term in the vocabulary of rhetorical theory. "Audience" is standard; so also are "speaker," "subject," "occasion," and "speech." If I were to ask, "What is a rhetorical audience?" or "What is a rhetorical subject?"—the reader would catch the meaning of my question.

When I ask, What is a rhetorical situation?, I want to know the nature of those contexts in which speakers or writers create rhetorical discourse: How should they be described? What are their characteristics? Why and how do they result in the creation of rhetoric? By analogy, a theorist of science might well ask, What are the characteristics of situations which inspire scientific thought? A philosopher might ask, What is the nature of the situation in which a philosopher "does philosophy"? And a theorist of poetry might ask, How shall we describe the context in which poetry comes into existence?

The presence of rhetorical discourse obviously indicates the presence of a rhetorical situation. The Declaration of Independence, Lincoln's Gettysburg Address, Churchill's Address on Dunkirk, John F. Kennedy's Inaugural Address—each is a clear instance of rhetoric and each indicates the presence of a situation. While the existence of a rhetorical address is a reliable sign of the existence of situation, it does not follow that a situation exists only when the discourse exists. Each reader probably can recall a specific time and place when there was opportunity to speak on some urgent matter, and after the opportunity was gone he created in private thought the speech he should have uttered earlier in the situation. It is clear that situations are not always accompanied by discourse. Nor should we assume that a rhetorical address gives existence to the situation; on the contrary, it is the situation which calls the discourse into existence. Clement Attlee once said that Winston Churchill went around looking for "finest hours." The point to observe is that Churchill found them—the crisis situations—and spoke in response to them.

No major theorist has treated rhetorical situation thoroughly as a distinct subject in rhetorical theory; many ignore it. Those rhetoricians who discuss situation do so indirectly—as does Aristotle, for example, who is led to consider situation when he treats types of discourse. None, to my knowledge, has asked the nature of rhetorical situation. Instead rhetoricians have asked: What is the process by which the orator creates and presents discourse? What is the nature of rhetorical discourse? What sorts of interaction occur between speaker, audience, subject, and occasion? Typically the questions which trigger theories of rhetoric focus upon the orator's method or upon the discourse itself, rather than upon the situation which invites the orator's application of his method and the creation of discourse. Thus rhetoricians distinguish among and characterize the types of speeches (forensic, deliberative, epideictic); they treat issues, types of proof, lines of argument, strategies of

Reprinted from *Philosophy & Rhetoric,* 1 (Winter, 1968), 1–15. Reprinted with permission of the author and editor of *Philosophy & Rhetoric.*

ethical and emotional persuasion, the parts of a discourse and the functions of these parts, qualities of styles, figures of speech. They cover approximately the same materials, the formal aspects of rhetorical method and discourse, whether focusing upon method, product or process; while conceptions of situation are implicit in some theories of rhetoric, none explicitly treat the formal aspects of situation.

I hope that enough has been said to show that the question—What is a rhetorical situation?—is not an idle one. I propose in what follows to set forth part of a theory of situation. This essay, therefore, should be understood as an attempt to revive the notion of rhetorical situation, to provide at least the outline of an adequate conception of it, and to establish it as a controlling and fundamental concern of rhetorical theory.

I

It seems clear that rhetoric is situational. In saying this, I do not mean merely that understanding a speech hinges upon understanding the context of meaning in which the speech is located. Virtually no utterance is fully intelligible unless meaning-context and utterance are understood; this is true of rhetorical and non-rhetorical discourse. Meaning-context is a general condition of human communication and is not synonymous with rhetorical situation. Nor do I mean merely that rhetoric occurs in a setting which involves interaction of speaker, audience, subject, and communicative purpose. This is too general, since many types of utterances—philosophical, scientific, poetic, and rhetorical—occur in such settings. Nor would I equate rhetorical situation with persuasive situation, which exists whenever an audience can be changed in belief or action by means of speech. Every audience at any moment is capable of being changed in some way by speech; persuasive situation is altogether general.

Finally, I do not mean that a rhetorical discourse must be embedded in historic context in the sense that a living tree must be rooted in soil. A tree does not obtain its character-as-tree from the soil, but rhetorical discourse, I shall argue, does obtain its character-as-rhetorical from the situation which generates it. Rhetorical works belong to the class of things which obtain their character from the circumstances of the historic context in which they occur. A rhetorical work is analogous to a moral action rather than to a tree. An act is moral because it is an act performed in a situation of a certain kind; similarly, a work is rhetorical because it is a response to a situation of a certain kind.

In order to clarify rhetoric-as-essentially-related-to-situation, we should acknowledge a viewpoint that is commonplace but fundamental; a work of rhetoric is pragmatic; it comes into existence for the sake of something beyond itself; it functions ultimately to produce action or change in the world; it performs some task. In short, rhetoric is a mode of altering reality, not by the direct application of energy to objects, but by the creation of discourse which changes reality through the mediation of thought and action. The rhetor alters reality by bringing into existence a discourse of such a character that the audience, in thought and action, is so engaged that it becomes mediator of change. In this sense rhetoric is always persuasive.

To say that rhetorical discourse comes into being in order to effect change is altogether general. We need to understand that a particular discourse comes into existence because of some specific condition or situation which invites utterance. Bronislaw Malinowski refers to just this sort of situation in his discussion of primitive language, which he finds to be essentially pragmatic and "embedded in situation." He describes a party of fishermen in the Trobriand Islands whose functional speech occurs in a "context of situation."

The canoes glide slowly and noiselessly, punted by men especially good at this task and always used for it. Other experts who know the bottom of the lagoon . . . are on the look-out for fish. . . . Customary signs, or sounds or words are uttered. Sometimes

a sentence full of technical references to the channels or patches on the lagoon has to be spoken; sometimes . . . a conventional cry is uttered. . . . Again, a word of command is passed here and there, a technical expression or explanation which serves to harmonize their behavior towards other men. . . . An animated scene, full of movement, follows, and now that the fish are in their power the fishermen speak loudly, and give vent to their feelings. Short, telling exclamations fly about, which might be rendered by such words as: "Pull in," "Let go," "Shift further," "Lift the net."

In this whole scene, "each utterance is essentially bound up with the context of situation and with the aim of the pursuit. . . . The structure of all this linguistic material is inextricably mixed up with, and dependent upon, the course of the activity in which the utterances are embedded." Later the observer remarks: "In its primitive uses, language functions as a link in concerted human activity, as a piece of human behaviour. It is a mode of action and not an instrument of reflection."[1]

These statements about primitive language and the "context of situation" provide for us a preliminary model of rhetorical situation. Let us regard rhetorical situation as a natural context of persons, events, objects, relations, and an exigence which strongly invites utterance; this invited utterance participates naturally in the situation, is in many instances necessary to the completion of situational activity, and by means of its participation with situation obtains its meaning and its rhetorical character. In Malinowski's example, the situation is the fishing expedition—consisting of objects, persons, events, and relations—and the ruling exigence, the success of the hunt. The situation dictates the sorts of observations to be made; it dictates the significant physical and verbal responses; and, we must admit, it constrains the words which are uttered in the same sense that it constrains the physical acts of paddling the canoes and throwing the nets. The verbal responses to the demands imposed by

this situation are clearly as functional and necessary as the physical responses.

Traditional theories of rhetoric have dealt, of course, not with the sorts of primitive utterances described by Malinowski—"stop here," "throw the nets," "move closer"—but with larger units of speech which come more readily under the guidance of artistic principle and method. The difference between oratory and primitive utterance, however, is not a difference in function; the clear instances of rhetorical discourse and the fishermen's utterances are similarly functional and similarly situational. Observing both the traditions of the expedition and the facts before him, the leader of the fishermen finds himself *obliged* to speak at a given moment—to command, to supply information, to praise or blame—to respond appropriately to the situation. Clear instances of artistic rhetoric exhibit the same character: Cicero's speeches against Cataline were called forth by a specific union of persons, events, objects, and relations, and by an exigence which amounted to an imperative stimulus; the speeches in the Senate rotunda three days after the assassination of the President of the United States were actually required by the situation. So controlling is situation that we should consider it the very ground of rhetorical activity, whether that activity is primitive and productive of a simple utterance or artistic and productive of the Gettysburg Address.

Hence, to say that rhetoric is situational means: (1) rhetorical discourse comes into existence as a response to situation, in the same sense that an answer comes into existence in response to a question, or a solution in response to a problem; (2) a speech is given *rhetorical* significance by the situation, just as a unit of discourse is given significance *as* answer or *as* solution by the question or problem; (3) a rhetorical situation must exist as a necessary condition of rhetorical discourse, just as a question must exist as a necessary condition of an answer; (4) many questions go unanswered and many problems remain unsolved; similarly, many rhetorical situations mature and decay without giving birth to rhetorical utterance; (5) a situation is rhetorical insofar as it needs and invites discourse capable of participating with situation and thereby altering its reality; (6) discourse is rhetorical insofar as it functions (or seeks to function) as a fitting response to a situation which needs and invites it. (7) Finally, the situation controls the rhetorical response in the same sense that the question controls the answer and the problem controls the solution. Not the rhetor and not persuasive intent, but the situation is the source and ground of rhetorical activity—and, I should add, of rhetorical criticism.

II

Let us now amplify the nature of situation by providing a formal definition and examining constituents. Rhetorical situation may be defined as a complex of persons, events, objects, and relations presenting an actual or potential exigence which can be completely or partially removed if discourse, introduced into the situation, can so constrain human decision or action as to bring about the significant modification of the exigence. Prior to the creation and presentation of discourse, there are three constituents of any rhetorical situation: the first is the *exigence;* the second and third are elements of the complex, namely the *audience* to be constrained in decision and action, and the *constraints* which influence the rhetor and can be brought to bear upon the audience.

Any *exigence* is an imperfection marked by urgency; it is a defect, an obstacle, something waiting to be done, a thing which is other than it should be. In almost any sort of context, there will be numerous exigences, but not all are elements of a rhetorical situation—not all are rhetorical exigences. An exigence which cannot be modified is not rhetorical; thus, whatever comes about of necessity and cannot be changed—death, winter, and some natural disasters, for instance—are exigences to be sure, but they are not rhetorical. Further, an exigence which can be modified only by means other than discourse is not rhetorical; thus, an exigence is not rhetorical when its modification requires merely one's own action or the application of a tool, but neither requires nor

invites the assistance of discourse. An exigence is rhetorical when it is capable of positive modification and when positive modification requires discourse or can be assisted by discourse. For example, suppose that a man's acts are injurious to others and that the quality of his acts can be changed only if discourse is addressed to him; the exigence—his injurious acts—is then unmistakably rhetorical. The pollution of our air is also a rhetorical exigence because its positive modification—reduction of pollution—strongly invites the assistance of discourse producing public awareness, indignation, and action of the right kind. Frequently rhetors encounter exigences which defy easy classification because of the absence of information enabling precise analysis and certain judgment—they may or may not be rhetorical. An attorney whose client has been convicted may strongly believe that a higher court would reject his appeal to have the verdict overturned, but because the matter is uncertain—because the exigence *might* be rhetorical—he elects to appeal. In this and similar instances of indeterminate exigences the rhetor's decision to speak is based mainly upon the urgency of the exigence and the probability that the exigence is rhetorical.

In any rhetorical situation there will be at least one controlling exigence which functions as the organizing principle: it specifies the audience to be addressed and the change to be effected. The exigence may or may not be perceived clearly by the rhetor or other persons in the situation; it may be strong or weak depending upon the clarity of their perception and the degree of their interest in it; it may be real or unreal depending on the facts of the case; it may be important or trivial; it may be such that discourse can completely remove it, or it may persist in spite of repeated modifications; it may be completely familiar—one of a type of exigences occurring frequently in our experience—or it may be totally new, unique. When it is perceived and when it is strong and important, then it constrains the thought and action of the perceiver who may respond rhetorically if he is in a position to do so.

The second constituent is the *audience.* Since rhetorical discourse produces change by influencing the decision and action of persons who function as mediators of change, it follows that rhetoric always requires an audience—even in those cases when a person engages himself or ideal mind as audience. It is clear also that a rhetorical audience must be distinguished from a body of mere hearers or readers: properly speaking, a rhetorical audience consists only of those persons who are capable of being influenced by discourse and of being mediators of change.

Neither scientific nor poetic discourse requires an audience in the same sense. Indeed, neither requires an audience in order to produce its end; the scientist can produce a discourse expressive or generative of knowledge without engaging another mind, and the poet's creative purpose is accomplished when the work is composed. It is true, of course, that scientists and poets present their works to audiences, but their audiences are not necessarily rhetorical. The scientific audience consists of persons capable of receiving knowledge, and the poetic audience, of persons capable of participating in aesthetic experiences induced by the poetry. But the rhetorical audience must be capable of serving as mediator of the change which the discourse functions to produce.

Besides exigence and audience, every rhetorical situation contains a set of *constraints* made up of persons, events, objects, and relations which are parts of the situation because they have the power to constrain decision and action needed to modify the exigence. Standard sources of constraint include beliefs, attitudes, documents, facts, traditions, images, interests, motives and the like; and when the orator enters the situation, his discourse not only harnesses constraints given by situation but provides additional important constraints—for example his personal character, his logical proofs, and his style. There are two main classes of constraints: (1) those originated or managed by the rhetor and his method (Aristotle called these "artistic proofs"), and (2) those other constraints, in the situation, which may be operative (Aristotle's "inartistic proofs"). Both classes must be divided so as to separate those constraints that are proper from those that are improper.

These three constituents—exigence, audience, constraints—comprise everything relevant in a rhetorical situation. When the orator, invited by situation, enters it and creates and presents discourse, then both he and his speech are additional constituents.

III

I have broadly sketched a conception of rhetorical situation and discussed constituents. The following are general characteristics or features.

1. Rhetorical discourse is called into existence by situation; the situation which the rhetor perceives amounts to an invitation to create and present discourse. The clearest instances of rhetorical speaking and writing are strongly invited—often required. The situation generated by the assassination of President Kennedy was so highly structured and compelling that one could predict with near certainty the types and themes of forthcoming discourse. With the first reports of the assassination, there immediately developed a most urgent need for information; in response, reporters created hundreds of messages. Later as the situation altered, other exigences arose: the fantastic events in Dallas had to be explained; it was necessary to eulogize the dead President; the public needed to be assured that the transfer of government to new hands would be orderly. These messages were not idle performances. The historic situation was so compelling and clear that the responses were created almost out of necessity. The responses—news reports, explanations, eulogies—participated with the situation and positively modified the several exigences. Surely the power of situation is evident when one can predict that such discourse will be uttered. How else explain the phenomenon? One cannot say that the situation is the function of the speaker's intention, for in this case the speakers' intentions were determined by the situation. One cannot say that the rhetorical transaction is simply a response of the speaker to the demands or expectations of an audience, for the expectations of the audience were themselves keyed to a tragic historic fact.

Also, we must recognize that there came into existence countless eulogies to John F. Kennedy that never reached a public; they were filed, entered in diaries, or created in thought.

In contrast, imagine a person spending his time writing eulogies of men and women who never existed: his speeches meet no rhetorical situations; they are summoned in existence not by real events, but by his own imagination. They may exhibit formal features which we consider rhetorical—such as ethical and emotional appeals, and stylistic patterns; conceivably one of these fictive eulogies is even persuasive to someone; yet all remain unrhetorical unless, through the oddest of circumstances, one of them by chance should fit a situation. Neither the presence of formal features in the discourse nor persuasive effect in a reader or hearer can be regarded as reliable marks of rhetorical discourse: A speech will be rhetorical when it is a response to the kind of situation which is rhetorical.

2. Although rhetorical situation invites response, it obviously does not invite just any response. Thus the second characteristic of rhetorical situation is that it invites a *fitting* response, a response that fits the situation. Lincoln's Gettysburg Address was a most fitting response to the relevant features of the historic context which invited its existence and gave it rhetorical significance. Imagine for a moment the Gettysburg Address entirely separated from its situation and existing for us independent of any rhetorical context: as a discourse which does not "fit" any rhetorical situation, it becomes either poetry or declamation, without rhetorical significance. In reality, however, the address continues to have profound rhetorical value precisely because some features of the Gettysburg situation persist; and the Gettysburg Address continues to participate with situation and to alter it.

Consider another instance. During one week of the 1964 presidential campaign, three events of national and international significance all but obscured the campaign: Khrushchev was suddenly deposed, China exploded an atomic bomb, and in England the Conservative Party was defeated by Labour. Any student of rhet-

oric could have given odds that President Johnson, in a major address, would speak to the significance of these events, and he did; his response to the situation generated by the events was fitting. Suppose that the President had treated not these events and their significance but the national budget, or imagine that he had reminisced about his childhood on a Texas farm. The critic of rhetoric would have said rightly, "He missed the mark; his speech did not fit; he did not speak to the pressing issues—the rhetorical situation shaped by the three crucial events of the week demanded a response, and he failed to provide the proper one."

3. If it makes sense to say that situation invites a "fitting" response, then situation must somehow prescribe the response which fits. To say that a rhetorical response fits a situation is to say that it meets the requirements established by the situation. A situation which is strong and clear dictates the purpose, theme, matter, and style of the response. Normally, the inauguration of a President of the United States demands an address which speaks to the nation's purposes, the central national and international problems, the unity of contesting parties; it demands speech style marked by dignity. What is evidenced on this occasion is the power of situation to constrain a fitting response. One might say metaphorically that every situation prescribes its fitting response; the rhetor may or may not read the prescription accurately.

4. The exigence and the complex of persons, objects, events and relations which generate rhetorical discourse are located in reality, are objective and publicly observable historic facts in the world we experience, are therefore available for scrutiny by an observer or critic who attends to them. To say the situation is objective, publicly observable, and historic means that it is real or genuine—that our critical examination will certify its existence. Real situations are to be distinguished from sophistic ones in which, for example, a contrived exigence is asserted to be real; from spurious situations in which the existence or alleged existence of constituents is the result of error or

ignorance; and from fantasy in which exigence, audience, and constraints may all be the imaginary objects of a mind at play.

The rhetorical situation as real is to be distinguished also from a fictive rhetorical situation. The speech of a character in a novel or play may be clearly required by a fictive rhetorical situation—a situation established by the story itself; but the speech is not genuinely rhetorical, even though, considered in itself, it looks exactly like a courtroom address or a senate speech. It is realistic, made so by fictive context. But the situation is not real, not grounded in history; neither the fictive situation nor the discourse generated by it is rhetorical. We should note, however, that the fictive rhetorical discourse within a play or novel may become genuinely rhetorical outside fictive context—if there is a real situation for which the discourse is a rhetorical response. Also, of course, the play or novel itself may be understood as a rhetorical response having poetic form.

5. Rhetorical situations exhibit structures which are simple or complex, and more or less organized. A situation's structure is simple when there are relatively few elements which must be made to interact; the fishing expedition is a case in point—there is a clear and easy relationship among utterances, the audiences, constraints, and exigence. Franklin D. Roosevelt's brief Declaration of War speech is another example: the message exists as a response to one clear exigence easily perceived by one major audience, and the one overpowering constraint is the necessity of war. On the other hand, the structure of a situation is complex when many elements must be made to interact: practically any presidential political campaign provides numerous complex rhetorical situations.

A situation, whether simple or complex, will be highly structured or loosely structured. It is highly structured when all of its elements are located and readied for the task to be performed. Malinowski's example, the fishing expedition, is a situation which is relatively simple and highly structured; everything is ordered to the task to be performed. The usual courtroom case is a good example of situation which is complex and highly structured. The jury is not a random and scattered audience but a selected and concentrated one; it knows its relation to judge, law, defendant, counsels; it is instructed in what to observe and what to disregard. The judge is located and prepared; he knows exactly his relation to jury, law, counsels, defendant. The counsels know the ultimate object of their case; they know what they must prove; they know the audience and can easily reach it. This situation will be even more highly structured if the issue of the case is sharp, the evidence decisive, and the law clear. On the other hand, consider a complex but loosely structured situation, William Lloyd Garrison preaching abolition from town to town. He is actually looking for an audience and for constraints; even when he finds an audience, he does not know that it is a genuinely rhetorical audience—one able to be mediator of change. Or consider the plight of many contemporary civil rights advocates who, failing to locate compelling constraints and rhetorical audiences, abandon rhetorical discourse in favor of physical action.

Situations may become weakened in structure due to complexity or disconnectedness. A list of causes includes these: (a) a single situation may involve numerous exigencies; (b) exigences in the same situation may be incompatible; (c) two or more simultaneous rhetorical situations may compete for our attention, as in some parliamentary debates; (d) at a given moment, persons comprising the audience of situation A may also be the audience of situations B, C, and D; (e) the rhetorical audience may be scattered, uneducated regarding its duties and powers, or it may dissipate; (f) constraints may be limited in number and force, and they may be incompatible. This is enough to suggest the sorts of things which weaken the structure of situations.

6. Finally, rhetorical situations come into existence, then either mature or decay or mature and persist—conceivably some persist indefinitely. In any case, situations grow and come to maturity; they evolve to just the time when a rhetorical discourse would be most fit-

ting. In Malinowski's example, there comes a time in the situation when the leader of the fishermen should say, "Throw the nets." In the situation generated by the assassination of the President, there was a time for giving descriptive accounts of the scene in Dallas, later a time for giving eulogies. In a political campaign, there is a time for generating an issue and a time for answering a charge. Every rhetorical situation in principle evolves to a propitious moment for the fitting rhetorical response. After this moment, most situations decay; we all have the experience of creating a rhetorical response when it is too late to make it public.

Some situations, on the other hand, persist; this is why it is possible to have a body of truly *rhetorical* literature. The Gettysburg Address, Burke's Speech to the Electors of Bristol, Socrates' Apology—these are more than historical documents, more than specimens for stylistic or logical analysis. They exist as rhetorical responses *for us* precisely because they speak to situations which persist—which are in some measure universal.

Due to either the nature of things or convention, or both, some situations recur. The courtroom is the locus for several kinds of situations generating the speech of accusation, the speech of defense, the charge to the jury. From day to day, year to year, comparable situations occur, prompting comparable responses; hence rhetorical forms are born and a special vocabulary, grammar, and style are established. This is true also of the situation which invites the inaugural address of a President. The situation recurs and, because we experience situations and the rhetorical responses to them, a form of discourse is not only established but comes to have a power of its own—the tradition itself tends to function as a constraint upon any new response in the form.

IV

In the best of all possible worlds, there would be communication perhaps, but no rhetoric— since exigencies would not arise. In our real world, however, rhetorical exigences abound; the world really invites change—change conceived and effected by human agents who quite properly address a mediating audience. The practical justification of rhetoric is analogous to that of scientific inquiry: the world presents objects to be known, puzzles to be resolved, complexities to be understood—hence the practical need for scientific inquiry and discourse; similarly, the world presents imperfections to be modified by means of discourse— hence the practical need for rhetorical investigation and discourse. As a discipline, scientific method is justified philosophically insofar as it provides principles, concepts, and procedures by which we come to know reality; similarly, rhetoric as a discipline is justified philosophically insofar as it provides principles, concepts, and procedures by which we effect valuable changes in reality. Thus rhetoric is distinguished from the mere craft of persuasion which, although it is a legitimate object of scientific investigation, lacks philosophical warrant as a practical discipline.

Lloyd F. Bitzer

Lloyd F. Bitzer is Professor of Communication Arts at the Unversity of Wisconsin, Madison.

Notes

1. "The Problem of Meaning in Primitive Languages," sections III and IV. This essay appears as a supplement to Ogden and Richards' *The Meaning of Meaning.*

The preceding discussions which have described rhetoric as a relevant field of study grounded in the humane tradition and deriving its impetus from a situation are vital introductory materials for understanding the nature of this volume. As essential as these analyses are, however, they do not go far enough in explaining the full rationale of our method in organizing the parts and chapters that follow. The added key to open up our panoramic view of Western thought, we feel, may be found in Douglas Ehninger's essay "On Systems of Rhetoric." Rejecting the notion that a single, clear-cut definition of the term rhetoric can be developed, Ehninger borrows from systems theory to show that what we have are three great rhetorics which he labels Classical, British or Continental, and Contemporary. This study, as you will see, delineates the special communication characteristics of each of the systems. The practical relevance of this model for us is that it provides a framework in which we can concentrate almost exclusively on the major western theorists without sacrificing what is significant and unique in the body of rhetorical literature. A final point to be observed here is this: if we perceive rhetoric from the vantage point of a systems approach, we not only come to a further appreciation of rhetoric as a humanity but will also see its roots in the social and behavioral sciences.

On Systems of Rhetoric

I

In this paper I shall be concerned with rhetorical systems as systems.

A rhetoric I define as an organized, consistent, coherent way of talking about practical discourse in any of its forms or modes. By practical discourse I mean discourse, written or oral, that seeks to inform, evaluate, or persuade, and therefore is to be distinguished from discourse that seeks to please, elevate, or depict. An organized, consistent, coherent way of talking about something, in line with my present purpose, I call a system. In this sense, not only the rhetoric embodied in a single treatise, but also the rhetoric embodied collectively in the treatises of a given place or period constitutes a system, and may be spoken of as such.

In the remarks that follow I shall be concerned with the second of these possibilities. Specifically, I shall attempt to describe the rhetorics of three historical periods in terms broad enough to exhibit their essential characteristics as systems, and then to suggest certain practical uses of an analysis conducted at this level.

It would be naive to suppose that in the characterizations I offer it will be easy to walk a line between the obvious on the one side and the disputable or false on the other. Nor do I expect that the formulations I advance or the inferences I draw will escape criticism. Because not all of the rhetorical treatises of a period fall into a mold, an attempt to treat that period as a system means that one must select from diverse possibilities the trends and emphases that are dominant. Because any one treatise, insofar as it pretends to completeness, is a complex construct, involving a delicate balance among ethical, aesthetic, semantic, and pragmatic elements, attempts to fit it into a pattern inevitably invite refutation by the citation of isolated passages.

But while the hazards are sizable the rewards beckon. Unlike microscopic sightings, which atomize and divide, a macroscopic view extending over an entire genus of treatises submerges differences and details so as to call forth the common characteristics of rhetorical

Reprinted from *Philosophy & Rhetoric,* 1 (Summer, 1968), 131–144. Reprinted with permission of the author and editor of *Philosophy & Rhetoric.*

systems as organized wholes—the parts of which they are composed, the joints at which they are articulated, and the weaknesses to which they are prone.

Of these advantages, however, I shall speak further in the final section of this paper. Initially, I turn to the task of characterizing the rhetorics of three historical periods in terms broad enough to display their common nature as systems. I chose as case studies for my investigation what I regard as the three crucial eras in the development of Western rhetorical thought—the classical period, the late eighteenth century, and the period extending from the early 1930s to the present time.

II

The rhetoric of the classical period arose out of a two-fold problem or need.

First, with the development of democratic institutions in the city states of Sicily and Greece, speechmaking as an activity found new avenues of expression and gained in importance until it came to be regarded as an art form as well as a social instrument. What was this phenomenon upon which men depended for the making of laws, the administration of justice, and the honoring of heroes? What was the essential nature of the speech act? Of what parts did this act consist? Upon what faculties or arts did it depend? How could it systematically be described and talked about? And, second, how could proficiency in the important business of performing this speech act be taught in a society where every man must act as his own lawyer and his own legislator? How might instruction in speechmaking be methodized and imparted to the masses?

These two needs, as limited and shaped by the social and intellectual milieu in which the new activity of speechmaking found itself, were the decisive factors in determining the nature of the classical rhetoric. Because this rhetoric operated in an aural world it became the art or science of oral rather than of written discourse. Because its principal functions were to argue the relative merits of laws and policies and to attack or defend from attack in the

courtroom, it became primarily the art of persuasion. Because skill in speaking had to be imparted to the masses rhetoric was written with an eye to easy prescription and stressed the development of mechanical or "artificial" procedures and routines. Because speaking was regarded as a fine art as well as a practical tool, rhetoric was given both aesthetic and pragmatic dimensions.

But while all of these properties and others must be recognized in a full description of the classical rhetoric, the one characteristic which perhaps most adequately distinguishes it as system is its basically grammatical nature. For, without denying other achievements, it still must be said that the central concern and principal contribution of the classical rhetoric were the development of the syntax of the speech act—the delineating and naming of the parts of that act and the tracing of the permutations and combinations of which these parts permit. And this emphasis is entirely understandable. Before the classical writers could consider the pragmatic or aesthetic aspects of speechmaking, they first had to determine what the act of speaking entailed and to devise a grammar for talking about its parts and their relationships.

The work of the classical rhetoricians in devising such a grammar was admirable. So well, indeed, did they perform this task that even today any system of rhetoric which fails to encompass the basic terms and relationships which they isolated is properly regarded as incomplete. They defined or located the speech act itself in two important ways: first, methodologically, by distinguishing rhetoric from grammar, logic, and poetic; and second, substantively, by exploring the relations rhetoric bears to politics and ethics. They divided the speech act into its functional parts of speaker, speech, and audience-occasion, and speculated upon the relative importance of each of these parts in determining the success of the whole. They distinguished among the kinds or types of speeches which they found in the world about them—the legislative, judicial, and epideictic—and described the characteristic uses of each. They recognized the various arts or "offices" upon which oral communication depends—invention, disposition, style, memory, and delivery—and they assigned a specific function to each. As sub-classifications within the various *officia,* they devised vocabularies for discussing types of proofs, characters of style, and the parts of a speech. And, finally, they arranged this grammar into a pattern which permitted its easy acquisition by the aspiring student.

But while as a grammatically centered and pedagogically oriented system the classical rhetoric had strengths, its focus on grammar and pedagogy also made for weaknesses.

First, in their desire to draw lines between phenomena which by nature blend into another—to divide, compartmentalize, and name—the ancients gave if not a false, at least a painfully over-simplified picture of the relationships between invention and disposition and invention and style. Indeed, save perhaps in the case of delivery—and even here modern studies in paralanguage give grounds for doubt—the divisions among all the *officia* tend to be artificial rather than real.

Second, in their desire to render the art of speaking teachable, and teachable to the average man, the classical writers were led to depend too much on preprocessed materials and modes of expression; to reduce to formula or routine, matters inherently incapable of such reduction; to provide, as in the *status* and the topics, purely "artificial" substitutes for knowledge and cogitation—substitutes which by converting *noesis* to rote might equalize individual differences in industry and ability.

Third, and most important, in their emphasis upon the speech act as such and hampered by the primitive psychology and epistemology with which they worked, as a group the classical writers tended either to scant or to present a patently naive account of the relation between the speech act and the mind of the listener.

III

Whereas the rhetoric of the classical period was basically "grammatical" in nature, the rhetoric of the period we now are to examine is best described as "psychological." For it was the major contribution of the "new British rhetoric" of the later eighteenth century, as embodied principally in such works as Lord Kames' *Elements of Criticism* (1761), John Ogilvie's *Philosophical and Critical Observations* (1774), George Campbell's *Philosophy of Rhetoric* (1776), and Joseph Priestley's *Lectures on Oratory and Criticism* (1777), that it corrected the major deficiency of the classical system by working out a series of detailed statements concerning the relation between the communicative act and the mind of the listener-reader.

And here, too, the new emphasis or interest arose in response to a felt need and was shaped by the environment in which that need emerged. For as Locke and his successors among the British empiricists began to develop more sophisticated systems of psychology and epistemology, not only did the ancients' lack of attention to the message-mind relationship seem a more glaring deficiency, but many of the traditional assumptions concerning how men know or are persuaded no longer were acceptable.

So far as the student of rhetorical systems is concerned, it is immaterial that most of the doctrines which the new rhetoricians chose as groundings for their work—the faculty and associational psychologies, the common sense philosophy, and the like—no longer are fashionable. What is important is that, taking these doctrines as premises, the British rhetoricians of the period worked out a more sophisticated statement of the message-mind relationship than had hitherto been possible, and that here again the statement was shaped by the environment in which the need arose.

In their effort to carry rhetoric beyond the grammar of the speech act, with its attendant pedagogical rules and cautions—to bring it, as Campbell said, to a "new country" where rules might be validated by checking them against those principles of the human understanding from whence they sprang[1]—the architects of the new system gave rhetoric an epistemological rather than a grammatical or a logical starting point. Instead of approaching rhetoric through an analysis of what might be said on behalf of a cause, as had the ancients, they approached it through an analysis of the mind of the listener-reader, premising their doctrine upon assumptions concerning the ways in which men come to know what they know, believe what they believe, and feel what they feel. From such an analysis, they assumed, the radical principles of rhetoric could be inferred and, as Campbell said, validated. In short, whereas the ancients had built a subject- or substance-centered rhetoric, the eighteenth-century theorists built an audience-centered one. They classified speeches in terms of the effect the speaker sought to produce upon his listener— "to enlighten the understanding, to please the imagination, to move the passions, or to influence the will."[2] They categorized proofs according to the ways in which listeners come to believe—by experience, analogy, testimony, and the calculation of chances.[3] They fused the traditional areas of invention and arrangement into the broader concept of this conduct or "management" of a discourse and included in this rubric all of the grosser resources, both substantive and methodological, by which the listener could be persuaded.[4] They rejected the view that rhetoric is a "counterpart" of dialectic or logic, and declared it to be an "offshoot" of logical studies. Then, with rhetoric dependent upon logic for its routines of analysis and proof, they took the bold step of ruling the tasks of search and discovery entirely out of the art, and of substituting in their stead a new doctrine of invention conceived of as the framing and use of proofs that had previously been derived.[5]

How shall we evaluate this "new" rhetoric? Although now largely dated, there can be little question, I think, but that on the whole it was a remarkable achievement and represented a level of sophistication not envisioned by the ancients. At the same time, however, it is equally clear that this new system, as had the classical rhetoric, suffered from too intense a preoccupation with one aspect of the communication spectrum. While the ancients had focused on the grammar of the speech act at the expense of exploring how that act is related to the listener, so the eighteenth-century writers focused on the speaker-listener relationship at cost of developing an improved grammar of the act itself. Consequently, as in the case of Priestley,[6] they gave the traditional concepts new tortured meanings, or like Campbell they accepted the ancient grammar and buried it in their works—deemphasized it until the parts of the speech act and the arts or offices upon which the act depends tended to lose identity as discrete units.

Even more important, however, in their preoccupation with the message-mind relationship the architects of the "new" rhetoric gave insufficient attention to another vital dimension of a complete and rounded theory of communication. And this is the role that practical discourse plays in society—the function it performs and should perform in promoting social cohesion and exercising social control.

In two different senses the "new" rhetoric of the eighteenth century was almost entirely an armchair construct—a product of the study rather than of the forum. First, it was largely unrelated to and uninterested in speaking and writing as they existed in the world about it. It was a hypothetical or "if, then" rhetoric— a self-contained theoretical study which might equally well exist if actual discourses never were or never had been composed. Campbell, who in the *Philosophy* defends the study of "eloquence" on the ground that it furnishes the quickest, surest, and pleasantest way to knowledge of the human mind, reserves most of his practical advice on speaking for the strangely unphilosophical *Lectures on Systematic Theology and Pulpit Eloquence* (1807). Joseph Priestley regards his *Lectures on Oratory* as a practical illustration of the associational psychology of David Hartley.[7] And Hugh Blair, by allying rhetoric with *belles lettres,* places that discipline at the service of the critic as well as of the speaker or writer.[8]

Finally, and more briefly, as one might imagine of a system that largely predates the development of experimental techniques of investigation and verification, the "new" rhetoric was armchair in the sense that for the most part it consisted of inferences drawn from premises based upon intuition or common sense.

IV

The third and last of the period systems we are to examine extends from the early 1930s to the present time, and encompasses developments which, for the most part, have occurred here in the United States.

If the classical rhetoric may be characterized as "grammatical" and the "new" rhetoric of the eighteenth century as "psychological," the rhetoric of our third period may best be described as "social" or "sociological." For while as a system contemporary rhetoric is unusually complex and embraces many specialized strands of interest, all of these strands find unity in the fact that at bottom they view rhetoric as an instrument for understanding and improving human relations.

Like systems of the past, the contemporary system arises out of a felt need and is shaped by the intellectual and social milieu in which rhetoric today finds itself. And here the need is simple but compelling. From the personal to the national and international levels tensions and breakdowns in human relations now, as never before, may result not only in maladjusted personalities or in misunderstanding among individuals, but in depressions, wars, and the suicide of the race itself.

Under such circumstances it is natural that rhetoric as a form of verbal interaction among persons and groups should be concerned with the part it can play in promoting human understanding and in improving the process by which man communicates with man.

This motive is reflected in the thinking of Kenneth Burke who argues that because language is symbolic action rhetorical analysis can throw light upon human relations and motives generally, while rhetoric as a social force arising out of an atmosphere of divisiveness can promote consubstantiality and peace through the process of identification.[9] Similarly, it underlies I. A. Richards' definition of rhetoric as a study of the causes and remedies of misunderstanding and accounts for his interest in metaphor and in "comprehending."[10]

Proponents of group discussion, under the influence of Dewey's instrumentalism and the explorations of the group dynamists, seek to implement the ideal of improved human relations by developing a specialized rhetoric of reflective problem solving. Students of communication theory, influenced by the terminology and insights of the electronics engineers, believe that an understanding of transmission systems will help to eliminate many of the blockages that occur when man speaks to man. The General Semanticists profess to find a neuter or feckless mode of communication a cure for many of the world's social ills. Writers on argument, aware that traditional proof patterns are inapplicable to disputes on moral issues, seek a logic of "ought propositions," drawn with a particular eye to the problems of "conflict resolution."

But these workers and others throughout the broad field of contemporary rhetoric do not find unity only in their concern with the social aspects of improved communication. They are bound still more closely together by their common belief that at the root of many of the misunderstandings which impair or block communications are man's language and his habits of using and abusing it—a conviction bolstered by the growing realization that language is not a pliable medium which through struggle may be molded to one's will, but rather is itself a shaping force which goes far toward determining how man will conceive of himself and of his world.

Therefore, while the ancients centered principally upon methods for analyzing the substance or subject matter of a "cause" and while the eighteenth-century framers of the "new" rhetoric emphasized the message-mind relationship, contemporary writers find a locus of interest in language as the vehicle by which the message is transmitted. Beyond this, however, they recognize that while language is the central instrument of human communication, other symbol systems, some of which lie beneath the sender's or receiver's threshold of awareness, also may carry messages which influence thought or behavior.

The new focus, no less than the ones which preceded it, has had both desirable and undesirable results. The encompassment within rhetoric of appeals which are at least partially "unconscious"[11] has extended the traditional range of that science, and in so doing has provided a more comprehensive picture of the role which rhetorical forces play in promoting social cohesion and effecting social control. On the other hand, since this extension carried to its fullest would render any stimulus-response situation rhetorical, rhetoric is in danger of losing its identity as a discrete discipline. Indeed, even today it is moot to dispute whether one may with profit talk of a rhetoric of clothes, or of social status, or, for that matter, of a rhetoric of the stoplight.[12]

And, second, the current interest in vehicles of message transmission, coupled with the premium which quantitative studies in communication research place upon ever more effective transmission, threatens the concern which a sound rhetoric should have for message content and for the ethical and aesthetic dimensions of communication. If a rhetoric is to pretend to completeness, it must be concerned not only with means, but with ends. Besides asking what does communicate and persuade, it must ask what should persuade and what that which persuades should persuade to. Moreover, because at bottom ethical and pragmatic considerations are inseparable from the problem of form, a complete rhetoric also must have an aesthetic dimension.

If, then, as there is reason to suspect, the present emphasis on the vehicle of transmission may threaten the integrity of rhetoric as a bounded discipline or impair those relations which guarantee its character as a humane subject, it may be well in the future to watch this development with more than ordinary care.

V

As I remarked at the outset, this paper has two purposes: (1) to attempt to describe the rhetorics of three periods in terms broad enough to exhibit their essential characteristics as systems, and (2) to suggest some of the uses of an analysis conducted at this level. Having described the three rhetorics, I now inquire into the uses which such analysis may have.

First, I would argue that attempts to characterize the rhetorics of various places or periods at the systems level are useful because they introduce a healthy and much needed relativism into studies still too much dominated by the notion of the classical rhetoric as a preferred archetype from which all departures are greater or lesser aberrations.

As our survey has suggested, the collective rhetorics of a period, as well as the rhetoric embodied in a single treatise, are time- and culture-bound. Systems of rhetoric arise out of a felt need and are shaped in part by the intellectual and social environment in which the need exists. No matter how sound internally or how imposing architecturally a given system may be—no matter how much its ethical or aesthetic groundings may arouse our admiration—to regard it as a universally applicable paradigm is to overlook a fundamental fact concerning the very nature of rhetoric.

From this it follows that the continuing dialogue on the question, What is rhetoric? except as an academic exercise, is largely profitless. If there is no one generic rhetoric which, like a Platonic Idea, is lurking in the shadows awaiting him who shall have the acuteness to discern it, the search for a defining quality can only end in error or frustration. It would serve the cause of rhetorical studies in general, I think, if instead of continuing this dialogue we openly adopted the plural of the noun and spoke of the history or theory of "rhetorics."

But more important than any reform in notation which might be effected by the laying of the one-rhetoric myth is the fact that a view which allows for many rhetorics rather than a single preferred one pointedly reminds us that in the final analysis the worth of a rhetorical system cannot be divorced from pragmatic considerations. It cannot be merely good or bad; it must be good or bad for something. Abstractly considered, a system geared to the Platonic ideal of communicating truth in order to make men better is to be ranked above one devoted to the ornamenting of language or the tricks of persuasion, and without doubt every "good" rhetoric has as its ultimate purpose the communication of "truth." But, at the same time, a rhetoric which conceives of truth as transcendent entity and requires a perfect knowledge of the soul as a condition for its successful transmittal automatically rules itself out as an instrument for doing the practical work of the world, and for this reason is less preferable than a system geared to the communication of contingent truths as established by probable rather than apodeictic proofs. In short, the problem of evaluating a rhetoric is a complex one, calling for a delicate balancing of the ideal with the utilitarian and for a precarious adjustment of ends to means. A study of rhetorical systems as systems, I believe, may contribute to our understanding of this fact.

Second, I would contend that analysis of the sort here attempted is useful because it helps to clarify the roles which form and substance play in the creation of a rhetoric. Our discussion appears to show that while the form a rhetoric assumes is a joint product of need and environment, its content or subject matter in each case is supplied by all or some of the constituents of the communication process. Indeed, if a system of rhetoric did not have these constituents as its subject matter, it would not be a system of rhetoric but a system of another sort.

Because systems of rhetoric share in part or in whole the same content or substance, no matter how much they vary in form or purpose they have inescapable elements of commonality. Therefore, looked at from one point of view they are different rather than alike, while from another they are alike rather than different. It is, I suggest a failure on the part of the disputants to make clear how they are viewing a rhetoric which lies at the basis of the wearisome controversy concerning the classical or non-classical orientation of the rhetorics of George Campbell or Kenneth Burke.[13] In any event, by making their respective points of view clear, the parties to this argument almost certainly would narrow the area of dispute.

Third, analysis of rhetorics at the systems level, I believe, is useful because it directs attention to the dangers and difficulties involved in constructing a rhetoric. And surely this information is helpful both in evaluating systems of the past and in building systems to meet the changing needs of the future.

Because even by the loose definition adopted here a system is an organized and coherent way of looking at something, unless an account of the communication process has a distinctive emphasis or focus—is ordered in terms of a hierarchy of ends and is marked by a distinguishing method—it is not a system but a random collection of observations and precepts. And yet it would appear from our discussion that emphasis in one direction may lead to unwarranted de-emphasis in another. For if the classical rhetoric focused on the grammar of the speech act at the expense of exploring the message-mind relationship, and if the "new" rhetoric of the eighteenth century emphasized the gramamar of the act, so the concern of contemporary theorists with the vehicle of transmission and its more efficient use threatens to detract interest from the crucial problem of message content.

In a different vein, our analysis underscores the fact that he who would construct a rhetoric of any sort must draw lines and erect boundaries where in fact none exist, and hence to this extent always must give an unreliable account of the territory and processes he attempts to map. On at least two counts practical discourse resists systematizing. First, human communication itself is a process—a fluid, on-going, circular movement without a definite beginning, middle, or end. In order to talk about communication at all not only must one arbitrarily slice off a segment of the whole, but he must momentarily stop or freeze motion within this segment, thus imposing a false stasis upon a kinetic phenomenon. And, second, discourse resists systematizing for the quite different reason that the several arts or skills upon which writing or speaking depends cannot be compartmentalized. Style glides imperceptibly into invention on the one hand and disposition on the other, while memory, as Ramus suggested,[14] is dependent on both, and invention and disposition, as the formulary rhetoric recognized, may perform interchangeable functions.[15] It is, I think, no exaggeration to say that a system of rhetoric never has and that very probably none ever will satisfactorily solve the foregoing problems.

And finally under this head, an analysis on the systems level confirms that while a distinctive grammar must lie at the basis of every rhetorical system a narrow focus upon a grammar is the least healthy and productive way of regarding rhetoric. Because rhetorical concepts may profitably be divided into only a limited number of parts and usefully combined or arranged in only a limited number of ways, after these possibilities have been exhausted innovation must consist of pointless elaborations and refinements. Hence, with the passage of time the distinctions drawn by a grammatically oriented rhetoric tend to become needlessly minute, its rules are multiplied beyond warrant, and ever growing areas of doctrine are reduced to formula and routine.[16] If rhetoric is to have status as a humane discipline, clearly it must develop its psychological and social dimensions. In proportion as it does so, however, our analysis also indicates that rhetoric may become a challenging and illuminating field for study—one worthy of attention by the best minds of an age. The great rhetorical systems of the past and present stand as testimony to this fact.

Fourth and last, I would argue the usefulness of examining rhetorics as systems for what such study may suggest concerning a possible metasystem of rhetorics and the promise which this metasystem holds for the future. For as our analysis suggests—and as I believe an examination of additional systems would confirm—while in one sense the major rhetorics of the Western world may properly be described as revolutionary, in another sense they may perhaps be regarded as evolutionary. Although each of the systems we have examined overthrew the premise or starting point of its predecessor for a premise that was radically different and distinctively its own, it also appears that in each case the new starting point not only corrected a deficiency in the preceding system but encompassed that system to pass beyond it. Just as the "new" rhetoric of the eighteenth century, though it accepted

much of the classical grammar, raised its sights above the grammatical to develop an account of the message-mind relationship, so contemporary theorists, accept the crucial position which this relationship must occupy in a fruitful rhetoric, and entertain the still broader purpose of exploring the social significance of the communication act in all its forms and uses.

Whether in the long view all major systems of rhetoric tend to correct deficiencies in their predecessors and tend to pass beyond them is a complex question, and one which cannot be divorced from a careful consideration of the social and intellectual environment in which each system arises. It would seem, however, that through the ages, and despite occasional setbacks, rhetorics have constantly become both richer in content and more embracing in scope. Perhaps the central lesson to be learned from an analysis of the rhetorics of various periods considered as systems is that while the final word on rhetorics never has and probably never will be said, there is reason for optimism concerning the future of rhetoric as a discipline—reason to believe that as man's knowledge grows and his attempts to talk about practical discourse in a coherent and consistent fashion improve, rhetorics ever will become more penetrating and more fruitful.

Douglas Ehninger

The late Douglas Ehninger was Professor of Speech and Dramatic Art at the University of Iowa.

Notes

1. George Campbell, *The Philosophy of Rhetoric,* ed. Lloyd Bitzer (Carbondale, Ill., 1963), p. 1i.
2. *Ibid.,* p. 1.
3. *Ibid.,* pp. 50–58. Cf. Richard Whately, *Elements of Rhetoric,* ed. Douglas Ehninger (Carbondale, Ill., 1963), pp. 46–108.
4. Hugh Blair, *Lectures on Rhetoric and Belles Lettres,* ed. Harold Harding, 2 vols. (Carbondale, Ill., 1965), II, 127–155, etc.
5. Whately, pp. 4, 35–167 *passim.*
6. Joseph Priestly, *Lectures on Oratory and Criticism,* ed. Vincent M. Bevilacqua and Richard Murphy (Carbondale, Ill., 1965), *Lectures,* II–IV, VI—VII, etc.
7. *Ibid.,* Preface, p.i.
8. See Blair, *Lectures* XX–XXIV, XXXV–XLVII *passim.*

9. Kenneth Burke, *A Rhetoric of Motives* (New York, 1950), pp. xiv–xv.
10. I. A. Richards, *The Philosophy of Rhetoric* (New York, 1936), pp. 3, 89–138; *Speculative Instruments* (Chicago, 1955), pp. 17–38.
11. See Kenneth Burke, "Rhetoric—Old and New," *Journal of General Education, V* (April 1951), 203. "If I had to sum up in one word the difference between the 'old' rhetoric and a 'new' (a rhetoric reinvigorated by fresh insights which the 'new' sciences contributed to the subject), I would reduce it to this: The key term for the old rhetoric was 'persuasion' and its stress was upon deliberate design. The key term for the new rhetoric would be 'identification,' which can include a partially 'unconscious' factor in appeal."
12. See Donald C. Bryant, "Rhetoric: Its Functions and Scope," *Quarterly Journal of Speech,* XXXIX (December 1953), 405.
13. See, for example, Douglas McDermott, "George Campbell and the Classical Tradition," *Quarterly Journal of Speech,* XLIX (December 1963), 403–409.
14. See *P. Rami Scholarum Dialecticarum, seu Animadversionum in Organum Aristotelis, libri XX,* Recens emendati perJoan. Piscatorem Argentinensem (Frankfurt, 1581), p. 593.
15. See Wilbur Samuel Howell, *Logic and Rhetoric in England, 1500–1700* (Princeton, N.J., 1956), pp. 138–145.
16. Besides the excessive refinements worked by the classical rhetoricians in the areas of invention and disposition, the sixteenth-century rhetoric of style may be taken as an example of this tendency; for this rhetoric, in its concern to distinguish and name all possible deviations from the normal and usual patterns of expression, was no less grammatical in nature than was the routinized rhetoric of the ancients.

....

Hopefully we have succeeded in the opening section of this volume in creating the framework upon which the rhetoric of Western thought has been built. The beginning chapter and accompanying essays have described the general nature of rhetoric as a humane, action-centered field of study involving enlightened choices that an audience assembled in a specific situation is morally obligated to make. This introductory material further has pictured rhetoric as an art or science concerned with generating understanding, emphasizing values, and producing persuasion; and used by members of all disciplines in communicating the content of their field. Finally, at least one of these essays has discussed the systemic nature of rhetoric, making it possible for us to view rhetoric from the perspective of three great systems: the classical, the British, and the contemporary.

From the vantage point of the above perspectives, the ensuing chapters will be treated. As they are developed, it is our belief that the following popular contemporary ideas pertaining to the true nature of rhetoric will be seriously challenged:

1. Rhetoric is an appearance, not a reality.
2. Rhetoric is a truncated art excessively concerned with ornate style and delivery.
3. Rhetoric deals exclusively with public communication.
4. Rhetoric is limited to the oral genre.
5. Rhetoric is a prescriptive study involving communication practicum, and containing little or no body of theory and literature.

Part Two Classical Rhetorical Theory

Probably no single term in current use in the United States enjoys so much prestige as the word "communication." Back in the 1950s whenever Americans faced a major problem they were assured that "education" or "more education" was the answer. Today "communication" is the panacea, mouthed with equal conviction by advertisers and marriage counsellors, educators and law enforcement officials.

If we were to conduct a public opinion poll on almost any city street in America and ask each passerby what "communication" meant, radio and televison would be among the most popular responses. Thus, a foreigner to the land might assume communication began with the advent of commercial radio in 1920 or commercial television in the late 1940s. Actually, its roots are much older.

Three thousand years ago and more, men and women were sending messages to each other, broadcasting ideas, listening, and like today, often misunderstanding what they read and heard. This book is about rhetoric and communication, past and present.

Our point of view is dictated by the ancient Greeks, the first Westerners to write down recommendations for making speech persuasive to others. If anyone could be said to have invented rhetoric, it would be they. Early Greek society like our own was oriented to the spoken word. To be sure, the Greeks had an alphabet and some knew how to read and write, but written communication in those times was slow and laborious, expensive and often stilted. Some of the early speeches of the Greek orator, Demosthenes, were promptly criticized when delivered: "they smell of the lamp," listeners cried in derision.

"The Rhetoric of Western Thought" is a richly rewarding topic for study. Besides the insatiably curious Greeks its history includes practical, well-organized Romans; Christians consumed with a desire to convert others and later, to ward off heresy; philosophers, scientists, and literary analysts from Britain and the continent; along with contemporary specialists in aesthetics, ethics, and media analysis. Add for flavor a goodly number of opportunists, charlatans, and demagogues. The story is, in short, a saga of good and bad, of achievement and blind alleys, and of various cultural approaches to the use of words to affect behavior.

Since it all began in ancient times, we start our narrative with the world of Greece and Rome.

2

The World of Greece and Rome

Douglas Ehninger tells us that the collective rhetorics of a period are culture-bound. Consequently if we mean to understand the major rhetorical theories of classical civilization—a civilization quite different from our own—we must first examine Greek and Roman culture.

Let us begin with a consideration of geography and climate, two important cultural determinants. The land of the Greeks is a rugged, mountainous peninsula in eastern Europe, jutting southward into the Mediterranean Sea. Although countless islands in the Aegean and the Adriatic have from time to time been under Greek control, what interests us most is the Greek mainland, a land mass of some 40,000 square miles, about the size of the state of Ohio.

In Greece, you are never far from the mountains or the sea. The crisp, clear air and the bright, blue skies of the eastern Mediterranean are a delight to tourists and cameramen alike. Even amateurs return home with marvelous colored slides for both the scenery and atmosphere are spectacular.

What is not spectacular is the limited productivity of Greek soil. Tillable soil is at a premium here. Olive trees are carefully tended on hillside slopes because there is no other place for them to grow. Farmers struggle to eke out a living today as in ancient times. The modern visitor to Greece still sees coarse-garbed peasant women weeding their crops by hand, bent over as their forbears were centuries before. Donkeys haul precious twigs and prunings for fuel, along with hay to feed the cattle. The importation of food from abroad is a fact of life familiar to every Greek.

It was trade from abroad in fact which provided Athens with its opportunity to lead the ancient world. While Sparta, her primary rival, is ringed by snow-capped peaks even in May, Athens is an easy dozen miles from a large natural harbor, the Piraeus. It was the Athenian navy which destroyed the Persians at sea in 480 B.C., after their city had been sacked. And it was the Athenians who replaced the Phoenicians as the leading traders of the Mediterranean world.

Scattered islands and isolated mountain communities had one thing in common in ancient times; both preferred strong local government. The Greeks formed between two and three hundred city states, with Athens and its population of 200,000 being by far the largest. These mini-states shared much in common: all spoke the same language; all shared a common history and literature; all worshiped the same gods; each participated whenever it could in athletic games and in music, drama, and oratory contests.

Yet, strangely enough, these miniature city states rarely joined together in common defense. Local rivalries often seemed more threatening to them than distant barbarians in the north and east. The pleas of countless orators for pan-Hellenism, for a single Greek state, were of no avail. Only military dictators like Philip of Macedon and his son, Alexander the Great, would eventually force unification. What the city states seemed to want most was simply to be left alone.[1]

Culture is more than the sum of its parts. Oftentimes there is a spirit, an esprit de corps, a unique way of life which transcends geography, climate, agriculture, and government. In *The Greek Way,* Edith Hamilton tried to capture this thread, by contrasting the civilizations of East and West, of Egypt and Greece.[2] The Kingdom of the Nile was a vast, rich land area controlled by the pharoah, his priests, and his soldiers. An army of slaves made specialized vocations possible. There was ample sustenance for all and extended periods of peace. Yet Hamilton tells us that Egyptian society was preoccupied with death. The pharoahs erected giant monuments to themselves to impress future generations. As a result, Egypt became the land of tombs and pyramids. Priests counselled the downtrodden that they could look forward to an afterlife; regardless of their present state, a brighter future lay ahead. Given such advice, acceptance of servitude was widespread.

Athens was a world apart from such thinking. Individual perfection of mind and body dominated Greek thought; hence, the Greeks excelled at philosophy and sports. Life in all its exuberant potential was the keynote to Greek civilization. The free citizen of Athens was trained to be a generalist, able to do many things well. He might be asked at any time to judge a murder trial or oversee the strengthening of city fortifications, embark on an embassy abroad or participate as a member of the Executive Council in city government. Citizens were expected to join in Assembly debates on topics ranging from war and peace, to finance, legislation, national defense, and commerce.[3] Probably the historian Thucydides summed up Athenian civic responsibility best when he wrote: "We do not say that a man who takes no interest in politics is a man who minds his own business; we say that he has no business here at all."[4]

The early Greeks worshiped perfection. It was, they thought, the domain of the gods. If man were to approach godliness, he must strive always to do his best, to be as perfect as he was able. The Greeks thought every object had a character of its own, an essence which they called *ethos.* Modern sociologists often speak of a society's ethos when they mean its distinctive flavor. Everything the Greek saw about him appeared to have just such a character. A perfect speaker, for example, was conceived of as a man of honesty, intelligence and good will.[5] The speaker did not himself necessarily possess such qualities; rather, others perceived such qualities in him. It was the appearance of perfection which mattered.

In Greek society, form often seemed to be more important than reality. The perfect statue revealed a superb, muscular body and a faultless face, devoid of human emotion. It is only later in the days of the Romans that a smile appears upon faces cut in stone. The perfect story conformed to a literary ideal rather than to factual accuracy. The way a soldier died in battle seemed to be more important in the eyes of his relatives than whether the battle was won or lost. Ritual and procession typified Greek religion rather than sermons and the worship of a personal God.

Greek society, like our own, was oriented to the spoken word. Take Homer's great epic poems, the *Illiad* and the *Odyssey,* for example. These works constitute the poetic cornerstone of Greek culture—part history, part mythology, part oratory, part patriotism.[6] It was as if a single great genius wrote the *Bible,* Chaucer's *Canterbury Tales,* and Shakespeare's plays all in one. Homer's epics involved events which took place about 1300 B.C. An Asian prince violated the Greek code of hospitality and had to be punished; ten years of bitter warfare followed. About six centuries later, a blind wanderer began to collect and narrate the many tales of the conflict. Homer's tales passed from generation to generation by word of mouth until at last they became so much a part of Greek heritage that Homerology was taught to every schoolboy. Years later, at Olympia, Delphi, and Epidaurus, when a Greek citizen heard Homer's tales repeated, he would at any moment pick up the narrative himself if the story-teller paused unduly. Known throughout history as the first great work of European literature, Homer's epic poems were not finally written down until the third century, B.C. Oral tradition was as much a part of Greek culture as it is today in modern Africa or India.

The Greeks depended upon trade for survival. Because of their geographic isolation, they were committed to strong local government. These independent city states shared much in common however—language, religion, history, literature, the persistent drive to seek perfection in mind and body. Theirs was an oral society dedicated to self-actualization. Thus the theory and practice of speechmaking came to flourish among them.

The first written rhetoric in the Western world was composed about 465 B.C. at the Greek colony of Syracuse in Sicily. A change of government resulted when a tyranny was displaced by a democracy. In the aftermath, property holders presented conflicting claims to various parcels of land. Who were the true owners? An enterprising bystander by the name of Corax realized that if a claimant could establish a more plausible case than his opponent, he would win title to the disputed property. With this insight, the rhetoric of probability was born. Corax devised a system of rules for arranging and arguing a legal case and promptly made this knowledge available to others, for a fee.[7] His system was later introduced to Athens and other city states on the mainland.

Legal suits were an everyday occurrence in ancient Greece. In cases involving major crimes, the jury usually included five hundred members. Thus, oratory often was more critical to legal success than factual evidence. Greek law did not provide for an advocate system like the one we know in America.[8] Every free citizen spoke for himself. But it was possible to secure the services of a good speechwriter if one had the necessary means. Many of the leading orators of ancient Greece, such as the great Demosthenes, amassed considerable fortunes by serving as forensic logographers, legal ghost-writers for the well-to-do.

Since the city state of Athens was a democracy governed by some 40,000 free citizens, the power of every citizen to speak effectively was highly valued. Rule by precinct, or *deme* as the Greeks called it, meant that on almost any day one might be called upon to speak on a matter of public policy.[9] Except for generals, all city officials were chosen annually by lot. The ruling Executive Council of Fifty was chosen anew each month.

Jury panels of 6,000 were regularly on call. In any given day, one out of every five Athenian citizens was engaged in some form of public service. The ability to speak, to listen critically to the arguments of others, and to utter appropriate response were deemed valuable skills by all.

At the foot of the Acropolis, the three hundred foot limestone hill which dominates the central city of Athens, stands the *agora* or marketplace. Here traders came to buy and sell. Here were located the minor courts, side by side with merchant stalls, and here was the *stoa* or porch where the philosophers liked to stroll. The agora was an international marketplace for goods and ideas—colorful, noisy, varied, unique in the world of the ancient Greeks. While most other city states had their acropolis and agora, none attracted the clientele, foreign and domestic, like Athens did.

Greek mythology tells us that a maiden named Cassandra possessed the power to prophesy the future, but the god Apollo decreed that her prophesies should never be believed. A prophet the Greeks (and later the Romans) *did* believe was the oracle at Delphi. For a thousand years men came to an isolated mountainside in central Greece to seek her advice. Petitioners presented their questions to the priests of the Temple of Apollo. The priests would then disappear into the bowels of the Temple to consult with the oracle herself, a peasant woman from a nearby village. In a semi-trance, the oracle mumbled a reply which was later relayed to the questioner. In gratitude, he would leave valuable gifts of goods and money. One such petitioner, a wealthy prince from Thrace, asked if his contemplated invasion of Persia would prove successful. The response was that as a result of the action he was about to undertake, a great empire would fall. The prince confidently led his army into battle and was badly defeated. Ruined and disillusioned he returned to Delphi and demanded to know what went wrong. As a result of your action, a mighty empire fell, the priest replied; we did not say that it would be the *Persian* Empire.

From 776 B.C. until the Christians took over the Roman Empire some thousand years later, competitive athletic contests were held every four years at the village of Olympia in southern Greece. Besides sports, Greeks from all over the Mediterranean world vied with one another for trophies in drama, music, and oratory. Distinguished visitors from foreign lands, such as the Sicilian, Gorgias of Leontini, were invited to address the assembled multitude.[10] Each city state had its own treasure house for the series of events often took weeks at a time. So much a part of the Greek world were these Olympic games that warring cities would declare a truce so they could compete peacefully with one another and resume battle once competitive activities ceased.

Of the many uses of the spoken word in ancient Athens, none was more important than education. Athenian boys were trained orally by private tutors. They learned music, reading, writing, and gymnastics in this way.[11] The dialogue method of question and answer was reserved for advanced work. At the start of the fifth century, B.C., an information explosion took place in Ionia and on the islands near Asia Minor. In Athens, there was keen interest in higher education and in the new discoveries. The need to disseminate this knowledge and to offer advanced work was met by a band of wandering teachers who travelled by foot from one city state to another offering short courses for a fee.[12] These itinerant professors were called *sophists,* after the Greek word *sophos* meaning knowledge. Their function was to supplement the elementary instruction of the day. Fluent lecturers with excellent memories, the Greek sophists offered courses in rhetoric, grammar, art, drama, architecture, mathematics, poetry, literature, and various other branches of knowledge. The later fall of the sophists was partly due, Plato tells us in one of his dialogues, to the use of rhetoric as mere flattery and as a vehicle for misleading others.[13] If happiness meant a life founded on truth, sophists who disregarded the truth and made the worse appear the better cause were evil-doers, clever but specious reasoners. Sophistic education was also an expensive luxury few common citizens could afford. Some sophists were suspect as agnostics who preferred man rather than god as the measure of all

things. Others offered instruction on any subject at all for a fee and many promised more than they could deliver. For all these reasons sophistic education declined in importance early in the fourth century, B.C.

Athenian society was oriented to the spoken word; hence the study of rational discourse, of oral persuasion, and of drama was a natural outgrowth of Greek curiosity and inventiveness. Dialectic, rhetoric, and poetics were the terms the Greeks used for such studies. As we would expect in such a society, Greek rhetoric encompassed a variety of speech settings. Legal speaking in the law courts was referred to as forensic discourse; political speaking such as that which occurred in the Athenian Assembly was called deliberative; occasional ceremonial speeches were labelled epideictic. Greek interest in the language with which to clothe ideas produced a plain, middle, and grand style of address.[14] The perfect speaker was conceived of as bright, honest, and socially responsible, a man of truth and reason who could, when occasion demanded, move the mind and passions of his listeners.

The orator-general, Pericles, was just such a leader. Remarkably adept at political persuasion, Pericles succeeded in having the war treasury of the Delian defense league transferred from its island home to Athens for safekeeping. He then convinced his fellow Athenians to use these war funds for peaceful purposes by re-building the Acropolis, earlier destroyed by a Persian army. Pericles' dream was of structures made to last centuries, marble temples to dazzle and fascinate mankind for thousands of years. He secured the services of the best artisans known to man. And he presided over the entire grand operation for the better part of thirty years. If we would know what the Golden Age of Pericles was like, we need only look at the Parthenon in downtown Athens. A temple dedicated to the patron goddess Athena (whose forty-foot ivory and gold statue it housed), the Parthenon is one of the man-made wonders of the world—a living testimonial to the power of the spoken word.

Of the many Greek orators of note, two particularly merit our attention. The first was a man of great natural talent, a soldier-athlete, who began life as a teacher's aide in his father's school. Aeschines by name, this eloquent Greek was a professional actor of considerable ability. He was chosen as court clerk, a position of responsibility, and represented Athens in an important diplomatic mission to Philip of Macedon. Aeschines was graceful of movement, an easy, fluent speaker to whom success seemed to come without effort. He was, in short, naturally talented. As one who chose the course of political expediency, Aeschines was often in the public eye, a popular, if not always credible, leader.

In contrast stood Demosthenes, acclaimed by many as the world's greatest orator.[15] Demosthenes began life so inauspiciously we would today think of him as a "born loser." He was a sickly child who could not participate in athletic games like other youths. His patrimony was squandered by unscrupulous guardians and though he ultimately defeated them after five separate trials, he was penniless at the time of the final verdict. Demosthenes yearned to play a major role in the affairs of his city state but he labored under an awesome series of handicaps: a weak voice, awkward movement, sloppy diction, a lateral lisp, shortness of breath, and a tendency to compose long sentences, ill-suited for oral presentation. It is said that when he first spoke in the Athenian Assembly, men laughed at his fumbling ways and he retired in shame. Failure might deter a lesser man but not Demosthenes. He dreamed of fame and fortune and he meant to have both.

Legend tells us that an actor instructed him in voice and physical action.[16] To overcome his lisp, Demosthenes spoke with pebbles in his mouth. To project his voice, he delivered speeches by the seashore, shouting above the crashing waves. To strengthen his breath, he declaimed orations while running uphill. To strengthen his will to succeed, he shaved half his head so that he could no longer appear in public and could thus undertake his studies unmolested in a hidden cave. Demosthenes, to a large degree, represented the triumph of nurture over nature.

Demosthenes and Aeschines were political and oratorical rivals whose final confrontation came in 330 B.C. in a famous trial known as the case "On the Crown." A well-meaning friend proposed that the Athenian Assembly award Demosthenes a golden crown for public service to the state.[17] The friend recommended that the crown be bestowed at the Theater of Dionysius where a large assembly of citizens and foreigners could observe the ceremony. Aeschines, who barely won a bribery suit brought against him by Demosthenes several years before, now saw his chance for revenge. He contested the crown on three bases: first, that Demosthenes could not receive such an award because the books he kept as a financial offical had not yet been audited; second, that Athenian law required citizen honors to be given before the Assembly rather than at the Theater specified; and third, that Demosthenes did not deserve such an award for he had not always had Athens' best interests in mind.

Technically, Aeschines was in the right on the first two charges. Athenian law stipulated that unaudited officials were not eligible to receive public honors and that when public awards were given, they were to be awarded before the Assembly itself. But the critical issue was the third and it was here that Demosthenes was to score his greatest victory. His problem was one of self-vindication: how does a public man defend himself when his advice proves costly in men and property? For many years Demosthenes urged his fellow citizens to oppose Philip of Macedon—the father of Alexander the Great. Finally, they did so and were soundly defeated. How then could this advocate of defeat win an audience to his cause when many of his listeners counted relatives among the fallen?

The case Demosthenes devised has won the admiration of such diverse contemporary leaders as Ted Kennedy and Richard Nixon. Knowing that his listeners would be annoyed by self-praise, Demosthenes coupled his political career with the course taken by their ancestors. What he advised, their parents endorsed. To reject Demosthenes meant to reject what most recognized as the best of the Athenian past. The vindictive oratory of Aeschines was simply no match for Demosthenes' brilliant strategy. Heavily fined because he failed to get even one fifth of the jury's vote, Aeschines retired in defeat to Rhodes. Exile from the mother city, Athenians believed, was a fate worse than death.

The military defeat of the Greek city states by Philip of Macedon in 338 B.C. brought with it a dramatic change in Greek thinking. Forced at last into a pan-Hellenic mold, the Greeks now found themselves part of a much larger world. In the new Macedonian society, the individual citizen was no longer king. Greek philosophers sought to ease this dissonant situation in two ways.[18] The first involved reducing the importance of the world around the Greeks. This approach was championed by a thinker named Epicurus. By non-involvement in public affairs, the individual Greek could achieve a state of tranquility, of apathy or nonconcern. He could avoid pain simply by entering a non-feeling state. Epicureans defined pleasure not as physical indulgence and sexual license but as the absence of pain in the body or trouble in the mind. Satisfying momentary needs was essential; community involvement was not.

A second popular philosophy of the day was called stoicism, after the porch where Zeno and his followers roamed. Wisdom and self-control lay at the heart of this school of thought. The stoics declared there was a basic order to the universe, knowable to man. An individual achieved happiness by discovering this order or pattern and conforming to it. At various times, the pattern was referred to as nature, providence, the cosmos, god, reason, and law. The stoic was unaffected by such externals as wealth, beauty, and power. Conformity to the plan of the universe, even if this involved suffering, guided his behavior.

Greek stoics interpreted the Roman conquest of the Mediterranean world as the divine plan of life. Later when Christianity became the state religion in Rome, its ready acceptance throughout the Roman Empire was assured. Thus, a pagan Greek philosophy paved the way for the expansion of the Christian religion.

If the culture of Greece contributed to the development of a viable and enduring rhetoric, so, too, did the setting which surrounded the Romans. Central Italy is blessed with a warm climate and fertile plains. Life is easy there as it had been earlier in ancient Egypt. Captive slaves did a thousand manual tasks, freeing the wealthy for entertainment and capricious whim. One of the Caesars, for example, liked horse races so much he set legions of workers to the task of creating a hippodrome in his back yard—a five story excavation and race course viewable to the tourist today on Palatine Hill. The Romans founded a vast empire that lasted a thousand years. Their mother city became the dominant center of Western civilization, a far more powerful metropolis than Athens had ever been.

Practicality dominated Roman thought. In order to control a vast empire from the steppes of Russia to the shores of the Atlantic the Romans created a powerful army, an efficient bureaucracy, and a set of universal laws. They also constructed a connecting network of all-weather roads and a system of aqueducts to carry water to inland towns far from river or sea. The Caesars sought to provide the citizens of Rome itself with spectacular diversions, so they built eight coliseums in addition to the one which still stands at one end of the Forum.[19] Here the people witnessed such spectacles as chariot races, naval battles, fights to the death among powerful animals and, of course, the confrontation of lions and early Christians. Inside plumbing and outside sewers were Roman inventions, too.[20] Remnant Greek temples were refurbished to become modern Roman temples and later, Christian churches. No structure went to waste when the Romans controlled the Mediterranean world.

The Romans found much to admire in Greek culture and they borrowed generously. Rhetoric struck them as a more practical art than philosophy, for their Republic was modeled after the Athenian city state. The twelve Greek gods became twelve Roman gods. Roman youth were taught by Greek tutors, thus insuring the preservation of much of earlier Greek civilization. Homer's epic poems inspired Virgil's *Aeneid*. Roman dramatists copied Greek dramatists. Roman history, architecture, philosophy—all contained much that was Greek in origin.

But the Romans were more than just borrowers. They were classifiers and refiners. They preserved and transmitted the heart of Hellenic civilization to the wide world they conquered, and later this same Roman network served the cause of Christianity, for it was the Romans who brought the new religion to Britain and Africa, Babylon and Scandinavia.

In the realm of education, Isocrates' Greek system of liberal arts wedded to the spoken word became the pattern everywhere. In Rome as in Athens earlier, the philosopher-orator became the ideal citizen. Cicero was the Latin embodiment of the ideal. A brilliant speaker, a lifelong student of philosophy and liberal studies, a clever politician, ambitious, expedient, marvelously literate and articulate, Cicero epitomized the Roman Republic a half century before Christ. When he desired to study rhetoric and philosophy, he sailed east to Athens and Rhodes. Demosthenes, he perceived as the greatest of the Greek orators; men would later debate whether Cicero himself surpassed Athens' favorite son. Greek teachers, Greek ideals, Greek philosophy, Greek gods adopted with little or no change—that was the Roman way.[21]

The treatment presented here of Roman culture is admittedly brief. A helpful overview of that culture can be found in Edith Hamilton's *The Roman Way to Western Civilization* (1932; available in recent paperback reprint), a companion volume to her *Greek Way* mentioned earlier. M. L. Clarke's *Rhetoric at Rome* (1953) provides the interested reader with a coherent specialized treatment.

In 292 B.C. Egyptian and Greek scholars at the great library at Alexandria began the mammoth job of preservation, classification, and refinement of Greek culture. Here for the first time ever an authoritative text of Homer's *Iliad* was written down. Here were deposited and catalogued Aristotle's encyclopedic studies, including the *Rhetoric* salvaged by a Roman general from a cellar in Asia Minor. The concept of stock issues applicable in trial settings was identified here for the first time. Such central turning points in a criminal case included the following: that an alleged crime was committed, that the alleged act caused harm, that the harm was less than the prosecution charged, and that the alleged act was justified.

The *Rhetorica ad Herenium,* written in the first century, B.C., is the earliest Latin rhetoric of which we have knowledge. Characteristically, it is Greek to the core and tersely practical.[22] Here in this schoolboy manual we encounter for the first time the five great canons of classical rhetoric: *inventio, dispositio, elocutio, memoria,* and *pronuntiatio.* In order to compose an effective speech, the speaker must first choose an appropriate topic. Then he must identify the whole range of relevant ideas and supporting evidence available. This initial process of discovery the Romans labelled *inventio;* modern rhetoricians call it invention. Next the speaker must select from the whole spectrum of ideas available to him those which best meet the needs of purpose, audience, and occasion. Further, he must arrange them in a sequence both clear and memorable. Then the speaker must determine the amount of detail needed for the proofs he intends to employ. Selection, sequence, and apportionment were what the Romans call *dispositio;* modern speech communication scholars prefer the term speech organization. *Elocutio* refers to style, to the words and rhetorical devices the speaker uses to clothe his ideas. *Memoria* or memory embraces the mental process of recall. In a day when manuscript speeches were drafted *after* a speech was delivered, when the question demanded discourse hours in length, memorization was a necessary skill for the orator. The Greeks and Romans like today's college students recognized the value of code words, mnemonic devices designed to aid instant recall. Finally, the Romans stressed *pronuntiatio* or delivery. Here they meant the speaker's voice and physical action. To Roman theorists rhetoric was one great art, composed of five lesser arts.

The Romans made other contributions to rhetorical theory as well. In contrast to Aristotle and the Greeks, they stressed the impact of the speaker's prior reputation upon his listeners.[23] The speaker, they noted should adjust his material to the audience *while speaking* rather than serving as a slave to a set speech memorized earlier. In a court of law, the speaker should focus his attention upon the key issue in the case rather than provide equal stress to each argument he advanced. Like the Greeks, the Romans recognized the importance of emotion in persuasion, but what was new was their emphasis upon a moving peroration, an end to the speech deliberately calculated to influence the feelings of listeners throughout the audience.

The Roman lawyer-rhetorician, Quintilian, compiled a four-volume work on rhetoric which embodied a system of education from the cradle to the grave. So systematic was Quintilian's *Institutes of Oratory* that it served as the model for much of medieval education throughout Europe.[24] Clarity of language was stressed to the point where misunderstanding was virtually impossible. The apprenticeship of student speakers to master orators was encouraged in much the same way as masons and carpenters learned their trade. As a rule, Roman rhetoricians were better at amplification than innovation. Greek ideas became Roman ideas, often with little or no credit being given to the original source.

Broadly speaking, speech theorists in Greece and Rome viewed the subject of rhetoric in one of three ways: as a moral instrument for conveying truth to the masses, as a culturally important subject which merited scientific classification and analysis, and as practical training essential for the active citizen. Plato typified the first view; Aristotle, the second; and Isocrates, Cicero, and Quintilian, the third.[25] Let us turn now to a sampling of the views of each.

Notes

1. The above description is based on the following sources: Professor Berquist's travels in Greece in the spring of 1971; Walter Agard, *What Democracy Meant to the Greeks* (Madison, Wisconsin: University of Wisconsin Press, 1960 reprint of 1942 edition); C. M. Bowra et al, *Classical Greece* (New York: Time, Inc. Great Ages of Man series, 1965); *Greece and Rome: Builders of Our World* (National Geographic Book Service, 1968).
2. Cf. especially chaps. I and XVI in E. Hamilton, *The Greek Way to Western Civilization* (New York: Mentor reprint of 1930 edition; 1960).
3. R. C. Jebb, *The Rhetoric of Aristotle: A Translation* (Cambridge: University Press, 1909), pp. 16–18. Unless otherwise noted, further quotations from Aristotle's *Rhetoric* come from this source.
4. C. C. Arnold, D. Ehninger and J. C. Gerber, *The Speaker's Resource Book* (Chicago: Scott, Foresman, 1961), p. 218.
5. Cf. William M. Sattler, "Conceptions of Ethos in Ancient Rhetoric," *Speech Monographs,* 14 (1947), 55–65.
6. Some observers assumed Homer's poems were fiction. For a quite different view, see M. B. Grosvenor, "Homeward with Ulysses," *Nat. Geog. M.,* 144, 1 (July, 1973), 1–39.
7. For a fuller account of Corax's activities, see Bromley Smith, "Corax and Probability," *Quarterly Journal of Speech,* 7, 1 (Feb., 1921), 13–42.
8. Cf. James G. Greenwood, "The Legal Setting of Attic Oratory," *Central States Speech Journal,* 23, 3 (Fall, 1972), 182, *et passim.*
9. Agard, *What Democracy Meant to the Greeks,* p. 70, *et passium.*
10. Cf. Bromley Smith, "Gorgias: A Study of Oratorical Style," *Quarterly Journal of Speech,* 7, 4 (Nov., 1921), 335–59.
11. D. L. Clark, *Rhetoric in Greco–Roman Education* (New York: Columbia University Press, 1957), p. 21.
12. Bromley Smith's studies of the sophists, published in the *Quarterly Journal of Speech,* included the following: Protagoras (Mar., 1918), Prodicus (Apr., 1920), Corax (Feb., 1921), Gorgias (Nov., 1921), Hippias (June, 1926), Thrasymachus (June, 1927), and Theodorus (Feb., 1928).
13. Plato, *Gorgias,* trans. by W. R. M. Lamb (Cambridge, Massachusetts: Harvard University Press, 1967), *passim.*
14. George Kennedy, *The Art of Persuasion in Greece* (Princeton, N.J.: Princeton University Press, 1963), p. 12, *et passim.* Cf. also the comprehensive work of R. C. Jebb, *The Attic Orators from Antiphon to Isaeus* (London: Macmillan, 2nd ed., 1893, 2 vols.).
15. For an enlightening account of the rivalry between Aeschines and Demosthenes, see *Demosthenes' On the Crown: A Critical Case Study of a Masterpiece of Ancient Oratory,* ed. by James J. Murphy (New York: Random House, 1967).
16. *Plutarch's Lives,* trans. Bernadotte Perrin (Cambridge, Mass.: Harvard University Press, 1967), p. 17ff
17. Demosthenes' friend, Ctesiphon, proposed the crown in 336 B.C. but the trial was repeatedly postponed.
18. The authors are indebted at this point to the research of Mr. James Dennison.
19. The other eight were destroyed because Christians were sacrificed to lions in their arenas.
20. The best view of a restored Roman city we have is ancient Pompeii, south of Naples. This thriving Roman

community was buried under volcanic ash in 79 A.D., and later discovered at the time of the American Revolution. Even today there remains considerable work for the archaeologist at Pompeii.

21. Cf. Edith Hamilton, *The Roman Way to Western Civilization* (New York, N.Y.: Mentor, 1961 reprint of 1932 ed.).

22. *Rhetorica ad Herennium,* trans. Harry Caplan (Cambridge, Mass.: Harvard University Press, 1968).

23. Jebb, *Aristotle's Rhetoric,* p. 6.

24. Cf. Harold F. Harding, "Quintilian's Witnesses," *Speech Monographs,* 1 (1934), 1–20.

25. The authors are indebted to Donald Lemen Clark for this three fold designation of classical rhetorical theory. See his *Rhetoric in Greco-Roman Education,* pp. 24–25.

3

Plato's Moral-Philosophical View of Rhetoric

Plato was the father of Western philosophy, a wealthy Athenian who rejected the customary practices of his own society. He perfectly symbolized the Greek spirit of inquiry and the Academy which he founded in 387 B.C. was to continue functioning for a thousand years. When Plato started his school, the prevailing mode of higher education in Athens was sophistic. The new professor was anxious, therefore, to establish his uniqueness, to distinguish his brand of learning from that already offered. A talented literary artist, Plato chose the medium of the dialogue. What he did was to compose a series of fictional conversations based on philosophical problems he deemed important. These dialogues which invariably featured his friend, Socrates, as the questioning hero were advertisements for the Academy, persuasive previews of the instruction which awaited the interested student. Apparently they accomplished this end for the Academy soon had a goodly number of students.[1]

The Gorgias: A Study of False Rhetoric. One of Plato's earliest dialogues was that known as the *Gorgias*. The principal character, Gorgias of Leontini, was a famous Sicilian sophist who introduced argument from probability and a florid style of rhetoric to Athens. Legend has it that Gorgias was sent to Athens as an ambassador and so charmed the Athenians that they persuaded him to remain in their city and instruct their sons in rhetoric. Using literary license, Plato makes Gorgias and his friends the butt of Socrates' ridicule. The Sicilian sophist was pictured as a speaker more concerned with form than content, one who recommended a rhetoric of appearance rather than of reality.

In the *Gorgias,* Plato "undertakes to refute the claims made for rhetoric by Gorgias, Polus, and Callicles."[2] He then proceeds to define the rhetorical practice of his day as "the art of persuading an ignorant multitude about the justice or injustice of a matter, without imparting any real instruction."[3] As the dialogue unfolds, Socrates presents four arguments attacking the utility of rhetoric:

1. "Rhetoric is not an art."
2. "Rhetoric does not confer power."
3. "Rhetoric as a protection against suffering wrong is of little importance."
4. "Rhetoric as a means of escaping a deserved punishment is not to be commended."[4]

Quite clearly what Plato sought to accomplish in this dialogue was to set forth the parameters of false rhetoric that typified much of Greek public discourse in the 4th century, B.C.

In order to see how the arguments establishing the nature of false rhetoric unfold in the *Gorgias,* we present the following passages featuring a discussion between the youthful Polus and Socrates.

Polus: I will ask; and do you answer me, Socrates, the same question which Gorgias, as you suppose, is unable to answer: What is rhetoric?

Socrates: Do you mean what sort of an art?

Polus: Yes.

Socrates: Not an art at all, in my opinion, if I am to tell you the truth, Polus.

Polus: Then what, in your opinion, is rhetoric?

Socrates: A thing which, in the treatise that I was lately reading of yours, you affirm to have created art.

Polus: What thing?

Socrates: I should say a sort of routine or experience.

Polus: Then does rhetoric seem to you to be a sort of experience?

Socrates: That is my view, if that is yours.

Polus: An experience of what?

Socrates: An experience of making a sort of delight and gratification.

Polus: And if able to gratify others, must not rhetoric be a fine thing?

Socrates: What are you saying, Polus? Why do you ask me whether rhetoric is a fine thing or not, when I have not as yet told you what rhetoric is?

Polus: why, did you not tell me that rhetoric was a sort of experience?

Socrates: As you are so fond of gratifying others, will you gratify me in a small particular?

Polus: I will.

Socrates: Will you ask me, what sort of an art is cookery?

Polus: What sort of an art is cookery?

Socrates: Not an art at all, Polus.

Polus: What then?

Socrates: I should say a sort of experience.

Polus: Of what? I wish that you would tell me.

Socrates: An experience of making a sort of delight and gratification, Polus.

Polus: Then are cookery and rhetoric the same?

Socrates: No, they are only different parts of the same profession.

Polus: And what is that?

Socrates: I am afraid that the truth may seem discourteous; I should not like Gorgias to imagine that I am ridiculing his profession, and therefore I hesitate to answer. For whether or no this is that art of rhetoric which Gorgias practices I really do not know: from what he was just now saying, nothing appeared of what he thought of his art, but the rhetoric which I mean is a part of a not very creditable whole.

Gorgias: A part of what, Socrates? Say what you mean, and never mind me.

Socrates: To me then, Gorgias, the whole of which rhetoric is a part appears to be a process, not of art, but the habit of a bold and ready wit, which knows how to behave to the world: this I sum up under the word 'flattery'; and this habit or process appears to me to have many other parts, one of which is cookery, which may seem to be an art, and, as I maintain, is not an art, but only experience and routine: another part is rhetoric, and the art of tiring [i.e. attiring, dress] and sophistic are two others: thus there are four branches, and four different things answering to them. And Polus may ask, if he likes, for he has not as yet been informed, what part of flattery is rhetoric: he did not see that I had not yet answered him when he proceeded to ask a further question,—Whether I do not think rhetoric a fine thing? But I shall not tell him whether rhetoric is a fine thing or not, until I have first answered, 'What is rhetoric?' For that would not be right, Polus; but I shall be happy to answer, if you will ask me, What part of flattery is rhetoric?

Polus: I will ask, and do you answer: What part of flattery is rhetoric?

Socrates: Will you understand my answer? Rhetoric, according to my view, is |the shadow of a part of politics.

Polus: And noble or ignoble?

Socrates: Ignoble, as I should say, if I am compelled to answer, for I call what is bad ignoble. . . .[5]

Initially, then, Plato rejected rhetoric as a knack comparable to cookery, and as a form of flattery designed to gratify the mob. Rhetoric, in short, was a pseudo-art of appearances rather than a vehicle for conveying truth.[6] In a way his criticism is still relevant. All of us can think of instances in which speech is used to deceive and disguise. The demagogue who pursues his own goals instead of the best interests of his followers is a case in point. So, too, is the salesman who is more interested in making a commission than in satisfying the needs of his customers.

The model which appears on p. 48 should help the reader visualize the essential elements of this dialogue.

The Phaedrus: A Study of True Rhetoric. Plato's second dialogue on rhetoric, the *Phaedrus,* is of greater importance to us for it is here that the most eminent of the Greek philosophers articulates what he terms a "true rhetoric" in contrast to the "false rhetoric" he ridiculed earlier. Before proceeding to an analysis of this dialogue, let us review briefly Plato's theory of truth. To Plato, truth was the only reality in life. Truth existed, he thought, as an idea in the minds of gods; thus truth partook of the divine. He illustrated this notion in his most famous philosophical work, *The Republic.* There are, Socrates observes in this dialogue, three types or levels of beds or tables. First in priority ranking is the concept of bed or table which exists in pure form in the minds of gods. Second is that created by the carpenter. Third is the picture of bed or table portrayed by the artist. Since the painter, therefore, is two steps removed from the perfect idea upheld by deity, he tends to rely on imperfect images of reality. What applies to painters and other artists also applies to poets and rhetoricians, for they, too, are two steps from certain knowledge. Thus they are ruled out of the ideal republic.[7] There truth articulated by "philosopher kings" would guide every decision.

The format of the *Phaedrus* is based on a series of three speeches about love. The technique Plato used here was the literary device known as the allegory, a story with a double meaning. Plato's phrase "love" is identified with rhetoric; thus the main theme of this dialogue is " the art of speaking."[8]

The scene involves two characters, Socrates and Phaedrus, who chance to meet one day on the outskirts of Athens. Phaedrus has just heard what he considers to be an exceptional speech on love and is anxious to share its contents with his older friend, Socrates. The two agree to sit beneath a shade tree by a stream where they may pursue their discussion in leisurely comfort.

The speech which caught Phaedrus' attention, Plato tells us, was presented by Lysias, a well-known Athenian orator of the day. Lysias took the position that "people should grant favors to non-lovers rather than lovers," that is that we ought to prefer a neuter brand of speech or rhetoric to that which arouses our thoughts or feeling.[9] So, the best language is that which generates no response or interest at all, according to this view. The value judgments of good and bad we daily pronounce should be eliminated from our language so that our discourse becomes semantically pure. Scientific report writing and the prose style used in business letters become the ideal; connotative language and the language of abstraction are to be avoided at all cost. Lysias' non-lover becomes the modern day objective reporter whose task is to describe and record, not to interpret or evaluate.

In his essay entitled, "The *Phaedrus* and the Nature of Rhetoric," Richard Weaver notes "there are but three ways for language to affect us. It can move us toward what is good; it can move us toward what is evil; or it can in hypothetical third place, fail to move us at all."[10] Plato's non-lover is the speaker who fails "to move us at all."

A second speech on love which appears in the dialogue is delivered by Socrates who feels Lysias' speech is so specialized as to be misleading. Accordingly the theme of this second speech is that love is a form of exploitation. The evil lover seeks to make the object of his attentions depend upon him and is jealous of any possible outside influence. Rhetorically speaking, the evil lover is one who uses language to enslave and deceive another. The mortician who sells a widow a casket for her husband more expensive than she can afford and the real estate agent who sells customers houses some thousand of dollars above their capacity to pay are cases in point. The evil lover, the base rhetorician, is out to serve him-

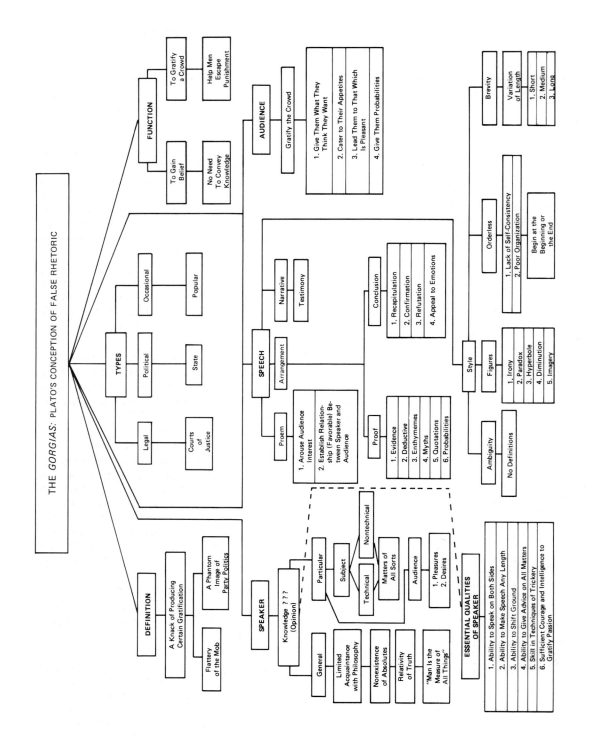

THE *GORGIAS*: PLATO'S CONCEPTION OF FALSE RHETORIC

FUNCTION

To Gratify a Crowd
- Help Men Escape Punishment

To Gain Belief
- No Need To Convey Knowledge

AUDIENCE

Gratify the Crowd
1. Give Them What They Think They Want
2. Cater to Their Appetites
3. Lead Them to That Which Is Pleasant
4. Give Them Probabilities

TYPES

Legal
- Courts of Justice

Political
- State

Occasional
- Popular

SPEECH

Arrangement

Proem
1. Arouse Audience Interest
2. Establish Relationship (Favorable) Between Speaker and Audience

Proof
1. Evidence
2. Deductive
3. Enthymemes
4. Myths
5. Quotations
6. Probabilities

Narrative
Testimony

Conclusion
1. Recapitulation
2. Confirmation
3. Refutation
4. Appeal to Emotions

Style

Ambiguity
- No Definitions

Figures
1. Irony
2. Paradox
3. Hyperbole
4. Diminution
5. Imagery

Orderless
1. Lack of Self-Consistency
2. Poor Organization
- Begin at the Beginning or the End

Brevity

Variation of Length
1. Short
2. Medium
3. Long

DEFINITION

Flattery of the Mob

A Knack of Producing Certain Gratification

A Phantom Image of Party Politics

SPEAKER

Knowledge ? ? ? (Opinion)

General
- Limited Acquaintance with Philosophy
- Nonexistence of Absolutes
- Relativity of Truth
- "Man Is the Measure of All Things"

Particular

Subject
- Technical
- Nontechnical
- Matters of All Sorts

Audience
1. Pleasures
2. Desires

ESSENTIAL QUALITIES OF SPEAKER
1. Ability to Speak on Both Sides
2. Ability to Make Speech Any Length
3. Ability to Shift Ground
4. Ability to Give Advice on All Matters
5. Skill in Techniques of Trickery
6. Sufficient Courage and Intelligence to Gratify Passion

self. Colorful language laden with emotional appeal and spurious arguments are the tools he uses to sell his product. Distortion and delusion typify his approach. Anything goes as long as he gets *his* way. It is this type of lover, this abusive user of rhetoric who gives persuasion its devilish, manipulative image. Those who make the worse appear the better cause, bad men skilled in speech, receive our condemnation today as they did in Plato's time. To cite only one recent example, governmental officials who make firm declarations and later label them "inoperative" insure our distrust and contempt.

In the first two speeches, Plato's view of love is incomplete, for most Greeks believed love to be a quality possessed by the gods. There must, therefore, be a third speech and indeed there is. Socrates proceeds to describe the noble lover, the skillful user of language, as one who seeks that which is best for his listeners rather than for himself. The attitude of the noble lover is the antithesis of that of the evil lover. His is a kind of "inspired madness," Plato tells us, for he ignores self-interest. Instead he uses language to teach and inspire, to reveal rather than conceal truth and value. Here, for example, is the wartime rhetoric of Winston Churchill or the presidential wisdom of an Abraham Lincoln. Here is virtue conjoined with eloquence, sublime oratory, superlative prose. The noble lover is Plato's ideal speaker, a rhetorician at once welcome in his ideal state. He is the conveyor and preserver of truth and morality. Moral users of language may never exist in great number but they are the pillars of a healthy society. Indeed in Plato's view, the noble lover approached divinity.

At the close of the lengthy dialogue on the three lovers and their corresponding relationship to three types of speakers, Socrates and Phaedrus attempt to put true rhetoric into perspective. The flow of thought may be seen in the ensuing excerpt:

Phaedrus: Let us talk.

Socrates: Shall we discuss the rules of writing and speech as we were proposing?

Phaedrus: Very good.

Socrates: Is not the first rule of good speaking that the mind of the speaker should know the truth of what he is going to say?

Phaedrus: And yet, Socrates, I have heard that he who would be an orator has nothing to do with true justice, but only with that which is likely to be approved by the many who sit in judgment; nor with the truly good or honorable, but only with public opinion about them, and that from this source and not from the truth come the elements of persuasion.

Socrates: Any words of the wise ought to be regarded and not trampled under foot, for there is probably something in them, and perhaps there may be something in this which is worthy of attention.

Phaedrus: Very true.

Socrates: Let us put the matter thus: Suppose that I persuaded you to buy a horse and go to the wars. Neither of us knew what a horse was like, but I knew that you believed a horse to be the longest-eared of domestic animals.

Phaedrus: That would be ridiculous.

Socrates: There is something more ridiculous coming. Suppose, now, that I was in earnest and went and composed a speech in honor of an ass, whom I entitled a horse, beginning: "A noble animal and a most useful possession, especially in war, and you may get on his back and fight, and he will carry baggage or anything."

Phaedrus: That would be most ridiculous.

Socrates: Ridiculous! Yes; but is not even a ridiculous friend better than a dangerous enemy?

Phaedrus: Certainly.

Socrates: And when the orator instead of putting an ass in the place of a horse, puts good for evil, being himself as ignorant of their true nature as the city on which he imposes is ignorant; and having studied the notions of the multitude, persuades them to do evil instead of good,—what will be the harvest which rhetoric will be like to gather after the sowing of that fruit?

Phaedrus: Anything but good.

Socrates: Perhaps, however, Rhetoric has been getting too roughly handled by us, and she might answer: What amazing nonsense is this! As if I forced any man to learn to speak in ignorance of the truth! Whatever my advice may be worth, I should have told him to arrive at the truth first, and then come to me. At the same time I boldly assert that mere knowledge of the truth will not give you the art of persuasion.

Phaedrus: There is reason in the lady's defense of herself.

Socrates: Yes, I admit that, if the arguments which she has yet in store bear witness that she is an art at all. But I seem to hear them arraying themselves on the opposite side, declaring that she speaks not true, and the Rhetoric is not an art but only a dilettante amusement. Lo! a Spartan appears, and says that there never is nor ever will be a real art of speaking which is unconnected with the truth.

Phaedrus: And what are these arguments, Socrates? Bring them out that we may examine them.

Socrates: Come out, children of my soul, and convince Phaedrus, who is the father of similar beauties, that he will never be able to speak about anything unless he be trained in philosophy. And let Phaedrus answer you.[11]

Following the above exchange, Socrates offers a summary of his principal arguments delineating a true rhetoric.

Until a man knows the truth of the several particulars of which he is writing or speaking, and is able to define them as they are, and having defined them again to divide them until they can be no longer divided, and until in like manner he is able to discern the nature of the soul and discover the different modes of discourse which are adapted to different natures, and to arrange and dispose them in such a way that the simple form of speech may be addressed to the simpler nature, and the complex and composite to the complex nature—until he has accomplished all this, he will be unable to handle arguments according to rules of art, as far as their nature allows them to be subjected to art, either for the purpose of teaching or persuading; that is the view which is implied in the whole preceding argument.[12]

Two twentieth-century scholars have summed up the *Phaedrus* in a clear and precise manner. "The central idea [of the *Phaedrus*]," Richard Weaver observed, "is that all speech, which is the means the gods have given man to express his soul, is a form of eros, in the proper interpretation of the word. With that truth the rhetorician will always be brought face to face as soon as he ventures beyond the consideration of mere artifice and device."[13] Twenty-eight years before Weaver's analysis, Everett Lee Hunt, then Dean of Swarthmore College, presented the following seven points as a summary statement of Plato's suggestions in the *Phaedrus* "for the organization of rhetoric into a scientific body of knowledge":

1. "The first rule of good speaking is that the mind of the speaker should know the truth of what he is going to say." This cannot be interpreted as an injunction to speak the truth at all times. It is rather to *know* the truth in order (a) to be persuasive by presenting to the audience something which at least resembles truth, and (b) to avoid being oneself deceived by probabilities. In order to know the truth, the rhetorician must be a philosopher.

2. The rhetorician must define his terms, and see clearly what subjects are debatable and what are not. He must be able to classify particulars under a general head, or to break up universals into particulars. The rhetorician, then, must be a logician.

3. Principles of order and arrangement must be introduced. "Every discourse ought to be a living creature, having its own body and head and feet; there ought to be a

middle, beginning and end, which are in a manner agreeable to one another and to the whole."

4. The nature of the soul must be shown, and after having "arranged men and speeches, and their modes and affections in different classes, and fitted them into one another, he will point out the connection between them—he will show why one is naturally persuaded by a particular of argument, and another not." In other words, the rhetorician must be a psychologist.

5. The rhetorician must "speak of the instruments by which the soul acts or is affected in any way." Here we have the division under which comes practically all of rhetoric when viewed more narrowly and technically. The "instruments" by which rhetoric affects the soul are style and delivery. Plato believed style to be acquired, however, as Pericles acquired it, by "much discussion and lofty contemplation of nature."

6. The art of writing will not be highly regarded; nor will continuous and uninterrupted discourse be regarded as equal to cross-examination as a means of instruction. This is Plato's way of saying that any method of attempting to persuade multitudes must suffer from the very fact that it is a multitude which is addressed, and that the best of rhetoric is unequal to philosophic discussion.

7. The rhetorician will have such a high moral purpose in all his work that he will ever be chiefly concerned about saying that which is "acceptable to God." Rhetoric, then, is not an instrument for the determination of scientific truth, nor for mere persuasion regardless of the cause; it is an instrument for making the will of God prevail. The perfect rhetorician, as a philospher, knows the will of God.[14]

A diagram of Plato's conception of true rhetoric as depicted in the *Phaedrus* may take the form as shown on p. 52.

In sum, Plato in these well known works conceived of two different types of rhetoric. The first or "false rhetoric," he perceived as all too common in the Athenian society around him. This rhetoric he rejected as showy in appearance, self-serving, and artificial. The second or "true rhetoric" he himself exemplified. The rhetoric he embraced was truthful, self-effacing, and real. Plato's noble lover was part philosopher, part logician, part psychologist. He must know the truth. He must be a master of dialectic, the Platonic instrument for the discovery and dissemination of the truth. And he must understand the human soul in order that he may appeal to the better side of mankind. The moral rhetoric of Plato as conceived in the *Phaedrus* continues to represent an ideal for all of us, even though history demonstrates the ideal is seldom achieved.

Plato's Other Dialogues. As the foregoing discussion suggests, Plato turned his full attention to rhetoric, pointing out both its shortcomings and its potential in the *Gorgias* and the *Phaedrus*. But it would be a mistake to consider these dialogues as constituting all that Plato had to say about rhetoric as a field of study. We have found that the general subject of rhetoric is featured with varying degrees of emphasis in every dialogue that Plato wrote.[15] In these writings he touched on all aspects of human discourse. Insights on the nature of eloquence, the need for ethics in communication, and the use of pathos are discussed in the *Apology;* rhetoric as a means of generating meaning and knowledge in *Cratylus;* criticism and taste, speech introductions, ethos, humor, and persuasion in *Laws;* learning as recollection in *Meno;* first principles and dimensions of intrapersonal communication in *Phaedo;* types of speech forms and recommendations concerning the length of speeches in *Protagoras;* the cardinal virtues, ideal forms, audience analysis and adaptation, and the notion of conversion in *The Republic;* genuine and sophistical discourse, and refutation in the *Sophist;* model speeches on love by Agathon and Socrates in the *Symposium;* the use of examples and analogies, and appeals to the motives in *Statesman;* and the noble lover, probablility, and knowledge vs. opinion in *Theaetetus.* Moreover, in these works Plato often dealt with the canon of rhetoric that Aristotle tended to neglect—delivery. Note, for

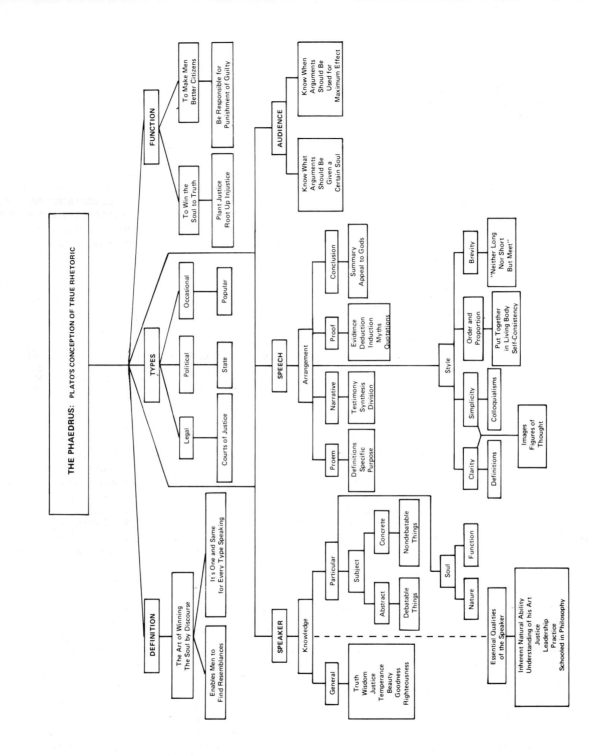

THE PHAEDRUS: PLATO'S CONCEPTION OF TRUE RHETORIC

DEFINITION

The Art of Winning The Soul by Discourse

It's One and Same for Every Type Speaking

Enables Men to Find Resemblances

TYPES

Legal — Courts of Justice

Political — State

Occasional — Popular

FUNCTION

To Make Men Better Citizens

Be Responsible for Punishment of Guilty

To Win the Soul to Truth

Plant Justice Root Up Injustice

AUDIENCE

Know When Arguments Should Be Used for Maximum Effect

Know What Arguments Should Be Given a Certain Soul

SPEECH

Arrangement

Proem — Definitions Specific Purpose

Narrative — Testimony Synthesis Division

Proof — Evidence Deduction Induction Myths Quotations

Conclusion — Summary Appeal to Gods

Style

Clarity — Definitions

Simplicity — Colloquialisms

Images Figures of Thought

Order and Proportion — Put Together in Living Body Self-Consistency

Brevity — "Neither Long Nor Short But Meet"

SPEAKER

Knowledge

General — Truth Wisdom Justice Temperance Beauty Goodness Righteousness

Particular — Subject

Abstract — Debatable Things

Concrete — Nondebatable Things

Soul — Nature, Function

Essential Qualities of the Speaker

Inherent Natural Ability Understanding of his Art Justice Leadership Practice Schooled in Philosophy

52

example, the views he expressed in the *Cratylus* for adapting one's voice control and bodily activity to the basic characteristics of the object or thing being described:

We should imitate the nature of the thing; the elevation of our hands to heaven would mean lightness and upwardness; heaviness and downwardness would be expressed by letting them drop to the ground; if we were describing the running of a horse, or any other animal, we should make our bodies and their gestures as like as we could to them. . . . For by bodily imitation only can the body ever express anything. . . . And when we want to express ourselves, either with the voice, or tongue, or mouth, the expression is simply their imitation of that which we want to express.[16]

Plato's preoccupation with a fully developed rhetorical theory led him beyond the oratorical form of public speaking that had so captivated the Greeks of his day. The type of communication method which he most earnestly wished to develop was dialectic. This was the pattern he used in constructing most of his dialogues; and it is the one he repeatedly recommended in his writings for philosophical conversation. Described as the essence of science and the guide for all discourse, dialectic chooses as its subject matter such abstract and enduring notions as knowledge and being. It is through dialectic that a participant glimpses the noble verities and the eternal truths of ideal forms.

The sequence and rhetorical strategies that are used give dialectic its uniqueness and scientific thrust. Adhering to a chronological pattern, it begins with a definition of terms and proceeds through analysis and synthesis to an ultimate conclusion based on enlightened understanding. The particular communication strategies also unfold in a sequential manner that utilizes four steps. One of the participants initiates the discussion by phrasing one or more questions. Among the points considered here will be the defining of appropriate terms. This is followed by the presentation of a response that sets forth hypotheses which are developed through demonstration. As soon as these answers are introduced, the third step, comprised of refutation and cross-examination,

takes place. The final phase hopefully will consist of a modification of the original position held by each participant.[17] The desired end result is shared meaning and enlarged understanding. Plato's theory of dialectic bears a resemblance to John Dewey's reflective thinking process, and, as will be seen in our analysis of the contemporary period, contains striking similarities to some of the principal ideas advanced in the current popular trend: "rhetoric as a way of knowing." In all, the innovative ideas he set in motion were to have an evolutionary power rarely matched by subsequent authors.

Notes

1. Plato, *Gorgias,* trans. by W. R. M. Lamb (Cambridge, Mass.: Harvard University Press, 1967), p. 250.
2. Everett Lee Hunt, "Plato and Aristotle on Rhetoric and Rhetoricians," *Studies in Rhetoric and Public Speaking in Honor of James Albert Winans* (New York: The Century Co., 1925), p. 25. Hereafter cited as "Plato and Aristotle."
3. *Ibid.,* p. 26.
4. *Ibid.,* p. 27.
5. B. Jowett, tr., *The Dialogues of Plato,* 4 vols. (New York: Scribner, Armstrong, and Co., 1874), III, 47–49.
6. "Plato and Aristotle," p. 28.
7. Cf. *The Republic,* trans. by Paul Shorey (Cambridge, Mass.: Harvard University Press, 1963).
8. "Plato and Aristotle," p. 32.
9. Richard M. Weaver, "The *Phaedrus* and the Nature of Rhetoric," reprinted in *Language is Sermonic,* ed. by R. L. Johannesen, R. Strickland, and R. T. Eubanks (Baton Rouge: Louisiana State University Press, 1970), p. 60.
10. *Ibid.* The reason for the use of the term "hypothetical" in the above passage is that Weaver took the position that language virtually always affects the reader or listener. See his "Language is Sermonic" in Part III of this work.
11. Jowett, *The Diaglogues of Plato, I,* 564–565.
12. *Ibid.,* 582–583.
13. *Language is Sermonic,* p. 83.
14. "Plato and Aristotle," pp. 37–38.
15. This claim is covered at length in the following essay to be published by Southern Illinois University Press in its volume honoring Edward P. J. Corbett, Jr.: James L. Golden, "Plato Revisited: A Theory of Discourse for All Seasons."
16. Edith Hamilton and Huntington Cairns, eds., *Plato: The Collected Dialogues* (New York: Bollingen Foundation, 1961), pp. 457–58.
17. See Michel Meyer, "Dialectic and Questioning: Socrates and Plato." *American Philosophical Quarterly,* 17 (October 1980), 283.

4

The Scientific Approach of Aristotle

Of all the students educated at Plato's Academy, none was so distinguished as Aristotle. The son of the court physician at the kingdom of Macedonia to the north of Greece, Aristotle was trained as a field biologist. He was an expert at observing all living and non-living things and in classifying such data for the use of others.[1] Unlike today's scientists, Aristotle's investigations were not limited to specialties like botany and zoology. Instead he took the whole Greek world as his laboratory. Thus we find works by Aristotle on law and political science, ethics and drama as well as what we currently think of as "the sciences." Every subject to which an Athenian turned his attention received the diligent attention of Aristotle as well, and among these was rhetoric, the art of effective speaking. So comprehensive and fundamental were Aristotle's views on rhetoric that it is no exaggeration to say that his treatise on the subject is the most important single work on persuasion ever written.

General Nature of Rhetoric. Rhetoric, like dialectic, is common to all men. Yet the art of persuasion like the art of reasoned discourse belongs to no one field of study. "All men in a manner use both; for all men to some extent make the effort of examining and of submitting to inquiry, of defending or accusing."[2] Earlier works on rhetoric, Aristotle maintained, dealt with only part of the field. They concerned themselves, he declared, with irrelevant appeals to the emotions of a jury, while they neglected reason in public discourse. They prescribed how a speech should be organized but ignored the speaker's role in creating proof.

Further, they stressed legal speaking while neglecting the deliberative rhetoric of the political assembly, a branch of the art "nobler and worthier of a citizen," Aristotle noted, "than that which deals with private contracts."[3]

Aristotle perceived this subject to be both significant and challenging and when he established his own school, he made it part of the regular curriculum. Rhetoric is useful, Aristotle wrote,

first, because truth and justice are naturally stronger than their opposites; so that, when awards are not given duly, truth and justice must have been worsted by their own fault. This is worth correcting. Again, supposing we had the most exact knowledge, there are some people whom it would not be easy to persuade with its help; for scientific exposition is in the nature of teaching, and teaching is out of the question; we must give our proofs and tell our story in popular terms, — as we said in the *Topics* with reference to controversy with the many. Further, — one should be able to persuade, just as to reason strictly, on both sides of a question; not with a view to using the twofold power — one must not be the advocate of evil — but in order, first, that we may know the whole state of the case; secondly, that, if anyone else argues dishonestly, we on our part may be able to refute him. Dialectic and Rhetoric, alone among all arts, draw indifferently an affirmative or a negative conclusion: both these arts alike are impartial. The conditions of the subject-matter, however, are not the same; that which is true and better being naturally, as a rule, more easy to demonstrate and more convincing. Besides it would be absurd that, while incapacity for physical self-defense is a reproach, incapacity for mental defense should be none; mental effort being more distinctive of man than bodily effort. If it is objected that an abuser of the rhetorical faculty can do great mischief, this, at any rate, applies to all good things except virtue, and especially to the most useful things, as strength, health, wealth, generalship. By the right use of these things a man may do the greatest good, and by the unjust use, the greatest mischief.[4]

The foregoing passage clearly shows that rhetoric, in Aristotle's opinion, has an important four-fold function: (1) to uphold truth and justice and play down their opposites; (2) to teach in a way suitable to a popular audience; (3) to analyze both sides of a question; and (4) to enable one to defend himself. Viewed from this perspective, rhetoric is a moral, but practical art grounded in probability or the contingent nature of things.

Aristotle's analytical approach to rhetoric is most apparent in his definition of the term: "the faculty of discovering in every case the available means of persuasion."[5] It was not enough that a speaker conceive of a single approach to persuasion. He must examine *all* the means available. Only then would he be likely to choose the best course of action rather than that which first came to mind. A *comprehensive* view of one's subject and audience is much to be preferred over a narrow one, Aristotle told his students.

Forms of Proof. Proof is either invented for the occasion or already existent, "artistic" or "nonartistic," Aristotle tells us.[6] A speaker may create support for his ideas or he may use documents or depositions already at hand. Of the first type, proofs artistically created by the speaker, there are three kinds: those which demonstrate that a thing is so *(logos)*, those which depend for their effectiveness on the believability of the speaker *(ethos)*, and those designed to sway a listener's feelings *(pathos)*. Logical proof, Aristotle declared, "is wrought

through the speech itself when we have demonstrated a truth or an apparent truth by the means of persuasion available in a given case." Ethical proof, he wrote, "is wrought when the speech is so spoken as to make the speaker credible; for we trust good men more and sooner, as a rule, about everything; while, about things which do not admit of precision, but only guess-work, we trust them absolutely." Lastly, "the hearers themselves become the instruments of proof when emotion is stirred in them by the speech; for we give our judgments in different ways under the influence of pain and joy, of liking and of hatred."[7] Aristotle's threefold analysis of proof is every bit as appropriate to persuasion today as it was when written twenty-three centuries ago.

The enthymeme. The heart of Aristotle's theory of logical proof was the rhetorical syllogism or enthymeme. Because Aristotle believed that "enthymemes are the very body and substance of persuasion,"[8] we will treat this concept in detail, first by summarizing its nature, and then by applying it to a portion of one of Shakespeare's plays. Although many approaches to the study of the enthymeme have appeared in our literature in recent years, the one we will use is in keeping with the traditional interpretation presented by James McBurney of Northwestern University.[9]

Aristotle regarded the enthymeme as a method of persuasion which has the same relationship to rhetoric that the syllogism has to logic. Both of these forms of reasoning begin with a general premise and proceed to a particular case. The ideas may be presented in three steps: a major premise, a minor premise, and a conclusion. The initial or major premise was usually a categorical statement such as *All Athenians love to argue.* A second or minor connecting premise might be *Socrates is an Athenian.* The conclusion which then follows is *Socrates loves to argue.* It is significant to note that while the enthymeme and syllogism are structurally the same, they differ in one major respect: that is, the degree of certainty of the sources from which they draw their premises. The enthymeme deals with probable knowledge, whereas the syllogism is concerned with scientific truths. Consider, for instance, the following argument:

All men are mortal.   (Major Premise)
Socrates is a man.   (Minor Premise)
Socrates is mortal.   (Conclusion)

The degree of certainty in this major premise is stronger than that in the previously cited statement: "All Athenians love to argue." The degree of probability, therefore, constitutes an essential difference between enthymematic and syllogistic reasoning. Some writers have overlooked this fact, and, consequently, have defined the enthymeme as a truncated syllogism. There is, of course, some justification for this point of view. For nowadays rarely does one give formal speeches using all three steps of an enthymeme. Nor did the Greek orators. Usually the persuasive speaker would omit one or even two of the parts of the rhetorical syllogism, for they already existed in the minds of the listeners. As Aristotle put it, "if one of these elements is something notorious, it need not even be stated, as the hearer himself supplies it."[10] But while a characteristic of the enthymeme is its capacity to suppress one of its parts, the point which we are here stressing is that the enthymeme is a rhetorical syllogism "drawn, not from universal principles belonging to a particular science, but from probabilities in the sphere of human affairs."[11]

The three sorts of premises from which enthymemes are drawn are probabilities, signs [fallible and infallible], and examples. By probability Aristotle meant arguments that are generally true and contain an element of cause. For example, since "sons tend to love their mothers, Orestes will love his mother." In this connection McBurney has observed that "when one concludes that Orestes loves his mother, because 'love [usually] attends the objects of affection,' the argument does not attempt to prove [to give a sign] that Orestes actually does love his mother; but rather [assuming it probable that he loves his mother] attempts to account for or explain this phenomenon."[12]

The sign, which is the second premise of the enthymeme, is a proposition setting forth a reason for the existence of a particular fact.

No attempt is made to explain what has caused the fact.[13] According to Aristotle there are two types of signs: the fallible and the infallible. When a speaker, in seeking to demonstrate the truth of the statement that "wise men are just," asserts that "Socrates was wise and also just," he is employing a fallible sign because the conclusion does not establish with certainty. Further, to observe that one has "a fever for he is breathing rapidly" does not necessarily indicate illness. If, on the other hand, a speaker states that a woman "has had a child because she is in milk," he is relying on an infallible sign; for, in every instance, an assumption of this kind can be scientifically verified.

Aristotle is not so specific in his discussion of the example, the third premise of the enthymeme. He made it evident, however, that the enthymeme can be formed either from historical or invented examples. In Book II he tells us that enthymemes taken from examples are those which proceed by induction from one or more parallel cases until the speaker abstracts a general rule, from which he argues to the case in point.[14] Let us assume, for instance, that a speaker wishes to establish the relationship between military ingenuity and political acumen. He first examines the life of General Grant and immediately discovers that the Civil War hero is regarded as one of America's worst presidents. Next he finds that General De-Gaulle failed to organize a strong political party in France. He then sees that Colonel Peron, as a political leader, alienated Argentina from the free world. Finally he notes that Dwight Eisenhower is ranked by contemporary historians in the lower one-fifth of American presidents. From these parallel examples he may conclude that military leaders make poor politicians. The speaker is now ready to argue the case in point. Thus he claims that Alexander Haig should not be elected President in 1984.

Not only was Aristotle interested in analyzing the premises of the enthymeme but also in a consideration of its proper subject matter. Here he was concerned with the problem of the sources or places which furnish arguments. The rhetorician may draw his material from either universal or particular *topoi*. Universal topics are broad, general sources which are equally applicable to physics or politics. The four common topics are the possible and impossible, past fact, future fact, and size. Special topics, on the other hand, are associated with a "particular species or class of things." They provide the speaker with a thorough insight into a specific problem. Aristotle advises his readers that most enthymemes are formed from special subjects such as ethics and politics.

After the speaker has chosen his premises from the available special and universal *topoi,* he must next turn to what Aristotle calls "lines of argument." These topics are to be interpreted as "methods of reasoning rather than material propositions."[15] Twenty-eight types of valid arguments and nine which are referred to as "sham" are discussed in Book II. They are as follows:

Valid Lines of Argument

1. Opposites
2. Inflections
3. Correlative terms
4. More and less
5. Time
6. Definition
7. Induction
8. Existing decisions
9. Turning the tables
10. Part to whole
11. Simple consequences
12. Criss-cross consequences
13. Inward thoughts, outward show
14. Proportional results
15. Identical results and antecedents
16. Altered choices
17. Attributed motives
18. Incentives and deterrents
19. Incredible occurrences
20. Conflicting facts
21. Meeting slander
22. Cause to effect
23. Meaning of names
24. Actions compared
25. Course of action
26. Previous mistakes
27. Division
28. Ambiguous terms

Sham Enthymemes

1. Diction (Structure of and homonyms)
2. Fallacious combination and separation
3. Indignation
4. A "sign"
5. The accidental
6. Consequence
7. Post hoc propter hoc
8. Time and manner
9. Substituting the absolute for the particular

Whenever one of these lines of argument is combined with a premise derived from a general or special topic an enthymeme is formed.[16]

The *Rhetoric* also distinguishes between the two primary species of the enthymeme, the demonstrative and the refutative. The demonstrative begins with consistent propositions and reaches affirmative conclusions. The converse is true of the refutative enthymeme. Since its purpose is to controvert the demonstrative the conclusions are obtained from "inconsistent propositions," and its purpose is not to affirm but to destroy a premise. One should remember, however, that both the enthymeme and the counter syllogism are constructed from the same *topoi.*

In discussing the question of refutation Aristotle carefully emphasizes the fact that the enthymeme is not properly refuted by simply pointing out the existence of probability in one of the premises. For by its very nature the enthymeme embraces the probable and, as a result, cannot be expected to set forth conclusions of scientific certainty. The same is true with respect to refutation of any argument from sign. It is not a question, therefore, of the presence of probability in either the premise or the conclusion, but rather one of how closely the probability or the sign resembles truth.

It would appear from the discussion thus far that Aristotle was thinking of the enthymeme only as a mode of logical proof. If this were true, however, the organizational pattern of the *Rhetoric* cannot be adequately understood.[17] If Aristotle were sincere in assuming that the enthymeme is "the body and substance of persuasion," he would not have given such spatial emphasis to ethical and pathetic appeals, unless he felt these proofs were directly related to the rhetorical syllogism.

In his explanation of the maxim, which is a shortened enthymeme, Aristotle suggests two advantages produced by this type of general truth. First, the audience will be delighted in hearing an expression of an oft repeated generalization which corresponds to their own beliefs. Thus, an audience comprised exclusively of men, would react favorably to the assertion that women drivers are poor drivers. While the form of the argument is enthymematic the degree of pathos is strong.

Secondly, by employing maxims the speaker often enhances his own character in the eyes of his auditors. Aristotle, commenting on this point, observed that "maxims always produce the moral effect, because the speaker in uttering them makes a general declaration of ethical principles (preferences); so that, if the maxims are sound, they give us the impression of a sound moral character in him who speaks."[18] Only by recognizing the relationship of the enthymeme to ethos and pathos can we fully comprehend the integral part which that mode of persuasion played in Aristotle's rhetorical system.

In summary, the enthymeme may be defined as a rhetorical syllogism which draws its premises from probabilities, signs, and examples. It has two species, the demonstrative and refutative, both of which derive their materials from particular or universal *topoi,* and then combine that material with the various lines of argument. Further, while the enthymeme is technically a form of logical proof, it frequently produces an emotional and ethical effect.

Most of the principles which we have discussed are clearly illustrated in Shakespeare's historical play, "Julius Caesar." An analysis of Mark Antony's speech on the death of Caesar should suffice to show that Shakespeare was evidently acquainted with the theory of the enthymeme. Moreover, it will tend to demonstrate how the enthymeme is a vital component of practical argument.

Antony's address was delivered primarily for the purpose of counteracting the influence of a previous oration by Brutus. Antony knew that he must refute the charge that Caesar was ambitious. To do this he used enthymematic reasoning based on Aristotelian principles both to disarm his hearers and motivate them to action.

The introduction contains two maxims which adequately express the sentiment of the audience. "The evil that men do lives after them; the good is oft interred with their bones." This statement is, in effect, a truncated enthymeme constructed from probable knowledge. Antony next states that "the noble Brutus hath told you Caesar was ambitious; if it were so, it was a grievous fault, and grievously hath Caesar answered it." Such an assertion may be restated in enthymematic form as follows:

Ambition is a grievous fault.	(Major Premise)
Caesar had ambition.	(Minor Premise)
Caesar had a grievous fault.	(Conclusion)

Of course Antony did not accept the minor premise or the conclusion of this argument, but since the audience concurred with Brutus it was necessary to give them sufficient proof to show the fallibility inherent in the reasoning. He chose to do this by developing a counter syllogism utilizing signs. Caesar could not have been ambitious, he argued, because

1. "He hath wrought many captives home to Rome, whose ransoms did the general coffers fill."
2. "When the poor have cried Caesar hath wept."
3. "You all did see that on the Lupercal I thrice presented him with a kingly crown which he did thrice refuse."

The orator naturally concluded that these signs are the substance of non-ambition.

Antony next turned to the line of argument based on "time." "You all did love him once not without cause; what cause withholds you then to mourn for him?" The following enthymeme is implied in this plea:

We should mourn for   (Major Premise)
those we once had
cause to love.
We once had cause to   (Minor Premise)
love Caesar.
We should, therefore,   (Conclusion)
mourn for Caesar.

Antony's persuasion was complete as he demonstrated the enormity of Brutus' crime. "For Brutus as you know was Caesar's angel. Judge O you Gods how dearly Caesar loved him! This was the most unkindest cut of all." Actually he was telling his listeners that

Those who kill their friends are the unkindest of men.
Brutus killed his friend.
Brutus is the unkindest of men.

This is an enthymeme expressing the argument of "more or less."

The rhetorical syllogisms which Antony used are consonant with the teachings of Aristotle. All of the premises of the enthymemes are drawn from the particular *topoi* of ethics and politics, those branches of knowledge dealing with the conduct of man in human affairs. In addition, many of the twenty-eight lines of argument suggested by Aristotle can be seen. They may be summarized as follows:

1. Antony succeeds in "turning the utterances" of Brutus against him.
2. The question of "time" is noted in the reference that "you all did love him once."
3. Throughout the oration there seems to be an ambiguity with respect to the meaning of the term "ambition." To Brutus it had one connotation; to Antony it had another.
4. The enthymeme constructed from signs is an argument "from part to whole."
5. The "consequence" of envy and hate as seen in Casca is murder.

6. Although Brutus professed to love Caesar his testimony is not sincere. It is nothing more than "inward thoughts and outward show."
7. The problem of "incentives and deterrents" permeates the discussion.
8. It seems "incredible" that Brutus would commit such a crime.
9. The doctrine of "more or less" is implicit in the charge that there is no greater crime than that of killing your friend.

By combining the special *topoi* of ethics and politics with these lines of arguments, Antony strengthened his own character and obviously aroused the emotions of his hearers. In short, his persuasion, which is expressed through the media of ethos, logos, and pathos, originates with the enthymeme.

Ethical and Pathetic Appeals. In Book II of his three book treatise, Aristotle focuses his attention on the listener. It is here that he describes ethos as the hearer's perception of a speaker based on the speech itself. The Greeks conceived of the perfect speaker as one who possessed intelligence, a virtuous character, and good will. They judged the soundness of the speaker's ideas in terms of their own experience and the evidence he presented to support his proposal. The speaker's integrity was judged on the basis of the apparent truthfulness of the statements made. Good will was judged in terms of the best interests of the listening audience. Despite the fact Aristotle's inclination to assume the basic rationality of man led him to stress logical proof, he came to believe that in a typical rhetorical situation involving a general audience ethical appeals are perhaps the most influential single element in persuasion.[19]

Since Aristotle equated rhetoric with the whole man, he also analyzed human emotions. The method he used was that of contrast as he discussed the following pairs: anger and mildness, friendship and enmity, fear and boldness, shame and shamelessness, gratitude and ingratitude, pity and indignation, envy and emulation.[20] As he probed into the nature of these emotions and related them to the challenge facing a rhetor, Aristotle revealed his orderly mind and scientific technique. He asked such questions as these: What type of person feels a given emotion? What is the state of mind of one experiencing a particular emotion? Under what circumstances is the emotion aroused or allayed? Out of the response to these inquiries, Aristotle was able to define the emotion. Typical explanations used in describing the emotions are the following statements:

1. "Anger (is) an appetite, attended with pain, for revenge, on account of an apparent slighting of things which concern one, or of oneself, or of one's friends, when such slighting is improper."
2. "Friendship (is) wishing for a person those things which one thinks good—wishing them for his sake, not for one's own—and tending, in so far as one can, to effect these things."
3. "Fear (is) a pain or trouble arising from an image of coming evil, destructive or painful; for men do not fear all evils—as, for instance, the prospect of being unjust or slow; but only such evils as mean great pain or losses, and these, when they seem not distant, but close and imminent."
4. "Shame (is) a pain or trouble about those ills, present, past or future, which seem to tend to ignominy; shamelessness is a kind of negligence or indifference about these things."
5. "Pity (is) a pain for apparent evil, destructive or painful, befalling a person who does not deserve it, when we might expect such evil to befall ourselves or some of our friends, and when, moreover, it seems near."[21]

Taken as a whole this early analysis of human nature merits the attention of those interested in psychology.

Forms of Discourse or Speaking Occasions. Aristotle classified speaking in ancient Athens in three ways: forensic discourse—that which deals with happenings in the past as in the case of alleged criminality; epideictic—that which deals with praise and blame as in the case of a ceremonial address; and deliberative—that which deals with future policy as in the case of legislative debate. Crucial to an understanding of Aristotle's theory of forensic speaking is his treatment of wrongdoing. Criminal acts, he said, are either voluntary or involuntary and are caused by such forces as chance, nature, reason, and passion.[22] Since the major concern of both the prosecution and the defense focuses on whether or not an act was committed and the causes that were operative, forensic discourse emphasizes fact past. The forensic addresses Lysias wrote for wealthy patrons parallel the later rhetoric of Clarence Darrow and Edward Bennett Williams. Notwithstanding its usefulness as a practical art in the Western world, however, forensic discourse did not have a strong appeal for Aristotle because of its susceptibility "to unscrupulous practices."[23]

Epideictic speaking occasions are those in which an orator praises or blames an individual, an idea, or organization, a locale, or a nation. In view of the fact that the substance of epideictic discourse is drawn largely from the field of ethics, "we have in the *Rhetoric* . . . a summary view of the needed ethical material—happiness, goods, virtue and vice, wrongdoing and injustice, pleasure, equity, laws, and friendship."[24] Of particular importance to this type of rhetorical occasion is the subject of cardinal virtues. Plato doubtless influenced Aristotle with his summary of the four virtues which he believed to be essential for the formation of an ideal republic—courage, temperance, wisdom, and justice. The trait Plato held to be the great integrating virtue which could only exist if the other three were present is justice.[25] When Aristotle turned to an analysis of epideictic discourse, he discussed these four cardinal virtues of Greek culture and added five others including magnanimity, liberality, gentleness, prudence, and magnificence.[26] The epideictic speaker's task is to relate the virtues to the theme being discussed. Evidence would be cited, for example, to show that a praiseworthy individual exemplified specific virtues, while a blameworthy person practiced vices. Pericles' Funeral Oration is the ancestor of Lincoln's Gettysburg Address and Douglas MacArthur's Farewell Speech to Congress. Demosthenes' attacks on Philip of Macedon established the pattern for Cicero's philippics against Mark Antony and Winston Churchill's addresses on Adolph Hitler. Epideictic discourse eulogizing the founding fathers typified much of the speaking during the bicentennial celebration.

Of the three types of discourse, Aristotle was most interested in the deliberative. Partly because other writers had ignored this speaking form, and partly because it embraces all of those subjects dealing with fact future, Aristotle felt justified in giving to deliberative speaking his major attention. If ethics permeated all aspects of the epideictic genre, politics performed the same function for the deliberative. Thus a rhetor using this speaking form must be a student of each type of government—an aristocracy, an oligarchy, a monarchy, and a democracy. Only in this way can he adapt to the political views of his hearers. From our contemporary American perspective it is instructive to note that the chief subjects about which all men debate in a democracy, Aristotle observed, are these: ways and means (i.e. public revenue), war and peace, national defense, commerce (i.e., imports and exports), and legislation.[27] No modern political scientist would disagree.

Aristotle's discussion of the forms of address is significant for several reasons. First, he implies that the speaker's starting point is the occasion. Secondly, he notes that epideictic discourse is primarily concerned with fact present, forensic discourse with fact past, and deliberative discourse with fact future. Thirdly, he reinforces the notion that the principal subject matter fields utilized by rhetoric are ethics and politics.

To summarize Aristotle's notions on types of speeches and occasions, we reprint below the chart developed by Forbes Hill in his essay on "The Rhetoric of Aristotle."[28]

Organization of Ideas and Audience Analysis and Adaptation. In his discussion of forms of proof and the types of speaking occasions, Aristotle developed his views on the message—a canon of rhetoric described by the Romans as *inventio*. The arrangement and adaptation of the speaker's ideas became a second canon, which later was labeled *dispositio*. Any speech, Aristotle observed, has four parts which unfold in a chronological order: proem or introduction, statement, argument, and epilogue or conclusion.[29] Most essential to Aristotle were the statement and argument; for it is in these parts of the discourse that logical appeals are used. Proems and epilogues are included in an address in order to arouse the attention of or create good will with a popular audience in the beginning of a speech and to stir their emotions in the conclusion.

Another facet of *dispositio* was audience analysis and adaptation. On this point Plato and Aristotle held widely divergent views. "Aristotle did not share Plato's notion that a true art of rhetoric would enable a speaker to adapt himself to each of the persons of an audience as the dialectician adjusts himself to one deuteragonist."[30] What should concern the rhetor, argued Aristotle, was not "a given individual like Socrates or Hippias, but with what seems probable to men of a given type."[31]

Kind of Speech	Kind of Auditor	Time	Ends	Means
Forensic	Decision-maker	Past	The unjust and just	Accusation and defense
Deliberative	Decision-maker	Future	The advantageous and disadvantageous	Persuasion and dissuasion
Epideictic	Spectator	Present	The noble and the shameful	Praise and blame

Because of his preoccupation with the characteristics of groups as a whole rather than with the special traits of a particular person, Aristotle approached audience analysis in a comprehensive way. To begin with, he pointed out, all men seek happiness. Speakers must, if they mean to be persuasive, propose those things which either create or enhance the happiness of their listeners. Aristotle listed the following traits as those most treasured by his fellow Greeks: good birth (as measured by the eminence of one's family), numerous children, wealth, good repute, honor, health, physical beauty, strength, size, long life, many friends, good fortune, and virtue.[32] The wise speaker related his proposals to those goods which bring happiness to his listeners. Thereby, he adapted to his audience.

A second dimension of audience analysis involved the traits one associates with audiences of different ages. Compare, for example, Aristotle's description of the young with America's male college students:

Young men are lustful in character, and apt to do what they lust after. Of the bodily desires, they are most apt to indulge, and to exceed in, the sexual. They are changeable and fickle in their desires, which are violent but soon appeased; for their impulses are rather keen than great, like the hunger and thirst of the sick. They are passionate, quick to anger and apt to obey their impulse; and they are under the dominion of their passion, for, by reason of ambition, they cannot bear to be slighted, and they are indignant, if they think they are wronged. They are ambitious, or rather contentious; for youth covets pre-eminence, and victory is a form of pre-eminence. They are both ambitious and contentious rather than avaricious; this they are not at all, because they have not yet experienced want—as goes the saying of Pittakos about Amphiaraos. They think no evil, but believe in goodness, because as yet they have not seen many cases of vice. They are credulous, because, as yet, they have not been deceived. They are sanguine, because they are heated, as with wine, and also because they have not had many disappointments. They live for most part by hope; for

hope is of the future, as memory of the past, and for young men the future is long and the past short; since, on the first day of a life, there is nothing to remember and everything to hope. They are easily deceived, for the same reason,—since they hope easily. They are comparatively courageous; for they are passionate and hopeful, and passion keeps men from being fearful, while hope makes them bold: no one fears while he is angry, and to hope for a good thing is emboldening. They are shy; for, as yet, they have no independent standard of propriety, but have been educated by convention alone. They are high-minded; for they have not yet been abased by life, but are untried in its necessities; and to think oneself worthy of great things is high-mindedness; and this is characteristic of the hopeful man. They choose honourable before expedient actions; for they live by habit rather than by calculation; and calculation has the expedient for its object, as virtue has the honourable. They are fond of their friends, their relations, their companions, more than persons of the other ages, because they delight in society, and because, as yet, they judge nothing by the standard of expediency, and so do not apply it to their friends. All their mistakes are on the side of excess or vehemence—against the maxim of Chilon; they do everything *too much;* they love too much, hate too much, and so in all else. They think they know everything and are positive; this, indeed, is the cause of their overdoing all things. Their wrong deeds are done insolently, not viciously. They are ready to pity, because they think all men good, or *rather* good; for they measure their neighbours by their own innocence, and so conceive that these are suffering wrongfully. And they are lovers of laughter,—hence also lovers of wit; for wit is educated insolence.[33]

How does the following analysis of senior citizens accord with your view of, say, your grandparents?

As they have lived many years, and have been deceived or have erred more often, and as most things are disappointing, they are positive about nothing, and do all things much too feebly. They *think,* but are never *sure;* in their uncertainty, they always add 'maybe,'—'perhaps'; they speak thus on all subjects, and positively about nothing. They think evil; for evil-thinking is to put the worst construction upon everything. Further, they are suspicious through their incredulity, being incredulous through their experience. For these reasons they neither like nor hate strongly, but, according to the advice of Bias, like, as if they would afterwards hate, and hate, as if they would afterwards like. They are meansouled, through having been abased by life; for they desire nothing great or extraordinary, but only the appliances of life. They are illiberal; for property is one of the necessaries; and, at the same time, they know from their experience, that it is hard to acquire, but easy to lose. They are cowardly, and afraid of everything; for they are of the opposite temperament to youth; they are chilled, while youth is hot; and so old age has prepared the way to cowardice, since fear is a chill. They cling to life, and the more on their latest day, since the object of desire is the absent, and since, too, men most desire that in which they are deficient. They are unduly selfish; for this, too, is a meanness of soul. And, because they are selfish, they live too much for the expedient, too little for the honourable; the expedient being a relative good, the honourable an absolute good. They are not shy, but rather shameless; for, as they do not care, in the same degree, for what is honourable, as for what is expedient, they disregard appearances. They are slow to hope, owing to their experience,—since most things which happen are unsatisfactory and turn out for the worse,—and also from their cowardice. They live in memory more than in hope; for the remainder of their life is small, and the past part large—and hope is of the future, as memory of the past. This is the reason of their talkativeness;—they are for ever speaking of the past, since the retrospect gives them pleasure. Their fits of passion are sharp, but feeble; hence they are not lustful, nor apt to act after lust, but rather for gain.

Hence men of this age appear temperate, their desires have become slack, and they are slaves to lucre. And their life is regulated by calculation rather than by moral instinct; calculation having expediency for its object, while moral instinct has virtue. Their wrong deeds are done viciously, not insolently. Old men, like young, are compassionate, but not for the same reason as young men; the latter are so from benevolence, the former from weakness; for they think that every possibility of suffering is near themselves, and this, we saw, was a condition of pitying. Hence they are given to lamentation, and are not witty or lovers of mirth; for the love of lamentation is opposite to the love of mirth.[34]

Unlike our own culture in which youth is worshipped, the Athenians admired a period they termed the "prime of life." Aristotle described that ideal state this way:

Men in their prime will evidently be of a character intermediate between these, abating the excess of each;—neither excessively bold, for this is rashness, nor over-timid, but rightly disposed in both respects, neither trusting nor distrusting all things, but rather judging by the true standard, and living neither for the honourable alone, nor for the expedient alone, but for both; inclining neither to frugality nor to extravagance, but to the just mean. And so, too, in regard to passion and desire, they will be courageously temperate and temperately courageous. Young men and old men share these qualities between them; young men are courageous and intemperate, old men are temperate and cowardly. To speak generally—those useful qualities, which youth and age divide between them, are joined in the prime of life; between their excesses and defects, it has the fitting mean. The body is in its full vigour from thirty to five and thirty; the mind at about forty-nine.[35]

Aristotle's partiality for the "golden mean" prompted him to suggest that whenever a speaker addresses an audience comprised of all three groups, he should gear his remarks to the prime of life. In this way he would not deviate too far from the interests of the young and the old.

Style and Delivery. In the preceding analysis we have seen how Aristotle was a message-centered rhetorician whose principal concern was to help his student discover, organize, and adapt the available means of persuasion to a particular rhetorical situation or occasion. But he also recognized that a speaker must reinforce his invention and disposition with a compelling style and delivery. Even though these canons held a subordinate position, they, like the spectacle in a dramatic production, are essential tools in persuasion. Thus style (the use of language to express ideas) and delivery (the management of the voice) form part of the focus of Book III.

In his treatment of style, Aristotle deals with the traditional elements of language such as accuracy of word choice, clarity, appropriateness, and vividness. He was especially interested in delineating the characteristics of the metaphor or implied comparison. "Metaphor," said Aristotle, "is the application of a strange term either transferred from the genus and applied to the species or from the species and applied to the genus, or from one species to another or else by analogy."[36] Aristotle then clarifies this definition by giving an example of each type of metaphor. A transferral of a term from genus to species can be seen in the statement, "Here *stands* my ship." When we say that a ship stands we actually mean that it is "riding at anchor," for the latter is a species of standing. The sentence, "Indeed *ten thousand* noble things Odysseus did," is an example of transference from one species to another. The term "ten thousand" is akin to "many." since they are both members of the same species, one can be substituted for the other.

The fourth and most commonly used method of deriving metaphors is that of analogy. Here we have four terms which have a proportional relationship to each other, such as B is to A as D is to C. By analogy the D may be substituted for the B and the B for the D. Replacing these letters with names, we let A be Plato, B a goblet, C Ares, and D a shield.

By definition the goblet is to Plato as the shield is to Ares. A metaphor is obtained by referring to the goblet as a shield of Plato or the shield as a goblet of Ares. Since the shield and the goblet are both characteristic of deity, they come under the same genus and can therefore be interchanged.[37]

In developing his theory of style, Aristotle further observed that one of the most important functions of a metaphor in public address is to teach. If words are strange, foreign, or archaic, they are not known to all and, consequently, do not give any new information. Proper and ordinary words, on the other hand, are already known by the audience. It is the metaphor, more than any other figure of speech, therefore, that increases our knowledge. When Homer calls old age a stubble, he conveys learning and knowledge through the medium of the genus, because they are both withered.[38]

The metaphor, Aristotle states, teaches by bringing into view resemblances between things which appear on the surface as dissimilar. It is most effective when it is drawn from objects that are related, but not too obvious to everyone at first sight. Whenever the significance of the metaphor is comprehended at first glance, the mind is not stirred into action. If people are to engage in reflective thinking, the figure must arouse curiosity.

Similarly Aristotle suggests that metaphors should also "be derived from something beautiful. . . ."[39] When a speaker plans a speech of praise he must take his metaphors from the superior things that fall under the same genus. Thus it makes a difference whether we say "rosy-fingered morn" or "red-fingered morn" because the rose reminds us of something that is agreeable to sight and smell. It is essential, therefore, that the forms of the word express an agreeable sound.

Aristotle, finally emphasizes the point that metaphors cannot be derived from anyone else.[40] This does not imply that one writer or speaker cannot borrow a metaphor from another; but that the invention of metaphor is an innate talent, and therefore cannot be taught. Although metaphors are not confined to men of genius, they do show originality and are definite marks of natural ability. It is obvious, then, that a proportional relationship exists between one's intellect and his success in using metaphors.

Aristotle was far less enthusiastic about analyzing delivery. It was to him a necessary but low priority canon that does not lend itself to philosophical speculation or scientific inquiry. As a result he subordinates it to style— a fact which disturbed the Roman rhetoricians.

The *Rhetoric* of Aristotle is not a well organized textbook by modern standards. Rather it appears to be Aristotle's own lecture notes collected over a twelve year period. Topics are treated briefly, dropped, and reconsidered elsewhere. Illustrative material is limited, perhaps because Aristotle resorted to impromptu examples at the time of utterance, examples which undoubtedly changed over the years. Clearly Aristotle himself made no effort to edit this material for later publication. What we have instead are rough lecture notes used intermittently when needed. But despite these reservations the *Rhetoric* remains the most significant rhetorical work in Western thought. Indeed, as Lane Cooper correctly points out, "Aristotle's treatise on Rhetoric is one of the world's best and wisest books."[41]

In order to make Aristotle's comprehensive treatise more manageable to the reader, we have provided a detailed outline of the parts comprising the whole, along with brief explanatory material in the right-hand margins. We are indebted to Professor Herbert James of Dartmouth College for portions of this material.

I. *General Nature of Rhetoric*
   A. Rhetoric is the counterpart of dialectic.
   B. Rhetoric is the faculty of discovering in the particular case all the available means of persuasion.
   C. The functions of rhetoric are to make truth prevail, to instruct, to debate, to defend.

Rhetoric, which seeks to discover all types of verbal and non-verbal means of persuasion appropriate to a given situation, deals with probable knowledge designed to promote truth and justice. It recognizes the contingent nature of propositions, and the need to speak in self-defense.

II. *Kinds of Hearers, corresponding to Kinds of Oratory*
   A. Deliberative speaking
      1. Audience seeking advice
      2. Divisions = persuasion and dissuasion concerning advantage and injury with respect to the future
      3. Subject matter
         a. Happiness
            1. Good birth
            2. Good children
            3. Many children
            4. Good friends
            5. Many friends
            6. Health
            7. Beauty
            8. Strength
            9. Stature
            10. Good old age
            11. Athletic ability

Speakers in legislative bodies and/or related groups recommend actions which an assembly should take in order to guarantee success in the future. Elements of happiness and good are emphasized.

        12. Wealth
        13. Honor
        14. Fame
        15. Good fortune
        16. Virtue
        17. Power
        18. Avoid opposites
    b. Goods
        1. Happiness
        2. Virtues of Soul
        3. Excellence of body
        4. Wealth
        5. Friends
        6. Honor-Reputation
        7. Power in speaking
        8. Power of action
        9. Memory
        10. Aptness in learning
        11. Quickness of thought
        12. Arts and Sciences
        13. Life
        14. Justice
    c. Deliberations
        1. Ways and Means
        2. War and Peace
        3. National Defense
        4. Imports and Exports
        5. Legislation

These five political and economic issues constitute the major subjects that are to be discussed in making legislative decisions.

    d. Forms of Government
        1. Democracy
        2. Oligarchy
        3. Aristocracy
        4. Monarchy

The deliberations will be affected by the form of government.

B. Forensic speaking
    1. Audience seeking justice
    2. Divisions = accusation and defense involving justice and injustice as it relates to the past
    3. Subject matter
        a. Human Actions
            1. Causes of Human actions
                a. Chance
                b. Nature
                c. Compulsion
                d. Habit
                e. Reasoning
                f. Anger
                g. Desire

The forensic speaker, whether a member of the prosecution or the defense, stresses justice or injustice with respect to an accused person's alleged action.

Acts are committed from one or more of these seven causes.

2. Aims
    a. Good (See list
       under Deliberative
       speaking)
    b. Pleasant
b. Nature of Wrong-doing
    1. Disposition of wrong-
       doers

       a. Believe action
          possible
       b. Escape detection
       c. Penalty less than
          pain

It is important for a speaker and judge to know the characteristic traits inherent in or associated with potential wrong-doers and victims of wrong-doing.

    2. Victims
       a. Possess needed
          things
       b. Distant and near
       c. Unsuspecting
       d. Easy going, retiring
       e. Frequently wronged
       f. Unpopular
       g. Friends, Enemies
       h. Lacking friends
       i. Lack speaking
          ability
       j. Foreigners
       k. Criminals
    3. Special Law (Written)
    4. Universal Law
       (Unwritten Equity)

C. Epideictic speaking
  1. Audience seeking praise
  2. Divisions = praise and blame
    as they pertain to honor and
    dishonor in the present
  3. Subject matter
    a. Virtue

       1. Justice
       2. Temperance
       3. Courage
       4. Magnificence
       5. Magnanimity
       6. Liberality
       7. Gentleness
       8. Prudence
       9. Wisdom

An individual who exemplifies these cardinal virtues is an honorable person meriting praise. One who violates these virtues deserves blame.

    b. Acts of nobleness
       1. Act of courage
       2. Just deeds

Noble acts are those which are grounded in virtue.

  3. Honor
  4. Unselfish deeds
  5. Absolute goods
  6. Gifts of nature
  7. Goods for after-life
  8. Goods done for others
  9. Goods not beneficial to doer
  10. Deeds opposite of shame
  11. Concern without fear
  12. Virtues of a class
  13. Gratification for others
  14. Avenge against enemy
  15. Memorable things
  16. Unique possessions
  17. Non-yielding possessions
  18. Special traits of people
  19. Distinctive marks of habit
  20. Independence
  21. Opposites for blame
  22. Victory

III. *The Elements of Persuasion*
  A. Basic Ideas
    1. Sources
      a. Lines of Argument
        1. Materials of Enthymemes
          a. Probabilities
          b. Examples
          c. Infallible Signs
          d. Fallible Signs

An enthymeme, which is a rhetorical syllogism based on probability, may make use of both fallible and infallible signs.

        2. Universal
          a. Genuine
          b. Spurious
        3. Substantive Items
          a. Commonplaces
            1. Possible and Impossible
            2. Past Fact
            3. Future Fact
            4. Size

A line of argument may be derived from a broad general topic or from a special topic area or field of study.

          b. Special Topics
            1. Ethics
            2. Physics
            3. Politics
            4. Philosophy
            5. Other Special Sciences

2. Proof
   a. Ethical Proof
      1. Intelligence
      2. Character
      3. Good Will
   b. Logical Proof
      1. Rhetorical Syllogisms or Enthymemes
         a. Demonstrative = draw conclusions from admitted propositions
         b. Refutative = draw conclusions inconsistent with adversary's
            1. Sham enthymemes
            2. Maxims
      2. Refutation of Enthymemes
         a. Counter-syllogisms
         b. Objection based on attacking premise, adducing similar premise, adducing contrary premise, and adducing previous decisions
      3. Rhetorical Induction— Examples
         a. Historical parallel
         b. Invented parallel (Comparison, Fable)
   c. Pathetic Proof
      1. Emotions
         a. Anger–Mildness
         b. Love–Hatred
         c. Fear–Boldness
         d. Shame–Shamelessness
         e. Benevolence–Unkindness
         f. Pity
         g. Indignation
         h. Envy
         i. Emulation–Contempt

Proof may be of two types: artistic (reasoning) and inartistic (evidence)

These three traits are the constituent elements of ethical or personal proof.

The most important aspect of logical proof is enthymematic reasoning. Enthymemes may be constructed for the purpose of demonstrating or refuting a claim

Although an enthymeme may be constructed from examples, reasoning by example may also be a form of inductive reasoning.

For a speaker to arouse or allay a particular emotion in the audience, he must understand the nature of the emotion and its opposite, as well as the type of person who is inclined to experience the emotion.

2. Adapting to emotional traits of the audience
   a. Time of Life = Youth, Prime of Life, Old
   b. Varieties of Fortune = good birth, wealth, power

Since a person's emotional attitude is affected by his age level, it is necessary to know and appreciate the motivating forces of each age group.

Our heritage, wealth, and power also influence our emotional well-being.

B. Arrangement
   1. Proem
      a. Function is to state end and object
      b. Epideictic discourse
         1. Entrance alien or akin to theme
         2. Knit proem to theme
         3. Topics include praise, blame, advice
         4. Appeal for indulgence
      c. Forensic discourse
         1. State subject
         2. Appeal for indulgence
      d. Deliberative discourse
         1. Proem rare
         2. Excite or remove prejudice
         3. Amplify facts; adornment

Although not a very important part of arrangement, the proem sometimes is needed. The type of proem depends upon the form of discourse being employed.

   2. Statement
      a. Reveal necessary facts
      b. Depict character and emotional traits observing proper mean
      c. Epideictic = use of intermittent approach
      d. Forensic = ethical appeal, brief in defense, continuous
      e. Deliberative = refresh memory; least important part

The statement, which is a crucial part of the discourse, contains the narrative needed to construct the argument.

On the whole, the statement is not a vital part here.

   3. Argument
      a. Function is to prove, refute, interrogate
      b. Epideictic discourse
         1. Amplification is best
         2. Proof of facts rarely given
      c. Forensic discourse
         1. Enthymeme is best

The principal claims are incorporated into the argument. They may be designed to prove, refute, or question. Generally speaking, argument is less important for epideictic discourse than for the other two forms.

 2. Determine stasis or
    status
    a. Act not committed
    b. Act not harmful
    c. Harm less than
       reward
    d. Act justified
 d. Deliberative discourse
    1. Example is best
    2. Thing cannot be done
    3. Thing is unjust
    4. Thing is harmful
    5. Thing is of minor
       importance
 4. Epilogue
    a. Ethical appeal
    b. Magnify and depreciate
    c. Pathetic appeal
    d. Recapitulation
C. Style and Delivery
 1. Delivery
    a. Pitch
    b. Volume
    c. Rhythm
 2. Diction
    a. Choice of Words
       1. Lucidity
          a. Current terms
          b. Distinctive names
          c. Metaphors
       2. Propriety (Deviations
          from ordinary usage)
       3. Impressiveness
          a. Metaphors
          b. Epithets
          c. Simile
    b. Sentence movement
       1. Purity
          a. Connecting words
          b. Specific words
          c. Avoid ambiguity
          d. Proper gender
          e. Correct number
       2. Appropriateness
          a. Emotional
          b. Ethical
          c. Suited to theme

The stasis is the turning point of an issue or the central point being disputed. Thus it may consist of one or more of these four points.

By suggesting that a thing cannot be done, or is minor or harmful, the speaker may either persuade or dissuade an audience regarding a course of action to be taken.

As in the case of the proem, the epilogue is not always required. When it is needed, it may contain both ethical and pathetic appeals and/or a summary of the argument.

Delivery, which may be viewed as a subordinate part of style, makes use of pitch, volume, and rhythm.

Clarity, correctness, appropriateness, and vividness should be evident in a speaker's choice of words and sentence structure. Special care should be taken in the handling of metaphors.

In sentence movement, as in the case of word choice, the doctrine of usage in style constitutes an important guideline.

3. Dignity
   a. Description
   b. Metaphors and Epithets
   c. Plurals
   d. Repeat definite article
   e. Connective particles
   f. Negatives
   g. Antithesis
   h. Actuality
   i. Deceptive surprise

Notes

1. For a more extended analysis of Aristotle's methodology, see Donal J. Stanton and Goodwin Berquist, "Aristotle's *Rhetoric:* Empiricism or Conjecture?", *Southern Speech Communication Journal,* 41, 1 (Fall, 1975), 69–81.
2. *The Rhetoric of Aristotle: A Translation* (Cambridge: University Press, 1909), p. 1.
3. *Ibid.,* p. 3.
4. *Ibid.,* pp. 4–5.
5. *Ibid.,* p. 5.
6. The use of the terms "artistic" and "non-artistic" comes from the Lane Cooper translation of *"The Rhetoric* (New York: Appleton-Century-Crofts, 1932), p. 8. These terms seemed to the authors more meaningful than Jebb's "artificial" and "non-artificial."
7. *The Rhetoric,* trans. by Jebb, p. 6.
8. Rhetorical scholars now generally seem to agree that what distinguishes the enthymeme from the syllogism is its *probable* nature and that some enthymemes may include a statement of all three terms, rather than one or two.
9. James H. McBurney, "The Place of the Enthymeme in Rhetorical Theory," *Speech Monographs,* 3 (1936), 49–74.
10. *The Rhetoric,* trans. by Jebb, p. 9.
11. Everett Lee Hunt, "Plato and Aristotle on Rhetoric and Rhetoricians," *Studies in Rhetoric and Public Speaking in Honor of James Albert Winans* (New York: The Century Co., 1925), p. 50.
12. McBurney, "The Enthymeme," p. 57.
13. *Ibid.,* p. 56.

14. *The Rhetoric,* trans. by Cooper, p. 147
15. McBurney, "The Enthymeme," p. 61.
16. *Ibid.,* p. 62.
17. *Ibid.,* p. 63.
18. *The Rhetoric,* trans. by Cooper, p. 154.
19. *Ibid.,* p. 9.
20. *Ibid.,* pp. 90–131.
21. Jebb, *The Rhetoric of Aristotle,* pp. 71–89.
22. *The Rhetoric,* trans. by Cooper, pp. 56–67.
23. Hunt, "Plato and Aristotle," p. 52.
24. *Ibid.*
25. See *The Republic.*
26. *The Rhetoric,* trans. by Cooper, p. 47.
27. *Ibid.,* pp. 21–23.
28. James J. Murphy, ed. *A Synoptic History of Classical Rhetoric* (New York: Random House, 1972), p. 24.
29. *The Rhetoric,* trans. by Cooper, pp. 221–241.
30. Hunt, "Plato and Aristotle," p. 58.
31. *Ibid.*
32. *The Rhetoric,* trans. by Cooper, pp. 24–29.
33. *The Rhetoric,* trans. by Jebb, pp. 99–100.
34. *Ibid.,* pp. 100–102.
35. *Ibid.,* p. 102.
36. Aristotle, *Poetics,* trans. by W. Hamilton Fyfe (Cambridge, Mass.: Harvard University Press, 1955), p. 81.
37. *Ibid.*
38. *The Rhetoric,* trans. by Cooper, pp. 206–207.
39. *Ibid.,* p. 189.
40. *Poetics,* p. 91.
41. *The Rhetoric,* trans. by Cooper, p. vii.

5

The Education of the Citizen-Orator

In Chapters Three and Four we saw how Plato's dialogues and Aristotle's treatise constitute major contributions to the rhetoric of Western thought. The first provided moral guidelines for the persuasive speaker so timeless in appeal no one has improved upon them since. The second circumscribed the field of rhetoric so broadly modern writers on persuasion inevitably become constant borrowers. But Plato and Aristotle were not the only early thinkers to write on this subject. The insights of dozens of other theorists, practitioners, and critics have survived as well.[1] Our purpose here is not to provide a compendium of the thoughts of every Greek and Roman who ever wrote about rhetoric but to survey important representative contributions to the field. In particular, we will focus in this chapter on what might be called the educational philosophical school of thought as seen in the writings of Isocrates, Cicero, and Quintilian.

Isocrates of Athens

Well educated but early deprived of his patrimony, Isocrates began his career as a logographer or speech writer for wealthy Athenians. He wanted desperately to play a leading role in the affairs of his city state but was unable to do so for two reasons. First, he had a weak voice; he was unable to be heard by large groups out-of-doors, and this after all was how the Athenian Assembly conducted its business. Further, he was naturally timid; he had what we would today call an advanced case of stage fright. In a society oriented to the practice of oratory, Isocrates was a man of ambition without promising prospects.

At age forty-three, he finally found a solution to his dilemma. If he could not himself become an outstanding citizen orator, then he would do the next best thing: he would train Athens' future leaders. In 392 B.C., some five years before Plato established his Academy, Isocrates founded a school of speech, the first permanent institution of higher learning in his native city. For over fifty years, he conducted his school single-handedly. Here he tutored as many as one hundred students at a time, setting forth his ideas for the future leaders of Athens and much of the Greek world. And here he became "the foremost speech teacher of the ancient world."[2]

In a society dominated by the spoken word, rhetoric was of critical importance. No one before or since, we submit, has put the matter as well as Isocrates did in the passage that follows:

We ought . . . to think of the art of discourse just as we think of the other arts, and not to form opposite judgments about similar things, nor show ourselves intolerant toward that power which, of all the faculties which belong to the nature of man, is the source of most of our blessings. For in the other powers which we possess . . . we are in no respect superior to other living creatures; nay, we are inferior to many in swiftness and in strength and in other resources; but, because there has been implanted in us the power to persuade each other and to make clear to each other whatever we desire, not only have we escaped the life of wild beasts, but we have come together and founded cities and made laws and invented arts; and, generally speaking, there is no institution devised by man which the power of speech has not helped us to establish. For this it is which has laid down laws concerning things just and unjust, and things honourable and base; and if it were not for these ordinances we should not be able to live with one another. It is by this also that we confute the bad and extol the good. Through this we educate the ignorant and appraise the wise; for the power to speak well is taken as the surest index of a sound understanding, and discourse which is true and lawful and just is the outward image of a good and faithful soul. With this faculty we both contend against others on matters which are open to dispute and seek light for ourselves on things which are unknown; for the same arguments which we use in persuading others when we speak in public, we employ also when we deliberate in our own thoughts; and, while we call eloquent those who are able to speak before a crowd, we regard as sage those who most skillfully debate their problems in their own minds. And, if there is need to speak in brief summary of this power, we shall find that none of the things which are done with intelligence take place without the help of speech, but that in all our actions as well as in all our thoughts speech is our guide, and is most employed by those who have the most wisdom.[3]

Speech separates men from all other animals; speech underlies all of the important institutions of our society—law, education, morality. We use speech to debate public policy; we also use speech to resolve problems in our own minds. Nothing of substance in society is accomplished without the aid of speech. Those who use speech best are the men of greatest wisdom among us. These were Isocrates' views on the subject he taught for over half a century. Is it any wonder that a subject so conceived should form the nucleus of a whole system of education in both Greece and Rome?

Students were admitted to Isocrates' school of speech at age fifteen. To be accepted, they had to demonstrate competence in science and mathematics and promise in voice control, intellect, and nerve. Their master felt that geometry and astronomy served as a sort of mental gymnastics which prepared the mind for philosophy and civics.[4] Further, he knew by his own experience that lung power and self-confidence were crucial ingredients to oratorical success. To be a leader in a democratic state meant to be a capable if not outstanding speaker. The tuition for a three to four-year course of study was roughly $200, a large sum for those days when the normal curriculum might extend six weeks and cost far less.

Isocrates maintained that there were three essentials for learning: natural ability, training, and practice. Those who were unwilling to work hard at developing their talents soon dropped out.

Instruction began with introductory lectures on writing, speaking, and Greek culture. The sole texts available were a set of "speeches" written by the master himself. These set pieces, together with student essays were studied, criticized, revised, rewritten, and reexamined again and again. Students were sent to the Assembly and the law courts to study the compositions of experienced orators as well.

The core of Isocrates' curriculum was public speaking, for he belived speech was the best available instrument for sharpening human judgment. To find the right expression demanded a sensitivity to both thought and language no other method then in use required. The right word, Isocrates declared, was a sure sign of good thinking. Taken in its broadest sense, learning to speak properly was tantamount to learning to think properly. Isocrates advised his students that the liberally educated man was conspicuous for his eloquence rather than for his wealth or valor. Note that effective speech-making was the sign of sound training, *not* its principal goal.

The curriculum also included writing, debate, classical prose and poetry, philosophy, mathematics, and history. The brand of education Isocrates offered was literary in its stress upon the development of a graceful style, psychological in its emphasis upon influencing human behavior, political in its use of contemporary issues in government, and pragmatic in its preparation of students to serve as citizen leaders in Greek society. Isocrates had no interest in idle speculation, in a search for knowledge unrelated to human conduct. Nor did he believe in the existence of absolute truth. Rather, he recommended that his students pursue that conduct which all Greeks acknowledged to be good. To him, the moral man was one who chose wisely in a given situation. Education in "the wisdom of choice" was as essential an exercise for the soul, he believed, as gymnastics was for the body. Thus a sharp contrast existed between the truth-seeking of students at Plato's Academy and the practical training in civic leadership offered by Isocrates.

Isocrates' set speeches, the texts his students studied with care, were propagandistic in nature for they mirrored the master's lifelong belief in pan-Hellenism. Like many thinkers in his day, Isocrates was justly proud of the many cultural accomplishments of the Greek people. But he was dismayed by the endless squabbling of the various city states. He yearned for a united Greece, a goal achieved only at his life's end with the military conquests of the Macedonians.

Unlike other teachers of his time, Isocrates did not pretend to have a monopoly on wisdom. He often sent his students to learn from others, from whomever was best qualified to teach them. Even though his own curriculum was richly diverse, he recognized special talent in others.

Isocrates' approach to education was innovative in that he made widespread use of imitation and models. He insisted on providing each of his students with individual attention. Pupils came from every corner of the Mediterranean world. At the end of their extended stay in Athens, many wept. Some initiated a life-long correspondence with the master and some erected a statue to his memory at the Temple of Apollo at Delphi.

The aim of Isocrates' system of education was the development of citizen orators, not of orators *per se.* Graduates of his school became prominent generals, philosophers, historians, and statesmen. Isocrates attracted more students than all the other sophists and philosophers combined.

Plato perceived "something of philosophy" in Isocrates' work and predicted he would excel all those who studied rhetoric and "leave them farther behind than children."[5] *Against the Sophists,* Isocrates' attack on the itinerant and often immoral professors of his day, served as the prototype of Plato's *Gorgias,* the dialogue he wrote several years later.

Isocrates' name is cited more often than that of any other rhetorician in Aristotle's *Rhetoric.* And his broad influence may well exceed even this enviable record. Consider, for example, his treatment of the character of a speaker, written when Aristotle was still a student at Plato's Academy:

Mark you, the man who wishes to persuade people will not be negligent as to the matter of character; no, on the contrary, he will apply himself above all to establish a most honourable name among his fellow citizens; for who does not know that words carry greater conviction when spoken by men of good repute than when spoken by men who live under a cloud, and that the argument which is made by a man's life is of more weight than that which is furnished by words?[6]

Cicero, with his notable gift for imagery, summed up the impact of the great Athenian teacher best: "Then behold Isocrates arose, from whose school as from the Trojan horse, none but real heroes proceeded."[7]

The Roman Rhetoricians: Cicero and Quintilian

Practical, thorough, intellectually diverse—Isocrates' version of rhetorical education stimulated the thinking of Roman philosophers and educators two centuries later. Rhetoric at Rome began with the mastery of Greek rhetoric.

Young Romans were "expected to memorize the system and might be subjected to a thorough catechism on it."[8] The Greek language was taught in Roman schools and oftentimes the teachers themselves were Greek so there was no way around the "system"—the student had no choice but to learn.

The Greeks invented rhetoric but the Romans perfected it. Consonant with their stress on thoroughness and practicality, the Romans believed in an early start. Before all things let the talk of the child's nurses be grammatical, Quintilian counseled.

To their morals, doubtless, attention is first to be paid; but let them also speak with propriety. It is they that the child will hear first; it is their words that he will try to form by imitation. We are by nature more tenacious of what we have imbibed in our infant years; as the flavour, with which you scent vessels when new, remains in them . . . those very habits, which are of a more objectionable nature, adhere with the greater tenacity; for good ones are easily changed for the worse, but when will you change bad ones into good? Let the child not be accustomed, therefore, even while he is yet an infant, to phraseology which must be unlearned.[9]

Elementary education was placed in the hands of a teacher called a *grammaticus:* his duties involved correcting spelling, grammar and punctuation together with reading and interpreting poetry and history. He provided students with a solid introduction to language and culture; others were responsible for instruction in arithmetic, geometry, music, and astronomy.

Advanced rhetorical education involved a rich variety of skills perhaps the most distinctive of which was declamation. The instructor would present a case similar to those debated in the Roman Forum and the students would argue its merits as closely as possible to reality.[10] If we were to walk into a Roman classroom where rhetoric was being taught we might hear a debate on the following typical themes:

1. A certain commander, being surrounded by the enemy and unable to escape, came to an agreement with them, by which he was to withdraw his men, leaving behind their arms and equipment. This was done, and so his men were saved from a hopeless situation with the loss of arms and equipment. The commander was accused of high treason. . . .

2. The law forbids the sacrifice of a bull calf to Diana. Some sailors caught by a storm on the high seas vowed that if they reached a harbour which was in sight they would sacrifice a bull calf to the diety of the place. It so happened that at the harbour there was a temple of Diana, the very goddess to whom a bull calf might not be sacrificed. Ignorant of the law, they made their sacrifice on reaching shore and were brought to trial.[11]

The mastery and skillful use of argument and language were nutured through such exercises, along with those in writing, paraphrase, translation, imitation, and memorization. Students were also assigned readings in poetry, history, and oratory and they undertook as well the study of law and politics.

The ultimate goal of such training was the production of the philosopher-orator-statesman. Cicero, the greatest of the Roman orators, articulated the ideal program in his most famous rhetorical work, *de Oratore.*

In my opinion . . . no man can be an orator possessed of every praiseworthy accomplishment, unless he has attained the knowledge of every thing important, and of all liberal arts, for his language must be ornate and copious from knowledge, since, unless there be beneath the surface matter understood and felt by the speaker, oratory becomes an empty and almost puerile flow of words.[12]

Cicero himself was a life-long student and would travel anywhere in the Mediterranean world at his own expense to enhance his education.

Forms of Proof: Stasis as an Element of Logos. To be thus widely read and broadly educated insured the speaker ample subject matter for his speeches. But the Romans went further by amplifying Greek concepts in fill-

stasis

ing in gaps on various aspects of the canons. Consider, for example, some of their notions on the forms of proof. They went beyond Aristotle and most Greek authors in their discussion of *stasis*. This element of logos came to mean the central turning point in a case—the issue upon which a debate may hinge. Cicero and Quintilian argued that the state of any case could be determined by asking certain questions: whether a thing is, what is is, and of what kind it is. Did a case turn on a question of fact, definition, or quality? Quintilian analyzed Cicero's defense of Milo as an example: "First (fact), Did Milo kill Clodius? Yes, fact admitted. Second (definition), Did Milo murder Clodius? No. Claudius lay in wait and attacked Milo. Therefore, the killing was not premeditated. It must be defined as self-defense, not as murder. Third (quality), Was the act good or bad? Good, because Claudius was a bad citizen, and the Republic was better off with him dead."[13] Let the student examine the nature of the cause with these questions in mind, Cicero wrote, and the point at issue becomes immediately apparent.[14]

When we apply the Roman theory of stasis to representative controversial issues in the 1960's and 1970's, it is easy to see its relevance. Observe, for example, the heated debates generated during the Vietnam War. Here are a few typical central turning points that led to division among Americans.

1. Was the Vietnam War essentially a Civil War? (Stasis of Definition)
2. Were the My Lai killings justified? (Stasis of Quality)
3. Did the South Vietnamese Army or the Viet Cong first violate the cease fire agreements? (Stasis of Fact)

How these questions were answered frequently determined whether members of the Administration and Congress would be identified as "Hawks" or "Doves."

Arguments and information were to be found in certain "places," as the Romans metaphorically phrased it. Quintilian described the process this way: "I now come to *things*, among which *actions* are most closely connected with

persons, and must therefore be first considered. In regard, then to everything that is done, the question is, either *why*, or *where*, or *when*, or *in what manner*, or *by what means*, it was done. Arguments are consequently derived from *the motives for actions done* or *to be done*"[15] The ancient student of rhetoric, like the modern student of journalism, used these questions to guide him in the discovery of a case. "The places pointed to by Quintilian's questions were cause, place, time, manner, means."[16]

Ethical Proof. In the area of ethical proof the Romans also expanded the concept of *inventio*. Aristotle, you may recall, spoke of the constituent elements of ethos as being intelligence, character, and good will. But his interest in these notions was largely limited to the period of speech presentation itself. He did not feel that the listener should concern himself unduly with the orator's actions outside of the immediate rhetorical situation. The Romans, however (perhaps influenced by Isocrates' earlier view), broadened ethical proof to include the thrust and image of the speaker's life as a whole. Thus they constructed a theory consistent with their notion of the "perfect orator." Because this aspect of Roman thinking was to have importance for centuries to come, let us turn to the personification of this idea of antecedent ethical proof—Quintilian's "good man theory."

In Book XII of his *Institutes of Oratory*, Quintilian develops his concept of the perfect orator. First, he is a good man and after that he is skilled in speaking, Quintilian declared.[17] Although technical skill is important, it is subordinate to the moral strength of the speaker. So strong were Quintilian's convictions on this subject that he believed "no man can be an orator unless he is a good man." It is not difficult to understand this strong emphasis on the character of the speaker if we analyze Quintilian's views on the function of a speech. "Oratory," he tells us, "is in the main concerned with the treatment of what is just and honorable." A speech which does not exemplify these traits is suitable only to a "hireling pleader" or a "hack advocate." The orator "is sent by heaven to be a blessing to all mankind." Consequently, he is not only a leader but a servant of the people. When he speaks in the forum he pleads with the judge to acquit the innocent defendant. As he speaks in the senate in time of war he encourages the citizens to abandon their fear. As he orates on special occasions he inspires his hearers to emulate the great heroes of the past. In short, whether the speech is forensic, deliberative, or epideictic in nature, it is designed for the sole purpose of guiding the hearers along a righteous path.

Quintilian, therefore, concludes that only the individual "who is a good man skilled in speaking" can hope to perform these essential duties of the orator. Who is this good man? What traits does he possess? Quintilian answers that he is a man who is free from all vice, a lover of wisdom, a sincere believer in the cause which he advocates, and a servant of the state and the people.

Quintilian believed that "vileness and virtue cannot jointly inhabit in the selfsame heart." A man is either good or evil. It is impossible for him to yield to the lusts of the flesh and, at the same time, carry out the great responsibility which belongs to the orator. "Surely the advocate who is called upon to defend the accused," asserts Quintilian, "requires to be a man of honor, honor which greed cannot corrupt, influence seduce, or fear dismay."

Quintilian, like Aristotle, Plato, and Cicero, stressed the importance of knowledge as an essential requisite of the orator. To acquire understanding of the subject matter of a particular case, the speaker must assiduously study all pertinent material. Since study, however, requires considerable effort the heart and mind must be free from those distractions which turn the attention of the orator away from the "object of preparation." Arguing from less to greater, Quintilian points out that if many of the necessary daily activities interfere with our speech preparation, how much more will such violent passions as "envy," "avarice," and "greed" hamper serious contemplation.

Further, the orator cannot hope to achieve his end unless he sincerely believes in the cause which he advocates. First, be inspired yourself, advises Quintilian, then you are ready to "inspire such good feelings in others." Quintilian disagrees with those who state that a speaker may have the ability to simulate an attitude of sincerity. "For however we try to conceal it," he noted, "insincerity will always betray itself, and there was never in any man so great eloquence as would not begin to stumble and hesitate as soon as his words ran counter to his inmost thoughts."

The ideal orator, likewise, places the interests of the people before his own welfare. His actions will not be motivated by ambition, but rather his duty to his countrymen. It is clear, Quintilian argues, that the evil man is a slave to his own fleshly desires. In time of emergency he may sacrifice the people at the altar of cowardice or greed. The good man, on the other hand, even in the moments of greatest adversity, remains just and honorable.

Not content with a philosophical explanation alone of the nature of the good man, Quintilian turns to more practical considerations. He answers his critics who charge that his theory is impractical and inconsistent. The ideal orator must know how to speak on both sides of a question, and, in addition, may frequently be forced to tell a falsehood in defence of a good cause. We cannot understand the nature of virtue until we have seen vice. Since it is incumbent on the orator to teach honor and justice, he must analyze the opposite traits of dishonor and injustice. In this connection, Quintilian observes that "the schemes of his adversaries should be no less known to the orator than those of an enemy to a commander in the field."

How can the orator express untruths and still be a virtuous man? Quintilian points out that the end, rather than the means, is the leading principle of life. Any methods which the orator might use are acceptable if the cause which he defends is just. In each of the following situations, for example, a lie would, in Quintilian's opinion, serve a more useful purpose than the truth:

1. To divert an assassin from his victim.
2. To deceive an enemy to save our country.
3. To convince an unjust judge that certain righteous acts were never done.

4. To forgive enemies who may serve the state to advantage.
5. To comfort a child who is sick.

Quintilian next considers the problem of teaching the prospective orator how to become a good man. He is careful to note that virtue is not an innate gift from God. Instead it is something that comes from study, contemplation, and training. The student would be wise, therefore, to concentrate on the subject of ethics and logic; "for no one will achieve sufficient skill in speaking, unless he makes a thorough study of all the workings of nature and forms his character on the precepts of philosophy and the dictates of reason." Although the powers of a particular student are "inadequate to such an achievement," his efforts will not be in vain. For he will be rewarded according to the distance which he travels toward that goal.

What is distinctive in this theory is the stress upon "goodness" as the Romans understood that word. "Goodness," to them, meant dutiful service to family and state. Thus Quintilian, as the chief propagator of the "good man theory," felt content in upholding an ends-means philosophy. Situational ethics which typified Roman morality was later ignored by the Christian Church when it sought an educational system for its believers. Quintilian's comprehensive system of education with its central focus on the "good man" appealed at once to ethical Christians: no matter that Roman and Christian ideas of morality failed to coincide. From the fifth century, A.D. to the Renaissance, the educational concepts of Quintilian dominated Western thought.

Pathetic Proof. As we turn from ethical to pathetic proof, we again see that the Romans both reinforced and extended Aristotle's theories. Accepting the view that man is basically rational, they agreed with Aristotle that emotional proof should be used as a reinforcement of logos. But they went far beyond Aristotle and Isocrates in highlighting the value of pathos. In the *Orator,* Cicero suggested that impressive pathetic appeals must be used to strengthen the logos.[18] The speaker, he said, who inflames the court accomplishes far more than the one who merely instructs it. Nonemotional speech produces yawning, gossiping, and poor eye contact. Only when a speaker stirs the audience to pity or hate and has them hang on every word is a genuine orator present.

Cicero further observed that he owed his reputation as an outstanding orator to his ability to appeal to sympathy and pity. It is for this reason, he noted, that he frequently was selected as the speaker to deliver a closing plea to a jury. Moreover, he freely participated in rhetorical acts designed to arouse emotions. On one occasion Cicero and other members of a defense team told a defendant to stand up and raise his small son so that all could see. The result was "a wailing and lamentation" thoughout the forum.[19]

Cicero set the stage for Quintilian's theory of pathetic proof. Fully convinced of the need for compelling pathos, Quintilian observed: "There is room for addresses to the feelings. The nature of the feelings is varied, and not to be treated cursorily; nor does the whole art of oratory present any subject that requires greater study."[20]

With Cicero, Quintilian viewed humor and laughter as important emotions which have the power to dispel hatred or anger. The following statements taken from Quintilian's theory of humor, we feel, are timely and useful suggestions for twentieth-century speakers:

1. "There are three things out of which we may seek to raise a laugh, to wit, others, ourselves, or things intermediate."
2. "There is such a thing as a humorous look, manner or gesture. . . ."
3. Humor should "never be designed to wound, and we should never make it our ideal to lose a friend sooner than lose a jest."

Dispositio. The Roman rhetoricians sought to amplify the other four divisions of classical rhetoric as well. The four parts of a speech outlined by Aristotle—proem, statement, argument, and epilogue—were enlarged to five—exordium, narration, proof, refutation, and peroration. In developing these points, Cicero gave practical suggestions that still have a contemporary relevance. The purposes of an exordium or introduction, he said, are to arouse attention, to orient the listeners regarding the theme, and to conciliate. If the proof or body portion of the discourse contains three main ideas, he added, the strongest argument should come first and the weakest should be placed in the middle. Finally, the peroration or concluding action step is the appropriate section to use forceful emotional appeals.[21]

Cicero's inclusion of refutation as a separate element of *dispositio* foreshadows later theories of argumentation and debate. Both he and subsequent writers held that the weight of an argument is often sustained unless it is countered by strong reasoning and evidence. Cicero himself offers us a splendid model of persuasive refutation in his historically significant essay "On Old Age." First, he lists the following arguments which are frequently used to relegate older people to a position of inferiority and unhappiness: (1) elderly citizens are inactive; (2) they lack physical vitality and stamina; (3) they are unable to experience "sensual pleasures"; and (4) they are rapidly approaching death.

Cicero next turns to each of the four indictments against old age and presents a point-by-point refutation. The inactivity of older people, he argued, does not prevent them from engaging in intellectual pursuits. Nor does it keep them from remembering what is important in maintaining the good life. Secondly, the loss of physical vigor due to age is more than offset by an improvement in vocal melody and a mastery of a subdued style. Thirdly, an older person, by being deprived of sensual pleasures becomes more temperate, refrains from engaging in unrewarding activities, and strengthens his appetite for conversation. Fourthly, the issue of death not only confronts the elderly but also the young. More importantly one's success in life is not determined by the number of years spent on earth but by the quality of his existence. Nor can we overlook the fact that since death is followed by immortality, grief is unwarranted.[22]

By the time that Cicero finishes his refutation, he has successfully established the claim that old age has positive merits as well as shortcomings. For this reason his argument not only gives us a valuable insight concerning the use of refutation, but provides comfort and encouragement to senior citizens in the 20th century.

Cicero also amplified the classical notion that *dispositio* embraces audience analysis and adaptation as well as arrangement.[23] Prudence and judgment, he stated, must be used by the orator in choosing and organizing arguments and speech details so that they will be suitable to the listeners and occasion. This implies the need, in some instances, to make major adjustments on an impromptu basis.

Quintilian approached speech organization from the viewpoint of a defendant in a legal case. He considered the methods for responding to single and multiple accusations, the importance of ordering arguments to best advantage, the order of speakers, and the nature of one's defense. Himself a courtroom pleader of note, Quintilian relied partly on personal experience and partly on the wisdom of those who preceded him. The Romans devoted more attention to forensic speaking than to any other type. This explains in part why refutation became one of the five parts of a speech.

Elocutio. The Roman tendency to amplify and fill in gaps was also evident in their handling of the canon of style or language control. In his discussion of style, Cicero declared the speaker's purpose would determine his use of language: *to prove* he will resort to the "plain" style typified by Greek orators in the province of Attica; *to please* he will enjoy a "middle" style championed by Isocrates; *to persuade* he will choose the "grand" style of discourse first used by Gorgias. In his dialogue, *Orator*, Cicero described the ideal orator as one who mastered all three styles "He in fact is eloquent who can discuss commonplace matters simple, lofty subjects impressively, and topics ranging between in a tempered style."[24]

The "plain" speaker had as his main concern, propriety. He talked in a subdued voice and used the most common of words. His attention was directed to thought rather than language, so he disregarded rhythm and smoothness and avoided ornamentation. His goal was to speak adroitly and neatly, clearly and properly. He might employ mild metaphors and maxims, but only when they enhanced understanding, never for effect. His discourse, then, was plain and direct, expeditious and ordinary.

The speaker who sought to entertain his listeners would choose a "middle" style. Vigor was sacrificed for charm. Any and every form of ornamentation was appropriate, including the use of wit and humor. Such a speaker possessed the skill to develop arguments with breadth and erudition; he was master at amplification. His words were chosen for the effect they would produce on others. Harsh sounds were avoided. Euphony and imagery were cultivated. The overall effect was one of moderation and temperance, of polish and urbanity. This style of discourse more than any other typified Cicero himself and would later influence us in English through the marvelous prose style of Edmund Burke.

The "grand" style of oratory Cicero described was magnificent, stately, opulent, and ornate. The grand orator was fiery, impetuous; his eloquence "rushes along with the roar of a mighty stream."[25] Such a speaker might sway thousands if conditions were right. But if he resorted to dramatic delivery and majestic speech without first preparing his listeners, he would be "like a drunken reveller in the midst of sober men." Timing and a clear understanding of the speaking situation were critical. The grand orator must be familiar with the other two forms of style or his manner would strike the listener as "scarcely sane." The "eloquent speaker" was Cicero's ideal. No one ever achieved the eminence he had in mind but like Plato's philosopher king, the ideal sometimes motivated man's best efforts.

Memoria. The canon of memory which goes unmentioned in Aristotle's *Rhetoric* was also viewed by the Romans as an area the orator must master. A Greek by the name of Simonides was the first to teach this mental discipline, according to Quintilian. The story goes that Simonides was attending an athletic banquet when he was informed that two messengers on horseback wished to speak with him. While he was absent from the banquet hall, the building collapsed, crushing the guests so horribly "that those who went to look for the bodies of the dead, in order to bury them, were unable to recognize by any mark, not only their faces, but even their limbs." Then Simonides, by the aid of his memory, "pointed out the bodies to the friends in the exact order in which they had sat."[26]

The essential rule recommended as a first requisite by Simonides, Cicero, and Quintilian was the association of words with visual images which could be remembered against some familiar background. The common system was to identify words or topics with physical objects and place. Convinced that it is chiefly order that gives distinctness to memory, Cicero suggested that certain places must be firmly fixed in the mind; then symbols to be used in a discourse should be mentally arranged in those places. Thus "the order of places would preserve the order of things, and the symbols of the things would denote the things themselves; so that we should use the places as waxen tablets, and the symbols as letters."[27]

Quintilian was more specific in developing the method of association. He asked potential speakers to familiarize themselves with a series of visual images such as the rooms of a house and furniture in each room. They should associate part of what they have written or planned with each chair, statue, or the like in a room. Then when they speak they can imagine they are going into the vestibule of the house so as to be reminded of words or thoughts associated with it.

Let us consider the following hypothetical speech using Quintilian's method. The specific purpose of the address is to discuss the principal causes of cheating in academic institutions. With such a theme, the speaker might come into the classroom and concentrate upon five places and things: (1) chairs; (2) blackboard; (3) lectern; (4) hallway; and (5) windows. He would then be ready to associate these objects with the ensuing potential main ideas:

1. The *chairs* = an overemphasis on grades.
2. The *blackboard* = unfair testing procedures.

3. The outside *hallway* = peers who cheat in order to survive academically.
4. The *lectern* = poor teaching and lectures.
5. The *windows* = the general public that cheats on such matters as income taxes.

Other suggestions for improving the memory were also given. Although Cicero argued that nature actually endows us with a good, average, or poor memory, he nevertheless gives several hints. Chief among these are the need to use a proper sequence that has a logical structure, and to imprint ideas firmly in our mind through the senses.

Quintilian spelled out some rules for memorizing a manuscript speech or a part in a dramatic production. These he summarized as follows:

1. Learn the manuscript "piecemeal."
2. Mark those sections that prove difficult to learn.
3. Practice the passages aloud. ("The mind should be kept alert by the sound of the voice, so that the memory may derive assistance from the double effort of speaking and listening.")
4. Test frequently, repeating passages which tend to slip from memory.
5. Use an artistic sequence so that if interruption occurs in the middle of a speech the train of thought will not be lost.[28]

The best overall method of improving the memory, argued Quintilian, is through practice and industry.

Pronunciatio. The Greeks were aware that a speaker's manner of presentation was important to his success. Indeed, Cicero tells us that when Demosthenes was asked to name the three most important qualities an orator must have, his reply was "Delivery, Delivery, Delivery."[29] But Aristotle, as we have observed, was message-oriented. He considered the management of the speaker's voice largely extraneous to his main business. It remained for the Romans, therefore, to explore this canon in depth.

Complaining that no previous rhetorician had ever undertaken a systematic treatment of delivery, the Roman author of *Rhetorica ad Herennium* observed: "I believe (that it) deserves serious consideration."[30] Included in this author's system is a discussion of three speaking tones—the conversational, the debating, and the pathetic. The debating tone is "sustained or broken," and characterized by "an occasional quick gesture of the arm, a mobile countenance, and a knowing glance." Moreover, it often features pacing, stamping of the foot, and a "look of intense concentration." The pathetic tone frequently is accompanied by slapping "one's thigh" and beating "one's head." The author concludes his analysis of delivery by ensuring that what the orator is saying should appear to come from the heart.

Cicero stood high among those rhetoricians who gave a significant position to delivery. In his *Brutus,* one speaker is rebuked for his lackadaisical manner. "Did you smite your brow, slap your thigh, or at least stamp your foot? No! In fact, so far from touching my feelings, I could scarcely refrain from going to sleep then and there."[31] Despite this extreme, Cicero elevated delivery to a respectable place in rhetorical practice. He defined it as the control of the voice and body in a manner suited to the dignity of the subject and style of the speech. Holding that nature and training go hand in hand in producing a specific voice for each emotion, he declared: The whole "frame of a man, and his whole countenance, and the variations of his voice, sound like strings in a musical instrument, just as they are moved by the affections of the mind."[32] He then added that while we look to nature for a musical voice, clarity can be improved by practice.

Quintilian agreed with Cicero and other predecessors that a good delivery comes largely from nature but that it can be enhanced by nurture. Similarly, he, too, placed emphasis on the association of the emotions with delivery, and gave suggestions concerning the voice. It should be easy, powerful, fine, flexible, firm, sweet, well sustained, clear, pure, and one that cuts the air and penetrates the ear. One should not hiss, pant, cough, wheeze, or sing. Most of all, vocal tones should be suited to the occasion and to the speech.

Quintilian was the first rhetorician to provide an extensive treatment of gesture and facial expression. Here are some of his suggestions:

1. Gesture of the head can indicate humility, haughtiness, languor, or rudeness.
2. The face can be suppliant, menacing, soothing, sad, cheerful, proud, humble.
3. With your arms and hands, ask, promise, threaten, supplicate; show fear, joy, grief, doubt, acknowledgment, penitence; indicate measure, quantity, number, time.
4. Strike the thigh to indicate indignation, but do not stamp the foot too often.
5. As for the speech as a whole, open calmly and gain fire and momentum as you go.
6. The fingers may be used to designate specific ideas.

In utilizing an educational-philosophical approach to rhetoric, the Romans, following in the tradition of Isocrates, were influential and relevant. They are to be commended for seeing the relationship between nature and nurture, for identifying and stressing all five classical canons of rhetoric, for alerting students regarding the significance of antecedent ethical proof, and for filling in vital gaps concerning memory and delivery. They also recognized that since rhetorical situations may have permanence, a speech too should have permanence.

Notes

1. For an overview of the varied contributions of Greek and Roman rhetoricians, see L. Thonssen, A. C. Baird, and W. Braden, *Speech Criticism,* 2nd. ed. (New York: The Ronald Press Co., 1970. Excerpts of representative classical works in rhetoric appear in T. Benson and M. Prosser, *Readings in Classical Rhetoric* (Boston: Allyn and Bacon, Inc., 1969).
2. For the principal objectives which guided Isocrates' school, see G. Berquist, "Isocrates of Athens: Fore-most Speech Teacher of the Ancient World," *The Speech Teacher,* 8 (September 1959), 253–255.
3. "Antidosis," *Isocrates,* trans. by George Norlin (Cambridge: Harvard University Press, 1929; reprinted 1956), II, 327–329.
4. "Antidosis," II, 333.
5. *Phaedrus,* trans. by Lane Cooper (London: Oxford University Press, 1938), pp. 70–71.
6. "Antidosis," II, 339.
7. *Cicero on Oratory and Orators,* trans. by J. S. Watson (New York: Harper and Brothers, 1860), p. 108.
8. M. L. Clarke, *Rhetoric at Rome* (London: Cohen and West Ltd., 1953), p. 15.
9. Quintilian's *Institutes of Oratory,* trans. by J. S. Watson (London: George Bell and Sons, 1875). I, 9–10.
10. So long as the Roman Republic existed, this form of training continued, but once the Caesars came to power, the themes declaimed became fictitious or hypothetical.
11. Cited in Clarke, *Rhetoric at Rome,* p. 18.
12. *Cicero on Oratory and Orators,* p. 11.
13. Cited in D. L. Clark, *Rhetoric in Greco-Roman Education* (New York: Columbia University Press, 1957), pp. 72–73.
14. *Cicero on Oratory and Orators,* p. 119.
15. *Institutes of Oratory,* I. 340.
16. Clark, *Rhetoric in Greco-Roman Education,* p. 76.
17. The references used in this discussion of ethos are taken from *The Institutio Oratoria of Quintilian,* trans. by H. E. Butler (London: William Heinemann, 1961), IV, Book XII.
18. Cicero, *Orator,* trans. by H. M. Hubbell (London: William Heinemann, 1962), pp. 403–409.
19. *Ibid.,* p. 405.
20. *Institutio Oratoria,* I, 421.
21. Cicero, *De Oratore,* trans. by E. W. Sutton (Cambridge, Mass.: Harvard University Press, 1959), II, 78.314.
22. Moses Hadas, ed. *The Basic Works of Cicero* (New York: The Modern Library, 1951), pp. 127–158.
23. Russell Wagner, "The Meaning of *Dispositio."* *Studies in Speech and Drama in Honor of Alexander Drummond* (Ithaca, New York: Cornell University Press, 1944), pp. 285–294.
24. *Orator,* XXIX, 100.
25. *Ibid.,* XXVIII, 97.
26. *Institutio Oratoria,* XI, 2, 11–14.
27. *Cicero on Oratory and Orators,* p. 187.
28. *Institutio Oratoria,* XI, 2, 27–50.
29. *Orator,* XVII, 56.
30. *Ad Herennium,* trans. by Harry Caplan (Cambridge, Mass.: Harvard University Press, 1964), III, XI, 19. It is generally believed that Cicero was the author of this work.
31. *Brutus,* trans. by G. L. Hendrickson (Cambridge, Mass.: Harvard University Press, 1942), IXXX, 278.
32. *Cicero on Oratory and Orators,* p. 256.

In the foregoing treatment of the educational philosopohical approach to rhetoric which formed one of the major trends in the classical period, we have sought to develop general concepts and guidelines as articulated in representative treatises and in the classrooms. To see more graphically how Roman rhetorical scholars provided specific and detailed suggestions for achieving the goal of constructing enduring speeches, we reprint the ensuing essay, "Cicero and Quintilian on the Formation of an Orator." Among the points emphasized in this paper are the relationships that exist between speaking, reading, and writing, and the reciprocal influence that each of these communication forms has on the other. Cicero and Quintilian, as we will see, display a strong preference for those orators who excel in all three categories. In sum, it is our hope that this essay will function as a summary statement of the classical concern for teaching public communication as a field of study.

Cicero and Quintilian on the Formation of an Orator

The theory of culture approach to rhetoric has long been identified with the name of Isocrates. For decades in his highly successful school which attracted potential orators, historians, and political leaders, he taught that rhetoric "ought to be a work of art as complete and as substantive as the utterance of poetry. . . ."[1] In doing so he demonstrated faith in prose rhythm as a literary form and recommended its use as a means of preparing the student of communication to take part in political affairs.

Isocrates, who described his system as philosophical, built his concept of oratory around four major characteristics. To be effective, he argued, a speaker or writer must have a broad view of nature and society; he must root his ideas in an elevated moral tone; he must adhere to a thorough and well structured method of practice and scholarship; and he should strive to create works that would have permanent rather than ephemeral value.[2] The communicator who hoped to achieve these ends would, of necessity, have a firm grasp of the humanities and social sciences, project a strong moral dimension, and reveal a commitment to scholarship. He would, in short, have an appreciation for culture.

This cultural and pragmatic emphasis in rhetorical instruction held a special appeal for Cicero and Quintilian. "The brilliancy of Isocrates" which, observes Jebb, came "to Cicero through the school of Rhodes" contributed

significantly to the development of Cicero's rhetorical theory and practice,[3] and this, in turn, helped shape the philosophy of Quintilian. With Isocrates the two leading Roman rhetoricians saw the relationship of art, nature, reading, and practice in producing the orator. To sketch this correlation and to show some of its implications is the burden of this essay.

An important first step in understanding Cicero's method of forming an orator is to note his interest in constructing a philosophy of scholarship which could serve as a framework for producing rhetorical works that have artistic form. In his *Tusculan Disputations,* written a few weeks before the Ides of March in 44 B.C., Cicero observed that an author who publishes his thoughts expressed in faulty content, arrangement, and style is guilty of "an unpardonable abuse of letters and retirement."[4] A few months later, following the murder of Caesar, Cicero sought to protect the scholarly reputation as well as the physical safety of his friend Brutus. In a letter to Atticus he noted: "Brutus has sent me his speech that he delivered before the Assembly on the Capitol. He wants me to correct it frankly before he publishes it." Cicero then added: "I should like you to read the speech . . . and to

Reprinted from *Speech Journal,* "Cicero and Quintilian on the Formation of an Orator" Vol. VI, 29–34, 1969, by James L. Golden. Reprinted with permission.

let me know what you think of it."[5] The interest which both Brutus and Cicero expressed on this occasion concerning the need for careful scrutiny of speeches designed to be published doubtless epitomizes the prevailing fear which gripped the real and suspected opponents of Caesar. But more importantly it reveals the high status of Latin scholarship during the generation of Cicero and the immediately subsequent Augustan Age. As a man of letters who was, according to Chester Starr, "the most important single cultural leader in the thousand years of Roman development,"[6] Cicero conducted a lifelong campaign to create a philosophical vocabulary in Latin and to establish standards for a concise, varied, vivid, and informal style which would appeal to the literati. But he also set for himself the task of enriching his native tongue so that it could become suitable as a spoken language.[7] His conscious attempt to mobilize the Latin language led Cicero to write numerous letters, essays, dialogues, poems, and speeches that were filed for publication. Moreover it prompted him to see strong similarities between a speaker's devotion to careful scholarship and his ability to express ideas orally and in writing.

This Isocratic tendency to view rhetoric and other prose forms as an artistic production which should win the approval of men of culture not only influenced Cicero's *De Oratore* but constitutes a major thrust in Quintilian's *Institutio Oratoria*. But the ideal orator both men sought to create must meet three additional requirements. He should have an inherent ability to speak, a comprehensive reading knowledge of philosophy and other liberal arts, and intense practice in writing. So closely related are these forms of communication, Quintilian held, that if one were separated the others would lose their power. He observed in his *Institutio Oratoria*:

They are so intimately and inseparably connected, that if any one of them be neglected, we shall but waste the labor which we have devoted to the others. For eloquence will never attain to its full development or robust health, unless it acquires strength by frequent practice in writing, while such

practice without the models supplied by reading will be like a ship drifting aimlessly without a steersman. Again, he who knows what he ought to say and how he should say it, will be like a miser brooding over his hoarded treasure, unless he has the weapons of his eloquence ready for battle and prepared to deal with every emergency.[8]

Largely because of the high standards inherent in a cultural view of rhetoric, Cicero and Quintilian, like their Greek predecessors, concluded that nature was a more influential force than nurture in shaping an orator. For it is nature which gives to the speaker his inventive ability, his talent to arrange and adapt arguments in a judicious manner, his potential power in language control, and his basic vocal and physical mechanism. Without these innate essentials one cannot appreciate the role of culture in rhetoric, nor can he develop a facility in the arts of reading and writing which form the essence of oratory.

But if nature is needed to provide the raw materials for effective rhetorical performance it is nurture that takes the materials and moulds them into a meaningful pattern. One of the fruits of nurture is to open the doors of knowledge through a thorough and steady program of reading and study. "No man can be an orator complete in all points of merit," said Cicero, "who has not attained a knowledge of all important subjects and arts. For it is from knowledge that oratory must derive its beauty and fullness, and unless there is such knowledge, well-grasped and comprehended by the speaker, there must be something empty and almost childish in the utterance."[9] As the search for the perfect orator unfolds in the subsequent pages of *De Oratore*, Cicero strives mightily to show that learning and eloquence must go together.

In formulating a pragmatic educational view of rhetoric based on a theory of culture which stressed the value of nature and knowledge, Cicero and Quintilian, standing squarely in the tradition of Isocrates, said little that was new. As they turned to the function and importance of writing as a tool for developing an orator they were refreshingly innovative and influential. In the early stages of an orator's preparation, Quintilian held that an endowed speaking talent is first in importance, while reading ranks second. As the student of rhetoric progresses, however, the relative value of these points will shift. With the maturing of the educational process, writing assumes a steadily significant role. In his *De Oratore* and *Brutus,* Cicero asserted that writing is not only an "eminent . . . teacher of eloquence,"[10] but the most impressive single influence on speaking practices.[11]

Cicero and Quintilian were not content to give testimonials concerning the general value of writing in relation to speech. They proceeded to examine the specific contribution of the pen as an implement of oratory. This was especially evident in the area of extemporaneous speech. Some Roman speakers frequently wrote out their addresses in complete manuscript form, then committed the language to memory. But they attempted to deliver the oration in such an off-hand manner that even the judge could not detect the amount of labor which went into the construction of the work. Such a practice, however, failed to fortify the speaker against unpredictable emergencies. Moreover, particularly in forensic speaking, it was often too time-consuming to be useful. Cicero and other successful pleaders before the bar, therefore, usually wrote certain portions of their orations, such as the introduction, conclusion, and select passages in the discussion. The effectiveness of the speech, then, depended largely upon their ability to improvise.

Through his experiences as a peformer and an observer of forensic opponents, Cicero also had come to believe that whenever a person can express unpremeditated thoughts in a style that resembles what is written, he may be considered a master of extempore speech. That the means of gaining this facility is through diligent practice in writing is also clear. As Cicero put it in *De Oratore:*

. . . he too who approaches oratory by way of long practice in writing, brings this advantage to his task, that even if he is extemporizing, whatever he may say bears a likeness to the written word; and moreover

if ever, during a speech, he has introduced a written note, the rest of his discourse, when he turns away from the writing, will proceed in unchanging style. Just as when a boat is moving at high speed, if the crew rest upon their oars, the craft herself still keeps her way and her run, though the driving force of the oars has ceased, so in an unbroken discourse, when written notes are exhausted, the rest of the speech still maintains a like progress, under the impulse given by the similarity and energy of the written word.[12]

Quintilian echoed a similar sentiment when he said:

For without the consciousness of such preliminary study our powers of speaking extempore will give us nothing but an empty flow of words, springing from the lips and not from the brain. It is in writing that the eloquence has its roots and foundations, it is writing that provides the holy of holies where the wealth of oratory is stored, and whence it is produced to meet the demands of sudden emergencies.[13]

If writing skill contributes significantly to one's extemporaneous speaking style, it is also useful as a means of measuring the validity of an orator's reputation and long range effectivenss. In fulfilling this challenge of rhetorical criticism, Cicero and Quintilian classified Greek and Roman orators into three categories: (1) persuasive speakers who wrote little or ineffectively; (2) good writers who spoke rarely or inadequately; and (3) scholarly writers who spoke well.

Hortensius, Sulpicius, Galba, and Pericles were articulate speakers, yet they either lacked the ability to write or the will to do so. Hortensius, a contemporary of Cicero, early in his career mastered the Asiatic style, and developed a dynamic delivery. As he cultivated these talents, he became one of the leading orators of Rome. Indeed his prestige remained unchallenged until Cicero's eloquence reached maturity. Notwithstanding his success as a speaker, Hortensius was a deficient writer. "His writings," said Quintilian, "fall so far short of the reputation which for so long secured him the first place among orators."[14]

Sulpicius likewise was an effective speaker who had an elevated and flowing style, a vibrant and resonant voice, and a graceful and theatrical manner. Yet he failed to achieve permanent distinction as an orator, for, as Cicero regretfully observed: "No oration from the mind of Sulpicius . . . is extant. I often heard him comment on the fact that he had never cultivated the habit of writing and found it impossible."[15]

That Pericles was similarly a persuasive speaker, Socrates, Plato, and Cicero concurred. For forty years the Athenians applauded his eloquence. But when Quintilian examined Pericles' written works, he concluded that some other pen had composed them. "I have been unable to discover anything," he said, "in the least worthy of his great reputation for eloquence, and am consequently the less surprised that there should be some who hold that he never committed anything to writing and that the writings circulating under his name are the works of others."[16]

Cicero, when asked by Brutus to explain how Galba's reputed speaking effectiveness was not apparent in his printed works, suggested three reasons why certain orators did not write as well as they spoke or did not write at all. Since it was often customary, first of all, to write out speeches after they had been delivered, the orators, when writing, were in a different physical environment and psychological mood. The inspiration which they had received from the cheering multitudes in the forum was not present in their private studies at home. Hence they no longer had the urge to call forth the necessary energy that is needed to write with vividness and force. Under such circumstances the written composition doubtless was inferior to the spoken word. Secondly, since some orators were primarily concerned with their immediate audience they had no compulsion to influence posterity. Others, finally, refrained from writing, as we have seen, because they recognized their natural deficiency or inadequate training.[17]

If Cicero and Quintilian were disappointed in orators who lacked training or talent in writing, they also criticized writers who could not or did not communicate ideas orally. The two leading members of this group were Isocrates and Lysias. Although Cicero called Lysias an almost perfect orator, and described Isocrates as a "consummate orator" and "an ideal teacher," he deplored the tendency of these speakers to shrink "from the broad daylight of the forum."[18] Implicit in Cicero's description of Isocrates and Lysias was an indictment of logographers who observed rather than experienced the rhetorical strategy they had created. Despite his enormous talents Isocrates could not be included "in the class of perfection," noted by Cicero in his *De Optimo Genere Oratorum*. "For his oratory does not take part in the battle nor use steel, but plays with a wooden sword. . . ."[19]

The ideal orator sought by Cicero and Quintilian would most likely be found in the third category of communicators who achieved excellence both in writing and speaking. Not the least of those who approximated this high standard of eloquence were Aeschines, Demosthenes, and Cicero himself. The following statement drawn from the *Brutus* stands as testimony of Desmosthenes' accomplishments: "For the perfect orator and the one who lacks absolutely nothing you would without hesitation name Demosthenes. Ingenuity however acute, however subtle, however shrewd, would fail to discover any point in the orations from his hand which he has overlooked."[20] In other rhetorical works Cicero was less laudatory, arguing that his Greek predecessor fell short of perfection, but he never altered his judgment that Demosthenes was unsurpassed in the history of oratory. It remained for Quintilian in Book X of *Instituio Oratoria* to establish the precedent of drawing a comparison between Demosthenes and Cicero. These two orators, Quintilian held, had two important points in common. They knew how to write as well as how to speak. A close analysis of their published speeches demonstrates that the touch of the hand was equal to the power of the voice. In short, they did what all good orators should do. They wrote as they spoke and spoke as they wrote. Such, observed Quintilian, is the essence of oratory.[21]

Once they had become convinced of the interrelationship between writing and speaking Cicero and Quintilian, as proponents of the philosophical-educational view of rhetoric, established guidelines for gaining facility in writing manuscripts that contain "the best thoughts in the choicest language."[22] Quintilian began his discussion of this theme by exhorting his students to avoid spending excessive time on the first draft. But he also warned them not to compose too rapidly. Thirdly he criticized the common procedure of dictating speeches to an amanuensis. To these prescriptive statements emphasizing what should not be done, he next presented positive suggestions for improvement. One should know when, where, and how fast to write; and he should, when necessary, employ the three methods of revision—"addition, excision, and alteration."[23]

Of the possible exercises that may be used to help develop writing skill the most important are imitation, translation, and paraphrasing. Whenever these practices are combined they stimulate the memory, increase the understanding, and enhance the flexibility and ease of expression. Hopefully what is learned from these exercises will tend to produce an eloquence which is similarly effective in the written and spoken word. The value of this approach is described in the following passages taken from *Cicero's De Optimo Genere Oratorum:*

I translated the most famous orations of the two most eloquent Attic orators, Aeschines and Demosthenes, orations which they delivered against each other. And I did not translate them as an interpreter, but as an orator, keeping the same ideas and the forms, or as one might say, the "figures" of thought, but in language which conforms to our usage. And in so doing, I did not hold it necessary to render word for word, but I preserved the general style and force of the language. . . . The result of my labour will

be that our Romans wil know what to demand from those who claim to be the atticists and to what rule of speech, as it were, they are to be held.[24]

Cicero also found it rewarding to translate and paraphrase the works of Xenophon and Plato.[25]

It would appear from this brief survey that the two leading Roman rhetoricians wanted prospective orators who had a natural talent for eloquence to embrace a theory of culture approach to rhetorical performance which emphasized the worth of reading and writing as important elements in forming the model speaker. Notwithstanding the fact that this philosophy was derived largely from Isocrates, Cicero and Quintilian are to be commended for their creative suggestions concerning the relationship between writing and speaking ability. The practitioner who stresses one of these communication forms and neglects the other may achieve temporary fame as a persuasive speaker or an enduring influence as an accomplished manuscript writer. But he can never approximate the ideal orator who must excel in both areas. The implications of his analysis are not without significance. First, in arguing that a facility in writing is needed to produce the necessary momentum for an extemporaneous speaker to address his immediate audience with rhythmical smoothness and force, Cicero and Quintilian, conscious of the importance of effect, constructed a practical system of rhetoric which viewed the orator as the prime motivator of a group of listeners on a specific occasion.

Oratory, however, must have a larger goal than to stimulate a listener in a particular situation at a designated moment in history. It should also address itself to a long range audience not bound by time and locale. In a sense, therefore, Cicero and Quintilian were not only rhetorical critics but literary critics as well. It is instructive at this point to recall Wichelns' classic treatise, "The Literary Criticism of Oratory." The literary critic, he observed, views a "work as the voice of the human spirit addressing itself to men of all ages and times. . . ."[26] This tradition of criticism which Wichelns found prevalent in the nineteenth century received an early impetus in the writings of Cicero and Quintilian. Convinced that long range effectiveness, as well as immediate impact, is an essential measurement of rhetorical success, they wished to elevate oratory to the level of literature. This prompted them to give a preeminent position not only to invention but to style which, in turn, made them wary of publishing manuscripts that had not been polished and honed to meet the taste of an educated populace. For this reason they alluded with approval to the great confrontation between Aeschines and Demosthenes in 330 B.C. as an example which both instructed and inspired the Romans of the first century B.C. and A.D. not merely because of the historic message and the renowned protagonists but because of the elegant and sublime style that gave the extant manuscripts permanence. In fashioning his own eloquence Cicero quite clearly kept one eye on his immediate audience and another on posterity. Thus he, like Demosthenes, provided models which could be imitated, translated, and paraphrased during subsequent centuries. Perhaps the author of *Ad Herennium* had the youthful Cicero in mind when he said: "Let orators devote their artistic power to this purpose—to win esteem as worthy themselves to be chosen as models by others, rather than as good choosers of others who could serve as models for them."[27]

Not to be overlooked is another influence derived from a writing-speaking centered rhetoric conceived by Isocrates and perpetuated by Cicero and Quintilian. In giving similar emphasis to the need for instructing students in the two forms of communication and in describing the effect each has upon the other, they, despite their attachment to an oral society which moulded them, anticipated the tradition of rhetoric and belles lettres that flourished in the eighteenth century. Adam Smith in his popular lectures in Edinburgh and later in his classroom discussions at the University of Glasgow, and Hugh Blair in his celebrated book in 1783 combined rhetoric with polite literature and criticism as a basis for teaching their students to develop proficiency in oral and written communication.

Similarly post-World War II courses combining units on reading, writing, speaking, and listening are at least indirectly traceable to Cicero and Quintilian. In maintaining, therefore, an abiding concern for creating an ideal orator who could produce works of immediate and permanent value, the Roman rhetoricians pointed the way toward a rhetoric of relevance for mid-twentieth century students of communication theory.[28]

James L. Golden

Notes

1. R. C. Jebb, *The Attic Orators from Antiphon to Isaeus*, 2 Vols. (New York, 1962), II, 52.
2. *Ibid.*, 36–53.
3. *Ibid.*, 73.
4. Cicero, *Tusculan Disputations*, ed., C. D. Yonge, I, 3.
5. Cicero to Atticus, Sinuessa, May 18, 44 B.C., in Moses Hadas, ed., *The Basic Works of Cicero* (New York, 1951), pp. 418–19.
6. Chester Starr, *A History of the Ancient World* (New York, 1965), p. 526.
7. See H. M. Hubbell, tr., *Orator* (Cambridge, Mass., 1942), p. 298; Hadas, *The Basic Works of Cicero*, x, xvii; H. J. Haskell, *This Was Cicero* (New York, 1942), p. 301; and Charles Baldwin, *Ancient Rhetoric and Poetic* (Gloucester, Mass., 1959), p. 39.
8. H. E. Butler, tr., *The Institutio Oratoria of Quintilian* (London, 1921–22), Book X, 1, 2. Hereafter cited as *I.O.*
9. E. W. Sutton and H. Rackham, tr., *Cicero De Oratore* (Cambridge, Mass., 1959), Book I, vi, 20.
10. *Ibid.*, I, 33, 150.
11. G. L. Hendrickson, tr., *Brutus* (Cambridge, Mass., 1942), xxiii, 92. Cited hereafter as *Brutus*.
12. *De Oratore*, I, 33, 152–53.
13. *I.O.*, Book X, 3, 2–3.
14. *Ibid.*, XI, 3, 8.
15. *Brutus*, 1vi, 205.
16. *I.O.*, III, 1, 12.
17. *Brutus*, 23, 91–95.
18. H. M. Hubbell, tr., *Cicero De Optimo Genere Oratorum* (Cambridge, Mass., 1960), V, 17. Cited hereafter as *De Optimo Genere Oratorum*. Also see *Brutus*, viii, 32 and 35.
19. *De Optimo Genere Oratorum*, v, 17.
20. *Brutus*, viii, 35.
21. *I.O.*, Book X, 7, 7.
22. *Orator*, 1xvii, 227.
23. *I.O.*, Book X, 3 and 4.
24. *De Optimo Genere Oratorum*, v, 14, 15.

25. Cicero was particularly impressed with Plato's ability to communicate. In his essay "On Moral Duties," he observed: "I indulge the fancy that Plato, had he chosen to practise oratory, would have made an impressive and eloquent pleader. . . ." *The Basic Works of Cicero*, p. 6. He reinforces this idea in *De Oratore*. Here he suggests that after reading the *Gorgias* "what impressed me most deeply about Plato in that book was, that it was when making fun of orators that he himself seemed to me the consummate orator." *De Oratore*, I, xi, 47.

26. Herbert Wichelns, "The Literary Criticism of Oratory," in *Studies in Rhetoric and Public Speaking in Honor of James Albert Winans* (New York, 1925), p. 213.
27. H. Caplan, tr., *Ad Herennium* (Cambridge, Mass., 1964), iv, 7.
28. They would have endorsed enthusiastically the strategy of John F. Kennedy who confessed that he prepared his inaugural address with the thought in mind that it would achieve a high place in United States history. See *New York Times*, January 13, 1961.

Although the major emphasis in this section has been on "the education of the orator," it is vitally important to note that Cicero, in particular, recognized the need to relate rhetoric to conversation or interpersonal communication. Indeed, in his famous essay "On Moral Duties," he not only called for an indepth analysis of the "science of conversation" but presented preliminary guidelines which have relevance for contemporary discourse. After observing that "speech is a great power in the world," he said:

It is of two kinds, formal discourse and conversation. Formal discourse is appropriate to judicial argument and to political and deliberative orations; conversation finds its natural place in social gatherings, learned discussions, and in friendly reunions and banquets. There is a science of rhetoric, and I am inclined to think a science of conversation possible though none exist. The demand for masters creates the supply, and though the world is full of students of rhetoric, there are neither students nor masters of conversation. Still the rules of rhetoric are equally applicable to conversation. Since the voice is the organ of speech, we should try to make it clear and pleasant. These qualities, it is true, are natural gifts, but the first may be improved by practice, the second by the imitation of calm and articulate speakers. There was nothing about the two Catuli to make you think they possessed a fine literary sense; for the culture they had was nothing extraordinary, and yet it was thought they spoke Latin with the greatest purity.

Their pronunciation was agreeable, the sounds were neither mouthed nor minced, obscure nor affected; and they spoke without effort, yet without monotony or excessive modulation. The diction of L. Crassus was more copious and not less brilliant, but the eloquence of the Catuli ranked as high as his. In wit and humour Caesar, the brother of the elder Catulus, was the first speaker of his time; even at the bar his easy conversational style surpassed the laboured speeches of his rivals. If, then, we aim at decorum in everything we do, we should strive to perfect ourselves in all these qualities. Forming our conversation on the admirable model of the disciples of Socrates, let us put forward our opinions in an easy tentative way and not without a spice of humour. Above all, we should never monopolize the conversation but allow every one in turn to have his fair share. First of all it is necessary to consider the subject, and, whether it be grave or gay, let our language correspond. Again it is important not to betray any defect of character, such as the malice of the slanderer who delights in attacking the absent either in jest or with the serious purpose of covering them with abuse and contumely. Conversation generally turns upon family affairs, politics or learning and culture. These are the subjects to which we must endeavor to bring it back if it has drifted into another channel, but we must always study the company; for tastes differ, and nothing pleases all men at all times or to the same degree. It is well to mark the moment when the subject palls and to end as we began with tact.

The sound principle, that in all our conduct we should be free from passion or wild irrational feeling, ought naturally to govern our conversation. Let us betray no symptom of anger, or intense feeling, or of apathy, listlessness, or similar defects, and endeavor to exhibit respect and consideration for those with whom we converse. If at times reproof is required, it may be necessary to speak in a louder tone and in stronger language and to assume the appearance of anger. But like the cautery and the lance, that is an extreme measure which we should seldom and reluctantly employ and only as a last resource. Anger itself we must put far away, for with it we can do nothing right or well-advised. Often it will suffice to administer a gentle, but calm, reproof and to exhibit sternness without insolence. Nay more, let us show that even the severity of our censure is only intended for the good of the offender. Again, in the quarrels we have with our bitterest enemies, it is proper to stifle our feelings and maintain our composure whenever insults may be offered to us. If we are under the dominion of excitement we lose our balance and forfeit the respect of the company. Another offence against decorum is to boast of oneself, especially without ground, and to expose oneself to derision byplaying the 'Braggart Captain.' (*Basic Works*, pp. 50–52)

Cicero, in sum, is telling us that in order to be an effective conversationalist, we should focus on a worthy and timely subject such as family affairs, politics, or the arts and sciences; know when and how long to speak; adapt to the interests of our guests and colleagues; exemplify decorum, tact, self-control, and rationality; utilize humor to liven the discussion; and channel our ideas through a clear, pleasant, and articulate vocal pattern. Above all, we should avoid playing the role of the braggadocio. Such procedures, we feel, constitute useful rules that may be applicable for present-day situations involving interpersonal communication.

The foregoing analysis of classical rhetorical theory may be summarized under three broad headings. First, we saw how the culture of ancient Greece and Rome provided the ambience for the flowering of rhetoric. All facets of Greek and Roman life suggested a strong need for knowledge of and skill in rhetorical theory and practice. The democratic political system in 4th Century-Greece and 1st Century-Rome (until the death of Cicero in 43 B.C.) encouraged the discussion of controversial issues affecting the state; the legal system called to the attention of the populace the role that rhetoric could play in self-defense; the literary, dramatic, and historical productions featured rhetorical strategies and techniques in communicating their subject matter; and the society, in general, promoted dialogue. Against this background of prevailing interest in communication, the sophists, schools, and academies found a rationale for giving instruction in rhetoric.

Secondly, we have observed that in the classical period three major approaches, all of which were related, dominated rhetorical theory and training. The moral-philosophical view represented by Plato established as its ideal the noble lover—a speaker who seeks to lead the audience to an understanding of truth centered in the will of the gods. The scientific-philosophical view epitomized by Aristotle described in specific detail a communication model comprised of speaker, speech, and audience; and recognized the vital notion that rhetoric deals almost exclusively with probability and contingent propositions. The educational-philosophical view typified by Isocrates, Cicero, and Quintilian admitted the superiority of nature over nurture in the formation of an orator, yet created an effective model for teaching rhetoric in the classroom.

Thirdly, our survey has demonstrated that there were several distinguishing characteristics of classical rhetorical theory which affected later thought. With varying degrees of emphasis the Greek and Roman scholars made these claims:

1. Rhetoric is a field of study worthy of scientific speculation and inquiry.
2. Rhetoric has a unique vocabulary and

category system consisting of such elements as forms of discourse and the canons of *inventio, dispositio, elocutio, memoria,* and *pronunciatio.*
3. Rhetoric, for the most part, is concerned with persuasion.
4. Rhetoric is essentially an oral activity.
5. Artistic proof, with its stress on enthymematic reasoning, is more important than inartistic proof comprised largely of evidence.

6. The ethical dimension is a central aspect of rhetoric.

Perhaps we should also add that while public speaking was the dominant rhetorical form preoccupying the attention of the ancients, there were telltale signs pointing to a developing theory of interpersonal communication. Illustrative of this emerging trend were Plato's reliance on dialectic and the Socratic method and Cicero's guidelines for constructing an "art of conversation."

6

Rhetoric in Transition

As we stated in the introductory section of this volume, our approach in dealing with the rhetoric of Western thought is to give a primary emphasis to the three major systems. Now that the overview of the classical system has been presented, we need to turn next to the second great system which was articulated by British and Continental theorists in the seventeenth, eighteenth, and nineteenth centuries. Before doing so, however, we would like to provide a brief summary of the evolution of rhetorical theory beginning with the Second Sophistic (50–400 A.D.) and ending with the Renaissance period (1400–1600 A.D.). In treating this section as a bridge or transition that leads to system two, we in no way mean to deemphasize the importance of the leading rhetorical works written by the medieval and Renaissance scholars. Our position is that these theories, while relevant for a changing society, do not constitute a separate system that is unique in its orientation and influential in its long range impact. We concur with Nancy Harper when she says: "Though there was little advance, and much decline, in human communication theory during the medieval and Renaissance periods, there were a number of developments important to the continuation of the discipline." (*Human Communication Theory*. Rochelle Park, N.J. Hayden Book Company, Inc., 1979), p. 135.)

J. Russell Corley, who for several years was a primary lecturer in a survey course in western rhetorical theory, has written the following essay. His goal is to demonstrate how in this transitional period the continuity of rhetoric as a field of study was maintained even though original and speculative thought were minimal.

The Second Sophistic (50–400 A.D.)

Culture and society influence the rhetorical action, theory, and education of an age. Rhetoric often plays an important role in shaping changes within a social system, but these societal transitions also constrain future rhetorical action. We now turn our attention to a brief overview of some major changes in rhetoric which occurred as the Roman Empire rose and declined and as Christianity became an accepted vision of reality through the Middle Ages and the Renaissance.[1]

It may be recalled that during the age of Plato and Aristotle there was a group of teachers who excelled in stylistic excesses. Men like Gorgias prided themselves on their ability to impress an audience with their use of language and their powerful delivery. Such men drew criticism from philosophers like Socrates, Plato, and Aristotle, yet sophistic artificiality has never been fully crushed and remains even today. The sophistic tradition has been influential during certain periods in the history of rhetoric; one such period was that of the Roman Empire. It is impossible to establish an exact date when rhetoric at Rome began its transition from a practical art intimately connected with political and legal issues in the Republic to a truncated art of style and delivery divorced from the civic affairs in the Empire. For our purposes we can consider the period of the Second Sophistic as spanning from about 50 to 400 A.D.[2]; our interest lies in some of the causes and characteristics of this phase of rhetorical history.

As the Republic died, freedom of speech was limited and rhetoric became an art concerned with ornate expression and polished delivery. It is important to note that the rise of the Caesars to power eventually led to the fall of rhetoric as a viable political and legal tool. Three changes in Roman oratory deserve consideration.[3] First, as the Caesars established their rule over Rome, democracy faded and political decisions were taken out of the citizens' hands and given to the politically elite. True deliberative oratory vanished as public discussions of political issues were virtually abolished. Any opportunity to address a political question was constrained by the fact that the speaker could be punished for taking a stand against Caesar's position. Such threats to an orator's freedom of expression obviously weakened eagerness to express opposition concerning controversial issues.

Second, the legal system in Rome had become increasingly technical and restrictive. The complexity of the laws demanded that pleading in courts be limited to legal specialists who knew the intricate details of jurisprudence; these specialists were close students of legal procedure but they were rarely great orators. Frequently forensic orators were unduly influenced by severe political pressures. This climate was not conducive to creative rhetorical action, and forensic oratory declined.

Third, the major form of rhetoric which was encouraged was epideictic oratory, but it, too, was constrained by political realities. Speeches of praise usually treated themes favorable to the reigning Caesar and the Empire; speeches of blame most often focused upon political "enemies of the state." Ceremonial speaking became the safest form of rhetoric, yet its very emphasis upon praise and blame encouraged stylistic excesses. Rhetoric removed from the crucial realities and issues of daily life moves toward an oratory which emphasized expression over content.

These constraints upon oratory obviously influenced the behavior of rhetorical practitioners and educators. As the opportunities for a relevant rhetoric decreased, the use of rhetoric as a mode of exhibition and entertainment increased. Baldwin argues that the sophists prided themselves on feats of fluency, improvisations, memory, and grand displays of linguistic dexterity.[4] Examples of these qualities can be found in the ancient work entitled *The Lives of the Sophists*. The writers describe the actions of one sophist named Prohaedresius who stood before a large crowd and requested that two of his enemies propose a theme upon which he would speak. These men suggested a subject which they felt would be impossible to treat eloquently. Prohaedresius accepted the challenge and asked that there be no applause for his performance. He spoke in an inspired manner using all of his rhetorical talent, and just as he was about to finish his argument he shifted his speech to the opposing stance and was even more eloquent than before. The audience was overwhelmed and could not restrain their applause; many rushed up and kissed his feet and others called him a god.[5]

During the Second Sophistic a popular form of oratorical entertainment was the declamation.[6] A declamation is a speech composed and memorized for presentation before an audience; the theme is either fictitious or historical and is thus removed from contemporary political affairs. Declamations had once been used as an integral part of the rhetorical education process; they had been the means by which orators like Cicero developed their speaking skills and prepared themselves for rhetoric in society. As the Caesars gained control, declamations became an end in themselves; they became a type of public entertainment by which an accomplished rhetorician, like Prohaedresius, could exhibit his skills before an audience. In the declamations of the Second Sophistic little attention was paid to argument; instead the emphasis was upon a moving performance. In short, style and delivery became primary in the teaching and practice of rhetoric. Rhetoric became a form of entertainment and escape for the Roman citizens; the skillful sophist could make a living by performing before audiences not unlike those who pay to see a contemporary rock star perform in concert.

It should be noted that the Second Sophistic made some positive contributions to Roman culture. Kennedy observes, "The sophists were like fashionable preachers who encouraged belief in inherited values of religion and morality in the most polished and elegant form, and they contributed significantly to the stability of a society whose major goal was preservation of the status quo in the face of barbarian attack and new religious movements."[7]

As far as significant advancements of rhetorical theory are concerned, the Second Sophistic contributed little. It is sufficient for our purposes to consider one work probably written during the latter half of the first century entitled *On the Sublime*.[8] This work explores the uses of language in "elevating" or "transporting" an audience to experience a strong emotional state of awe known as the sublime. The writer indicates that a creative use of language must be joined with powerful mental conceptions and a strong emotional state if the sublime is to be obtained.[9] The emphasis is not upon the mere manipulation of language to display linguistic ability; instead, the writer stresses the artistic use of style to express vivid ideas and emotions. It was rare to find this balanced combination in the practice of the sophists; even today the eloquent combination of language and thought is a rare occurrence.

St. Augustine and a Christian Rhetoric

The next important rhetorical development is a specific example of a general and enduring problem: the relationship between Christian faith and secular culture.[10] The specific problem centers around the question: "Can pagan rhetorical theory be used in the proclamation of the Christian message?"[11]

For early Christians their commitment to the life, teaching, and authority of Jesus Christ was uncompromising. Their singleminded loyalty led them to be persecuted in the pagan Roman empire. Over time Roman paganism declined and Christianity emerged as the predominant religion. In 313 A.D., Emperor Constantine gave Christianity equal status with the pagan cults and terminated the persecution of Christians. Later Theodosius abolished pagan cults altogether and Christianity became the official state religion. While officially terminated, paganism continued exerting a powerful influence upon the spirit of the times, and its presence alongside Christianity created an age of anxiety. It was during this time that St. Augustine addressed the problem of a Christian rhetoric.

St. Augustine's (354–430 A.D.) family reflected the societal tensions of the times: his mother was Christian and his father was pagan.[12] Born in northern Africa, he received most of his education at Carthage; later he became a professor of rhetoric. Augustine describes himself as one who thoroughly enjoyed sexual pleasures and worldly vices during his years as a young man. He showed little interest in his mother's Christian beliefs and found Christian sermons lacking in eloquence compared to those of the pagan writers and speakers. He also found the Latin translations of the Bible to be poor examples of writing and confusing in their meaning. He was attracted to philosophy and rhetoric rather than to religion.

Augustine taught rhetoric in Carthage, Rome, and finally in Milan, where he heard St. Ambrose preach. He was pleased with the sermons of this great Christian because they were intelligent, aesthetically pleasing, orderly, and convincing. In 386, Augustine became a convert to Christianity and returned to north Africa where he planned to live a monastic life. In 395, he became the Bishop of Hippo, an important city in the region; he held that position until his death. It was during this period that he wrote *On Christian Doctrine,*[13] his great work which applied Ciceronian rhetorical theory to preaching.

Augustine wrote the first three sections of this work around 396; they dealt with the interpretive problem of discovering sermon material from scripture. About 427, he wrote book four which dealt with the use of rhetoric in expressing ideas. This fourth section is a significant work in the history of rhetoric because it rejects the Second Sophistic and returns to Cicero's writings in order to find a rhetoric which can be adapted to the needs and mission of the Christian movement.[14]

An understanding of the historical context enables us to see Augustine's book as a response to an enduring rhetorical problem.[15] Christianity depends upon the spoken word for preaching and evangelism. Judaism held a central place for the dynamic proclamation of God's word: Moses and the prophets probably spoke their messages before they were recorded. Christianity grew out of this tradition of the spoken word. Much of the materials in the gospels consist of spoken lessons delivered by Jesus. Jewish and Christian speakers had not formalized a rhetorical theory. They were convinced of the authoritative truth of God's revelation and trusted less in oratorical techniques than in spiritual inspiration to lead them to deliver an appropriate message. In the first two chapters of I Corinthians, the apostle Paul contrasts his presentation of the gospel with the wisdom and eloquence of the age. He emphasizes the work of the Holy Spirit to convince an audience of the truth of God's revelation in Jesus.

Kennedy gives us insight into the central role of communication for the early Christians. He points out two major types of Christian oratory. First are messages addressed to a non-Christian audience, including *apologia,* the defense of the Christian faith. Second are addresses to Christian audiences including both messages to heretics and to orthodox Christians. Sermons to orthodox audiences had different functions: remind and strengthen the audience of their basic commitments, provide a prophetic word for a particular situation,

comment upon a chosen text of Scripture, or praise and/or blame a person or occasion in light of the Christian faith.[16] Such a dependence upon spoken and written messages implies the need for a rhetorical theory that enhances successful communication.

For many Christian preachers Paul's contrast between worldly eloquence and spiritual speaking increased with the growing societal acceptance of the second sophistic. These Christians felt that sophistic practices were deceitful, aimed at worldly success, and grounded in a philosophical acceptance of the relativity of truth. They believed that sophists took selfish pride in personal ability to impress an audience with rhetorical skills and to lead an audience away from a sincere desire to yield to the authority of truth. Yet some Christians found that the total abandonment of secular society was not an acceptable alternative. These Christians found aspects of pagan education, literature, and society that could be appreciated and possibly transformed into a Christian lifestyle. Yet such a relational strategy was often accompanied with intellectual and emotional tension. The problem of unacceptable compromise was a difficult one. The conflict between Christian purity and pagan culture is illustrated in Clarke's description of St. Jerome:

In a famous passage in one of his letters St. Jerome tells how when he was on his way to Jerusalem to adopt the life of the ascetic he found it impossible to do without his library. Fasting and penance alternated with the reading of Cicero and Plautus, and when he took up the prophets he was disgusted by their style. Then he fell ill, and in a feverish dream seemed to be brought before the seat of judgment. Asked to give an account of himself he replied: "I am a Christian." "You lie," answered the judge. "You are a Ciceronian, not a Christian. For where your heart is, there shall your treasure be." "I was silent at once," Jerome goes on, "and amid my stripes (for he had ordered me to be beaten) I was even more tortured by the burning of my conscience. . . ." Finally those present threw themselves at the feet of the judge and besought him to make allowances for youth and to allow time for penitence to the sinner, punishing me thereafter if I should ever read the books of the Gentiles again. And I who at this moment of crisis would have promised even more, began to swear an oath: "Lord, if ever I possess or read secular books, I shall have denied thee."[17]

Many Christians who rejected rhetoric as pagan took the position that the possession of Christian truth automatically enabled the preacher to communicate that truth clearly. They felt they needed no help from any rhetorician to express their ideas in a persuasive manner. St. Augustine entered this debate over a Christian rhetoric and attempted to resolve the conflict. He rejected the second sophistic, but he also refused to go to the extreme of calling all rhetoric "evil." He argued thus:

Now, the art of rhetoric being available for the enforcing either of truth or falsehood, who will dare to say that truth in the person of its defenders is to take its stand unarmed against falsehood? For example, that those who are trying to persuade men of what is false are to know how to introduce their subject, so as to put the hearer into a friendly, or attentive, or teachable frame of mind, while the defenders of the truth shall be ignorant of that art? That the former are to tell their falsehoods briefly, clearly, and plausibly, while the latter shall tell the truth in such a way that it is tedious to listen to, hard to understand, and in short, not easy to believe it? That the former are to oppose the truth and defend falsehood with sophistical arguments, while the latter shall be unable to defend what is true, or to refute what is false? That the former while imbuing the minds of hearers with erroneous opinions, are by their power of speech to awe, to melt, to enliven, and to arouse them, while the latter shall in the defence of the truth be sluggish, and frigid, and somnolent? Who is such a fool as to think this wisdom? Since, then, the faculty of eloquence is available for both sides, and is of very great service in the enforcing of wrong or right, why do not good men study to engage it on the side of truth when bad men use it to obtain the triumph of wicked and worthless causes, and to further injustice and error?[18]

In short, Augustine provided a rationale for the use of rhetoric in the Christian cause. After establishing a need for rhetoric, he turned to consider the dimensions of an appropriate communication theory for proclaiming the "truth found in Scripture."

Augustine argued that the preacher should not memorize long lists of rhetorical rules; instead he should study the great orators of Scripture and listen to the leading Christian speakers of the time. He felt that the close observation of excellent models would more quickly teach the Christian rhetorician the basic requirements of eloquence than would a rote memorization of figures of speech. He redefined eloquence because the Scriptures did not meet the requirements of pagan oratory. He asserted that divine oratory is distinctively different from secular speech and that what is desirable for secular speaking is unsuitable for the task of proclaiming a divine message. He cited scriptural examples of divine eloquence which moved an audience towards God; he ultimately created a fourth type of discourse: the sermon.

Augustine argued that the ideal Christian rhetorician is a defender of the faith, an enemy of error, and an expositor of scripture. He affirmed that God's grace is an important element in preaching, but he was quick to add that more than prayer is needed in the preparation and delivery of any sermon. He claimed that the preacher must work diligently to discover ideas and to arrange them in a moving manner. Finally, he cited Cicero's three ends of discourse and argued that there is a goal hierarchy in preaching. All Christian rhetoric must first teach the truth; this is the primary function of every sermon. Second, a sermon often attempts to move an audience to action; to do this the speaker has to motivate the listeners to commit themselves to live the truth they have been taught. The final end of discourse involves delighting an audience; this is never a primary goal in preaching, but it may serve an important function in maintaining an audience's attention.

St. Augustine's rhetorical theory is grounded in the classical theories of rhetoric; it provides an interpretation of Ciceronian theory which was adopted by many writers during the Middle Ages. *On Christian Doctrine* can be considered the first manual on preaching and an important bridge from classical to medieval rhetoric. For these reasons it is a significant work in the rhetoric of Western thought.

Rhetoric and the Middle Ages (400–1400 A.D.)

As we turn our attention to rhetoric during the Western Middle Ages our concern is to highlight briefly the major trends of this period. It should be understood that little innovation in rhetorical theory was made during the Middle Ages; instead, most scholars took Ciceronian theory and applied it to areas of practical need.[19] The three classical works which were most often paraphrased, commented upon, and even plagiarized were Cicero's *De Inventione,* Augustine's *On Christian Doctrine,* and *Ad Herennium.* We will briefly explore how rhetoric was adapted to the medieval world.

Miller, Prosser, and Benson describe three factors which influenced rhetoric in the Middle Ages.[20] First there was a continuing rejection of rhetoric as a pagan art. Even though Augustine addressed this issue, he had not resolved the conflict. Much of the rhetorical theory which was accepted came out of Augustine's application of Cicero to Christian concerns; in a sense Cicero received legitimation through Augustine. Second, Christianity began to lose much of its enthusiasm for evangelism and became monastic in its thrust. Education of citizens was limited and was primarily accomplished through cathedral and monastic schools; the monks were not as concerned with teaching their students how to proclaim truth as they were with moving their students towards a deeper and more personal experience of God. Also, some teachers felt that rhetoric was the science of speaking well

in secular situations; because secular life was not emphasized by the monks, rhetoric was taught not as a practical art but as a scholastic exercise. Finally, there was no democratic society in which secular rhetoric could flourish. Political leaders came to view rhetoric, not as a form of oratory, but as an administrative tool which provided rules for the composition of formal letters and official documents directed toward the passage and administration of laws.

There were at least four applications of rhetoric during the Middle Ages. First, writers like Cassiodorus (480–575) considered rhetoric as a liberal art and one of three great arts called the *trivium.*[21] The *trivium* consisted of logic (or dialectic): the art of reasoning, defining, investigating, and discovering truth; grammar: the art of syntax, meter, figures of speech, and the study of poetry; and rhetoric: the art of expression, style, and organization. These three arts were taught in the medieval schools and were important scholastic skills. During different periods the *trivium* was redefined and one art would be stressed over the others. For example, in the monastic schools, logic was often emphasized because it was a means by which a Christian could contemplate theological truth.[22]

A second area of application was the close alignment of rhetoric with logic by men like Boethius (c. 480–524).[23] Within his perspective rhetoric was contrasted and eventually assimilated to dialectic as a form of discourse:

1. Dialectic proceeds by interrogation and response; rhetoric has uninterrupted discourse.
2. Dialectic employs perfect syllogisms; rhetoric is satisfied with brief enthymemes.
3. Dialectic seeks to dislodge an adversary; rhetoric tries to move a judge or judges.[24]

Once rhetoric was closely allied to logic it was not a difficult step for later philosophers to assign invention and organization to logic and leave rhetoric with only style and delivery.

Third, rhetoric became allied with letter writing.[25] Medieval society placed little value on oratory outside of preaching; most political changes as well as religious ones were accomplished not through speeches but through letters. Scholars like Alberic of Monte Cassino saw rhetoric as important to the task of writing letters and argued that the Ciceronian parts of speech could be used as an organizing principle. An emphasis was placed upon a proper salutation and opening through which a writer attempted to create good will with an addressee. The rhetoric of letters also stressed correctness of language and dignity of style. This conscious adaptation of rhetoric is one of the most important applications of classical theory during the Middle Ages.

Finally, rhetoric played a role in preaching, the primary type of oral discourse during the Middle Ages.[26] Of course, St. Augustine was important in the development of the sermon, but another major figure was Rabonus Maurus (776–856). Murphy describes Maurus' method in selecting rhetorical concepts for preachers:

> When he turns to the subject of speaking . . . his whole approach is based upon the function of the priest as a divinely appointed preacher, and he chooses his doctrines from several sources instead of adopting the Ciceronian system whole. . . . He offers advice to the preacher gleaned sometimes from Cicero, and sometimes even from personal experience.[27]

Murphy argues that Maurus' selective approach to theory was unusual for medieval scholars. Before this time many writers had been slaves to a particular work or theorist; Maurus felt free to select from the classical writers in his effort to guide preaching. Although there were many preaching manuals, they did not create an exciting oratory; most sermons tended to be long, lacking in organization, intricately detailed, highly symbolic, and usually poor examples of effective rhetoric. McKeon adds that rhetoric became "the art of stating truths certified by theology."[28]

As we close our discussion of rhetoric in the Middle Ages we should point out that many important figures during this thousand year period have not been mentioned. Alcuin, Isidore of Seville, Priscian, Bede, John of Salisbury, Hugh of St. Victor, Geoffrey of St. Vinsauf, and St. Bonaventure, and others made contributions to medieval rhetorical theory. Readers interested in rhetoric during this period are referred to the works cited in the notes at the end of this section.

Renaissance Rhetoric (1400–1600 A.D.)

Renaissance rhetoric extended and refined many of the trends we saw in medieval rhetoric; once again we see a building upon classical writers with few conceptual innovations. Kennedy argues: "Italian civic life serves as the environment for a remarkable enthusiasm for classical rhetoric during the fourteenth, fifteenth, and sixteenth centuries. . . . A knowledge of Greek and works of Greek literature, including rhetorical treatises and orations, was recovered in the West."[29] He goes on to point out that many "lost" Latin rhetorical works were discovered in monasteries and that new translations and commentaries were made available.[30] The practice of public oratory seems to have expanded in some minor ways during this period, but it was yet to emerge as a driving social dynamic. Ehninger argues the rhetoric of this age can be characterized as a "aesthetically oriented art of ingratiation—a form of conscious flattery or supplication." He goes on to describe this art in greater detail:

> Its purpose was to teach a socially proper mode of expression, and *socially proper* meant the elegant or the unordinary—a way of ceremonially "talking up the social scale" in an effort to curry favor or to mark oneself as a member of a preferred class.

> Thus we find rhetoric defined as "the theory of speaking ornamentally" or as clothing thought in gay and aureate language, with its substance reduced to a catalogue of tropes and figures, the decorative aspect of *elocutio*. . . . We find rhetoric spilling over into . . . letter writing, and becoming, for all practical purposes, the art of addressing an

individual rather than the art of moving a mass audience. In short, rhetoric was treated as a branch or subdivision of etiquette, and may, in fact, be found in such works as Castiglione's *Courtier* or Peacham's *Complete Gentlemen*.[31]

Castiglione's *The Book of the Courtier* perhaps best illustrates this shift which Ehninger describes.[32] As a handbook for gentlemen, this work outlines the refined means for gaining advancement in the court of a prince. The characters of the book described the actions and manners expected of a courtier, whether it be in telling a joke, courting a lady, or advising the prince. The audience for a courtier's rhetoric was interpersonal and intimate in nature; his rhetorical action involved an effort to manage positive impressions and to increase status within an elite social system. Such a rhetoric included the proper use of spoken and written language, but it also embraced the actions of the individual as symbolic acts.[33] Whenever the courtier engaged in competition or in the display of talent, he was to do so in such a way that if he failed he was not embarrassed and if he succeeded he was greatly praised. The proper courtier was to watch his dress, his involvement with women, and his choice of companions. In a way *The Book of the Courtier* describes an expanded rhetoric which centers upon the creation of favorable image in the minds of a small but powerful audience.

During the Renaissance there was a move to subordinate rhetoric to logic. Peter Ramus is the best known of those scholars who limited rhetoric to style and delivery while giving invention and arrangement to the field of dialectic. He had little interest in emphasizing the civic and oral nature of rhetoric. Instead his work and that of his students continued the truncation of rhetoric that began during the second sophistic and was encouraged during the Middle Ages. Most rhetorical education was aimed at "boys at about the age of junior high school students today; clarity, simplicity, and a content which could be easily memorized were desirable features in such teaching."[34]

Rennaissance schools were usually run by priests who emphasized the rhetorics of Quintilian and Cicero which allowed for both moral and practical training.[35] A major revolution in rhetoric was created by the innovation of the printing press; gradually the printed page became a critical communication channel. Such a change implied that rhetoric became further removed from the live mass audience and more fully aligned with an audience which was separated in time and space from the source and from other audience members.[36]

Corbett characterizes Rennaissance rhetoric as persuasive discourse which attempted "to carry its point by reasoned, sustained, conciliatory discussion of the issues."[37] It was a classical rhetoric adapted to the spirit of the times; it was a rhetoric which emphasized both the aesthetic and social capacities of communication. Just as the rhetorics of the Second Sophistic, St. Augustine, and the Middle Ages were shaped by social, political, and theological forces, so Rennaissance rhetoric was influenced by the great changes in man's understanding of himself and his world.

This original essay was composed for this work by J. Russell Corley, Ohio State University.

Notes

1. This chapter is based upon the primary research of some major rhetorical scholars. Most important among them are James J. Murphy, *Rhetoric in the Middle Ages* (Berkeley, Calif.: University of California Press, 1974); George A. Kennedy, *Classical Rhetoric and its Christian and Secular Tradition From Ancient to Modern Times*, (Chapel Hill, N.C.: The University of North Carolina Press, 1980); Charles Sears Baldwin, *Medieval Rhetoric and Poetic* (Gloucester, Mass.: Peter Smith, 1959); M. L. Clarke, *Rhetoric at Rome* (London: Cohen and West, Ltd., 1953); and Richard McKeon, "Rhetoric in the Middle Ages," *Speculum*, 17 (1942), 1–32.
2. Murphy, p. 35.
3. Murphy, pp. 35–37; Kennedy, pp. 25–40; Baldwin, pp. 5–7; Clarke, pp. 99–102.
4. Baldwin, pp. 13–16.
5. Philostratus and Eunapius, *The Lives of the Sophists*, W. C. Wright, tr., (London and New York: Loeb Classical Library, 1922), pp. 493–499.
6. Clarke, pp. 88–108.
7. Kennedy, p. 38.

8. Longinus, *On the Sublime,* G. M. A. Grube, tr., (Indianapolis and New York: Library of Liberal Arts, 1957).

9. *Ibid.,* p. 10.

10. For a discussion of the general problem see H. Richard Niebuhr, *Christ and Culture* (New York, N.Y.: Harper and Row, Publishers, Inc., 1951); Etienne Gilson, *Reason and Revelation in the Middle Ages* (New York, N.Y.: Charles Scribner's Sons, 1938).

11. For details see Murphy, pp. 47–64; Kennedy, pp. 120–160.

12. For biographical details see St. Augustine, *Confessions;* Peter Brown, *Augustine of Hippo* (Berkeley, Calif.: University of California Press, 1967).

13. St. Augustine, *On Christian Doctrine* or *Christian Instruction,* J. F. Shaw, tr., (Edinburgh, 1883).

14. Baldwin, p. 51.

15. See Clarke, pp. 148–157.

16. Kennedy, pp. 132–143.

17. Clarke, p. 148.

18. Augustine, *On Christian Doctrine,* Book 4, Section 3, n.p.

19. See Joseph M. Miller, Michael H. Prosser, and Thomas W. Benson, eds., *Readings in Medieval Rhetoric* (Bloomington, Ind.: Indiana University Press, 1973), pp. xiii-xv. For extensive discussion see Murphy, Kennedy, McKeon, and Baldwin.

20. *Ibid.*

21. Murphy, pp. 62–67.

22. Prosser, et. al., p. xiv.

23. Murphy, pp. 67–71.

24. *Ibid.,* p. 70.

25. Baldwin, pp. 208–227.

26. Murphy, pp. 81–87.

27. *Ibid.,* p. 82.

28. *McKeon,* p. 15, 19–25.

29. Kennedy, p. 195.

30. *Ibid.*

31. Douglas Ehninger, "On Rhetoric and Rhetorics," *Western Speech,* 31 (1967), 244.

32. Baldesar Castiglione, *The Book of the Courtier,* George Bull, tr., (Baltimore, Md.: Penguin Books, Inc., 1967).

33. This interpretation follows Kenneth Burke, *A Rhetoric of Motives* (Berkeley, Calif.: University of California Press, 1969 edition), pp. 221–233.

34. Kennedy, p. 211; for his discussion of this process see pp. 207–213. For an extensive study of this trend see the standard work by Wilbur Samuel Howell, *Logic and Rhetoric in England, 1500–1700* (New York, N.Y.: Russell and Russell, 1961).

35. Edward P. J. Corbett, "The Rhetoric of the Open Hand and the Rhetoric of the Closed Fist," in Douglas Ehninger, ed., *Contemporary Rhetoric* (Glenview, Ill.: Scott, Foresman and Company, 1972), pp. 202–207.

36. *Ibid.,* p. 204.

37. *Ibid.,* p. 202.

Part Three
British
Rhetorical
Theory

In the preceding chapters we have seen how classical rhetorical theory flourished in Greece and Rome. So successful was the system of training used by the ancients that it constituted a model for rhetorical scholars in the Middle Ages, the Renaissance, and, to some extent, the seventeenth century. "At different periods, of course, the system was subjected to retrenchments, amplifications, shifts of emphasis, revitalizations, innovations, and changes in terminology, sometimes to suit the whim of a particular teacher or group, at other times to make the system more relevant to the needs and moods of the time."[1] Following the development of the printing press, for example, "and during periods when a great deal of political and mercantile business was carried on through the medium of letters, the emphasis both in the classroom and in the rhetoric texts shifted more and more from oral to written discourse."[2] The influence of Christianity and humanism also contributed to some modifications of classical theory. But these changes were primarily in degree rather than substance.

It seems evident that despite innovations which occasionally altered its scope or emphasis, rhetoric at the close of the sixteenth century was still primarily an integral part of an old and cherished system dating back to Socrates, Plato, Aristotle, Cicero, and Quintilian. The classical strain which dominated the period found expression in Thomas Wilson's *Arte of Rhetorique,* published in 1553. This historically significant study was the first modern English rhetoric text that gave full treatment to the basic tenets set forth by the ancients. Standing firmly in the classical tradition, Wilson discussed the canons of *inventio, dispositio, elocutio, memoria,* and *pronunciatio.* Similarly he dealt with three kinds of orations—demonstrative, judicial, and deliberative, and analyzed the three purposes of speech—to instruct, to delight, and to pesuade. In all, it was essentially an English version of the rhetorical theories of Cicero, Quintilian, and the author of *Ad Herennium.*

But if classical doctrine was a vital element in sixteenth-century British thought, it encountered a serious challenge in the early decades of the seventeenth century. With dramatic suddenness, revolutionary scientific, philosophical, and psychological developments modified traditional theories of knowledge, thereby creating the demand for a "new rhetoric" rooted not only in the past but in modern epistemology. These happenings gave rise to four rhetorical trends which interacted with each other during the next two hundred years: (1) neoclassicism; (2) the eclectic method of the belletristic scholars; (3) the psychological-epistemological school of rhetoric; and (4) the truncating approach of the elocutionists. In the following chapters we will examine each of these trends. In approaching the study of British rhetoric from the point of view of trends, we are fully aware of the fact that we must move back and forth in chronology. We feel, however, that this is necessary in order to see the flow of thought within a particular school. We begin with neoclassicism and belles lettres because they most clearly reflect the major teachings of the classical writers. We then move to the epistemologists whose interest in the social and behavioral sciences led them to go far beyond the ancients in exploring the human mind. Finally, we turn to the elocutionists whose tendency to focus primarily on the single canon of delivery set them apart from the other major trends. Hopefully by the time we have completed our survey, we will be able to appreciate both the diversity and the similarities in British rhetoric.

7

Neoclassicism and Belles Lettres

Neoclassicism

The period roughly covering from 1700 to 1740 represents the literary reign of neoclassicism in Britain. Frequently described as the Augustan Age in English thought, this era was under the dominating influence of Jonathan Swift, Alexander Pope, and John Dryden. These classicists, motivated to some degree by eminent French critics, happily joined the ranks of the ancients. Aristotle's *Poetics,* Horace's *Ars Poetica,* and Longinus' *On the Sublime* were to them the desiderata of effective literary composition. They came to believe that if the English language hoped to live as a virile instrument of expression, it must be patterned after the eternal precepts set forth in these works. Consequently, they had little sympathy for those who sought to establish an experimental methodology as a basis for criticism. Such an approach, they were convinced, minimized the importance of classical learning.

Taking their cue from Horace, the Augustans set up a standard for effective writing. The first crucial step that must be observed by all prospective authors is imitation; that is, after diligently studying the ancients, one should strive to imitate the classical precepts. This means that to be a good writer, there is no need for originality, except in the mode of expression. It is the duty of every writer, therefore, to develop a style which describes old truths in a new and interesting manner. The criteria upon which the success of this style depends are correctness and lucidity. It follows that ornate images, ambiguous words and phrases, and verbose expressions, have no place in good style.[3]

Jonathan Swift

One of the leading characteristics of the Augustans was their inflexible attitude toward those who questioned the value of classicism. Jonathan Swift was the first to voice his disapproval. He had witnessed the advance of experimental science and had envisioned it as a definite threat to all forms of art. Out of this feeling of fear and bitterness came the "Battle of the Books," a masterpiece of satirical criticism. In this account, Swift tells of a battle that occurred in the Public Library between the Ancients and Moderns. He vividly portrays scenes depicting the utter futility of the modern forces. Bacon, Descartes, Locke, and Boyle all received telling blows at the hands of Aristotle, Plato, and Horace. One of the highlights of the narration is an animated conversation carried on by the spider, a modernist, and the bee, an ancient—the latter revealing Swift's position in the conflict. This delightful episode does more than serve as a dramatic relief. It clearly states the issues that are involved.[4]

In the "A Tale of a Tub," Swift throws more light on the long literary controversy. He ridicules the modern methods of research by pointing out the tendency of contemporary scholars to read introductions, and prefaces rather than books. "I do utterly disapprove and declare against the pernicious custom, of making the Preface a bill-of-fare to the book," said Swift.[5] In an ironical vein, Swift next condemns the egotistical moderns who set themselves up as aesthetic authorities. "We of this age have discovered a shorter and more prudent method, to become scholars and wits, without the fatigue of reading or thinking."[6] Thus we have the paradoxical statement implied by the rebels that they, not the Greeks or Romans, are the true ancients. Swift concluded his indictment with these words: "Our illustrious moderns have eclipsed the weak glimmering lights of the ancients, and turned them out of the road of all fashionable commerce, to a degree, that our choice town wits, of most refined accomplishments, are in grave dispute, whether there have been ever any ancients or not. . . ."[7]

Alexander Pope

Probably the most popular Augustan was Alexander Pope who ruled for over fifty years as the dominant figure in English literature. His "Essay on Criticism," written at the age of twenty, was considered by his contemporaries as a model of critical theory. Samuel Johnson, in commenting on this work, said that if Pope had never written another line, the "Essay" would be sufficient to establish him as the foremost critic and poet of his day.[8] The "Essay on Criticism" played a significant part in the ancient-modern struggle. In this poem, Pope sets down certain rules which must be observed if a high standard of criticism is to be achieved. These tenets are built around the underlying principle of nature. Follow nature, says Pope, and then frame your judgments by her standards.[9] A writer cannot hope to succeed unless he absorbs this spirit and willingly accedes his will to the will of nature. True art, therefore, is an imitative art—nature being the original, art the copy.

But how is the poet to determine what is "natural" in poetry? Pope answers by saying that it is to be found in the best works of the ancients.

You then whose judgment the right course would steer,
Know well each ancient's proper character.
His fable, subject, scope in every page.
Religion, country, genius of his age
Without all these at once before your eyes,
Cavil you may, but never criticize.[10]

Herein lies Pope's strong classical leanings. It is a clear, terse statement of the respective genius of the two schools. If the modernist is to understand the universal truths of nature, he must call upon the ancients to intercede on his behalf. It is like Plotinus' "One," the first member of the Trinity, which fills up and overflows, then emanates into the second member of the Trinity and this, in turn, into the third member. Nature is the *One,* the classical writers are the second part of the Trinity, and the true modern genius, the third. The effulgence of nature descends upon the ancients, and they in turn radiate the way for us. Thus there is a hierarchical arrangement in which the moderns, as third members of the Poetical Trinity, are dependent upon their ancient masters. This can be further illustrated by showing the relationship of Homer and Virgil. The former looked directly to nature for his source of inspiration; the latter looked to Homer. In Pope's opinion, both poets imitated nature. Homer chose the direct method, Virgil the indirect. The fact that Virgil was not original in his approach did not mean that he possessed inferior genius. It simply meant that he saw nature through his master's eyes.[11]

The combined efforts of the Augustans in supporting the classical tradition were instrumental in temporarily preventing an encroachment of scientific methodology in the field of art. Once again men's minds were turned back to the cherished teachings of the past. But while generating a renewed feeling of reverence for the classics, Pope and his school failed to appreciate the challenge of the scientific philosophical thinkers who prevailed in the seventeenth century.

John Lawson

Notwithstanding the fact that neoclassicism began to wane in the middle of the century, some rhetoricians were not yet ready to alter either the content or the structure used by the ancients in their analyses of oral discourse. Chief among these authors were John Lawson and John Ward whose books were published at the time when Hugh Blair was beginning his lectures at the University of Edinburgh. Lawson's *Lectures Concerning Oratory,* which appeared in Dublin in 1758, was little more than an Anglicized version of the theories of Aristotle, Cicero, and Quintilian. Although he often drew upon English literature for illustrative material, attempted to incorporate a few of the concepts of Baconian faculty psychology in his discussion of emotions, and sought to make adaptations for students seeking a career in preaching, Lawson seemed content to summarize and apply classical rhetorical doctrines. He turned primarily to Aristotle for guidelines on invention, and to Cicero and Quintilian for ideas on disposition, style, and delivery.[12] The end product was an unimaginative and sterile work which not only was ignored by Blair and Campbell but by subsequent scholars.

John Ward

If Lawson's *Lectures* were an unoriginal and tedious summary of classical views, so too was John Ward's *Systems of Oratory,* published one year later. This two volume study, which covers more than eight hundred pages, is the most extensive treatment of classical rhetoric theory in the English language.[13] Without criticism, Ward accepts the format and treatment employed by the ancients. Like them, he equates rhetoric with persuasion; recognizes the three forms of oratory—deliberative, forensic, and epideictic; and highlights the numerous elements of invention, disposition, style, and delivery. Early in Volume I he objects to the inclusion of memory as one of the five canons because it was not a unique aspect of rhetoric. Yet at the close of Volume II he apparently changes his mind and decides to devote a chapter to it. So firm is Ward's commitment to the ancients that he, unlike Lawson, derives most of his illustrations from classical documents. At heart he is a Roman. He thus turns principally to Cicero and Quintilian, rather than to Aristotle, for guidance and inspiration. His work, in short, is a comprehensive summary of the best of Roman rhetorical thought and practice. Despite its obvious lack of originality, it had considerable appeal for students and professors in American colleges and universities during the nineteenth century.[14]

What set the neoclassicists apart from their contemporaries such as Hume, Campbell, and, as we will later note, the belletristic scholars was not their admiration for classical notions but their slavish devotion to them and their tendency to reject newly developing trends. This failure to incorporate relevant social and behavioral science data into their theories of discourse prevented the neoclassicists from advancing our knowledge of rhetoric.

Belles Lettres

A second major trend in British rhetorical thought was the work of the belletristic scholars. Consistent with the practice of the epistemologists, these students of communication theory borrowed heavily from the ancients and the modernists in producing a "new" type of rhetoric. From Aristotle they derived a communication model comprised of source, message, and receiver; an understanding of ethical, logical, and pathetic proof; a recognition of the effect of the occasion on a speaker's choice of material and development of themes; and an appreciation for perspicuity in style. From Cicero and Quintilian they accepted the definition of rhetoric as one great art consisting of five lesser arts (invention, disposition, style, memory, and delivery); the tripartite separation of the ends of discourse into instructing, pleasing, and moving, and of style into plain, medium, and grand; and the role of nature, imitation, and the use of models in the formation of an orator or writer. Finally, from Longinus they learned the value of combining rhetoric and poetics into a single, coherent system; and the meaning and significance of taste and sublimity. The professors of rhetoric and belles lettres were unwilling to rely on classical ideas and models alone. From modern works they derived principles of faculty psychology, a knowledge of the function of reason in criticism, insights into genius, and examples of eloquence depicting the potentialities inherent in the native idiom.

Among the unique features of the belletristic movement was the tendency to broaden rhetoric to include writing and criticism, along with speaking, as forms that should be studied in a single course or text. The student, therefore, received training not only in oral discourse but in poetry, drama, historical and philosophical writing, and, occasionally, in miscellaneous matters pertaining to education. This technique of joining rhetoric and polite literature, and in employing classical and contemporary models, proved to be, as we shall see in the case of Hugh Blair, a pedagogically attractive approach to the study of communication.

The principal works employing the belletristic approach can be understood only against the background of an important movement that began in the latter part of the seventeenth century. Longinus' celebrated treatise *On the Sublime,* virtually unknown to modern rhetoricians, suddenly appeared in 1674 with a translation and commentary by Boileau. Almost at once the essay caught the imagination of French and English scholars, stimulating in them a strong interest in taste, sublimity, and genius as potentially useful criteria to be employed in criticism. In his brief but penetrating analysis, Longinus made several points with telling effect. He set the tone of his study by asserting that the goal of genius "is not to persuade the audience but rather to transport

them out of themselves."[15] Observing that this aim could not be attained by using language that was inflated or frigid, he listed the five genuine sources of the sublime: (1) "the command of full blooded ideas"; (2) "the inspiration of vehement emotion"; (3) figures of thought; (4) figures of speech; and (5) "dignity and elevation."[16] Here Longinus was suggesting that when a communicator unites profound ideas with strong emotion and nobility of phrase, he transports or lifts the audience. So essential is this ability, he added, that one may redeem "all his mistakes by a single touch of sublimity and true excellence."[17]

Joseph Addison

The subject of sublimity, along with its related theme of taste, commanded the attention of Joseph Addison, an English essayist and poet. What is it, he asked, that gives pleasure to the imagination when we survey outward objects? The pleasure results from viewing what has the characteristics of greatness, novelty, and beauty. Greatness, by which Addison meant the sublime, was the perceiving of an object in its fullest view. It is present during those moments when the eye or the imagination focuses on open country, vast uncultivated deserts, lofty mountain ranges, high rocks and precipices, wide expanses of water, and a spacious horizon. "Our imagination loves to be filled," said Addison, "with an object, or to grasp anything that is too big for its capacity."[18] To the grandeur stemming from greatness may be added beauty and novelty. Together they make their way to the soul of man through his imagination.

Addison defined taste as "that faculty of the soul, which discerns the beauties of an author with pleasure and the imperfections with dslike."[19] Convinced that taste was to a certain degree innate, he nevertheless argued that it could be improved and cultivated by those who gained a knowledge of the writings of the best authors and critics, and who conversed with men of genius. Addison was not reluctant to apply his theory of taste to contemporary British works which he found to be overly partial to epigrams, turns of wit, and forced conceits.

John Baillie

Students of taste in the middle of the century moved steadily in the direction of psychology as they sought to draw their precepts from human nature. Locke's treatment of the senses and Hume's discussion of associationism became driving forces for Dr. John Baillie who wrote *An Essay on the Sublime* that was published posthumously in 1747. Starting with the premise that nature conveys the sublime to our senses, Baillie then used an analogy to the works of art, saying that they likewise may produce a similar experience. An appealing object of nature or of art in and of itself may activate immediately the senses causing sublimity. This does not preclude, however, a second possibility. For those objects which lack this power when standing in isolation may when united with other concepts through association become a stimulus for the sublime.[20]

Edmund Burke

Two other essays in the late 1750's similarly relied extensively upon psychology. The first volume was Edmund Burke's *A Philosophical Enquiry into the Origin of our Ideas of the Sublime and Beautiful,* to which was attached an introductory discourse on taste. Burke accepted the hypothesis that the mind is comprised of faculties, and that taste results from the senses, the imagination, and judgment. Since all men have these traits, they have taste. Differences that arise among observers are due to natural sensibility, knowledge, and training—those elements that strengthen the judgment.[21]

The discussion of taste formed the rationale for Burke's comprehensive analysis of the sublime and beautiful. After speaking of general emotions, he described the effect upon the senses of such passions as astonishment, ter-

ror, obscurity, vastness, infinity, uniformity, magnitude, difficulty, darkness, color, and loudness. These passions have in common the power to create strong impressions upon the imagination of the beholder. Some of Burke's favorite terms to pinpoint the meaning of sublime were "vast," "rugged," "dark," "gloomy," "solid," "massive," and "terror." If these qualities caused pain, that is part of the cost that one must pay in order to experience the sublime.[22]

More gentle and pleasant than sublimity is the beautiful which has as its object love. Contrary to popular opinion, Burke suggested, proportion, fitness, and perfection are not causes of beauty. The following traits are the real causes: smallness, smoothness, variation, delicacy, color, physiognomy, and clarity. The sublime and beautiful, therefore, are built on different principles: the one has terror for its basis and leads to astonishment; the other depends on pleasure to stimulate the affection of love.

Burke's theory of the sublime is noteworthy not only because of his stress on emotion, but because of his unusual faith in the power of words to arouse the senses needed to promote the sublime and beautiful. Words, he said, are generally more motivating than pictures or scenes. With such a belief he found it easy to claim: "Eloquence and poetry are . . . more capable of making deep and lively impressions than any other arts, and even than nature itself in very many cases."[23] In evaluating the worth of Burke's discussion, Samuel Monk has observed that the *Enquiry,* despite its shortcomings, was "one of the most important aesthetic documents that eighteenth-century England produced."[24]

Alexander Gerard

In 1759, two years after the appearance of Burke's *Enquiry,* Alexander Gerard published a similarly significant volume, entitled *An Essay on Taste.* Like his predecessors, Gerard equated taste with ideas relating to the powers of the imagination. His major sources were Locke, Hume, and Baillie. From them he gained an enthusiasm for the doctrines of reductionism and associationism which became the key for his aesthetic theory. Gerard broke down taste into the simple principles of novelty, grandeur and sublimity, beauty, imitation, harmony, ridicule, and virtue. Throughout his analysis the impact of association is evident. Objects which are not by nature sublime, he argued, may possess this quality when united with other concepts in a proper manner. Examples of this may be seen in the fine arts, in color combinations, and in all aspects of imitation.

Gerard endorsed the views of earlier writers who spoke of the development and improvement of a standard of taste. "Goodness of taste," he said, "lies in its maturity and perfection. It consists in certain excellencies of our original powers of judgment and imagination combined." These may be reduced to the elements of sensibility, refinement, correctness, and "proportion or comparative adjustment of its separate principles."[25] To eliminate a defect in taste, Gerard recommended a strengthening of the internal senses and of judgment, and the need for establishing general precepts that conform to "the common feelings of men."[26]

Another important facet of Gerard's theory was his discussion of the relationship between taste and genius and the influence of taste on criticism. A man of genius, Gerard pointed out, has a comprehensive and perceptive imagination which enables him to see associations or connections between ideas regardless of their remoteness. This talent to unite concepts quickly is a product not of practice but of imagination. Genius, the leading quality of invention, "is the grand architect which not only chooses the materials, but disposes them into a regular structure."[27] The function of taste, on the other hand, is to guide, moderate, and give the finishing touches to the efforts of genius. Without genius one cannot perform, but he may be able to judge. For taste provides the critic with a discernment that assists him in interpreting his own feelings with accuracy, and in explaining these sentiments to others.

These descriptions of taste, genius, and criticism—strongly rooted in eighteenth-century psychology—anticipated the philosophy of Hugh Blair.

Charles Rollin

It was within the context of a renewal of interest in the classics, of revolutionary advances in epistemological thought, and of an evolving theory of taste that the trend toward belletristic rhetoric developed. Of the many works that were belletristic in function and scope, three stand out: Charles Rollin's *The Method of Teaching and Studying the Belles Lettres* (1726–28); Adam Smith's *Lectures on Rhetoric and Belles Lettres* (1762–63); and Hugh Blair's *Lectures on Rhetoric and Belles Lettres* (1783). Rollin's four volume study, which was translated into English in 1734,[28] doubtless was influenced by early French rhetorics. Consciously avoiding any real pretense of originality, Rollin confesses at the outset that the ideas espoused in his volumes represent the combined thinking of classical rhetoricians and seventeenth and eighteenth-century scholars at the University of Paris.[29] Despite this disclaimer, Rollin departed markedly from his predecessors in his selection and development of materials.

The Method of Teaching and Studying the Belles Lettres was designed to improve the understanding, manners, and religious affections of students, and possibly their parents and friends. The work is separated into six parts: grammar, poetry, rhetoric, history, philosophy, and educational administration and procedures. In the amplification of these units, all of the elements of the belletristic tradition to be covered later by Smith and Blair are present. Rollin establishes guidelines for future studies by analyzing taste, sublimity, the rhetorical canons, ends of discourse, forms of proof, and the eloquence of the bar, pulpit, and sacred writings.[30] It is, in fine, a comprehensive bringing together of the major tenets of communication under the rubric of a single discipline. For his efforts Rollin won the praise of Bishop Atterbury and Voltaire who regarded the book as "one of the completest Treatises ever published on the Subject of polite literature."[31]

Adam Smith

The English counterpart to Rollin was Adam Smith whose *Inquiry into the Nature and Causes of the Wealth of Nations* (1776) earned for him the reputation as "father of political economy." In 1748, Smith began under the sponsorship of Lord Kames a series of public lectures in Edinburgh on rhetoric and belles lettres which were repeated during the following two years. Largely as a reward for the popularity of these lectures, Smith received a coveted appointment in 1751 as Professor of Logic at the University of Glasgow. One year later he moved to the discipline of Moral Philosophy, an academic specialty which he taught for thirteen years. Steeped in the classics and well versed in French and Italian as well as in English history, literature, and psychology, Smith sought both in his lectures and in his writings to present a systematic analysis of style, oratory, and criticism.

Crucial to an understanding of Smith's rhetorical lectures was his emphasis on the various forms of discourse. Whenever he developed one of the traditional canons, he related his discussion to oratorical, poetical, dramatic, and historical writing. He compared the function, ends, structure, and substance of each, demonstrating wherein each conformed to and deviated from the other. Since the common element present in all methods of communication is style, Smith gave to this canon a central position. Throughout the lectures he summarized the origin and progress of language, trumpeted the virtues of perspicuity in style, and cited the danger of an excessive reliance on tropes and other figures of speech and thought.

In his discussions of the purposes and ends of discourse and of the three forms of eloquence—demonstrative, judicial, and deliberative—Smith hewed closely to classical teachings. Persuasion, epitomized by well reasoned arguments and moving emotional appeals, he regarded as the primary aim of rhetoric. But Smith, who was also a student of the faculty psychologists, made room in his system for a secondary purpose—to inform. This method, which he called didactic, adheres to the narrative form and is designed to instruct.[32]

Interspersed throughout the lectures are numerous comments on literary criticism. Smith's aesthetic theory was an outgrowth of his philosophy of taste which had deep roots in the classical and modern psychological traditions. A proper taste, he remarked, is one that conforms to the fashions and customs of a particular age and locale, and to a majority sentiment. Since a thorough understanding of the nature of man is an essential requisite for one who seeks to make delicate and discriminating judgments, the critic must begin his task by searching his own mind in order to assess his genuine feelings. But if he stops here, he is in danger of measuring perfection against the yardstick of his own interests and sensibilities. So he needs, secondly, to come to an appreciation of the feelings of others. "We must look at ourselves," he argued, "with the same eyes with which we look at others; we must imagine ourselves not the actors, but the spectators of our own character and conduct. . . ."[33]

The most fitting summary of Smith's views on taste is found in his *Lectures on Justice, Police, Revenue and Arms*. Here he suggested that the three essential ingredients of beauty, which he held to be the principal substance of taste, are "proper variety," "easy connexion," and "simple order."[34] These traits, which combine to form the general neoclassic concept of "decorum" or "propriety," pervade Smith's approach to all phases of rhetorical criticism. With Dryden, the first great English poet to discuss this doctrine at length, he embodied extensively in his criticism the principles of "refinement," "correctness," "strict unity," and "simple clarity."[35] Smith's impatience with the Greek dramatists grew out of his belief that they had violated these rules by placing an undue emphasis on bodily pain.

Shakespeare annoyed him by constantly violating the unity of place: his practice of making one scene in France, the following one in
London, and the next in York, warned Smith,
creates distances of such magnitude that we
wonder what has happened in the intervals. No
such fault, he added, could be found in the
plays of Racine and Sophocles who were content to concentrate on one place.[36] But if Smith
showed impatience with a work that lacked
decorum or propriety, he applauded those productions that exemplified these traits. He thus
placed John Dryden, Alexander Pope, and
Thomas Gray upon pedestals because of the
conciseness, beauty, harmony, and movement
of their poetry. Pope, he held, was the "most
correct, as well as the most elegant and harmonious of all the English poets." In Gray he
recognized but one fault, namely that he wrote
too little. Although he viewed Swift as basically more talented than these three poets because of his superior style and sentiment, he
regretted that the articulate and clever doctor
frequently descended to the level of "a gossi-
per writing for the entertainment of a private
circle."[37]

Smith's lectures as reported in his students'
notes are not, on the whole, well organized or
profound. All too often he relied on the Roman
rhetoricians and the neoclassicists to buttress
his evaluations. Such a procedure led Wordsworth to say with biting sarcasm that Smith
was "the worst critic, David Hume not ex-
cepted, that Scotland, a soil to which this sort
of weed seems natural, has produced."[38] Yet
Smith's importance as a major rhetorician is
incontrovertible. His treatment of the ends of
discourse, his rejection of commonplaces, his
recognition of arguments from the essential
nature of things, his stress on passions and
sympathy, and, most of all, his belletristic
methodology triggered the imagination of
Hugh Blair who achieved permanent fame for
his remarkably successful attempt to blend the
best elements of rhetoric and poetics.

Hugh Blair

In 1759, eleven years after Smith delivered his
first public lectures, Lord Kames assisted
Hugh Blair in setting up a similar series of discourses. Though the initial lectures were presented at the University of Edinburgh, no
college credit was given. In the following year,
the Town Council appointed Blair Professor
of Rhetoric, making his course a recognized
part of the college curriculum.[39] It was not until
1762, however, that he officially received the
title of Regius Professor of Rhetoric and Belles
Lettres. After serving in this capacity for more
than twenty years, Blair retired in 1783, and
immediately thereafter published his *Lectures
on Rhetoric and Belles Lettres*. This work was,
for the most part, a reproduction of the discussions he had delivered at the University
since 1759. Blair explains in the preface that
many students, relying on superficial notes,
were circulating imperfect copies of his lectures. The purpose of the volume, therefore,
was to give to the public an accurate account
of his teachings.[40]

When Blair's lectures appeared, they received a warm reception. Schools in England
and America introduced them into their cur-
ricula, and within a short time "half of the educated English-speaking world studied" the
rhetorical theories of Blair with approbation.[41]
The immediate reaction proved more than a
passing fancy. From the beginning the public
demand was so great that the first edition was
followed by many other editions in England,
in America, and on the continent. From 1783
to 1873, sixty-two complete editions and fifty-
one abridgments were published. In addition,
there were ten translations in French, Italian,
Russian, and Spanish. Ten textbooks containing representative lectures were also used in
English and American schools.

It is difficult to appreciate Blair's position
as a rhetorician unless the extrinsic and intrinsic sources of his enormous popularity are

understood.[42] The general resurgence of interest in culture and human nature, the restoration of rhetoric to its earlier status, and Blair's reputation as an eloquent divine, perceptive critic, and stylist were factors that contributed to the success of his *Lectures on Rhetoric and Belles Lettres.* But there were at least three other causes with still greater import. First, the organizational structure and educational philosophy were appealing to students who, with little prior background study, wanted a comprehensive, coherent, and rational overview of rhetoric, literature, and criticism. Taken in their entirety, Blair's lectures—forty-seven in all—were systematic discussions of five major subject areas. Five of the discourses dealt with criticism, taste, and genius; four with language; fifteen with style; ten with eloquence; and thirteen with literary themes such as poetry and historical and philosophical writing. The lectures begin with the construction of a base consisting of the ingredients of taste, and, then moving in an upward spiral, they survey the history of language and analyze the nature and constituent parts of style. In a total of twenty-four lectures, or slightly more than one half of the course, the foundation was laid for a consideration of eloquence and polite literature.

If Blair's hierarchical structure had popular appeal, so, too, did his pedagogical technique and pleasing style. He was pragmatic enough to realize that abstract statements lacking concrete evidence were, at best, dry and uninteresting. Consequently, whenever he made an important observation, he substantiated it with a specific example. The lectures, therefore, contain exemplary models from the works of leading authors past and present. Additionally, Blair expressed his ideas in language that exemplified the precision, propriety, and perspicuity he held to be essential to good style.

A second cause responsible for Blair's effectiveness was the fact that his brand of eclecticism epitomized the dynamic, developing nature of rhetoric. Determined to avoid the extremes of classicism on the one hand and excessive novelty on the other, he wanted to demonstrate the continuity as well as the changing aspects of rhetoric. He had come to believe that a rhetorical system grounded only in the classics was static and sterile, while one based exclusively on modernism was without historical roots. He met this challenge by bringing together "the best ancient and contemporary thought on rhetoric and belles lettres."[43] The influence of the Roman rhetoricians and Longinus is at all times evident. The lectures on the conduct of the discourse in all its parts, for example, are modern versions of the ideas of Cicero and Quintilian on organization; the sections on style incorporate many of the precepts of Quintilian; and the discussions on taste and sublimity reveal a keen awareness of Longinus' *On the Sublime.*[44] Similarly, Blair made frequent use of modern teachings. His analysis of the ends of discourse and his belief in the conviction-persuasion duality, the notion that a reader or listener could be convinced that a thing was true without feeling compelled to act on this belief, grew out of his reading of the faculty psychologists; his attack on the commonplaces and his acceptance of the managerial function of invention stemmed from contemporary theories of logic; his appreciation of the tenets of neoclassicism, romanticism, rationalism, and common sense philosophy shaped the direction of his critical theories; his partiality for Thomas Sheridan's emphasis on the natural method and the conversational pattern affected his recommendations on delivery; and his favorable response to the course structure outlined by Rollin and Smith gave him a philosophy and format that he could strive to perfect. The versatility and range which Blair displayed in making his lectures derivative constituted proof of the existence of an ongoing quality in rhetorical thought.

To suggest that Blair was primarily a masterful synthesizer of the ideas of others is to imply that he lacked originality.[45] A careful scrutiny of the lectures, however, yields compelling evidence to refute this claim. As a result, a third major factor contributing to Blair's popularity was his innovative treatment of key principles of rhetoric and criticism. He modified, for instance, the traditional practice of placing all forms of oratory in the categories of epideictic, deliberative, and judicial. He endorsed the classical concept of judicial eloquence, but combined demonstrative and deliberative speaking under one head which he called the eloquence of the public assembly, and added to these, the eloquence of the pulpit. He then discussed the purpose of each communication form and its rank in the trilogy. The first division of demonstrative speaking, which Blair designated special occasional oratory, has as its function to please. Judicial rhetoric has a higher aim, the convincing of the intellect. The supreme goal in communication, that of persuasion, characterizes the purpose of deliberative speaking and of pulpit oratory. In making a distinction between convincing and pesuading, Blair affirmed his faith in the faculty psychology notion of a conviction-persuasion duality. In writing his essay on "pulpit oratory," moreover, he made one of his most original contributions to rhetorical theory. As a prominent minister in the Scottish Presbyterian Church, he knew first hand the problems confronting a preacher in preparing a sermon. Because the lecture he delivered on this theme was the result of an empirical study covering many years, it has permanent relevance.

Blair's handling of invention, though sketchy in detail, was, like his analysis of the nature and function of discourse, fresh and imaginative. He was innovative in the way he phrased his indictment against commonplaces, in his tendency to relate genius to inventive ability, and his attitude toward rules. The ancient doctrine of "Loci Communes" or topics, he felt, was of little aid to the speaker in preparing either the introduction or the line of reasoning. He supported the view by pointing out that "knowledge and science must furnish the materials that form the body and substance of any valuable composition."[46] To those who believed that knowledge of the commonplaces would increase their inventive talent, Blair recommended the reading of Aristotle, Cicero, and Quintilian. But when one is faced with the task of preparing a persuasive speech, he continued, he should disregard the ancient topics and concentrate on his subject. Blair clinched his argument with the following allusion: "Demosthenes, I dare say, consulted none of the loci, when he was inciting the Athenians to take arms against Philip; and where Cicero has had recourse to them, his orations are so much the worse on that account."[47]

Blair's discussion of invention was similar to his treatment of genius. Although these terms were not synonymous, they shared a similar meaning. To say that a man possesses genius, Blair asserted, is to imply that he has unusual inventive and creative powers.[48] Invention, on the other hand, requires a thorough knowledge of the subject, and the ability to reason adequately concerning the theme. It is clear, then, that the man of genius has a greater capacity to analyze the particular problem.

A defect in genius or invention, Blair further held, cannot be supplied by art. The only source from which these powers can be derived is nature. All that rhetoric or art can do is to guide genius in the proper direction or to assist the speaker in arranging arguments that invention discovers. Because rhetorical rules, therefore, have little, if any, effect on the improvement of invention, Blair apparently felt justified in giving this subject a minimum amount of space in his lectures.

Many of the conclusions Blair reached, such as his recognition of the managerial nature of invention and the limited value of topics, were a part of the teachings of the epistemologists. But it was Blair's innovative approach in applying and phrasing these ideas that gave them a prominent place in the "new rhetoric" of the eighteenth century.

Blair must be credited, finally, with being one of the first modern writers to think of rhetoric as a form of criticism. Indeed, the lectures, to a large degree, are composed of a series of critical precepts pertaining to the arts of writing and speech. This preoccupation with criticism has motivated some recent authors to study Blair as a critic rather than a rhetorician. In sanctioning this method of approaching the study of communication, George Saintsbury asserted that Blair "is to be very particularly commended for accepting to the full the important truth that 'Rhetoric' in modern times really means 'Criticism.' "[49] If Saintsbury's assessment is correct, Blair is to be praised for his use of a critical method that was soundly conceived and executed. The principles he established and their application to nature and works of art constituted the base, as we have seen, upon which all of his judgments on taste derived. Refusing to limit himself to a single school of critical thought, he was part neoclassicist, part rationalist, part epistemologist, and part romanticist. His genius in drawing these varied philosophies together in an innovative and coherent manner gave to his lectures and to the belletristic movement an enduring fame seldom equaled in rhetorical history.[50]

Since Blair personifies the high degree of effectiveness associated with the belles lettres aproach to rhetoric, we would like to single out several important concepts and recommendations he discussed which influenced the direction rhetoric was to take both in Europe and America for many years. First was his clear and concise treatment of taste—the rhetorical element forming the base upon which much of Blair's theory was constructed. Taste, which he described as "the power of receiving pleasure from the beauties of nature and of art,"[51] is a faculty of the mind common to all men and women and can be influenced by exercise and reason. Taste, like the body, responds to exercise. Diligent practice, for example, enables a polisher to improve his sense of touch or an instrument-maker his sense of vision. Using the same line of reasoning, Blair proceeds to show that one who assiduously studies the compositions of approved models will improve his taste.

Taste is also influenced by reason. Although these qualities are separate faculties of the mind, they are closely related. Taste produces pleasure; reason explains the nature of that pleasure. It is the duty of reason to determine the accuracy of a production of nature. Whenever a pleasure derived from nature or art is consonant with sound judgment, the taste is perfected.

Blair realized that taste is a fluctuating quality which varies with the nature and cultural background of an individual. It is conceivable that two people may react differently to the virtues of a given writer. One might be impressed by Virgil's style; another, by his thought. Such differences are not inconsonant with reason. If, however, one denies the existence of any virtues in Virgil, then the views of the critics are diametrically opposed. Who is going to decide, in such cases, which judgment is the better? Blair answers this question by stating that "his taste must be esteemed just and true, which coincides with the general sentiments of men."[52]

The two main souces of the pleasure of taste are sublimity and beauty. Sublimity may be found in inanimate objects and in human nature. It implies vastness, force, and power. Nature, with its oceans, its heavens, and its infinite space, pleases the imagination. That which is most effective, however, is mighty power and strength. Ideas which express solemnity, obscurity, disorder, and above all, the Supreme Being, exemplify force.

The sublime is often seen in human nature. A magnanimous or heroic spirit instills in the mind a feeling of admiration. When a story is told of a courageous warrior, the grandeur of character displayed usually produces the noblest form of pleasure. Sublimity in writing or speaking is characterized by simplicity, conciseness, and strength. The truly sublime passage is an expression of bold, pathetic thoughts in language that is not profuse nor superfluous, not bombastic nor frigid, but at the same time, is sufficiently strong to give a clear and full impression of the object described.

Beauty is a calmer, but more lasting quality than the sublime. It is portrayed in nature in the form of color, figure, and motion. Color simply implies these sensory stimuli which come to us through one source only, the structure of the eye. Figure is composed of two categories: regularity and variety. The truly beautiful object is one which combines regularity, variety, and motion. The human countenance is an excellent illustration of this pleasing combination.

To understand more specifically how Blair constructed his arguments on taste, and at the same time to appreciate how his lectures unfolded in general, we present here the following discourse entitled "Lecture II."

Lecture II

Taste

The nature of the present undertaking leads me to begin with some inquiries concerning taste, as it is this faculty which is always appealed to, in disquisitions concerning the merit of discourse in writing.

There are few subjects on which men talk more loosely and indistinctly than on taste; few which it is more difficult to explain with precision; and none which in this course of Lectures will appear more dry or abstract. What I have to say on the subject, shall be in the following order. I shall first explain the Nature of Taste as a power or faculty in the human mind. I shall next consider, how far it is an improvable faculty. I shall show the sources of its improvement, and the characters of taste in its most perfect state. I shall then examine the various fluctuations to which it is liable, and inquire whether there be any standard to which we can bring the different tastes of men, in order to distinguish the corrupted from the true.

Taste may be defined "The power of receiving pleasure from the beauties of nature and of art." The first question that occurs concerning it is, whether it is to be considered as an internal sense, or as an exertion of reason? Reason is a very general term; but if we understand by it, that power of the mind which in speculative matters discovers truth, and in practical matters judges of the fitness of means to an end, I apprehend the question may be easily answered. For nothing can be more clear, than that the taste is not resolvable into any such operation of reason. It is not merely through a discovery

of the understanding or a deduction of argument, that the mind receives pleasure from a beautiful prospect or a fine poem. Such objects often strike us intuitively, and make a strong impression, when we are unable to assign the reasons of our being pleased. They sometimes strike in the same manner the philosopher and the peasant; the boy and the man. Hence the faculty by which we relish such beauties, seems more nearly allied to a feeling of sense, than to a process of the understanding; and accordingly from an external sense it has borrowed its name; that sense by which we receive and distinguish the pleasures of food, having, in several languages, given rise to the word taste, in the metaphorical meaning under which we now consider it. However, as in all subjects which regard the operations of the mind, the inaccurate use of words is to be carefully avoided; it must not be inferred from what I have said, that reason is entirely excluded from the exertions of taste. Though taste, beyond doubt, be ultimately founded on a certain natural and instinctive sensibility to beauty, yet reason, as I shall show hereafter, assists taste in many of its operations, and serves to enlarge its power.

Taste, in the sense in which I have explained it, is a faculty common in some degree to all men. Nothing that belongs to human nature is more general than the relish of beauty of one kind or other; of what is orderly, proportioned, grand, harmonious, new,

From Hugh Blair's *Lectures on Rhetoric and Belles Lettres.* (Philadelphia: T. Ellwood Zell, 1862.) p. 16–37, 212–215, 377–387.

or sprightly. In children, the rudiments of taste discover themselves very early in a thousand instances; in their fondness for regular bodies, their admiration of pictures and statutes and imitations of all kinds; and their strong attachment to whatever is new or marvellous. The most ignorant peasants are delighted with ballads and tales, and are struck with the beautiful appearance of nature in the earth and heavens. Even in the deserts of America, where human nature shows itself in its most uncultivated state, the savages have their ornaments of dress, their war and their death songs, their harangues and their orators. We must therefore conclude the principles of taste to be deeply founded in the human mind. It is no less essential to man to have some discernment of beauty, than it is to possess the attributes of reason and of speech.

But although none be wholly devoid of this faculty, yet the degrees in which it is possessed are widely different. In some men only the feeble glimmerings of taste appear; the beauties which they relish are of the coarsest kind; and of these they have but a weak and confused impression; while in others, taste rises to an acute discernment, and a lively enjoyment of the most refined beauties. In general, we may observe, that in the powers and pleasures of taste, there is a more remarkable inequity among men than is usually found in point of common sense, reason, and judgment. The constitution of our nature in this, as in all other respects, discovers admirable wisdom. In the distribution of those talents which are necessary for man's well-being, nature hath made less distinction among her children. But in the distribution of those which belong only to the ornamental part of life, she hath bestowed her favours with more frugality. She hath both sown the seeds more sparingly; and rendered a higher culture requisite for bringing them to perfection.

This inequality of taste among men is owing, without doubt, in part, to the different frame of their natures; to nicer organs, and finer internal powers, with which some are endowed beyond others. But, if it be owing in part to nature, it is owing to education and culture still more. The illustration of this leads to my next remark on this subject, that taste is a most improvable faculty, if there be any such in human nature; a remark which gives great encouragement to such a course of study as we are now proposing to pursue. Of the truth of this assertion we may easily be convinced, by only reflecting on that immense superiority which education and improvement give to civilized, above barbarous nations, in refinement of taste; and on the superiority which they give in the same nation to those who have studied the liberal arts, above the rude and untaught vulgar. The difference is so great, that there is perhaps no one particular in which these two classes of men are so removed from each other, as in respect of the powers and the pleasures of taste; and assuredly for this difference no other general cause can be assigned, but culture and education. I shall now proceed to show what the means are by which taste becomes so remarkably susceptible of cultivation and progress.

Reflect first upon that great law of our nature, that exercise is the chief source of improvement in all our faculties. This holds both in our bodily, and in our mental powers. It holds even in our external senses, although these be less the subject of cultivation than any of our other faculties. We see how acute the senses become in persons whose trade or business leads to nice exertions of them. Touch, for instance, becomes infinitely more exquisite in men whose employment requires them to examine the polish of bodies, than it is in others. They who deal in microscopical observations, or are accustomed to engrave on precious stones, acquire surprising accuracy of sight in discerning the minutest objects; and practice in attending to different flavours and tastes of liquors, wonderfully improves the power of distinguishing them, and of tracing their composition. Placing internal taste therefore on the footing of a simple sense, it cannot be doubted that frequent exercise, and curious attention to its proper objects, must greatly heighten its power. Of this we have one clear proof in that part of taste, which is called an ear for music. Experience every day shows, that nothing is more improvable. Only the simplest and plainest compositions are relished at first; use and practice extend our pleasure; teach us to relish finer melody, and by degrees enable us to enter into the intricate and compounded pleasures of harmony. So an eye for the beauties of painting is never at all once acquired. It is gradually formed by being conversant among pictures, and studying the works of the best masters.

Precisely in the same manner, with respect to the beauty of composition and discourse, attention to the most approved models, study of the best authors, comparisons of lower and higher degrees of the same beauties, operate towards the refinement of taste. When one is only beginning his acquaintance with works of genius, the sentiment which attends them is obscure and confused. He cannot point out the several excellencies or blemishes of a performance which he peruses; he is at a loss on what to rest his judgment; all that can be expected is, that he should tell in general whether he be pleased or not. But allow him more experience in works of this kind, and his taste becomes by degrees more exact and enlightened. He begins to perceive not only the character of the whole but the beauties and defects of each part; and is able to describe the peculiar qualities which he praises or blames. The mist dissipates which seemed formerly to hang over the object; and he can at length pronounce firmly, and without hesitation, concerning it. Thus in taste, considered as mere sensibility, exercise opens a great souce of improvement.

But although taste be ultimately founded on sensibility, it must not be considered as instinctive sensibility alone. Reason and good sense, as I before hinted, have so extensive an influence on all the operations and decisions of taste, that a thorough good taste may well be considered as a power compounded of natural sensibility to beauty, and of improved understanding. In order to be satisfied of this, let us observe, that the greater part of the productions of genius are no other than imitations of nature; representations of the characters, actions, or manners of men. The pleasure we receive from such imitations or representations is founded on mere taste: but to judge whether they be properly executed, belongs to the understanding, which compares the copy with the original.

In reading, for instance, such a poem as the *Aeneid,* a great part of our pleasure arises from the plan or story being well conducted, and all the parts joined together with probability and due connexion; from the characters being taken from nature, the sentiments being suited to the characters, and the style to the sentiments. The pleasure which arises from a poem so conducted, is felt or enjoyed by taste as an internal sense; but the discovery of this conduct in the poem is owing to reason; and the more that reason enables us to discover such propriety in the conduct, the greater will be our pleasure. We are pleased, through our natural sense of beauty. Reason shows us why, and upon what grounds, we are pleased. Wherever in works of taste, any resemblance to nature is aimed at, wherever there is any reference of parts to a whole, or of means to an end, as there is indeed in almost every writing and discourse, there the understanding must always have a great part to act.

Here then is a wide field for reason's exerting its powers in relation to the objects of taste, particularly with respect to composition, and works of genius; and hence arises a second and a very considerable source of the improvement of taste, from the application of reason and good sense to such productions of genius. Spurious beauties, such as unnatural characters, forced sentiments, affected style, may please for a little; but they please only because their opposition to nature and to good sense has not been examined, or attended to. Once show how nature might have been more justly imitated or represented; how the writer might have managed his subject to greater advantage; the illusion will presently be dissipated, and these false beauties will please no more.

From these two sources then, first, the frequent exercise of taste, and next the application of good sense and reason to the objects of taste, taste as a power of the mind receives its improvement. In its perfect state, it is undoubtedly the result both of nature and of art. It supposes our natural sense of beauty to be refined by frequent attention to the most beautiful objects, and at the same time to be guided and improved by the light of the understanding.

I must be allowed to add, that as a sound head, so likewise a good heart, is a very material requisite to just taste. The moral beauties are not only themselves superior to all others, but they exert an influence, either more near, or more remote, on a great variety of other objects of taste. Wherever the affections, characters, or actions of men are concerned, (and these certainly afford the noblest subjects to genius,) there can be neither any just or affecting description of them, nor any thorough feeling of the beauty of that description, without our possessing the virtuous affections. He whose heart is indelicate or hard, he who has no admiration of what is truly noble or praise-worthy, nor the proper sympathetic sense of what is soft and tender, must have a very imperfect relish of the highest beauties of eloquence and poetry.

The characters of taste, when brought to its most improved state, are all reducible to two, Delicacy and Correctness.

Delicacy of taste respects principally the perfection of that natural sensibility on which taste is founded. It implies those finer organs or powers which enable us to discover beauties that lie hid from a vulgar eye. One may have strong sensibility, and yet be deficient in delicate taste. He may be deeply impressed by such beauties as he perceives; but he perceives only what is in some degree coarse, what is bold and palpable; while chaster and simpler ornaments escape his notice. In this state, taste generally exists among rude and unrefined nations. But a person of delicate taste both feels strongly, and feels accurately. He sees distinctions and differences where others see none; the most latent beauty does not escape him, and he is sensible of the smallest blemish. Delicacy of taste is judged of by the same marks that we use in judging of the delicacy of an external sense. As the goodness of the palate is not tried by strong flavours, but by a mixture of ingredients, where, notwithstanding the confusion, we remain sensible of each; in like manner delicacy of internal taste appears, by a quick and lively sensibility to its finest, most compounded, or most latent objects.

Correctness of taste respects chiefly the improvement which that faculty receives through its connexion with the understanding. A man of correct taste is one who is never imposed on by counterfeit beauties; who carries always in his mind that standard of good sense which he employs in judging of every thing. He estimates with propriety the comparative merit of the several beauties which he meets with in any work of genius; refers them to their proper classes; assigns the principles, as far as they can be traced, whence their power of pleasing flows, and is pleased himself precisely in that degree in which he ought, and no more.

It is true, that these qualities of taste, delicacy and correctness, mutually imply each other. No taste can be exquisitely delicate without being correct; nor can be thoroughly correct without being delicate. But still a predominancy of one or other quality in the mixture is often visible. The power of delicacy is chiefly seen in discerning the true merit of a work; the power of correctness, in rejecting false pretensions to merit. Delicacy leans more to feeling; correctness, more to reason and judgment. The former is more the gift of nature; the latter, more the product of culture and art. Among the ancient critics, Longinus possessed most delicacy; Aristotle, most correctness. Among the moderns, Mr. Addison is a high example of delicate taste; Dean Swift, had he written on the subject of criticism, would perhaps have afforded the example of a correct one.

Having viewed taste in its most improved and perfect state, I come next to consider its deviations from that state, the fluctuations and changes to which it is liable; and to inquire whether, in the midst of these, there be any means of distinguishing a true from a corrupted taste. This brings us to the most difficult part of our task. For it must be acknowledged, that no principle of the human mind is, in its operations, more fluctuating and capricious than taste. Its variations have been so great and frequent, as to create a suspicion with some, of its being merely arbitrary; grounded on no foundation, ascertainable by no standard, but wholly dependent on changing fancy; the consequence of which would be, that all studies or regular inquiries concerning the objects of taste were vain. In architecture, the Grecian models were long esteemed the most perfect. In succeeding ages, the Gothic architecture alone prevailed, and afterwards the Grecian taste revived in all its vigour, and engrossed the public admiration. In eloquence and poetry, the Asiatics at no time relished any thing but what was full of ornament, and splendid in a degree that we should denominate gawdy; whilst the Greeks admired only chaste and simple beauties, and despised the Asiatic ostentation. In our own country, how many writings that were greatly extolled two or three centuries ago, are now fallen into entire disrepute and oblivion. Without going back to remote instances, how very different is the taste of poetry which prevails in Great Britain now, from what prevailed there no longer ago than the reign of King Charles II, which the authors too of that time deemed an Augustan age: when nothing was in vogue but an affected brilliancy of wit; when the simple majesty of Milton was overlooked, and *Paradise Lost* almost entirely unknown; when Cowley's laboured and unnatural conceits were admired as the very quintessence of genius; Waller's gay sprightliness was mistaken for the tender spirit of love poetry; and such

writers as Suckling and Etheridge were held in esteem for dramatic composition?

The question is, what conclusion we are to form from such instances as these? Is there anything that can be called a standard of taste, by appealing to which we may distinguish between a good and a bad taste? Or, is there in truth no such distinction? and are we to hold that, according to the proverb, there is no disputing of tastes; but that whatever pleases is right, for that reason that it does please? This is the question, and a very nice and subtle one it is, which we are now to discuss.

I begin by observing, that if there be no such thing as any standard of taste, this consequence must immediately follow, that all tastes are equally good; a position, which, though it may pass unnoticed in slight matters, and when we speak of the lesser differences among the tastes of men, yet when we apply it to the extremes, presently shows its absurdity. For is there any one who will seriously maintain that the taste of a Hottentot or a Laplander is as delicate and as correct as that of a Longinus or an Addison? or, that he can be charged with no defect or incapacity who thinks a common newswriter as excellent an historian as Tacitus? As it would be held downright extravagance to talk in this manner, we are led unavoidably to this conclusion, that there is some foundation for the preference of one man's taste to that of another; or, that there is a good and a bad, a right and a wrong in taste, as in other things.

But to prevent mistakes on this subject, it is necessary to observe next, that the diversity of tastes which prevails among mankind, does not in every case infer corruption of taste, or oblige us to seek for some standard in order to determine who are in the right. The tastes of men may differ very considerably as to their object, and yet none of them be wrong. One man relishes poetry most; another takes pleasure in nothing but history. One prefers comedy; another, tragedy. One admires the simple; another, the ornamented style. The young are amused with gay and sprightly compositions. The elderly are more entertained with those of a graver cast. Some nations delight in bold pictures of manners, and strong representations of passion. Others incline to more correct and regular elegance both in description and sentiment. Though all differ, yet all pitch upon some one beauty which peculiarly suits their turn of mind; and therefore no one has a title to condemn the rest. It is not in matters of taste, as in questions of mere reason, where there is but one conclusion that can be true, and all the rest are erroneous. Truth, which is the object of reason, is one; beauty, which is the object of taste, is manifold. Taste, therefore, admits of latitude and diversity of objects, in sufficient consistency with goodness or justness of taste.

But then, to explain this matter thoroughly, I must observe farther that this admissible diversity of tastes can only have place where the objects of taste are different. Where it is with respect to the same object that men disagree, when one condemns that as ugly, which another admires as highly beautiful; then it is no longer diversity, but direct opposition of taste that takes place; and therefore one must be in the right, and another in the wrong, unless that absurd paradox were allowed to hold, that all tastes are equally good and true. One man prefers Virgil to Homer. Suppose that I, on the other hand, admire Homer more than Virgil. I have as yet no reason to say that our tastes are contradictory. The other person is more struck with the elegance and tenderness which are the characteristics of Virgil; I, with the simplicity and fire of Homer. As long as neither of us deny that both Homer and Virgil have great beauties, our difference falls within the compass of that diversity of tastes, which I have showed to be natural and allowable. But if the other man shall assert that Homer has no beauties whatever; that he holds him to be a dull and spiritless writer, and that he would as soon peruse any old legend of knight-errantry as the *Iliad;* then I exclaim, that my antagonist either is void

of all taste, or that his taste is corrupted in a miserable degree; and I appeal to whatever I think the standard of taste, to show him that he is in the wrong.

What that standard is to which, in such opposition of tastes, we are obliged to have recourse, remains to be traced. A standard properly signifies, that which is of such undoubted authority as to be the test of other things of the same kind. Thus a standard weight or measure, is that which is appointed by law to regulate all other measures and weights. Thus the court is said to be the standard of good breeding; and the scripture of theological truth.

When we say that nature is the standard of taste, we lay down a principle very true and just, as far as it can be applied. There is no doubt, that in all cases where an imitation is intended of some object that exists in nature, as in representing human characters or actions, conformity to nature affords a full and distinct criterion of what is truly beautiful. Reason hath in such cases full scope for exerting its authority; for approving or condemning; by comparing the copy with the original. But there are innumerable cases in which this rule cannot be at all applied; and conformity to nature, is an expression frequently used, without any distinct or determinate meaning. We must therefore search for somewhat that can be rendered more clear and precise, to be the standard of taste.

Taste, as I before explained it, is ultimately founded on an internal sense of beauty, which is natural to men, and which, in its application to particular objects, is capable of being guided and enlightened by reason. Now were there any one person who possessed in full perfection all the powers of human nature, whose internal senses were in every instance exquisite and just, and whose reason was unerring and sure, the determinations of such a person concerning beauty, would, beyond doubt, be a perfect standard for the taste of all others. Wherever their taste differed from his, it could be imputed only to some imperfection in their natural powers. But as there is no such living standard, no one person to whom all mankind will allow such submission to be due, what is there of sufficient authority to be the standard of the various and opposite tastes of men? Most certainly there is nothing but the taste, as far as it can be gathered, of human nature. That which men concur the most in admiring, must be held to be beautiful. His taste must be esteemed just and true, which coincides with the general sentiments of men. In this standard we must rest. To the sense of mankind the ultimate appeal must ever lie, in all works of taste. If any one should maintain that sugar was bitter and tobacco was sweet, no reasonings could avail to prove it. The taste of such a person would infallibly be held to be diseased, merely because it differed so widely from the taste of the species to which he belongs. In like manner, with regard to the objects of sentiment or internal taste, the common feelings of men carry the same authority, and have a title to regulate the taste of every individual.

But have we then, it will be said, no other criterion of what is beautiful, than the approbation of the majority? Must we collect the voices of others, before we form any judgment for ourselves, of what deserves applause in eloquence or poetry? By no means; there are principles of reason and sound judgment which can be applied to matters of taste, as well as to the subjects of science and philosophy. He who admires or censures any work of genius, is always ready, if his taste be in any degree improved, to assign some reasons for his decision. He appeals to principles, and points out the grounds on which he proceeds. Taste is a sort of compound power, in which the light of the understanding always mingles, more or less, with the feelings of sentiment.

But though reason can carry us a certain length in judging concerning works of taste, it is not to be forgotten that the ultimate conclusions to which our reasonings lead, refer at last to sense and perception. We may speculate and argue concerning propriety of conduct in a tragedy, or an epic poem. Just

reasonings on the subject will correct the caprice of unenlightened taste, and establish principles for judging of what deserves praise. But, at the same time, these reasonings appeal always in the last resort, to feeling. The foundation upon which they rest, is what has been found from experience to please mankind universally. Upon this ground we prefer a simple and natural, to an artificial and affected style; a regular and well-connected story, to loose and scattered narratives; a catastrophe which is tender and pathetic, to one which leaves us unmoved. It is from consulting our own imagination and heart, and from attending to the feelings of others, that any principles are formed which acquire authority in matters of taste.

When we refer to the concurring sentiments of men as the ultimate taste of what is to be accounted beautiful in the arts, this is to be always understood of men placed in such situations as are favourable to the proper exertions of taste. Every one must perceive, that among rude and uncivilized nations, and during the ages of ignorance and darkness, any loose notions that are entertained concerning such subjects, carry no authority. In those states of society, taste has no materials on which to operate. It is either totally suppressed, or appears in its lower and most imperfect form. We refer to the sentiments of mankind in polished and flourishing nations; when arts are cultivated and manners refined; when works of genius are subjected to free discussion, and taste is improved by science and philosophy.

Even among nations, at such a period of society, I admit that accidental causes may occasionally warp the proper operations of taste; sometimes the taste of religion, sometimes the form of government, may for a while pervert; a licentious court may introduce a taste for false ornaments, and dissolute writings. The usage of one admired genius may procure approbation for his faults, and even render them fashionable. Sometimes envy may have power to bear down, for a little, productions of great merit; while popular humour, or party spirit, may, at other times, exalt to a high, though short-lived reputation, what little deserved it. But though such casual circumstances give the appearance of caprice to the judgments of taste, that appearance is easily corrected. In the course of time, the genuine taste of human nature never fails to disclose itself and to gain the ascendant over any fantastic and corrupted modes of taste which may chance to have been introduced. These may have currency for a while, and mislead superficial judges; but being subjected to examination, by degrees they pass away; while that alone remains which is founded on sound reason, and the native feelings of men.

I by no means pretend, that there is any standard of taste, to which, in every particular instance, we can resort for clear and immediate determination. Where, indeed, is such a standard to be found for deciding any of those great controversies in reason and philosophy, which perpetually divide mankind? In the present case, there was plainly no occasion for any such strict and absolute provision to be made. In order to judge of what is morally good or evil, of what man ought, or ought not in duty to do, it was fit that the means of clear and precise determination should be afforded us. But to ascertain in every case with the utmost exactness what is beautiful or elegant, was not at all necessary to the happiness of man. And therefore some diversity in feeling was here allowed to take place; and room was left for discussion and debate, concerning the degree of approbation to which any work of genius is entitled.

The conclusion, which it is sufficient for us to rest upon, is, that taste is far from being an arbitrary principle, which is subject to the fancy of every individual, and which admits of no criterion for determining whether it be false or true. Its foundation is the same in all human minds. It is built upon sentiments and perceptions which belong to our nature; and which, in general, operate with the same uniformity as our other intellectual principles. When these sentiments are perverted by ignorance and prejudice, they are capable of being rectified by reason. Their sound

and natural state is ultimately determined, by comparing them with the general taste of mankind. Let men declaim as much as they please concerning the capric and the uncertainty of taste; it is found, by experience, that there are beauties; which, if they be displayed in a proper light, have power to command lasting and general admiration. In every composition, what interests the imagination, and touches the heart, pleases all ages and all nations. There is a certain string to which, when properly struck, the human heart is so made as to answer.

Hence the universal testimony which the most improved nations of the earth have conspired, throughout a long tract of ages, to give to some few works of genius; such as the Iliad of Homer, and the Aeneid of Virgil. Hence the authority which such works have acquired, as standards in some degree of poetical composition; since from them we are enabled to collect what the sense of mankind is, concerning those beauties which give them the highest pleasure, and which therefore poetry ought to exhibit. Authority or prejudice may, in one age or country, give a temporary reputation to an indifferent poet or a bad artist; but when foreigners, or when posterity examine his works, his faults are discerned, and the genuine taste of human nature appears. *Opinionum commenta delet dies; naturae judicia confirmat.* (Time overthrows the illusions of opinion, but establishes the decisions of nature.)[53]

In the next lecture Blair dealt with the related theme of criticism. The application of reason and good sense to the pleasures of nature and art, he said, is the criterion by which the merit of a production can be determined. True criticism, he further held, is not based on abstract reasoning; rather it is the result of a careful analysis of facts. To substantiate this belief, Blair pointed out that Aristotle's opinions concerning the three unities were formed after a thorough examination of the works of the great writers of antiquity. Criticism is an empirical art, therefore, which is never independent of facts and observations. In all, the purpose of critical rules is to help the writer or speaker avoid faults in his compositions; beyond this, criticism cannot go.

What Blair said on taste and criticism not only cuts to the heart of his rhetorical doctrine, but it lays the foundation for subsequent modern ideas on rhetoric grounded in judgment and evaluation. As a final consideration in our attempt to show the contemporaneity of several of Blair's major theories, we will now summarize what we perceive to be the advice he would give to twentieth-century students of rhetoric enrolled in American colleges and universities. The suggestions presented here are derived primarily from that portion of Lecture XIX dealing with "Directions for forming a Proper Style," and from Lecture XXXIV focusing on "Means of Improving in Eloquence."

Before summarizing Blair's recommendations, however, let us review briefly the challenging situation he would find in the last quarter of twentieth-century America. Unlike his own era in which the fortunate few were sent to the university and the vast majority of the citizenry were illiterate, he would be shocked with the magnitude of college enrollments. But he would feel quite at home with the visible desire for educated persons to be able to read, write, and speak effectively. At the same time he would not be surprised to learn that the goal of achieving widespread student proficiency in basic communication skills had fallen far short of the mark.

Here is what Blair would soon come to know. A 1977 nationwide poll of 4,400 college faculty members employed at 161 colleges and universities indicated that a sizable majority find their students "seriously underprepared" in oral and written communication.[54] Additionally a midwestern university student newspaper reported that four out of ten incoming freshmen were unable to write a coherent paragraph and must consequently enroll in remedial English.

As an eighteenth-century visitor to modern America, Blair would have difficulty in understanding the role that the electronic media would play in causing a sharp decline in the quality of communication practice. Among the data that would come to his attention are the following:

1. American preschool children "watch television 6,000 hours before they spend a single hour in the classroom."[55]
2. By the time students "graduate from high school, they will have spent 16,000 hours in front of television sets and only 11,000 hours in the classroom."[56]
3. An increasing number of United States citizens rely on television as their principal information source.
4. The television viewer is a passive observer who typically turns on the tube to amuse himself rather than to engage his mind.
5. Thirty and sixty second television advertisements endlessly repeated have more staying power than an in-class discussion of an eloquent speech or a thoughtful essay by renowned political and literary leaders.
6. It is faster and easier to call by telephone than to take the time to compose a letter.

These facts doubtless would cause Blair to reflect that time spent in this way is time taken away from standard communication-oriented activities such as reading, writing, speaking, or critical listening.

More disturbing to Blair than the deleterious effect of the electronic media on communication skills would be the knowledge that the current tendency to endorse the "social pass" in the public school system ultimately means that a high school diploma is more a certificate of attendance than a measure of achievement. But he would take comfort in learning from the *Chronicle of Higher Education* that the thirty-four high schools nationwide whose test averages have not dramatically declined in the past ten years have continued to require basic instruction in communication.

Against this background that would prove both familiar and strange to Blair, he would deliver his universal and timely lecture on forming a good style and in improving eloquence. The presentation would proceed in the following vein.

The effective writer should begin with clear ideas. Not to know what one means to say is to guarantee reader confusion. If it takes several drafts of an essay before the author has satisfied himself on this point, so be it. Further, the student writer needs practice, the more the better. Admittedly, English composition classes are costly to the university because they must necessarily be small in size; yet how else can sustained individual attention be ensured? Also of importance is the need to read the best literary works available. In doing so, however, the prospective communicator should avoid slavish imitation, for a good written style is a personal asset nontransferable to others.

It is necessary, Blair continues, to adapt ideas to a specific target audience; thus a speaker or writer should consider the purpose and the occasion. In adhering to these suggestions, one should remember that thought precedes style; substance comes before form or ornamentation. The goal at all times should be correctness, precision, propriety, and lastly, polish.

In turning to a consideration of methods for achieving eloquence, Blair prescribes a similar pattern. First of all, a beginning speaker, he says, should put forth his best effort by reading and studying widely, and striving never to be at a loss for selecting an appealing subject. Once this is done the following rules should prove helpful:

1. Speak regularly and often for speakers require practice every bit as much as do athletes.
2. Study the best models, not necessarily those you hear most frequently.
3. Learn from the mistakes of others.
4. Let your aim be verbal fluency; do not be governed by a set of mechanical rules as a grammarian is.
5. Remember that repetition is both necessary and appropriate in oral discourse for a listener cannot re-read.

Notwithstanding the fact that the above advice was first given at the University of Edinburgh during the time of the American Revolution, there can be little doubt concern-ing its continuing relevance for modern students. The college senior who misspells words in his letter of application or reveals himself to be inarticulate in a job interview will learn the hard way that few skills in our society are more valuable and useful than those which involve communication.

Notes

1. James L. Golden and Edward P. J. Corbett, Jr., eds., *The Rhetoric of Blair, Campbell, and Whately* (New York: Holt, Rinehart and Winston, Inc., 1968), p. 5.
2. *Ibid.*
3. A. Bosker, *Literary Criticism in the Age of Johnson,* 2nd ed. (New York: Hafner Publishing Co., 1952), pp. 1–7.
4. Jonathan Swift, "The Battle of the Books," in Sir Walter Scott, ed., *The Works of Jonathan Swift,* 19 vols. (Boston: Houghton Mifflin and Co., 1883), X, 221–25.
5. "A Tale of the Tub," in *ibid.,* 124.
6. *Ibid.,* 136.
7. *Ibid.,* 120.
8. Arthur Murphy, ed., *The Works of Samuel Johnson,* 12 vols. (London: Thomas Tegg, et. al., 1824), XI, 176.
9. Alexander Pope, "Essay on Criticism," in *Works,* 10 vols. (London: C. and J. Rivington, 1824), V, 68–69.
10. *Ibid.,* 118–24.
11. *Ibid.,* 130–38.
12. John Lawson, *Lectures Concerning Oratory* (Dublin: George Faulkner, 1758). For a detailed analysis of Lawson's rhetorical theories, see Ray E. Keesey, "The Rhetorical Theory of John Lawson," Ph.D. Dissertation, The Ohio State University, 1950.
13. W. P. Sandford, *English Theories of Public Address, 1530–1828* (Columbus, Ohio, 1931), p. 110. For Ward's full work, see *A System of Oratory,* 2 vols. (London: John Ward, 1759).
14. Warren Guthrie, "Rhetorical Theory in Colonial America," in Karl Wallace, ed., *History of Speech Education in America* (New York: Appleton-Century-Crofts, Inc., 1954), p. 54.
15. *On the Sublime,* 1.4.
16. *Ibid.,* VIII.1.
17. *Ibid.,* XXXVI.1.–2.
18. Richard Hurd, ed., *The Works of the Right Honorable Joseph Addison,* 6 vols. (London: T. Cadell and W. Davies, Strand, 1811), IV, 340.
19. *Ibid.,* 330.
20. For a brief but penetrating overview of Baillie's philosophy, see Samuel H. Monk, *The Sublime* (Ann Arbor: The University of Michigan Press, 1960), pp. 73–77.
21. Edmund Burke, *The Works and Correspondence of the Right Honourable Edmund Burke,* 8 vols. (London: Francis and John Rivington, 1852), II, 566–77.

22. *Ibid.,* 598–620.
23. *Ibid.,* 679.
24. Monk, p. 87.
25. Alexander Gerard, *An Essay on Taste,* Walter J. Hipple, ed. (Gainesville, Fla.: Scholars-Facsimilies & Reprints, 1963), p. 95.
26. *Ibid.,* p. 249.
27. *Ibid.,* p. 166.
28. Charles Rollin, *The Method of Teaching and Studying the Belles Lettres,* 4 vols. (London: A Bettesworth and C. Hitch, 1734).
29. *Ibid.,* I, 63.
30. Most of these discussions appear in volume II.
31. *Ibid.,* I, A 2.
32. Adam Smith, *Lectures on Rhetoric and Belles Lettres,* John M. Lothian, ed. (London: Thomas Nelson, 1963), p. 140.
33. Adam Smith, *The Theory of Moral Sentiments* (London: A Millar, 1759), p. 257.
34. *Lectures on Justice, Police, Revenue and Arms,* Edward Cannan, ed. (New York: Kelly & Millman, 1956), p. 171.
35. See Walter Jackson Bate, ed., *Criticism: The Major Texts* (New York, 1952).
36. Smith, *Lectures on Rhetoric and Belles Lettres,* p. 119.
37. James Anderson, *The Bee or Literary Weekly Intelligencer, consisting of original Pieces and Selections from Performances of Merit, Foreign and Domestic,* 18 vols. (London, 1791), III, 4.
38. William Wordsworth, "Essay Supplementary to Preface," in Charles W. Eliot, ed., *Prefaces and Prologues to Famous Books* (New York, 1909), p. 338 n. For more favorable views of Smith's contributions as a rhetorician, see the following essays: Vincent Bevilacqua, "Philosophical Influences in the Development of English Rhetorical Theory, 1748 to 1783," *Proceedings of the Leeds Philosophical and Literary Society Literary and Historical Section,* XII (April, 1968), 191–215; Bevilacqua, "Adam Smith and Some Philosophical Origins of Eighteenth-Century Rhetorical Theory," *The Modern Language Review,* 63 (July, 1968), 559–68; and Wilbur S. Howell, "Adam Smith's Lectures on Rhetoric: An Historical Assessment," *Speech Monographs,* XXXVI (November, 1969), 393–418.
39. Sir Alexander Grant, *The Story of the University of Edinburgh,* 2 vols. (London: Longman, Green and Company, 1884), I, 276. For an informative essay on the history of this chair, see Henry W. Meikle. "The Chair of Rhetoric and Belles Lettres in the University of Edinburgh." *University of Edinburgh Journal,* XIII (1945), 89–103.
40. Hugh Blair, *Lectures on Rhetoric and Belles Lettres* (Philadelphia: T. Ellwood Zell, 1862), p. 3.
41. William Charvat, *The Origins of American Critical Thought,* 1810–1835, (Philadelphia: University of Pennsylvania Press, 1936), p. 44.
42. For an analysis of these influences, see Douglas Ehninger and James L. Golden, "The Intrinsic Sources of Blair's Popularity," *The Southern Speech Journal,* XXI (Fall, 1955), 12–30; and "The Extrinsic Sources of Blair's Popularity," *The Southern Speech Journal,* XXII (Fall, 1956), 16–32.
43. Robert Schmitz, *Hugh Blair* (New York: King's Crown Press, 1948), p. 66.
44. Blair's view on sublimity and taste also reflect the teachings of Burke and Gerard.
45. As late as 1948, one of the authors expressed the prevailing view concerning Blair's status as a rhetorician in the following manner: ". . . it is clear that the *Lectures on Rhetoric and Belles Lettres,* for the most part, is not an original work. Many writers have condemned Blair for his lack of originality." James L. Golden, "The Rhetorical Theory and Practice of Hugh Blair," M. A. thesis, The Ohio State University, 1948, p. 167.
46. Blair, *Lectures on Rhetoric and Belles Lettres,* p. 11.
47. *Ibid.,* p. 354.
48. *Ibid.,* p. 29.
49. George Saintsbury, *A History of Criticism and Literary Taste in Europe,* 3 vols. (New York: Dodd, Mead, and Company, 1902), II, 462.
50. Blair's long range influence may be seen in D. Josef Gomez Hermosilla, *Arte De Hablar, En Prosa Y Verso* (Paris: Liberia De Garnier Hermanos, 1866). This volume, first published in 1842 and revised in 1866, relies so heavily on Blair that the author confesses he often actually uses the words that appear in the *Lectures on Rhetoric and Belles Lettres;* and he does so without the use of quotation marks in many instances.
51. Blair, *Lectures on Rhetoric and Belles Lettres,* p. 16.
52. *Ibid.,* p. 24.
53. *Ibid.,* pp. 16–26.
54. E. C. Ladd, Jr., and S. M. Lipset, "The Faculty Mood; Pessimism is Predominant," *The Chronicle of Higher Education,* October 3, 1977, p. 14.
55. Ernest L. Boyer and Arthur Levine, *A Quest for Common Learning: The Aims of General Education* (Washington, D.C.: Carnegie Foundation, 1981), p. 37.
56. *Ibid.,*

8

The Epistemologists

We place those authors in the psychological-philosophical or epistemological school of thought whose principal concern was to relate communication theory to the basic nature of man. With determination and skill, reinforced by painstaking research in the natural and social sciences, they set for themselves the task of unraveling the mystery of man's mind and soul. Notwithstanding the fact that their fame was derived primarily from writings generally associated with psychology and philosophy, these epistemologists left an indelible imprint upon the direction rhetoric was to take for generations to come.

Our discussion of this trend will be divided into two parts. First we will deal with four great innovators of Western thought who made their contributions during the period from 1600 to 1725: Francis Bacon, René Descartes, John Locke, and Giambatista Vico. What these great thinkers had to say about knowledge in general and communication theory in particular remains provocative and challenging to contemporary students.

The Four Innovators, 1600–1725

Francis Bacon

Shortly after Copernicus made the startling discovery that the earth with clockwise precision rotates around the sun, his European followers—including Kepler, Gilbert, Galileo, Bacon, Descartes, and Boyle—initiated a scientific movement that challenged the classical preoccupation with deduction, and stressed the value of an experimental method based on the inductive process. Of this group of modern thinkers, Bacon and Descartes had the most impact on rhetoric. Described as "the greatest poet of science" and the "herald of the scientific movement," Bacon, who had come to realize the importance of the recent discoveries—"printing, gunpowder, and the compass"—recommended to his contemporaries "a total reform of human knowledge, a true advancement of learning, and a revolution in the conditions of life."[1] Convinced that progress was an inherent principle of life, he sketched in 1605 a philosophy of optimism in his first monumental work, the "Advancement of Learning." In this treatise may be found Bacon's innovative discussion of the faculties of the mind.[2] "The parts of human learning," he argued, "have reference to the three parts of Man's Understanding which is the seat of learning: History, to his Memory, Poesy to his Imagination, and Philosophy to his Reason."[3] To the faculties of understanding, reason, imagination, and memory, he then added will and appetite. These categories explaining the mind of man led to Bacon's celebrated statement that "the duty and office of Rhetoric is to *apply Reason to Imagination* for the better moving of the will."[4]

An integral part of Bacon's rhetorical theory was his concept of invention. Unlike the ancients, he played down the role of discovery in the formulation of arguments and the gathering of source data, emphasizing instead the element of "remembrance." A speaker, in effect, reaches back into his memory to summon forth knowledge that he already knows; then he applies it to the rhetorical situation at hand.[5]

How, it might be asked, does the communicator get the knowledge that is to be stored in the memory for appropriate use in a given situation? Bacon's response to this question is both traditional and original. He is strikingly similar to the classical scholars in suggesting that knowledge may be obtained from general and special or particular topics. But he is innovative in his discussion of four commonplaces as aids to invention. The first, he calls "Colours of Good and Evil." "The persuader's labour," Bacon argues, "is to make things appear good or evil, and that in higher or lower degree. . . ."[6] To assist potential speakers in the use of this commonplace, Bacon provided a "Table of Colours or appearances of Good and Evil" which contains shades of meaning and a list of possible accompanying fallacies associated with a particular argument.[7] Since the commonplace of "Colours of Good and Evil" often deals with premises that appear on the surface to be true, Bacon warns us to examine such claims critically. Consider, for instance, the following statement: "What men praise and honour is good; what they dispraise and condemn is evil." At first glance the thought expressed in this argument seems to be a high level "good" grounded in the idea that public sentiment is infallible. But to Bacon this argument in a sophism which deceives people by appealing to their ignorance, factional spirit, prejudices, and "natural disposition" to "praise and blame."[8]

The second commonplace, which is labeled "antitheta," consists of theses which may be argued pro and con. In his *De augmentis,* Bacon lists forty-seven theses expressed both in affirmative and negative terms. Similar to a modern day debate brief, this technique helps the advocate answer possible objections to his claims; it is also useful in making decisions. Assume, for example, that we are confronted with the difficult and challenging task of rendering a decision on a controversial issue. If we use Bacon's method of "antitheta," we might take a sheet of paper, draw a vertical line down the middle of the page, and then place the affirmative contentions on the left side and the negative counter claims on the right. By weighing all of the arguments for and against, Bacon implies, we should be able to reach a thoughtful conclusion.

"Formulae" constitute a third type of commonplace or aid to invention. They are "small parts of a speech, fully composed and ready for use. . . ."[9] They may take the form of a stock phrase, sentence, or paragraph designed to serve as a transition or summary; or a humorous thrust devised for the purpose of blunting the attack or image of an adversary. Here Bacon, perhaps drawing upon his own rich experiences in law courts and in Parliament, illustrates how "formulae" may be employed to diminish the impact of an opponent's argument. "When one's adversary declares, 'you go from the matter,' you reply: 'But it was to follow you.' When he demands that 'you come to the point,' you answer: 'Why, I shall not find you there.' If he says, 'You take more than is for granted,' you retort: 'You grant less than is proved.' "[10] Admittedly, such examples appear contrived and artificial. But this kind of rhetorical strategy is still prevalent in contemporary political, forensic, and religious discourse.

The fourth and final commonplace discussed by Bacon is that of "apothegms." These are "pointed speeches" or pithy statements which may be "interlaced in continued speech" or "recited upon occasion of themselves." Like salt, they can be "sprinkled where you will."[11] In compiling a list of "apothegms," Bacon alluded to the classics, British and continental history, and to his own works. The ensuing examples are representative:

1. When the oracle of Delphi pronounced Socrates to be the wisest man in Greece, Socrates is reputed to have said: "I am not wise, and know it; others are not wise, and know it not."
2. "Queen Isabella of Spain used to say, 'Whosoever hath a good presence and a good fashion, carries continual letters of recommendation.' "[12]

Nor was Bacon content to describe the nature and utility of the commonplaces; he also gave three useful hints for collecting them.

First, he asserted, we should *observe* the world around us, taking special note of particular instances, similarities and contrasts in events, and the "utterances of others."[13] Secondly, we should *converse* freely in order to generate fresh insights. The well-known political leaders—Charles James Fox of the eighteenth century and Robert Kennedy—relied on this method, more than any other, for gaining the knowledge needed to cope with knotty domestic and international problems. Thirdly, Bacon adds, we should *study* widely, especially in the area of history.

Bacon next turns to a consideration of how to record the data gathered from the process of observing, conversing, and studying. His advice was the use of commonplace "note books or phrase books." To make certain that the source material in these books be etched in the memory, Bacon suggested: "One man's notes will little profit another. . . ."[14] The act of writing one's own notes, he felt, contributed importantly to the practice of recall. Among those contemporary figures we have known who used a commonplace book for preparation of speeches was John F. Kennedy.

Perhaps more vital in appreciating Bacon's contribution to knowledge is to examine his analysis of sense perception. Motivated by a desire to establish progressive stages of certainty, he rejected the widely practiced inductive method that moved from particular instances to general premises, and then proceeded to "judgment and the discovery of middle axioms." Instead, he observed, we should derive "axioms from the senses and particulars, rising by a gradual and unbroken ascent, so that it arrives at the most general axioms last of all."[15] Bacon's interest in psychology led him to conclude that faulty sense perception could hinder man's quest for establishing reliable and valid conclusions through the method of induction. He was particularly concerned with the need to clear the human mind of four potential fallacies which he called the "Idols of the Tribe," "Idols of the Cave," "Idols of the Market Place," and "Idols of the Theatre."[16] These terms used to designate the fallacies were both novel and meaningful. The "Idols of the Tribe" represented the inherent

limitations in the general nature of man. As a whole, suggested Bacon, mankind shared a homogeneous spirit that often exemplifies obsessions, narrowness, restlessness, and excessive emotionality. Moreover it is a spirit formed in part by an inadequate response to sense messages that may be blurred or inaccurate. Thus it is wrong, asserted Bacon, to argue "that the sense of man is the measure of things."[17]

If the "Idols of the Tribe" stem from human nature itself as seen in the generality of man, the "Idols of the Cave" are derived from those unique qualities and experiences of the individual man. One's basic personality, intellectual capacity, educational training, occupation, or value system may serve as "a cave or den of his own, which refracts, and discolours the light of nature."[18] The life style that results from these elements significantly affects an individual's attempt to interpret his sense impressions.

Not only is a man influenced by his general and particular nature, but by his close associations with others in the "Market Place." Here Bacon, anticipating the twentieth-century semanticist, warned of the pitfalls confronting those who failed to use words with precision and care while communicating with others. Such writers and speakers, he said, confuse words with things, and hastily conceived definitions with reality. This idol, consequently, is the most troublesome fallacy because "the ill and unfit choice of words wonderfully obstructs the understanding."[19]

The final idol, that of the Theatre, describes how untested information that has "immigrated into men's minds from the various dogmas of philosophy, and also from wrong laws of demonstration," are "but so many stage-plays, representing worlds of their own creation after an unreal and scenic fashion."[20] Bacon used this idol to attack those philosophical systems that have been handed down from generation to generation with no effort on the part of the recipients to apply scientific criteria for the purpose of judging their validity.

To conclude his perceptive analysis of the idols, Bacon stressed its meaning for his theory of knowledge. Since his purpose was to construct an epistemological system that would lead men to an earthly kingdom "founded on the sciences," he saw the idols as barriers that would block the entrance. Thus these fallacies "must be renounced and put away with a fixed and solemn determination, and the understanding thoroughly freed and cleansed." In fine, man in search of scientific certainty must assume the purity and simplicity of a little child which Christianity holds to be essential for "entrance into the kingdom of heaven."[21]

To gain further insight into Bacon's notions on the Idols, consider the following passage drawn from his *Novum organum:*

There are four classes of Idols which beset men's minds. To these for distinction's sake I have assigned names—calling the first class *Idols of the Tribe;* the second, *Idols of the Cave;* the third, *Idols of the Market-place;* the fourth, *Idols of the Theatre.*

The formulation of ideas and axioms by true induction is no doubt the proper remedy to be applied for the keeping off and clearing away of idols. To point them out, however, is of great use; for the doctrine of Idols is to the interpretation of Nature what the doctrine of the refutation of Sophisms is to common logic.

The Idols of the Tribe have their foundation in human nature itself, and in the tribe or race of men. For it is a false assertion that the sense of man is the measure of things. On the contrary, all perceptions as well of the sense as of the mind are according to the measure of the universe. And the human understanding is like a false mirror, which, receiving rays irregularly, distorts and discolours the nature of things by mingling its own nature with it.

The Idols of the Cave are the idols of the individual man. For everyone (besides the errors common to human nature in general) have a cave or den of his own, which refracts and discolours the light of nature; owing either to his own proper and peculiar nature; or to his education and conversation with others; or to the reading of books, and the authority of those whom he esteems and admires; or to the differences of impressions, accordingly as they take place in a mind preoccupied and predisposed or in a mind indifferent and settled; or the like. So that the spirit of man (according as it is meted out to different individuals) is in fact a thing variable and full of perturbation, and governed as it were by chance. Whence it was well observed by Heraclitus that men look for sciences in their own lesser worlds, and not in the greater or common world.

There are also idols formed by the intercourse and association of men with each other, which I call Idols of the Marketplace, on account of the commerce and consort of men there. For it is by discourse that men associate; and words are imposed according to the apprehension of the vulgar. And therefore the ill and unfit choice of words wonderfully obstructs the understanding. Nor do the definitions or explanations wherewith in some things learned men are wont to guard and defend themselves, by any means set the matter right. But words plainly force and overrule the understanding, and throw all into confusion, and lead men away into numberless empty controversies and idle fancies.

Lastly, there are idols which have immigrated into men's minds from the various dogmas of philosophies, and also from wrong laws of demonstration. These I call Idols of the Theatre; because in my judgment all the received systems are but so many stage-plays, representing worlds of their own creation after an unreal and scenic fashion. Nor is it only of the systems now in vogue, or only of the ancient sects and philosophies, that I speak; for many more plays of the same kind may yet be composed and in like artificial manner set forth; seeing that errors the most widely different have nevertheless causes for the most part alike. Neither again do I mean this only of entire systems, but also of many principles and axioms in science, which by tradition, credulity, and negligence have come to be received.

Two other aspects of Bacon's philosophy are not without significance for the role they played in helping to mold eighteenth-century rhetorical theory. First was his rejection of the syllogism as a productive means for establishing principles. That the syllogism with its emphasis on opinion and probability and its usefulness in checking reasoning was important to popular arts such as rhetoric, Bacon was willing to admit. Indeed, he, like Aristotle, recognized the function of topics and commonplaces in constructing arguments. But he excluded the syllogism as a part of his scientific method on the grounds that it had little correspondence to the essential nature of things. He put it this way in his essay on "The Great Instauration," written in 1620—fifteen years after "The Advancement of Learning."

The syllogism consists of propositions; propositions of words; and words are the tokens and signs of notions. Now if the very notions of the mind . . . be improperly and overhastily abstracted from facts, vague, not sufficiently definite, faulty in short in many ways, the whole edifice tumbles. I therefore reject the syllogism; and that not only as regards principles . . . but also as regards middle propositions; which, although obtainable no doubt by the syllogism, are, when so obtained, barren of works, remote from practice, and altogether unavailable for the active department of the sciences. Although therefore I leave to the syllogism and these famous and boasted modes of demonstration their jurisdiction over popular arts and such as are matter of opinion (in which department I leave all as it is), yet in dealing with the nature of things I use induction throughout, and that in the minor propositions as well as the major. For I consider induction to be that form of demonstration which upholds the sense, and closes with nature, and comes to the very brink of operation, if it does not actually deal with it.[22]

In later discussions we will observe how Bacon's reservations concerning the syllogism prepared the way for similar attacks by Descartes, Locke, Hume, and Campbell.

Secondly, it is instructive to note that Bacon was among the early English prose authors who sought to replace the copious style, then in vogue, with a language control featuring Attic simplicity. He was content to break with the Elizabethan tradition even though it led to a "schizm of eloquence" because of his conviction that scientific ideas may best be expressed in a clear, unadorned style.[23] Bacon thus contributed importantly to the doctrine of perspicuity that was to become a benchmark of eighteen-century rhetorical thought.

Bacon's pioneering theories set into motion a movement toward a new empiricism that achieved focus and symbolic effect in the experimental studies of the Royal Society. In his history of the Society published in the 1660s, Thomas Sprat eulogized Bacon for providing the inspiration and direction of his "Enterprize, as it is now set on foot. . . ."[24] Additionally he praised him for his cogent defense of "Experimental Philosophy" and his model of excellence in style. Sprat's assessment of Bacon's accomplishments has been widely shared by subsequent writers.

René Descartes

While the theories of Bacon and the Royal Society were being disseminated throughout England, similar probings into the nature of man and methods of study were taking place in France. These inquiries began in earnest in 1637 with the publication of Descartes' celebrated *Discourse on Method*. Partly autobiographical, this study contains the heart of Descartes' philosophy. He relates that when he had completed his studies, he resolved to devote his remaining years to an analysis of himself rather than to the reading of books. By then, however, Descartes already had formed strong convictions concerning branches of learning that were a part of the humane tradition. He regarded "eloquence highly, and was in raptures with poesy (i.e. poetry)," but thought that "both were gifts of nature rather than fruits of study."[25] He complained that the syllogism was incapable of investigating the unknown and separating truth from error. It was, instead, useful only in communicating "what we already know."[26] Most of all, he was "delighted with the mathematics, on account of the certitude and evidence of their reasonings."[27] The remarkable similarity between these views and those expressed by George Campbell in his *Philosophy of Rhetoric* will be observed later.

This preference for mathematical certainty as opposed to syllogistic probability may be seen in Descartes' four-fold study method. With unwavering resolution he was determined to accept only those claims which could be verified with proof containing no ground for doubt; to divide all difficult aspects of a subject into as many segments as possible; to follow a pattern of inquiry utilizing a climactic order and a cause to effect sequence; and to use an all-inclusive system of enumeration that prevents omissions.[28]

Central to Descartes' study design was his faith in the power of reason to determine truth and to discipline the imagination. The mind of man, he suggested, was capable of reaching unchallenged conclusions such as: "I think, therefore I am"; and "God exists." Similarly the mind had the ability to regulate the senses in such a way that the fallacy of the idols could be brought under control. Like Bacon, he further believed in an advancement of learning made possible for an enlightened society through the means of experiments.[29] But he went beyond his predecessor's grasp of understanding abstract scientific principles and in appreciating the full implications of rationalism for the experimental process.[30]

Despite his apparent indebtedness to Bacon, Descartes was, in many respects, unique and prophetic. In arguing that experiment takes precedence over disputation, inquiry over communication, and action over speculation, he broke with the logicians of the past.[31] His mathematical contribution to science and his stress on reasoning enabled him to make bold predictions "which became the assumptions of nineteenth-century science."[32] This overall impact prompted Leon Roth to observe that the *Discourse on Method* "marks an epoch. It is a dividing line in the history of thought. Everything that came before it is old; everything that came after it is new."[33] What is more relevant for this study is the fact that Descartes' work influenced the direction and thrust

of the French Academy and, indeed, became a textbook for the Port-Royal logicians and rhetoricians who, in turn, influenced British thought.

Descartes' impact on later scholars can best be seen by turning to the publication of the second edition of Arnauld and Nicole's *Logique of Port-Royal*. This provocative edition contained from the beginning to end the cardinal tenets of Cartesian philosophy and shook the foundations of traditional rhetorical theory. With Descartes and Boileau, Arnauld and Nicole held that truth is the transcendent goal in life. Thus the only acceptable communication model is one which adheres to the principles of geometry requiring demonstration based on clear definitions, axioms, and cause to effect relations. In such a system there could be no place for the scholastic art of syllogizing, commonplaces which substitute verisimilitude for reality, or highly emotional appeals. Nor was there a need for a method of expression or invention because of man's natural facility in these areas. In short, since rhetoric cannot produce truth it is, at best, relegated to the simple task of communicating principles that logic and experimentation can discover.[34] These views, as we shall later note, produced a strong counter response from the brilliant Italian scholar, Giambattista Vico.

John Locke

Many of the ideas of Bacon and Descartes, as well as those of the members of the French Academy and Royal Society, found eloquent expression in John Locke's monumental *Essay of Human Understanding* written in 1690. To a large extent Locke succeeded in summarizing the central features of seventeenth-century scientific thought. Additionally, however, he presented novel and penetrating insights into the nature of man. Although Locke is well known for his claim that rhetoric was a "powerful Instrument of Error and Deceit,"[35] he had a positive influence on the psychological philosophical theories of discourse that evolved in the eighteenth century, culminating in Campbell's *Philosophy of Rhetoric*. Of the many concepts included in Locke's *Essay*, four have special meaning for students of rhetorical theory. They are his treatment of the faculties of the mind, association of ideas, pathetic proof, and the syllogism.

Locke concluded that since the mind has the power to *perceive* and *prefer,* it must be comprised of two major faculties, the understanding and the will.[36] In explaining the nature of the faculty of understanding, Locke developed his famous theory of ideas. Reflection upon sensory experience, he observed, produces ideas which are, in turn, held together in a meaningful pattern through the talent of the mind to trace relationships that show natural correspondence and connection. Reason likewise enables us to unite ideas that are apparently unrelated by relying on the laws of association. Here we may observe from past experiences that whenever a particular idea reaches the understanding an "associate appears with it." Under such conditions, the doctrine of association permits us to connect these concepts so that they will form an inseparable unit in our minds.[37]

Locke's thesis caused him to reject the syllogism on the grounds that it neither demonstrates nor strengthens the connection that two ideas may have with each other. Nor does it advance an argument or lead to moral truth. The power of inference, a gift presented to man by God, makes it possible for us to perceive associations and to determine whether or not ideas are coherent or incoherent. Thus the understanding, concludes Locke, "is not taught to reason" by the "methods of syllogizing."[38] Quite clearly Locke gave a new dimension to the reservations pertaining to the syllogism articulated by Bacon, Descartes, and the Port-Royal logicians.

As one of the early proponents of faculty psychology, Locke came to believe that an idea which reaches the understanding does not necessarily have the power to motivate the will. The rational process, he argued, must be reinforced by a pathetic appeal that ultimately becomes the major determinant of action. All of the emotions have one common element which Locke called "uneasiness," and described as the absence of some good. Whenever the mind experiences "uneasiness," it feels pain and generates the compelling desire to remove it.

The will, in short, may be influenced when the passions are stirred, for the arousal of an emotion inevitably causes pain. There is little opportunity for persuasion, however, if the mind is at ease since the desire for happiness has already been achieved.[39] To some extent Locke's views anticipated the twentieth-century theory of cognitive dissonance.[40]

Giambattista Vico

By the time Locke's probings into the human mind had attracted attention in England and on the Continent, another European epistemologist, the Italian rhetorician and social scientist Giambattista Vico was elaborating his theory of ideas at the University of Naples.[41] Launching his career in 1699, he immediately began a series of annual lectures which formed the germinal seed of his innovative philosophy.[42] Steeped in the classics—especially in the works of Homer, Plato, Cicero, and the Roman historian, Tacitus—Vico turned to the origin of language and to ancient rhetoric and poetics as a starting point in his quest to unlock the mysteries of man's nature, culture, and history. When he wished to improve his own style, "on successive days he would study Cicero side by side with Boccaccio, Virgil with Dante, and Horace with Petrarch, being curious to see and judge for himself the differences between them."[43] But the two classicists he admired above all others were Plato and Tacitus. He explains this preference in the following manner: "For with an incomparable metaphysical mind Tacitus contemplates man as he is, Plato as he should be,"[44] In the writings of these two ancient authors, Vico saw the model he hoped to imitate—that which presented both the virtues of pragmatism and idealism.

But if he derived much of his early basic philosophy and method from Plato and Tacitus, he received his greatest help in the area of communication from Homer and Cicero. From the readings of Homer who represented much of the early knowledge of the Greeks, Vico first saw a close relationship between rhetoric and human nature. Man alone, he came to believe, knows with a high degree of accuracy his own feelings and attitudes and expresses these sentiments to others with a wide range of universal communication procedures such as verbal and non-verbal symbols, art, and music. Since people of all ages adhere to this practice of communicating a language that can be interpreted, each person through sympathy can know, at least approximately, the feelings of his contemporaries. Equally important, by studying the communicative patterns of earlier societies, one may similarly come to appreciate what they have believed and experienced.[45]

The prime source of Vico's rhetorical theory was Cicero who held that rhetoric is a useful art designed to help men adjust to the exigencies of life, thereby rendering them more productive and influential. It was Cicero who taught him that rhetoric, a form of practical knowledge based on probability, is as significant in the sphere of human relations and conduct as a mathematical truth stemming from geometry is to the physical world. Cicero's orations, moreover, persuaded him that the generality of mankind cannot be motivated unless the passions are stirred.[46] Most of all, it was Cicero who convinced him that verisimilitudes constructed from topics or lines of arguments, rather than a recitation of physical facts, constituted the pivotal element needed to alter one's behavior through speech.[47]

Vico, it would appear, equated invention with the topics, and regarded the Ciceronian theory of the verisimilar with its emphasis on probability as the key to knowledge.[48] He did so with the conviction that "absolute truth, as preached by the Cartesians, does not appeal to all the faculties of the mind."[49] By supplanting certainty with verisimilitude, Vico pointed the way to the social scientist's use of the concept of "hypothesis," and "illustrated the practical end toward which knowledge should tend."[50]

Up to this point the analysis tends to suggest that Vico was an uncompromising classicist who was preoccupied with the obsession to use ancient doctrines to diminish the appeal of Descartes and other seventeenth-century modernists. Such an assessment is not responsive to the evidence. For Vico's early devotion to Homer, Plato, Tacitus, and Cicero was matched by his later zeal for Bacon. Indeed,

he found the "esoteric wisdom" of Plato and the "common wisdom" of Tacitus both present in the comprehensive and ingenious mind of Bacon.[51] After making this discovery, he developed an abiding belief in the premise that the "constant of human nature" could be "reduced to scientific principles."[52] He admired the successes of Galileo and Newton in systematizing and explaining the scientific characteristics inherent in the world of nature, and became convinced that he could, by using the tools of social and behavioral science, discover similar valid axioms pertaining to the world of nations.[53] What he found was to have far reaching significance for historiography and anthropology. His researches led him to conclude that there was "an ideal eternal history traversed in time by the history of every nation in its rise, development, maturity, decline, and fall."[54] In observing that every nation goes through a series of stages beginning with inception and concluding with disintegration, Vico became the first major proponent of the cyclical view of history.[55] Moreover, in suggesting that a society begins with a primitive belief in magic and progresses to an advanced commitment to philosophy, he gave support to the sociological tenet that nature is not static, but an on-going process of growth. Whatever occurs in the historical evolution of a nation, therefore, takes place at the appropriate point in the cyclical pattern.[56]

After Vico had established the essential principles of his new science, he enthusiastically compared it with the natural sciences. In fact, he was willing to argue that the geometrical propositions which Descartes and his followers held to be the key to our understanding of the physical world were merely creations of man. It is easy, concluded Vico, to demonstrate mathematical principles because they are man-made concepts designed to conform to our perception of the universe. As such, these propositions are no more reliable than the knowledge derived from scientific historical methods depicting the story of man.[57] In thus avoiding the polarities of rationalism on the one hand and empiricism on the other, Vico developed for himself the task of providing a synthesis of the two approaches to knowledge.

At this juncture it is useful to summarize the arguments which Vico used in his attempt to refute some of the major tenets advanced in Descartes' *Discourse on Method*. To make these ideas salient, we present the following brief containing the central arguments both of Descartes and of Vico. Three points should be remembered as you examine Descartes' contentions and Vico's rejoinder. First, the sequence of the arguments has been determined by us in order to ensure clarity and to see appropriate relationships. Secondly, Vico, in constructing his response approximately seven decades after Descartes had written his treatise, had the advantage of hindsight. Thirdly, it is of interest to note that the opposing views articulated here are often reproduced in the 1980s with a group of philosophers on one side and the rhetoricians on the other.

Descartes Vs. Vico: Debate on the Theory of Knowledge

Descartes

I. The Cartesian Method is grounded in Mathematical Certainty.
  A. It insures a systematic and orderly process guided by rules.
    1. Through intuition we have a vision of clarity and truth.
    2. Through deduction we make inferences from truth.
  B. Observe how the method is modeled after Mathematics.
    1. It is based on axioms which are known directly and clearly. (Intuition)
    2. It uses mathematical reasoning from axioms to the unknown. (Deduction)
  C. We must discover the one absolute truth with certainty and then move step by step without losing clarity and certainty along the way.
    1. We should accept only those claims which can be verified with proof containing no grounds for doubt.
    2. We should divide all difficult aspects of a subject into as many parts as possible.
    3. We should follow a pattern of inquiry utilizing a climactic order and cause to effect structure.

Vico

I. There are inherent limitations in Descartes' attempt to equate truth with Mathematical propositions.
  A. Consider his claim that we should only accept that which can be proved beyond any reasonable doubt.
  B. Mathematical certainty has nothing to do with the following subject areas that influence our daily lives.
    1. Politics
    2. Military Science
    3. Medical Science
    4. Jurisprudence
    5. History and Religion
  C. The Mathematical formal logic approach also runs counter to man's nature.
    1. It deemphasizes the faculty of memory.
    2. It ignores imagination, thereby thwarting our genius for invention.
II. Despite his commitment to Mathematics, Descartes' use of reasoning and evidence is unduly subjective. Thus he is inconsistent.
  A. The mind, he argues, is the criterion of truth.
    1. The mind, not the senses, he says, gives us knowledge of the external world.

4. We should use an all-inclusive system of enumeration that prevents omissions.

Note: The following statement, which is the cornerstone of my philosophy, meets the above criteria: "I think, therefore I am."

II. My theories have led me to conclude that rhetoric is not a worthy field of study.
   A. It makes use of the scholastic art of syllogizing.
   B. Rhetoric fails to rely exclusively on reason.
      1. Reason determines truth and disciplines the imagination.
      2. Experimentation is the key to knowing.
   C. Rhetoric is non-philosophical.
      1. It uses verisimilitude; that is, appearances of being real.
      2. By relying on commonplaces and topics, it deals only with probabilities.
      3. It is incapable of producing truth.
   D. Rhetoric is limited to communicating what is already known.

2. His argument, "I think, therefore I am," is a subjective claim.
3. So, too, is his argument that "God exists."
   B. Furthermore, in his preoccupation with Mathematics, he overlooks the subjective nature of that discipline.
      1. Mathematics was created by man.
      2. In effect, Mathematics is not on as high a level as Descartes claims.

III. Descartes is an enemy of rhetoric.
   A. He errs in faulting rhetoric on these grounds.
      1. It is beneath the level of philosophical speculation.
      2. It places undue stress on pathos.
      3. It can only communicate what is already known.
   B. Rhetoric, contrary to what Descartes believes, is rooted in a probability-based reality.
      1. By using topical philosophy, it has the power to create knowledge.
      2. Rhetorical invention precedes demonstration; and rhetorical discovery precedes truth.
      3. Rhetoric creates data and hypotheses.
      4. Only through rhetoric can we communicate our ideas and impressions to others.

The immediate failure of Vico to attract widespread support for his creative attempt to synthesize classical and modern precepts is surprising. René Wellek has argued that Vico's supposed impact on England and Scotland in the eighteenth century is, at best, marginal.[58] Yet so pervasive was his influence on the social sciences during the nineteenth and twentieth centuries that Sir Isaiah Berlin— President of Oriel College at Oxford—calls him "one of the boldest innovators in the his-

tory of human thought." Berlin further adds that Vico,

virtually invented the idea of culture; his theory of mathematics has to wait until our own century to be recognized as revolutionary; he anticipated the esthetics of both romantics and historicists, and almost transformed the subject; he virtually invented comparative anthropology and philology and inaugurated the new approach to history and the social sciences that this entailed; his notions of language, myth, law, symbolism, and the relationship of social to cultural evolution, embodied insights of genius; he first drew that celebrated distinction between the natural sciences and human studies that has remained a crucial issue ever since.[59]

When it is remembered that Vico's social science philosophy was developed during his long tenure as a Professor of Rhetoric at the University of Naples, his status as a pioneering communication theorist is remarkable. To him we are indebted for his reaffirmation of the role of probability in rhetoric and for his brilliant attempt to place rhetoric squarely in the tradition of the emerging field of social and behavioral science.

It is difficult to overestimate the impact that Bacon, Descartes, Locke, and Vico had on the development of rhetorical thought. Approaching their study of the nature of man from similar starting points, they did not always reach the same conclusions. This was particularly true of Descartes who alone among the four innovators tended to embrace a form of absolutism patterned on the model of mathematics. Yet Descartes was an influential figure in the history of British and continental rhetorical theory because he created a rhetorical situation which demanded Vico's response upholding the value of probability and the integrity of the social sciences. Taken as a whole the imaginative writings of these epistemologists served as a model and inspiration for later authors representing the psychological-philosophical school of rhetoric.

Eighteenth-Century Epistemologists

At the time of Vico's death in 1744, the philosophy of rationalism, which had received its major impetus from the writings of Descartes and Locke, began to take hold among many of the leading literati in Britain and on the continent. In varying degrees the works of David Hume, David Hartley, Lord Kames, Adam Smith, Joseph Priestley, Samuel Johnson, Edward Gibbon, Francois Voltaire, Jean Jacques Rousseau, and Thomas Paine reflect this emphasis. As rationalism unfolded in the eighteenth century there were three clearly delineated features. First, there was a heightened consciousness for the need of logic in the study of man and his institutions. Secondly, there was an absolute belief in the attainability of reliable knowledge. Thirdly, there was a faith in the capacity of man to make society better. Reason, in sum, was no longer the property of philosophers but a weapon for social improvement.[60]

The telltale signs of rationalistic thought were highly visible. Despite the enormous appeal of traditional Christianity promulgated by John Wesley, religion, for instance, contracted sharply in the eighteenth century. Prior to 1660, the world was viewed as a place of sin, peopled with men who were wicked. God and the devil haunted man. But from 1660 onward religion was less influential. The messages of Bishop Tillotson reflected changing attitudes induced by rationalism. To him, religion was a matter of right behavior; and since there was nothing evil in riches, places, or profits, the world was a happy spot in which to live.[61] As the ideas of rationalism began to secularize society, many prominent thinkers embraced a highly generalized deism. Some felt that they no longer had a need to look to God; others made a polite nod to the unknown. It was against this background of declining interest in orthodox religion in the latter part of the century that Hugh Blair delivered his popular sermons at St. Giles Church in Edinburgh.[62] The fact that Blair gained such prominence as a Protestant divine was not due to his eloquence or to his grasp of theology, but to his talent to construct relevant and inoffensive moral discourses that kept alive the latent religious sentiment of his audience.[63]

Another sign of the steadily increasing impact of rationalism was its influence in governmental and social affairs. In the 1690s Locke and Newton advised the government on currency affairs. Of still greater significance was the fact that a realistic attitude toward experimentalism developed. Statistics were used in decision-making, and a rational approach to social and economic matters began to be introduced.

A third sign could be observed in the continued advance of the scientific revolution which had been initiated in the seventeenth century. Even though there was an active decline in the number of scientists by 1730, science nevertheless continued to move forward. By the 1740s and 1750s scientific societies and lectures prepared for large popular audiences became the order of the day. These public discourses were designed for adults who wished to explore the physical world through scientific methods. The undiminished thirst for knowledge produced an age of circulating libraries, encyclopedias, and dictionaries.[64] In addition, it brought on an era in which young people alarmed their elders by wanting to read radical writers like Thomas Paine.[65] It was the age of Josiah Wedgwood's scientific approach to pottery-making—an enterprise whose products stand for quality to this very day.

To what extent did the rhetoricians make use of the basic tenets of rationalism? How did they view the classical tradition? What were the immediate and long range influences of this modern epistemology on the rhetoric of Western thought? The answers to these questions should provide an insight into what might be called the eighteenth-century British version of the psychological-philosophical theory of discourse.

One of the distinguishing characteristics of the rationalists, as noted earlier, was a compelling desire to study human nature. Their probings convinced them of man's *unique* power to engage in abstract thought and to communicate on the level of symbolism. To understand the mind of man, they came to believe, was to recognize the nature and function of discourse. Consequently, writers of diverse orientation developed a considerable interest in rhetoric. The works of David Hume and David Hartley, in particular, demonstrate how a philosopher and a physician could be rhetoricians.

Before proceeding to an analysis of the theories of the British epistemologists rhetoricians, we should observe briefly their method and sources. With a goal to construct a rhetoric consistent with the principles of man's nature, they brought to their task a knowledge of and appreciation for the elements of classicism that had a permanent relevance, and precepts of modernism that possess contemporary scientific and social value. They were, in essence, synthesizers who applied scholarly criteria in evaluating the worth of all information handed down to them. In doing so, they strove hard to free themselves from the four fallacies of sensory experience and educational training outlined by Bacon.

The principal British epistemologists concerned with rhetoric were David Hume, David Hartley, Lord Kames, Joseph Priestley, George Campbell, and Richard Whately. Although we will discuss each of these representative authors, far greater attention will be given to Campbell and Whately because of the substantial influence they exercised. Thus, a later chapter will be devoted to their theories and contributions.

David Hume

If John Locke was the pillar of rational thought, David Hume, a close disciple, was the leading world philosopher and interpreter of humanism to write in English.[66] In any analysis of the writings of Hume it is important to remember that he, like his associates Blair and Campbell, was a native of Scotland—a small country which experienced "unrivaled literary brilliance" during the period from 1739 to 1783.[67] Among those who initiated the "second golden age" of Scottish letters were Hume and Thomas Reid in philosophy, William Robertson in history, Adam Smith in political economy, Robert Burns in poetry, and Sir Joshua Reynolds in art. The hub of Scottish literary activity was the capital city of Edinburgh. Described by contemporary observers as "a hotbed of genius" and the "Athens of the North,"[68] Edinburgh was a cultural center which could take just pride in its celebrated educational institution, the University of Edinburgh. To city and college came students from England, America, and the continent. Thus Blair was able to write to Hume on July 1, 1764: "Our education here is at present in high reputation. The English are crowding down upon us every season."[69]

To Hume must go the major credit for setting the literary revolution in motion. In 1739 he wrote his greatest work, *A Treatise on Human Nature*. Within a few years he published *An Enquiry Concerning Human Understanding* and *An Enquiry Concerning the Principles of Morals*. In these psychological-philosophical works, Hume showed a remarkable capacity to synthesize classical and modern thought, and to generate fresh ideas. Just as Vico had combined a devotion to Plato and Tacitus with an enthusiasm for Bacon, Hume traced his intellectual heritage to Cicero and Locke. Early in his career Hume turned to the writings of Cicero for both instruction and entertainment.[70] Nursing this interest throughout his life, he freely included quotations from and footnotes to Cicero's moral essays, rhetorical works, and orations. By 1742 he had become so familiar with Cicero's speeches that he wrote a critique of them in a letter to Henry Home (Lord Kames).[71] In his *Enquiry Concerning the Principles of Morals* published a few years later, he used a lengthy excerpt from *De Oratore* to illustrate his theory of virtue; and he patterned his *Dialogues* so closely after the model of *De Natura Deorum* that he all but lost his originality.[72] It is not surprising, therefore, that he could at the middle of the century take comfort in affirming that "the fame of Cicero flourishes at present; but that of Aristotle is utterly decayed."[73]

What makes Hume a central figure in the history of British rhetorical thought, however, was not his admiration for Cicero but his strong pull toward Locke's philosophy of ideas. He was intrigued by Locke's tendency to compartmentalize the faculties, his theory of association, and his belief in the primacy of the emotions. The teachings of Locke and the example of Issac Newton, who achieved far-reaching success in applying the experimental method to natural science, spurred Hume to become "the first to put the whole science of man upon an empirical footing, and to appeal to experience exclusively and systematically in reaching his results."[74] The researches that ensued enabled him to conclude that the mind of man moves from one idea to another through the three qualities of "resemblance, contiguity in time or place, and cause to effect."[75] In his discussion of cause and effect, Hume was original and influential. The mind which he held to be a bundle of sense perceptions united by association, may be subdivided into two faculties, impressions and ideas—the former constituting the cause and the latter the effect. From this premise Hume derived the definition of belief as "a lively idea related to or associated with a present impression."[76]

Since Hume held that human motivation stems from man's emotional nature, he, as Locke had done earlier, argued that appeals to the passions of pleasure and pain are necessary to persuade the will to act. But he went beyond Locke when he claimed that "reason is and ought only to be the slave of the passions, and can never pretend to any other office than to serve and obey them."[77] Because of Hume's strong belief that impressions have greater force than ideas and that the experimental method is vastly superior to deduction, he joined Descartes and Locke in excluding the syllogism as an effective tool in exploring human nature.

In still another area Hume contributed vitally to the evolution of rhetorical thought. Whereas Aristotle had relegated nonartistic proof (oaths, witnesses, documents, etc.) to a subordinate position, Hume, who doubtless was influenced by his role as historian as well as philosopher and psychologist, elevated evidence—especially testimony—to a high plane. What he had to say about testimony as a form of rhetorical proof grounded in experience is clearly delineated in his controversial discussion of miracles. The following passages on this theme are included here not only for the purpose of revealing Hume's theory of testimony but because they also triggered a strong response from two later rhetoricians, George Campbell and Richard Whately. Moreover, we need only look around us to see that the question of what constitutes religious evidence is still being debated among certain Christian groups in the 1970s.

A miracle is a violation of the laws of nature; and as a firm and unalterable experience has established these laws, the proof against a miracle, from the very nature of the fact, is as entire as any argument from experience can possibly be imagined. Why is it more than probable that all men must die, that lead cannot of itself remain suspended in the air, that fire consumes wood and is extinguished by water, unless it be that these events are found agreeable to the laws of nature, and there is required a violation of these laws, or in other words a miracle, to prevent them? Nothing is esteemed a miracle if it ever happen in the common course of nature. It is no miracle that a man, seemingly in good health, should die on a sudden, because such a kind of death, though more unusual than any other, has yet been frequently observed to happen. But it is a miracle that a dead man should come to life, because that has never been observed in any age or country. There must, therefore, be a uniform experience against every miraculous event, otherwise the event would not merit that appelation. And as a uniform experience amounts to a proof, there is here a direct and full *proof,* from the nature of the fact, against the existence of any miracle; nor can such a proof be destroyed or the miracle rendered credible but by an opposite proof which is superior.

The plain consequence is . . . that no testimony is sufficient to establish a miracle unless the testimony be of such a kind that its falsehood would be more miraculous than the fact which it endeavors to establish. And even in that case there is a mutual destruction of arguments, and the superior only gives us an assurance suitable to that degree of force which remains after deducting the inferior. When anyone tells me that he saw a dead man restored to life, I immediately consider with myself whether it be more probable that this person should either deceive or be deceived, or that the fact which he relates should really have happened. I weigh the one miracle against the other, and according to the superiority which I discover I pronounce my decision, and always reject the greater miracle. If the falsehood of his testimony would be more miraculous than the

event which he relates, then, and not till then, can he pretend to command my belief or opinion. . . .

For first, there is not to be found in all history any miracle attested by a sufficient number of men of such unquestioned good sense, education, and learning as to secure us against all delusion in themselves, of such undoubted integrity as to place them beyond all suspicion or any design to deceive others, of such credit and reputation in the eyes of mankind as to have a great deal to lose in case of their being detected in any falsehood, and at the same time attesting facts performed in such a public manner and in so celebrated a part of the world as to render the detection unavoidable; all which circumstances are requisite to give us full assurance in the testimony of men.

Secondly, we may observe in human nature a principle which, if strictly examined, will be found to diminish extremely the assurance which we might, from human testimony, have in any kind of prodigy. The maxim by which we commonly conduct ourselves in our reasonings is that the objects of which we have no experience resemble those of which we have; that we have found to be most usual is always most probable; and that where there is an opposition of arguments, we ought to give the preference to such as are founded on the greatest number of past observations. But though, in proceeding by this rule, we readily reject any fact which is unusual and incredible in an ordinary degree, yet in advancing further, the mind observes not always the same rule, but when anything is affirmed utterly absurd and miraculous, it rather the more readily admits of such a fact upon account of that very circumstance which ought to destroy all its authority. The passion of *surprise* and *wonder,* arising from miracles, being an agreeable emotion, gives a sensible tendency toward the belief of those events from which it is derived. And this goes so far that eventually those who cannot enjoy this pleasure immediately, nor can believe those miraculous events of which they are informed, yet love to partake of the satisfaction at second hand or by rebound, and place a pride and delight in exciting the admiration of others. . . .

The many instances of forged miracles and prophecies and supernatural events which, in all ages, have either been detected by contrary evidence or which detect themselves by their absurdity, prove sufficiently the strong propensity of mankind to the extraordinary and the marvelous, and ought reasonably to beget a suspicion against all relations of this kind. This is our natural way of thinking, even with regard to the most common and most credible events. For instance, there is no kind of report which arises so easily and spreads so quickly, especially in country places and provincial towns, as those concerning marriages, insomuch that two young persons of equal condition never see each other twice, but the whole neighborhood immediately joins them together. The pleasure of telling a piece of news so interesting, of propagating it, and of being the first reporters of it spreads the intelligence. And this is so well known that no man of sense gives attention to these reports till he find them confirmed by some greater evidence. Do not the same passions, and others still stronger, incline the generality of mankind to believe and report, with the greatest vehemence and assurance, all religious miracles?

Thirdly, it forms a strong presumption against all supernatural and miraculous relations that they are observed chiefly to abound among ignorant and barbarous nations; or if a civilized people has ever given admission to any of them that people will be found to have received them from ignorant and barbarous ancestors, who transmitted them with that inviolable sanction and authority which always attend received opinions. When we peruse the first histories of all nations, we are apt to imagining ourselves transported into some new world, where the whole frame of nature is disjointed and every element performs its operations in a different manner from what it does at present. Battles, revolutions, pestilence, famine, and death are never the effect of those natural causes which we experience. Prodigies, omens, oracles, judgments quite obscure the few natural events that are intermingled with them. But as the former grow thinner every page, in proportion as we advance nearer the enlightened ages, we soon learn that there is nothing mysterious or supernatural in the case, but that all proceeds from the usual propensity of mankind toward the marvelous, and that, though this inclination may at intervals receive a check from sense and learning, it can never be thoroughly extirpated from human nature.

It is strange, a judicious reader is apt to say upon the perusal of these wonderful historians, *that such prodigious events never happen in our days.* But it is nothing strange, I hope, that men should lie in all ages. You must surely have seen instances enough of that frailty. You have yourself heard many such marvelous relations started, which being treated with scorn by all the wise and judicious, have at last been abandoned even by the vulgar. Be assured that those renowned lies which have spread and flourished to such a monstrous height arose from like beginnings, but being sown in a more proper soil shot up at last into prodigies almost equal to those which we relate. . . .

I may add as a fourth reason which diminishes the authority of prodigies, that there is no testimony for any, even those which have not been expressly detected, that is not opposed by an infinite number of witnesses, so that not only the miracle destroys the credit of testimony, but the testimony destroys itself. . . .

Upon the whole, then, it appears that no testimony for any kind of miracle has ever amounted to a probability, much less to a proof; and that, even supposing it amounted to a proof, it would be opposed by another proof derived from the very nature of the fact which it would endeavor to establish. It is experience only which gives authority to human testimony, and it is the same experience which assures us of the laws of nature. When, therefore, these two kinds of experience are contrary, we have nothing to do but subtract the one from the other and embrace an opinion either on one side or the other with that assurance which arises from the remainder. But according to the principle here explained, this subtraction, with regard to all popular religions, amounts to an entire annihilation; and therefore we may establish it as a maxim that no human testimony can have such force as to prove a miracle, and make it a just foundation for any such system of religion. . . .

I am the better pleased with the method of reasoning here delivered, as I think it may serve to confound those dangerous friends or disguised enemies to the *Christian religion* who have undertaken to defend it by the principles of human reason. Our most holy religion is founded on *faith,* not on reason, and it is a sure method of exposing it to put it to such a trial as it is by no means fitted to endure. To make this more evident, let us examine those miracles related in Scripture, and not to lose ourselves in too wide a field, let us confine ourselves to such as we find in the *Pentateuch,* which we shall examine according to the principles of these pretended Christians, not as the word of testimony of God himself, but as the production of a mere human writer and historian. Here then we are first to consider a book presented to us by a barbarous and ignorant people, written in an age when they were still more barbarous, and in all probability long after the facts which it relates, corroborated by no concurring testimony, and resembling those fabulous accounts which every nation gives of its origin. Upon reading this book we find it full of prodigies and miracles. It gives an account of a state of the world and of human nature entirely different from the present, of our fall from that state, of the age of man extended to near a thousand years, of the destruction of the world by a deluge, of the arbitrary choice of one people as the favorites of heaven, and that people the countrymen of the author, of their deliverance from bondage by prodigies the most astonishing imaginable. I desire any-

one to lay his hand upon his heart and after a serious consideration declare whether he thinks that the falsehood of such a book, supported by such a testimony, would be more extraordinary and miraculous than all the miracles it relates, which is, however, necessary to make it to be received, according to the measures of probability above established.

What we have said of miracles may be applied, without any variation, to prophecies, and indeed all prophecies are real miracles and as such only can be admitted as proofs of any revelation. If it did not exceed the capacity of human nature to foretell future events, it would be absurd to employ any prophecy as an argument for divine mission or authority from heaven. So that, upon the whole, we may conclude that the *Christian religion* not only was at first attended with miracles, but even at this day cannot be believed by any reasonable person without one. Mere reason is insufficient to convince us of its veracity. And whoever is moved by *faith* to assent to it is conscious of a continued miracle in his own person, which subverts all the principles of his understanding and gives him a determination to believe what is most contrary to custom and experience.

Because of the length of the preceding excerpt on miracles, and because of its significance in our later treatment of George Campbell's theories of reasoning and evidence, we offer the following brief of Hume's position:

I. *Miracles violate the law of nature*
   A. Only those events take place that are consistent with nature.
      1. Since man is mortal, he is predestined to die.
      2. A heavy object such as lead is incapable of being suspended in air.
      3. Fire has the power to burn wood but not to resist water.
      4. The laws of the universe prevent dead men from being restored to life.

B. The idea of a miracle is contradictory to observable evidence.
II. *We are unable to prove the existence of miracles through testimony.*
   A. No alleged miracle in history has been established by the testimony of a sufficient number of learned men.
   B. Witnesses to presumed miracles tend to be duped by the emotions of "surprise and wonder" and by the propensity to believe in the "marvelous."
   C. Those who say they experienced miracles generally come from "ignorant and barbarous nations;" thus they are unreliable witnesses.
   D. We have no meaningful testimony to show that miracles occur in the present day.
   E. Testimony upholding the existence of a specific miracle is always offset by counter testimony denying it occurred.
III. *Belief in miracles is the result of faith not of reason.*
   A. Since miracles described in the Old Testament were written by men for the uneducated masses long after the supposed events occurred, belief in these supernatural events runs counter to reason.
   B. When a happening such as a miracle is "contrary to custom and experience," faith is needed to produce belief.

Hume's position on miracles and on what constitutes convincing proof, it seems clear, is consistent with the high standards of scholarship he set for himself in his philosophical and historical works. But, as we shall see, it did not satisfy his pupil Campbell.

David Hartley

The conclusions reached by the physician David Hartley in his *Observations on Man, His Frame, His Duty, and His Expectations,* published in 1749—ten years after *The Treatise on Human Nature*— are strikingly similar to those set forth by Hume. Although he makes no reference to Hume's works, Hartley doubtless is indebted to them. Throughout his volume he draws upon general classical rhetorical principles and upon Locke, seeking "to do for human nature what Newton did for the solar system."[78] Thus the doctrine of association, which was the basic element in Hartley's theory of knowledge, is as fundamental to man's intellectual nature as gravitation is to the planets. All ideas, he argued, are derived from sensations caused by vibrations in the nerves of the muscles. As ideas in their elementary form enter the mind they are gradually transformed through the power of association into complex beliefs and attitudes that stimulate human action.

An essential aspect of Hartley's system is the view that all developments in life, including persuasive communication events, "are links in an eternal chain of cause and effects."[79] The subject of pleasure and pain illustrates how causal relationships are a part of one's daily life. From the basic starting point of sensation six other pleasures and pains are generated, each dependent upon those that precede it. The seven classes and the order in which they occur are sensation, imagination, ambition, self-interest, sympathy, theopathy, (i.e. religious emotion), and moral sense.

In formulating his psychological and moral theories, Hartley, unlike Vico and Hume, rarely alluded to specific rhetoricians or their works. Yet his debt to classical rhetorical precepts is unmistakable. When analyzing propositions and the nature of assent, he urged that a plain didactic style should be used to appeal to the understanding, and figurative language to stimulate the passions.[80] More importantly he recognized the role of rhetoric in producing the pleasures and pains of imagination. Convinced that rhetoric like history conforms to reality, he defined invention as "the art of producing new Beauties in Works of Imagination, and new Truths in Matters of Science."[81] To describe how the communicator stirs the imagination, Hartley turned to traditional rhetorical doctrines. He advocated an inventive process characterized by forceful logical, emotional, and ethical appeals. Further he recommended that these available means of persuasion should be properly arranged and expressed in moving language designed to excite the passions. Out of such an approach human conduct is altered.[82]

In still another important respect Hartley found a helpful ally in rhetoric. More than most of his contemporaries, he used classical persuasive strategies to outline his book and to argue his thesis. Employing many of the Aristotelian and Ciceronian elements of logos, he attempted to show, for example, the relevancy and reliability of Christianity. Repeatedly he relied upon cause to effect reasoning, the argument from sign, and indirect testimony. Additionally he incorporated refutation in his discussion in an effort to demonstrate the good consequences of Christian piety. It would appear, then, that Hartley's elaborate system of associational psychology, which was to have a noticeable impact on Campbell and Priestley as well as on nineteenth-century writers, used traditional rhetorical theory and modern epistemological thought as important sources.

Lord Kames

The attempts of Hume and Hartley to produce a philosophy of human nature based upon classical theories and modern science gave a new dimension to psychological and sociological thought, and created a challenge for literary critics to employ a similar method. One of the leading proponents of this approach was Henry Home [Lord Kames] whose efforts contributed to the "Age of Reason" in Scottish literature. That Kames was influenced by experimental methodology is observable in his rigid adherence to the Newtonian theory and to Locke's doctrine of the association of ideas. In his work *Elements of Criticism,* published in 1762, Kames combines the analytical and synthetic methods. He begins with effects and by tracing a series of particular causes, reaches a general concept. From here he descends slowly, explaining consequences by the universal law which he has established.

Kames was especially intrigued with Locke's principle of connections; that is, "per-

ceptions and ideas in a train." There is, he believed, a definite connection of ideas in one's mind. "It is required [in every work of art]," said Kames, "that, like an organic system, its parts be orderly arranged and mutually connected, bearing each of them a relation to the whole."[83] Working from this premise, Kames found fault with many of the ancients. Homer, Pindar, Horace, and Virgil are criticized for not observing the rules of connection, order, and arrangement."[84] He likewise was one of the first writers to fault Aristotle's *Poetics*. He agreed with Aristotle on the unity of action, but thought he put too much emphasis on the unities of time and place. On this point, he said, "we are under no necessity to copy the ancients; and our critics are guilty of mistake, in admitting no greater latitude of place and time than was admitted in Greece and Rome."[85]

Kames was willing to endorse any of the ancient teachings which were based on reason. He found it easy, therefore, to praise Aristotle's doctrine of tragedy because it "depends upon natural operations of the human mind."[86] But Kames was quick to condemn an unwarranted imitation of the classics. In all, Kames' wide ranging scholarship, his openness to new ideas, and his leadership capacity, made him a favorite in Edinburgh society and a literary model to be emulated by such men as Adam Smith, Hugh Blair, and James Boswell.

Joseph Priestley

Like many earlier epistemologists who turned their attention to rhetoric, Joseph Priestley was a man of many interests and accomplishments. He was a Unitarian preacher and theologian, as well as an educator. Most of all he was a renowned scientist who discovered oxygen and invented soda water. His major contribution to the rhetoric of Western thought was his *Course of Lectures on Oratory and Criticism.*[87] Published in 1777, this volume contains many of the benchmarks of belletristic rhetoric. In its basic thrust, however, it more correctly belongs to the epistemological school of thought. At least this was Priestley's intention, agreeing to put his lectures in print only after he had convinced himself that he would be the first author to apply Hartley's principles of association to the field of oratory and criticism. That he fulfilled his promise of relating Hartley's teachings to rhetoric cannot be denied. Even when Priestley is giving the appearance of subscribing to Aristotle's treatment of topics, he is actually superimposing upon them Hartley's doctrine of association. Topics and ideas, he argues, are tied in with experience and recollection which, in turn, are "associated by means of their connection with, and relation to one another."[88]

Hartley is again the source for Priestley's discussion of style and taste. After acknowledging that pleasure derived from a discourse results from a stimulation of the imagination and passions, he rejects the popular interpretation that those "delicate sensations" and "sensible feelings" experienced by the listener or reader are "reflex, or internal senses."[89] Priestley explains his own position as follows:

> According to Dr. Hartley's theory, those sensations consist of nothing more than a congeries or combination of ideas and sensations, separately indistinguishable, but which were formerly associated either with the idea itself that excites them, or with some other idea, or circumstance, attending the introduction of them. It is this latter hypothesis that I adopt, and, by the help of it, I hope to be able to throw some new light on this curious subject.[90]

In a subsequent lecture on imagination and taste, Priestley likewise alludes to Hartley to explain how the pleasures that are received from a "country landscape," a "rural scene," or a "romance" come from the mental principles of association.[91]

The *Lectures on Oratory and Criticism*, it should be pointed out, are more than a practical application of Hartley's psychology. Indeed, the study is so dependent upon other seventeenth and eighteenth-century works such as Locke's *Essay Concerning Human Understanding*, Hume's *Enquiry into the Principles of Morals*, Kames' *Elements of Criticism*, and John Ward's *Systems of Oratory* that Priestley has been called "more an

'index scholar' in rhetoric than an original thinker."[92] It is of interest to note, however, that the two critics who made this assessment also observed that Priestley's "psychological reinterpretation of traditional rhetorical principles in terms of associational psychology" gives him a permanent place in the history of Western rhetorical thought.[93]

What we have seen in the foregoing discussion are major contributions to rhetorical thought made by a group of epistemologists who achieved fame in a wide variety of scholarly areas. Well versed in Psychology, Philosophy, and Science, they drew ideas from their field of special knowledge, and applied them to theories of human communication. In doing so, they profoundly influenced George Campbell and Richard Whately, the writings of whom will constitute our principal focus in the next chapter.

Notes

1. Hugh C. Dick, ed., *Selected Writings of Francis Bacon* (New York: The Modern Library, 1955), X.
2. Karl Wallace has observed that the "central pillars" of the *Advancement of Learning* "are the psychological faculties." *Francis Bacon on the Nature of Man* (Urbana, Ill.: University of Illinois Press, 1967), p. 2.
3. *Selected Writings of Francis Bacon*, p. 230.
4. *Ibid.*, p. 309.
5. Francis Bacon, "Advancement of Learning," in *The Works of Lord Bacon*, 2 vols. (London, Bohn, 1871), I, 48.
6. *Ibid.*, 254.
7. *Ibid.*, 255.
8. Karl R. Wallace, *Francis Bacon on Communication & Rhetoric* (Chapel Hill, N.C., 1943), p. 66.
9. *Ibid.*, p. 71.
10. *Ibid.*, p. 73.
11. *The Works of Lord Bacon*, I, 310.
12. *Ibid.*, pp. 315, 319.
13. *Francis Bacon on Communication & Rhetoric*, p. 78.
14. *Ibid.*, p. 81. Also see pp. 82–83.
15. "Novum organum," in *ibid.*, p. 465.
16. See *ibid.*, pp. 469–487.
17. *Ibid.*, p. 470.
18. *Ibid.*
19. *Ibid.*
20. *Ibid.*, p. 471.
21. *Ibid.*, p. 487.
22. "The Great Instauration," in *ibid.*, pp. 441–42.
23. Dick makes this claim in the introduction of *ibid.*, XVII.

24. Thomas Sprat, *History of the Royal Society,* Jackson I. Cope and Harold W. Jones, eds. (St. Louis: Washington University Press, 1959), p. 35.

25. René Descartes, *A Discourse on Method* (London: J. M. Dent and Sons, 1941), p. 7.

26. *Ibid.,* p. 15.

27. *Ibid.,* p. 7.

28. *Ibid.,* pp. 15–17.

29. *Ibid.,* p. 50.

30. This conclusion appears in the editor's commentary in the introduction of *Discourse on Method,* XI.

31. Wilbur S. Howell, *Logic and Rhetoric in England, 1500–1700* (New York: Russell & Russell, Inc., 1961), pp. 346–49.

32. *Discourse on Method,* XI.

33. Cited in Howell, *Logic and Rhetoric in England,* p. 343.

34. Hugh Davidson, *Audience, Words, and Art: Studies in Seventeenth-Century French Rhetoric* (Columbus, Ohio: The Ohio State University, 1965), p. 82.

35. John Locke, *An Essay Concerning Human Understanding,* 2 vols. (London: D. Browne, et al., 1760), II, 106.

36. *Ibid.,* I, 192.

37. *Ibid.,* p. 367.

38. *Ibid.,* II, 290–99.

39. *Ibid.,* I, 203–210.

40. Leon Festinger, *A Theory of Cognitive Dissonance* (New York: Row, Peterson, 1957).

41. Vico was born in 1670 and died in 1744. In honor of the tercentenary year of his birth, the following comprehensive volume was published: Giorgi Tagliacozzo and Hayden White, eds., *Gambattista Vico: An International Symposium* (Baltimore: The Johns Hopkins Press, 1969).

42. The most famous of these lectures was presented in 1708 under the title *De nostri temporis studiorum ratione.* It was first published in English with the title: "On the Study Methods of our Time." See Elio Granturco, ed., Giambattista Vico, *On the Study Methods of our Time* (Indianapolis: Bobbs Merrill, 1965).

43. Max H. Fisch and Thomas G. Bergen, eds., *The Autobiography of Giambattista Vico* (Utica, N.Y.: Great Seal Books, 1963), p. 120.

44. *Ibid.,* p. 138.

45. Thomas G. Bergin and Max H. Fisch, eds., *The New Science of Giambattista Vico* (Ithaca, N.Y.: Cornell University Press, 1958), pp. 65, 755–76.

46. Grassi has observed: "The thinker who tried, at the end of the humanistic tradition, to overcome the dualism of *pathos and logos* . . . was Vico; and the basis of his effort was a discussion of the preeminence of topical versus critical philosophy." Ernesto Grassi, "Critical Philosophy or Topical Philosophy?" in *Giambattista Vico: An International Symposium,* pp. 41–42.

47. This is a major premise in *On the Study Methods of our Time.* For an instructive criticism, see Grassi's essay.

48. Alfonsina A. Grimaldi, *The Universal Humanity of Giambattista Vico* (New York: S. F. Vanni, 1958), p. 52.

49. *Ibid.*

50. *Ibid.,* p. 53.

51. *Autobiography,* p. 139. In addition to Plato, Tacitus, and Bacon, Vico selected Grotius as one of his four favorite authors. See Enrico De Mas, "Vico's Four Authors," in *Vico: An International Symposium,* pp. 3–14.

52. Grimaldi, p. 3.

53. *The New Science,* XXXIII.

54. *Ibid.,* p. 104.

55. Isaiah Berlin, "One of the Boldest Innovators of the History of Human Thought," *The New York Times Magazine,* November 23, 1969.

56. *The New Science,* pp. 104–105.

57. *Ibid.,* p. 104.

58. René Wellek, "The Supposed Influence of Vico on England and Scotland in the Eighteenth Century," in *Vico: An International Symposium.* pp. 215–23.

59. *The New York Times Magazine,* November 23, 1969.

60. J. H. Plumb, "Reason and Unreason in the Eighteenth Century," Unpublished address delivered at Ohio State University, April 9, 1969.

61. *Ibid.*

62. For an analysis of Blair's preaching techniques, see James L. Golden, "Hugh Blair: Minister of St. Giles," *Quarterly Journal of Speech,* XXXVIII (April, 1952), 155–60.

63. *Ibid.*

64. Samuel Miller, *A Brief Retrospect of the Eighteenth Century,* 2 vols. (New York: T. and J. Swords, 1803), II, 425; and Hugo Arnot, *History of Edinburgh* (Edinburgh: T. Turnbull, 1818), pp. 516, 567.

65. "Reason and Unreason in the Eighteenth Century in England."

66. V. C. Chappell, ed., *The Philosophy of David Hume* (New York: The Modern Library, 1963), VII.

67. James Golden and Douglas Ehninger, "The Extrinsic Sources of Blair's Popularity," *Southern Speech Journal,* XXII (Fall, 1956), 28.

68. Michael Joyce, *Edinburgh: The Golden Age* (London: Longmans, Green, 1951), pp. 1, 6.

69. John Hill Burton, *Life and Correspondence of David Hume* (Edinburgh: W. Tait, 1846), II, 229.

70. J. Y. T. Greig, *David Hume* (New York: Oxford University Press, 1931), p. 59.

71. David Hume to Henry Home, June 13, 1742, in John Burton, pp. 144–45.

72. The quotation was drawn from *De Oratore,* II, LXXXIV, 343–44. Greig criticized Hume for relying too heavily upon Cicero's *De Natura Deorum* when writing his *Dialogues.* Greig, *David Hume,* p. 231.

73. L. A. Selby-Bigge, ed., *Enquiries Concerning the Human Understanding and Concerning the Principles of Morals by David Hume* (Oxford: The Clarendon Press, 1936), p. 7.

74. Campbell, XV. It is important to note that the term "philosophy" in the eighteenth century was used to cover a broad range of disciplines including psychology.

75. David Hume, *A Treatise of Human Nature,* ed. by T. H. Green and T. H. Grose, 2 vols. (New York: Longmans, Green, and Co., 1898), I, 319.

76. *Ibid.,* 396.
77. *Ibid.,* II, 195.
78. Leslie Stephen, *History of English Thought in the Eighteenth Century,* 2 vols. (London: G. P. Putnam's Sons, 1876), II, 66.
79. *Ibid.,* 64.
80. David Hartley, *Observations on Man, His Frame, His Duty, and His Expectations* (1749) (Gainesville, Florida, 1966), p. 357.
81. *Ibid.,* p. 434.
82. *Ibid.,* p. 432.
83. Henry Lord Kames Home, *Elements of Criticism,* ed. by Abraham Mills (New York: Huntington & Savage, 1849), p. 23.
84. *Ibid.,* pp. 23–24.
85. See the discussion of "The Three Unities," in *ibid.,* pp. 429–440. See in particular, p. 432.
86. See chapter on "Three Unities."
87. Vincent M. Bevilacqua and Richard Murphy, eds., *A Course of Lectures on Oratory and Criticism by Joseph Priestley* (Carbondale, Ill.: Southern Illinois University Press, 1965).
88. *Ibid.,* p. 22.
89. *Ibid.,* p. 72.
90. *Ibid.,* pp. 72–73.
91. *Ibid.,* p. 130.
92. *Ibid.,* lii.
93. *Ibid.*

9

The Rhetorics of Campbell and Whately

George Campbell

The rhetorical trend we have chosen to call the epistemological school of thought reached its zenith in the writings of George Campbell, a Scottish Presbyterian minister and educator, and in the works of Richard Whately, Archbishop of the Anglican Church. In the epochal year of 1776, Campbell published his *Philosophy of Rhetoric.* Among the greatest books on communication theory written in the modern era, Campbell's work, more than any preceding volume devoted exclusively to rhetoric, brought together the best knowledge available to eighteenth-century scholars.[1] Few men could roam so freely over classical and contemporary thought, and sift from these ideas the most relevant concepts that would contribute significantly to the development of a theory of discourse rooted in human nature and interdisciplinary in its thrust.

As an admirer of the classics, Campbell reminded his theological students to immerse themselves in such specific works as Quintilian's *Institutio Oratoria,* Cicero's *De Inventione* and *De Oratore,* the *Ad Herennium,* Longinus' *On the Sublime,* and the critical essays of Dionysius. What he liked most of all was the classical emphasis on rules as an art form. In his *Lectures on Pulpit Eloquence,* Campbell taunted his contemporaries for their inability to extend the highly artistic approach to rhetoric developed by the ancients. "As to the rhetorical art itself," he said, "in the particular the moderns appear to me to have made hardly any advance or improvement upon the ancients. I can say, at least, of most of the per-

formances in the way of institute, which I have had an opportunity of reading on the subject, either in French or English, every thing valuable is servilely copied from Aristotle, Cicero, and Quintilian."[2]

Underlying Campbell's philosophy was the idea that rhetoric is a dynamic, developing process. He most earnestly wished, therefore, to incorporate into his inventional theory not only relevant classical precepts but the principal findings of the social and behavioral sciences and select experimental evidence from the natural sciences. In this way, he thought, could be avoided the sterility that results from an undue reliance upon the Greek and Roman rhetoricians.

Book I of the *Philosophy of Rhetoric* contains Campbell's most original contributions to rhetorical thought. Included in this section are basic elements of faculty psychology, the laws of association, sympathy, moral reasoning, and what the Scots called "common sense." Campbell began his inquiry by examining the nature of man. The writings of Bacon, Locke, and Hume, reinforced by his own observations and experience, taught him that the mind is separated into faculties. To Locke's categories of understanding and will, he added imagination and the passions. These were to be viewed not so much as discrete elements but as a hierarchy, ranging from the elementary faculty of the understanding to the more complex faculty of the will. Persuasion, therefore, is the final result of a four step process that starts with instruction, and proceeds through the imagination and passions until it motivates the will. Campbell explains these relationships in the following way:

In order to evince the truth considered by itself, conclusive arguments alone are requisite; but in order to convince me by these arguments, it is moreover requisite that they be understood, that they be attended to, that they be remembered by me; and in order to persuade me by them to any particular action or conduct, it is further requisite, that by interesting me in the subject, they may, as it were, be felt. It is not therefore the understanding alone that is here concerned. If the orator would prove successful, it is necessary that he engage in his service all these different powers of the mind, the imagination, the memory, and the passions. These are not the supplanters of reason, or even rivals in her sway; they are her handmaids, by whose ministry she is enabled to usher truth into the heart, and procure it there a favourable reception.[3]

From the general considerations Campbell moved to a more detailed discussion of the mental faculties and their relationship to rhetorical practice. Appeals to the understanding, he suggested, consist of explanation and proof. The communicator may have as his purpose to clarify an unknown doctrine or a complex idea. The predominant quality of this end of discourse is perspicuity in language. When the listener, however, approaches a rhetorical situation with an attitude of disbelief or doubt concerning a thesis, the speaker is constrained to use argument in such a way that conviction is achieved.

Campbell felt obliged to begin his discussion of imagination with a brief refutation of those who tended to regard this faculty as beneath the level of serious scholarly inquiry. He then defined imagination as "that faculty of mind, whereby it is capable of conceiving and combining things together, which in that combination have neither been perceived by the senses, nor are remembered."[4] It follows, therefore, that such communication forms as fables, parables, allegories, and poetry are addressed to the imagination; and that part of the discourse most suitable to this appeal is narration. For here the speaker or writer may employ vivid and impelling language, imitation, and resemblances to portray lively and beautiful representations of his subject.

The stimulation of the passions grows naturally out of the descriptions directed to the imagination. Through an association of images, Campbell observed, the emotions are stirred. These lively associations hurry the audience along into feelings of "love, pity, grief, terror, aversion or desire."[5] Campbell added that the emotions experienced by the auditor are especially strong when they are seen operating in the speaker.

The best means of influencing the will, which Campbell called the most difficult task facing a communicator, is to combine in an artful manner strong arguments designed to convince the judgment and graphic emotional appeals related to the passions.[6] In holding that conviction operates on the understanding and persuasion on the will and resolution, Campbell supported the notion that a conviction-persuasion duality exists. Such a dichotomy not only was endorsed by Blair but by rhetoricians for generations to come.

The significance of Campbell's belief in the faculties may be seen in his definition of eloquence as "that art or talent by which the discourse is adapted to its end."[7] In this system, the listener, rather than the occasion or speaker, becomes the starting point in the construction of a message.

Campbell's discussion of the forms of proof, long considered the substance of invention, is a comprehensive, yet uneven, analysis revealing his grasp of classical rhetoric, the Bible, and the principal writings of Bacon, Descartes, Locke, and Hume. The fact that Campbell was an orthodox Presbyterian divine, opposing the extremist views of the enthusiasts on the one hand and the scepticism of Hume on the other, is also visible in the development of his inventional theory. This influence is reflected in his treatment of the requirements of a speaker, his positioning of emotional proof, and his partiality for moral reasoning. How Campbell blended these ancient and modern secular and religious forces into a tightly knit, eclectic system of invention is our present concern.

There are no well defined sections in any of his works in which Campbell handles the subject of ethical proof. Yet it is possible to go to his *Philosophy of Rhetoric, Lectures on Systematic Theology,* and occasional sermons to pull out relevant passages that deal with this theme. On April 7, 1752, he delivered a sermon "The Character of a Minister of the Gospel as a Teacher and Pattern." In this address, Campbell asserted that a preacher trebles his effectiveness whenever his teachings correspond to his practice. Using an argument from less to greater, he pointed out that the minister, whose chief end is persuasion, must adhere to Quintilian's good man theory.[8] Twenty-four years later, in his *Philosophy of Rhetoric,* Campbell acknowledged the importance of intelligence, yet placed it on a lower plane than character. "Men generally will think themselves in less danger of being seduced by a man of weak understanding, but of distinguished probity," he said, "than by a man of the best understanding who is of a profligate life."[9] In making this claim, Campbell in no way meant to denigrate the worth of knowledge on the part of the speaker. He admonished all prospective ministers, for example, to steep themselves in the writings of the classical rhetoricians and orators, and to be conversant with modern authors including Rollin, Fenelon, and Hugh Blair.[10]

No summary of Campbell's attitudes toward ethical proof is complete without a reference to the doctrine of sympathy. Cicero, Hume, and Smith taught him to believe that genuine sympathy between the communicator and the listener can only exist when trust is present. It is for this reason that the speaker who demonstrates sincerity and good will has the best chance to create a bond with his audience, and thereby establish the necessary interaction that leads to the influencing of the will.

Campbell was more systematic and original in his treatment of pathetic proof. His conviction that Aristotle was right in assuming the basic rationality of man and in dissecting emotions for the purpose of showing how they may react upon logos was tempered by what he had learned from Locke and Hume about human nature. He accepted Locke's dichotomy of passions—the "pleasant" and the "painful," and his contention that passions are held together by an attraction or association. Pity, for instance, is a group of emotions "comprised of commiseration, benevolence, and love." Campbell further suggested "that pain of every kind generally makes a deeper impression on the imagination than pleasure does, and is retained longer in the memory."[11] Hume's notions are also present. Although his belief in the dominance of impressions over ideas did not cause Campbell to modify his hierarchy of ends progressing from the understanding to the will, it did persuade him to see the causal relationship betwen lively ideas and the imagination and passions.

A peripheral aspect of Campbell's views on pathetic proof was his penetrating discussion of wit and humor. The mind, he said, is agreeably surprised when a speaker presents novel ideas that debase pompous or seemingly grave things, aggrandizes small and frivolous concepts, or places in juxtaposition dissimilar objects or incongruous events. The process of debasing or aggrandizing a notion derives its strength from appeals to the imagination which may incorporate the method of burlesque. Incongruity, on the other hand, gets its thrust from unlikely associations that generate a surprise meaning. We do not, says Campbell, expect a well-dressed man to fall into a kennel. Thus when a rhetor describes such a happening, we are amused by the incongruity inherent in the situation.

Since wit essentially is a result of novelty and surprise, Campbell came down hard on the use of old jokes as a rhetorical technique. "Nothing is more tasteless, and sometimes disgusting," he asserted, "than a joke that has become stale by frequent repetition."[12] His belief that the surprise element is a central aspect of wit led him to conclude that "a witty repartee is infinitely more pleasing than a witty attack." Wit, in short, has as its primary aim to paint and divert. Consequently, it must be clothed in clever language employing figures of speech and thought that titillate the fancy.

Humor, Campbell goes on to observe, is more pathetic than wit, but since it addresses itself to contempt rather than to imagery and resemblances, it is inferior in nature and function. Notwithstanding this reservation, Campbell proceeds to give several practical hints for employing humor in discourse. Here are a few of his suggestions, all of which pertain to the foibles of human character:

1. Describe a person's "caprices, little extravagances, weak anxieties, jealousies, childish fondness, pertness, vanity, and self-conceit."
2. Relate familiar stories in a whimsical manner, sometimes assuming a particular character and relying on mimicry and "peculiarities in voice, gesture, and pronunciation."
3. Describe your own shortcomings and blunders.
4. A serious countenance may prove to be beneficial in order to conceal your art.

In his discussion of wit and humor, Campbell observed that these rhetorical strategies designed to produce laughter may have as their goal either to divert, "or to influence the opinions and purposes of the hearers. . . ." The related art of ridicule seeks more to dissuade than to persuade. "It is," he said, "fitter for refuting error than for supporting truth, for restraining from wrong conduct, than for inciting to the practice of what is right." Moreover, "it is not properly leveled at the false, but at the absurd in tenets."

What Campbell said about wit, humor, and ridicule grew out of his theory of human nature. To see how practical these insights have proved to be, we need only look at the writings and speeches of such well known British figures as Samuel Pepys, James Boswell, George Bernard Shaw, and Winston Churchill.

Throughout his famous *Diary,* written in the seventeenth century, Pepys engaged in self-disclosure, revealing himself as a humorous man who took great pleasure in describing his "caprices," "jealousies," "childish fondness," and "self-conceit." With a frankness matched only by Boswell a century later, Pepys lets the reader in on his combative dialogues and other encounters with his wife, his unpredictable and irreverent behavior in church during the preaching of a sermon, and the spying techniques he used to check up on his subordinates. On one occasion following a highly successful speech in the House of Lords, he fancied himself a reborn Cicero. But in order to protect his sudden fame as an eloquent orator, he contemplated an abrupt retirement from the podium so that he could savor his newly-discovered eminence.

If Campbell perhaps had Pepys in mind when he constructed his theories on wit, humor, and ridicule, he also had ample opportunity to learn of the antics of his fellow Scotsman, James Boswell, who had a unique talent for telling stories about himself and others. When he did so, he often employed mimicry and a whimsical manner as suggested by Campbell. Never was this more evident than in his vivid account of the evening when he and Hugh Blair sat "together in the pit of Drury Lane playhouse. . . ." "In a wild freak of youthful extravagance," said Boswell, "I entertained the audience prodigiously by imitating the lowing of a cow." He then added with some degree of enjoyment: "I was so successful in this boyish frolic that the universal cry of the galleries was, 'Encore the cow! Encore the cow!' In the pride of my heart I attempted imitations of some other animals, but with inferior effect. My reverend friend, anxious for my *fame,* with an air of utmost gravity and earnestness, addressed me thus: 'My dear sir, I would confine myself to the cow.' "

The humor in Boswell's story was enhanced by the presence of incongruity caused by Blair's participation in the event. The "Minister of St. Giles" was by nature both pompous and discreet. Moreover, since his conservative parishioners in Edinburgh did not permit him to attend a theatrical production, he had to escape to London in order to indulge his aesthetic tastes regarding drama.

Shaw and Churchill, like Pepys and Boswell, were also scintillating story tellers who could arouse the fancy of their audiences. But they also had a remarkable capacity for witty repartee designed to throw an opponent off balance. Their brilliant exchanges presented to each other have formed the basis for numerous dinner table conversations centering on the theme of humor.

The uniqueness of Campbell's theory of rhetorical proof may be measured not so much in terms of what he had to say on ethos and pathos as in his remarks on logos. His comments on this phase of invention exemplify the brilliant analytical powers he had sharpened through his reading, writing, and platform presentations. Never was he more prone to depart from the classical teachings and embrace modern psychological and philosophical theory. Notwithstanding the fact that Campbell's fresh approach led Whately to indict him for apparently failing to understand even the most rudimentary elements of logic,[13] he went beyond his contemporaries in synthesizing seventeenth and eighteenth-century scientific thought and applying it to rhetoric.

The heart of Campbell's theory of logical proof is found in his description of evidence. The first type, which he designates intuitive in nature, bears a close resemblance to the method of knowledge delineated by Bacon and Descartes. It consists of *mathematical axioms,* derived from intellection, *consciousness* kept alive by sensory messages, and *common sense* shared in varying degrees by all mankind. Almost instantly the mind can gain an insight into the meaning and worth of a principle or a reputed fact. But despite the high degree of reliability of this intuitive evidence, Campbell, like Descartes and other rationalists, grew impatient with those who accepted it without a probing analysis. Rarely was this more evident than in a fast day sermon on the duty of allegiance, delivered on December 12, 1776. Observe how he taunted the American colonists for their uncritical acceptance of certain axioms:

Indeed the most consistent patrons of the American cause deny that the legislative power of the British senate can justly extend to the colonies in any thing. . . . This appears to them an *axiom* in politics as clear as any in mathematics. And though for a first principle, it has been wonderfully late of being discovered, they are so confident of its self-evidence, that they never attempt to prove it; they rather treat with contempt every person who is so weak as to question it. These gentlemen, however, will excuse me, as I am not certain that I understand them, and am a little nice about first principles, when I ask, what is the precise meaning they affix to the term *consent?* For I am much afraid, that if they had begun with borrowing from the mathematicians, the laudable practice of giving accurate *definitions* of their terms, and always adhering to those definitions, we had never heard of many of their newfangled axioms. . . .[14]

In his *Philosophy of Rhetoric,* Campbell subdivided deductive evidence into scientific proof and moral reasoning. The former is, in effect, a restatement of Cartesian philosophy and, for the most part, resides outside the sphere of rhetoric. It deals with abstract independent truths, relies on a single coherent series, and excludes from its domain any demonstration which contains multiple degrees of certainty or contradictions.[15]

What, then, is the kind of evidence available to the speaker who seeks to convince or persuade? Moral reasoning is Campbell's answer. It stands above possibility and probability but below absolute certainty. In the highly important discussion that follows, Campbell draws heavily upon Bacon, Descartes, Locke, and Hume; but because of his religious orientation, he moves in other directions as well. There are four species of moral evidence: experience, analogy, testimony, and calculation of chances. Experience, Campbell points out, is based upon our own observation and provides a useful method of proceeding inductively from a particular example to a universal premise. Further it enables us to isolate the constituent elements of a fact. When an experience is replicated by experimental research, its persuasive appeal is substantially strengthened.

Analogy, in Campbell's view, is an "indirect experience, founded on some remote similitude."[16] The more distant or ambiguous the relationship between two objects or events, the less rewarding is the comparison. Because of this shortcoming the analogy generally is a weak form of support. To offset this inherent problem, Campbell recommends that numerous analogies be used, but primarily for defensive reasons. Thus while it cannot advance truth, it diminishes the power of an opponent's refutation.

Campbell's discussion of the third species of moral reasoning, testimony, constitutes a landmark in argumentation theory. In asserting that it was "an original principle of our nature,"[17] Campbell lifted testimony from the inartistic plane described by Aristotle to the level of artistic proof. In 1761, this subject became the theme of his first major work, *A Dissertation on Miracles*. Designed as a refutation to an earlier study on miracles by Hume, Campbell's *Dissertation* set out to prove the weakness of Hume's claim that "no testimony of a miracle could ever amount to a probability much less a proof."[18] The task, said Campbell, was not an easy one. The difficulty arose from the fact that Hume was more than a "subtle" and "powerful adversary"; he was also an instructor and friend. If he succeeded in answering his opponent, Campbell observed, it would be not merely because truth was on his side but because he had learned to use the very principles and methods taught to him by Hume. With this rationale Campbell stated the proposition that "miracles are capable of proof from testimony." He then attempted to demonstrate that nothing in human nature, the history of mankind, or common sense has refuted the Biblical account of the miracles. Moreover, he added, testimony has a special affinity with experience because it derives from the observations of others. What makes the Christian miracles believable is that they were corroborated by more than one witness. Such a combination of experiences, when unsuccessfully challenged by contrary evidence, produces moral certainty.[19]

Ten years later in a sermon delivered before the Synod of Aberdeen on April 9, 1771, Campbell developed similar views on the nature of testimony. After condemning religious enthusiasts for violating the dictates of common sense and the admonitions of their conscience, he drew a parallel between history and the Bible to show that both rely upon testimony for their prime source material.

The history of past ages we derive solely from testimony. Our knowledge of countries which we never saw, and the much greater part of natural history, must proceed to us entirely from the same source. It will be admitted, that on these topics, without such extraneous information, a man of the most enlightened reason, and the most acute discernment, could never investigate aught beyond the sphere of his corporeal senses. If then we receive from a book, pretending to contain a divine revelation, the account of what happened in a period preceding the date of civil history, can it be justly sustained an objection to the veracity of the writer, that he unravels a series of facts, which, by no use or improvement of reason, it would have been in our power to discover? This identical objection would operate equally against all the histories, natural or civil, foreign or domestic, and travels and voyages, that ever were, or ever will be in the world. Nor is this reasoning applicable only to such events as the creation, the fall, and the deluge. Its application to the discoveries revelation brings concerning the designs of Heaven for our recovery, and final happiness, stands precisely on the same footing.[20]

Campbell thus found in testimony the type of proof he needed to affirm his belief in the authenticity of the Bible. But he was quick to point out that every Biblical account must be subjected to a critical analysis before the evidence could be accepted. "The credibility of the facts related," he said, "is no proof of their truth, though it be a foundation for inquiry. The next province of reason is, to examine the evidence by which the veracity of the writer is supported. . . ."[21] Such a conclusion is similar to Descartes' *Discourse on Method*.

These well honed ideas on testimony which Campbell had formulated as part of his theology form the nucleus of his remarks on this subject in the *Philosophy of Rhetoric*. Again he argued that testimony is experiential in nature because it is based upon the observations of others. Similarly, he maintained that it provided the source material for many disciplines including philosophy, history, grammar, languages, jurisprudence, criticism, and revealed religion. But Campbell added a new dimension when he asserted that testimony is stronger for single facts than is experience. The latter has a higher position only when it leads to a generalized conclusion resulting from experimental studies. Even this advantage can be offset in part, Campbell added, with concurrent testimonies that support a particular observation.[22]

We reprint Campbell's full explanation of testimony both because of its historical significance and its present value.

The third tribe is the evidence of testimony, which is either oral or written. This also hath been thought by some, but unjustly, to be solely and originally derived from the same source, experience. The utmost in regard to this, that can be affirmed with truth, is that the evidence of testimony is to be considered as strictly logical, no further than human veracity in general, or the veracity of witnesses of such a character, and in such circumstances in particular, is supported, or perhaps more properly, hath not been refuted, by experience. But that testimony, antecedently to experience, hath a natural influence on belief, is undeniable. In this it resembles memory; for though the defects and misrepresentations of memory are corrected by experience, yet that this faculty hath an innate evidence of its own we know from this, that if we had not previously given an implicit faith in memory, we had never been able to acquire experience. This will appear from the revisal of its nature, as explained above. Nay, it must be owned, that in what regards single facts, testimony is more adequate evidence than any conclusions from experience. The immediate conclusions from experience are general, and run thus: 'This is the ordinary course of nature;'—'Such an event may reasonably be expected, when all the attendant circumstances are similar.' When we descend to particulars, the conclusion necessarily be-

comes weaker, being more indirect. For though all the *known* circumstances be similar, all the *actual* circumstances may not be similar; nor is it possible in any case to be assured, that all the actual circumstances are known to us. Accordingly, experience is the foundation of philosophy; which consists in a collection of general truths, systematically digested. On the contrary, the direct conclusion from testimony is particular, and runs thus: 'This is the fact in the instance specified.' Testimony, therefore, is the foundation of history, which is occupied about individuals. Hence we derive our acquaintance with past ages, as from experience we derive all that we can discover of the future. But the former is dignified with the name of knowledge, whereas the latter is regarded as matter of conjecture only. When experience is applied to the discovery of the truth in a particular incident, we call the evidence presumptive; ample testimony is accounted a positive proof of the fact. Nay the strongest conviction built merely on the former is sometimes overturned by the slightest attack of the latter. Testimony is capable of giving us absolute certainty (Mr. Hume himself being judge) even of the most miraculous fact, or of what is contrary to uniform experience. For, perhaps, in no other instance can experience be applied to individual events with so much certainty, as in what relates to the revolutions of the heavenly bodies. Yet, even this evidence, he admits, may only be counterbalanced, but destroyed by testimony.

But to return. Testimony is a serious intimation from another, of any fact or observation, as being what he remembers to have seen or heard or experienced. To this, when we have no positive reasons of mistrust or doubt, we are, by an original principle of our nature (analogous to that which compels our faith in memory), led to give an unlimited assent. As on memory alone is founded the merely personal experience of the individual, so on testimony in concurrence with memory is founded the much more extensive experience which is not originally our own, but derived from others. By the first, I question not, a man might acquire all the knowledge necessary for mere animal support, in that rudest state of human nature (if ever such a state existed) which was without speech and without society; to the last, in conjunction with the other, we are indebted for every thing which distinguishes the man from the brute, for language, arts, and civilization. It hath been observed, that from experience we learn to confine our belief in human testimony within the proper bounds. Hence we are taught to consider many attendant circumstances, which serve either to corroborate or to invalidate its evidence. The reputation of the attester, his manner of address, the nature of the fact attested, the occasion of giving the testimony, the possible or probable design in giving it, the disposition of the hearers to whom it was given, and several other circumstances, have all considerable influence in fixing the degree of credibility. But of these I shall have occasion to take notice afterwards. It deserves likewise to be attended to on this subject, that in a number of concurrent testimonies (in cases where there could have been no previous concert), there is a probability distinct from that which may be termed the sum of the probabilities resulting from the testimonies of the witnesses, a probability which would remain even though the witnesses were of such a character as to merit no faith at all. This probability arises purely from the concurrence itself. That such a concurrence should spring from chance is as one to infinite; that is, in other words, morally impossible. If therefore concert be excluded, there remains no other cause but the reality of the fact.

Now to this species of evidence, testimony, we are first immediately indebted for all the branches of philology, such as, history, civil, ecclesiastic, and literary; grammar, languages, jurisprudence, and criticism; to which I may add revealed religion, as far as it is to be considered as a subject of historical and critical inquiry, and so discoverable by natural means: and secondly, to the same source we owe, as we hinted above, a great part of that light which is commonly known under the name of experience, but which is, in fact, not founded on our own personal observations, or the notices originally given by our own senses, but on the attested experiences and observations of others. So that as hence we derive entirely our knowledge of the actions and productions of men, especially in other regions and in former ages, hence also we derive, in a much greater measure than is commonly imagined, our acquaintance with Nature and her works.—Logic, rhetoric, ethics, economics, and politics are properly branches of pneumatology, though very closely connected with the philological studies above enumerated.[23]

The inclusion of calculation of chances as the fourth species of moral reasoning gave Campbell pause because of its mixed nature. Sharing some of the characteristics of both demonstrative and moral evidence, it is difficult to categorize with precision. What Campbell hoped to do was to devise some type of method that would assist the communicator in establishing a strong probability when the elements of experience, analogy, and testimony were contradictory and incapable of further experimental validation. With the aid of mathematics, one might predict on the basis of past experiences stored in his memory what the likely statistical probability of an occurrence may be. In this sense it is demonstrative. But one might also use reason for the purpose of balancing all of the possibilities inherent in both sides of a question. The calculation of chances is then made on the grounds of degree of moral certainty. This kind of proof which relates mathematics and logic to experience and chance can be illustrated, concluded Campbell, "in the computations that have been made of the value of annuities, insurances, and several other commercial articles."[24]

A final elaboration of Campbell's theory of moral evidence appears in his discussion of the syllogism. Following in the tradition of Descartes, Locke, and Hume, he rebelled against what he called the scholastic art of syllogizing. In his attack he presented four indictments. First, the syllogism, in proceeding by synthesis and from universals to particulars, runs counter to moral reasoning which proceeds by analysis and from particulars to universals. Secondly, it has not been used by mathematicians as an appropriate means of demonstrating theorems. Thirdly, it is of little utility in applying knowledge stemming from experience. Lastly, since it is confined primarily to the adjustment of language to express previously known concepts, it contributes nothing to our understanding.[25]

Campbell's inventional theory, in sum, partook more of the modern scientific thought than of classical precepts. The investigatory nature of the Greek and Roman inventional system, with its stress on topics and commonplaces as a means of generating new arguments and evidence, was largely discounted. Since every man is endowed with a memory, he may begin construction of a discourse, not by following the road of inquiry in search of new materials, but by recalling the information that had come to him earlier by way of intellection and experience, and by familiarizing himself with the findings already engendered by logic. "As logic therefore forges the arms which eloquence teacheth us to wield," Campbell observed, "we must first have recourse to the former, that being made acquainted with the materials of which her weapons and armour are severally made, we may know their respective strength and temper, and when and how each is to be used."[26] This decision to accept the Baconian distinction between inquiry and transmission gave to invention a managerial rather than an investigatory function.

If Campbell's provocative notions on inventional theory stand as his greatest single contribution to rhetorical thought, his notions on audience analysis and adaptation and on language control and style perhaps have had the longest range influence on rhetorical practice and pedagogy. With considerable foresight he told prospective speakers what they need to know about audiences in general and audiences in particular. We can assume as a starting point in speech preparation, he argued, that all men and women are endowed with an understanding, an imagination, a memory, and

passions. It behooves persuasive speakers, therefore, to use arguments that can be understood, to employ language that is vivacious and lively, to provide an organizational pattern and form of repetition that stimulate the memory, and to utilize appeals that arouse the emotions. Concluding that "passion is the mover to action" and "reasoning the guide," Campbell listed the following seven "circumstances that are chiefly instrumental in operating on the passions":

1. Probability
2. Plausibility
3. Importance
4. Proximity of Time
5. Connexion of Place
6. Relation to the Persons addressed
7. Interest in the Consequences

From these general considerations, he moved to an analysis of the things which a speaker should know about his particular audience. These include such matters as educational level, moral culture, habits, occupation, political leanings, religious affiliation, and locale. The excerpt which follows, while revealing some of Campbell's biases, nevertheless is a useful reminder regarding the speaker's need to know the characteristics of a particular audience. "Now, the difference between one audience and another is very great, not only in intellectual but in moral attainments. That may be clearly intelligible to a House of Commons, which would appear as if spoken in an unknown tongue to a conventicle of enthusiasts. That may kindle fury in the latter, which would create no emotion in the former but laughter and contempt. . . . Liberty and independence will ever be prevalent motives with republicans, pomp and splendour with those attached to monarchy. In mercantile states, such as Carthage among the ancients, or Holland among the moderns, interest will always prove the most cogent argument; in states solely or chiefly composed of soldiers, such as Sparta and ancient Rome, no inducement will be found a counterpoise to glory. Similar differences are also to be made in addressing different classes of men. With men of genius the most successful topic will be fame; with men of industry, riches; with men of fortune, pleasure."[27]

Campbell's discussion of language and style was similar to that expressed by Blair and other belletristic scholars. He supported the element of perspicuity because of its importance in developing appeals to the faculty of understanding. Similarly, figurative language performs an essential role in stimulating the imagination and the passions. The use of language, therefore, has a strong correlation with invention. While it is not our purpose here to present a thorough review of Campbell's theory of style, we feel it is appropriate to highlight his doctrine of usage. We do so because of the tremendous impact which this theory has exerted on subsequent rhetorical literature. As can be seen from an examination of the following passages, Campbell upholds the notion that language should conform to the criteria of "reputable," "national," and "present" use.[28] Later we will observe how the contemporary rhetorician I. A. Richards rejects this approach.

Section I—Reputable Use

In what extent then must the word be understood? It is sometimes called *general use;* yet is it not manifest that the generality of people speak and write very badly? Nay, is not this a truth that will be even generally acknowledged? It will be so; and this very acknowledgment shows that many terms and idioms may be common, which nevertheless, have not the general sanction, no, nor even the suffrage of those that use them. The use here spoken of, implies not only *currency,* but *vogue.* It is properly *reputable custom.*

This leads to a distinction between good use and bad use in language, the former of which will be found to have the approbation of those who have not themselves attained it. The far greater part of mankind, perhaps ninety-nine of a hundred, are, by reason of poverty and other circumstances, deprived of the advantages of education, and condemned to toil for bread, almost incessantly, in some narrow occupation. They have neither the leisure nor the means of attaining any knowledge, except what lies within the contracted circle of their several professions. As the ideas which occupy their minds are few, the portion of the language known to them must be very scanty. It is impossible that our language of words should outstrip our knowledge of things. It may, and often doth, come short of it. Words may be remembered as sounds, but cannot be understood as signs, whilst we remain unacquainted with the things signified.

Hence it will happen, that in the lower walks of life, from the intercourse which ranks occasionally with one another, the people will frequently have occasion to hear words of which they never had occasion to learn the meaning. These they will pick up and remember, produce and misapply. But there is rarely any uniformity in such blunders, or any thing determinate in the senses they give to words which are not within their sphere. Nay, they are not themselves altogether unconscious of this defect. It often ariseth from an admiration of the manner of their superiors, and from an illjudged imitation of their way of speaking, that the greatest errors of the illiterate, in respect of conversation, proceed. And were they sensible how widely different their use and application of such words is, from that of those whom they affect to imitate, they would renounce their own immediately.

But it may be said, and said with truth, that in such subjects as are within their reach, many words and idioms prevail among the populace which, notwithstanding a use pretty uniform and extensive, are considered as corrupt, and like counterfeit money, though common, not valued. This is the case particularly with those terms and phrases which critics have denominated *vulgarisms.* Their use is not reputable. On the contrary, we always associate with it such notions of meanness, as suit those orders of men amongst whom chiefly the use is found. Hence it is that many, who have contracted a habit of employing such idioms, do not approve them; and though, through negligence, they frequently fall into them in conversation, they carefully avoid them in writing, or even in a solemn speech on any important occasion. Their currency, therefore, is without authority and weight. The tattle of children hath a currency, but, however universal their manner of corrupting words may be among themselves, it can never establish what is accounted use in language. Now, what children are to men, that precisely the ignorant are to the knowing.

From the practice of those who are conversant in any art, elegant or mechanical, we always take the sense of the terms and phrases belonging to that art; in like manner, from the practice of those who have had a liberal education, and are therefore presumed to be best acquainted with men and things, we judge of the general use in language. If in this particular there be any deference to the practice of the great and rich, it is not ultimately because they are greater and richer than others, but because, from their greatness and riches, they are imagined to be wiser and more knowing. The source, therefore, of that preference which distinguisheth good use from bad in language, is a natural propension of the human mind to believe that those are the best judges of the proper signs, and of the proper application of them, who understand best the things which they represent.

But who are they that in the public estimation are possessed of this character? This question is of the greatest moment for ascertaining that use which is entitled to the epithets reputable and good. Vaugelas makes them in France to be "the soundest part of the court, and the soundest part of the authors of the age." With us Britons, the first part at least of this description will not answer. In France, which is a pure monarchy, as the dependence of the inferior orders is much greater, their submission to their superiors, and the humble respect which in every instance they show them, seem, in our way of judging, to border even upon adoration. With us, on the contrary, who in our spirit, as well as in the constitution of our government, have more of the republican than of the monarchical, there is no re-

markable partiality in favour of courtiers. At least there being such rarely enhanceth our opinion either of their abilities or of their virtues.

I would not by this be understood to signify, that the primary principle which gives rise to the distinction between good use and bad language, is different in different countries. It is not originally, even in France, a deference to power, but to wisdom. Only it must be remarked, that the tendency of the imagination is to accumulate all great qualities into the same character. Wherever we find one or two of these, we naturally presume the rest. This is particularly true of those qualities, which by their immediate consequences strongly affect the external senses. We are in a manner dazzled by them.—Hence it happens, that it is difficult even for a man of discernment, till he be better instructed by experience, to restrain a veneration for the judgment of a person of uncommon splendour and magnificence; as if one who is more powerful and opulent than his neighbours were of necessity wiser too. Now, this original bias of the mind some political constitutions serve to strengthen, others to correct.

But without resting the matter entirely on the difference in respect of government between France and Britain, the British court is commonly too fluctuating an object. Use in language requires firmer ground to stand upon. No doubt, the conversation of men of rank and eminence, whether the court or not, will have its influence. And in what concerns merely the pronunciation, it is the only rule to which we can refer the matter in every doubtful case; but in what concerns the words themselves, their construction and application, it is of importance to have some certain, steady, and well-known standard to recur to, a standard which every one hath access to canvass and examine.

And this can be no other than authors of reputation. Accordingly, we find that these are, by universal consent, in actual possession of this authority; as to this tribunal, when any doubt arises, the appeal is always made.

I choose to name them authors of reputation, rather than good authors, for two reasons: first, because it is more strictly conformable to the truth of the case. It is solely the esteem of the public, and not their intrinsic merit (though these two go generally together), which raises them to this distinction, and stamps a value on their language. Secondly, this character is more definitive than the other, and therefore more extensively intelligible. Between two or more authors, different readers will differ exceedingly, as to the preference in point of merit, who agree perfectly as to the respective places they hold in the favour of the public. You may find persons of a taste so particular as to prefer Parnell to Milton; but you will hardly find a person that will dispute the superiority of the latter in the article of fame. For this reason, I affirm that Vaugelas' definition labours under an essential defect; inasmuch as it may be difficult to meet with two persons whose judgments entirely coincide in determining who are the sounder part of the court, or of the authors of the age. I need scarcely add, that when I speak of reputation, I mean not only in regard to knowledge, but in regard to the talent of communicating knowledge. I could name writers, who, in respect of the first, have been justly valued by the public, but who, on account of a supposed deficiency in respect of the second, are considered as of no authority in language.

Nor is there the least ground to fear that we should be cramped here within too narrow limits. In the English tongue there is a plentiful supply of noted writings in all the various kinds of composition, in prose and verse, serious and ludicrous, grave and familiar. Agreeably then to this first qualification of the term, we must understand to be comprehended under general use, *whatever modes of speech are authorized as good by the writing of a great number, if not the majority, of celebrated authors.*

Section II—National Use

Another qualification of the term *use* which deserves our attention, is that it must be *national*. This I consider in a twofold view, as it stands opposed both to *provincial* and to *foreign*.

In every province there are peculiarities of dialect which affect not only the pronunciation and the accent, but even the inflection and the combination of words, whereby their idiom is distinguished both from that of the nation and from that of every other province. The narrowness of the circle to which the currency of the words and phrases of such dialects is confined, sufficiently discriminates them from that which is properly styled the language, and which commands a circulation incomparably wider. This is one reason, I imagine, why the term *use,* on this subject, is commonly accompanied with the epithet *general.* In the use of provincial idioms, there is, it must be acknowledged, a pretty considerable concurrence both of the middle and of the lower ranks. But still this use is bounded by the province, county, or district, which gives name to the dialect, and beyond which its peculiarities are sometimes unintelligible, and always ridiculous. But the language, properly so called, is found current, especially in the upper and the middle ranks, over the whole British empire. Thus, though in every province they ridicule the idiom of every other province, they all vail to the English idiom, and scruple not to acknowledge its superiority over their own.

For example, in some parts of Wales (if we may credit Shakespeare), the common people say *goot* for good; in the south of Scotland they said *gude,* and in the north *gueed.* Wherever one of these pronunciations prevails, you will never hear from a native either of the other two; but the word *good* is to be heard everywhere from natives as well as strangers; nor do the people ever dream that there is anything laughable in it, however much they are disposed to laugh at the county accents and idioms which they discern in one another. Nay more, though the people of distant provinces do not understand one another, they mostly all understand one who speaks properly. It is a just and curious observation of Dr. Kenrick, that "the case of languages, or rather speech, being quite contrary to that of science, in the former the ignorant understand the learned better than the learned do the ignorant; in the latter, it is otherwise."

Hence it will perhaps be found true, upon inquiry, notwithstanding its paradoxical appearance, that though it be very uncommon to speak or write pure English, yet, of all the idioms subsisting amongst us, that to which we give the character of purity is the commonest. The faulty idioms do not jar more with true English, than they do with one another; so that, in order to our being satisfied of the truth of the apparent paradox, it is requisite only that we remember that these idioms are diverse one from another, though they come under the common denomination of *impure.* Those who wander from the road may be incomparably more than those who travel in it; and yet, if it be into a thousand different bypaths that they deviate, there may not in any one of these be found so many as those whom you will meet upon the king's highway.

What hath been now said of provincial dialects, may, with very little variation, be applied to professional dialects, or the cant which is sometimes observed to prevail among those of the same profession or way of life. The currency of the latter cannot be so exactly circumscribed as that of the former, whose distinction is purely local; but their use is not on that account either more extensive or more reputable. Let the following serve as instances of this kind. *Advice,* in the commercial idiom, means information or intelligence; *nervous,* in open defiance of analogy, doth in the medical cant, as Johnson expresseth it, denote, having weak nerves; and the word *turtle,* though pre-occupied time immemorial by a species of dove, is, as we learn from the same authority, employed by sailors and gluttons to signify a tortoise.

It was remarked, that national might also be opposed to foreign. I imagine it is too evident to need illustration, that the introduction of extraneous words and idioms, from other languages and foreign nations, cannot be a smaller transgression against the established custom of the English tongue, than the introduction of words and idioms peculiar to some precincts of England, or at least somewhere current within the British pale. The only material difference between them is, that the one is more commonly the error of the learned, the other of the vulgar. But if, in this view, the former is entitled to greater indulgence from the respect paid to learning; in another view, it is entitled to less, as it is much more commonly the result of affectation. Thus two essential qualities of usage, in regard to language, have been settled, that it be both *reputable* and *national.*

Section III—Present Use

But there will naturally arise here another question, "Is not use, even good and national use, in the same country, different in different periods? And if so, to the usage of what period shall we attach ourselves, as the proper rule? If you say *the present,* as it may reasonably be expected that you will, the difficulty is not entirely removed. In what extent of signification must we understand the word *present?* How far may we safely range in quest of authorities? or, at what distance backwards from this moment are authors still to be accounted as possessing a legislative voice in language?" To this I own it is difficult to give an answer with all the precision that might be desired. Yet it is certain, that when we are in search of precedents for any word or idiom, there are certain mounds which we cannot overleap with safety. For instance, the authority of Hooker or of Raleigh, however great their merit and their fame be, will not now be admitted in support of a term or expression not to be found in any good writer of a later date.

In truth, the boundary must not be fixed at the same distance in every subject. Poetry hath ever been allowed a wider range than prose; and it is but just that, by an indulgence of this kind, some compensation should be made for the peculiar restraints she is laid under by the measure. Nor is this only a matter of convenience to the poet; it is also a matter of gratification to the reader. Diversity in the style relieves the ear, and prevents its being tired with the too frequent recurrence of the rhymes, or sameness of the metre. But still there are limits to this diversity. The authority of Milton and of Waller, on this article, remains as yet unquestioned. I should not think it prudent often to introduce words or phrases of which no example could be produced since the days of Spenser and of Shakespeare.

And even in prose, the bounds are not the same for every kind of composition. In matters of science, for instance, whose terms, from the nature of the thing, are not capable of such a currency as those which belong to ordinary subjects, and are within the reach of ordinary readers, there is no necessity of confining an author within a very narrow circle. But in composing pieces which come under this last denomination, as history, romance, travels, moral essays, familiar letters, and the like, it is safest for an author to consider those words and idioms as obsolete, which have been disused by all good authors for a longer period than the age of man extends to. It is not by ancient, but by present use, that our style must be regulated. And that use can never be denominated present, which hath been laid aside time immemorial, or, which amounts to the same thing, falls not within the knowledge or remembrance of any now living.

This remark not only affects terms and phrases, but also the declension, combination, and the construction of words. Is it not then surprising to find, that one of Lowth's penetration should think a single person entitled to revive a form of inflection in a particular word, which had been rejected by all good writers, of every denomination, for more than a hundred and fifty years? But if present use is to be denounced for ancient, it will be necessary to determine at what precise period antiquity is to be regarded as a rule. One inclines to remove the standard to the distance of a century and a half; another may, with as good reason, fix it three

centuries backwards, and another six. And if the language of any of these periods is to be judged by the use of any other, it will be found, no doubt, entirely barbarous. To me it is so evident, either that the present use must be the standard of the present language, or that the language admits no standard whatsoever, that I cannot conceive a clearer or more indisputable principle, from which to bring an argument to support it.

Yet it is certain, that even some of our best critics and grammarians talk occasionally as if they had a notion of some other standard, though they never give us a single hint to direct us where to search for it. Dr. Johnson, for example, in the preface to his very valuable dictionary, acknowledges properly the absolute domination of custom over language, and yet, in the explanation of particular words, expresseth himself sometimes in a manner that is inconsistent with his doctrine. "This word," says he in one place, "though common, and used by the best writers, is perhaps barbarous." I have always understood a barbarism in speech to be a term or expression totally unsupported by the present usage of good writers in the language. A meaning very different is suggested here, but what that meaning is it will not be easy to conjecture. Nor has this celebrated writer given us, on the word *barbarous,* any definition of the term which will throw light on his application of it in the passage quoted. I entirely agree with Doctor Priestley, that it will never be the arbitrary rules of any man, or body of men whatever, that will ascertain the language, there being no other dictator here but use.

It is indeed easier to discover the aim of our critics in their observations on this subject, than the meaning of the terms which they employ. These are often employed without precision; their aim, however, is generally good. It is, as much as possible, to give a check to innovation. But the means which they use for this purpose have sometimes even a contrary tendency. If you will replace what hath been long since expunged from the language, and extirpate what is firmly rooted, undoubtedly you your-self become an innovator. If you desert the present use, and by your example at least, establish it as a maxim, that every critic may revive at pleasure old-fashioned terms, in-flections, and combinations, and make such alterations on words as will bring them nearer to what he supposeth to be the ety-mon, there can be nothing fixed or stable on the subject. Possibly you prefer the usage that prevailed in the reign of Queen Eliza-beth; another may, with as good reason, have a partiality for that which subsisted in the days of Chaucer. And with regard to etymology, about which grammarians make so much useless bustle, if every one hath a privilege of altering words, according to his own opinion of their origin, the opinions of the learned being on this subject so various, nothing but a general chaos can ensue.

On the other hand, it may be said, "Are we to catch at every new-fashioned term and phrase which whim or affectation may in-vent, and folly circulate? Can this ever tend to give either dignity to our style, or per-manency to our language? It cannot, surely. This leads to a further explanation and lim-itation of the term *present use,* to prevent our being misled by a mere name. It is pos-sible, nay, it is common, for men, in avoiding one error, to run into another and a worse. There is a mean in every thing. I have pur-posely avoided the expressions *recent use* and *modern use,* as these seem to stand in direct opposition to what is *ancient.* But I have used the word *present* which, in re-spect of place, is always opposed to *ab-sent,* and in respect of time, to *past* or *future,* that now have no existence. When, there-fore, the word is used of language, its proper contrary is not ancient but *obsolete.* Be-sides, though I have acknowledged lan-guage to be a species of *mode* or *fashion,* as doubtless it is, yet, being much more per-manent than articles of apparel, furniture, and the like, that, in regard to their form, are under the domination of that inconstant power, I have avoided also using the words *fashionable* and *modish,* which but too gen-erally convey the ideas of novelty and levity.

Words, therefore, are by no means to be ac-counted the worse for being old, if they are not obsolete; neither is any word the better for being new. On the contrary, some time is absolutely necessary to constitute that cus-tom or use, on which the establishment of words depends.

If we recur to the standard already as-signed, namely, the writings of a plurality of celebrated authors; there will be no scope for the comprehension of words and idioms which can be denominated novel and up-start. It must be owned that we often meet with such terms and phrases in newspa-pers, periodical pieces, and political pam-phlets. The writers of the times rarely fail to have their performances studded with a competent number of these fantastic orna-ments. A popular orator in the House of Commons hath a sort of patent from the public, during the continuance of his popu-larity, for coining as many as he pleases. And they are no sooner issued, than they ob-trude themselves upon us from every quarter, in all the daily papers, letters, essays, ad-dresses, &c. But this is of no significancy. Such words and phrases are but the insects of a season at the most. The people, always fickle, are just as prompt to drop them, as they were to take them up. And not one of a hundred survives the particular occasion or party-struggle which gave it birth. We may justly apply to them what Johnson says of a great number of the terms of the laborious and mercantile part of the people, "This fu-gitive cant cannot be regarded as any part of the durable materials of a language, and therefore must be suffered to perish, with other things unworthy of preservation."

As use, therefore, implies duration, and as even a few years are not sufficient for as-certaining the characters of authors, I have, for the most part, in the following sheets, taken my prose examples, neither from liv-ing authors, nor those who wrote before the Revolution; not from the first, because an author's fame is not so firmly established in his lifetime; nor from the last, that there may be no suspicion that the style is super-an-nuated. The vulgar translation of the Bible I must indeed except from this restriction. The continuance and universality of its use throughout the British dominions affords an obvious reason for the exception.

Thus I have attempted to explain what that *use* is, which is the sole mistress of language, and to ascertain the precise import and extent of these her essential attributes, *reputable, national,* and *present,* and to give the directions proper to be observed in searching for the laws of this empress. In truth, grammar and criticism are but her minister; and though, like other ministers, they would sometimes impose the dictates of their own humor upon the people, as the commands of their sovereign, they are not so often successful in such attempts as to encourage the frequent repetition of them.

Campbell, it is clear, stood at the transitional period in the evolution of rhetorical thought. The full force of the classical tradition and modern science made a deep imprint upon his mind. In the general area of rules and in his lengthy treatment of language control and style, he followed closely the ancients. But it was the modernists who directed his attention to the study of the nature of man. Out of this interest came his historic discussion of the ends of discourse, the nature of proof, and the meaning of rhetorical invention.

Richard Whately

Although George Campbell's *Philosophy of Rhetoric* is often viewed as the benchmark of the psychological-philosophical trend in British rhetorical thought, it was Richard Whately who carried this approach "to its logical completion."[29] First published in 1828—fifty-two years after the appearance of Campbell's work, Whately's *Elements of Rhetoric* is significant both as an historical document and as a moulder of contemporary argumentation theory.

As in the case of the twentieth-century authors Stephen Toulmin and Chaim Perelman, Whately limited the scope of rhetoric to a study of argumentation. "I propose in the present work," he said in the introduction to *Ele-*

ments, "to treat of 'Argumentative Composition,' *generally* and *exclusively.* . . ."[30] Later in his discussion of the parameters of rhetoric, he observed that "the only province that Rhetoric can claim entirely and exclusively is 'the art of inventing and arranging arguments. . . .' "[31] In his analysis of invention, however, Whately subscribed to Campbell's notion that rhetoric is less concerned with investigation and discovery than with "management."[32] It is the function of logic and inquiry to provide the substance of truth out of which reasoning is formed and conveyed to others by means of the rhetorical process.[33] "The orator," in short, "approaches the process of rhetorical invention not as an investigator but as a communicator" who is "already armed with a general proposition he will advance and with a knowledge of the substantive resources, factual and inferred, by which that proposition may be established."[34]

If argumentation is the central focus of Whately's rhetorical system, what, we might ask, did he say on this subject that was distinctive? To answer this question let us turn first to his categorization of two classes of argument—*a priori* and sign. An *a priori* argument, according to Whately, is reasoning from cause to effect which he describes as "an accounting for." To be effective this type of argument should contain a sufficiently strong cause to establish plausibility.[35] In modern parlance, to establish an *a priori* case is to present a case which will stand unless challenged.

More important from historical point of view is Whately's second classification—the argument from sign. Whereas an *a priori* argument proceeds from a cause to an effect, an argument from sign moves in the direction of an "effect to a condition." Of significance here is Whately's inclusion of testimony as "a kind of sign." In his discussion of testimony, he distinguishes between "matters of fact and opinion," and emphasizes the impact that character has upon the persuasibility of witnesses.[36]

Three specific types of testimony highlighted by Whately deserve special mention. First is that called "undesigned." This incidental and unplanned testimony gains its strength and uniqueness from the fact that it has the appearance of genuineness and disarming simplicity. Second is that labeled "negative testimony." If an advocate is challenged to deal with a particular question or charge that is widely known by the general public, his failure to contradict the claim constitutes negative testimony. For it is assumed that the uncontradicted statement has validity. The third testimonial form to be singled out here is termed "concurrent." When several witnesses who have had no contact with each other affirm a similar conclusion, the independent nature of their claims has greater force.

Whately advises his readers that a given kind of testimony when presented is less effective than the use of a combination of several types. Thus the advocate who can offer varied testimony including undesigned, negative, and concurrent, and who can demonstrate that the witnesses he cites have a strong character and are large and representative in number, significantly enhances the strength of his claims. It follows, therefore, that a "progressive approach" is the ultimate aim of every advocate. On this point, Whately observes: "The combined force of the series of Arguments results from the *order* in which they are considered, and from their *progressive* tendency to establish a certain conclusion." He then proceeds to show how progressive arguments may be used to establish the law of inertia, the "being and attributes of God," and tolerance.[37] Observe how Whately utilizes the progressive argumentative pattern to set forth the nature of God.

Again, in arguing for the existence and moral attributes of the Deity from the authority of men's opinions, great use may be made of a like progressive course of Argument, though it has been often overlooked. Some have argued for the being of God from the universal, or at least, general, consent of mankind; and some have appealed to the opinions of the wisest and most cultivated portion, respecting both the existence and the moral excellence of the Deity. It cannot be denied that there is a presumptive force in each of these Arguments; but it may be answered, that it is conceivable, an opinion common to almost all the species, may possibly be an error resulting from a constitutional infirmity of the human intellect; that if we are to acquiesce in the belief of the majority, we shall be led to Polytheism; such being the creed of the greater part:—and that more weight may reasonably be attached to the opinions of the wisest and best-instructed, still, as we know that such men are not exempt from error, we cannot be perfectly safe in adopting the belief they hold, unless we are convinced that they hold it *in consequence* of their being the wisest and best-instructed. . . . Now this is precisely the point which may be established by the above-mentioned progressive Argument. Nations of Atheists, if there are any such, are confessedly among the rudest and most ignorant savages: those who present their God or Gods as malevolent, capricious, or subject to human passions and vices, are invariably to be found (in the present day at least) among those who are brutal and uncivilized; and among the most civilized nations of the ancients, who professed a similar creed, the more enlightened members of society seem either to have rejected altogether, or to have explained away, the popular belief. The Mahometan nations, again, of the present day, who are certainly more advanced in civilization than their Pagan neighbors, maintain the unity and the moral excellence of the Deity; but the nations of Christendom, whose notions of the Divine goodness are more exalted, are undeniably the most civilized part of the world, and possess, generally speaking, the most cultivated and improved intellectual powers. Now if we would ascertain and appeal to, the sentiments of Man as a rational Being, we must surely look to those which not only prevail most among the *most* rational and cultivated, but towards which also a *progressive* tendency is found in men in *proportion* to their degrees of rationality and cultivation. It would be most extravagant to suppose that man's advance towards a more improved and exaulted state of existence should tend to obliterate true and instil false notions. On the contrary, we are authorized to conclude, that those notions, would be the most correct, which men would entertain, whose knowledge, intelligence, and intellectual cultivation should have reached comparatively the highest pitch of perfection; and that those consequently will approach the nearest to the truth, which are entertained, more or less, by various nations, *in proportion* as they have advanced towards this civilized state.[38]

What comes through in the above passage is not only Whately's faith in the power of the progressive approach as an argumentative strategy, but his extreme devotion to Christianity. He could not forget his role as a Christian minister who would achieve the position of Archbishop of the Anglican Church. Such a commitment went far to formulate what might be designated an ecclesiastic rhetoric.[39] The whole fabric of Whately's system of argumentation reflects this influence. In no instance is this more evident than in his famous discussion of presumption and burden of proof. Motivated by his Christian beliefs and stimulated by his study of law, he constructed a theory of presumption that is largely upheld by modern textbooks on argumentation and debate. The heart of this influential theory, we feel, is contained in the following passages drawn from the *Elements of Rhetoric*.[40]

Presumption and Burden of Proof

It is a point of great importance to decide in each case, at the outset, in your own mind, and clearly to point out to the hearer, as occasion may serve, on which side the *Presumption* lies, and to which belongs the *(onus probandi) Burden of Proof*. For though it may often be expedient to bring forward more proofs than can be fairly demanded of you, it is always desirable, when this is the case, that it should be known, and that the strength of the cause should be estimated accordingly.

According to the most correct use of the term a "Presumption" in favour of any supposition, means not (as has been sometimes erroneously imagined) a preponderance of probability in its favour, but, such a *preoccupation of the ground* as implies that it must stand good till some sufficient reason is adduced against it; in short, that the *Burden of proof* lies on the side of him who would dispute it.

Thus, it is a well-known principle of the Law, that every man (including a prisoner brought up for trial) is to be *presumed* innocent till his guilt is established. This does not, of course, mean that we are to *take for granted* he is innocent; for if that were the case, he would be entitled to immediate liberation: nor does it mean that it is antecedently *more likely than not* that he is innocent; or, that the majority of these brought to trial are so. It evidently means only that the "burden of proof" lies with the accusers;—that he is not to be called on to prove his innocence, or to be dealt with as a criminal till he has done so; but that they are to bring their charges against him, which if he can repel, he stands acquitted.

Thus again, there is a "presumption" in favour of the right of any individuals or bodies-corporate to the property of which they are in *actual possession*. This does not mean that they are, or are not, *likely* to be the rightful owners: but merely, that no man is to be disturbed in his possessions till some claim against him shall be established. He is not to be called on to prove his right; but the claimant, to disprove it; on whom consequently the "burden of proof" lies.

Importance of Deciding on Which Side Lies the *Onus Probandi*

A moderate portion of common-sense will enable any one to perceive, and to show, on which side the Presumption lies, when once his attention is called to this question; though, for want of attention, it is often overlooked: and on the determination of this question the whole character of a discussion will often very much depend. A body of troops may be perfectly adequate to the defence of a fortress against any attack that may be made on it; and yet, if, ignorant of the advantage they possess, they sally forth into the open field to encounter the enemy, they may suffer a repulse. At any rate, even if strong enough to act on the offensive, they ought still to keep possession of their fortress. In like manner, if you have the "Presumption" on your side, and can but *refute* all the arguments brought against you, you have, for the present at least, gained a victory: but if you abandon this position, by suffering this Presumption to be forgotten, which is in fact *leaving out one of, perhaps, your strongest arguments,* you may appear to be making a feeble attack, instead of a triumphant defence.

Such an obvious case as one of those just stated, will serve to illustrate this principle. Let any one imagine a perfectly unsupported accusation of some offence to be brought against himself; and then let him imagine himself—instead of replying (as of course he would do) by a simple denial, and a defiance of his accuser to prove the charge,—setting himself to establish a negative,—taking on himself the burden of proving his own innocence, by collecting all the circumstances indicative of it that he can muster: and the result would be, in many cases, that this evidence would fall far short of establishing a certainty, and might even have the effect of raising a suspicion against him, he having in fact kept out of sight the important circumstance, that these probabilities in one scale, though of no great weight perhaps in themselves, are to be weighed against absolutely nothing in the other scale.

The following are a few of the cases in which it is important, though very easy, to point out where the Presumption lies.

Presumption in Favour of Existing Institutions

There is a Presumption in favour of every *existing* institution. Many of these (we will suppose, the majority) may be susceptible of alteration for the better; but still the "Burden of proof" lies with him who proposes an alteration; simply, on the ground that since a change is not a good in itself, he who demands a change should show cause for it. No one is *called on* (though he may find it advisable) to defend an existing institution, till some argument is adduced against it; and that argument ought in fairness to prove, not merely an actual inconvenience, but the possibility of a change for the better.

Presumption of Innocence

Every book again, as well as person, ought to be presumed harmless (and consequently the copyright protected by our courts) till something is proved against it. It is a hardship to require a man to prove, either of his book, or of his private life, that there is no ground for any accusation; or else to be denied the protection of his Country. The Burden of proof, in each case, lies fairly on the accuser. I cannot but consider therefore as utterly unreasonable the decisions (which some years ago excited so much attention) to refuse the interference of the Court of Chancery in cases of piracy, whenever there was even any *doubt* whether the book pirated *might* not contain something of an immoral tendency.

Presumption against a Paradox

There is a "Presumption" against any thing *paradoxical,* i.e. contrary to the prevailing opinion: it may be true; but the Burden of proof lies with him who maintains it; since men are not to be expected to abandon the prevailing belief till some reason is shown.

Hence it is, probably, that many are accustomed to apply "Paradox" as if it were a term of reproach, and implied absurdity or falsity. But correct use is in favor of the etymological sense. If a Paradox is unsupported, it can claim no attention; but if false, it should be censured on *that* ground; but not for being *new.* If true, it is the more important, for being a truth not generally admitted. *"Interdum vulgus rectum videt; est ubi peccat."* Yet one often hears a charge of "paradox and nonsense" brought forward, as if there were some close connexion between the two. And indeed, in one sense this is the case; for to those who are too dull, or too prejudiced, to admit any notion at variance with those they have been used to entertain, *that* may appear nonsense, which to others is sound sense. Thus "Christ crucified" was "to the Jews, a stumbling-block," (paradox) "and to the Greeks, foolishness;" because the one "required a sign" of a different kind from any that appeared; and the others "sought after wisdom" in their schools of philosophy.

Christianity, Presumptions Against and For

Accordingly there was a Presumption against the Gospel in its first announcement. A Jewish peasant claimed to be the promised Deliverer, in whom all the nations of the Earth were to be blessed. The Burden of proof lay with Him. No one could be fairly called on to admit his pretensions till He showed cause for believing in Him. If He "had not done among them the *works* which none other man did, they had not had sin."

Now, the case is reversed. Christianity *exists;* and those who deny the divine origin attributed to it, are bound to show some reasons for assigning to it a human origin: not indeed to prove that it *did* originate in this or that way, without supernatural aid; but to point out some conceivable way in which it *might* have so arisen.

It is indeed highly expedient to bring forward evidences to establish the divine origin of Christianity: but it ought to be more carefully kept in mind than is done by most writers, that all this is an argument "ex abundanti," as the phrase is,—over and above what can fairly be called for, till some hypothesis should be framed, to account for the origin of Christianity by human means. The Burden of proof, *now,* lies plainly on him who rejects the Gospel: which, if it were not established by miracles, demands an explanation of the greater miracle,—its having been established, in defiance of all opposition, by human contrivance.

The Reformation

The Burden of proof, again, lay on the authors of the Reformation: they were bound to show cause for every *change* they advocated; and they admitted the fairness of this requisition, and accepted the challenge. But they were *not* bound to show cause for *retaining* what they left unaltered. The Presumption was, in those points, on their side; and they had only to reply to objections. This important distinction is often lost sight of, by those who look at the "doctrines, &c. of the Church of England as constituted at the Reformation," in the mass, without distinguishing the altered from the unaltered parts. The framers of the Articles kept this in mind in their expression respecting infant-baptism, that it "ought by all means to be *retained.*" They did not introduce the practice, but left it as they found it; considering the burden to lie on those who denied its existence in the primitive church, to show *when* it did arise.

The case of Episcopacy is exactly parallel: but Hooker seems to have overlooked this advantage: he sets himself to *prove* the apostolic origin of the institution, as if his task had been to *introduce* it. Whatever force there may be in arguments so adduced, it is plain they must have far *more* force if the important Presumption be kept in view, that the institution had notoriously existed many ages, and that consequently, even if there had been no direct evidence for its being coeval with Christianity, it might fairly be at least supposed to be so, till some other period should be pointed out at which it had been introduced as an innovation.

Tradition

In the case of any *doctrines* again, professing to be essential parts of the Gospel-revelation, the fair *presumption* is, that we shall find all such distinctly declared in Scripture. And again, in respect of commands or prohibitions as to any point, which our Lord or his Apostles did deliver, there is a presumption that Christians are bound to comply. If any one maintains, on the ground of Tradition, the necessity of some additional article of faith (as for instance that of Purgatory) or the propriety of a departure from the New Testament precepts (as for instance in the denial of the cup to the Laity in the Eucharist) the burden of proof lies with him. We are not called on to prove that there is no tradition to the purpose;—much less, that no tradition can have any weight at all in *any* case. It is for *him* to prove, not merely generally, that there is such a thing as Tradition, and that it is entitled to respect, but that there is a tradition relative to each of the points which he thus maintains; and that such tradition is, in each point, sufficient to establish that point. For want of observing this rule, the most vague and interminable disputes have often been carried on respecting Tradition, generally.

It should be also remarked under this head, that in any one question the Presumption will often be found to lie on different sides, in respect of different parties. E.G. In the question between a member of the Church of England, and a Presbyterian, or member of any other Church, on which side does the Presumption lie? Evidently, to each, in favour of the religious community to which he at present belongs. He is not to separate from the Church of which he is a member, without having some sufficient reason to allege.

A Presumption evidently admits of various degrees of strength, from the very faintest, up to a complete and confident acquiescence.

Deference

The person, Body, or book, in favour of whose decisions there is a certain Presumption, is said to have, so far, "Authority"; in the strict sense of the word. And a recognition of this kind of Authority,—an *habitual* Presumption in favour of such a one's decisions or opinions—is usually called "Deference."

It will often happen that this deference is not recognized by either party. A man will perhaps disavow with scorn all deference for some person,—a son or daughter perhaps, or an humble companion,—whom he treats, in manner, with familiar superiority; and the other party as readily and sincerely renounce all pretension to Authority; and yet there may be that "habitual Presumption" in the mind of the one, in favour of the opinions, suggestion, &c. of the other, which we have called Deference. These parties however are not using the *words* in a different sense, but are unaware of the state of the *fact*. There is a Deference; but *unconscious*.

Transferring the Burden of Proof

It is to be observed, that a Presumption may be *rebutted* by an opposite Presumption, so as to shift the Burden of proof to the other side. E.G. Suppose you had advised the removal of some *existing* restriction: you might be, in the first instance, called on to take the Burden of proof, and allege your reasons for the change, on the ground that there is a Presumption against every Change. But you might fairly reply, "True, but there is another Presumption which rebuts the former; every *Restriction* is in itself an evil; and therefore there is a Presumption in favour of its removal, unless it can be shown necessary for prevention of some greater evil: I am not bound to allege any *specific* inconvenience; if the restriction is *unnecessary, that* is reason enough for its abolition: its defenders therefore are fairly called on to prove its necessity."

Again, in reference to the prevailing opinion, that the *"Nathanael"* of John's Gospel was the same person as the Apostle *"Bartholomew"* mentioned in the others, an intelligent friend once remarked to me that *two* names afford a *prima facie* Presumption of two persons. But the name of *Bar*tholomew, being a "Patronymic," (like Simon Peter's designation *Bar*Jona, and Joseph's surname of *Bar*sabas, mentioned in Acts;—he being probably the same with the Apostle "Joseph Barnabus," &c.,) affords a Counter-presumption that he must have had *another* name, to distinguish him from his own kindred. And thus we are left open to the arguments drawn from the omission, by the other Evangelists, of the name of Nathanael,—evidently a very eminent disciple,—the omission by John of the name of the Apostle Bartholomew,—and the recorded intimacy with the Apostle Philip.

Presumption against Logic

In one of Lord Dudley's (lately published) letters to Bishop Copleston, of the date of 1814, he adduces a presumption against the Science of Logic, that it was sedulously cultivated during the dark periods when the intellectual powers of mankind seemed nearly paralysed,—when no discoveries were made, and when various errors were widespread and deep-rooted: and that when the mental activity of the world revived, and philosophical inquiry flourished, and bore its fruits, Logical studies fell into decay and contempt. To many minds this would appear a decisive argument. The author himself was too acute to see more in it than—what it certainly is—a fair Presumption. And he would probably have owned that it might be met by a counter-presumption.

Counter-Presumption

When any science or pursuit has been unduly and unwisely followed, to the neglect of others, and has even been intruded into their province, we may presume that a *re-action* will be likely to ensue and an equally excessive contempt, or dread, or abhorrence, to succeed. And the same kind of reaction occurs in every department of life. It is thus that the thraldom of gross superstition, and tyrannical priest-craft, have so often led to irreligion. It is thus that "several valuable medicines, which when first introduced, were proclaimed, each as a panacea, infallible in the most opposite disorders, fell, consequently, in many instances, for a time, into total disuse; though afterwards they were established in their just estimation, and employed conformably to their real properties."

So, it might have been said, in the present case, the mistaken and absurd cultivation of Logic during ages of great intellectual darkness, might be expected to produce, in a subsequent age of comparative light, an association in men's minds, of Logic, with the idea of apathetic ignorance, prejudice, and adherence to error; so that the legitimate uses and just value of Logic, supposing it to have any, would be likely to be scornfully overlooked. Our ancestors, it might have been said, having neglected to raise fresh crops of corn, and contented themselves with vainly thrashing over and over again the same straw, and winnowing the same chaff, it might be expected that their descendants would, for a time, regard the very operations of thrashing and winnowing with contempt, and would attempt to grind corn, chaff, and straw, altogether.

Such might have been, at that time, a statement of the counter-presumptions on this point.

Presumption Overthrown

Subsequently, the presumption in question has been completely done away. And it is a curious circumstance that the very person to whom that letter was addressed should have witnessed so great a change in public opinion, brought about (in great measure through *his own* instrumentality) within a small portion of the short interval between the writing of that letter and its publication, that the whole ground of Lord Dudley's argument is cut away. During that interval the Article on Logic in the *Encyclopaedia Metropolitana* (great part of the matter of it having been furnished by Bishop Copleston) was drawn up; and attracted so much attention as to occasion its publication in a separate volume: and this has been repeatedly reprinted both at home and in the United States of America, (where it is used as a textbook in, I believe, every College throughout the Union,) with a continually increasing circulation, which all the various attempts made to decry the study, seem only to augment: while sundry abridgements, and other elementary treatises on the subject, have been appearing with continually increased frequency.

Certainly, Lord Dudley, were he *now* living, would not speak of the "general neglect and contempt" of Logic at present: though so many branches of Science, Philosophy, and Literature, have greatly flourished during the interval.

The popularity indeed, or unpopularity, of any study, does not furnish, alone, a decisive proof as to its value: but it is plain that a presumption—whether strong or weak—which is based on the fact of general neglect and contempt, is destroyed, when these have ceased.

It has been alleged, however, that "the Science of Mind" has not flourished during the last twenty years; and that consequently the present is to be accounted such a dark period as Lord Dudley alludes to.

Supposing the statement to be well-founded, it is nothing to the purpose; since Lord Dudley was speaking, not, of any one science in particular, but of the absence or presence of intellectual cultivation, and of knowledge, generally;—the depressed or flourishing condition of Science, Arts, and Philosophy on the whole.

But for the state of the "science of mind" at any given period, *that* is altogether a matter of opinion. It was probably considered by the Schoolmen to be most flourishing in the ages which we call "dark." And it is not unlikely that the increased attention bestowed, of late years, on Logic, and the diminished popularity of those Metaphysicians who have written against it, may appear to the disciples of these last a proof of the low state (as it is, to Logical students, a sign of the improving state) of "the Science of Mind." That is, regarding the prevalence at present of logical studies as a sign that ours is "a dark age," this supposed darkness, again, furnishes in turn a sign that these studies flourish only in a dark age!

Presumptions for and Against the Learned

Again, there is a presumption, (and a fair one) in respect of each question, in favour of the judgement of the most eminent men in the department it pertains to;—of eminent physicians, *e.g.* in respect to medical questions,—of theologians, in theological, &c. And by this presumption many of the Jews in our Lord's time seem to have been influenced, when they said, "have any of the Rulers, or of the Pharisees believed on Him?"

But there is a counter-presumption, arising from the circumstance that men eminent in any department are likely to regard with jealously any one who professes to bring to light something unknown to themselves; especially if it promise to *supersede,* if established, much of what they have been accustomed to learn, and teach, and practise. And moreover, in respect of the medical profession, there is an obvious danger of a man's being regarded as a dangerous experimentalist who adopts any novelty, and of his thus losing practice even among such as may regard him with admiration as a philosopher. In confirmation of this, it may be sufficient to advert to the cases of Harvey and Jenner. Harvey's discovery of the circulation of the blood is said to have lost him most of his practice, and to have been rejected by every physician in Europe above the age of forty. And Jenner's discovery of vaccination had, in a minor degree, similar results.

There is also this additional counter-presumption against the judgment of the proficients in any department; that they are prone to a bias in favour of everything that gives the most palpable *superiority* to themselves over the uninitiated, (the Idiotae) and affords the greatest scope for the employment and display of their own peculiar acquirements. Thus, *e.g.* if there be two possible interpretations of some Clause in an Act of Parliament, one of which appears obvious to every reader of plain good sense, and the other can be supported only by some ingenious and far-fetched legal subtlety, a practised lawyer will be liable to a bias in favour of the latter, as setting forth the more prominently his own peculiar qualifications. And on this principle in great measure seems founded Bacon's valuable remark; *"harum artium saepe pravus fit usus, ne sit nullus."* Rather than let their knowledge and skill lie idle, they will be tempted to misapply them; like a schoolboy, who, when possessed of a knife, is for trying its edge on everything that comes in his way. On the whole, accordingly, I think that of these two opposite presumptions, the counter-presumption has often as much weight as the other, and sometimes more.

No Necessary Advantage to the Side on Which the Presumption Lies

It might be hastily imagined that there is necessarily an advantage in having the presumption on one's side, and the burden of proof on the adversary's. But it is often much the reverse. *E.G.* "In no other instance perhaps" (says Dr. Hawkins, in his valuable "Essay on Tradition,") "besides that of Religion, do men commit the very illogical mistake, of first convassing all the objections against any particular system whose pretensions to truth they would examine, before they consider the direct arguments in its favor." (p. 82.) But why, it may be asked, *do*

they make such a mistake in *this* case? An answer which I think would apply to a large proportion of such persons, is this: because a man having been brought up in a Christian-Country, has lived perhaps among such as have been accustomed from their infancy to *take for granted* the truth of their religion, and even to regard an *uninquiring* assent as a mark of commendable *faith;* and hence he has probably never even thought of proposing to himself the question,—Why should I receive Christianity as a divine revelation? Christianity being nothing *new* to him, and the *presumption* being in favour of it, while the burden of proof lies on its opponents, he is not stimulated to seek reasons for believing it, till he finds it controverted. And when it *is* controverted,—when an opponent urges— How do you reconcile this, and that, and the other, with the idea of a divine revelation? these objections strike by their *novelty,*— by their being opposed to what is generally received. He is thus excited to inquiry; which he sets about,—naturally enough, but very unwisely,—by seeking for answers to all these objections: and fancies that unless they can all be satisfactorily solved, he ought not to receive the religion. "As if (says the Author already cited) there could not be truth, and truth supported by irrefragable arguments, and yet at the same time obnoxious to objections, numerous, plausible, and by no means easy of solution." "There are objections (said Dr. Johnson) against a *plenum* and objections against a *vacuum;* but one of them must be true." He adds that "sensible men really desirous of discovering the truth, will perceive that reason directs them to examine first the argument in favour of that side of the question, where the first presumption of truth appears. And the presumption is manifestly in favour of that religious creed already adopted by the country. . . . Their very earliest inquiry therefore must be into the direct arguments, for the authority of that book on which their country rests its religion."

But reasonable as such a procedure is, there is, as I have said, a strong temptation, and one which should be carefully guarded against, to adopt the opposite course;—to attend first to the objections which are brought against what is established, and which, for that very reason, rouse the mind from a state of apathy. Accordingly, I have not found that this "very illogical mistake" is by any means peculiar to the case of religion.

When Christianity was first preached, the state of things was reversed. The Presumption was against it, as being a novelty. "Seeing that these things *cannot be spoken against,* ye ought to be *quiet,*" was a sentiment which favoured an indolent acquiescence in the old Pagan worship. The stimulus of novelty was all on the side of those who came to overthrow this, by a new religion. The first inquiry of any one who at all attended to the subject, must have been, not,—What are the objections to Christianity?—but on what grounds do these men call on me to receive them as divine messengers? And the same appears to be the case with those Polynesians among whom our Missionaries are labouring: they begin by inquiring—"Why should we receive this religion?" And those of them accordingly who *have* embraced it, appear to be Christians on a much more rational and deliberate conviction than many among *us,* even of those who, in general maturity of intellect and civilisation, are advanced considerably beyond those Islanders.

I am not depreciating the inestimable advantages of a religious education; but, pointing out the *peculiar* temptations which accompany it. The Jews and Pagans had, in their early prejudices, greater difficulties to surmount than ours; but they were difficulties *of a different kind.*

Thus much may suffice to show the importance of taking this preliminary view of the state of each question to be discussed.

It is difficult to overestimate the importance of Whately's pioneering analysis of presumption and burden of proof. What makes his discussion a significant landmark in the rhetoric of Western thought is the reminder that presumption rests not on the side where a "preponderance of probability" exists, but on that side which consists of a "preoccupation of the ground." (i.e. that side which the majority of a given audience favors at the outset of a speech.) And he also was on target in reminding his students that no meaningful debate on a controversial question can proceed intelligently unless it is first determined where the presumption lies. Finally, Whately contributed vitally to argumentation theory when he pointed out that, in most circumstances, there is a presumption in favor of "existing institutions," "innocence," "tradition," and people who command "deference." Such insights paved the way for modern high school and college debate practices. Since a negative team often begins with an initial presumption in favor of the status quo, the affirmative team has the burden of proof to overthrow the prevailing presumption. To counter this starting point, the affirmative debaters are given the right to begin and end the contest. This type of format supports Whately's contention that there is "no necessary advantage to the side on which the presumption lies."[41]

As we conclude our treatment of the psychological-philosophical approach to rhetoric, two major inferences seem appropriate. First the epistemologists ranging from Bacon to Whately constructed a psychological, audience-centered rhetoric grounded in the nature of man. Secondly, because they brought to their task a knowledge of the scientific method and religion, they found the need to elevate evidence to a position comparable to reasoning. Campbell and Whately, especially, permitted their Christian bias to affect their claims and choice of examples and illustrations. Yet this very commitment compelled them to restore a needed balance between artistic and non-artistic proof.

Notes

1. One of the most important recent publications on Campbell is Lloyd F. Bitzer, ed., *The Philosophy of Rhetoric by George Campbell* (Carbondale, Ill.: Southern Illinois University Press, 1963).

2. George Campbell, *Lectures on Systematic Theology and Pulpit Eloquence* (Boston: Lincoln and Edwards, 1832), p. 99.

3. George Campbell, *The Philosophy of Rhetoric* (Boston: Charles Ewer, 1823), p. 101.

4. *Lectures on Systematic Theology and Pulpit Eloquence,* p. 131.

5. *Ibid.,* p. 132.

6. *Ibid.* Also see *The Philosophy of Rhetoric,* pp. 23–30.

7. *The Philosophy of Rhetoric,* p. 23.

8. George Campbell, "The Character of a Minister of the Gospel as a Teacher and Pattern," A Sermon preached before the Synod of Aberdeen at Aberdeen, April 7, 1752 (Aberdeen, Scotland, 1752).

9. *The Philosophy of Rhetoric,* p. 129.

10. *Lectures on Systematic Theology and Pulpit Eloquence,* pp. 99–100.

11. *The Philosophy of Rhetoric,* pp. 165–168.

12. All quotations on wit and humor are taken from *The Philosophy of Rhetoric,* pp. 30–33; 39–42; 43–48.

13. Douglas Ehninger, ed., *Elements of Rhetoric by Richard Whately* (Carbondale, Ill.: Southern Illinois University Press, 1963), p. 9.

14. George Campbell, "The Nature, Extent, and Importance of the Duty of Allegiance," A Sermon preached at Aberdeen, December 12, 1776, Being the Fast Day Appointed by the King, on account of the Rebellion in America," in George Campbell, *A Dissertation on Miracles* (London, 1824), p. 275.

15. *The Philosophy of Rhetoric,* p. 70.

16. *Ibid.,* p. 80.

17. *Ibid.,* p. 83.

18. *A Dissertation on Miracles,* p. 25.

19. *Ibid.,* p. 134.

20. "The Spirit of the Gospel, a Spirit Neither of Superstition Nor of Enthusiasm," *ibid.,* pp. 152–53.

21. *Ibid.,* p. 154.

22. *The Philosophy of Rhetoric,* pp. 82–84.

23. *Ibid.*

24. *Ibid.,* p. 86.

25. *Ibid.,* pp. 90–99. This discussion resembles closely earlier attacks on the syllogism cited above.

26. *Ibid.,* p. 59.

27. *Ibid.,* pp. 127–128.

28. *Ibid.,* pp. 178–188.

29. *Elements of Rhetoric* by Richard Whately, XXVIII. (Boston and Cambridge: James Munroe and Co., 1855).

30. *Ibid.,* p. 4.

31. *Ibid.-,* p. 40.

32. *Ibid.,* xxviii.

33. *Ibid.,* xxviii–xxix.

34. *Ibid.,* xxix.

35. *Ibid.,* p. 46.

36. *Ibid.,* pp. 60–62.

37. *Ibid.,* p. 82.

38. *Ibid.,* pp. 106–107.

39. *Ibid.,* ix.

40. *Ibid.,* pp. 139–146; 152–160.

41. In our analysis of Whately we have dealt almost entirely with his theories of argument. What he had to say on delivery will be briefly examined in our forthcoming discussion of the Elocutionary Movement.

10

The Elocutionary Movement

A final group of British scholars responsible for initiating a major trend in rhetorical thought in the eighteenth century were the elocutionists who devoted their attention primarily to delivery. In their practice of singling out a particular canon for emphasis, they used a strategy similar to that of the sixteenth-century stylists. Functioning as truncators who separated a specific canon from the other four treated by the ancients, both the elocutionists and the stylists reflected the influence of Peter Ramus and his disciple Omar Talon. In the second half of the sixteenth century, Ramus, a French philosopher, sought to realign logic and rhetoric. Under logic or dialectic, he argued, belonged the canons of invention and disposition. Since rhetoric, on the other hand, should not be permitted to share the same subject matter, it should consist merely of style and delivery. Wilbur Samuel Howell gives the following rationale which apparently motivated Ramus to truncate rhetoric:

It seemed clear to Ramus that his law of justice was violated at the point where invention and disposition were claimed both by dialectic and by rhetoric. This law really meant that two arts could not share the same subject matter, and that, when they did, learning was to be accused of an egregious blunder, even as the arts were to be condemned for redundancy and untidiness. As he saw it, he had no recourse but to detach invention and disposition either from the one or the other of the arts which treated them. What he therefore did was to constitute dialectic as the theory of invention and disposition, rhetoric as the theory of style and delivery. Memory, the fifth part of ancient rhetoric, he regarded as a faculty to be assisted and strengthened by what dialectic says on the subject of disposition and method.[1]

Although Ramus "is not the originator of the idea" that rhetoric should be limited to style and delivery, he proved to be such a popular and influential persuader that he won the devotion of numerous followers who proclaimed him as a seminal thinker.[2] What makes him particularly significant in this historical survey is the fact that the Ramistic dichotomy not only provided the rationale for rhetorical works on style such as Henry Peacham's *Garden of Eloquence* (1577) but established a framework in which the elocutionary movement could build.

Eighteenth-Century Elocutionists

Although the first book written in English limiting itself to the subject of delivery appeared as early as 1617,[3] the elocutionary movement did not progress in earnest until the following century. In the 1700s and in subsequent decades, students of speech and polite literature saw three pressing needs which, they believed, had to be met before effective oral communication in English could develop.

First, their research of ancient and modern works proved much to their dismay that no previous writer had come to grips adequately with delivery. The author of *The Art of Speaking* observed in 1768 that Greek, Roman, French, and Italian scholars had spoken copiously of invention, disposition, and style, but had neglected the last canon.[4] Four decades earlier John Henley noted that Aristotle, in considering delivery a gift of nature, gave no rules on the subject. Moreover, he added, many of the helpful hints appearing in Quintilian's *Institutio Oratoria* were more appropriate for eloquence of the bar than for other forms of public address, and more suitable for the classical period than the modern era.[5] These elocutionists found it hard to understand why a subject reputed to be Demosthenes' favorite rhetorical canon had been so poorly handled.

Thomas Sheridan, perhaps the most famous British elocutionist,[6] took special notice of the failure of contemporary authors to analyze delivery. Locke, he said regretfully, wrote in a brilliant and speculative manner about the theoretical nature of man, but completely ignored the challenge to apply his doctrines to a practical theme such as voice and gesture.[7]

The elocutionists saw a second major need that made the study of delivery a fertile field for future research. Everywhere they looked they could see an increased demand for expressing ideas in oral English. Speaking opportunities were developing rapidly in parliament, at the bar, in the pulpit, and in public recitations and polite conversation. The pulpit in particular fascinated the elocutionists. Thus they often wrote their treatises with the minister in mind.

The interest in private and public speech was matched by a corresponding concern for the study of language and pronunciation. The time had come, the elocutionists believed, not only for a comprehensive English dictionary such as that of Samuel Johnson's, but for a rhetorical grammar setting forth a standard of punctuation. Both Sheridan and John Walker wrote books dealing exclusively with this theme.[8] What they hoped to accomplish in doing so was to lift oral English to the high status level enjoyed by written English.

As the elocutionists became aware of the omissions in rhetorical literature with respect to delivery, and as they witnessed expanding opportunities in public speaking and oral reading and a developing interest in language study, they surveyed contemporary practices in oral presentation. What they saw was disheartening. In the church, at the bar, and in parliament they could find no Demosthenes or Cicero who could move the passions with a dynamic voice control and properly motivated bodily activity. Two neoclassicists, Addison and Swift, made commentaries on this weakness that were to be quoted often in the middle of the century. Additionally, they compared the ancients with the moderns, and they concluded that "had we never so good an ear, we have still a faultering tongue, and a kind of impediment in our speech."[9] After condemning preachers who "stand stock-still in the pulpit, and will not so much as move a finger to set off the best sermons in the world," Addison gave a ringing indictment against speaking practices at the bar.

How cold and dead a figure . . . does an orator often make at the British bar, holding up his head with the most insipid serenity, and stroking the sides of a long wig that reaches down to his middle? The truth of it is, there is often nothing more ridiculous than the gestures of an English speaker; you see some of them running their hands into their pockets as far as ever they can thrust them, and others looking with great attention on a piece of paper that has nothing written on it; you may see many a smart rhetorician turning his hat in his hands, moulding it into several different cocks, examining sometimes the lining of it, and sometimes the button, during the whole course of his harangue. . . . I remember, when I was a young man, and used to frequent Westminister-hall, there was a counsellor who never pleaded without a piece of pack-thread in his hand, which he used to twist about a thumb, or a finger, all the while he was speaking: the wags of those days used to call it the thread of his discourse, for he was not able to utter a word without it.[10]

Nor had the situation improved by 1762, the publication date of Sheridan's *Lectures on*

Elocution. It is common knowledge, said Sheridan, that British natives as a whole do not have the ability to speak or read with grace and propriety in public; nor have they had to date a methodology to overcome this difficulty. He later taunted his English contemporaries with the claim that a country with a limited vocabulary has an inadequate supply of ideas, and a nation with a limited system of tones and gestures has an inferior use of feelings.[11]

Apart from the three major needs outlined above, the elocutionists noted several subsidiary reasons for concentrating on the area of delivery. While these factors were not as urgent, they, along with the others, helped create the rationale for focusing on one canon of rhetoric. First, the study of delivery, the elocutionists argued, would extend our knowledge of human nature. Whatever we learn about symbolic vocal expression and gesture assumes importance because these characteristics belong exclusively to man. In this regard they thought of themselves as empiricists who derived their conclusions from observation, experience, and social science methodology. They used the information resulting from their investigations to study the effects of delivery on the mental faculties. Some used an approach similar to that employed by twentieth-century students of speech and hearing science. In his *Introduction to the Art of Reading,* for instance, John Rice considered the relationship between sense and sound, and discussed vocal anatomy.[12] Sheridan, moreover, used scientific instruments as a part of his public demonstrations. James Boswell reports that in April, 1781, he, along with fifty men and twenty ladies, went to hear Sheridan discuss his favorite subject. There he was impressed with the apparatus which was used to "clear and smooth and mellow" the voice.[13]

Secondly, delivery was the only major canon, the elocutionists pointed out, that had not yet been under a concerted attack during the modern era. The inventional system of topics and the stylistic movement's stress on schemes and tropes, for example, had received a withering indictment from the Port-Royal logicians, the Royal Academy, and Locke.

Similarly, Ramus and his English followers had separated invention and disposition from rhetoric. No one thus far, however, had succeeded in launching a campaign against the canon of delivery.[14] Finally, the elocutionists believed that English was peculiarly suited to public speaking and oral reading. James Burgh summarized the attitude of his colleagues on this point. "Whoever imagines the English tongue unfit for oratory, has not a just notion of it. . . . And in oratory, and poetry, there is no tongue, ancient, or modern, capable of expressing a greater variety of humours, or passions, by its sounds than the English. . . ."[15]

Once the elocutionists had demonstrated a need and articulated their rationale, they proceeded to discuss the theory of delivery and offer practical suggestions for improving voice control and bodily activity. They defined elocution in essentially the same manner. John Henley referred to his book *The Art of Speaking in Public* as "An Essay on the Action of the Orator as to his Pronunciation and Gesture." In their introductory remarks the editors explained that the work "treats of Pronunciation and Gesture in particular, which are the very life, soul and quintessence of Rhetoric. . . ."[16] Expressing a comparable opinion, Sheridan described elocution as "the just and graceful management of the voice, countenance, and gesture in speaking,"[17] Included within the sphere of elocution were both oratory and oral reading. The former was identified with persuasion; the latter with "that system of rules, which teaches us to renounce written composition with justness, energy, variety, and ease. . . ."[18]

That the elocutionary movement as it developed in the eighteenth century was firmly entrenched in the principles of faculty psychology there can be little doubt. Sheridan noted that much of the world was still in the dark about the understanding and the imagination, and was unaware that "the passions and the fancy have a language of their own, utterly independent of words"; and this language can be instrumental in bringing forward the four faculties of the mind with such force that persuasion ensues.[19] Later, in his

"Two Dissertations on the State of Languages," Sheridan reaffirmed his belief in the faculties and asserted that they should be strengthened. Rice also incorporated the tenets of faculty psychology into his elocutionary system. Adhering to the conviction-persuasion duality, he deplored the practice of political speakers and ministers who bypassed appeals to the understanding and moved directly to a stimulation of the passions. Eleven years before the publication of Campbell's *Philosophy of Rhetoric,* Rice called for a type of public speaking that progressed in a hierarchical order beginning with the understanding and ending with the influencing of the will. It was wrong, he added, for parliamentary leaders like Lord Chatham to stir the emotions without first instructing the intellect.[20]

Burgh and Walker similarly reinforced their theories with principles drawn from psychology and the related school of taste. The faculties, Burgh observed, are always responsive to elegant speakers who with the aid of a pleasing voice and gesture transport the mind to the lofty plane of the sublime and beautiful.[21] Walker turned to Burke's *Enquiry* for information pertaining to emotional proof. He praised Burke for recognizing the connection between the internal feeling of a passion, and the external expression of it. "Hence it is," concluded Walker, "that though we frequently begin to read or express, without feeling any of the passion we wish to express, we often end in full possession of it."[22]

This reliance on the psychological theories then in vogue prevented the elocutionists from playing down the significance of invention as a vital element in the communication process. They were upset, as noted earlier, with the practice of circumventing the understanding. But they were even more disturbed with orators who had inferior content and superior vocal skill and gesture, for such communicators had an impressive power to persuade without providing thoughtful and relevant information to an enlightened auditory. This was the basis for Sheridan's tendency to denigrate the Methodists. He confessed their effectiveness in delivery but castigated them for using what he perceived to be shallow ideas. Placing

them in the category of "wild orators," he nevertheless cited them as an example of how a dynamic delivery pattern could influence the reception of a message.

Sure I am, that the advantages which the Methodist teachers have obtained over the regular clergy, in seducing so many of their flocks from them, have been wholly owing to this. For were they to read their nonsense from notes, in the same cold, artificial manner, that so many of the clergy deliver rational discourses, it is to be presumed, that there are few of mankind, such idiots, as to become their followers; or who would not prefer sense to nonsense, if they were cloathed in the same garb.[23]

It would appear that Sheridan's caricature of the Methodists was motivated to some degree by prejudice, but also by a sincere desire to illustrate to the Anglican clergy the role that delivery can play in affecting the faculties.

The practical application of knowledge which Sheridan found missing in the writings of Locke was a central feature of the works on elocution. Within their method of instruction was the underlying belief that theory had no value unless it was accompanied by carefully arranged training periods in front of a critical observer. This theory-practice pedagogical system had three distinctive characteristics. It recommended the natural manner, along with prescriptive rules for achieving it, and taught the need to know the internal and external traits of a passion. Students who wished to use the natural method were told to study the normal dispositions and affections of themselves and others, and to observe people in action during conversational situations. Whatever is considered natural in informal face-to-face communication sessions was the model to be followed on the platform either for public speaking or oral reading. It was a technique, in sum, that urged prospective orators and interpreters to be true to their own genuine feelings and to avoid imitating the performance of others.[24]

The elocutionists were quick to advocate rules for the management of the voice and gesture. Sheridan's practice was typical. He consistently advised speakers to learn their shortcomings in vocal control and to work on these defects in the presence of an auditor. Here are a few representative rules that show his prescriptive method:

1. To get more force a communicator should "fix his eyes upon that part of his auditory which is farthest from him," and "mechanically endeavour to pitch his voice so as that it may reach them."
2. In striving for more force one should "never utter a greater quantity of voice, than he can afford without pain to himself, or any extraordinary effort."
3. To correct an excessive speed in utterance, "the most effectual method will be, to lay aside an hour every morning, to be employed in the practice of reading aloud, in a manner, much slower than is necessary."
4. To improve the pronunciation of vowels and consonants, these sounds should be repeated over and over again.
5. The rule to be remembered concerning the proper use of accent "is to lay the accent always on the same syllable, and the same letter of the syllable, which they usually do in common discourse, and to take care not to lay any accent or stress, upon any other syllable."[25]

More detailed and artificial were the rules for bodily activity presented by Walker. He gave suggestions, first of all, to oral readers.

When we read to a few persons only in private, it may not be useless to observe, that we should accustom ourselves to read standing; that the book should be held in the left hand; that we should take our eyes as often as possible from the book, and direct them to those that hear us. The three or four last words, at least, of every paragraph, or branch of a subject, should be pronounced with the eye pointed to one of the auditors. When any thing sublime, lofty, or heavenly, is expressed, the eye and the right hand may be very properly elevated; and when any thing low, inferiour, or grovelling is referred to, the eye and hand may be directed downwards; when any thing distant or extensive

is mentioned, the hand may naturally describe the distance or extent; and when conscious virtue, or any heartfelt emotion, or tender sentiment occurs, we may as naturally clap the right hand on the breast, exactly over the heart.[26]

In turning to public speaking, Walker advised that this type of communication requires more action than oral interpretation. His detailed, mechanical suggestions contained in the following passage, at first glance, appear to be inconsistent with his conviction that gestures should comply with the taste of a society, and with his commitment to the natural manner of delivery.

In speaking extempore, we should be sparing of the use of the left hand, which may not ungracefully hang down by the side, and be suffered to receive that small degree of motion which will necessarily be communicated to it by the action of the right hand. The right hand, when in action, ought to rise extending from the side, that is, in a direction from left to right; and then be propelled forwards, with the fingers open, and easily and differently curved: the arm should move chiefly from the elbow, the hand seldom be raised higher than the shoulder, and when it has described its object, or enforced its emphasis, ought to drop lifeless down to the side, ready to commence action afresh. The utmost care must be taken to keep the elbow from inclining to the body, and to let the arms, when not hanging at rest by the side, approach to the action we call *a-kimbo;* we must be cautious, too, in all action but such as describes extent or circumference, to keep the hand, or lower part of the arm, from cutting the perpendicular line that divides the body into right and left; but above all, we must be careful to let the stroke of the hand, which marks force, or emphasis, keep exact time with the force of pronunciation; that is, the hand must go down upon the emphatical word, and no other.[27]

Walker's ideas undoubtedly were influenced by what he had observed in music and dancing, and, to some extent, by what he had seen in theatrical productions. If his rules were too artificial and prescriptive for a natural mode of delivery, they had the saving merit of attempting to make gesturing a science.

The habit of establishing rules for voice production and bodily activity was perhaps most noticeable in the field of pronunciation. Sheridan, who was the leader in an effort to have a fixed, universal standard of pronunciation for English, devised a system of visible marks to designate how a particular word should be articulated. Rice, in supporting Sheridan's goal of producing an acceptable standard, included an appendix in his *Art of Reading* which he subtitled: "The Sketch of a Plan for establishing a criterion, by which the Pronunciation of Languages may be ascertained; and, in particular that of the English Tongue, reduced to a certain fixt Standard."[28]

Not content to limit their investigations to an analysis of the natural method and to rules and standards, the elocutionists also sought to determine the connection between bodily movement and the passions. Burgh was one of the first to become persuaded that each internal emotion has an accurate external manifestation that could be detected by any discerning eye. As he put it in his *Art of Speaking:* "Nature has given every emotion of the Mind its proper outward expression, in such a manner, that what suits one, cannot, by any means, be accommodated to another. . . ."[29] He next undertook to list and discuss seventy-one emotions ranging from "tranquility" and "cheerfulness" to "fainting" and "death." Observe the description of the emotion he labels "persuasion." "Persuasion," he said, "puts on the looks of moderate love. Its accents are soft, flattering, emphatical and articulate."[30]

Burgh's method of describing and illustrating the passions impressed Walker, prompting him to use the same plan. Here is a typical sampling of the passions appearing in the *Elements of Elocution:*

Tranquility appears by the composure of the countenance, and general repose of the whole body, without the exertion of any one muscle. The countenance open, the forehead smooth, the eyebrows arched, the mouth just not shut, and the eyes passing with an easy motion from object to object, but not dwelling long upon any one. To distinguish it, however, from insensibility, it seems necessary to give it that cast of happiness which borders on cheerfulness.

A pleasing emotion of mind, on the actual or assured attainment of good, or deliverance from evil, is called *Joy.* Joy, when moderate, opens the countenance with smiles, and throws, as it were, a sunshine of delectation over the whole frame: When it is sudden and violent, it expresses itself by clapping the hands, raising the eyes towards heaven, and giving such a spring to the body as to make it attempt to mount up as if it could fly: When Joy is extreme, and goes into transport, rapture, and ecstasy, it has a wildness of look and gesture that borders on folly, madness, and sorrow.

Pity is benevolence to the afflicted. It is a mixture of love for an object that suffers, and a grief that we are not able to remove those sufferings. It shows itself in a compassionate tenderness of voice, a feeling of pain in the countenance, and a gentle raising and falling of the hands and eyes, as if mourning over the unhappy object. The mouth is open, the eyebrows are drawn down, and the features contracted or drawn together.

Fear is a mixture of aversion and sorrow, discomposing and debilitating the mind upon the approach or anticipation of evil. When this is attended with surprise and much discomposure, it grows into terror and consternation. Fear, violent and sudden, opens wide the eyes and mouth, shortens the nose, gives the countenance an air of wildness, covers it with deadly paleness, draws back the elbows parallel with the sides, lifts up the open hands, with the fingers spread, to the height of the breast, at some distance before it so as to shield it from the dreadful object. One foot is drawn back behind the other, so that the body seems shrinking from the danger, and putting itself in a posture for flight. The heart beats violently, the breath is quick and short, and the whole body is thrown into a general tremour. The voice is weak and trembling, the sentences are short, and the meaning confused and incoherent.[31]

Walker's procedure, notwithstanding its obvious superficiality, emanated from the belief that covert bodily activity should be consistent with overt behavior, and that well planned and meaningful gestural motions can generate an accurate inner feeling and outward expression of the passion being displayed.

Gilbert Austin's Chironomia

In their scope, scientific grounding, and use of specific notational or marking systems, none of the eighteenth-century works on elocution could equal Gilbert Austin's *Chironomia*, published in 1806. This monumental study, which was to exert a strong influence "upon the history and teaching of rhetoric and oral interpretation in Europe and America,"[32] was impressive in its design and goals. The following complete title of the text suggests the wide range of Austin's interest in elevating the fifth canon of rhetoric to the level of a science: "Chironomia;" or a *Treatise on Rhetorical Delivery:* Comprehending Many Precepts, Both Ancient and Modern, For the Proper Regulation of the *Voice, the Countenance, and Gesture.* Together With An *Investigation of the Elements of Gesture, and a New Method for the Notation Thereof: Illustrated by Many Figures.*"

As he begins his task Austin expressed the hope that he would complete the rules needed "for the better study and acquisition of rhetorical delivery. . . ." It soon becomes quite clear, however, that what the Irish author and clergyman wished to stress was not so much delivery as a whole but the science of gesturing. He devotes two chapters to the voice and one each to the countenance, reading, declamation, oratory, and acting. At the same time he sets aside fifteen chapters to a consideration of gesture. Here are but a few of the topics he considers:

Of Notation and Gesture
Of the Position of the Feet and Lower Limbs
Of the Positions, Motions, and Elevation of the Arms
Of the Positions and Motions of the Hands
Of the Head, the Eyes, the Shoulders, and Body

An essential element in Austin's detailed system was the creation of a marking method to show proper facial expressions, eye contact, hand or bodily action, and stance. Had such notations been used in the classical period or in the time of Shakespeare or Milton, he said, prospective orators or actors in the present day would have models to emulate and rules to follow. Thus instead of relying on conjecture we would know how Demosthenes and Cicero performed and how Shakespeare and Milton wanted their writings to be read orally.

Austin's complicated method of teaching delivery, along with its impact on the elocutionary movement, cannot be fully appreciated unless we see the visual drawings and markings he used. What follows, therefore, on pp. 184–187 is a reproduction of four of the eleven plates he used to depict appropriate posture and stance, the systematic positions of the arms and hands, and complex significant gestures. The plates, in all, contain 122 separate items which constitute a reference chart alluded to in the last half of the volume. Robb and Thonssen have observed:

(The plates) explain that Austin's system of gesture and movement is based upon the speaker's position in an imaginary sphere, and that notations are made to indicate changes of position, especially of the arms as they move in the sphere. The notations for arms, hand, and head are placed above the line of literature to be read, and the movement about the stage indicated below; for example, AR2 means that the speaker advances two steps to the right.[33]

The elocutionary movement, on balance, has left an influence on Western rhetorical thought which is both detrimental and fruitful. While expressing a preference for the natural method, many of the elocutionists unwittingly gave prescriptive mechanical rules which frequently led to excesses—a practice soundly condemned by Whately.[34] Moreover, by centering their attention primarily on delivery, elocutionists were inclined to ignore the close relationship between the message and the channel. This tendency prompted Howell to observe

that voice and gesture seem much more trivial when studied by themselves than they are when studied within the context of the best possible conceptions of invention, arrangement, and style. It was the solidest virtue of Cicero's and Quintilian's rhetorical writings that they saw delivery as an activity allied with but never separable from, the speaker's need to know his subject, to arrange it properly, and to give it effective expression. Indeed, Cicero and Quintilian had learned this virtue from Aristotle, and the lesson should never be forgotten. . . .[35]

Howell concludes his indictment of the elocutionists by suggesting that they mistakenly "sought to save classical rhetoric by rediscovering its precepts of delivery and by emphasizing them by themselves, whereas in reality classical rhetoric could best have been saved by modernizing those precepts and by teaching them only within the context of philosophically reconstituted theories of invention, arrangement, and style."[36]

Despite the shortcomings outlined by Howell, the elocutionists exerted a positive effect in several respects. Sheridan's "principles of elocution," for example, "lie somewhere at the roots of much of the present teaching of oral interpretation."[37] Perhaps even more important, Austin's comprehensive notational system "anticipated the electronic wizardry of tape and disc that today preserves the images and the voices of poets, actors, orators, and public officials who record memories for the archives of oral history projects."[38] The elocutionists, in sum, showed a strong preference for applying science and the scientific method to their study of human communication. On this crucial point, Frederick Haberman notes:

It is the elocutionists' primary claim to fame in rhetorical history that they applied the tenets of science to the physiological phenomena of spoken discourse, making great contributions to human knowledge in that process. The spirit of the elocutionary movement, like that of science, was one of independence, of originality, of a break with tradition. The methodology of the elocutionary movement, like that of science, was a combination of observing and recording. Just as the astronomer observed the movements of the planets and recorded them in special symbols, so the elocutionists observed certain phenomena of voice, body, and language, and recorded them in systems of notation. The elocutionists who contributed most to the movement are those whose work is characterized by exhaustive analysis based on observation, by systematic organization, and by the invention of systems of symbolic representation. The philosophy of the elocutionary movement, like that of the scientific-rationalistic creed, was a conception of man controlled by natural law. The elocutionists believed that the nature of man was governed by the same law and order which seventeenth-century science had discovered in the nature of the universe. They could claim that their rules and principles and systems represented the order that is found in nature; they were 'nature still, but nature methodized.' The phrase 'follow nature' meant in general that the rational order found in the universe should be reproduced in books; and it meant in the field of delivery that the laws of elocution must approximate as closely as possible the laws of life.[39]

Scholars who have debated the worth of the elocutionary movement, as we can see, have marshalled strong arguments on one side or the other of the issue. All agree, however, that the elocutionists hold an important place in Western rhetorical thought because of their attempt (though artificial at times) to derive a theory of delivery based on science and human nature, and because of the great influence which their efforts had on the teaching of speech in the American classroom for more than a century.

In our survey of British and Continental Rhetoric, which covered the period roughly from 1600 to 1828, we have observed how distinguished figures renowned in other fields turned their attention to the study of human communication, thereby leaving their mark on Western rhetorical thought. Francis Bacon, René Descartes, Giambattista Vico, David Hume, and Adam Smith were among the leading philosophers and/or social scientists of the modern era. Edmund Burke was a celebrated political leader. Hugh Blair, George Campbell, and Archbishop Richard Whately were influential protestant divines. Because of the eminence these scholars and practitioners achieved in their professional occupations, and the courage they possessed in applying their wide knowledge to an analysis of rhetoric, they were able to contribute new insights which both reinforced and modified the classical heritage.

Most of the rhetorical notions emanating from the British period fall under the major categories of neoclassicism, belles lettres, the psychological-epistemological school of thought, and the elocutionary movement. Except for neoclassicism, which tended to use traditional classical symbols, the other trends featured six emphases which gave fresh impetus to the idea that rhetoric is a dynamic developing process. These may be summarized as follows:

1. Rhetoric should be broadened to include the written genre and criticism.
2. Communicators should use a variety of ends of discourse rather than limit themselves to persuasion.
3. The audience, including their general human traits and their particular conditioning forces, should become a starting point in preparation for a rhetorical transaction.
4. Invention should be treated as a managerial function instead of a discovery process.
5. Inartistic proof or evidence deserves a place of importance comparable to artistic proof or reasoning.
6. The canon of delivery, long relegated to a state of "benign neglect," is worthy of scientific analysis.

How many of these emphases worked their way into contemporary rhetorical theory will be evident as we consider the next chapters of this volume.

Notes

1. Wilbur S. Howell, ed., *Fenelon's Dialogues on Eloquence* (Princeton, Princeton University Press, 1951), pp. 10–11.
2. *Ibid.*, pp. 11–12.
3. Warren Guthrie, "The Elocution Movement—England," in Joseph Schwartz and John A. Rycenga, eds., *The Province of Rhetoric* (New York: The Ronald Press Company, 1965), p. 257. This essay first appeared in *Speech Monographs* (March, 1951).
4. James Burgh, *The Art of Speaking* (London: T. Longman and J. Buckland, 1768), pp. 1–2.
5. John Henley, *The Art of Speaking in Public*, 2nd. ed., (London: N. Cox, 1727), p. 9.
6. The most impressive study of Sheridan's theories may be found in Wallace A. Bacon, "The Elocutionary Career of Thomas Sheridan," *Speech Monographs*, XXXI (March, 1964), 1–53.
7. Thomas Sheridan, *A Course of Lectures on Elocution*, 1762 (Menston, England: The Scholar Press Limited, 1968), VI–VII.
8. See Thomas Sheridan, *A Rhetorical Grammar of the English Language*, 1781 (Menston, England: The Scholar Press Limited, 1969); and John Walker, *A Rhetorical Grammar* (Boston: Cummings and Hilliard, 1822). This volume first appeared in 1785.
9. Joseph Addison, *The Works of the Right Honorable Joseph Addison*, ed. by Richard Hurd, 6 Vols. (London: T. Cadell and W. Davies, Strand, 1811), VI, 452.
10. *Ibid.*, IV, 328.
11. Thomas Sheridan, "Two Dissertations on the State of Languages," in *A Course of Lectures on Elocution*, pp. 168–69.
12. John Rice, *An Introduction to the Art of Reading with Energy and Propriety* (London: J. and R. Tonson, 1765).
13. James Boswell, *Private Papers of James Boswell from Malahide Castle*, ed. Geoffrey Scott, 18 vols. (Mount Vernon, N.Y.: W. E. Rudge, privately printed, 1928–34), I, 70.
14. Wilbur S. Howell, "Sources of the Elocutionary Movement in England," *Quarterly Journal of Speech* XLV (February 1959), 1–18.
15. Burgh, p. 4.
16. Henley, xvii.
17. Sheridan, *A Course of Lectures on Elocution*, p. 19.
18. John Walker, *Elements of Elocution* (Boston: D. Mallory & Co., 1810), p. 18.
19. Sheridan, *A Course of Lectures on Elocution*, X.
20. Rice, pp. 288–89.
21. Burgh, p. 30.
22. Walker, *Elements of Elocution*, p. 311.

23. Sheridan, *A Course of Lectures on Elocution,* p. 128.
24. *Ibid.,* pp. 119–20.
25. *Ibid.* pp. 32–38, 55–56, and 85–88.
26. Walker, *Elements of Elocution,* pp. 304–305.
27. *Ibid.,* p. 305.
28. Rice, p. 307.
29. Burgh, p. 12.
30. *Ibid.,* p. 22.
31. Walker, *Elements of Elocution,* pp. 317–36. The most comprehensive analysis dealing with Walker's methods is M. Leon Dodez, "An Examination of the Theories and Methodologies of John Walker with Emphasis upon Gesturing," Ph.D. Dissertation, The Ohio State University, 1963.
32. Mary Margaret Robb and Lester Thonssen, eds., *Chironomia or A Treatise on Rhetorical Delivery by Gilbert Austin* (Carbondale, Ill.: Southern Illinois University Press, 1966), V.
33. *Ibid.,* IX–X.
34. In the last chapter of *Elements of Rhetoric,* Whately articulated the need for a natural mode of delivery, and criticized the elocutionists for devising a mechanical marking system that promoted artificiality.
35. Howell, "Sources of the Elocutionary Movement in England," pp. 17–18.
36. *Ibid.,* p. 18.
37. Bacon, "The Elocutionary Career of Thomas Sheridan," p. 46.
38. *Chironomia,* 1x.
39. Frederick W. Haberman, "English Sources of American Elocution," in Karl Wallace, ed., *History of Speech Education in America* (New York: Appleton-Century-Crofts, Inc., 1954), pp. 109–110.

Plate 1.

Positions

Fig 7

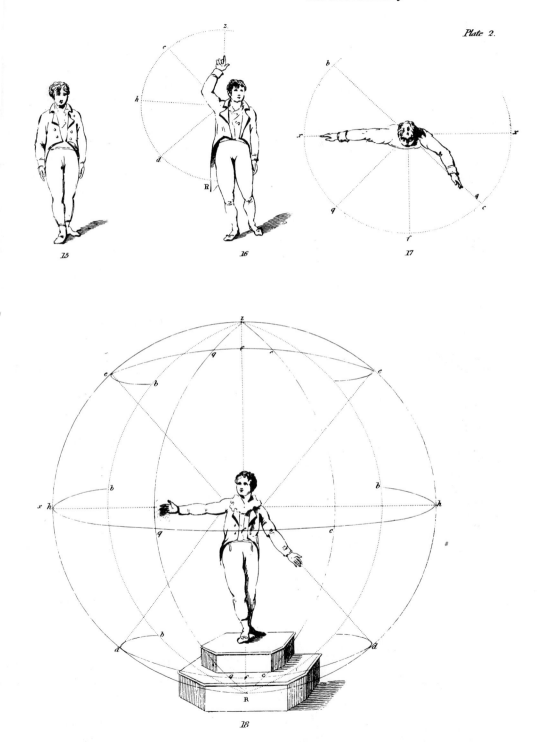

Plate 2.

Kelly del.

Warner sc.

Plate. 10.

Complex Significant Gestures.

Kelly del.

Warner sc.

Plate, 11.

Complex Significant Gestures.

Kelly del.

Warner sc.

Part Four
Contemporary
Rhetorical
Theory

The last major rhetorician we discussed in the British period was Richard Whately whose seven editions of the *Elements of Rhetoric* appeared during the years from 1828 to 1846. As we move from Britain to America where most, but not all, of contemporary rhetorical theory was spawned, it is important to note that the works of Blair and Whately, along with those of the elocutionists, had some influence on rhetorical training in American colleges and universities.* Even so, up until 1890 "the writings in rhetoric," emanating primarily from scholars in grammar and literature, "were concerned with written forms of communication."[1] By 1893–1894, however, the trend began to change. With the opening of that academic year, fifty-two colleges could boast separate departments of speech.[2] Twenty-one years later in 1914, seventeen men met for the purpose of creating a national organization of speech teachers—a decision which was to go a long way toward providing academic respectability to speech programs.

In these formative years numerous prominent scholars taught courses and wrote textbooks on varying aspects of rhetoric. Of this group we would like to mention three who were both representative and influential: Thomas Trueblood, James Winans, and Charles Woolbert. Trueblood, who served as Chairman of the Department of Elocution and Oratory at the University of Michigan from 1902 to 1926, emphasized the classical canon of *pronunciatio.* His volume on *Practical Elements of Elocution* (1893), co-authored with Robert Fulton, helped revitalize the elocutionary movement in the United States.

While Trueblood devoted most of his energy to the study of a single canon, James Winans, who taught first at Cornell University and later at Dartmouth College, combined traditional and modern theories in his efforts to formulate a broad-based relevant rhetoric suitable for twentieth-century students. His pioneering work on *Public Speaking,* written in 1915, is exemplary in its use of classical precepts and the application of contemporary principles of psychology. Students found it profitable to turn to his volume for valuable insights on traditional doctrines, on the conversational pattern of delivery, and on methods for gaining attention and maintaining interest. Just as Campbell had borrowed heavily from Locke and Hume to develop his ideas on faculty psychology and moral reasoning, Winans borrowed freely from William James to devise

*There were, for example, thirty two separate printings of Blair's work published in America between 1784 and 1873. Nor did these include the numerous abridgements as well as the extensive cuttings which appeared in other texts.

his theory of persuasion. His scholarly, eclectic approach helped make Cornell University the undisputed center of rhetorical inquiry and research during the first quarter of the twentieth century.

Meanwhile Charles Woolbert, like Trueblood, was advancing the cause of rhetorical training in the Middle West. First at the University of Illinois and then at the University of Iowa, Woolbert, utilizing behavioral psychology, dealt at length with the subject of persuasion. In a series of widely publicized articles in the *Quarterly Journal of Speech,* and in the revised edition of *The Fundamentals of Speech* (1927), he highlighted the role of logic in persuasion, challenged the value of adhering to belief in a conviction-persuasion duality, and described the important part that bodily activity played in oral communication.

Winans and Woolbert, far more than Trueblood, set the stage for a resurgence of interest in rhetoric as a field of study beginning in the 1930s. Theories which were to evolve in the next five decades form the core of what we call our third great system of rhetoric. As we examine the enormous amount of literature pertaining to rhetorical theory in the contemporary period, we see four themes under which most material can be classified: (1) rhetoric as meaning, (2) rhetoric as value, (3) rhetoric as motive, and (4) rhetoric as a way of knowing.

I. A. Richards and Marshall McLuhan highlight "meaning" as an inherent communication problem in social relations. Richard Weaver cogently reminds us of the impact of values on our language systems. Kenneth Burke bases his rhetorical system largely on human motivation. In fact, he entitled two of his most important treatises *The Grammar of Motives* and *The Rhetoric of Motives.* Finally, Chaim Perelman and Stephen Toulmin approach rhetoric as an instrument for the creation and advancement of knowledge.

In developing these four subject areas, we will divide the material into fourteen chapters. It will be our plan to discuss the representative ideas associated with the rhetorician we have chosen to feature first, and then to present exploratory essays springing, at least in part, from these generative insights. In order to sharpen our focus and enhance clarity, we will keep the appropriate theme words in the title of each chapter. Overall, four chapters will be devoted to the rhetoric of meaning, three to value, three to motive, and four to a way of knowing.

Admittedly, the selection of our four themes and the primary emphasis on six major contemporary rhetoricians is somewhat arbitrary. We are conscious of the fact that each rhetorician could be placed in more than one category. Perelman, for instance, repeatedly speaks of rhetoric as a means of "gaining adherence for values." Burke and Weaver, moreover, are heavily involved in the notion of the role of rhetoric in generating meaning and understanding. We are further aware of the fact that many of the other current authors whose partial works we have reproduced in this volume, could themselves be the subject of a probing analysis. In the selection and development of our categories and in the choice of rhetorical theorists, our purpose merely is to provide some of the leading perspectives on contemporary rhetorical thought. It is hoped that while these perspectives are limited in scope they still may show the dynamic, developing nature of Western rhetorical theory.

11

Rhetoric as Meaning: I. A. Richards, Significant Symbols, Speech Acts

The exploration into contemporary rhetorical trends begins with the question of meaning. Although several modern theorists could easily be included in this discussion, we have chosen to focus in the next two chapters upon the ideas of I. A. Richards and Marshall McLuhan. At first glance, it seems as if these two individuals, separated by a half century in time, are quite dissimilar in their theoretical positions. They are. But, at several crucial points, the construct of "meaning" mysteriously serves to unite Richards and McLuhan. Thus, we have sorted out the "meaning" theme and have highlighted this issue as a significant bridge between the thoughts of McLuhan and Richards.

Marshall McLuhan opens his provocative text, *Understanding Media: The Extension of Man,* with the following insight.

In a culture like ours, long accustomed to splitting and dividing all things as a means of control, it is sometimes a bit of a shock to be reminded that, in operational and practical fact, the medium is the message. This is merely to say that the personal and social consequences of any medium—that is, of any extension of ourselves—result from the new scale that is introduced into our affairs by each extension of ourselves, or by any new technology.[3]

Thus, McLuhan begins his intellectual search for the nature of meaning in the various media which engulf men in a technological society.

In *The Meaning of Meaning*—a work jointly compiled by I. A. Richards and C. K. Ogden, a similar idea is echoed.

Language, though often spoken of as a medium of communication, is best regarded as an instrument; and all instruments are extensions, or refinements, of our sense organs. The telescope . . . the microscope . . . are . . . capable . . . of introducing new relevant members into the contexts of our signs. And as receptive instruments extend our organs. . . .

Both Richards and McLuhan are concerned with the social consequences and inherent nature of meaning characteristic of media. Richards narrows his focus to the language medium, the meanings elicited by words, and the implications thereof to human thinking, and ultimately to social relationships. McLuhan, on the other hand, widens his emphasis to include the meanings which occur in all the diverse media abounding in our atomic age.

So, both McLuhan and Richards attack a portion of the psycho-philosophical problem of meaning. Each, however, launches his own personal strategy, tactics, and assumptions into the arena. The results of such inquiry are intriguing and thought-provoking. It must be remembered, however, that Richards and McLuhan have been selected as representatives of the "meaning school" for pedagogical purposes only. That is, Richards and Mc-Luhan have each woven theories and hypotheses far "richer" than is evident in the following pages. Nevertheless, the meaning issue is functional in that it serves as an intellectual handle or key into the thinking of two unique writers of the twentieth century who are concerned with sociological aspects in human communication.

Chapter 12 will consider Marshall Mc-Luhan's thoughts on communication by reviewing his major ideas on media and reprinting an essay he authored in 1973. Further ideas on the media and meaning issue will be considered in essays on television and politics which appear in Chapter 13. The immediate discussion, however, focuses on I. A. Richards. After a review of Richards' theory, an article published in 1972 is reprinted. Following Richards' essay are sections on the rhetoric of the significant symbol and speech act theory which, we feel, are natural outcomes of a meaning-centered theory of rhetoric.

Richards' Rhetoric of Meaning

Ivor Armstrong Richards has extensively inquired into the impact which language and symbols have on human relationships. His chief concern is with *meaning:* how language and words come to mean. Richards' contribution to rhetorical thought is predicated on the ideas of Francis Bacon concerning perception—specifically Bacon's Idols of the Market Place. Although Bacon is classified as a British theorist, his metaphor of the Market is, as we now see, distinctly modern:

There are Idols formed by the intercourse and association of men with each other, which I call Idols of the Marketplace on account of the commerce and consort of men there. For it is by discourse that men associate, and words are imposed according to the apprehension of the vulgar. And therefore the ill and unfit choice of words wonderfully obstructs the understanding . . . words plainly force and overrule the understanding, and throw all into confusion, and

lead men away into numberless empty controversies and idle fancies.[5]

Bacon, then, considers man's use of language as a potential barrier to human understanding and relationships. As he puts it: ". . . the Idols of the Marketplace are the most troublesome of all, idols which have crept into the understanding through the alliances of words and names."[6]

I. A. Richards has considered the language issue raised by Bacon perhaps more seriously than any contemporary author. In the ensuing discussion of Richards' contribution to modern rhetorical theory, we shall focus on two of his major works. The first, *The Meaning of Meaning,* was published in 1923 in conjunction with C. K. Ogden. The second work considered herein is Richards' *Philosophy of Rhetoric* (1936).

These texts and their theoretical contribution have been chosen because they provide, we think, a brief but meaningful introduction into Richards' thinking. Richards' contribution to the field of rhetoric certainly goes far beyond the concepts discussed in the ensuing pages. For those who wish to further their study of Richards' ideas, we recommend the following works: *The Foundations of Aesthetics* (with C. K. Ogden and James Woods, 1922), *Principles of Literary Criticism* (1924), *Science and Poetry* (1926), *Practical Criticism* (1929), *Basic Rules of Reason* (1933), *How to Read a Page* (1942), and *Speculative Instruments* (1955).

Richards' theoretical bias is quickly discerned in his unique definition of rhetoric which appears in the *Philosophy of Rhetoric:*

Rhetoric, I shall argue, should be a study of misunderstanding and its remedies. We struggle all our days with misunderstandings and no apology is required for any study which can prevent or remove them.[7]

With this premise, Richards launches into a discussion of the context theorem of meaning, the interinanimation of words, the Proper Meaning Superstition, and the metaphor. A brief consideration of each of these rhetorical concepts ensues.

Perhaps the integrating conceptual dimension of Richards' system is his "Context Theorem of Meaning." To understand this central theorem it is necessary to sketch Richards' theory of abstraction—or *how* words come to mean.

Richards postulates that as human beings we are all responsive to incoming data; hence, man continually responds to "things" in his perceived environment. Furthermore, man's *reactions to* and *interpretations of* environmental stimuli or data are dependent on past confrontations and experiences with *similar* stimuli. Accordingly, effects from more or less similar happenings in the past give our responses their character or meaning.[8] In conclusion, the *meanings* we attach to the stimuli in our environments are thus rooted far in our past and grow out of one another.[9] Richards, then, underscores the importance of the *context* in relation to past experience with similar stimuli. In this connection, he observes:

Our interpretation of any sign is our psychological reaction to it, as determined by our past experience in similar situations, and by our present experience.

If this is stated with due care in terms of causal contexts or correlated groups we get an account of judgment, belief and interpretation which places the psychology of thinking on the same level as the other inductive sciences. . . .

A theory of thinking which discards mystical relations between the knower and the known and treats knowledge as a causal affair open to ordinary scientific investigation, is one which will appeal to common sense inquirers.[10]

Therefore, while we live in the present, our reactions to the here and now world are directly correlated to our individual and collective histories. We are engaged in perpetual *sorting* activity whereby we *perceive* incoming bits of information (Richards denies that we have "sensations" or datum which "stand on their own"), *compare* them with our past, *analyze* them, *classify* and *process* them, and attach *meaning* accordingly—hence, we come to understand the data bits. So, our reactions

and decisions in the here and now situation are tied to our past histories. All *perceived* events and things are automatically processed by the mind which continuously *compares* the here and now with the individual's past.

We have perceptions, responses whose character comes to them from the past as well as the present occasion. A perception is never just of an *it;* perception takes whatever it perceives as a thing of a certain sort. All thinking from the lowest to the highest— whatever else it may be—is sorting.[11]

In the *sorting* process, stimuli within the present field of awareness are analyzed and classified with similar past stimuli: categories of contexts are thus created and maintained by each individual. The issue of *how* meaning develops in individuals is therefore a complex phenomenon rooted in personal histories. Summarizing Richards to this point, we may say: man is a *perceiving* being who responds to the present stimuli in his environment by interpretations based on past contexts and experience.[12]

We need to mention at this point, however, an essential characteristic of the human sorting process which Richards considers. Given the nature of thinking and sorting, Richards states that when any *part* of a context appears (a context is "a set of entities—things or events—related in a certain way. . . .")[13] the possibility exists that the *entire* context will be remembered and the organism will act *as if* the total context were present. In other words, the *part* has the power to elicit the *whole*. Richards cites the case of a chicken who, when attempting to bite into a striped yellow and black caterpillar, found its taste offensive and immediately dropped the small creature. From that time hence, the chicken refused to touch any yellow and black striped caterpillar for the mere sight of it conjured up the previous bitter taste context. Richards elaborates:

This simple case is typical of all interpretation, the peculiarity of interpretation being that when a context has affected us in the past the recurrence of merely a part of the context will cause us to react in the way in which we reacted before. A sign is always a stimulus similar to some part of an original stimulus and sufficient to call up the engram (i.e., 'to call up an excitation similar to that caused by the original stimulus') formed by that stimulus.[14]

A further illustration of this ability to "abridge" from the immediate external context to previous and similar contexts when only one segment or part of the whole is perceived may also prove helpful. Several years ago a young boy was playing on the front lawn of his home—a small, quiet, Midwestern town. He was lying on his back clutching his neighbor's small black kitten—holding it above his face. With his arms extended the boy was trying to shield the sun from his eyes by placing the kitten between him and the fiery ball. Alas, however, the game was cut short. It seems that the young boy became so engrossed in his hide and seek game with the sun and kitten that he clenched the poor creature a bit too firmly. And, as the kitten had just eaten a large breakfast, she reacted naturally to the young man's grip by expelling the contents of her stomach on the young man's once smiling, gleeful face. This strange episode took place almost twenty-five years ago and to this day, the young man has avoided all kittens and, as expected, becomes very anxious in their presence. Thus the mere perception of a kitten at once evokes the former context.

We have detailed Richards' theory of abstraction precisely because it is the foundation of his rhetorical theory. In essence, man's sorting activity is basic to an understanding of his rhetorical behavior. Thus far, Richards has considered only man's response to things and events in his environment. However, *words* and *symbols* are also important stimuli; accordingly, Richards turns his attention to the character and uniqueness of symbols.

Words are symbols and unique, says Richards, in that they are "substitutes exerting the powers of what is not there."[15] That is, words and symbols transcend the here and now and *stand for* that which is missing. Richards terms the study of words and symbolism the science of Symbolism. However, he further narrows

the traditional definition of "symbol" to include only words which refer to verifiable "things" in our environment. Symbols are "words that refer, through thoughts, to things. Everything inside the skin that relates to feelings, attitudes, hopes, dreams, etc., is excluded. This is the distinguishing characteristic of the science of symbolism."[16] Richards' focus, then, is *only* on words which have a definite referent in reality. Words which do not refer to "things," are termed "emotive language" and are *not* the locus of Richards' theory. It is important to keep this distinction in mind throughout the ensuing discussion. Marie Nichols provides an instructive illustration:

Let us take the following three sets of symbols to illustrate Richards' analysis of language and the classification of its uses:

1. Winston Churchill is eighty-three years old.
2. The grand old man who occupied 10 Downing Street during the Second World War is eighty-three years old.
3. Four-score and three he counts his years, proud England's mighty son.

The first sentence Richards would identify as a purely referential statement, and, therefore, a *scientific* use of language. The context out of which the symbol grew would include recurrent experiences with the process of explicit naming and counting. The referent is the person bearing the name and having those years.

The second sentence represents a change in symbolization. The references, or psychological context, out of which the symbols were composed might include an affectionate attitude on the part of the composer of the symbol, a remembering of the events of the war, a recollection of others who had occupied the house at 10 Downing Street, in addition to a strict reference to the number of years of life. The referent is still to a person. The symbol, however, has not been produced for merely referential uses. Attitudes, reminiscences, and perhaps other factors have exerted strong influence. This use of language Richards labels 'emotive' or 'mixed,' hence, 'rhetorical.'

The third set of symbols represents still further change in symbolization. The purely referential function of language has almost completely vanished. Who is being talked about is no longer definite. The psychological context out of which this symbolization grew might contain feelings about age and England and some queries about relations, sonship, fatherhood. It might even include feelings about Lincoln at Gettysburg. This use of language represents almost completely the "emotive" function of language and would be regarded as poetry, good or bad.

When Richards and his collaborator published *The Meaning of Meaning*, they claimed among their peculiar contributions the following: 'An account of interpretation in causal terms by which the treatment of language as a system of signs becomes capable of results,' and second, 'A division of the functions of language into two groups, the symbolic and the emotive.' The symbolic use of words is 'statement; the recording, the support, the organization and the communication of references.' The emotive use of words is the 'use of words to express or excite feelings and attitudes.' There are, in other words, 'two totally distinct uses of language.'[17]

With this distinction in mind, Richards begins his analysis of symbolic language.

How, then, do words which refer to "things" in our environments come to *mean?* Similar to our previous discussion on *how* stimuli come to mean, the meaning attached to words also depends on past encounters with the word and what it correspondingly *stands for.* The summation of past experience with a symbol together with the present instance of the word determine meaning. Thus, the immediate external context together with past psychological contexts determine meaning. Richards labels this *total* of past and present experience the *technical context.* So, in Richards' terms, words attain meaning through the technical context which surrounds them.

If we sum up thus far by saying that meaning is *delegated efficacy*, that description applies above all to the meaning of words, whose virtue is to be substitutes exerting the powers of what is not there. They do this as other signs do it, though in more complex fashions, through their contexts.[18]

Consider the word-symbol "kitten." Suppose you hear this word in a conversation with a colleague. To interpret the immediate event (i.e., the hearing of the word "kitten"), you abstract from the technical context (the psychological context plus the external context) and arrive at a meaning for the symbol "kitten." So, you *abridge* from the immediate instance of the symbol back through your past "kitten" contexts—i.e., you sort through your category of "kitten." In so doing, you attach a meaning to the word "kitten"—a meaning which is actually the missing part of the context.

Richards' theory of *how* words *mean,* then, is based on the concept of context and the sorting process. With these thoughts underlying Richards' thinking, it is logical that he would be critical of the doctrine of usage discussed by the British rhetorician, George Campbell. Whereas Campbell believed that every word has a "proper" and "correct" usage or meaning, such thinking is foreign to Richards who insists that meanings are in people, not words or symbols. So, Richards discusses the Proper Meaning Superstition.

A chief cause of misunderstanding, I shall argue later, is the Proper Meaning Superstition. That is, the common belief . . . that a word has a meaning of its own (ideally, only one) independent of and controlling its use and the purpose for which it should be uttered. This superstition is a recognition of a certain kind of stability in the meanings of certain words. It is only a superstition when it forgets (as it commonly does) that the stability of the meaning of a word comes from the constancy of the contexts that give it its meaning. Stability in a word's meaning is not something to be assumed, but always something to be explained. And as we try out explanations, we discover, of course, that— as there are many sorts of constant contexts—there are many sorts of stabilities.[19]

Thus, contexts determine and shape the meaning of words and symbols. It follows that since every human being is a unique entity who has had different past and immediate experiences (contexts), everyone will attach slightly different meanings to symbols. That is, we operate from personal contexts—therefore, meaning becomes individualized precisely because it is context dependent.

How, then, do we happen to understand one another? How do we agree on meanings? Richards partly answers these questions when he considers the literary context "as the other words before and after a given word which determines how it is to be interpreted. . . ."

The familiar sense of 'context' can be extended further to include the circumstances under which anything was written or said; wider still to include, for a word in Shakespeare, say, the other known uses of the word about that time, wider still finally to include anything whatever about the period, or anything else which is relevant to our interpretation of it.[20]

Thus, the literary context is certainly an essential component which enables us to determine "collective" meaning and understanding. In sum, words never appear in isolation but in literary contexts, which in turn provide clues as to possible responses.

The result of literary contexts is "interinanimation." Richards states that "no word can be judged as to whether it is good or bad, correct or incorrect, beautiful or ugly, or anything else that matters to a writer, in isolation."[21] So, it follows that words in a sentence, a phrase, or a paragraph are *dependent* upon one another and their *interaction* (interinanimation) provides the literary context. "But in most prose, and more than we ordinarily suppose, the opening words have to wait for those that follow to settle what they shall mean—if indeed that ever gets settled."[22] Interinanimation, then, refers to the mutual dependency and interaction which links words and symbols together in a literary relationship.

The best known rhetorical device developed in the *Meaning of Meaning* is perhaps the "semantic triangle." Ogden and Richards concluded that a major problem in human communication is man's tendency to treat words as if they were *things in reality*. So, in saying the word "dog" we tend to behave as if the three letter symbol **DOG** is an actual four legged animal that barks, growls, runs, eats, and sleeps. That is, as the general semanticists argue, we confuse the symbol or word with the "thing" or object in reality; Richards and Ogden, in turn, say that we tend to make a one-to-one correspondence or a *necessary connection* between the word and reality object (referent). Ogden and Richards argue that there is only an *indirect* relationship between symbol and reference since the symbol is merely an *abstraction* of reality rather than reality itself. Recall that words and symbols *stand for* "things" in the real world, according to Richards.

Thus, humans communicate with symbols which in turn stand for or refer to verifiable "things." But, there is a third element involved in the semantic triangle. Besides the symbol and referent Ogden and Richards consider the *thought* or *reference*. Often when we use words we are tempted to conclude that our partner in communication is operating from *our* thought/reference perspective. That is, we assume that our *references* are identical or universal—something which in all probability seldom occurs because of the individual's abstraction process. Such an assumption can effectively obstruct communication between individuals. Now, recall the earlier discussed incident of the young man and the kitten. As stated, this event took place years ago, but the young man of our story will vividly remember that traumatic moment in his youth. In fact, to this day, he avoids all kittens. He rarely touches them and becomes quite uncomfortable in their presence. We might diagram this situation as follows.

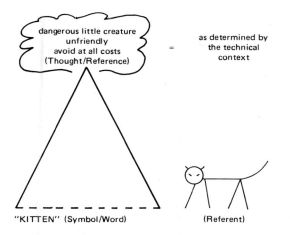

"KITTEN" (Symbol/Word)   (Referent)

In this situation, the meaning of the symbol "kitten" has been determined by the context and the sorting activity inherent in the abstraction process. So, meaning is delegated efficacy. Thus, there is *not* a necessary connection between symbol and referent. This is an impossibility in Richards' rhetorical system.

Now, what happens when the young man is engaged in a conversation with another individual who has a quite different Thought or Reference for "kitten"?

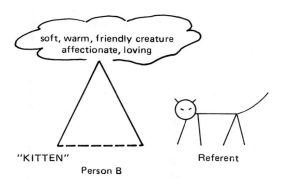

"KITTEN"   Referent

Person B

When the young man and person B are discussing kittens they are (a) using the identical symbol: "Kitten," and (b) they are reacting to a similar referent, *but* (c) their thought/references are quite different. Such an incongruence can easily lead to a misunderstanding between these two individuals discussing cats. The semantic triangle is thus a practical tool because it makes clear the relationship of thought, reference, and referent and demonstrates that meanings exist not in symbols or words but in people. Stated differently, the identical symbol or word does not often evoke *identical* meanings from two or more participants in human communication.

Richards' theory of abstraction leads him to consider meaning as the "missing parts of a context." This leads to a discussion of the nature of context (external and psychological) and the importance of the literary aspects of context and interinanimation. The semantic triangle makes clear the distinction between symbol, reference, and referent—describing the *lack* of necessary connection between symbol and referent. This indirect relationship is a logical conclusion of the delegated efficacy concept central to Richards' thinking. Finally, we need to examine briefly the *metaphor* whereby Richards' ideas are brought to culmination

As we have seen, Richards maintains that all human thinking is a matter of sorting—i.e., the individual's mind is continually engaged in establishing and refining categories of stimuli. Incoming data are quickly processed, analyzed, compared, and classified. Thus, Richards' theory of abstraction leads him to conclude that the metaphor is really the heart of our language systems.

We early begin to use language in order to learn language, but since it is no mere matter of the acquisition of synonyms or alternative locutions, the same stressing of similarities between references and elimination of their differences through conflict is required. By these means, we develop references of greater and greater abstractness, and metaphor, the primitive symbolization of abstraction, become possible. Metaphor, in the most general sense, is the use of one reference to a group of things between which a given relation holds, for the purpose of facilitating the discrimination of an analogous relation in another group.

In the understanding of metaphorical language one reference borrows part of the context of another in an abstract form.[23]

Richards continues this line of inquiry.

The view that metaphor is onmipresent in speech can be recommended theoretically. If you recall what I said in my second lecture about the context theorem of meaning; about meaning as the delegated efficacy of signs by which they bring together into new unities the abstracts, or aspects, which are missing parts of their various contexts, you will recollect some insistence that a word is normally a substitute for (or means), not one discrete past impression but a combination of general aspects. Now that is itself a summary account of the principle of metaphor. In the simplest formulation, when we use a metaphor we have two thoughts of different things active together and supported by a single word, or phrase, whose meaning is a resultant of their interaction.[24]

Therefore, within Richards' theory of abstraction, the metaphor "is a borrowing between and intercourse of *thoughts,* a transaction between contexts. *Thought* is metaphoric, and proceeds by comparison, and the metaphors of language derive therefrom."[25]

Richards believes that we need to examine the metaphorical nature of language more closely. Thus, he proposes two concepts which enable us to speak intelligently about metaphor.

We need the word 'metaphor' for the whole double unit, and to use it sometimes for one of the two components in separation from the other is as injudicious as that other trick by which we use 'the meaning' here sometimes for the work that the whole double unit does and sometimes for the other component— the tenor, as I am calling it—the underlying idea or principal subject which the vehicle or figure means.[26]

So, the vehicle and tenor become conceptual tools helpful in analyzing our language. Perhaps an illustration would prove beneficial. In Monday morning coffee breaks in the fall, the normal conversation centers on the "big" football game. In the course of the discussion it is not uncommon to hear these words about your favorite linebacker. "He was a real animal last Saturday, wasn't he Tom?" The tenor (underlying idea to which the vehicle refers) in this metaphor is "he" or the linebacker. The vehicle ("animal") attributes the characteristic of "savage or ferocious" behavior to the brutal play of the linebacker. Daniel Fogarty summarizes Richards' thinking on the metaphor and its importance or centrality to human language and social relationships.

Richards' most emphatic contention about metaphor, thus explained, is that language is naturally metaphor. Since metaphor is just abstraction for the purpose of clearer and more vivid communication, since it seems to be the nature of our thinking to be perpetually busy with sorting and classifying references and comparing contexts and their parts, and since our language symbolizes this thinking, it seems to Richards that our language must be highly, habitually, and even naturally metaphoric.[27]

Since language is metaphoric in nature, an understanding of the basic nature of metaphors (tenor and vehicle interaction) will help one to comprehend better the "workings" of language.

I. A. Richards provides us with a unique philosophy of rhetoric founded on his theory of abstraction, the semantic model, the context theorem of meaning, interinanimation, and metaphor. He is chiefly concerned with how words mean and how they work in discourse. With such an analysis of language, Richards believes that we can begin to understand *how* misunderstanding occurs. By appreciating the complexities of meaning, perhaps we can begin to break down the communication barriers which exist in human discourse: we can begin to understand one another. An understanding of contexts as the basis for human thinking is thus developed to the logical conclusion concerning the metaphorical nature of language. Therefore, context, delegated efficacy, interinanimation, semantic triangle, and metaphor are all inextricably related.

In conclusion, Richards claims that we can study *how* man thinks by examining *how* he uses language. Conversely, one can study how man uses language by studying how he thinks. In either case, we can study both language use and thinking through an understanding and appreciation of the metaphor.

Notes

1. Giles W. Gray, "Some Teachers and the Transition to Twentieth-Century Speech Education," *A History of Speech Education in America*, Karl R. Wallace, ed. (New York: Appleton-Century-Crofts, Inc., 1954), p. 424.
2. *Ibid.*, p. 422.
3. Marshall McLuhan, *Understanding Media: The Extension of Man* (New York: Signet Books, 1964), p. 23.
4. C. K. Ogden and I. A. Richards, *The Meaning of Meaning: A Study of the Influence of Language Upon Thought and of the Science of Symbolism*, 4th ed. (New York: Harcourt, Brace and Company, 1936), p. 98.
5. Francis Bacon, *Idols of the Mind*, in Richard Hughes and P. Albert Duhamel, *Rhetoric: Principles and Usage*, 2nd ed. (Englewood Cliffs, New Jersey: Prentice-Hall, Inc., 1967), pp. 361–362.
6. *Ibid.*, p. 365.
7. I. A. Richards, *The Philosophy of Rhetoric* (New York: Oxford University Press, 1965), p. 3.
8. *Ibid.*, pp. 29–30.
9. *Ibid.*, p. 30.
10. *Meaning of Meaning*, pp. 244–245.
11. *Philosophy of Rhetoric*, p. 30.
12. Richards' ideas concerning perception and sortings differentiate him from the Nominalists and Realists of the Eighteenth-Century controversy concerning "about whether we have and how we come by abstract ideas and what they are. This theorem alleges that meanings from the very beginning, have a primordial generality and abstractness. . . . It is behaving of thinking with a concept—not, of course *of* one. . . . The theorem holds that we *begin* with the general abstract anything, split it, as the world makes us, into sorts and then arrive at concrete particulars by the overlapping or common membership of these sorts." *Philosophy of Rhetoric*, pp. 30–31.
13. *Meaning of Meaning*, p. 58.
14. *Ibid.*, p. 53.
15. *Philosophy of Rhetoric*, p. 32.
16. Bess Sondel, *The Humanity of Words: A Primer of Semantics* (New York: The World Publishing Company, 1958), p. 56.
17. Marie H. Nichols, "I. A. Richards and the New Rhetoric," *Quarterly Journal of Speech*, XLIV (February 1958), in Richard L. Johannesen, ed., *Contemporary Theories of Rhetoric: Selected Readings* (New York: Harper and Row, 1971), pp. 131–132.
18. *Philosophy of Rhetoric*, p. 32.
19. *Ibid.*, p. 11.
20. *Ibid.*, pp. 32–33.
21. *Ibid.*, p. 51.
22. *Ibid.*, p. 50.
23. *Meaning of Meaning*, p. 213.
24. *Philosophy of Rhetoric*, p. 93.
25. *Ibid.*, p. 94.
26. *Ibid.*, pp. 96–97.
27. Daniel Fogarty, *Roots for a New Rhetoric* (New York: Russell and Russell, 1959), p. 38.

The following essay authored by Richards provides an excellent overview of the key concepts presently used in the fields of semantics and linguistics. These major terms—such as "code," "context," "message," and "referent"—have been employed elsewhere in this book. Since this article was published in 1972, it is a more mature statement of Richards' thinking and, as such, may have a slightly different slant than his earlier works quoted in the preceding analysis.

The Richards essay addresses several issues, but for our present purposes the reader should focus on the key linguistic concepts carefully delineated by the author. He approaches his subject creatively by examining a literary specimen written by Roman Jakobson. After reproducing Jakobson's original paragraphs, Richards offers an alternative wording—an Everyman's English version. He then proceeds to analyze the two under three headings: (1) the types of control under which choice is made, (2) the principles guiding comparings that are made, and (3) the discriminative process.

Throughout, Richards is concerned mainly with "the process of making out meanings."

After preliminary considerations, Richards examines the control factors or those things that ultimately decide the nature of the communicative act. For instance, corresponding emphases on the addresser, addressee, context, message, contact, or code will shape the communication in definite ways. In rewording the Jakobson paragraphs, Richards maintains that the addressee was the controlling factor in the development and end product of the Everyman's version. Richards notes that all six factors play a role in our utterances; some are compromised over others, but they all exert control.

Richards next examines the principles of comparings. He claims that the meaning of a particular utterance is in large measure determined by comparing it with possible alternatives of constructing the same utterance. So, the Everyman's version is compared to Jakobson's original—a process that helps provide meaning to both versions. Utterances, sentences, paragraphs, and larger language units attain meaning by comparisons—by direct or indirect examination of likenesses with differences. Richards views the process of composition as competition among alternative ways of uttering the same thing, that is, the process of comparing.

The final section of the essay considers the details of the discriminative process. Herein, Richards considers the means of metalingual elucidation: exposition (defining) and exemplification (providing instances). The terms "referent," "context," "code," "message," "signal," and the poetic function are discussed in some detail focusing on the role each plays in the meaning process.

Functions of and Factors in Language

I propose to examine minutely a famous formulation summarizing what language does and relating this systematically to the means through which language does it. Six basic functions are there cursorily described and a corresponding scheme of six fundamental factors is put forward. This clear and succinct account is that offered by Roman Jakobson in his concluding statement: "Linguistics and Poetics", closing the Conference on Style[1] held at Indiana University in Bloomington, April 17–19, 1958. The subject matter of the passage is clearly of central importance to literary semantics, amounting to a draught constitution for that study. It is condensed enough to justify and reward unusually close attention even at some cost in tedium.

The techniques tried out in this examination may also deserve explicit description and systematic exploration. This can set out from Jakobson's reminder[2] of Pierce's seemingly revolutionary doctrine of the *Interpretant:* "For us, both as linguists and as ordinary word-users, the meaning of any linguistic sign is its translation into some further, alternative sign, especially a sign 'in which it is more fully developed' as Pierce, the deepest inquirer into the essence of signs, insistently stated." Such translation into other signs of the same language, such RE-WORDING, to use Jakobson's label, will be the means here employed. The aim is to gain as deep, as wide, as full an awareness of WHAT WE ARE DOING as possible, as many-angled a set of views of that as we can. The three paragraphs we so consider were addressed to an audience composed of linguists, psychologists, literary critics, and theorists in literary criticism. Such diversity among their approaches may be expected to entail difference between their interpretations. And naturally the high compression of the account makes it, at first glance, seem to many readers somewhat cryptic. It thus poses a finely exacting challenge to sympathetic exploratory paraphrase, gloss and commentary.

We will be returning to Pierce's doctrine. But let us first give a preliminary reading to Jakobson's three paragraphs.

I will then offer a number of RE-WORDINGS (intra-lingual translations). I do so not in the least to suggest that Jakobson's sentences are in any need of change. Or of explanation, except in so far as any attempt to bring out the meanings of a discourse entails experimental change and comparison with possible alternative phrasing. My hope is to focus attention upon the process of making out meanings and thereby to raise the question: Are not procedures in this crucial activity capable of far more systematic development than has in general hitherto been attempted? As I weigh these various Re-Wordings I will take occasion to point out, as explicitly as I can (1) the types of control under which choice of the alternatives is being made; (2) the principles guiding the comparings that occur; (3) details of the discriminative process. The version[3] will be followed by a commentary organized under these three headings: 1. Control; 2. Principles; 3. Detail.

Language must be investigated in all the variety of its functions. Before discussing the poetic function we must define its place among the other functions of language. An outline of these functions demands a concise survey of the constitutive factors in any speech event, in any act of verbal communication. The ADDRESSER sends a MESSAGE to the ADDRESSEE. To be operative the message requires a CONTEXT referred to ("referent" in another, somewhat, ambiguous, nomenclature), seizable by the addressee, and either verbal or capable of being verbalized; a CODE fully, or at least partially, common to the addresser and addressee (or in other words, to the encoder and decoder of the message); and, finally, a CONTACT, a physical channel and psychological connection between the addresser and the addressee, enabling both of them to enter and stay in communication. All these factors in-

alienably involved in verbal communication may be schematized as follows:

CONTEXT

MESSAGE

ADDRESSER ——————— ADDRESSEE

CONTACT

CODE

Each of these six factors determines a different function of language. Although we distinguish six basic aspects of language, we could, however, hardly find verbal messages that would fulfill only one function. The diversity lies not in a monopoly of some one of these several functions but in a different hierarchical order of functions. The verbal structure of a message depends primarily on the predominant function. But even though a set *(Einstellung)* toward the referent, an orientation toward the CONTEXT—briefly the so-called REFERENTIAL, "denotative", "cognitive" function—is the leading task of numerous messages, the accessory participation of the other functions in such messages must be taken into account by the observant linguist.

(After four intervening pages)

Now that our cursory description of the six basic functions of verbal communication is more or less complete, we may complement our scheme of the fundamental factors by a corresponding scheme of the functions:

REFERENTIAL

EMOTIVE POETIC CONATIVE

PHATIC

METALINGUAL

RE-WORDED VERSION

Language has many different things to do. Before going into 'poetic' work we must say what place this has among the other sorts of work it does. We need a short, over-all account of the conditions which come together whenever anything is said. There must be:

1. an **Addresser** (someone directing, sending)
2. a **Message** (what is sent) to

3. an **Addressee** (person or persons to whom the message is sent).

For this to work out there must be:

4. a **Context** (something the addresser is thinking of, talking about; which the addressee can think of, more or less, as the addresser does)

5. a **Code** (system of sounds, marks, related to parts that can make up messages) and this must be fully or in part the same for 1 and 2

6. a **Contact** (physical and mental conditions which let 1 and 2 come into and keep in communication.)

```
                CONTEXT
                MESSAGE
ADDRESSER  _____  ADDRESSEE
                CONTACT
                 CODE
```

Each of these six conditions has chiefly to do with a different sort of work that language does. Though there are these separate angles from which we can look into language, few if any messages do only one sort of work. Language can do different things not through each side having only one sort of undertaking but through different organizations in which the sides may control or be controlled by one another. The structure (make-up) of a message depends, firstly, on the chief thing it is doing. It is true that, for many messages, their most important work is to represent the context; even so, the other things they may be doing must be noted by anyone wishing to see what is going on.

(After four intervening pages)

Having given a short outline of the six sorts of work language does, we may add a parallel picture of these:

```
               REFERENTIAL
EMOTIVE        POETIC        CONATIVE
               PHATIC
               METALINGUAL
```

Commentary

1. Control

The character of this version, it will be evident,[4] has been governed by a wish to make its message simple, non-technical and accessible to readers unaccustomed to learned language. In view of the importance for all users of language of what Jakobson's summary has to say, some study of how such things can be said so as to be maximally intelligible to all interested persons, no matter what their scholarly training and experience may be, should need no apology. As will be seen below, alternative versions of Jakobson's sentences can be given that are more penetrating, illuminative, and precise than these in Everyman's English. But most of those—for the ADDRESSEES that this version has in view—would hardly be more readily comprehensible to them than the original. One of the most fundamental axioms or assumptions ('constitutive factors',[5] if you like) of literary semantics is here being illustrated. For any 'speech event or act of communication' the character and resources of the Addressee(s) is plainly of first order importance.[6] Most Addressers will of course feel divided loyalties: all the six factors have their claims, and rivalry and conflict often arise. Fidelity to the Context (a dual term always, covering both what-is-talked-of and what-is-being-said-about-it); to the Contact (Let us not lose the Addressee's attention; may we be audible or legible!); to the Message itself (Let us not say too much or too little); to the Code (due respect for the dictionary, for usage, for linguistic decorum, for keeping verbal resources up); and to the Addresser too (concern for his proper interests and/or image): all six, in degrees varying with the situation and occasion, have to be satisfied. Between them, and through clever compromises, they CONTROL the how of our utterances.

I will juxtapose here for convenience in comparing Jakobson's two depictions and my own yantra—a diagram cross-section of a type-specimen Message. For two related explanations of it, see *Speculative Instruments,* "Toward a Theory of Comprehending" and *Poetries and Sciences,* "How does a Poem know when it is finished?", p. 110.

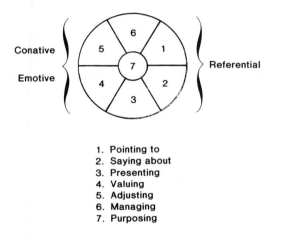

1. Pointing to
2. Saying about
3. Presenting
4. Valuing
5. Adjusting
6. Managing
7. Purposing

The centrality of 7 is important: 1, 2, 3, 4, 5, 6 are its means. So too with the work of 6—controlling the often conflicting endeavors of 1, 2, 3, 4, 5. Activity 3 has to do with realizing or not what the utterance is doing.

2. Principles of our comparings

Plainly enough, bookfuls might be poured out under this heading. The mention of compromises met above points to a leading Section. No living sentence can do all that it might have done. Something has been given up for something in its framing. (Sentences within Logic, Mathematics, purely expository Physics . . . etc. are exceptions. Perhaps we should not call them living? Their Addressees are ideal recipients, qualified by specifiable ability and training.) The comparing of any feature with any possible alternative proposed for it is a weighing of gains and losses.

We can go further. Whether it is already selected or merely considered for selection, what any feature in any utterance is (or can do) comes to it from its relations to the possible alternates. It is what is is (can do what it can do) by NOT being any of a number of other possibles. This principle rules throughout—from minimal 'distinctive features'[7] on up through all the varieties and hierarchies of linguistic units—up to paragraphs and chapters in discourse.[8] Comparing is taking account of, or participating in, this oppositional texture of being. Wittingly or unwittingly, we select in all that happens in and to us. The degree in which we may be said TO SELECT actively or to be, screen-wise, passively selective, varies and there are frequently cases in which what we are consciously trying to do differs greatly from what is brought about. In any case selection entails likeness-with-difference in what is present when we choose one course rather than some rival. COMPOSITION indeed is competition.[9] What is chosen pushes past the other competitors, as being more compatible, more consonant, with what has gone before, with what is, at the moment, directive, and with what is divined as being likeliest to come. In brief, composition is purposive, it is seeking what will suit later developments (as it tries to foresee them) as well as paying for promises entered upon by what it has already done.

All this is, of course, deeply familiar to us all. What we want *x* FOR determines which *x* we use—in any course of action in which we are alert enough, vigilant enough, awake enough, for USE and CHOOSE to become equivalents. The rest is habit, the acquired mechanical, a conserving, though sometimes potentially disastrous, legacy from past choices. This is true universally in behavior. Not surprisingly it rules most evidently in verbal composition—the most typically purposeful of our activities.

Whenever two or more candidates for selection are being compared our consideration of any one of the influences and is influenced by our considerings of the others. At every point, for example, my Everyman's Version seems simpler, and more obvious and less ambiguous, than it otherwise would, BECAUSE IT IS BEING COMPARED WITH JAKOBSON'S SENTENCES. It takes from them a continuous stream of decisions through an inter-related sequence of choice-points. It is being guided (its readers too) by Jakobson's original decisions. And they, too, I hope and believe, will seem in the comparison more lucid, more penetrable, kinder to the teeth, than they would alone. They convey more and penetrate further—unless I am mistaken. But I have to remember as I write this that I have just been through the elaborate process of composing an Everyman's Version (EV), involving me in multiple comparings of Jakobson's phrasing with a wide variety of candidates for substitution. In fact, I have been reading him with an unusual degree of attention and weighing against one another several ways of taking him—imagining too, as fully as I can, YOUR possible re-weighings, my Addressees, who will of course include here Jakobson himself, and what sort of a showing as a reader I may be making. These comparings, if reported explicitly enough, entail a good deal of showing up of the reader. Among the principles guiding comparings may be proposed, as highly desirable, constant assistance from a modicum of reflective doubt.

3. *Details of the discriminative process*

The six words selected by Jakobson as names for his six factors, for which the rest of the passage is serving as explication, mark the cardinal points (the pivots or hinges) on which the account turns. On how selectively (choosily) we take these six our understanding of it depends. They are, together with 'FUNCTION' and 'FACTOR' themselves, being 'technicalized' (fixed as to their senses) in this passage—and in the four brilliant pages of explanation and exemplification developed between the two diagrammatic schemes. This process of technicalization by which these terms are related to one another and the two

schemes put into parallel order repays further exploration and description. We could hardly find a better example, or type-specimen, showing how systematic treatment is made possible.

The six names of the factors and the six names of the functions are retained in my Everyman's Version, though FUNCTION and FACTOR are replaced by substitute phrases. The Metalingual purpose ('pre-dominant function') of the passage requires this. What it is primarily doing is ˢʷ'telling us how'ˢʷ [10] these words are here being, and will hereafter be, used. That we should know this is essential if what will be said with their aid in ensuing paragraphs is to be rightly understood. Let us see here all we can of how this 'telling us how' is done.

There are two main means of metalingual elucidation: exposition and exemplification. We can either offer the Addressee DEFINITIONS or place before him INSTANCES of what we are referring to, chosen as especially revealing the characteristics we want him to note. Both these, we may note, are predominantly conative in function. Our definitions will usually look like statements of fact made in the indicative mood. But 'essentially'[11] they are disguised imperatives or prayers or optatives: commands, or hope-generated invitations to the Addressee to behave with the terms in certain ways rather than in others.[12]

As usual here, this 'essentially' is as much a reinforcement of the conative intent of the sentences as it is a furthering of the referential task: to describe, that is, what we 'really'[13] do in definitions. This 'essentially' is, it is to be noted, an illustration of our second mode of metalingual clarification. To use Pierce's terms it is a token of that TYPE of procedure. And, while we are thinking of Pierce, we may pause to consider further the 'it' in Jakobson's quotation from him with which we began.

Not only may any 'further, alternative sign' into which a sign may be translated be 'more developed' (or less developed: to enlarge the field of Addressees, the signs used in the Everyman's Version are on the whole LESS developed than those in Jakobson's original) but they may be developed in different directions to bring out different possibilities, (potentials) in the meaning. Corresponding to Jakobson's two parallel schemes, six such potentials or vectors may be proposed. An alternative sign may affect.

(1) The Addresser-Emotive component (Factor-Function) that is, it may make the utterer's concern clearer or less clear, more noticeable or less.

(2) The Addressee-Conative component. That is, it may make what is being attempted through the utterance more evident or less.

(3) The Context-Referential component. That is, it may make what is being spoken OF and what is said ABOUT it more ʳseizableʳ or less.

(4) The Code-Metalingual component. That is, it may show better or worse (by its explications or through its example) how terms are being used.

(5) The Contact-Phatic component. That is, it may bring and keep the parties in touch more successfully or less. (ʳInsistenceʳ, incidentally, often switches the Addressee off. Pierce might have had more students earlier if he had not tried so hard to gain and hold them.)

(6) The Message-Poetic component, with which we come to the chief point that Jakobson has it at heart and in mind to make: the point to prepare for and frame which he has drawn this outline of the other factors and functions. It is also the point which Addressees in general may be least likely to take in without confusions.

To guard against these, some further attempts to provide alternative signs, ʳrewordingsʳ, developing especially the Context-Referential and the Code-Metalingual components will be in place. Jakobson rightly remarks that the nomenclature of "referent" is ʳsomewhat ambiguousʳ. It is. But so too is that of "context" and that of "code" and those of "message" and of "meaning" themselves. These are topics for which it often seems that any terms which may be introduced to deal with them become quickly infected with ambiguity whatever precautions are taken. And

of these topics, that which we approach through this cluster of related verbal signs has some claim to be rated the most virulent of all promoters of confusion. It is as though the **signata** themselves here are especially corruptive—an impression perhaps due to their being so ʳinalienably involvedʳ in whatever attempts we may make to order them.

Some of the sources of these ambiguities are not hard to point out. The difficulty rather is to keep and protect in our usage the distinction we have observed: "Observe the 'No Smoking' Sign!" This is a case where knowledge is not necessarily virtue. Noting an injunction and doing accordingly need not be the same thing. To take these terms in turn: ʳREFERENTʳ: "that which is being thought of, spoken about, that on which truth tests depend". Such a definition looks straight enough—until we observe that 'referent', so defined, is dual: both a bare denotation (extension AND the character being ascribed to it. The truth test takes account of both. Has the referent in fact the character ascribed? That is the question. Two translations arise: Is the ʳreferentʳ what would be, were it as the statement represents it as being? Or is it what would make that representation true, if true, and false, if false? The trouble can be detected **within,** I believe, every attempt either to give some account of it or to account for it.

Context links this trouble with at least two others. Any attempt to describe how we come to know anything through experience, become able to refer to it, think of it, talk of it, point to it, etc., has somehow to connect present thinkings of, pointings to, etc., with past originative occasions. Through one nomenclature or another it has to take account of recurrence. Perhaps I may best recur to a past attempt of my own to deal with a chief ambiguity.

A word, like any other sign, gets whatever meaning it has through belonging to a recurrent group of events, which may be called its context. Thus a word's context, *in this sense,* is a certain recurrent pattern of *past* groups of events, and to say that its meaning depends upon its context would be to point to the process by which it has acquired its meaning.

In another, though a connected, sense, a word's context is *the words which surround it in the utterance,* and the *other contemporaneous* signs which govern its interpretation

Both senses of 'context' need to be kept in mind if we are to consider carefully how interpretations succeed or fail. For clarity we may distinguish the second sort of context by calling it the *setting.* It is evident that a change in the setting may change the context (in the first sense) in which a word is taken. We never, in fact, interpret single signs in isolation. (The etymological hint given by *inter* is very relevant here.) We always take a sign as being *in some setting,* actual or supplied, as part of an interconnected sign-field (normally, with verbal signs, a sentence and an occasion). Thus, insufficient attention to the accompanying signfield (the setting and occasion) which controls the context (recurrent groups of events in the past) is a frequent cause of mistaken understanding. But equally, no care, however great, in observing the setting will secure good interpretation if past experience has not provided the required originative context.

(Preface to *Interpretation in Teaching,*
London, 1937, p. viii.)

For further details I must refer to *The Meaning of Meaning* (1923), more specifically to Appendix B, "On Contexts", in that volume: a formulation in which Frank Ramsey, when still a boy at Winchester, took an active part.

Two other ingredients should be noticed in considering how CONTEXT has acquired its present equivocal role in semantics.[14] O.E.D enters: "Concretely, the parts which immediately precede or follow any particular passage or text and determine its meaning" (cf. 'setting' above), adding that there are transferred and figurative uses. It is one of these to which Malinowski gave extended currency in his Supplement to *The Meaning of Meaning:* by

introducing *"context of situation,* if I may be allowed to coin an expression which indicates on the one hand that the conception of *context* has to be broadened and on the other that the *situation* in which words are uttered can never be passed over as irrelevant" (p. 360). He followed this up, two pages later, with "It is obvious that the *context of situation,* on which such a stress is laid here, is nothing else but the *sign-situation* of the Authors". They, however, were not so sure of that, and would rather stress the metaphor of weaving behind the word. The immediate situation within which the utterance occurs is principally important because through this the required linkages with past experience are activated. It is these linkages which weave into one vast web all the illimitable possibilities we cover so calmly with the word 'meaning'. The contexture which structures this web is not one of events or objects (except in very special senses[15]). It is a knitting together of what Pierce christened TYPES, instances of which are what he called TOKENS. He takes this nomenclature from the printed page.

There will ordinarily be about twenty 'the's' on a page, and, of course, they count as twenty words. In another sense of the word 'word,' however, there is but one word 'the' in the English language; and it is impossible that this word should lie visibly on a page, or be heard in any voice, for the reason that it is not a Single thing or Single event. It does not exist; it only determines things that do exist. Such a definitely significant Form I propose to call a *Type . . .* this or that word on a single line of a single page of a single copy of a book, I will venture to call a *Token.*

For our present purpose, the taking account of some ambiguities of the word **context,** what is most needed is a sustained act of realizing imagination of the extent and degree to which words as **types** are interconnected. It is not hyperbolic but literally the case that every word we can use is related, either directly or mediately, through one or other chain of links, with every other word in our vocabulary, and potentially every occasion in our past of passive and active use of any word, as Addressee or Addresser, can enter into the guiding contexts of present and future use. Ordinarily there need be little or no awareness of these influences, though occasionally the normal veil is in part, for a moment, lifted. It should be added further that these connexities are far from fixed and static. Later experience can shift them, it may develop them or impair and seemingly obliterate them. Typically, as we learn more about a matter or come to think differently of it, our contexts, the references we make, are changed. And since any Message is what it is thanks (in part and among the other factors) to its Context, we should not be surprised if Messages are inherently hard to identify and if communications are normally defective. Full and complete reproduction at the destination of what was selected at the source is no more than an ideal, a mathematical fiction. We don't expect to meet in this life points or straight lines or circles. No more should we hope for perfect understanding. The wonder is that Messages are so often conveyed so well.

The term **Message** too has its troubles. Chief among them is confusion with the Signal. A Message is a Meaning selected from the limitless possible field through (among other factors) the operation of a subsystem of references, its Context. It is conveyed (more or less) by use of a Signal. This, we should realize, is an entity of quite another order of being. In speech, the Signal consists of sounds and pauses; in writing it is made up of marks on a ground. These are physical events. For good reasons they are among the most fully and exactly observable events that can be found. That is why they are so useful in communication. With suitable apparatus, high enough magnification, sensitive enough recording, we can carry the identification process further with them than any need can call for. The contrast with Messages could hardly be stronger. This Essay has been one long attempt, far from successful I fear, to help in the identification of some fourteen central meanings of linguistics. Few literates with normal sight, facing a properly printed sentence, are uncertain whether they are reading **Contact** or **Context**: the differences between them can be

described as precisely as we please. Who, however normal his intelligence, will be quite certain where **Contact Ends and Context Takes Over,** or whether this emphasized word-group makes any sense, or how to settle such a question? None the less, as we shall shortly see, we have to try.

On the cover of the paperback edition of the second printing, 1965, of *Psycholinguistics,* edited by Charles E. Osgood and Thomas A. Sebeok (Indiana University Press), appears the middle part of that word —*ycholinguist*—out of focus and eye-strainingly distorted. I take it that the designer of the cover had been reading the opening pages and was making a valid and witty comment on the outcome. For there, in the course of defining the subject, message and signal are as openly and as thoroughly confused as could be. On page 2, after mentioning "at least two communicating units, a **Source Unit** (speaker) and a **Destination Unit** (hearer)" the authors continue:

Between any two such units, connecting them into a single system, is what we may call the *message.* For purposes of this report, we will define message as that part of the total output (responses) of a source unit which simultaneously may be a part of the total input (stimuli) to a destination unit. When individual A talks to individual B, for example, his postures, gestures, facial expressions and even manipulations with objects (e.g., laying down a playing card, pushing a bowl of food within reach) may all be part of the message, as of course are events in the sound wave channel.

and on the opposite page, as explicitly, an identification of the two is attempted.

Microlinguistics (or linguistics proper) deals with the structure of messages, the signals in the channel connecting communicators, as events independent of the characteristics of either speakers or hearers. Once messages have been encoded and are "on the air", so to speak, they can be described as objective, natural science events in their own right. In an even stricter sense, the linguist is concerned with determining the *code* of a given signal system, the sets of distinctions which are significant in differentiating alternative messages.

Turning the page over, we find "Psycholinguistics is that one of the disciplines studying human communication which is most directly concerned with the processes of decoding and encoding".

This is surely very odd behavior, probably best accounted for by what is said in the closing paragraph of the preface:

The actual thought and discussion of each topic was so thoroughly shared within the seminar that it would be difficult if not impossible to properly assign either credit or responsibility as the case might be. Therefore, we wish the reader to view this report as truly a joint product. We also hope the reader will keep in mind that this represents the result of only eight weeks' work. It is an exploratory survey of an interdisciplinary area, not a scholarly exposition of well-mapped territory.

Can one help being reminded of the definition of a platypus as an animal designed by a committee? I must return however to contexts and contacts. The chief thing we have to do is to unscramble them and keep them, if we can, unscrambled. It is not easy. The topic strongly invites, indeed tempts, us to mix them up.

Messages are generated by Contexts; they are conveyed by signals. Messages are living. They are animated instances of meaning, determinations from the context field; the signals which convey them are dead. My thinking, doubting, wondering at this moment is living activity; so is the nerve-muscle-joint process guiding my pen as I compose my Message. But the motions of the pen itself are inanimate, as are the configurations its point is tracing on the paper, the signals. The typist, the printer, the library, etc. put the page before you. As you read the inanimate lines of print, a living activity of thinking, doubting, wondering . . . despairing perhaps . . . arises in you. That is the Message coming into being again. It was not in the pen or on the page. So too with a speaker: ʼhis postures, gestures, facial expressionsʼ, actions and the rest, together with what

his voice does ʼin the sound wave channelʼ . . . anything that videotape can take down: all that is signal, merely. Not until it is interpreted by some living recipient does anything that should be called the Message appear. It is essential to a Message that what forms in the Addressee (or other recipient) should be of the same order of being with what has formed in the Addresser. He may get it all wrong (and often does) but there is an IT. The two apparitions are both meanings. But a sound track and a system of meanings are not things of a sort, able to agree or disagree. The distinction between Message and signal (Context and physical channel) is indeed a *pons asinorum* in linguistics. This point is discussed at length in my essay "The Future of Poetry", first printed as Appendix to *The Screens* and later included in *So Much Nearer*.

I have lingered and labored with this point because Jakobson's central terms in his two schemes: MESSAGE and POETIC, and the correspondence between them he points out, are the heart of the passage we are examining. His own formulation (on page 356) is:

We have brought up all the six factors involved in verbal communication except the message itself. The set *(Einstellung)* toward the message as such, focus on the message for its own sake, is the POETIC function of language. This function cannot be productively studied out of touch with the general problems of language, and, on the other hand, the scrutiny of language requires a thorough consideration of its poetic function. Any attempt to reduce the sphere of poetic function to poetry or to confine poetry to poetic function would be a delusive oversimplification. Poetic function is not the sole function of *verbal art* but only its dominant, determining function, whereas in all other verbal activities it sets as a subsidiary, accessory constituent. This function, by promoting the palpability of signs, deepens the fundamental dichotomy of signs and objects. Hence, when dealing with poetic function, linguistics cannot limit itself to the field of poetry.

The key phrase here is ʼverbal artʼ (they are my italics). A ʼmore developedʼ translation and analysis of this paragraph would nearly double the length of this essay. Even the sentence in which 'verbal art' occurs invites many pages. However, we may here postpone explication and be content with exemplification, with one of Jakobson's most gem-like and compelling illustrations:

The political slogan "I like Ike" /ay layk ayk/, succinctly structured, consists of three monosyllables and counts three diphthongs /ay/, each of them symmetrically followed by one consonantal phoneme / . . .l. . .k. . .k/. . . . Both cola of the trisyllabic formula "I like/Ike" rhyme with each other, and the second of the two rhyming words is fully included in the first one (echo rhyme), /layk/-/ayk/, a paronomastic image of a feeling which totally envelops its object. Both cola alliterate with each other, and the first of the two alliterating words is included in the second: /ay/ /ayk/, a paronomastic image of the loving subject enveloped by the beloved object. The secondary, poetic function of this electional catch phrase reinforces its impressiveness and efficacy.

In conclusion, may I point to the impressiveness and efficacy of the work done by the Poetic function in his two schemes themselves, and in their coordination. They constitute paronomastic images of communication: their symmetries, horizontal and vertical, are, to use one of his favorite expressions, particularly palpable: **context-contact-code** (the alliteration framing the **message**); **emotive-conative** (their rime hinting at how the first prepares for the second); **referential-metalingual** (the outer rime framing again the central function). POETIC (the 'dominant determining function of verbal art') having its own rime with **phatic**; the means, up through all levels, from "Hullo!" to *Hamlet,* to the **contact**, the meeting of minds, which is the least alienable condition of all that language may attempt to do. Can we find a better example of verbal art in the **poetic** function helping us more unexpectedly?

Magdalene College, Cambridge

Notes

1. Reported in *Style in Language,* edited by Thomas A. Sebeok (New York and London, Technology Press of M.I.T. and John Wiley and Sons Inc., 1960). See pages 353–358.
2. "On Linguistic Aspects of Translation" in *On Translation,* Reuben A. Brower (ed.), pp. 232–3.
3. As John Hollander perceptively remarks, "It is usually assumed from the start that, keeping an original text in mind, there is going to be *something* queer about a version of it, whether a French version, or a shortened one, or a version leaning strongly toward the views of Professor von Braun, or even a garbled version". "Versions, Interpretations, Performances", in *On Translation,* Reuben A. Brower (ed.), p. 221.
4. Those familiar with the literature of language-control will recognize that it is written in a limited English (Everyman's) deriving from Basic English, keeping to the Basic English Word List (except for a very few additions, of which CAN and MUST are typical) but using selected verbs appearing as nouns (or within them) on that List.
5. 'r . . .r' A specialized quotation mark meaning "Refer to a passage in which word or phrase has above appeared". Here the reference is to line 4 of the Jakobson excerpt. Specific directives can evidently be added to the *r* mark.
6. Others than the Addressees may be also concerned. The bystander, the possible critic, the detached observer frequently, and rightly, can take part in the shaping of the utterance.
7. '. . .' A specialized quotation mark meaning: "the expression is a technical term and as such is anchored to definitions and specimens which should strictly limit how it is used". See Jacobson and Halle, *Fundamentals of Language* (Mouton, 1956), p. 59.
8. See Jakobson and Halle, *Fundamentals of Language,* p. 60. "Any linguistic sign involves two modes of arrangement. (1) Combination. Any sign is made up of constituent signs and/or occurs only in combination with other signs. This means that any linguistic unit at one and the same time serves as a context for simpler units and/or finds its own context in a more complex linguistic unit. Hence any actual grouping of linguistic units binds them into a superior unit; combination and contexture are two faces of the same operation. (2) Selection. A selection between alternatives implies the possibility of substituting one for the other, equivalent to the former in one respect and different from it in another. Actually, selection and substitution are two faces of the same operation." CONTEXT here has a different use from CONTEXT (p. 26) above. The two are distinguished below (p. 34).
9. I have twice recently found myself to have written COMPETITION in place of COMPOSITION (ETI for OSI).
10. ᶳᵂ. . .ˢᵂ. Specialized quotation marks meaning that what may be said with the word or phrase (*step warily*) is not necessarily as we will ordinarily take it.
11. '. . .' Specialized quotation mark meaning that the enclosed term needs metalingual questioning.

12. For a fuller discussion of this position, see my *Interpretation in Teaching.*
13. Shrieks suggesting that such use of the words may be absurd (a jointly emotive and conative gesture). We may indeed fairly question (so I read the last sentence of Jakobson's second paragraph) whether, with many sentences, two or more functions may not rightly be considered to be co-equally in control.
14. A third may well be a doubt whether Emotive and Conative functions are not mediated as fully through Contexts as the Referential. See Jakobson's discussion on page 354 of *Style in Language* and his comment there on "Saporta's surmise". We would however still have to find a means of distinguishing Referential

from Emotive and Conative components in a message.
15. Two of these are Pierce's *Immediate Object* and *Dynamical Object* which correspond to the two senses of 'referent' touched on above. "We have to distinguish the *Immediate Object,* which is the object as the Sign itself represents it . . . from the Dynamical Object, which is the Reality which by some means contrives to determine the Sign to its Representation". (From "Prologomena to an Apology for Pragmaticism", *Monist,* 1906, quoted in Appendix D of *The Meaning of Meaning,* p. 280, where the passage from the same article on the type-token distinction will also be found.)

The Significant Symbol

The works of I. A. Richards, especially the volume on *The Meaning of Meaning,* stimulated considerable interest in the study of the nature of symbols and how they may be used to generate meaning and produce action. Soon numerous authors, from a wide variety of disciplines and orientations, began to build upon the theories of Richards. Of particular relevance to us here are the ideas developed by George Herbert Mead and his student Charles Morris regarding "significant symbols."

What Mead has in mind in using the term "significant symbol," was a communicator's use of signs for the purpose of arousing meaning in himself at the same time it occurs in another. "The significant symbol," he said, "is the gesture, the sign, the word which is addressed to the self. . . ."[1] Mead put it more graphically when he observed: "A person who is saying something is saying to himself what he says to others; otherwise he does not know what he is talking about. . . ."[2] Any communication which occurs that does not lead to a shared meaning between the speaker and the listener falls short of significance.

In addition to enabling a speaker to convey an intended meaning to himself as well as to one or more other listeners in a specific situation, "significant symbols" are a means by which a universe of discourse is established. Drawing upon the logicians, Mead gives the following definition of this phenomenon:

A universe of discourse is always implied as the context in terms of which, or as the field within which, significant gestures or symbols do in fact have significance. The universe of discourse is constituted by a group of individuals carrying on and participating in a common process of experience and behavior, within which these gestures or symbols have the same or common meanings for all members of that group. . . . A universe of discourse is simply a system of common or social meanings.[3]

The effect of the creation of a universe of discourse on socialization and the democratic process as a whole is clear. For the very existence and preservation of a society are fully dependent upon the capacity of the members of that group to employ "significant symbols."[4]

Morris, whose behavioral approach owes much to Mead's philosophy of the act, ably summarizes his colleague's interpretation of "significant symbols."

For Mead, it is characteristic of the human being that he can react to his own (or some of his) actions as other human beings will react. . . . Mead calls these symbols to which their producer is disposed to react like their receiver 'significant symbols.' He equates mind with the operation of such symbols. Mentality is thus for him a kind of behavior or disposition to behavior. . . . This capacity to respond by significant symbols is an intelligible basis for the analysis of the term 'freedom' and for the conception of man as a moral agent. Mead thus brings within his behavioral analysis what the traditional behaviorist ignores or denies or what the more complicated behaviorism of the present is still seeking after—a psychology equated to the full person.[5]

What is the procedure, we may next ask, that should be employed in order to produce "significant symbols?" This query may be answered in part by turning to the advice which Hugh Blair gave to prospective ministers two centuries ago. Observe how Blair anticipated Mead in his lecture on the "Eloquence of the Pulpit:"

In studying a sermon he (the preacher) ought to place himself in the situation of a serious hearer. Let him suppose the subject addressed to himself; let him consider what views of it would strike him most; what arguments would be most likely to persuade him; what parts of it would dwell most upon his mind. Let these be employed as his principal materials; and in these, it is most likely his genius will exert itself with the greatest vigour. . . .[6]

To approach from a different but related angle the question of formulating a method to develop "significant symbols," we may use a hypothetical illustration involving Blair's city of Edinburgh. Let us assume, for example, that you are a Scottish native standing on the corner of Princes Street and Waverly Bridge and an American tourist approaches you to ask: "Could you please tell me how to get to the Church of St. Giles?" Immediately you turn to the south and point to a large steeple several blocks away. You then tell the tourist to cross Waverly Bridge and continue south until he reaches a series of steep outdoor steps. You then instruct him to climb the steps, several hundred in number, and proceed through a close at the top which leads to the famous Royal Mile. The Church of St. Giles, you conclude, stands several hundred yards to the left on the right side of the block. What is required in this rhetorical transaction if a "significant symbol" is to be used is a need for the speaker to place himself in the perspective of the tourist and to respond to the signs he generates from the perspective. The communicator thus

also functions as one of the communicatees as he hears the combination of signs that sets forth the directions. "In the process of communication," Mead observes, "the individual is an other before he is a self. It is in addressing himself in the role of the other that his self arises in experience."[7]

The most far reaching implication of the notion of the "significant symbol," apart from its power to reduce misunderstandings, is the effect it has on the concept of audience. Many scholars have held that a person cannot persuade himself; nor can he be a part of the audience he is addressing. An attempt to persuade one's self, it is pointed out, is nothing more than an ideational process which does not qualify as communication. To embrace the idea of "significant symbols," however, is to argue that a communicator, by regarding himself as a candidate for action, experiences the meaning and alteration in behavior that his message, or sign usage, is intended to convey. This fact is convincing testimony of the shortcomings associated with the practice of ghostwriting techniques which permit a speaker to mouth, almost mechanically, the words of others. For whenever the encoder is not the source of the message being articulated, the signs he uses may not be achieving significance.

Speech Acts

The concept of "meaning" also has been studied by a unique group of scholars who focus not on individual words or significant symbols, but rather on the *acts* of speaking. Among those who have turned their attention to this theme are J. L. Austin, John Searle, Karl Wallace, and Douglas Ehninger.

Austin's provocative book *How to Do Things with Words*[8] is an excellent starting point to get at the notion of speech acts. He begins his analysis with a challenge to the traditional view that a statement is always an utterance which describes or reports, meets the requirements of a fact, and conforms to the criteria of truth and falsity. In many instances, he argues, words are used not for the purpose merely of "saying something" but for "the performing of an action." Consider the following examples:

1. " 'I do' (sc. take this woman to be my lawful wedded wife)—as uttered in the course of the marriage ceremony."
2. " 'I name this ship the Queen Elizabeth'—as uttered when smashing the bottle against the stern."
3. " 'I give and bequeath my watch to my brother'—as occurring in a will."
4. " 'I bet you a sixpence it will rain tomorrow.' "[9]

What is important in each of these utterances is not the question of fact or truth, but the performance of an act. The words, in short, become speech acts because they "do things." In developing this idea, Austin perceptively notes that if a marriage vow, the christening of an object, the bequeathing of a gift, or the making of a bet fails in any vital respect, the utterance should not be labeled false. Instead it should be characterized as "unhappy." On this point he observes: ". . . we call the doctrine of *the things that can be and go wrong* on the occasion of such utterances, the doctrine of the *Infelicities.*"[10]

Frequently these "infelicities" are caused by a violation of the ensuing speech act rule developed by Austin: "There must exist an accepted conventional procedure having a certain conventional effect, the procedure to include the uttering of certain words by certain persons in certain circumstances."[11] In assessing the importance of the rhetorical situation in which symbols are used, Austin allies himself, at least partially, with the contextual theory of meaning emphasized by Richards.

There are numerous implications of Austin's theory for students of communication. Not the least of these are the following three inferences which Rosenfield feels can be drawn from Austin's "performative conception of utterance as tactical behavior:"

For one, utterance, rather than linguistic units such as the word or sentence, comprises the minimal tactical unit of analysis.

For another, an utterance differs from a simple statement in that it needn't describe or report; it is not pertinent to assess its truth value. Thirdly, the utterance may itself be the totality of the social act.[12]

Expressing similar views to those of Austin, Searle begins his discussion of the speech act with remarks about language, claiming that "speaking a language is engaging in a rule-governed form of behavior."[13] In other words, "Talking is performing acts according to rules."[14] Searle elaborates:

Speaking a language is performing speech acts, acts such as making statements, giving commands, asking questions, making promises, and so on; and more abstractly, acts such as referring and predicting; and, secondly, that these acts are in general made possible by and are performed in accordance with certain rules for the use of linguistic elements.[15]

Thus, the appropriate study of meaning must focus not on words or symbols alone, but must consider the act of speech—which includes words, sentences, rules, and contexts. Regarding this idea, Searle observes: "The unit of linguistic communication is not, as has generally been supposed, the symbol, word or sentence . . . but rather the production or issuance of the symbol or word or sentence in the performance of the speech act."[16]

Wallace also considered the speech act as the appropriate unit of study for the communication scholar. Echoing the views of Searle, Wallace stressed that meaning is found/created by the *act*, not the word. He gives the following explanation:

The emphasis here is upon *unit* or a *whole.* It is an event having terminals. Part of it is internal to the speaker and is accessible to sense; part of it is external and is available to ear and eye. This fact makes the event impossible to describe unless we regard it as an act. . . . What grammarian, logician, linguistician, and psycholinguist study are the last stages of a creative act. What the poet and rhetorician try to do, aided by students of language behavior, is to understand all stages of a creative act.[17]

Consequently, meaning is revealed in the act itself. "To see this is to see that the symbolic features of utterance do not lie in words alone."[18] Continuing, Wallace states: "What we call meaning thus seems to arise from, or be a function of, the entire field of experience that is brought into play by a communication context. . . . It is implicit in every stage of utterance and becomes explicit upon the completion of utterance."[19]

Those who, like Austin, Searle, and Wallace, hold that meaning resides in the act of utterance, further suggest that words or sentences—even paragraphs—are not the proper unit for investigation (unless, of course, they are in themselves acts of utterance). Rather, the speech act—with its underlying assumptions and rules—is the generator of meaning. In brief, this perspective provides the bridge from the rhetorical to the interpersonal.

Along with Wallace, the scholar who has made the most useful attempt to relate speech act theory to rhetoric, we feel, is Douglas Ehninger. In his former seminar course on this subject at the University of Iowa and in his unpublished paper entitled, "Toward a Taxonomy of Prescriptive Discourse," Ehninger examined several speech acts and the corresponding conditions which define each action. Such an examination is essential, said Ehninger, if the rhetorician intends to formulate meaningful theory. We will briefly summarize a few of the speech acts which are considered in the Ehninger study.

To begin, Ehninger claims that instructing is that form of discourse that tells someone *how* to do something. For example, the instructions telling you how to assemble your new charcoal grill are representative of instructive discourse—discourse aimed at a defined goal. It becomes a means, then, of accomplishing that goal or desired end. A major characteristic is that the receiver (who wishes to attain some goal) lacks certain expertise and so needs instruction of how to do so. Thus, instructing is

a "means" rather than a goal-oriented act.[20] The assumptions accompanying the act include: (a) the listener *contracts* in advance to *perform as directed,* and (b) if he performs as directed, he will reach the defined and established goal.

A second speech act is advising or *telling* someone that he *ought* seriously to *consider* doing something. Such an act requires a unique rhetorical stance wherein the speaker must take a "superior" posture in relation to the listener. By definition, the proclamation of "ought" statements necessitates "special knowledge" in the form of advice. Subsequently, possession of "special knowledge" brings a moral obligation to the speech act of advising which is not found in instructing. The speaker, then, risks his name and reputation in the act of advising and must keep the best interests of the listener in mind at all times.

A further dimension of advising is the free choice assumption. In other words, the listener is free to decide whether to accept or reject the message. Obviously, the act of instructing does not possess such a latitude of freedom because the hearer *must* follow the instructions (and carefully) if he is to reach his goal.

During the speech act of arguing, the speaker aims at *providing reasons* which justify why the listener should *reconsider* the correctness of something he is doing, plans to do, or believes in.[21] Several assumptions define this speech act. First, arguing assumes that the listener is mistaken or wrong about something and needs to be corrected. Second, the speaker is obligated to provide reasons for the listener. This obligation is absent in instructing and advising. Thirdly, whereas advising is directed only to something a listener is doing, arguing may be directed to beliefs as well as actions. Finally, the speech act of arguing is generally initiated by the speaker. In advising, the transaction is initiated by the listener.

The speech act of arguing propounds reasons for reconsidering a belief or behavior. The act of persuading, on the other hand, is to "cause a hearer to *decide* to behave or to do as the speaker desires."[22] Persuading, then, demands a commitment from the listener in the form of a change of mind or behavior. Such a commitment is lacking in the act of arguing. Thus, someone may argue with you without persuading you. So, the speech act of persuading does not necessarily require the use of reasons or rational discourse.

Rhetoricians, adhering to a speech act theory approach, need to study more than the words uttered during a communication transaction. Indeed, the assumptions, norms, roles, and stances taken by the speaker and listener need to be thoroughly described and categorized. Such an undertaking is a viable and necessary direction for the rhetorician wishing to have a firm understanding and appreciation of discourse.

Notes

1. "Significant Symbol," in *Selected Writings* (Indianapolis: The Bobbs-Merrill Co., 1964), p. 246.
2. *Mind, Self, and Society* (Chicago: University of Chicago Press, 1934), p. 147.
3. *Ibid.*, pp. 89–90.
4. Duncan has noted: "Symbols are the most easily, and most directly observable 'facts' in human relationships, for they are the forms in which relationships take place." Hugh Dalziel Duncan, *Symbols in Society* (New York: Oxford University Press, 1968), p. 152.
5. *Signification and Significance*, p. 30.
6. Hugh Blair, *Lectures on Rhetoric and Belles Lettres* (Philadelphia: S.C. Hayes, 1860), pp. 317–318.
7. *Selected Writings*, p. 312.
8. (Cambridge, Mass.: Harvard University Press, 1977).
9. *Ibid.*, p. 5.
10. *Ibid.*, p. 14.
11. *Ibid.*, p. 26.
12. Larry W. Rosenfield, "A Game Model of Human Communication," in *What Rhetoric (Communication Theory) is Appropriate for Contemporary Speech Communication?*, David Smith, ed., Minnesota Symposium, p. 34.
13. John S. Searle, *Speech Acts: An Essay in the Philosophy of Language* (London: Cambridge University Press, 1976), p. 16.
14. *Ibid.*, p. 22.
15. *Ibid.*, p. 16.
16. *Ibid.*
17. Karl Wallace, *Understanding Discourse: The Speech Act and Rhetorical Action* (Baton Rouge, Louisiana: Louisiana State University Press, 1970), p. 123.
18. *Ibid.*, p. 125.
19. *Ibid.*, pp. 127–128.
20. Douglas Ehninger, "Toward a Taxonomy of Prescriptive Discourse," unpublished paper, University of Iowa, p. 3. We also are indebted to Ehninger's former student Norman Elliott for his contributions to our thinking.
21. *Ibid.*, p. 6.
22. *Ibid.*, p. 9.

12

Rhetoric as Meaning: Marshall McLuhan and the Relationship between the Medium and the Message

Few authors in the 1960's captured the fancy of the Western world more than did Marshall McLuhan. Trained as a Renaissance scholar and Professor of English, he nevertheless became aware of the declining influence of the print media in an age of electronics. This prompted him to make numerous probes into the field of mass media communication. These probles called to our attention the enormous impact of modern technology on our lives, and led to the introduction of a new vocabulary, including such descriptive terms as "hot" and "cool," "high definition" and "low definition," and "medium as message" and "massage."

McLuhan is an important figure in any survey of the rhetoric of Western thought because of his provocative insights on communication media. Early in the 1960s, he was among the first to tell us that man's image of the world is changed significantly by various media which have proved to be dominant during a given period of history. There have been, in McLuhan's opinion, four important periods with special significance for students of rhetoric and culture. First was the preliterate, tribal society which relied exclusively on rudimentary face-to-face communication patterns. Secondly was the period of manuscript technology extending from the classical world of Socrates, Plato, and Aristotle through the first fourteen hundred years A.D. Thirdly was the era of the Guttenberg Galaxy embracing the years from the discovery of movable type in the fifteenth century to the latter part of the nineteenth century. Finally is the period of electric circuitry which received its initial impetus from the development of the telegraph,

and its subsequent thrust from the telephone, radio, television, and the computer.

In a series of popular books, McLuhan described in graphic detail how the prevailing media operating at a particular time has stimulated man's senses.[1] His definition of media is so broad and encompassing that it includes such elements as "the spoken word," "the written word," "roads," "comics," "wheels," "bicycles," "airplanes," "photographs," "the press," "motor cars," "ads," "games," "the telegraph," "typewriters," "telephones," "phonographs," "movies," "radio," "television," "weapons," and "automation."[2] All of these media, or technologies, McLuhan argues, both extend and amputate our sensory perceptions. "The wheel," for example, "is an extension of the foot"; "the book is an extension of the eye"; "clothing is an extension of the skin"; and "electric circuitry is an extension of the central nervous system."[3] Moreover, whenever one of these senses is extended, others experience amputation. If we extend the eye, for instance, we may at the same time amputate the ear.

The application of the extension-amputation principle is easy to make when we examine the four periods mentioned earlier. In the preliterate, tribal society, the oral genre which predominated extended the ear and diminished the influence of the eye. The manuscript period launched by the phonetic alphabet gave an important extension to the eye, causing a break with the ear and "between semantic meaning and visual code. . . ." Phonetic writing, in short, "has the power to translate man from the tribal to the civilized sphere, to give him an eye for the ear."[4]

But it was not until Gutenberg's invention of movable type in the fifteenth century that the use of the eye was maximized to the point that other senses virtually were cut off. The effect on man was dramatic. In the preface of his most creative work, *The Gutenberg Galaxy,* McLuhan states:

Printing from movable types created a quite unexpected new environment—it created the Public. Manuscript technology did not have the intensity or power of extension necessary to create publics on a national scale. What we have called "nations" in recent centuries did not, and could not, precede the advent of Gutenberg technology. . . . The unique character of the 'public' created by the printed word was an intense and visually oriented self-consciousness, both of the individual and the group. The consequences of this intense visual stress with its increasing isolation of the visual faculty from the other senses are presented in this book. Its theme is the extension of the visual modalities of continuity, uniformity, and connectiveness to the organization of time and space alike.[5]

It would appear then that the print-oriented society, responding to the technology of movable type, became so independent, isolated, and self-reliant that there was progressively less need for social communion.

By far the greatest impact on man's senses, McLuhan proceeds to argue, came with the onset of the electronic age. The whole nervous system of man has undergone a radical change. In breaking the hold that the Gutenberg galaxy had on man for more than four centuries, "electric circuitry has overthrown the regime of 'time' and 'space' and pours upon us instantly and continuously the concerns of all other men. It has reconstituted dialogue on a global scale. . . ."[6] This enormous influence will be seen more clearly when we turn later to a discussion of radio and television.

Out of the foregoing general views, which constitute McLuhan's starting point, he reached his most celebrated conclusion: "The medium is the message." On November 12, 1967, an article dealing with "McLuhan and His Critics" appeared in the *Washington Star.* At the top of the page we see McLuhan seated on a swivel chair in front of twelve TV monitors, eight of which have superimposed upon the screen the words: "The Medium is the Message."[7] This recurring theme, grown stale by its repetition, wends its way through all of McLuhan's probes. The meaning that we experience in a communication transaction, he asserts, is more dependent upon the medium than upon content. To gain a better perspective of this revolutionary concept, let us observe the following distincton which he makes between "hot" and "cool" media:

There is a basic principle that distinguishes a hot medium like the movie from a cool one like TV. A hot medium is one that extends one single sense in 'high definition.' High definition is the state of being well filled with data. A photograph is, visually, 'high definition.' A cartoon is 'low definition,' simply because very little information is provided. Telephone is a cool medium, or one of low definition, because the ear is given a meager amount of information. And speech is a cool medium of low definition, because so little is given and so much has to be filled in by the listener. On the other hand, hot media do not leave so much to be filled in or completed by the audience. Hot media are, therefore, low in participation, and cool media are high in participation or completion by the audience. Naturally, therefore, a hot medium like radio has very different effects on the user from a cool medium like the telephone. . . .[8]

Of all of the above distinctions between "hot" and "cool" media, perhaps the most controversial is the designation of movies as "hot." Film, it has been argued, has the same characteristics which are present in television. McLuhan's position is that there are noticeable differences both in the scanning principle and size of the screen, and in the effect on the viewer. The latter claim is illustrated with a reference to members of the African culture who tend to respond less favorably to film than to television. "With film," McLuhan suggests, "you are the camera and the nonliterate man cannot use his eyes like a camera. But with TV you are the screen. And TV is two-dimensional and sculptural in its tactile contours."[9]

Because of the pervasive influence of radio and television on modern culture, it will be fruitful for us to examine more fully how "hot" and "cool" apply to these two media. To say that a radio is a "high definition" medium implies that it contains considerable specific data designed to stimulate the auditory sense, thus making it unnecessary for the audience to supply details or their own version of meaning. Since so much information is present, the listeners find it easy to respond even though the level of their participation is minimal. It is for this reason, McLuhan suggests, that radio is very effective as a tool for persuasion in an oral tribal society so characteristic of many African communities in the mid-twentieth century.

By contrast television is a "cool" medium, providing limited data and requiring an intense degree of audience participation. As in the case of a cartoon, a television picture permits the listener to produce much of the message. Consequently, in political situations calling for decision-making, such as in the War in Vietnam and Watergate, a person sitting in front of a TV set in his/her living room becomes part of a unified whole. The situation is experienced feelingly because not only the eye and the ear are sensitized but also the tactile sense as well. In explaining this phenomenon, Carey observes: "Television, as a result of the scanning system on which it operates, is capable of conveying or eliciting a sense of touch."[10] According to McLuhan, color television creates even more listener involvement than does black and white.[11]

If radio and television illustrate the differences between "hot" and "cool" media, so, too, do glasses and sunglasses. On this point, McLuhan says:

The principle that distinguishes hot and cool media is perfectly involved in the folk wisdom: 'Men seldom make passes at girls who wear glasses.' Glasses intensify the outward-going vision, and fill in the feminine image exceedingly. . . . Dark glasses, on the other hand, create the inscrutable and inaccessible image that invites a great deal of participation and completion.[12]

There can be little doubt that McLuhan's belief in the notion that "the medium is the message," or as he says in one of his books the "massage," is the central aspect of his theory of communication. This claim, more than any other conclusion we have analyzed in this survey of Western thought, is a revolutionary thesis which runs counter to prior studies on meaning. Consistently we have demonstrated that the language symbols we use form the content of the message and generate meaning. But McLuhan has given us an antithetical interpretation of meaning by arguing that the medium, more than the content, is the essence of a message. Unfortunately, McLuhan's most widely publicized claim has made him an occasional victim of ridicule. Kenneth Burke's indictment typifies the problem. After criticizing McLuhan for placing an undue stress "upon the role of instruments (means, agencies) in shaping human dispositions, or attitudes and habits," Burke observed with telling sarcasm:

The medium is the message. Hence, down with content analysis. We should at least pause en route to note that the formula lends itself readily to caricature. Primus rushes up breathlessly to his friend Secundus, shouting, 'I have a drastic message for you. It's about your worst enemy. He is armed and raging and is—'whereupon Secundus interrupts: 'Please! Let's get down to business. Who cares about the content of a message? My lad, hasn't McLuhan made it clear to you? The *medium* is the message. So quick, tell me the really crucial point. I don't care what the news is. What I want to know is: Did it come by telegraph, telephone, wireless, radio, TV, semaphore signals, or word of mouth?'[13]

McLuhan's probes into the nature and effects of media on our sensoria are, Burke argues, often overdrawn. Other critics claim that McLuhan is an armchair theorist and clever coiner of phrases whose ideas do not lend themselves to experimental verification.[14] Still others note that McLuhan rose to fame in the decade of the turbulent 1960s, only to see his influence and relevance wane in the present decade.[15]

McLuhan is not without fault in creating doubts about the value of his probes. His background as a literary scholar has done little to help express his ideas in a clear and precise manner. Consequently he often is vulnerable to the charge that he uses vague, conflicting, and exaggerated language that belies his true purpose. In response to these criticisms, McLuhan reputedly said: "I don't agree with everything I say," and "If there are going to be McLuhanites, I am certainly not going to be one of them"[16]

But if McLuhan has his detractors he also has an astonishingly large number of admirers. His two most important books, *The Gutenberg Galaxy* and *Understanding Media,* have become required reading in many college courses; and they have won for McLuhan invitations to address executives in large corporations such as General Electric, I.B.M., and Bell Telephone. Moreover, he has been a frequent guest on the network television shows. In the face of his wide acceptance as a seminal thinker, we raise the following question: What are the implications of McLuhan's theories for a contemporary rhetorical theory grounded in meaning? There are, we feel, four responses to this query.

First, although we agree with Burke's claim that McLuhan has gone too far in equating the medium with the message, *we are indebted to him for alerting us to the great extent in which a medium affects the message and its reception.* One of the examples McLuhan uses to make this point was the Kennedy-Nixon debates in 1960. The verbal content of the message was the same for those who heard the presentations on radio and those who saw them on television. Yet in the crucial first debate the meaning was affected significantly by the medium. Kennedy was the acknowledged winner in the eyes of the television viewers, and Nixon the victor in the opinion of those who heard the debate on radio. These two groups found

it difficult to witness the *same* rhetorical event. Nixon's point-by-point debate style, buttressed by numerous speech details, gave to the radio listener all the arguments he needed. The high definitional material extended the ear, and reduced the amount of audience involvement.

Kennedy, on the other hand, was less interested in offering a detailed rebuttal to Nixon's specific contentions and in directing his remarks to his opponent. Instead, he spoke self-confidently and engagingly to the American people, inviting them, as it were, to participate as an equal partner in the formulation of his arguments. His "cool" manner, strengthened by a youthful appearance, presented a dramatic contrast with the more stern, austere, and "hot" image projected by Nixon. Even Kennedy's full hair line and bronzed look, McLuhan would say, gave added force to the tactile image.[17] Thus the television audience tended to share Kennedy's view that he, not the Republican candidate, was the type of leader required in the 1960s.

A second rhetorical implication stemming from McLuhan's probes is that since the nature of the medium affects the message reception, speakers should either choose that medium most suitable to their natural style or modify the style so as to make it appropriate to the medium. If we again apply this principle to radio and television, we may conclude that a communicator whose manner is "hot" will perhaps be more effective on radio; and a speaker who exemplifies "coolness" will probably be more persuasive on television. McLuhan's examples illustrating this principle are instructive. Hitler, who was able to galvanize German sentiment by utilizing the "hot" medium of radio, would doubtless have failed as a persuader had he projected his high degree of intenseness on the "cool" medium of television. The same was true of former Senator Joseph McCarthy of Wisconsin. His aggressive anti-Communist crusade, which aroused the radio audience in the early 1950s, ended abruptly and disastrously when it began to be transmitted on the emerging "cool" medium of television.[18] Finally, McLuhan would add, if it can be said that Franklin D. Roosevelt was made for radio, rather than for television, it can also be asserted that John F. Kennedy was a child of television who was less persuasive on radio.[19]

McLuhan, we feel, does not mean to suggest that a speaker's use of radio or television is completely dependent upon his/her natural personality, style, or appearance. His probe into the area of "hot" and "cool" encourages a speaker, at least implicitly, to alter the style and manner in order to make them suitable to a particular medium. A similar modification is also possible in the format that is to be used on radio and television. On the day following the first televised debate between Jimmy Carter and Gerald Ford in 1976, McLuhan said on the Today Show that the format should be modified. The stand-up debate technique featuring formal opening statements, planned questions by newsmen, and lengthy responses, he argued, was a "hot" approach presented in a "cool" medium which required an informal give-and-take between the participants, and involving the audience.

A third rhetorical implication related to McLuhanism is the resurgence of the oral mode of communication due to the influence of the electronic media.[20] While we cannot concur with McLuhan's belief that the print medium with its eye-oriented emphasis is dead, our experience supports his claim that the oral genre during the age of television has gained so rapidly in popularity that it has contributed to the retribalization of man. Moreover, with this developing interest in orality accompanied by a decline in writing and reading skills has come an increased preference for the study of and practice in interpersonal communication.[21] Here McLuhan points out that the rhetoric of the classroom, if it is to keep pace with the change in the perception of our youth caused by the impact of the electronic media, should emphasize the seminar approach or other modes of informal dialogue rather than the sustained, uninterrupted lecture.[22]

The fourth and final rhetorical implication pertaining to McLuhan's ideas "concerns the structure of public oral discourse," as Ehninger puts it, "and the modifications which may have to be made in our conceptions of that structure as we move into the electronic age." Ehninger goes on to state the importance of McLuhan's contribution to the canon of *dispositio:*

Traditionally, of course, influenced by print culture or not, we have taught and used a linear pattern of speech development, whether the particular pattern in question be the classical parts of exordium through peroration, the Ramistic analysis and synthesis, the geometric or demonstrative development of the Port Royalists, or the reflective thinking process of John Dewey. All of these patterns, in one way or another, have assumed that if a discourse is to be organized properly some sort of ground work must be laid, a forward-moving thought line developed step by step in accordance with the logical demands of the subject or the psychological demands of the listeners, and, finally, a summarizing or applicative conclusion added. But if McLuhan is right, and the configurational all-at-once mode of presentation characteristic of television is changing our perceptual habits—or if, as he repeatedly suggests, it is the mosaic arrangement of the front page of our newspaper, with its stories developed according to the rule that makes the lead paragraph an all-at-once nutshell or capsule summary of what is to follow—if these and the similar configurational stimuli of contemporary art and literature are indeed affecting us as he suggests—then may not we as rhetoricians be called upon to follow suit by developing nonlinear patterns of speech organization, as well as to evaluate anew our predominantly linear systems of proof as couched in the enthymeme and example? At least, this seems to me to be worth thinking about, especially in the face of some of the evidence which the communication researchers now are gathering concerning the relative effectiveness of climactic and anticlimactic order.[23]

The four implications of McLuhanism singled out above, we believe, are worthy of the attention of students of rhetorical theory interested in the impact of technology on human communication practices. McLuhan, despite his frequent excesses and unsupported claims, has gone far beyond most of his predecessors and peers in describing the relationship between the medium and the message, and in challenging traditional views regarding the canons. More than any other rhetorician analyzed in this book, he helps us understand and appreciate the reciprocal relationships between rhetoric and the mass media and the influence of the latter on our sensory perceptions.[24]

Notes

1. The following are representative: *The Gutenberg Galaxy* (Toronto, 1962); *Understanding Media* (New York, 1964); *The Medium is the Message* (New York, 1967); *War and Peace in the Global Village* (New York, 1968); and *From Cliche to Archetype* (New York, 1970).
2. See chapter headings of *Understanding Media.*
3. *The Medium is the Message,* pp. 26–40.
4. *The Gutenberg Galaxy,* p. 38.
5. *Ibid.,* p. 7.
6. *The Medium is the Massage,* p. 16.
8. "McLuhan and His Critics: Hot, Cool, and Baffling," F-3.
8. *Understanding Media,* p. 36.
9. *The Gutenberg Galaxy,* p. 52.
10. James W. Carey, "Harold Adams Innis and Marshall McLuhan," Douglas Ehninger, ed., *Contemporary Rhetoric* (Glenville, Ill.: Scott, Foresman and Co., 1972), p. 315.
11. *War and Peace in the Global Villge,* p. 77.
12. *Understanding Media,* p. 44.
13. *Language as Symbolic Action* (Berkeley, Cal.: University of California Press, 1966), p. 414.
14. His writings, suggests one critic, are "impure nonsense, nonsense adulterated by sense." Another observes: "Marshall McLuhan . . . continually risks sounding like the body-fluids man in 'Doctor Strangelove.' " Richard Kostelanetz, "Understanding McLuhan," *New York Times Magazine,* January 29, 1967, p. 18.
15. One recent author has noted: "The fact that contemporary students of communication are only vaguely conversant with McLuhan's ideas is testimony of the failure of McLuhanism to exert a significant impact upon communication as a field of scholarly inquiry." B. Aubrey Fisher, *Perspectives on Human Communication* (New York: Macmillan Publishing Co., 1978), pp. 238–39. It should be noted, however, that as the decade of the 1970's comes to a close, McLuhan's ideas are being picked up by the French Structuralists who have a strong interest in forms and structures as suggested by McLuhan. Interview with Joseph Pilotta, Columbus, Ohio, January 30, 1978. Pilotta enrolled in McLuhan's University of Toronto year-long course, "Myth and Media."
16. Charles Cooke, "McLuhan and His Critics: Hot, Cool, and Baffling." *Washington Star,* November 12, 1967, F-3. Equally surprising is McLuhan's confession to his students at the University of Toronto that "he gets his insights from inspiration resulting from prayers to the Blessed Mary." Interview with Pilotta.
17. Interview with Pilotta.
18. It is necessary to observe, however, that McCarthy's tactical error of making a frontal attack on President Eisenhower and on the United States Army was also a factor in McCarthy's demise.
19. Even in death Kennedy's television appeal was enormous. Said McLuhan: "The Kennedy funeral . . . manifested the power of TV to involve an entire population in a ritual process." *Understanding Media,* p. 293.
20. See Douglas Ehninger, "Marshall McLuhan: Significance for the Field of Communication," (Connecticut) *Speech Journal,* Vol. VI (1969), 17–24.
21. At the annual meeting of the ten Western Conference Chairmen of Departments of Communication in Detroit, Michigan, April, 1977, all of those present reported a steady increase in their undergraduate enrollments during recent years. This trend has continued through the early 1980's.
22. *Understanding Media,* p. 39.
23. "Marshall McLuhan: Significance for the Field of Speech Communication," VI, 22–23.
24. For a comprehensive analysis of McLuhan's theories and influence, see the symposium on "The Living McLuhan," *Journal of Communication,* 31 (Summer 1981), 116–198.

The following article, written by McLuhan in 1973, is representative both of his writing style and original thinking about media. Herein McLuhan considers a few aspects of the information age which was born with the launching of Sputnik in October of 1957. This launching of technical hardware has brought about a revolution in communications that affects the way we perceive and behave in the world. In brief, according to McLuhan the information age alters *how* meaning is attained as well as the *nature* of meaning itself. Thus, the author considers the impact of such developments as the new journalism and its emphasis on immersing consumers in situations, the xerox machine that can make anyone an instant publisher, the data banks that lead to a diminution of private identity, the nature of larger publics and their effect on the communication process, and the instant replay that narrows the gap between experience and meaning. The Spaceship Earth, McLuhan argues, will undergo significant changes as the information revolution unfolds in the years ahead. During the decade that has passed since these claims were made, the impact of technology on rhetorical and communication theory has steadily increased.

At the Moment of Sputnik the Planet Became a Global Theater in Which There Are No Spectators But Only Actors

Declining to write for the *Revue Européenne* in 1831, Lamartine said to its editor:

Do not perceive in these words a superb disdain for what is termed journalism. Far from it: I have too intimate a knowledge of my epoch to repeat this absurd nonsense, this impertinent inanity against the Periodical Press. I know too well the work Providence has committed to it. Before this century shall run out journalism will be the whole press—the whole human thought. Since that prodigious multiplication which art has given to speech—multiplication to be multiplied a thousand-fold yet—mankind will write their books day by day, hour by hour, page by page. Thought will be spread abroad in the world with the rapidity of light; instantly conceived, instantly written, instantly understood at the extremities of the earth—it will spread from pole to pole. Sudden, instant, burning with the fervor of soul which made it burst forth, it will be the reign of the human soul in all its plentitude. It will not have time to ripen—to accumulate in a book; the book will arrive too late. The only book possible from today is a newspaper.
(5)

Perhaps the largest conceivable revolution in information occurred on October 17, 1957, when Sputnik created a new environment for the planet. For the first time the natural world was completely enclosed in a man-made container. At the moment that the earth went inside this new artifact, Nature ended and Ecology was born. "Ecological" thinking became inevitable as soon as the planet moved up into the status of a work of art.

Ecological thinking and planning have always been native to preliterate man, since he lived not visually but acoustically. Instead of having external goals and objectives, he sought to maintain an equilibrium among the components of his environment in order to ensure survival. Paradoxically, electronic man shares much of the outlook of preliterate man, because he lives in a world of simultaneous information, which is to say, a world of resonance

Marshall McLuhan was director of the Centre for Culture and Techology at the University of Toronto and author of several books on communications media, the latest being *Take Today: The Executive as Dropout* (the effects of electric information speed on decision-making and social institutions).

in which all data influence other data. Electronic and simultaneous man has recovered the primordial attitudes of the preliterate world and has discovered that to have a specialized goal or program merely invites conflict with all other specialized enterprises. "All the arts aspire to the condition of music," said Walter Pater, and under conditions of instant information the only possible rationale or means of order involves us in the musical structuring of experience.

Gutenberg man, in the sixteenth century, had achieved a new kind of detachment, thanks to the new intensity of visual experience deriving from the innovation of the printed word. This new visual stress impelled the men of that time to follow their individual goals, whether of learning or of travel and discovery to the utmost extremes. A new race of visually oriented explorers of space and time emerged from the "caves" of the Gutenberg technology. The Gutenberg innovation enabled men to retrieve antiquity as never before. The new speed of the printing press created vast new political spaces and power structures based on the creation of new reading publics. The matrix of the press, with its assembly lines of movable types, provided the archetypes of the industrial revolution and universal education.

The typical virtues of industrial and typographic man are radically revised and reformed when information moves at the speed of light. Whereas visual man had dreamed of distant goals and vast encyclopedic programs of learning, electronic man prefers dialogue and immediate involvement. Since nothing on earth can be distant at the speed of light, electronic man prefers the inner to the outer trip and the inner to the outer landscape.

Simultaneous man is, paradoxically, traditional and simple in his tastes, preferring the human scale to the ancient grandeurs which are no longer difficult to achieve. Simultaneous man is acoustically rather than visually oriented, living in a world whose center is everywhere and whose margin is nowhere. Not for him the spirit of geometry or the spirit of quantity; instead of distant goals, he seeks pattern recognition, and instead of specialized jobs he prefers role-playing, with its flexibility and diversity. Indeed, at the moment of Sputnik the planet became a global theater in which there are no spectators but only actors. On Spaceship Earth there are no passsengers; everybody is a member of the crew. These facts do not present themselves as ideals but as immediate realities.

To Give Both Sides Tends to Ignore the Possibility That There May Be Many More Sides Than Two

It is noteworthy that the popular press as an art form has often attracted the enthusiastic attention of poets and aesthetes while rousing the gloomiest apprehensions in the academic mind. Let us look at the image of the newspaper as it still is today after a century of the telegraph. That image is organized not according to a story line but according to a date line. Like a symbolist poem, the ordinary newspaper page is an assembly of unconnected items in abstract mosaic form. Looked at in this way, it is plain that the newspaper had been a corporate poem for many years. It represents an inclusive image of community and a wide diversity of human interests. Minus the story line of the connected narrative, the newspaper has long had an oral and corporate quality which relates it to many of the traditional art forms of mankind. On every page of the newspaper, in the discontinuous mosaic of unrelated human items, there is a resonance that bespeaks universality even in triviality. Robert Louis Stevenson said, "I could make an epic from a newspaper if I knew what to leave out."

The telegraph press was born in the age of symbolist poetry, the age of Edgar Allen Poe. Poe had confronted the poetic process in a way entirely consistent with the new electric speed of events and reporting. He simply pointed to the possibility of writing poetry backwards, starting with the effect desired and then proceeding to discover the "causes" or means for the desired effect.

Snyder and Morris (8) pointed to the same structural revolution in news writing that Poe and the Symbolists had discovered for poetry:

Over the past hundred years the structure of the news story has undergone drastic modification. It is today a commonplace of American journalism that a news story must illustrate hind-to-end writing. Unlike other literary forms, the climax is at the beginning. The lead, or opening paragraph or paragraphs, gives the reader the essential facts. The body of the story is merely detailed expository material, its paragraph structure a series of separate units without transitions connecting them with what went before or what is to follow, and arranged in decreasing importance.

Symbolist art is the art of the rip-off. It is the experience of this active stripping that is the effect of symbolism. Merely as classified, separate items, things do not achieve symbolic status. It is so in the newspaper.

In the past decade there has come a recognizable change in the styles of reporting, now referred to as the "old journalism" and the "new journalism." The "old journalism" had sought objectivity; in presenting people and events it tried to achieve this by giving "both sides" at once. To give the pro and the con, the good and bad, has been, for a century at least, the approved way of attaining judicial balance and fairness. To give both sides, however, tends to ignore the possibility that there may be many more sides than two, and as the means of access to information improved and as the means of processing information speeded up, the mere chiaroscuro of the light and the dark, the pro and the con, has tended to yield to nonvisual and subjective patterns of depth involvement by immersion in total situations. However, if the "old journalism" tended toward the salience of *figures* in men and events, the "new journalism" can be discerned as a preference for *ground* rather than *figure*. The "new journalism" offers not so much a view of men and events but a means of immersion in situations which involve many people simultaneously. Thus, Norman Mailer's account of

the 1968 political conventions in Miami and Chicago is less concerned with the policies and the parties than with the experience of the hurly-burly of the conventions. (4) After all, the "you are there" immersion approach in journalism is only natural in the new surroundings of TV imagery: for TV brings the outside into the intimacy of the home, as it takes the private world of the home outside into the forum. The bounding line between the old and the new journalism seems to have been the popular line: "A funny thing happened to me on the way to the forum."

If the telegraph and the telephone revolutionized the patterns of information and speech in poetry and journalism, the advent of TV may carry us beyond speech altogether. One plausible projection by Gattegno (2) goes:

Sight, even though used by all of us so naturally, has not yet produced its civilization. Sight is swift, comprehensive, simultaneously analytic and synthetic. It requires so little energy to function, as it does, at the speed of light, that it permits our minds to receive and hold an infinite number of items of information in a fraction of a second. With sight, infinities are given at once; wealth is its description. In contrast to the speed of light, we need *time* to talk and to express what we want to say. The inertia of photons is nil compared to the inertia of our muscles and chains of bones.

Man has functioned as a seer and embraced vastnesses for millenia. But only recently, through television, has he been able to shift from the clumsiness of speech (however miraculous and far reaching) as means of expression and therefore of communication, to the powers of the dynamic, infinite visual expression, thus enabling him to share with everybody immense dynamic wholes in no time.

Even if for some time speech will remain the most common way of letting others know what we know, we can foresee the coming of an era where the processing of visual material will be as easy as our comprehension of talk but swifter because of the former's lack of inertia; and through its spatialization by electrons, we shall be able to share vast conscious experiences at once. Today large novels are needed for this.

Xerox Comes as a Reverse Flip as the End of the Gutenberg Cycle; Whereas Gutenberg Made Everybody a Reader, Xerox Makes Everybody a Publisher

Without trying to look ahead one hundred years—without looking even one year ahead, if we merely *Take Today* (6) for a look at the changing nature of human organization as reflected in things and in newspapers—it is possible to see some striking new patterns. The release of the Pentagon papers and the Ellsberg investigation point to one of these patterns, one directly related to the matter of Xerox. Xerox, as a new service in connection with printed and written materials, is so decentralized, accessible, and inexpensive that it results in making the ordinary person a publisher, if he so chooses.

Quite apart from its threat to the publishing business and to copyright regulations, Xerox has two other features. On the one hand, it has created the large committee as a new means of decision-making, because it permits uniform briefing and *position papers* for all. On the other hand, it has created, also on a large scale, the *underground press.* [In passing, it might be helpful to mention apropos the underground press that its relation to the public, or above-ground press, is somewhat similar to the old and new journalism. Speaking in Gestalt psychology terms, the press can be seen in relation to *figure* and *ground,* and in psychology as well as in journalism, the *ground* is usually subliminal, relative to the *figure.* Under conditions of electric simultaneity the *ground* of any *figure* tends to become more and more noticeable. Perhaps it all began with cubism and the discovery that by eliminating the merely visual or rational relations between services, by presenting the inside and the underside at the same time as the outside, the public became totally involved and aware in a multisensuous way. As new media continue to proliferate, the nature of "news" will naturally change too, along with the perpetually renewed revolution in information speeds and patterns.]

Position papers are secret or confidential documents for the attention of committees, and any office boy can publish these, no matter how top secret they may be. The Pentagon Papers were position papers which may or may not have been studied or discussed by a Congressional committee. They are "the news behind the news," which used to be considered muckraking but has now become an ordinary dimension of journalism, such as nourishes the underground press and which, in turn, affects the forms and publics of the regular press. What has happened since the old muckraking days of the 1920s is that espionage, whether political or commercial, has become the largest business in the world, and we take it for granted that the modern newspaper depends on "bugging" the whole community. In fact, we expect the press to "bug" the world and to challenge and penetrate all privacy and identity, whether private or corporate.

Among the unexpected features of the information revolution are the extraordinary diminution of private identity and egotistic conviction, as a result of major involvement in the lives of other people, and the extraordinary enlargement of the public sector. We have moved into an age in which everybody's activities affect everybody else, and therefore the whole matter of privacy is suspect, even as it is impractical. One result has been a relaxing of private morals (sometimes referred to as "permissiveness") and at the same time an extraordinary new intensity in public morals. This change is well reflected in the Watergate affair. In Washington, as elsewhere, laxity of private standards is expected, but the same private standards no longer extend to the image of the President. Under electric conditions it is not possible to extend the laxity of private life into the public domain; rather, a new absolutism in the public domain is felt to be mandatory.

The U.S. happens to be the country in which the private and specialized had been allowed the utmost development. Quite dramatically, therefore, the "bugging" of private lives, long taken for granted in the commercial, the political, and the military establishments, has suddenly become the means of revealing the bankruptcy of public morals.

A spectacular paradigm of the information revolution has been developed for the world at large by the Watergate affair. While it seems to specialize in matters of political espionage and image-building, it also draws attention to the fact that the entire educational and commercial establishments, as much as the political and military establishments, depend on data banks of total information concerning both producers and consumers, both the governors and the governed. The Watergate affair makes it quite plain that the entire planet has become a whispering gallery, with a large portion of mankind engaged in making its living by keeping the rest of mankind under surveillance. The FBI includes among its responsibilities keeping under surveillance individual members of the CIA. We thus have a complete scheme of baby-sitters for the baby-sitters—chaperones for chaperones—and it is the business of every commercial establishment to keep all other commercial establishments under surveillance as a minimal condition of survival.

Xerox is a new kind of decentralized service which dissolves privacy and creates many new forms of human association, whether in the classroom or in the legislature or in the press. Whereas Gutenberg had created a service that extended to whole nations, he had at the same time invented a form of hardware that fostered new forms of central organization, including a price system and the markets that came with it. What Arnold Toynbee had discerned as "etherealization"—the tendency in our time to do more and more with less and less—is part of the electronic information revolution of "software," which has the opposite effect of decentralizing. While hardware requires uniformity of product to pay for a centralized operation, the electronic form of information service permits not only decentralizing of organizations but a wide diversity of products without additional expenditure.

If book and hardware sales need to be large to defray expenses, electronic publishing by Xerox can dispense with large-scale publics and markets almost entirely. Even more easily than by hand-press, a writer can publish a few copies of his work for his friends by simply multiplying the typescript. In fact, Xerox completes the work of the typewriter. A poet composing at the typewriter is "publishing" his work, as it were, while composing. Xerox gives to this fact a new meaning.

Electric Speed May Already Have Violated Human Scale, Tending as It Does to Transport Man Instantly Everywhere

In the early days of the book, Montaigne thought of printing as a kind of flip from the confessional to the expressional:

Letter writing . . . is a kind of work in which my friends think I have some ability. And I would have preferred to adopt this form to publish my sallies, if I had had someone to talk to. I needed what I once had, a certain relationship to lead me on, sustain me, and raise me up. . . . I would have been more attentive and confident, with a strong friend to address, than I am now, when I consider the various tastes of a whole public. And if I am not mistaken, I would have been more successful. . . . Amusing notion: many things that I would not want to tell anyone, I tell the public; and for my most secret knowledge and thoughts I send my most faithful friends to a bookseller's shop. (1)

Montaigne here draws attention to the book as a kind of message in a bottle: secretly dispatched, to an unknown public of potential acquaintances. His thoughts on this subject help to reveal an aspect of the newspaper as well, because there is a special meaning in publication as a form of "put on"; the writer, whether of a diary or a newspaper column, is engaged in a very special way in putting on his public as a mask.

ERSILIA: Why wasn't it true? I wanted to kill myself!

LUDOVICO: Yes! But in doing so you created an entire novel—

ERSILIA (fearfully): What do you mean, created? Do you think I made it all up?

LUDOVICO: No, no, I meant, in me. You created it in me, without knowing it, by telling your story.

ERSILIA: When they found me in that park—

LUDOVICO: Yes, and then later, in the hospital. Forgive me, but how can you imply you were nobody? For one thing, you existed in the pity everyone felt for you when they read your story in the paper. You can't imagine the impression it made when it was published, the interest you aroused all over the city.

ERSILIA (anxiously): Do you still have it?

LUDOVICO: Yes, I think so. I must have saved it.

ERSILIA: Find it, find it! Let me see it!

LUDOVICO: No, why should you get all upset again?

ERSILIA: Let me see it! Please! I want to read it, I want to read what they wrote about me. (7)

The most secret diary, even that of Samuel Pepys, written in a code which remained unbroken for centuries—even such a diary is for the writer a mask, or a vortex of energy which increases his power over the language; for our mother tongue is itself a corporate mask of energy which is stepped up by the act of writing and, once again, by the act of publication. In the early days of printing, Montaigne saw this action as both putting on the public and the taking off his privacy:

I owe a complete portrait of myself to the public. The wisdom of my lesson is wholly in truth, in freedom, in reality . . . of which propriety and ceremony are daughters, but bastard daughters. . . .

. . . Whoever would wean man of the folly of such a scrupulous verbal superstition would do the world no great harm. Our life is part folly, part wisdom. Whoever writes about it only reverently and according to the rules leaves out more than half of it.

Montaigne had discovered the paradox that the larger public, the greater the premium on the second-confessional.

There is something rather mysterious about the process of the "put on" which is insep arable from communication. Baudelaire's famous phrase *"hypocrite lecteur mon semblable, mon frere"* captures the entire process. The reader is *hypocrite* in the very act of putting on the author's poem as his mask, for in reading the poem he is perceiving the world in a very special way, using what another poet, S. T. Coleridge, called "a willing suspension of disbelief for the moment." When we put on any man-made mask such as painting, poem, or music, or when we read a book or a newspaper, we are looking at the world in a very special way, altering our own perceptions by an artistic act of faith in the process in which we are engaged.

The second part of Baudelaire's phrase, *"mon semblable, mon frere,"* draws attention to the reciprocal part of the action. Whereas the reader or the user of any form puts it on as his mask, as an extension of his own perception and energy, the author or marker has also to put on his public, the potential reader or user of whatever he has made. The maker tends to project his own image as the mask of the user or reader which he endeavors to "put on." This complex process of communication, by which the medium is "put on" by its users in order that they may experience some alteration and extension of their own perceptions or powers, includes the "putting on" of the user by the medium. Commercially, this latter operation is referred to as "giving the public what it wants" or "the customer is always right." The complexity of this process is such that even literary critics have despaired of ever unravelling it. Critics of the press, on the other hand, are accustomed to labeling the whole thing as degrading, even as Shakespeare did with his own profession of acting.

One thing that needs to be noted in both connections is the great increase of the sense of power on the part of the maker and the user. Since the process in question is at the very heart of the communication activity, it is certain to remain central to the issue so long as the readers are human and not merely robots. Since "human scale" is indispensable for human satisfactions, the future of the press must inevitably retain this dimension. At present, electric speed may already have violated human scale, tending as it does to transport man instantly everywhere. When you are "on

Montaigne

the air" you are simultaneously here and in many other places in a manner that is discarnate and angelic, to say the least.

At Instant Speeds . . . the Public Begins to Participate Directly in Actions Which It Had Previously Heard About at a Distance in Place or Time

It is time to ask ourselves: "What is news?" When a visitor stepped into an antique store, he asked: "What's new?" His jocular query draws attention to the fact that we live in the age of the fake antique, which is itself a form of the replay. Is not "news" itself a replay in the newspaper medium of events that have occurred in some other medium, and does not this replay quality in reporting urge us to narrow the margin between the event and the replay? Does not this make us define news as "the latest"?

However, in the new age of instant replay, news takes on a totally new dimension that is almost metaphysical. A ball game or a horse race can now be replayed for its meaning, as it were, minus the experience. During the actual experience the issue may have been in doubt, but, as the poet explains, "we can have the experience and miss the meaning." In fact, such is the nature of experience that it is almost inevitable that we do miss the meaning. The "meaning," or the relation to ourselves of a particular event, may not come home to us until much later. However, with the instant replay of our own or others' experiences, it is now possible to have the meaning without the experience. Referees and judges may wait for the replay in order to render a decision. They have had the experience and are merely waiting for the meaning or the relation of the experience to themselves and to others.

The quality of the instantaneous in the replay of experience is somewhat like the difference between cognition and recognition. Recognition may come somewhat after the event and is a form of awareness in which we say: "Oh, I didn't realize it was you" or "Oh, now I see what it's all about." Recognition is an altogether higher order of awareness from

cognition, and yet it is now taken for granted as a normal feature of daily life in the electric age. Newspapers have long used this instant dimension in experience, at least since the time of the telegraph and the telephone, which have been with us for many decades. The mysterious thing about this kind of speed-up of information, whereby the gap is closed between the experience and the meaning, is that the public begins to participate directly in actions which it had previously heard about at a distance in place or time. At instant speeds the audience becomes actor, and the spectators become participants. On Spaceship Earth or in the global theater the audience and the crew become actors, producers rather than consumers. They seek to program events rather than to watch them. As in so many other instances, these "effects" appear before their "causes." At instant speeds the cause and effect are at least simultaneous, and it is this dimension which naturally suggests, to all those who are accustomed to it, the need to anticipate events hopefully rather than to participate in them fatalistically. The possibility of public participation becomes a sort of technological imperative which has been called "Lapp's Law": "If it can be done, it's got to be done"—a kind of siren wail of the evolutionary appetite.

References

1. Frame, Donald M. *Biography of Montaigne*. New York: Harcourt, Brace & World, 1965, p. 83.
2. Gattegno, Caleb. *Towards a Visual Culture*. New York: Outerbridge and Dienstsfrey, 1969, p. 4.
3. Longford, Elizabeth. *Victoria R. I.* London: Weidenfeld & Nicolson, 1964, p. 562.
4. Mailer, Norman, *Miami and the Siege of Chicago*. New York: New American Library, 1968.
5. McLuhan, Marshall. "Joyce, Mallarme, and the Press." In *Interior Landscape: The Literary Criticism of Marshall McLuhan*, cited by Eugene McNamara. New York: McGraw-Hill, 1969, p. 5.
6. McLuhan, Marshall, and Barrington Nevitt. *Take Today: The Executive as Dropout*, New York: Harcourt, Brace, Jovanovich Inc., 1972.
7. Pirandello, Luigi. "To Clothe the Naked." In *To Clothe the Naked and Two Other Plays*, translated by William Murray. New York: E. P. Dutton, 1962.
8. Synder, Louis L., and Richard B. Morris (Eds.). *A Treasury of Great Reporting*. New York: Simon & Schuster, 1962.

Journal of Communication, 24 (Winter 1974), 48–58.

13

Rhetoric as Meaning: Case Studies of Two Televised Events

In this third chapter on "Rhetoric as Meaning," our principal emphasis will be on two celebrated television events, and how the American people perceived them as a form of social reality. The first is an original essay written by William R. Brown for the third edition of this volume; and the second is a reprint of an article dealing with the 1980 televised presidential debates. These works, we feel, are a natural extension of McLuhan's thesis that the message is significantly influenced by the medium through which it is transmitted.

Brown's paper on "The Televised Watergate Hearings: A Case Study in Information Overload" comes on the tenth anniversary of one of the most remarkable electronic media events in American history. During the period of the gavel-to-gavel coverage, extending from May through the summer of 1973, an average audience of twenty million viewers watched at least some portion of the hearings each day. As a result both the president's men and the members of the Senate Select Committee, along with some of their staff, became instant stars—both tragic and comic players—in an unfolding drama which pushed many of the soap operas in the background. The fact that

Brown was present at some of the hearings, not only interviewing members of the Select Committee and representatives of the press and electronic media but observing the proceedings live in the Caucus Room, lends poignancy to his remarks.

What Brown attempts to do in this study is to ferret out the meanings of which the American citizens attributed to the participants of the "Presidential party" and of the "Senatorial party." The two archetypes that are used to evaluate the contributions of members of each group are traditional ones that date back to the era of the founding fathers: (1) "conspiracy-against-the-state," and (2) "virtue-in-the-service-of-the-state." The two protagonists, Brown suggests, both sought to label their opponents on the other side as conspirators seeking to undermine the federal government, while at the same time portraying themselves as highly moral people who devoted their full energies to the welfare of the state. Out of these confusing images caused by information overload, the author concludes, the public came to believe that representatives of the "Senatorial party," not the president and his aides, were the true friends of the people.

The Televised Watergate Hearings: A Case Study in Information Overload

More than a decade after Watergate, the student at that chapter in American history who comes to it with a fresh mind appreciates anew its tangled web of circumstances, even though the end of the story is now clear in a way that it could not have been apparent to the American public contemporary with the scandal. To today's student, struggling to become acquainted with the Watergate labyrinth of personae and events, it will not seem strange that at the height of public attention to the investigation, during the summer of 1973, reporters openly strove with the mass of Watergate details in the effort to bring perspective into their stories.

Daniel Schorr, for instance, distinguished commentator then with prestigious CBS News, sat in the hearings chamber with a TV monitor conferring a camera-eye angle on the very scene which he was viewing live. Cameras for the network feed, placed along the outside wall of the Senate Caucus Room, created a dais effect for the investigating senators and singled out witness and counsel for a dramatic confrontation not visually apparent to other newspersons nor to the standing-room-only audience of citizens at the far end of the long, narrow room.

Douglas Kiker, then and for many years later a familiar face on NBC News, relaxed long enough during a lunch recess in the proceedings to explain his own labors in coping with the myriad pieces of the Watergate mosaic:

I . . . agree with anybody who says that the sheer weight of facts and figures and numbers and characters of this whole thing has become so great as to be bewildering; you are really lost in the forest, in a jungle of facts. . . . My head is so packed with facts that I find myself really having to listen inordinately when an important point comes up in a testimony—and I know what's coming up, and I know what [chief committee counsel] Sam Dash is leading up to—but you

really have to think back and say, that meeting, when was that meeting, when was it, and how is it going to contradict, why is this important? So I think the average viewer might tend to lose the trail because it is a very complicated story. . . .[1]

Most Americans, obviously, could not spend their waking moments attending to such details. Yet they did more than simply accept the reports of professionals like Schorr and Kiker who were adept in managing information overload: The gavel-to-gavel television coverage of the hearings attracted millions of viewers each day. How could they bring order to that experience? This essay urges that they did so by invoking ordering patterns, which I call archetypes, in response to "prompting" to do so by mass-mediated scene setters. These political artists, henceforward called the "Presidential party" and the "Senatorial party," each offered Watergate enactments aimed at associating themselves with one cultural archetype and at dissociating themselves from the other. In the process, the American public hypothetically projected an interpretation upon the morass of Watergate details which at once organized and simplified them.

Succeeding sections of this paper, accordingly, (1) sketch the significance-giving archetypes and political *scenarios* designed to tap into them and (2) suggest the way televised actions by real-life players invited public attribution to them of one or another of the overload-coping patterns.

I

In the early months of 1973, two political artists set about creating scenarios, one of which was to be ratified as "reality" by American publics. In March, President Richard M. Nixon advised members of his staff to "name" administration resistance to the upcoming Senate investigation as a battle to save the Constitution: "He emphasized several times that the President has the constitutional responsibility to preserve the separation of powers, a responsibility he cannot disregard."[2] Over in the Sentate Office Building, Sam Dash, majority counsel for the Senate Select Committee, had concluded his study of the effectiveness of other investigating committees and had decided that the upcoming Watergate hearings "had to present . . . a narrative that began in the beginning and ended at the end and built toward a climax," in order to "recreate the . . . Town Hall through the medium of television. . . ."[3] Both sides, then, intended to endow their activities with democratic meanings that would lend significance to Watergate beyond the immediate context of a bungled burglary, presidential recalcitrance, and senatorial curiosity. These meanings were to depend upon public association of Watergate with certain interpretative frameworks or archetypes. By "archetype," I mean a cultural model or "memory" on which to fit events and thus form an interpretation of them that becomes thereby a patterned and disambiguated social "reality." Confronting each other within the emergent Watergate gestalt were to be two historical syndromes of belief.

On the one hand, both the Select Committee and the Presidency could invoke the centuries-old American conspiracy theory as an archetype. Such an approach to "reality" building has had its attractions since a half-century preceding the American Revolution, when the colonists had socially perceived a growing conspiracy against the "liberty" promised and promulgated in the English Constitution.[4] Later, Abraham Lincoln had utilized the paradigm of the covert plot in his famous "House Divided" speech, "proving" an effort to extend slavery to all states by inviting hearers to "trace" with him "the evidences of design, and concert of action among [the] chief bosses [of the design], from the beginning."[5] Muckrakers, Democratic and Polpulist candidates, and sober historians alike had decried monopolistic and exploitational collusion among "the interests" during post-Civil War decades; and Woodrow Wilson, that master of touching all the chords of sentiment in popular American audiences, had referred darkly

to an impending world Communist plot as stimulus to the supposedly counteracting League of Nations.[6] Not only had such demagogues as Joseph McCarthy and such radical rightists as Robert Welch, founder of the John Birch Society, been drawn to the conspiratorial archetype, thereby creating versions of the American scene to compete with others for ratification as "reality."

On the other hand, Americans historically had also gravitated toward another pole for synthesizing their shared national ethos: America had been the place where whatever goodness people possessed could express itself in the building of an ideal community. Liberals had sung poetically of innate virtue in the breast of the common man and woman and of their power to make politics and politicians instruments for the national good. Conservatives had mistrusted the individual as a repository of virtue—whether common citizen or ruler—and had sought to balance interest against interest in order to give virtue a needed support. But both had found in national integirty the antipode to conspiracy in the American world view. Sometime-liberals like Thomas Jefferson had seen in the tillers of the earth the virtues necessary to the life of the state;[7] pragmatic campaigners like Andrew Jackson had included the stalwart city toilers among the sources of national morality.[8] Men of money, liberal often enough only to test the rule that possession of wealth produces conservatism, had related private to group virtue in their ideal and practice of enlightened philanthropy.[9] And the collection of men made legendary as "the Founding Fathers," conservative by temperament and tilted toward liberalism by force of the Revolution, had produced that admixture of liberal and conservative visions of human goodness operationalized in the Federal Constitution, itself once memorialized by a liberal English statesman as "the most wonderful work ever struck off at a given time by the brain and purpose of man."[10]

Such are the cultural "memories" of "conspiracy" and "virtue-in-the-service-of-the-state," each containing not only formal, orderly powers but also effective charges of meaning. Each contending party in the Watergate drama potentially could be degraded or ennobled, respectively, to the extent that one or the other pattern gave shape to the public interpretation of its scenario. Such degrading or ennobling, significantly, would depend upon public attention to *some,* but not to the mass of, Watergate details. At the outset, both parties potentially related to each archetype. Specifically, each of the contending communication forces could be seen either as "conspiracy-against-the-state" or as "virtue-in-service-to-the-state."

Viewed through the overload-coping dimensions of the *conspiracy* paradigm, the party of the Presidency could take on the appearance of a pejorated "Mission Impossible," without the presumably laudable motives of its operatives for cleverly subverting totalitarian governments or schemes. In the Watergate affair, the staging of events, the confounding of opponents' operations, the creation of appearances, and the refinement of surveillance by means of technological wizardy could appear to have been directed, rather, against the *American* political system and populace. Replacing the "Mission Impossible" overtones could be the emergence of a "Gestapo Mentality" on the part of participants in the cover-up and in other activities related to Watergate.

On the other hand, equally potential in the early months of 1973 was another public projection of the Presidential party as *"virtue-in-service-of-the-state."* Over time it could appear as the defender of freedom in two major senses—as protector of the national security and, more pervasively, as preserver of the balance of powers between the executive and legislative branches ordained by the American Ark of the Covenant, and Federal Constitution.

On its part, the Senate Select Committee could also have been assigned a "conspiracy" interpretation. A liability was the Committee potentiality for appearing to be a witch hunt, a 1973 example of the grisly burlesque of justice seen earlier in the Salem Witchcraft trials and, in more recent memory, within the macabre movements of McCarthyism.[11] With an emotional key of group hysteria, with evidence of denunciation, and with guilt by accusation, the witch hunt ultimately would damn its perpetrators and sanctify its intended victims.

In another guise, however, the Senatorial party could appear over time as *"morality-in-support-of-the-ideal-state"* in at least three senses: protector of privacy and individual rights; provider of relief from coercion; and, most pervasively, restorer of the balance of powers between branches of the federal government.

In broad strokes, then, these are the alternative, potential social judgments in the two parties to the Watergate communication event. On behalf of each it was necessary to be dissociated from the conspiracy archetype and to associate the opponent with it; it was necessary also to be associated with the archetype of "virtue-in-service-of-the-state" and to dissociate it from the opponent. How to effect or prevent these linkages, in general and in particular, is the next topic.

In general, the scenario of each rhetorical camp was constructed to invite or "prompt" the public's *attribution,* based on each party's actions, of "virtue" to itself and of "conspiracy" to its competitor. Such interpretations would put the scandal into perspective "scenically," with less attention needed to "fine strokes" of Watergate details. Scenic interpretations, in turn, would depend upon cultural values.

In our culture, a variety of deeds are taken as outward signs of inward commitment to national virtues.[12] Important for this essay are two such "action corollaries" of national-value adherence: the practice of fair play, defined usually as playing by the rules,[13] and defense of the underdog, by which the rights of all may be assured if guaranteed to the weaker contender in any societal encounter. In general, as one beholds a practitioner of fair play and/or a defender of the underdog, one ascribes virtue, both as morality *and* strength, to the "real-life" actor; as one beholds an *unfair* player and/or oppressor of the underdog, one imputes evil, both as immorality *and* weaknesses, to the agent, who thereby becomes "perpetrator."

Moreover, such behaviors are no less deeds if carried out more by use of symbols than by use of large muscles. As Martin Maloney has argued convincingly, Clarence Darrow defended the underdog against legal penalty,[14] as surely as American manufacture and sale of rockets and jets have protected/endangerd Israel. Rhetorical acts are deeds. As with all deeds, they make possible the imputing of motive to the doer. When these deeds are *action* corollaries of cultural values, they invite categorization of their agents by archetypes partaking of virtue; when they violate the taken-for-granted of action corollaries, they invite publics' classifying of their agents by condemnatory archetypes. Such in general are the means of linking scenarios and agents; such linkages resolve ambiguity in public issues like Watergate without requiring scrutiny of all details relevant to public inquiry.

In particular, with regard to Watergate both rhetorical parties planned actions of fair play which would transcend, as though by Black's argumentative synthesis,[15] not only potential charges against themselves of conspiracy but also masses of Watergate details. The party of the Presidency, for example, announced a posture of scrupulous regard for the "rules" in the upcoming investigation. In his new conference of April 17, the President revealed plans both to cooperate with the Senate Committee and to go by the letter and spirit of the "rules" in the Constitution. His aides would voluntarily testify, the President promised, but "executive privilege," he insisted, was "expressly reserved," and might "be asserted during the course of the questioning as to any questions."[16] During his April 30 apologia, the President enlisted himself in the movement of electoral reforms which united all those who condemned such excesses as the acts associated with Watergate; he "sacrificed" his closest advisors, presumably to the Committee; he "purified" his administration by the addition of the morally impeccable Eliot Richardson as Attorney-General for the resigned Richard Kleindienst; he urged that the investigation should proceed in the courts, presumably under the strict *legal* rules of evidence and argu-

ment.[17] Clearly, the Presidential party not only planned to "play fair" but also to insist that the other contenders do the same.

The Senatorial party also laid its plans for enacting fair play and thus inviting public attention of virtue to it. Overall, its doing of fair play was the adapting of appropriate procedural principles of the law court. In place of the legal pleadings of pre-trial motions, the Committee planners substituted lengthy prepublic staff interviews with witnesses, during which each side was to be made aware of the stances to be taken by the other; further, the format provided opportunity for opening statements from witnesses in lieu of the usual friendly courtroom defense questioning; queries from Senators and staff would serve as equivalents of cross-examination; it was noted that even in court hearsay evidence was admissible in cases dealing with conspiracy charges; finally, each witness would be able to have at his or her side legal counsel for on-the-spot consultation and protection of witness rights.[18] The Senatorial party also planned to "play fair" and invite the public's attribution of virtue.

Who, in addition, was to be cast as the "underdog" in the competing scenarios whom the public, itself, would eventually defend—and thus disambiguate Watergate? Both sides enjoyed potentialities, just as they had for embodying fair play.

The Presidency could be underdog in that the President stood alone, except for a few trusted, loyal aides; in that the full investigative powers of the Congress and of the press could fall upon him; in that mass media could be seen as generating a distorted amplification of Watergate-related developments; and, finally, in that the President had already suffered victimization at the hands of his own followers and subordinates.

On its part, the Senatorial party could also be underdog as it confronted the awesome and centralized power of the Presidency, accelerating in its accumulation since the days of FDR; in the sense that it scrutinized a President re-elected by a landslide less than a year before; and in the sense that as a bi-partisan entity it could not speak with the seemingly single voice available to the executive branch. It would have to settle matters internally at the same time that it would have to deal with what could be seen as the "machinations" of the Presidency.

In the Watergate Hearings, as publics witnessed the practice of fair play (or its negation) and as they found themselves defining and defending the underdog rhetorical camp, these action corollaries of American values would prompt the assigning of "virtue" to one contender and the association of "conspiracy" with the other. In addition, as I move next to the parties' enactment of the televised Watergate drama, such association/dissociation with cultural archetypes is seen to depend upon the creation and protection of still another potential underdog in the Watergate affair, the public itself.

As the fleshing-out of Watergate scenarios proceeded in the hearings themselves, Watergate "victims" appeared at the beginning to have been only a group of defeat-doomed Democrats, even when chief Watergate burglar James McCord on the second day alleged that high echelons in the White House had reached him through two different intermediaries; victims were still only the hapless Democrats as testimony from workers at the Committee to Re-Elect the President detailed the message of code-named "Gemstone" documents to CREP Director and former Attorney General Mitchell and to H. R. Haldeman, White House Chief-of-Staff; purely spectatorial interest accrued as CREP Treasurer Maurice Stans and former CREP official Herbert Porter spoke of CREP spymaster Gordon Liddy's funding of the Watergate operation and of Porter's perjury to avoid "embarrassing" the "President . . . and . . . Mr. Mitchell and Mr. Haldeman and others"; that interest intensified as Deputy CREP Director Jeb Stuart Magruder pointed to John Mitchell as the authorizer of the break-in and to Haldeman as a likely monitor of the operation.[19]

However, significantly for assigning/assuming the underdog role, considerable widening of the White House "Mission Impossible" targets occurred with former White House Counsel John Dean's testimony of June 25–29, one of the peak periods of audience attention. Watergate, said Dean, had followed "a climate of excessive concern over leaks, an insatiable desire for political intelligence, all coupled with a do-it-yourself White House staff, regardless of the law."[20] During the morning session of June 27, Dean turned over a memorandum by him dated August 16, 1971, in which he had proposed that "we can use the available federal machinery to screw our political enemies."[21] Altogether, some 200 names appeared; on the priority list were journalists such as Ed Gutman, managing editor of the *Los Angeles Times;* columnist Mary McGrory; and Daniel Schorr of CBS News; politicians like Black Congressman John Conyers of Michigan and Allard Lowenstein of New York, a practitioner of the "new politics"; entertainment figures, including Paul Newman; labor leaders, among them Leonard Woodcock of the UAW; various people associated with private corporations; and the top Democratic advertising firm, the Doyle, Dane, and Bernback agency.[22] That "list" appeared to extend to thousands of ordinary Americans as Dean revealed, further, that he had never seen any document rescinding the 1970 "Huston Plan" of domestic intelligence, which he had been instructed to make operational and which presumably would lead to increased electronic shadowing of "individuals and groups in the United States who pose a major threat to national security," as well as increased mail surveillance, increased use of surreptitious entry, and development of "campus sources" who would coordinate their efforts with the intelligence agency "in order to forestall widespread violence."[23] After John Dean, viewers had some difficulty in viewing the Watergate as an isolated incident in a Presidential election, for Dean also provided the opening for a highly visible member of the Committee, himself, to assume the underdog role on behalf of the Committee and the people.

When Dean revealed that attempts had been made to influence his own testimony before the Watergate Committee, Connecticut Republican Lowell Weicker, who as committee member had already asked Special Watergate Prosecutor Archibald Cox to investigate whether White House questions raised about Weicker's 1970 campaign constituted "obstruction of proceedings before special committees,"[24] challenged, on camera, the Presidential party to play fair in his famous outburst that mixed fury and fear at becoming current, existential quarry for the domestic "Mission Impossible":

Whether it is you in that witness chair or it is me in this committee chair or any other man in back of this table or any other witness who is going to come before this committee, there are going to be no more threats, no intimidation, no innuendo, no working through the press to go ahead and destroy the credibility of individuals. If the executive branch of Government wants to meet the standards that the American people set for it in their mind, then the time has come to stop reacting and stop playing this type of a game, and either disavow it completely or make the very specific charges that apparently are being leaked. . . .

....

Republicans do not cover up; Republicans do not go ahead and threaten; Republicans do not go ahead and commit illegal acts; and God knows Republicans don't view their fellow Americans as enemies to be harassed but rather, I can assure you, this Republican, and those that I serve with, look upon every American as human beings to be loved and wanted.[25]

No testimony to past fact was this; here on television screens across the country appeared the image of a single Select Committee Senator who as real-life action agent performed at that moment the deed of warning and cast himself as the underdog at the hands of Presidential tormentors. To the extent that viewers identified with Weicker as underdog, they could pattern the entire Watergate story and not need to place in perspective the mass of testimony in order to do so. With this *on-stage*

rhetorical deed, a "Watergate conspiracy" had targeted "victims" in the hearings *themselves* before the eyes of viewers; the "verdict" of those viewers would protect the Committee; in turn, the Committee, as will be seen shortly, would protect the people.

Meanwhile, before, during and following such televised incidents, fleshing-out of the Presidential scenario had labored under the handicap of being off-camera (and therefore *off*-stage) as that party likewise enacted fair play and behaved like an underdog. Seeming as if they came from the wings (if they were noticed at all) were these rhetorical deeds: the June 6 message-event of naming—as a cooperative President's peace-offering to Congress—of highly-respected former Congressman Melvin Laird to replace John Ehrlichman as Chief Presidential Counsel for Domestic Affairs; Ehrlichman's June 8 press conference in Los Angeles attacking the credibility of John Dean's upcoming testimony by blaming the former Presidential counsel, himself, for the cover-up; Vice-President Spiro Agnew's attacking on June 11 the "Perry Masonish" impact of the televised hearings, which threatened "a gross perversion of justice": Nixon's urging on June 15 in Pekin, Illinois, that "it would be a tragedy if we allowed the mistakes of a few to obscure the virtues of most who are in the profession of politics. . . ."; Melvin Laird's promising that a cooperative President would answer "all questions" about Watergate after the major witnesses had gone before the Ervin Committee; Presidential Press Secretary Ziegler's repeating that promise during his own news conference of July 2, reaffirming that the President intended to "address" the Watergate Issue "in an appropriate forum or forums" after major witnesses were heard; Presidential Speechwriter Patrick Buchanan's making the same promise on August 6.[26]

On the other hand, when the Senatorial Party performed the "fair play" action corollary to "virtue-in-service-of-the-state," it did so in iconic form in the living rooms of an average of twenty million viewers a day.[27]

More frequent than televised instances of Committee members bickering with each other or with witnesses were message-events constituting fair play by the Senators that occurred within the hearings format for "fairness" already outlined. During the second day, Chairman Sam Ervin, a Democrat, limited the "admissibility" of McCord's hearsay evidence involving President Nixon in any illegal clemency discussions for convicted Watergate burglars: The testimony could not be "accepted" to "connect the President with what Mr. Caulfield [McCord's contact] was doing."[28] On May 24, Democrat Daniel Inouye, Senator from Hawaii, recommended that the Committee seek from the Justice Department any evidence of election irregularities or criminal conspiracies involving Democrats.[29] During the questioning of Maurice Stans, CREP Treasurer, on June 12, the Committee announced its unanimous decision not to question the witness on any matters pertaining to his impending trial in the Vesco affair involving possible illegal campaign contributions; moreover, Republican Weicker declined altogether to question the witness in order to make clear that he was not seeking revenge for Stans' earlier lack of support for Weicker's 1970 Senate race.[30] On June 13, Committee Vice-Chairman Howard Baker, Republican from Tennessee, moved to obtain financial records of the Democrats, and on June 14 Democrat Ervin signed the subpoena for the records.[31] By June 27, Democrat Inouye was on camera, reading the "Buzhardt Memorandum" from the Presidential party offering the "hypothesis" that John Dean and his "patron" John Mitchell were responsible for the Watergate burglary and cover-up.[32] The next day, Democrat Inouye finished asking Dean the cross-examination questions submitted by Presidential Counsel Fred Buzhardt; Republican Baker was searching in his own cross-examination.[33] When the President had refused to testify, the Committee chairman nevertheless was publicly hopeful of cooperation from him when the Senators unanimously asked for tapes relevant to the inquiry, on July 17.[34] Vice-Chairman Baker defended the "fair-committee" enactment; "We are trying to find facts, to establish circumstances, to divine the causes, and to ascertain the relationshps that make up in toto the so-called Watergate affair."[35] When on July 30, H. R. Haldeman, former White House Chief of Staff, testified that *as a private citizen* he had gained access to tapes denied the Committee, Ervin on July 31 was willing to be "scrupulous" in accepting the witness's version of them, admitting the Haldeman testimony on the taped conversations as the best the Committee could obtain at that time.[36] At the same time, the Committee behaved even-handedly in demanding documentation of Haldeman's own charges of Democratic dirty tricks in his opening statement.[37] As the major witnesses followed each other, the Committee voted to expedite the hearings, thus disarming "offstage" Presidential charges of "wallowing in Watergate." By such communication deeds, together with procedures designed to accommodate legal rules of evidence and courtroom cross-examination, the Senators practiced fair play—on the basis of which viewers could ascribe "virtue-in-service-to-the-state" to the Committee—simultaneously (1) transcending any potential appearance as conspiratorial witch hunt and (2) minimizing the necessity for attention to many other details of Watergate-related information.

Also "onstage" were the Committee's defense of its members and of the people as underdogs. After former White House Security Agent Alexander Butterfield's revelation of the White House tapes, it became increasingly "clear" that a Constitutional confrontation between the executive and legislative branches had come into being.

The Butterfield revelation bcame the dramatic hinge on which the two competing versions of reality turned: Repeated efforts of the Committee to obtain the Presidential tapes made "real" the Committee's struggle to redress or maintain the balance of power between the two branches of government. By July 17, the Committee voted unanimously to request access to the recordings; on July 23, the Presidential party argued both executive privilege and separation of powers in refusing access to "private presidential papers" and tapes; a day after Baker and Ervin had suggested a private hearing of the tapes by themselves and

Special Watergate Prosecutor Archibald Cox, Special Presidential Counsel Charles Wright was saying that he knew of no compromise that would remove the need for litigation—it was important that "no damaging precedent" be set for future White House-Congressional relations.[38]

Coupled with audience perceptions of Presidency-as-encroachment-on-citizens'-rights, such a defense probably seemed less a Presidential effort to maintain a *balance* of powers among the Federal branches and more one to enhance the *advantage* in power enjoyed by the executive. After all, why could not the Presidential party *voluntarily* have released the tapes, as it had earlier allowed White House aides "voluntarily" to testify, without bringing into play the Constitutional issue of separation of powers?

Presidential "usurpation," further, may have been made real by audience inference during the July 24 testimony of John Ehrlichman, defending the power of the President to order break-ins for purposes of national security such as that of the office of Daniel Ellsberg's psychiatrist, and telling an interrogating Herman Talmadge, Democrat from Georgia, that the legal principle of every man's home being his castle had badly "eroded."[39] In the person of Sam Ervin, the Committee acted as defender of privacy and Constitutional rights in other exchanges with Ehrlichman and his attorney, John Wilson: When Wilson argued that Congress had granted powers to the Presidency to control subversives, Ervin replied—as "old country lawyer"—that Ellsberg, not his psychiatrist, was the subject for investigation.[40] Following this, while being told that national security prevented discussing an heretofore undisclosed mission of the "Plumbers" (the White House unit empowered to stop leaks to the press), Republican Baker stated for the Committee and its viewers the suspicion that such withholding, in the name of "national security," in actuality could be intended to cover up wrongdoing.[41]

Climactically, in the midst of such legal interpretations and ascription of motives, the televised Committee made present and "real"

the Constitutional crisis by transacting its official business in "executive" session in full public view. In a scene that foreshadowed the succession of solemn votes by the House Judiciary Committee to impeach the President, six of the Senators, later joined by a then-absent Herman Talmadge, voted on July 26 to support ranking Republican Baker's motion to go to court to win access to documents and tape pertinent to the Watergate inquiry.[42] Here was a communication event which not only officially transformed the Watergate incident into a Constitutional confrontation, but one which was the apex of the Senatorial party's efforts to prompt audiences to attribute virtuous motives to the Committee's "defense" of the Constitution. Watergate, in its scenic sense, was becoming a struggle between Senatorial "principle" and Presidential "expediency."

The conspiratorial archetype had been assigned, in the developed scenario, to the Presidential party. A Harris poll taken between July 18–22 and published on July 25 showed by a landslide sixty to thirty per cent margin that Nixon was seen to be "more wrong" than right to refuse to turn over White House files;[43] similar opinions could have been reasonably expected in relation to the tapes. Such Presidential-party deeds were seen as negating fair play; as defensive rhetorical acts, they were protecting the President, not the Constitution nor the national security.

On the other hand, the archetype of "virtue-in-service-of-the-state" had been invoked on behalf of the Senatorial party, as shown by a Harris poll published on August 2: The Committee enjoyed a "favorable" evaluation by sixty-two per cent of the sample, with its leaders, Ervin and Baker, rated as "excellent" or "good" at their duties by sixty-two and fifty-seven per cent, respectively.[44] The Committee had been convincing in its enactment of fair play: A telephone survey completed at the close of Phase I of the hearings showed that sixty per cent of the systematically-selected respondents in a Midwestern test-market city believed the Senatorial party to have been "fair and impartial."[45] Given the Committee's practice of fair play that transcended any tinge of conspiracy, it had dissociated itself from the latter archetype and had associated itself with that of virtue-in-service-of-the-state. Given that archetype, its aggressive questioning of the Mitchells and the Ehrlichmans, its frequent leaks to the press, its disregard for "executive privilege," and its widening of the originally authorized scope of its investigation all failed to make it a "witch hunt" and blur the "truth" of its defense of the republic. Such an encompassing interpretation subsumed millions of words of testimony, easing the strain on viewers to make sense of the complicated twists and turns in the Watergate affair.

III

Only a final word remains.

When media professionals spoke of their own difficulties in perspectivizing the mass of detailed testimony, the same overload experience was shared by viewers of the gavel-to-gavel coverage. For the Senators and staff, on the other hand, testimony was stored in and cumulated by computer, to be called up in detail at any time that it was relevant to the testimony of new witnesses. Viewing the hearings without that technological capability, viewers coped with such information overload by attributing, via the Committee's rhetorical enactment of "fair play" and "defense of the underdog," the cultural archetypes of "conspiracy" and "virtue-in-service-of-the-state"—respectively—to the Presidential and Senatorial parties. Such ordering and disambiguation of mediated experiences depend ultimately on the claim for archetypes expressed by political scientist Robert MacIver's view that "every society is held together by . . . a complex of dominating thought-forms that determines and sustains all its activities."[46] Added to the role in rhetorical scene painting of archetypes, the presence of computer-assisted memory encourages us to modify Aristotle's distinction between rhetoric addressed to popular juries and that finely-grained argumentation addressed to precision-seeking judges. In the Watergate communication event, first in its developed scenario for television audiences and later with the turning over of computer-stored Watergate evidence to the House Judiciary Committee that voted to bring impeachment charges against the President, the Senatorial party's "text" did both.[47]

Notes

1. Interview with Kiker by The Ohio State University research team, Washington, D.C., July 31, 1973. The author's thanks are due the other members, including Michael Adams, Richard Crable, James Golden, Paul Keckley, and Charles Ottinger.
2. *Hearings Before the Select Committee on Presidential Campaign Activities of the United States Senate,* 93rd Cong. 1st Sess., Book V, p. 1943. Future references to this source will be shortened to a volume number and a page number.
3. Interview of Dash by James Golden, Washington, D.C., December 9, 1975.
4. Bernard Bailyn, *The Ideological Origins of the American Revolution* (Cambridge, Mass.: The Belknap Press of the Harvard University Press, 1967), pp. 34–35.
5. "The House Divided," Springfield, Illinois, June 16, 1858, in Roy P. Basler, ed., *The Collected Works of Abraham Lincoln* (New Brunswick, N.J.: Rutgers University Press, 1953), II, 462.
6. Speech at Des Moines, Iowa, September 6, 1919, in Albert Shaw, ed., *The Messages and Papers of Woodrow Wilson* (New York: Review of Reviews Corporation, 1924), II, 789. For another survey of conspiracy rhetoric, see G. Thomas Goodnight and John Poulakos, "Conspiracy Rhetoric: From Pragmatism to Fantasy in Public Discourse," *Western Journal of Speech Communication,* 45 (Fall 1981), 299–316.
7. William R. Brown, *Imagemaker: Will Rogers and the American Dream* (Columbia: University of Missouri Press, 1970), p. 107.
8. *Ibid.,* p. 108.
9. *Ibid.,* p. 168.
10. William Gladstone, quoted in Robert Oliver, *History of Public Speaking to America* (Boston: Allyn and Bacon, Inc., 1965) p. 65.
11. See Dale G. Leathers, "America Confronts the Internal Communist Menace," in DeWitte Holland, ed., *America in Controversy: History of American Public Address,* (Dubuque, Iowa: William C. Brown Company Publishers, 1973), pp. 351–370.
12. Brown, *Imagemaker,* pp. 45–47; 167–169; 218–220; 101–104.
13. *Ibid.,* pp. 103–104.
14. Martin Maloney, "Clarence Darrow," in Marie Hochmuch, ed., *History and Criticism of American Public Address,* Vol. III (New York: Russell and Russell, 1965), 262–312.

15. Edwin Black, *Rhetorical Criticism: A Study in Method* (New York: The Macmillan Company, 1965), pp. 155–159.
16. *The Washington Post*, April 18, 1973, p. A-24.
17. *The New York Times*, May 1, 1973, p. 31. See also *Weekly Compilation of Presidential Documents*, Vol. IX, No. 18 (May 7, 1973) 433–38. For Nixon's rhetoric throughout the Watergate period see William L. Benoit, "Richard M. Nixon's Rhetorical Strategies in his Public Statements on Watergate," *The Southern Speech Communication Journal*, 47 (Winter, 1982), 192–211 and Jackson Harrell, B. L. Ware, and Wil Linkugel, "Failure of Apology in American Politics," *Speech Monographs*, 42 (November, 1975), 245–261. For a group-dynamics based analysis of Administration decisions affecting the cover-up, see Dennis Gouran, "The Watergate Cover-up: Its Dynamics and its Implications," *Communication Monographs*, 43 (August, 1976), 176–186.
18. Interviews by Ohio State research team with the following members of the Select Committee Staff: Fred Thompson, Washington, D.C., August 2, 1973; Arthur Miller, Washington, D.C., August 1, 1973; Barry Schochet, August 3, 1973; Rufus Edmiston, August 3, 1973.
19. II, 494; 499; 503–504; 635–637; 787–795; 797–798; 799–804; 807; 819; 822; 827.
20. III, 915.
21. Exhibit no. 48, IV, 1689; IV, 1349–1350; see also III, 1973 and IV, 1411.
22. Exhibit no. 49, IV, 1693–1696; see also IV, 1498–1499.
23. IV, 1458; see also III, 1066–1067; III, 1319–1323; *The New York Times*, June 7, 1973, pp. 1, 36, 37.
24. IV, 1503.
25. IV, 1503–1504.
26. For all these "offstage" actions, see, respectively, *The New York Times*, June 7, 1973, p. 1; *The Los Angeles Times*, June 9, 1973, (unpaged clipping); *The New York Times*, June 9, 1973, p. 14; *The Washington Post*, June 12, 1973, pp. A-1 and A-9; *The New York Times*, June 16, 1973, p. 28; *The Washington Post*, June 28, 1973, p. A-1; *ibid.*, July 3, 1973, p. A-1; CBS interview as reported in *ibid.*, August 7, 1973, pp. A-1, A-16.
27. The figure was reported by Douglas Kiker, NBC reporter, in an interview with The Ohio State University research team, Washington, D.C., July 31, 1973.
28. I, 132.
29. I, 348.
30. II, 685, 694.
31. II, 766–767; *The Washington Post*, June 16, 1973, p. A-8.
32. IV, 1412–1429.
33. IV, 1431–1451; 1465–1488.
34. V, 2135–2137.
35. VI, 2481.
36. VIII, 3065, 3067.
37. VII, 2876; VIII, 3079–3081; 3173–3174; 3205–3207.
38. *The Washington Post*, July 24, 1973, pp. A-1 and A-17; *The New York Times*, July 30, 1973, pp. 1, 22.
39. VI, 2601.
40. VI, 2575–2579.
41. VII, 2709.
42. VII, 2659–2661. Recent research indicates that the most important factor in relating television viewing to social reality is receivers' perceptions of *realism* in programming content. See Dan Slater and William R. Elliott, "Television's Influence on Social Reality," *The Quarterly Journal of Speech*, 68 (February, 1982), 69–79.
43. *The Washington Post*, July 25, 1973, p. A-13.
44. *Ibid.*, August 2, 1973, p. A-15. Polling was completed July 12–22.
45. James Greenwood and William R. Brown, " 'Watergate': The Received Message," in William R. Brown and James L. Golden, *The Watergate Communication Event*, unpublished manuscript, p. 167. Conducted with the aid of the Ohio State research team, telephone calls to a systematically selected sample of Columbus, Ohio, residents were placed between the hours of 10:00 a.m. and 9:00 p.m. October 1–14, 1973. N was 392, of whom forty-five per cent were male. According to Ohio Bell eleven percent of Columbus telephone subscribers had unlisted numbers; approximately ninety-seven per cent of Columbus households had telephones.
46. Robert M. MacIver, *The Web of Government* (New York: The Macmillan Company, 1947), p. 4.
47. Interview with Sam Dash, Washington, D.C., December 9, 1975.

Seven years after the Senate Select Committee Hearings on Watergate, another electronic media event occurred which was to have an important influence on contemporary American politics. It was the televised debates between Ronald Reagan and third party candidate John Anderson and between Reagan and President Jimmy Carter. These three candidates were fully aware that the Kennedy-Nixon debates in 1960 and the Ford-Carter confrontation in 1976 had unmistakenly shown the power of television in shaping meanings. The same kind of effect was evident in 1980. The authors of the ensuing essay— "Media Rhetoric, Criticism and the Public Perception of the 1980 Presidential Debates"—advance a series of six propositions showing how the media promoted and evaluated the debates; how a speaker's style and manner as filtered through the television screen were more persuasive than the quality of his arguments; how an incumbent president now operates with a presumption against him; and how the currently used debate format aids the speaker more than the public interest. These premises, along with those developed by McLuhan and Brown, give a partial insight into the impact of technology on rhetoric.

Media Rhetoric, Criticism and the Public Perception of the 1980 Presidential Debates

The two televised debates of the 1980 presidential campaign were the most important media events of the election year.[1] An estimated fifty to fifty-five million voters watched the encounter between Ronald Reagan and John Anderson on September 21, and over one hundred million Americans apparently witnessed the confrontation between Reagan and President Jimmy Carter on October 28.[2] Although the Reagan-Anderson debate drew about thirty million fewer viewers than the first Ford-Carter debate in 1976, it was nevertheless the best attended media event since the start of the campaign three weeks earlier.[3]

What role did the American print and electronic media play in promoting and evaluating these debates? Our analysis and evidence suggests that six claims may be made. Taken together, they provide a composite view of the influential contribution media anchormen, editors, and reporters played in giving meaning to the debates.[4]

Claim 1. Prior to each debate, the media functioned as a promoter of the event and established expectations regarding the probable outcome.

The Reagan-Anderson debate at Baltimore, MD on September 21 received only moderate coverage in the print and electronic media. This general apathy was due primarily to two reasons, First, Jimmy Carter, the incumbent president whose record was the principal campaign issue, refused to participate on the grounds that he would be competing against two Republicans.[5] Second, the debate was scheduled quite early in the fall, and it was natural to assume that more important events would occur closer to election day in November.

The success of the first presidential clash, however, removed the initial reservations concerning the need for the press to function as an active promoter of future debates. As soon as the first confrontation had ended, newspaper editors began to call for a similar exchange between Carter and Reagan, and, indeed, between Carter and Anderson. The Anderson-Reagan debate was widely praised as an important step in the democratic process. We need more of these encounters, argued the *Baltimore Evening Sun* on September 22.[6] A day later the editors of the *New York Times* chastised President Carter for not participating in the first debate and challenged him to present his ideas "effectively; face to face."[7]

The interval between September 21 and October 18 when both Carter and Reagan agreed to a one-on-one debate was marked by frustration and false starts. Thinking he had won the first debate, John Anderson immediately sought a second. But opinion polls showed Reagan the victor and Anderson's strength cut in half from fifteen to eight per cent.[8] The League of Women Voters scheduled presidential debates in Portland, OR and Cleveland, OH and a vice-presidential encounter in Louisville, KY and then was forced to cancel all three.[9] October opinion polls indicated that Reagan was now ahead of Carter but not by

Mr. Berquist is Professor of Communication and Mr. Golden is Chairperson and Professor of Communication at The Ohio State University, Columbus, OH 43210.

a sufficient margin in seven key states to withstand an anticipated last minute Carter surge. The polls also revealed that an uncommonly large number of voters had simply not made up their minds.[10] For a while Carter and Reagan concentrated their attention on television commercials and local issues; neither seemed anxious to break the deadlock on a second debate. Then on October 15, the League of Women Voters removed President Carter's objection to a three way debate by concluding that John Anderson was no longer a major candidate. The following day the President extended a new invitation to debate and this time the challenge was accepted by the California governor.[11]

Once the date was finally set for the Carter-Reagan debate, the media engaged in an extensive promotional campaign to highlight its significance. Typical of the headlines appearing in the national press were these:

"High-Risk Chips on One Debate,"[12]

"The White House May Be Won or Lost Tonight in Cleveland,"[13]

"The Debate Between Carter and Reagan Could Make the Difference Between Victory and Defeat,"[14]

"President Carter and Ronald Reagan Meet in Cleveland Tonight for the Long Awaited Debate that Could be the Crucial Event in Determining Who Will be the Next President of the United States."[15]

Reporter panelists were chosen for the second debate two days before the event. One of the four selected, Harry Ellis of the *Christian Science Monitor,* told us he received approximately twenty telegrams and numerous phone calls urging him to ask particular questions. Special interest groups stressed the importance of "saving the Whales," "ERA," and "One World Citizenship." Ellis became an instant celebrity: local and network television stations contacted him for interviews and autograph seekers sought him out.[16] Two others among the October panelists had similar experiences to that of Soma Golden, a *New York Times* reporter panelist at the Reagan-Anderson debate in September. "The phone rang ceaselessly with unsolicited advice," Golden

noted; "ask about Agent Orange, about the Mafia, about the future of black universities. . . ."[17] Media-induced interest in the debates was widespread and unmistakable.

Television anchormen and reporters were anxious to arouse viewer interest as well but their attempts to do so were principally confined to the two or three days preceding each debate.[18] In his introduction to the Cleveland debate in October, for example, Walter Cronkite of the Columbia Broadcasting System declared: "It's not inconceivable that the election could turn on the next ninety minutes."[19] John Chancellor, anchorman for the National Broadcasting Corporation, heightened viewer interest by describing the hall where the debate was to be held as the "world's largest press room," and his colleague Tom Brokaw reminded listeners that the Cleveland electronic signal would circle the globe. Robert MacNeil of the Public Broadcasting System paraphrased Winston Churchill before the debate thus: "Never may so much have rested" on so little.

Media promotion on the day of the debate was not limited merely to describing the importance of the event; it carried out the larger purpose of alerting viewers to what actually might take place during the ninety-minute confrontation. A key concern of both sides was that their man avoid "any major blunder or misstep."[20] The editors of the *Los Angeles Times* held the opinion that the debate between Carter and Reagan "would help in delineating issues and personalities."[21] Maybe the majority of the still undecided ones will be doing their decision-making" on the evening of October 28, wrote Hal Gulliver of the *Atlanta Constitution.*[22] "Carter will be articulate, workmanlike, thorough. Reagan will be eloquent, slick and hard as blazes to pin down"; there may be no clear winner but the precedent is worth establishing said a group of southern editors.[23] Yet another source advised Governor Reagan to fulfill "a dual battle requirement" by attacking both Carter's economic record and his military pronouncements.[24]

The prospect of "a big evening or disaster" was affirmed by John Chancellor and Tom

Brokaw predicted that now at last we would get the "real views" of the candidates, ". . . something other than rhetoric"; "tempers will flare," he promised. Frank Mankiewicz, former adviser to several Democratic presidential contenders, argued that if Reagan seemed "presidential," the debate might work in his favor as an earlier one had for John Kennedy in September of 1960. John Deardorff, a 1976 adviser to Gerald Ford, noted that the forthcoming debate might well prove important "in a negative way"; the event, in short, could help the viewer decide who *not* to vote for.

Jack Hilton, a television consultant, sought to mold viewer expectations by drafting a set of "ten commandments" for each debater to follow. Presumably the candidate who adhered most successfully to these guidelines would emerge the winner:

1. Be yourself	6. Be correct
2. Be liked	7. Be anecdotal
3. Be prepared	8. Be a listener
4. Be enthusiastic	9. Build bridges
5. Be specific	10. Be cool[25]

Still another media technique for promoting citizen interest was employed the day before the Reagan-Anderson exchange. An Ohio newspaper invited its readers to "compare notes with the experts."[26] The ballot to be used by the Associated Press panel of judges at Baltimore was reprinted. One to five points were to be awarded in each of the following six categories: analysis, reasoning, evidence, organization, refutation, and presentation. Numerical scores correspond to quality judgments as follows: 1 = Poor, 2 = Fair, 3 = Average, 4 = Excellent, 5 = Superior. No special expertise was required.

According to these various media sources, the debates presented an incomparable opportunity for the candidates to take their cases to the American people. A "face-off" between Carter and Reagan, albeit late in the campaign, would create the most dramatic and decisive moment in an otherwise unexciting contest. Media promotion of the Cleveland encounter was principally confined to the three days which preceded it.

Claim 2. Once the debates were over, newspaper and television commentators became instant critics and reporters of listener response.

Consider, for example, what happened within minutes following the debate between Anderson and Reagan: "Political analysts and commentators," observed the editors of *Broadcasting,* "rushed to the telewriter or microphone as soon as the final handshake between the two candidates to tell the world who won and lost and what it all meant."[27]

To generate data for such instant reaction, media critics resorted to a variety of strategies. One of these was to appoint a national panel of geographically distributed debate coaches whose duty it was to identify "the winner" and to provide a rationale for their judgment. The Associated Press followed this practice; its panel used a variation of the standard American Forensic Association ballot.[28] Immediately after the first debate the AP panel announced that Anderson defeated Reagan by a margin of 169 to 154 points; the same seven-member panel later gave Reagan the edge over Carter 161 to 160.

Another strategy was to ask participating media personnel for their instant response. Bill Moyers, moderator of the Reagan-Anderson debate, initially rejected this approach; when asked who "won," he replied curtly "I don't play that game." Nevertheless, Moyers did say the debate "was not a bad beginning" because it gave viewers a "good sense" of how the two men handled themselves "under the conditions of this kind of debate."[29]

NBC television consulted its panel of campaign experts: Tom Pettit of NBC News, Jack Germond of the *Washington Star,* and David Broder of the *Washington Post.* Pettit called the Carter-Reagan debate "a scoreless tie." Germond told television viewers that he was sorry nothing new was said. Broder concluded that Governor Reagan talked to the country effectively while Carter "talked to his special constituencies even more effectively."

CBS News divided its instant coverage between anchorman, Walter Cronkite, and Bruce Morton, one of its regular reporters. Cronkite approached the task by drawing as sharp a distinction as he could between the two candidates. He described President Carter as "glib with facts and figures . . . humorless . . . stiff, formal, no warmth . . . not as good [as Reagan] in a one on one [confrontation]." In contrast, Governor Reagan was seen as "more informal . . . sharp in trying to deflect attacks . . . more fun, more at home with the audience." Carter never challenged Reagan's "facts," Cronkite declared, while Reagan relied heavily on charges he used earlier in the campaign.

Bruce Morton was obviously frustrated. The debate, he said, "didn't make or break anyone . . . a good matchup . . . not a debate . . . a funny kind of forum . . . [the candidates] more or less answered questions . . . no big blunders to help the challenger." Morton argued that Carter sought to portray Reagan as mean, rash, irresponsible; "in your living room" he didn't seem that way. Reagan came across as "a nice guy," Morton concluded, even though he appeared to be "insensitive" to racism early in his career.

ABC News chose to handle evaluative response in a quite different way. The only national network not to cover the Reagan-Anderson debate in September, ABC gambled on a novel plan to "scoop" the other networks. By arrangement with Bell Telephone, viewers could register their opinion as to who won the debate by calling a special number. Each call cost fifty cents. A record of 727,328 calls came in, with Governor Reagan receiving a two to one advantage.[30] The network chose the new method in lieu of conventional commentary by campaign reporters.

Ted Koeppel, moderator of ABC's "Nightline," repeatedly told viewers the poll was unscientific and was actually designed for entertainment purposes only. Yet the results were taken seriously; they were widely reprinted in the press and broadcast nationwide. The ABC poll was carried as a news story and doubtless influenced the attitude of some voters. A wave of criticism denouncing the new technique came from a host of editorial writers and such professional pollsters as George Gallup, Lou Harris, and Pat Caddell. Robert Kaiser of the *Washington Post* spoke for many

when he said: "ABC cooked up a new form of instant analysis that set a new standard for pernicious irrelevance."[31]

A fourth method used was to ask the candidates and their followers who won. The results were predictable: all three candidates made modest claims about their own presentations while their supporters boasted of victory. In each instance, "their" candidate was viewed as gaining needed momentum.[32] One could argue that such partisan response was hardly criticism at all. Yet it might well influence listeners leaning toward a particular candidate and strengthen the beliefs of fainthearted partisans.

Post-debate interviewers with listeners present in the Cleveland audience constituted yet another method for securing instant response to the debate. CBS adopted this approach at the end of its evening coverage and NBC employed it the following mornng on its "Today" show. The *Washington Post's* Robert Kaiser was unimpressed with this sampling technique. As he told readers in the nation's capital, "CBS decided to 'sample' public opinon by interviewing half a dozen of the only Americans who saw the debate without really seeing it—members of the public who had one of the rare tickets to sit inside Cleveland's Convention Center amid the klieg lights and cameras. On the 'Today' show yesterday NBC did the same. Just one of the people interviewed in Cleveland admitted that the debate had changed her vote. She refused to say how."[33]

Broadcasters for NBC and PBS used still another strategy, a refinement of the audience interview. Viewers far from the scene of the debate were invited to respond. Customers in a Houston pub praised the poise of the speakers while simultaneously maintaining that the candidates talked in circles. California undergraduates at UCLA applauded Carter's attack on Reagan's record as Governor but they preferred Reagan's views on the matter of inflation. Some students claimed the candidates resorted to "cheap shots" and at times "acted a little childish." All seemed to think that neither candidate "won." A frustrated New York executive admitted that she was looking for a miracle; she remained uncertain as to how she would vote. A Detroit housewife declared that the debate "crystallized" her position and that she was now "less undecided" than she had been before the debate. A Dallas priest told viewers the second debate proved to him that Reagan "can handle the pressure" of the presidency. No one really knows what effect these views had on television listeners, but it is probable that some of those interviewed put into words what others were thinking.

The motivation for providing readers and listeners with prompt reactions and instant criticism seems clear in retrospect. Both the electronic and print media wished to capitalize on the persuasive thrust of "presence."[34] Thus, commentators felt justified in telling Americans as a whole how a select group of Americans responded. Little effort was made to explain the limitations of such instant reaction, either critical or evaluative. Fortunately, however, a more thoughtful form of criticism followed soon after.

Claim 3. Media analysts contributed significantly to reader and viewer perception of the debates by participating in a "second wave" of more mature criticism.[35]

In the days following each dabate, media specialists sought to produce in-depth analyses based on scientific polls, interviews with political experts, dialogues with colleagues, study of debate transcripts and delayed reactions. Each of the major networks commissioned its own poll. ABC allied itself with the Lou Harris organization; CBS with the *New York Times;* and NBC with the Associated Press. Both President Carter and Ronald Reagan employed private pollsters. All of these polls, along with that conducted by George Gallup, tended to show that the conclusions of the instant analysts did not always agree with those of the public at large. The apparent stand-off between Reagan and Anderson and between Carter and Reagan, for instance, was later translated into a Reagan victory in each case.[36]

Not content to rely on scientific polls, editors and network officials consulted with experts who had specialized knowledge either as practitioners or theorists. Among these were such critics as John Sears, Reagan's former campaign manager; Robert Goodman, advertising executive; Bill Roberts of the California Spencer-Roberts consulting group; James Fallows, former Carter speechwriter; Mervin Field, Director of the Field polling agency; James D. Barber, Duke University authority on presidential character; and Nelson Polsby, University of California-Berkeley political scientist.[37] Examining the Reagan-Anderson debate two or three days after presentation, the experts had little difficulty in arguing that both contenders put on a "surprisingly good show."[38] They also agreed that President Carter lost ground in refusing to participate.[39] Perhaps Terence Smith of the *New York Times* captured the mood of experts best in this report: "The President's refusal to participate in the Baltimore debate produced a flock of critical placards at the airport at Springfield, Illinois, and an earlier stop today at Mr. Reagan's home state. Among the signs: 'Douglas wasn't afraid to Debate a Moderate Congressman from Ill.,' 'Hiding in the White House Again,' 'No Debate, No Votes,' and 'Carter is a Chicken.' "[40]

Actually such delayed criticism was more apparent in the aftermath of the Carter-Reagan debate. In a column written within twenty-four hours after the encounter, David Broder, political specialist for the *Washington Post,* used the following heading: "Both Debaters Did Well."[41] One week later, however, he stressed that the outcome depended upon two ostensibly minor episodes within the debate.

"The essence of the debate for many viewers was captured in the two seemingly irrelevant lines. Carter reducing his most telling argument about danger of nuclear war to the level of spurious campaign rhetoric by claiming the issue was raised by his young daughter, Amy. Reagan airily dismissing Carter's attack on his past positions with a patronizing 'There you go again.' "[42]

There can be little doubt that the quality of the criticism improved in the "second wave." Opinion polls, colleague interaction, and voter interviews all gave a firmer base upon which to construct criticism. Notwithstanding this advance, "second wave" analyses frequently fell short of the expectations set forth by political experts. John Sears put his reservations graphically:

"Most analyses first safely said they thought the debate was a draw, but then quickly stepped into the shoes of the people to say such things as Carter had more to prove or that Reagan, by avoiding outrageous statements, proved that he was capable of being President. . . ."[43] This limited perspective, both on the part of the instant analysts and "second wave" critics, may be explained in part, we feel, by the ensuing proposition which deals with the influence that television, in particular, had on the transmission of a message.

Claim 4. The presidential debates were electronic media events in which a speaker's delivery, appearance, and overall manner—as filtered through the television screen—proved to be more important than substance.

The significance of this claim can be seen when we compare and contrast the impact of reasoning and evidence with delivery and appearance. Informed observers argued that Anderson and Carter had stronger arguments and substance than did Reagan. The Associated Press panel, for example, maintained that Anderson had superior content as demonsrated by his logical appeals.[44] Similarly, two columnists for the *New York Times* praised Anderson for appealing to the intellect by buttressing his arguments with statistical data and citations from government documents.[45] If Anderson had the edge over Reagan in the area of substance, so, too, did Carter in his debate.[46]

But while Reagan apparently lost points due to his lack of hard core content, he more than offset this deficiency through his presentational skills and physical appearance. As David Broder of the *Washington Post* put it: "Substance aside, in all the important areas of the contest for public confidence, Reagan has the advantage. . . . Reagan had the physical presence, the size, the looks and, most important, the voice to dominate the proceedings. It is a supple, deep and trained voice, the more authoritative in contrast to Carter's breathy

squeaks. . . ."[47] Pleasing conversational tones, coordinated gestures, a friendly smile and an occasional toss of the head conveyed warmth and spontaneity to the television audience.

A *Newsweek* reporter supported Broder in his estimate of the Carter-Reagan exchange:

"What Carter achieved most effectively of all was to dominate the agenda—to keep Reagan pinned down on the defensive explaining himself and to deflect any sustained attack on his own record. . . . Yet Reagan's performance as a defendant made vastly more ingratiating television than Carter's as a prosecutor. His imperative was to look calm, cool, and Presidential and he brought it off with body language alone—and with an off—camera handshake that seemed to take Carter off guard and an innocent bystander smile that stood up under the President's heaviest fire. . . ."[48]

This perceived superiority of Reagan in the area of delivery, appearance, and manner was also evident in the debate with Anderson. James Kilpatrick, well-known syndicated columnist, observed: "Mr. Anderson came on too strong; he appeared strident, angry, uptight, ungracious. By contrast, Mr. Reagan—though palpably tense—seemed mellower, easier, less didactic."[49] Thus it would appear that in both debates Reagan benefitted greatly by his ability to operate in a medium which, according to Jim Lehrer of PBS, rewards a speaker for "mushy things" associated with delivery and manner.

The foregoing discussion suggests that the televised presidential debates enhance the power of style and delivery, deemphasize the importance of substance, and often obviate the need for a candidate to reveal his true identity and strongly held convictions. The grimace and the smile tend to count more than the quality of the arguments. It is instructive to note, however, that these characteristics which seem so essential in the televised presentation appear to be less appropriate for the live audience. Soma Golden, in her eyewitness account of the Reagan-Anderson debate, agreed with Anderson's advisers that their candidate projected an image of stiffness and intensity to the television viewer. But, she added, that was not the way he looked in Baltimore. Instead, "he was fascinating to watch—Howdy Doody grown up, an animated, provocative and bright politician. Up there on the podium, the flat and unconvincing Mr. Anderson I had ignored on television's nightly news for weeks became a surprisingly compelling figure."[50]

But if Anderson turned out to be an impressive debater before the live audience, the opposite was true for Reagan. "From ten yards away," noted Golden, "he was unconvincing. His responses were largely oratory. He did not merely duck questions but refused outright to answer some, including mine. It was hard to relate to him; he seemed to ignore the panel and arena audiences, concentrating, shrewdly, on the fifty million voters in television land."[51]

The fact that what a viewer sees as he sits in front of the television set is quite different from what a live audience experiences prompted Tom Brokaw and Richard Scammon of NBC to turn down an opportunity to be a part of the immediate audience. We did so, said Brokaw, because "it all seems so far away down there. You can't get any feel for it."[52] In short, the eyes of the camera told the story most Americans witnessed.

Claim 5. The 1980 presidential debates seemed to refute the notion that incumbency is an advantage.

Historically, incumbency has been considered to be a major asset in a presidential campaign. Usually the occupant of the Oval Office is better known than his challenger. He has access to a large number of prominent surrogates who can speak on his behalf and thus enlarge his campaign effectiveness.[53] As President of the United States, he has the power to grant timely favors and in so doing, to heal party wounds and bring the disgruntled back into the fold. Additionally, modern Presidents have enormous informational resources at their command. Presumably, therefore, at a crucial moment in a debate, an incumbent could say to a challenger: "Your facts simply are inaccurate," and proceed to overwhelm his opponent with specific evidence. Moreover, as President, the incumbent

has virtually unlimited, free access to network television. News conferences to announce developments of national importance are labeled "non-political" even though they may portray the President in a positive way.

For these reasons President Carter, early in September, was confident he would win reelection. The volatile hostage problem seemed to be nearing solution: the release of the fifty-two Americans in Iran would virtually guarantee Carter's return to the White House. Furthermore, the President fully intended to use the power of his office for political advantage as his predecessors had done. Consequently, Reagan forces braced themselves for an "October surprise."[54]

But these assets resulting from incumbency were accompanied by a remarkable liability. There was a widely held assumption that a President running for reelection must always appear to be a winner.[55] Any presidential debate judged "even," therefore, is in fact a perceived victory for the lesser known challenger. Aware of this limitation associated with the power of incumbency, Stuart Spencer, an important adviser to the California governor, announced on the eve of the Carter-Reagan debate: "All we want out of it is a tie."[56] Thus while President Carter was expected to win, Reagan could achieve "victory" with either a win or a tie. Clearly, Spencer's eleventh-hour pronouncement was designed to affect public perception of the forthcoming debate.

As the hour of the debate approached, another factor came into play which blunted the effect of incumbency. The President increasingly was forced to defend his record at a time when the economy worsened and American prestige abroad diminished. By contrast, Reagan, who was out of office at the time of his challenge, could assume the role of attacker rather than defender.[57] It is not surprising, therefore, that the early confidence in the Carter camp faded into apprehension by late October. Polls indicated Reagan was now ahead and news of a breakthrough in Iran was not forthcoming. The weekend before the Cleveland debate, Patrick Caddell, the president's own pollster, informed Carter that "the odds of his winning the debate were 2 in 10."[58] From the President's viewpoint, October 28th was a critical gamble.

The manner in which televised debates have weakened the influence of incumbency led Tom Wicker of the *New York Times* to write:

"It seems clearer than ever that on strictly political grounds Presidents are foolish to debate with their challengers. In the three major presidential debates held so far (1960, 1976, and 1980), the challenger . . . has profited the most, probably winning the election as a consequence. Merely appearing on the same platform and competing more or less equally with an incumbent seems to mean more than whatever debating points may be scored."[59]

In light of the powerful role played by the electronic media in a presidential campaign, an incumbent, it would appear, has a special challenge to become an effective manager of television. Unfortunately for President Carter, his skills in utilizing this medium were no match for those of Reagan.

Claim 6. Televised debate formats currently in use favor perceived candidate advantage rather than the public interest.

Criticism of the format used in the Reagan-Anderson debate was immediate and widespread. Letters to the editor of the *New York Times* complained that rhetoric as taught by the Greeks was replaced by "a video package" which did not permit genuine confrontation, "rebuttal and indepth questioning."[60] To call such an event a debate, observed one writer, "is patently absurd."[61] Other critics described the September format as "a license for evasive answers" and as a stimulus for restating worn-out campaign speeches.[62] In sum, since the panelists could not present follow-up questions, it was highly improbable that a participant would be responsive to the queries.

Displeasure with the September program format was not limited to newsmen and television viewers. Soma Golden, one of the panelists at Baltimore, described the frustration she and her fellow journal participants felt at the time:

I was surprised to learn just how much the format is the debate. Ideally, the candidates should have locked horns in a direct debate of substantial length on one or two important subjects. But they refused that and agreed instead to a series of very brief mini-debates, kicked off by reporters' questions. Worst of all, reporters were not allowed to follow up on their questions. Our frustration must have been obvious. We fought to change the format. Without follow-up questions, we said, one could not pursue an evasive response. But the league said no and we were left to interject stray comments, write exasperated notes to one another and shake our untelevised heads in disbelief at some of the responses.[63]

Although changes were implemented in the Carter-Reagan debate, the format again discouraged appropriate responses. A panelist asked two questions with one follow up each but the questions for each debater were identical, thereby reducing spontaneity and promoting sterility. The end result was not a debate but "a well managed and carefully planned press conference."[64] Of significance here is the fact that the candidates, in insisting "on a panel of reporters, as a sort of demilitarized zone between them,"[65] reduced the probability of having a strong clash of issues.

Discouraged by the format that was adopted for both debates, some observers began to call for specific reforms. Many Americans apparently agreed with Howard K. Smith, moderator of the Carter-Reagan debate, who urged the adoption of a "Lincoln-Douglas" format.[66] In support of this idea, James Kilpatrick recommended that the set for the debate should have a desk for each of the two candidates, along with "a lectern and a jug of water." A moderator should be placed "in the middle and a timekeeper at the side."[67]

In order to set his plan in motion, Kilpatrick suggested that a small committee comprised of knowledgeable persons, including political science professors, be established for the purpose of framing four resolutions. Each candidate would then speak twice on the affirmative side and twice on the negative. The constructive speech would take seven minutes and the rebuttal three.

What should the resolution be like? Two examples suffice to suggest what Kilpatrick had in mind: "Resolved, that the pending treaty on limitation of strategic arms should be abandoned, and that a new agreement should be sought with the Soviet Union. . . . Resolved, that the policies advocated by Mr. Carter would deal more successfully with inflation and unemployment than the policies advocated by Mr. Reagan. . . ."[68] In the first instance, Reagan would defend the affirmative and Carter, the negative. In the second example, these roles would be reversed.

In the foregoing propositions, we have argued that the print and electronic media actively promoted presidential debates as important media events and that they sought to establish certain expectations as to what such events would entail. Once a debate was held, commentators became instant critics as well as reporters of immediate listener response. A "second wave" of more mature criticism emerged in the days following.

We further concluded that in these televised debates, presidential skills were seen as more important than message content. An incumbent President, usually perceived as having an edge in a campaign for reelection, apparently has no special advantage in a televised debate, and indeed, may be at a distinct disadvantge in view of listener demands that he always be "a winner." Finally we noted that the current format of televised presidential debates tends to give priority to perceived candidate advantage rather than enlarging public understanding. One possible way to alleviate this problem is to adopt a "Lincoln-Douglas" type format in the future. In this way, issue-centered debates will once again help determine the outcome of an election.

The analytical techniques of rhetoricians interested in the mass media are not limited to those used in the preceding studies of Watergate and the 1980 presidential debates. In a 1979 text entitled THE RHETORIC OF TELEVISION (New York: Longman), Ronald Primeau advances the thesis that "Classical rhetoric can be applied particularily well to the electronic media because classical orators spoke to the people who had no books and depended entirely on the face-to-face delivery of messages" (p. 24).

Primeau's chapter headings reveal how he utlizes the five classical canons: invention— "Where Do They Get Those Ideas?"; organization— "It's the Order That Counts: Media Arrangement"; style— "Our Heroes Are Celebrities: Media Style"; delivery— "Delivering the Messages: TV Production from Working Script to 'On the Air' "; and memory—"Instant Replay and the Forgotten Art of Memoria." Primeau contends that the five classical canons can be as effectively applied to news and advertising as to game shows, sit coms, soap operas, sports and talk shows.

Contrary to McLuhan, content *does* matter: it is indeed possible to evaluate modern television from the fivefold perspective of classical rhetoric. If done carefully, such critiques combine both information and insight and provide the critic with a fresh look at a medium long taken for granted.

Notes

1. WGBH-Boston did televise a five-week series of surrogate "confrontations" involving Carter, Reagan, and Anderson advisers, but these public television broadcasts were not debates which involved the three leading candidates for the presidency. *New York Times,* 6 October 1980, p. A20.
2. *Broadcasting,* 29 September 1980, p. 48; *Washington Post,* 30 October 1980, p. A4. *Newsweek* set the figure at 105 million, while *Broadcasting* suggested a viewership of 120 million. *Newsweek,* 10 November 1980, p. 34; *Broadcasting,* 3 November 1980, p. 23.

   Television viewers in twenty-six countries in Western Europe, the Pacific, and South America also observed the proceedings of the second debate via communication satellite. *Los Angeles Times,* 29 October 1980, Pt. 1, p. 1.
3. Bill Peterson, *et al.,* "All 3 Candidates Have A Stake in Tonight's Debate," *Washington Post,* 21 September 1980, p. 86.
4. For a stimulating behind-the-scenes look at media involvement in the selection of a presidential candidate, see Laurence H. Shoup, *The Carter Presidency and Beyond: Power and Politics in the 1980's* (Palo Alto: Ramparts Press, 1980).
5. Another reason for Carter's reluctance to participate in the first debate was his disinclination to take part in an event which promised to "enhance Mr. Anderson's credibility as a major candidate. . . ." Terence Smith, "Carter Campaign is Seeking a Compromise with Reagan on Debates," *New York Times,* 7 September 1980, p. A12.
6. Ibid., p. A8.
7. "The Next Debate," p. A22.

8. Anderson told Chicago reporters two days later that he was "happy" with his performance. Warren Weaver, Jr., "A Confident Anderson Seeks A Second Debate," *New York Times,* 23 September 1980, p. B8. Six of seven forensic coaches "ruled Anderson the better debater; one called the show a draw on points." *Columbus Dispatch,* "Public Will Decide Who Was Winner in Challengers' Debate," 22 September 1980, p. A1. Although an Associated Press-NBC News Poll taken during the two days after the debate showed "no clear winner," the *New York Times*-CBS News Poll taken before and after the debate showed Reagan gaining four points while Anderson remained the same. "Campaign Report: Poll Finds No Clear Winner in Anderson-Reagan Debate," *New York Times,* 27 September 1980, p. 8; Hedrick Smith, "Poll Finds Reagan Leads After Debate," *New York Times,* 28 September 1980, p. 1. Between September 12–15 and October 10–12, Gallup reported that the Anderson vote slipped seven points. "Campaign Report: Gallup Poll Finds Anderson Loses Half of Support," *New York Times,* 15 October 1980, p. A23.

9. "Challengers Prepping for Debate." *Columbus Dispatch,* 21 September 1980, p. A3; *New York Times,* 30 September 1980, p. A20; 2 October 1980, p. B12.

10. *New York Times,* 1 October, p. A1; 5 October, p. 1; 12 October, p. 34; E. J. Dionne, Jr., "All Those 'Don't Knows' Are Crucial," *New York Times,* 12 October 1980, p. E1.

11. *New York Times,* 30 September 1980, p. A21; 1 October 1980, p. B7; 6 October 1980, p. A21; 15 October 1980, p. A23, p. B8; 18 October 1980, p. 1.

12. *The Atlanta Constitution,* 22 October 1980, p. A4.

13. *Louisville Courier-Journal,* 28 October 1980, p. A1.

14. *St. Louis Post-Dispatch,* 28 October 1980, p. A1.

15. *Washington Post,* 28 October 1980, p. A1.

16. Telephone interview, 23 January 1981, Ellis reported that "a blizzard of telegrams flowed in to each of the Cleveland panelists in the forty-eight hours preceding the debate. "Two Days in a Goldfish Bowl: What It was Like Being Debate Panelist," *Christian Science Monitor,* 30 October 1980, p. A10.

17. "The Editorial Notebook: Meanwhile, Inside the Debate," *New York Times,* 24 September 1980, p. A30.

18. A videotape was made out of the Reagan-Anderson debate and videotapes and audio cassettes were made of the NBC, CBS, ABC, and PBS debate coverage both before and after the Carter-Reagan debate. Quotations from television commentators which occur in this essay come from these recorded sources. The authors are indebted to Mr. Bruce Matthews of The Ohio State University Telecommunications Center for procuring these data. Funding came from an instructional research grant awarded to Professor Berquist by the University's Task Force on Learning Resources.

19. A week earlier a Reagan aide summed up the importance of the October debate thus: "There's an hour and half left in the campaign." "The Week in Review: Freedom Now? Hopes on Hostages Overshadow Final Week's Debate," *New York Times,* 26 October 1980, p. E1.

20. Thomas W. Ottendad, "Carter Has Advantage, Reagan the Opportunity in Debate," *St. Louis Post-Dispatch,* 28 October 1980, p. A6.

21. 16 October 1980, Pt. II, p. 6.

22. 22 October 1980, p. A4.

23. "At Last, the Debate," *Atlanta Constitution,* 27 October 1980, p. A4.

24. Martin Schram, "Carter Goes Into Debate With Gain in New Poll," *Washington Post,* 28 October 1980, p. A4.

25. *Washington Post,* 26 October 1980, p. C2.

26. "Here's How Judges Will Score Debate," *Columbus Dispatch,* 20 September 1980, p. B9.

27. *Broadcasting,* 29 September 1980, p. 48.

28. The Associated Press panel included James Unger, Georgetown University; Donn Parson, the University of Kansas; Barbara O'Connor, California State University-Sacramento; James Copeland, Marquette University High School; Jack Rhodes, University of Utah; Melissa Wade, Emory University; and William Southworth, University of Redlands.

29. *Baltimore Evening Sun,* 22 September 1980, p. A1.

30. *Broadcasting,* 3 November 1980, pp. 23, 25; *Los Angeles Times,* 31 October 1980, Pt. 1. p. 19; *St. Louis Post-Dispatch,* 29 October 1980, p. A5.

31. 30 October 1980, p. A4. Albert Cantril, President of the National Council for Public Opinion Research, noted that "despite ABC's disclaimers of the survey's reliability, getting 700,000 responses conveys a false impression of reliability, simply by the numbers." *Los Angeles Times,* 31 October 1980, Pt. 1, p. 19.

32. *Baltimore Evening Sun,* 22 September 1980. pp. A1, 3; *Cleveland Plain Dealer,* 30 October 1980, pp. B1, 4; *New York Times,* 23 September 1980, pp. A1, B8.

33. 30 October 1980, p. A4.

34. As an example of "presence" on the local scene, Professor Golden was contacted by UPI in Columbus to give an evaluation immediately after the Carter-Reagan debate.

35. The military metaphor, "second wave" criticism, was borrowed from CBS correspondent Dan Rather.

36. *Broadcasting,* 29 September 1980, p. 48; *Minneapolis Tribune,* 30 October 1980, pp. A1, 10; *Newsweek,* 10 November 1980, pp. 35, 37; *New York Times,* 28 September 1980, p. A11; *Wall Street Journal,* 30 October 1980, p. 2.

37. *Newsweek,* 10 November 1980, p. 36.

38. *Wall Street Journal,* 23 September 1980, p. 20.

39. Mary McGrory, "Neither Anderson Nor Reagan Lost," *Atlanta Constitution,* 24 September 1980,

p. A4; Louis Harris, "Skipping First Debate Hurt Carter's Popularity," *Atlanta Constituion,* 27 September 1980, p. A2; Flora Lewis, "The Jingo Issue," *New York Times,* 23 September 1980, p. A23; "Surprisingly Good Show," *Wall Street Journal,* 23 September 1980, p. 20; "Who Won, Who Lost," *St. Louis Post-Dispatch,* 23 September 1980, p. A8; "For Many in Iowa, Carter Lost the Debate," *New York Times,* 23 September 1980, p. B9.

40. "Carter, in California Visit, is Praised by Governor Brown," 23 September 1980, p. B8.

41. *New Orleans Times-Picayune,* 22 September 1980, Sect. 1, p. 11.

42. *Washington Post,* 5 November 1980, p. A18.

43. *Washington Post,* 30 October 1980, p. A23.

44. *Baltimore Evening Sun,* 22 September 1980, p. A8.

45. 23 September 1980, pp. B8, 9.

46. See *St. Louis Post-Dispatch,* 28 October 1980, p. A1; 29 October 1980, p. A10; *Washington Post,* 30 October 1980, p. A23.

47. "The 'Presidential' One Will Win," 26 October 1980, p. C7.

48. 10 November 1980, p. 36.

49. "One More Word on the TV Debates," *Atlanta Constitution,* 25 September 1980, p. A4.

50. *New York Times,* 24 September 1980, p. A30.

51. Ibid.

52. Michael Hill, "Television's Two-Ton Pencil Was Third Star of the Debate," *Baltimore Evening Sun,* 22 September 1980, p. A3.

53. Edward Walsh, "Carter Loads the Guns of Incumbency," *Washington Post,* 5 October 1980, pp. A1, 3. Walsh reported that "between now and election day, members of President Carter's Cabinet have been asked to reserve a total of 110 days for campaigning. . . ."

54. Hedrick Smith, "Reagan Camp Is Bracing For Final Push By Carter," *New York Times,* 3 October 1980,

p. A19; Lou Cannon and Edward Walsh, "The Debate: A Single Roll of the Dice With White House at Stake," *Washington Post,* 19 October 1980, p. A5.

55. "People expect too much of a President," Lloyd Cutler, Carter's legal counsel declared. Eleanor Randolph, "Role of Incumbent Hangs Heavily on the President," *Los Angeles Times,* 28 October 1980, Pt. 1, p. 1; *St. Louis Post-Dispatch,* 28 October 1980, p. A6.

56. *Washington Post,* 29 October 1980, p. A10. James Baker of the Reagan staff went even further: "We don't even have to tie. A close loss is a good performance." "Campaign Report: Face to Face Tonight," *New York Times,* 28 October 1980, p. A1.

57. Ellis informed us that "incumbency is tough in this television age." Often a question for the incumbent is built upon the negative. Reagan as challenger, on the other hand, did not have to deal with reporters who tend to "harp upon perceived failures and mistakes." Telephone interview, 12 January 1981.

58. *New York Times,* 9 November 1980, p. A18.

59. 9 November 1980, p. E21.

60. 28 September 1980, p. E20.

61. Ibid.

62. *New York Times,* 23 September 1980, p. B9; *Washington Post,* 24 September 1980, p. A27; 21 September 1980, p. D4.

63. *New York Times,* 24 September 1980, p. A30.

64. *Louisville Courier-Journal,* 30 October 1980, p. B2.

65. Ibid.

66. Tom Dorsey, "Is the American Electorate Served By TV Debate's 'No-Lose' Policy?," *Louisville Courier-Journal,* 30 October 1980, p. B2.

67. "Why Not Have a 'For Real' Debate?," *Atlanta Constitution,* 24 October 1980, p. A4.

68. Ibid.

14

Rhetoric as Meaning: Channeling the Message

In the preceding three chapters on meaning, we have examined some of the principal ideas of I. A. Richards, Marshall McLuhan, and of a group of theorists who have dealt with the related themes of significant symbols and speech acts. Additionally, we attempted to show in Chapter 13 how two influential televised political events stimulated millions of Americans to assign meanings to their experiences. In this final chapter on rhetoric as meaning, we will again highlight two case studies which have in common the goal of generating understanding through the process of channeling the message. The two channels consist of the traditional rhetorical canons: style or language control and delivery.

We begin our discussion by returning briefly to George Campbell's celebrated doctrine of usage. This doctrine, which had its roots in the classical period and was supported by Campbell's contemporaries, has become one of our strongest current legacies. With considerable devotion, a large majority of modern scholars both adhere to and trumpet the virtues of utilizing language that conforms to the criteria of "reputable," "national," and "present" use. Indeed, the chapters created by the authors of this textbook, along with the essays and reprints of others appearing in this volume, predictably have been guided by the rules of the doctrine of usage or standard English. In academia as a whole, seldom, if ever, have these rules been challenged despite the fact that they may shape meanings in a detrimental way—at least as it relates to a particular group in

our society. To offset this limitation, at least partially, we have commissioned the following essay, entitled "Linguistic Sexism: A Rhetorical Perspective."

The two authors, Susan Mura and Beth Waggenspack, have been instructors in a course in Western rhetorical theory. Moreover, they have had an abiding interest in the study of language and of human rights. It is against these background experiences and values that they seek to demonstrate how the doctrine of usage so ingrained in the mores of our social environment has created meanings unfavorable to women. Although Richards is not quoted directly, his influence is evident throughout the analysis. Here, as you will see, is the flow of the arguments they advance. First, our current practices are dominated by sexism. To establish this claim, they cite, with a large body of supporting data from linguists, our excessive reliance on the generic "he" and "man," and emphasize the debilitating effects of a non-parellelism based on "trivialization," unfortunate "word-pair" combinations, and "terms of address," all of which have the unhappy result of featuring sex roles that are harmful to women. Secondly, the authors demonstrate what they perceive to be the seriousness of this problem by pointing out the circular relationship between thought and language, and the effect that language usage has on the way we reason. Finally, they offer suggestions for reducing or eliminating sexism in language. To state whether or not this plan should be implemented or modified is beyond our purpose in this survey. What is of central importance as you read the ensuing arguments is to gain an appreciation of the part that language can play in affecting meaning and, in turn, the part that our desire for shared meaning can play in determining the words we use to channel our ideas.

Linguistic Sexism: A Rhetorical Perspective

What is the nature of the relationship between language and rhetoric? According to Kenneth Burke, "the basic function of rhetoric [is the] use of words by human agents to form attitudes or to induce actions in other human agents,"[1] while I. A. Richard asserts that "rhetoric . . . should be a study of misunderstanding and its remedies."[2] Both of these approaches lead us to look at our language and to investigate the meanings we would attribute to the symbols in it. One area in particular where such analysis is needed today is that of sexism in language, also known as linguistic sexism. The purpose of this essay will be to show that since the words we use form attitudes, in order to prevent misunderstandings, we must become aware of the impact of sexism in our language. To this end, the essay will (1) examine exactly what is meant when it is said that our language is sexist, (2) examine the impact of linguistic sexism in our attitudes and thoughts, and (3) suggest techniques to reduce or eliminate sexism from our language.

Is Our Language Sexist?

Sexism, in general, is the discrimination against a person on the basis of sex. As it relates to language, it is any verbal act that arbitrarily assigns roles or characteristics to people on the basis of sex alone.[3] Unfortunately, both of these terms carry sexist connotations of their own in that they are usually taken to refer only to women, but sexism exists just as surely against men. The most glaring instances of sexism are against women, for their role has been traditionally assigned a submissive and generally negative evaluation while men have traditionally been assigned a dominant and generally positive valuation; but as will be pointed out, many examples of linguistic sexism against males *do* exist.

Having established what is meant by linguistic sexism, the question now becomes one of whether or not the English language is sexist. According to Otto Jesperson, a prominent linguist in the early part of this century, the English language should be praised as it is "positively and expressly *masculine,* it is the language of a grown-up man and has very little childish or feminine about it."[4] It does appear that our language reflects the traditional male-female roles in our society; since males are traditionally the dominant sex, the flavor of the language is truly masculine. Within our language are many differing types of linguistic sexism, but these generally seem to fall into two primary categories: exclusion and nonparallelism.

Exclusion

The category of exclusion represents a type of sexism where one or the other of the sexes is eliminated, grammatically or connotatively, from consideration.

Generic "he." The term "generic" is a familiar one in this day of "un-brand" foods and "no-label" products; usually, generic items lack a specific company trademark. Generic refers to a whole kind, group, or genus (class) of items. The use of the generic "he" results from a stipulation in traditional English grammar that sex-indefinite referents call for the masculine pronoun "he," thus referring to the whole class of humans rather than only the male segment. The "proper" use requires that the following sentences use "he," although the referent or noun being represented may as likely be female as male.

> When a student takes an exam, *he* must study before hand.

> Prior to *his* presentation, the speaker expects an introduction.

> The teaching associate for this class is hard, isn't *he*?

Such use results in the average schoolbook having a four-to-one ratio of masculine to feminine pronouns, even in areas such as home economics which are traditionally considered to be feminine.[5] This ratio is carried over to everyday language and is odd in light of the fact that over fifty percent of our population is made up of females.

The use of the generic "he" is not quite as absolute as one might think. In cases where sex-role stereotypes are predominant, even the most fastidious grammarian would feel comfortable in switching to the use of "she." Therefore while we may have

> The professor should post *his* office hours;

> Before a doctor can practice, *he* must be licensed;

> The taxi driver drives as if *he* were a maniac;

we may also have

> If the secretary pleases *her* boss, *she* will succeed;

> A nurse must have *her* LPN to work in a hospital;

> The model constantly diets to look *her* best.

These uses are not thought of as strange or unusual, yet each contains an inherent bias as to the appropriate sex for each role, whether those involved fit the traditional sterotype or not. On the other hand, this use of the generic "he" may be stretched to a farce as two instances cited by Key suggest.[6] In the first, a female dancer had indecent exposure charges dismissed against her, because as the judge pointed out, the law specifically referred "to a person exposing an inappropriate part of *his* body." In the second, a state law is cited which reads, "No person may require another person to perform, participate in or undergo an abortion against *his* will." (Emphasis added)

Generic "man." Another example of exclusion as sexism is the use of generic "man." For example, it is common to see such terms and phrases as "mankind," "man-made," and "the man on the street." In Old and Middle English, this use was not exclusive, since "man" referred to a human being (irrespective of sex or age) while "wer" and "wif" were used for male and female, respectively. The use of generic "man" today, according to the *Oxford English Dictionary,* denotes primarily the male sex, with the generic sense being restricted to the "literary and proverbial." The use persists, albeit confusingly, as a generic in popular use, even though the terms are in fact perceived as being specific and *not* generic.[7] Take, for example, the word "manpower." Businesses claim that it includes women as well as men, but its use in a Boy Scout advertisement, "America's Manpower Begins with Boypower," makes the meaning all too clear.

In practice [then], the sexist assumption that man is a species of males becomes the fact. Erich Fromm certainly seemed to think so when he wrote that man's "vital interests" were "life, food, access to females, etc." Loren Eisely implied it when he wrote of man that "his back aches, he ruptures easily, his women have difficulties in childbirth."[8]

This bias is carried over to the word "people" at times, also, as evidenced by Samuel Eliot Morrison's (1965) summarization of the role of colonial women in only four lines in his book, *The Oxford History of the American People;* Nevins and Commanger's *Pocket History of the United States: The Story of a*

Free People also devotes only four sentences to the role of women.[9] One final example shows, as could be seen with the generic "he," that the use of the generic "man" may, indeed, be quite laughable in its inappropriateness. In this example, a 1975 radio news report stated "Archaeologists announced today that they have discovered evidence of *man's* existence as far back as 3,000,000 years ago, based on the dating of a *woman's* skeleton."[10]

An extension of the generic "man" may be found in the common use of man in occupational terms on titles when those holding the jobs may be of either sex. This includes such terms as businessman, mailman, foreman, chairman, policeman, patrolman, garbageman, etc. Examples of the specific connotations of these terms, despite objections to the contrary, are abundant. We see on television Farrah Fawcett's role as chair*man* of Women Against Cancer. Note the error in the general statement, "All the congressmen and their wives attended the festivities," and the incongruity found in "I think Margaret Thatcher is a true states*man.*" Due to the use of the generic, linguistic confusion easily may occur.

Non-Parallelism

The second major category of linguistic sexism is that of nonparallelism. The notion of parallelism is similar to Perelman's "rule of justice" which "requires giving identical treatment to beings or situations of the same kind."[11] Sexism arises when differing treatment is given to humans on the arbitrary basis of traditional sex roles, differences which appear to be due to socialization and not to inherent genetic differences.[12] At the root of nonparallelism are differing associations or connotations attached to males and females. For example, males' natural traits are assertiveness and control; females' are emotionality and passivity. Females' most frequent associations are domestically oriented, fashion-minded, and emotional; males' are delinquency, business, and money.[13] Neither of these roles is conducive to the maintenance of a mutually healthy individual.

The language used to describe both sexes is very restrictive. For the woman, she is the subordinate, the caretaker, the ornament, the immature. For the man, he is the powerful, the killer, the fighter, the business executive, the bread-winner, and the crook. The linguistic sanctions placed upon those who would engage in cross-sex-role behaviors is even more so. The phenomena referred to by Graham as "my virtue-is-your-vice," has it that the worst possible insult which can be given to a man is to call him "womanish, effeminate, or sissy"; for the woman, it is almost as bad to be called "a man or mannish" because this implies that she has overstepped her bounds, has unsexed herself, and has emasculated (made female) the men around her. Other types of non-parallelism seem to be outgrowths of an attempt to maintain this unjust but sharp distinction between the sexes. These types include trivialization, word pair non-parallelism, and terms of address.

Trivialization. This type of sexism in language operates through the use of diminuitive forms, such as poet*ess* and usher*ette,* and through a process which, through time, shifts a once neutral or positive term to a negative one. Diminution has a way of taking male-marked terms and making them less-than-male with a suffix such as "ette," "ix," or "ess." As such, we have actress, aviatrix, stewardess, waitress, authoress, and suffragette, all of which imply something deviant from and suggest something less than an actor, aviator, steward, waiter, author, or suffragist.

Other forms of trivialization come through the use of overt sex-marking or covertly-marked job titles; for example, (lady) doctor, (male) nurse, (male) secretary, (lady) lawyer, (male) teacher, (female) judge. In each of these cases, the overt sex-marking makes the term so labeled as a linguistic oddity, and the individual so designated as an anomaly in society, for they are less than what they "should" be.

Derogation takes a variety of words, originally neutral or positive in meaning, which now have many negative connotations. For example, we have girl (originally a child of either sex), whore (originally a polite term for a lover of either sex, deriving from the same Latin root as "dear"), harlot (a person of either sex), nymph (a beautiful young girl), wench (a child of either sex) and spinster (one who tended the spinning wheel).[14] Another trend is to attach animal names to trivialize one sex. Witness the use of "young pup" and "gorilla" to designate males and "chick" and "snow bunny" to refer to females. A recent example of this is a 1982 Borden Dairy's advertisement which proclaimed "1982 National Secretaries Week. Take a Heifer to Lunch."

Word-pair non-parallelism. This category, although similar to trivialization, refers specifically to pairs of words which were at one time equivalent. Take, for example, the differing connotations given to bachelor versus old maid, cook versus chef, teacher versus professor, master versus mistress, sir versus madam, governor versus governess, tailor versus seamstress. All were, at one time, parallel in connotation, denoting only sex differences, but all have shifted through an elevation of one and a derogation of the other. One may also look at such pairs as career man versus career woman or family man versus family woman. In these pairs, career man and family woman may seem to be redundant, for they express ideas which fit the normal expectations of society; they are, however, the logical but not practical equivalents of career woman and family man, both which imply a deviance from normal behavior. A further example may be seen in the wer and wif pair, originally meaning man and woman. Wer has changed to be used in werewolf and wif has shifted to mean wife. This shifting results in the non-parallel pair, man and wife (as opposed to husband and wife or man and woman) with a subtle implication of the wife being an attachment to the man.

Terms of address. This final category of linguistic sexism is one which has received much attention over the past few years with the acceptance of Ms. into general use. As a response to the non-parallelism of Mr. for any male and Miss or Mrs. as required signals of marital status for any female, Ms. is probably the best known example in the attempt to reduce or eliminate linguistic sexism. Other address patterns have not been so quick to change, however. Take, for example, a woman's taking of her husband's name upon marriage (in many instances, both given and surname), while he makes no change at all. Even when women do not adhere to this custom, few people will respect their wishes, and such simple things as getting a driver's license renewed or a loan application approved become major obstacles. This problem was recognized in 1840 when Elizabeth Cady Stanton, a founder of the Women's Rights Movement, declared on her wedding day that she wished to be known as Elizabeth Cady Stanton; she maintained:

There is a great deal in a name. It often signifies much and may involve a great principle. Why are slaves nameless unless they take that of their master? Simply because they have no independent existence . . . even so with women. The custom of calling women Mrs. John This or Mrs. Tom That is founded on the principle that white men are the lords of us all.[15]

Other problems crop up if the woman has a Ph.D. or M.D. In many instances, either she will not be granted the courtesy of her title (being labeled as Mrs. instead) or *he* will be assumed to hold the advanced degree.

The worlds of academia and business have their own inequities in this area. The common practice of addressing letters with unknown recipients to Sir ignores those people who aren't Sirs. The typical use of the title chairman is sexist in its connotations, leading at the extreme to such outlandish references as Madame Chairman. The use of chairperson is no better unless it is used for both males and females, for otherwise the gender marking is non-parallel and as biased as it ever was. Other examples of sexism in this area include (1) calling a female by a title and surname while calling a male by his surname only (Ms. Jones and Smith), (2) calling a female by her given name and a male by his last (Jane and

Mr. Worth), (3) calling a female by her husband's given and surname and a male by his own given and surname (Mrs. Peter Winston and Jim Barnes). In each of these instances, non-parallelism of reference prevails, maintaining a sexual bias (perhaps even in the guise of courtesy) against those individuals involved.

Does Linguistic Sexism Affect Our Attitudes and Thoughts?

Although the categories and examples of linguistic sexism presented here are not exhaustive, they do point out quite clearly that our language is most certainly sexist. The next question thus becomes one of impact. Does linguistic sexism matter? Does it affect our attitudes, the way we think about the world, the way we think about ourselves? In order to begin to answer this, we must digress momentarily to look at the nature of the relationship between language and thought.

Language and Thought

It is fairly well accepted today that a circular relationship exists between language and social thought such that "language both reflects and regulates social relationships; it shapes the environment and is itself shaped by it."[16] Thus, as a society develops, it creates a language reflective of what is important to that society. In so doing, the language begins to *"actively symbolize* the social system, representing metaphorically in its patterns of variation the variation that characterizes human cultures."[17] When children are socialized into a culture, their "thinking is heavily conditioned by *language,* by *custom,* and by *myth,"*[18] using these to construct pictures of the world around them and develop notions of the way things should be. "In this process," according to Halliday, "which is also a social process, the construal of reality is inseparable from construal of the semantic system in which the reality is encoded."[19] One can, of course, go to the extreme and postulate, as the Whorf-Sapir Hypothesis does, that language totally controls

our thoughts and therefore our society, but this theory, in its strong form, at least, is clearly unacceptable.[20]

The moderate and generally accepted version does make clear that while our speech system is a product of our social structure,[21] the same speech system inclines us to categorize the world in a particular way and thus maintain social reality. Another example from the 1982 National Secretaries Week presented a Cleveland Florists' Association advertisement with the following copy:

For years, "Secretaries Week" has meant Flowers for Secretaries. So FLOWER HER this year. But secretaries aren't the only women who deserve plenty of recognition. This year, let's recognize ALL WORKING WOMEN, understand their working needs, and support them. Secretary, bookkeeper, file clerk or receptionist, when they've done a great job, tell 'em "thanks" with fresh flowers.

Thus, "by their everyday acts of meaning, people act out the social structure, affirming their own statuses and roles, and establishing and transmitting the shared systems of value and knowledge."[22]

Linguistic Sexism and Thought

We know that our language does affect the way we think as it "actively creates an environment of its own,"[23] but how does this specifically relate to sexism and language? Linguistic sexism helps to maintain (if not create for new generations) a sexist society. Language lets us know that, at least semantically, men and women are entirely different creatures, rather than being the male and female of the human species. As Dr. Bobbye Sorrels Persing says,

sexist communication robs all people of full human potential. It often creates within more than half of the people of the world—women—the self-fulfilling prophecy of inferiority and failure. It often creates for the remainder—men—a frighteningly aggressive, insensitive, superioristic model of machismo.[24]

The semantic categories of our sexist language then organized our thought patterns, excluding one sex or the other from consideration, perpetuating the myth of non-equality in our thoughts.

Generic "man". Studies of the psychological perceptions of these semantic categories support this claim. For example, one may look at the use of generic "man." In a 1973 study, Schneider and Hacker asked college students to find pictures representative of the chapters in a major sociology text. One half of the students were assigned chapters entitled using generic "man," such as "Social Man," and "Industrial Man"; the other half were assigned chapters entitled "Society," and "Industrial Life." Analysis indicated that the titles using "man" resulted in sixty-four percent of the pictures being male only while the other chapter titles resulted in thirty to forty percent less male-only pictures. In fact, the title using generic "man" seemed to exclude women from primary consideration. Such exclusion seems to affect the authors and publishers of books, too. A study by Nilsen (1977) looked at fourteen randomly selected grade school texts using generic "man" in the title, e.g. *The First Men* (May), *Prehistoric Man* (Scheele), *Man and His Tools* (Burns), *Man and Magic* (Appel), among others. Of these, the illustrations represented 577 males and only 129 females, with a full one-third of the females being in one book, *The Color of Man* (Cohen). Perhaps, as Nilsen says, "it is significant that this book was illustrated not with drawings but with photographs. This is another example of the difference between the world that really exists, i.e. in photographs, and the world that we as adults perceive and present to children, i.e. in imaginative drawings."[25] What we end up with, therefore, is "the 'archetypical assumption' that all people are male until proven female."[26]

Another example is the mistranslation of the Bible, which for many stands as the very Word of God. When the word "man" is used, it is assumed to be the male of the species and is taken as evidence of the natural superiority of man over woman. The "man," however, which our current translations use, is based on a mistranslation of the Hebrew word "adam" which is generic for humankind.[27] It is obvious then the intent to be inclusive of both male and female as seen in Genesis 1:26–27: "So God created *man* in his own image, in the image of God he created him; male and female he created them." This mistranslation exists throughout the creation epic of Genesis 1 to 3, implying as it does a false role of man specific as master and sole symbol-maker.

Generic "he". The use of the generic "he" is equally as troublesome as the use of generic "man." It is suggested by Miller and Swift that "the generic pronoun (he) has an effect on personality development, implying that women are a human subspecies, whereas it bolsters male egos."[28] Logically, this is quite a reasonable notion. Children begin to pick up personal referents (the he/she and his/her) quite early and for a time seem to be fairly equal in their use. As the boy child grows, he will find that his personal referent is appropriate in a great many situations, while the girl child will find that her personal referent is a deviant and only appropriate for a restricted range of situations.[29] At an early age, it appears that children do use their respective personal pronouns to refer to neutral objects in about a 3:1 ratio, but as they enter school, the girl children are forced to reverse this ratio if they are to meet standard formal English criteria.[30]

Studies directed at discovering the use of her or she in relation to specific jobs indicated that he is not generic, as "he" was related to jobs such as doctor, plumber, and boss, while "she" was related to nurse, teacher, and dancer, even though the individuals were not specified and thus were grammatically indefinite.[31] A recent study by Wheeless, Berryman-Fink, and Serafini indicates that his breakdown of usage is still typical today, as well as the tendency to use "he" and "she" with respective sex-stereotyped occupations.[32] Again we find ourselves faced with the dilemma of being male, or at least neuter, unless proven female.

Connotative differences. Another area where sexism in language affects thought is in non-parallel treatment of the sexes. Women are faced with a linguistic description of themselves as childlike, passive, weak, dependent, fragile, serving, and flighty, a description which can easily lead to a degraded self-image. It has even led psychologists to view a healthy female as less balanced, less mature, and less self-actualizing than healthy adults (i.e. males).[33] On the other hand, men are faced with a description of themselves as tough, stoic, dominant, in charge, handy with tools, good at sports, and breadwinners. They must never cry or show any emotion save anger, must not appreciate the aesthetics, must not value family over career, and must not share in the housework lest they be labeled henpecked. So while in many ways the superiority of males may seem an ideal state, it is as harmful to males as are the inferiority stereotypes of females. For those who would disagree, a quick look at the high incidence rate of ulcers, heart attacks, and other stress-related ailments in males is evidence of this.

Our language, in its sexism, reflects unrealistic demands placed on males and females, perpetuating stereotypes which limit *human* potential, and, "as with racism, so with sexism; we all lose when another is diminished and belittled. We all have much to gain from fair and equal treatments under the language."[34]

Can Linguistic Sexism Be Reduced or Eliminated?

As we have seen, the English language is currently sexist in nature, and this sexism does have an impact on how we view the world due to the integral relationship between language and social structure. Unfortunately, as an extension of its "representativeness" of society, language tends to become stagnated. The words themselves become a representative of divine will and become reality in their own right—a part of "the 'objectivity' of the world of things."[35,36] Societies become enamoured by

the magic of language. The reason for this confusion which attends the growth of new organizations in society lies deep in the psy-

chology which concerns the effects of words and ceremonies on the habits of men [sic] in groups. Men [sic] always idealize these habits and the structure they give to society. The idealizing is done by magic words which at first are reasonably descriptive of the institutions they represent. At least they represent the dreams which we have of those institutions. When the institutions themselves disappear, the words still talk of the new organizations which have come to take the place of the old in the terms of these old words. The old words no longer fit. Directions no longer have the practical results which are expected. Realists arise to point this out and men [sic] who love and reverence these old words (that is, the entire God-fearing respectable element of the community) are shocked. Since the words are heavily charged with a moral content, those who do not respect them are immoral.[37]

Opponents to the elimination of sexism in language are responding to Arnold's notion, thinking of themselves as a part of this "respectable community," and they respond to proposed changes by citing several arguments. One argument states that language cannot be changed overnight, so no change should be encouraged. Opponents say that societal change must evolve over long periods of time and that language should reflect this evolution rather than act as an instigator for change. To counter this argument, we note that the relationship between society and language is circular, not linear. Entering the circle at any point should be an effective means of change. This does not imply that language can be altered overnight; any change will be gradual, but the end result should justify it. For example, one might examine the changes in the labels applied to Blacks over the years and note that the deliberate intervention into the language system caused a positive shift in the attitudes applied toward this race. The Black Rights Movement instigated a shift from the use of "nigger" to "colored" to "Negro" and finally to "Black." This resulted in changes in society's outlook as well as the self-image of the Black race.

Opponents also claim that the elimination of sexism forces changes in deeply ingrained language habits. They suggest that any such change is doomed to failure, just as the United States' change to the metric system was doomed to failure. We note that the majority of Western nations use metrics and the conversion to that system did not entail personal or social upheaval. With appropriate education and an attitude of acceptance, there is no reason why changes in language should result in social disruption.

Finally, opponents question the means to change. Several approaches have been suggested; some of these are acceptable and some are not. One example of the unacceptable is the ridiculous and unnecessary elimination of supposed sex references from our language, regardless of their derivation or current meaning (for example, person to perdaughter, management to personagement, amen to awomen, or hurricane to himmicane). These types of proposed changes are suggested only by those who would sabotage efforts to eliminate linguistic sexism as they make trivial the contribution of the change.[38] Other more well-intentioned yet no more acceptable changes include: (1) the creation of new pronoun forms to provide a generic singular (as in, she for she/he, herm for her/him, and heris for her/his; tey for he/she, tem for him/her, and ter/s for his/hers);[39] (2) creating a non-sexist generic term for humans (i.e. gen);[40] and (3) creating new courtesy titles for men which specify marital status, i.e. Mngl. (pronounced mingle) for single and Mrd. (pronounced murd) for married.[41] All of these changes have virtually no chance of becoming accepted and, in the face of more manageable alternatives, they should best be forgotten.

A Plan for Reducing Linguistic Sexism

To propose a change in our language, then, seems to some people to border on heresy, but to maintain the stifling stereotypes of sexism in language when the resources for change are easily available is to brand one's self as an irresponsible communicator and rhetorician. To be certain, the elimination of such sexism will not take the place of social change in reducing the stereotypes, but by becoming *aware* of the connotations of the symbols we do use, we may attempt to select those symbols which most closely fit with the reality of human nature. In turn, this should begin to have an impact on our thinking patterns as we cease to base our symbolic categorizations of people on sex alone and start to look at people as humans and individuals.

Generic "man". As an example of the readily available terms in use in eliminating sexism, generic "man" has as possibilities humanity, human beings, humankind, people, and persons. When it is used as a part of the occupational title, alternatives are also available. For example, chairman may go to chair, head, chairperson, co-ordinator, or moderator; businessman to businessperson or business executive; fireman to fire fighter; mailman to mail carrier; foreman to line supervisor; craftsman to crafter; and ombudsman to ombudser. The man in the street may easily become the person in the street or a passer-by; man-made may become synthetic; and man-hours may become workhours. In any of these cases, the substitutions are readily available and result in little more than a passing awkwardness as we adjust to a new usage.

Generic "he". The elimination of the generic "he" is a bit trickier than what we just saw with the generic "man," yet it can nonetheless be accomplished through any one of several alternatives.[42] The first is to recast the sentence into the plural, yielding something like "The students who study reap their rewards" rather than "The student who studies reaps his reward." Another possibility is to reword the sentence in order to eliminate unnecessary problems; for example, "Students who study reap rewards." Still another alternative is to use she or he (or s/he), although this should never be done in contexts where constant use within a single sentence may confuse the sense of the sentence. The result might be something like the following, if used correctly: The student who studies gets her or his reward." One may also alternate examples of male and female use, achieving something like

"Take responsibility for your students. Does he understand the material? Does she come to class regularly?" One final suggestion, supported by the National Council of Teachers of English (1974), is to use, except in strictly formal usage, plural pronouns as a substitute for the masculine singular.[43] Thus, one gets a sentence such as "Anyone who wants their final grade early should bring a postcard to the last class." This final suggestion is one which has stimulated much controversy with grammarians saying that the agreement in number is violated and humanists saying that the agreement in gender is more important than number. All authorities, however, do not condemn this particular use of the plural prououn, for even so authoritative a source as the *Oxford English Dictionary* (OED) defines *they* as "often used in references to a singular noun made universal by every, any, no, etc., or applicable to one of either sex." Examples of this use given by the OED include: "if a person is born of a gloomy temper . . . they cannot help it," or "he never forsaketh any creature unless they have forsaken themselves." The OED shows that historical precedence exists for this usage, for until the early 1800's, it provided the primary mode of reference to sex-indefinite subjects, whether singularly or in the plural. In casual conversation today this use predominates as it provides (as it always did) an easy and acceptable solution to the inaccuracy of the generic "he."

Non-parallelism. Variances in connotations due to non-parallel use of terms may be overcome in several ways. Terms which patronize or trivialize one sex should be avoided completely. It is just as easy to say "I'll have my secretary do it" as it is to say "I'll have my girl do it," and far less demeaning for the secretary. It is also quite easy to refer to people as authors, poets, sculptors, actors, etc. without specific gender marking being added. Special attention toward the use of parallel terms should be paid, such that we have men and women, not girls and men; man and woman, not man and wife; Jane Doe and Carl Smith, not Miss Doe and Smith; and so on. Care should be taken not to presume the sex of the person involved, as with secretaries, plumbers, bosses, doctors, or teachers, or to add inappropriate gender labels when our stereotypes aren't fulfilled, as with women doctors, male nurses, and the like. Other roles or behaviors should not presume sex by stereotype either, so rather than saying, "Have your Mom send cookies," it is preferable to say, "Have your parents send cookies."

Generally, the key toward reducing and eventually eliminating linguistic sexism is awareness—awareness of the psychological implications of one's language. While we cannot separate a symbol from its connotations, we can be aware of the connotations and how they function in discourse. Only then may we be prepared to select those symbols which will reduce misunderstanding and promote a higher level of communicative interaction by responsible rhetors.

Susan Mura is a graduate student in the Department of Communication at The Ohio State University; Beth Waggenspack is an Assistant Professor of Speech and Theater at The University of Missouri.

Notes

1. Kenneth Burke, *A Rhetoric of Motives* (New York: Prentice-Hall, Inc., 1950), p. 41.
2. I. A. Richards, *The Philosophy of Rhetoric* (New York: Oxford University Press, 1936), p. 3.
3. Guidelines for Nonsexist Use of Language in NCTE Publications," in *Sexism and Language,* ed. by Alleen Pace Nilsen, Haig Bosmajian, H. Lee Gershuny, and Julia P. Stanley (Urbana, Ill: National Council of Teachers of English, 1977), pp. 183–191; Bobbye Sorrels Persing, *The Nonsexist Communicator* (East Elmhurst, New York: Communication Dynamics Press, 1977), p. 1.
4. Otto Jesperson, *Growth and Structure of the English Language* (New York: The Free Press, 1968), p. 143. (First edition, 1905).
5. Alma Graham, "The Making of a Non-sexist Dictionary," in *Language and Sex: Difference and Dominance,* ed. by Barrie Thorne and Nancy Henley (Rowley, Mass: Newbury House Publishers, 1975), p. 58.
6. Mary Ritchie Key, *Male/Female Language* (Metuchen, N. J.: The Scarecrow Press, Inc., 1975), p. 89.
7. Joseph W. Schneider and Sally L. Hacker, "Sex Role Imagery and the Use of the Generic 'Man' in Introductory Texts," *American Sociologist,* VIII, 8 (1973), 18.

8. Alma Graham, "Non-sexist Dictionary," p. 62.
9. H. Lee Gershuny, "Sexism in Dictionaries and Texts: Omissions and Commissions," in *Language and Sex: Difference and Dominance,* ed. by Barrie Thorne and Nancy Henley (Rowley, Mass: Newbury House Publishers, 1975), p. 152.
10. Julia P. Stanley, "Gender-marking in American English: Usage and Reference," in *Sexism and Language,* ed. by Nilsen et al. (Urbana, Ill: National Council of Teachers of English, 1977), p. 56.
11. Chaim Perelman and L. Olbrechts-Tyteca, *The New Rhetoric: A Treatise on Argumentation* (London: University of Notre Dame Press, 1969), p. 218.
12. Eleanor E. Maccoby and Caro Nagy Jacklin, *The Psychology of Sex Differences* (Stanford, Ca: Stanford University Press, 1974), pp. 348–373.
13. H. Lee Gershuny, "Sexism in Dictionaries," p. 147.
14. Muriel R. Schulz, "The Semantic Derogation of Women," in *Language and Sex: Difference and Dominance,* ed. by Barrie Thorne and Nancy Henley (Rowley, Mass: Newbury House Publishers, 1975), pp. 66–69.
15. Theodore Stanton and Harriet Stanton Blatch, eds., "Elizabeth Cady Stanton to Rebecca R. Eyester, May 1, 1847," Elizabeth Cady Stanton as Revealed in Her Letters, *Diary and Reminiscences,* II (New York: Harper, 1922), 147–148.
16. Anthony D. Edwards, *Language in Culture and Class: The Sociology of Language and Education* (London: Heineman Educational Books Ltd, 1976), p. 34.
17. Michael A. K. Halliday, *Language as a Social Semiotic* (Baltimore: University Park Press, 1978), p. 3.
18. Gordon W. Allport, "The Historical Background of Modern Social Psychology," in *The Handbook of Social Psychology,* 2nd ed., Vol. 1, ed. by Gardner Lindzey and Elliot Aronson (Reading, Mass: Addison-Wesley, 1968), p. 49.
19. Michael A. K. Halliday, *Social Semiotic,* p. 1.
20. Benjamin L. Whorf, *Language, Thought, and Reality* (New York: John Wiley and Sons, 1956).
21. Basil Bernstein, "Elaborated and Restricted Codes," *American Anthropologist,* LXVI, 6 (1966), 56.
22. Michael A. K. Halliday, *Social Semiotic,* p. 2.
23. *Ibid.*
24. Bobbye Sorrels Persing, *Nonsexist Communicator,* p. 1.
25. Schneider and Hacker, "Sex Role Imagery," pp. 12–18; Alleen Pace Nilsen, "Sexism in Children's Books and Elementary Teaching Materials," in *Sexism and Language,* ed. by Nilsen et al. (Urbana, Ill: National Council of Teachers of English, 1977), p. 174.
26. Jessica Murray, "Male Perspective in Language," *Women: A Journal of Liberation,* III, 2 (1973), 50.
27. H. Lee Gershuny, "Sexism in Dictionaries," p. 111.
28. Casey Miller and Kate Swift, "De-sexing the English Language," *Ms.,* I (Spring 1972), 7.
29. Alleen Pace Nilsen, "Sexism in Children's Books," p. 176.
30. *Ibid.,* p. 178.
31. *Ibid.*
32. Virginia Eman Wheeless, Cynthia Berryman-Fink, and Diana Serafini, "The Use of Gender-specific Pronouns in the 1980's" (paper presented at the Fourth Annual Communication, Language, and Gender Conference, Morgantown, West Virginia, October, 1981).
33. Inge K. Broverman, Susan Raymond Vogel, Donald M. Broverman, Frank E. Clarkson, and Paul S. Rosenkrantz, "Sex-role Stereotypes: A Current Appraisal," *Journal of Social Issues,* XXVIII, 2 (1972), 59–78.
34. Johanna S. DeStefano, "Introduction from the NCTE Committee on the Role and Image of Women in the Council and the Profession," in *Sexism and Language,* ed. by Nilsen et al. (Urbana, Ill: National Council of Teachers of English, 1977), p. viii.
35. Max K. Adler, *Naming and Addressing: A Sociolinguistic Study* (Hamburg: Helmet Burske Verlag, 1978), p. 12.
36. Ernst Cassirer, *The Philosophy of Symbolic Forms,* Vol. I (New Haven, Conn: Yale University Press, 1957), 117.
37. William Arnold, *Folklore of Capitalism* (New Haven, Conn: Yale University Press, 1937), as quoted in Max K. Adler, *Naming,* p. 32.
38. Bobbye Sorrels Persing, *Nonsexist Communicator,* p. 8.
39. *Ibid.*: Miller and Swift, "Desexing."
40. Casey Miller and Kate Swift, "One Small Step for Genkind," *New York Times Magazine* (April 16 1972), p. 364.
41. Bobbye Sorrels Persing, *Nonsexist Communicator.*
42. "Guidelines for Nonsexist Use," pp. 183–191.
43. *Ibid.*

Since delivery, like language control, is a fundamental aspect of channeling a message, we turn now to this canon in an effort to see more clearly its function in producing meaning. Most helpful in this regard is Karl Wallace's provocative essay, "A Modern View of Delivery." What makes Wallace's approach so useful are the new insights he brings to this frequently misunderstood element of rhetoric. In his review of classical and British theories of delivery, Wallace faults the writers of these periods for treating this canon primarily from the standpoint of management of the body and voice and feeling and emotion; and for their tendency to separate the channel from the message. To follow this procedure, he argues, is to place delivery outside the province of meaning.

The last section of Wallace's paper is designed to show how a new interpretation of delivery is needed for a relevant rhetoric that is vital for the present day. Drawing upon his own notions of speech act theory with its concern for units of discourse, Wallace urges us to perceive delivery not as a separate canon but as an essential part of a single act "dominated by meaning." From beginning to end, he asserts, a speech act has but one overriding purpose—the creation of meaning. Because of its nature as a channeling medium, delivery occupies the final stage of a speech act which is a unified whole. Thus delivery functions in the dual capacity both as a moulder and as a reflector of meaning. Viewed from this perspective, delivery assumes a significant role in any theory of rhetoric that stresses the value of meaning.

A Modern View of Delivery

The endeavor to look anew at old concepts in often revealing and instructive. I hope to show that this is particularly true of a concept in rhetoric that has been variously, and sometimes loosely, called *delivery, pronuntiatio, actio, declamation,* and *elocution.* To some rhetoricians and teachers of speech, the "meaning" of *delivery* may be simple and self-evident; to others the word may be so vague and weasel-like that its significance can only be stipulated. For confirmation, each group may point to the same evidence, namely, that major theorists seem to avoid discussion of the nature of delivery—though most of them, like Cicero and Quintilian, are almost lyrical over *pronuntiatio* and *actio* as powerful influences in persuasion—or they omit mention of delivery altogether, as did George Campbell in his lectures on the philosophy of rhetoric.

I want to direct attention to the nature of delivery. Either its nature is not worth the trouble of thorough analysis and understanding, or delivery as a discernible part or component of a communicative act escapes analysis and upon probing vanishes into nothing of consequence. In looking at the concept anew, we shall first note briefly what the traditional rhetoricians and elocutionists have said, if indeed they said anything. We shall then proceed to see how delivery was understood when perceived in its original context as one of the five constituent parts, or divisions or operations of rhetoric. Finally, we shall suggest that it can properly be viewed as utterance that objectifies one's response to a context in which the respondent is functioning as a communicator. The physical basis is vocal and gestural (or bodily) behavior. This behavior is modified and shaped by words and word combinations that are subject to, and are dominated and refined by, the meaningful aspect of the utterance.

I

The difficulties inherent in dealing with the concept of delivery may be swiftly indicated.[1] Aristotle sets the stage, for his "definition" of delivery as well as his attitude toward it are reflected in the long history of rhetoric and still resonate in the pronouncements of modern teachers of English and speech.

[Delivery] is, essentially, a matter of the right management of the voice to express the various emotions—of speaking loudly, softly, or between the two; of high, low, or intermediate pitch; of the various rhythms that suit various subjects. These are the

Reprinted from *Essays in Honor of Claude M. Wise,* edited by A. Bronsteen C. L. Shaver and C. Stineno, pp. 153–166. Speech Communication Association, 1970.

three things—volume of sound, modulation of pitch, and rhythm—that a speaker bears in mind.[2]

In this passage it is clear that Aristotle recognized the physical aspects of *hypocrisis* and the regulation or management of those features of voice perceived as *megathos* ("volume," or the space-filling quality of utterance), *harmonia* (pitch and accentuation), and *rhythmos* (time and measure).[3] He is referring, too, to those meanings associated with the speaker's and listener's emotional state of being. He appears not to link vocal behavior with intellectual or mental activity; rather words and word combinations are the primary carriers of meaning.[4] We are told by implication that a speaker does not manipulate or "manage" his voice so as to reveal the meanings of words.[5] Aristotle makes no mention of gesture, as Cope admits.

Quintilian incorporates Cicero's view of delivery; so we shall be missing nothing if we let the *Institutes* speak for Cicero. Quintilian dutifully reports that "delivery [*pronuntiatio*] is often called action [*actio.*] But the first name is derived from the voice, the second from the gesture. For Cicero in one passage speaks of *action* as being *a form of speech* and in another as being *a kind of physical eloquence.*"[6] Prompted by Watson's rendition of the Latin, we should have Cicero saying that *actio* is as it were the speech of the body or the eloquence of the body.[7] Watson has Quintilian using *actio* as a generic term synonymous with *pronuntiatio.* Its "parts"—voice and motion (or movement)—are constituent parts, not discrete elements. Functionally, *pronuntiatio* directly reveals emotional meanings which rouse corresponding emotional meanings in listeners.[8]

The Ramists, as is well known, split the theory of rhetoric into invention and judgment on the one hand, and elocution and utterance or pronunciation on the other. Abraham Fraunce's understanding of *pronuntiatio* seems to represent the Ramists. Following Omar Talon, Fraunce described it as a "fit deliuering of the speech alreadie beautified," and

offers no more by way of definition.[9] He is obviously implying that in the prepared, premeditated oration the act of delivery follows composition. Fraunce implies darkly what Francis Bacon implies more plainly. In *The Advancement of Learning* Bacon uses *elocution, tradition,* and *delivery* as virtually equivalent terms. They all refer to the transmission, the delivering over, of one person's thoughts to another. In employing these words, he has in mind the physical basis of any act of communication, which for him meant speech, voice, gesture, and written characters.[10]

The better-known eighteenth-century rhetoricians and elocutionists either take no notice of delivery, as is true of Joseph Priestley and George Campbell, or regard it as the management of voice and body.[11] Hugh Blair devoted most of his discussion of "the pronunciation or delivery of a discourse" to voice, distinctness, slowness, and propriety.[12] In preparing the ground for his treatment of delivery, he reasserts that "tones and gestures" are the primary indicators of emotional experience. But he asserts, also, that the meanings embedded in ideas and words are enforced by vocal and gestural behavior. Thus Blair appears to imply that utterance possesses an intellectual quality as well as an emotional one.[13]

The father of the elocutionists, Thomas Sheridan, provides the significant evidence. "Elocution," he says, "is the just and graceful management of the voice, countenance, and gesture in speaking."[14] Sheridan's amplified version of this definition is more explicit:

A just delivery consists in a distinct articulation of words, pronounced in proper tones, suitably varied to the senses, and the emotions of the mind; with due observation of accent; of emphasis, in its several gradations; of rests or pauses of the voice, in proper places and well measured degrees of time; and the whole accompanied with expressive looks, and significant gestures.[15]

Although recognizing that *pronuntiatio* had "such a comprehensive meaning amongst the

[margin note: See ? Lambani]

ancients, as to take in the whole compass of delivery, with its concomitants of look and gesture," Sheridan observed that the meaning of the word by his day had been narrowed to denote chiefly articulation and accent. In looking at the elocutionary movement broadly, Frederick W. Haberman has observed that by 1725 the significations of *style, elocution* and *pronunciation* had changed markedly:

Whereas pronunciation once embraced the whole field of delivery, it later signified the correct phonation of words in isolation. *Elocution,* which once meant the manner of artistic composition, became identified with the manner of artistic delivery. *Style,* once a subsidiary synonym for elocution, later comphrehended the whole [art] of the choice and arrangements of words.[16]

In general it can be said that the elocutionist concentrated on bodily action, voice management, vocal production, and pronunciation, and that "delivery" referred to physical behaviors signified by these terms.[17] It can be said, also, that the elocutionists, like the ancients, assigned high value to vocal and gestural behavior because voice and bodily movement were charged with the power and revealed the subtleties of emotion and feeling. The vocabulary of those who write of the affective side of behavior varies somewhat, but the writers are all thinking of non-verbal meanings. James Mason, for example, speaks of "the full Sense and Spirit" and the "Sentiments" of the reader and speaker, and James Burgh of "the principal Passions and Humors."[18] Sheridan himself insisted that "the passions and the fancy have a language of their own, *utterly independent of words. . . .*[Italics mine.][19]

Until about the middle of the eighteenth century, then, the term "delivery" referred to vocal and gestural behavior that signaled the speaker's state of emotion and feeling. Nothing seems to have been said about the intellectual or symbolic aspect of experience that is associated with the primary, indicative meanings of words. During the century some rhetoricians and elocutionists began to claim

that delivery ought to be "natural" and sound like conversation. Certain qualities of vocal and bodily behavior were held to be unmistakable signs of what was going on when a speaker was *communicating* with someone. Between expressing and performing on the one hand, and communicating, or talking to and with, on the other, there was a real difference in voice or tone or style of utterance. Modern teachers of speech and rhetoric who know the history of their discipline are familiar with the controversy that boiled up over the proper way of achieving the conversational quality in delivery. The quality was evident in any mode of delivery open to the public speaker, the actor, and the interpretive reader. But how best to attain it? The controversy over method though it sheds strong light on the nature of delivery we cannot find space for here.[20]

Among teachers of public speaking in the twentieth century, James A. Winans was probably the first to probe searchingly into conversational quality. Even in the most formal circumstances, he said, speaking is an enlarged conversation in which the speaker's mental, vocal, and gestural activity reveal the the meanings of utterance as directly and immediately as it does in the most impromptu and spontaneous conversation. There is a difference between being aware of "the sound and feel" of words as is usually evident in a "memorized," or "reading," or absent-minded, or declamatory mode of delivery and being fully aware of meaning at the moment of utterance. There is a difference between the feeling or sense of communicating *with* an audience and the aloofness that marks soliloquizing.[21] In a word, during delivery a speaker is dominated by meanings prompted by the desire to communicate something appropriate to his hearers and for their benefit.

Despite Winans' contribution and despite the scientific analysis of speech and language behavior by students of linguistics, psycholinguists, and experimental phoneticians, there is *still no clear and commonly-accepted view of the nature of delivery.* In support of this statement, I shall reproduce a few "definitions" by the better known textbook writers on public speaking, speech fundamentals, communicative speaking, and the like. None of the quotations is earlier than 1951:

Delivery can be regarded as the whole of the speaker's overt behavior.
[Delivery] is the vital, physical means by which ideas are transmitted to a listener.
[Delivery] is *delivered* language.
Delivery is a comprehensive term for all aspects of a speaker's mental, audible, and visible behavior while addressing an audience.
Delivery is the total management of mind, voice, and body in the act of speaking. [And from the same page:] It is the moment of consummation of the communicative act.
[Delivery involves] the utterance of a message in the presence of other people. . . .

The amplification of the last of these definitions follows the Winans line. Involved in delivery is "a keen sense of communication and a vivid realization of your idea at the moment of utterance, and . . . control [over] all the channels of action—mental, physical, and vocal—to support and re-enforce ideas." The student is told that during delivery "you reactivate a subject and ideas to support it, that you regenerate the enthusiasm that led you to speak in the first place."
The "full and sharp realization of content . . . includes more than bare meaning; the implications and emotional content must also be realized." Moreover, "the reference here is not merely to . . . striking emotions . . . but to those attitudes and significances constantly present in lively discourse . . . the sense of one moment of meaning as being more important than another, awareness of query as opposed to assertion, concern as different from indifference," etc.[22]

II

The original rhetorical context in which *delivery* appeared may help in understanding our problem if not in solving it. The classical rhetoricians probably held that creative and analytical activity took place primarily, and perhaps entirely, within the speaker and that he resorted to voice and gesture in order to transmit to others what had been going on inside his head. The divisions or parts of rhetoric were *inventio, dispositio, elocutio, memoria,* and *pronuntiatio* (delivery). Concerned with the teaching of formal speechmaking and with the conditions that made an oration effective, the theorists saw the "parts" of rhetoric as operations indispensable to the production of a speech. Invention involved the finding of the materials of the speech, specifically the discovering of arguments, from the well of one's experience and from the circumstances calling for persuasion. Disposition was the selecting and ordering of the fundamental materials of the speech and thus the forming of it. Elocution was the wording, the putting into verbal symbols, of what had been invented and arranged, and memory involved the recalling of words in a sequence. Left to delivery, then, was the making of the vocal sounds associated with words and the indicating of the emotional context of words.

The five operations had a psychological basis. Their processes were categorized in terms of faculties or powers of the mind and soul. To see, if only briefly, what faculties were responsible for what operations is to see that delivery involved the emotional responses of the speaker, not the intellectual. When a speaker was said to invent and to dispose, two faculties were primarily at work: understanding and reason. The understanding, the abstracting power, searched about in man's storehouse of experience for materials having the simplest of abstract forms. The reason, closely allied with the understanding, was engaged in combining and synthesizing the simplest forms discovered and apprehended by the understanding; reason conducted the activities of composition and division. In these processes reason was also judging the consistency, the relevance, and perhaps the appropriateness, of what it was forming. The understanding was revealed in non-discursive mental activity as intelligence, wit, and insight; reason was revealed in discursive activity. It was the mind disposing, i.e., the mind engaged in moving about from one position to another the simple forms supplied by the inventive powers of the understanding. Thus the understanding and reason functioning together were held to account for discovering, selecting, and shaping that which was to be spoken. What was spoken were words and word patterns. Within the speaker—may we say, within the speaker's mind?—words were images, both auditory and visual. These were originally learned through sense experience and whenever man had to employ sensory channels through which to reach others he pulled on the language experience available to him. Reproducing words, so the classicists held, was the joint responsibility of memory and imagination. The symbolic, or meaningful, aspect of words was due to the joint efforts of the understanding and reason.[23] What we know about these operations, then, coupled with what is known about the habits of preparation of the great orators who illustrated the classical tradition—their occasional writing of the complete speech, their protracted oral practice and rehearsing, and the committing of the whole to memory—all suggest that composition was one thing and delivery another. A speech could exist, and did exist, undelivered orally, although it might be built for a definite audience, as were John Milton's speeches to Parliament. A speech, then, lived for its audience through print or through voice and gesture. Either channel of transmission revealed the speaker's intellectual operations, his linguistic meanings, equally well, but *pronuntiatio* and *actio* supplied power that print could not match, for they revealed the full emotional and affective experience of the orator. In post-classical times, the elocutionist was alive to this fact and his efforts to exploit it occasionally produced marvels of vocal and gestural gymnastics. Attention to the emotional resources of voice and gesture rather than to the meanings of words and word structures served to keep alive the notion that composition was one kind of thing and delivery another. Prior to the elocutionists, Peter Ramus and his followers claimed for logic the intellectual operations involved in inventing, disposing, and judging and relegated to rhetoric the activities of styling and delivering. The first three operations were sufficient to produce a composition in words; the last two provided ways of enhancing and embellishing speech and language for purposes of delighting and persuading. Perhaps it is not too extreme to say that in the hands of Ramean theorists delivery became quite unintellectual indeed.

Although the difficulties of interpretation are many, I think that rhetoricians in the classical tradition saw speechmaking as two different acts or events, the one bringing about a composition, the other transmitting the composition, the one consisting of the intellectual activities essential to the creating of a verbal product, the other consisting of vocal, gestural, and emotional behavior in response to what had been composed. Possibly the theorists regarded the external, palpable event as something more than the motor behavior necessary for conveying the inner impalpable event to the ears and eyes of an audience. Was the outer event the counterpart, or perhaps the correlative, of the inner event? Were vocal and gestural behaviors representing what had taken place internally? The historical evidence is too meager to cope with these problems. It is true that Aristotle clearly stated the presumption that is still central to any theory of communication, namely: ". . . spoken words are the symbols of mental experience . . . [and] the mental experiences which these directly symbolize are the same for all. . . ." On this evidence, the spoken word is an integral part of the mental experience it symbolizes. Yet the same statement implies that speech does not symbolize nonmental experience. The implication would appear to be inconsistent with Aristotle's definition of delivery as the management of the voice in ways that reveal emotion. The definition, however, may be intended to suggest their vocal qualities, overtones, intonations, inflections, and the like directly address the senses of the hearer and that the response to such stimuli is direct rather than mediated through symbols. So one would regard the phenomena of delivery as body speaking to body rather than mind speaking to mind.

III

The underlying reason for the historic difficulties in characterizing delivery is a psycholinguistic one. In what way, or ways, does one regard and describe the relationship of speech heard or language seen on the one hand, to the communicator's inner experience and activity, impalpable and unobservable by the exterior senses, on the other? Prior to committing this "sentence" to the eyes of others, something has gone on inside me. I need not here tackle that baffling question, *what* has gone on inside me. I need only say that something has occurred. So we can ask: How is the outer, observable event linked with the inner, unobservable event? Are we dealing with two events or with a single one? Is what is uttered and gestured a complete act with its own beginning and ending? Does the interior event immediately prior to it comprise a complete movement with its proper beginning and ending? Suppose we regard a speech act, or a communicative act, as a single event. And suppose outer behavior is simply the *objective* feature of the event— that which is the actualization, the culmination of an experience whose origin resides in the contextual situation to which the event is the communicative response. If this were the case, utterance is an aspect of an act, an integral feature of creative activity, and not a separate sensory event. A speech act is then an element, not further divisible into units.[24]

A modern view of delivery would regard vocal and gestural events and words uttered in communicative settings as integral parts of a single act. It is an act dominated by meaning and meaning therefore tinges every part of the act. In informal, dialogue-type circumstances, which classical theorists grossly neglected, the act can appropriately be called the speech act; in circumstances calling for formal discourse it can be called the rhetorical act, or perhaps rhetorical action. The essentials of the two acts are alike; so here we shall focus on the speech act. This act begins in a communicative setting that calls for an oral response. The oral response and accompanying gestures constitute the final and culminating stage of the response. Let us see.

In a setting calling for utterance, anyone who chooses to speak rather than not to speak has a reason. The speaker may or may not be aware of what prompts his utterance. In conversation he is typically unaware of what led

him to speak, and if pushed to account for his choice he may be able to do no more than to say, "It was the thing to do." The reason for utterance, technically speaking, lies chiefly in the concept of purpose. In some settings a more accurate term than *purpose is intention,* or *goal,* or perhaps *motive.* The notion of purpose—and of related but not synonymous concepts—is a property or feature of a communicative context shared by speaker and hearer. The contextual feature is that which invites speech and determines the direction or goal of utterance. The goal in turn prompts the selection of the materials and means by which the speaker expects to achieve his purpose. That is, there comes to the fore a segment of experience that is felt to be relevant and appropriate. The shaping of such a segment of experience under the influence of purpose constitutes the form of the act. Or perhaps one can say that internally a configuration of purpose and experience takes place. The configuration issues, or is figured, and is perceived by the speaker and his hearer as meaningful utterance. If this be the nature of an act of speech, it is evident that vocal and gestural behavior is functionally a part of the act. It is the culminating or terminal feature. If the act be thought of as a whole or a unit, it is the kind of whole to which utterance is essential. There is no speech act without utterance, and no utterance without events logically and naturally prior to it.[25]

Another property or essential quality of the speech act is meaningfulness, and delivery as a part of the speech act is marked by meaning. To define meaning is unnecessary here. It is important to recognize only that whatever we mean by meaning it appears as a function of the speech act as a whole. One does not speak unless the context of the communicative situation is in some way meaningful to him. It must make sense to him. Further, in his expectation and appraisal of the communicative moment, what he chooses to say must be likely to make sense, not nonsense, to his hearer. Meaning is roused, like the past itself, whenever a bit of experience is put to use and becomes active. In communicative speech that is indeed what happens; our experience works for us. In utterance, experience and its climate of meaning come into play precisely because the conditions of context, purpose, material, and form combine to utilize a portion of the speaker's past. It has often been said that we speak out of our experience to the experience of others; it makes deep sense also to say that we speak out of our meanings to the meanings of others. Hence a modern view of delivery must hold that vocal and gestural behavior is dominated and guided by meaning. Winans was close to the mark when he said that a speaker is engaged in the realization of ideas during the moments of utterance. If one objects to "idea," it might be better to say that a speaker is actualizing meaning. Or to say that experience that is potential, specific, and directed to the utterance of the moment is becoming actual and real to the speaker. And present during communicative utterance is always an edge of meaning revealed in the quality or "tone" of vocal behavior, saying that the speaker is talking *to* and *with his auditor and not merely to himself. This quality, as Winans said, is identical with a sense of communication,* something that is experienced by a speaker as a feeling-tone that pervades the utterance. A speaker who sounds the tone of communication is aware in the fringes of his attention field, that his success depends upon the understanding, respect, and good will of his listeners. He knows that *by* saying something he is trying to satisfy both himself and others.[26]

If it be true that informal, extempore utterance and that the prepared utterances of public speeches no matter how simple or elaborate are the final stages of creative, communicative acts and are the objective actualizations of inner, communication-directed activity, it is equally, though less obviously, true that the vocal and gestural behaviors of the oral reader and the actor are the culminations of creative acts. It is commonly held that a poem is incomplete unless read aloud. The reader who is other than the poet brings his experience to the understanding and interpretation of the text. Thus to some extent he shares in a creative enterprise that is completed and actualized by his utterance. Actors and director actualize through the resources of theatre the script of the playwright. The term, "living theatre," is apt.

The speech act and the rhetorical act are unitary wholes. They exist for the sake of meaning-to-be-communicated. They are indivisible except for purposes of analyzing, teaching, and learning. As one of the parts or aspects of such acts, delivery is permeated with the meaning of these acts.

That meaning must be regarded as an integral feature of delivery is an idea that is recognized more or less clearly by some students of speech behavior. They may, or may not have been directly influenced by the Winans tradition. S. S. Curry, for example, asserted that "expression is subjective as well as objective . . ." and that "the objective phenomena are manifestive of subjective experience."[27] Without caring to define delivery, Parrish said:

> We have held steadily before us the conception that one speaks not merely to express himself, but to accomplish some purpose with relation to a given audience, and *this conception must determine the nature of the speaker's delivery,* just as it must determine his choice of a subject and his selection of materials. [Italics mine.][28]

Waldo Braden and Giles Gray deplore the notion that a speech and its delivery have been considered two different things.[29] Keith St. Onge writes that "delivery is the total management of mind, voice, and body in the act of speaking." It marks "the moment of consummation of the communicative act."[30] William P. Sandford and W. Hayes Yeager are aware of the difficulties of definition, and allude to the views of Winans, Charles H. Woolbert, James M. O'Neill, Andrew Weaver, and Ray K. Immel, and then remark: "Delivery is obviously something more than the mere manipulation of external movements of the body and management of tones and inflections of the voice."[31] Huber Ellingsworth and Theodore Clevenger, Jr., state their position unequivocally: " 'Delivery' is not an object or an event, but is instead an aspect of the speech act. It never occurs outside the context created by a speaker addressing an auditor on some occasion in certain language concerning a particular idea."[32]

Surely today delivery cannot be properly described nor defined in terms that are exclusively physical. Nor can it be associated primarily or exclusively with the "expression" of emotion. It is saturated with the meaning for which a particular act of speech exists.

Karl Wallace

The late Karl Wallace was a distinguished professor of speech communication at the University of Massachusetts.

Notes

1. Doubtless some graduate student scholar should assemble and survey the evidence exhaustively. I hope that my choices from the historical record are not unrepresentative. For penetrating criticism and helpful suggestions in the preparation of this paper, I am indebted to my colleagues, Professors Jane Blankenship and Herman Cohen.
2. *Rhetorica* 1403 b 28–32, trans. by W. Rhys Roberts. *The Works of Aristotle Translated into English under the Editorship of W. D. Ross,* 12 vols., XI (Oxford: At the Clarendon Press, 1924), Roberts' translation should be compared with that of John Henry Freese in the Loeb Classical Library: *Aristotle: The "Art" of Rhetoric* (Cambridge: Harvard University Press, 1959).
3. Perhaps E. M. Cope's interpretation and renderings of the Greek are sharper and more revealing to the modern student than the translation of others. See *An Introduction to Aristotle's Rhetoric* (London and Cambridge: Macmillan and Co., 1867), pp. 277–278. Cf. *The Rhetoric of Aristotle with a Commentary by . . . Edward Meredith Cope, Revised and Edited . . . by John Edwin Sandys,* 3 vols. (Cambridge, England: At the University Press, 1877), III, 1–3.
4. Although today we would not care to distinguish sharply the meanings carried by words as they are used in utterance from those meanings borne by other features of utterance, we must understand that all learned men, as well as rhetoricians, once accepted such a distinction. Intellectual experience and an intellectual state of being were different from emotional experience and an emotional state of being; the indicative functions of language, attributed chiefly to what we call nouns, verbs, adjectives, and adverbs (i.e., the substantive aspects of utterance), and the indicative mood seemed obviously different from the non-indicative functions of language revealed in the other "moods" of utterance.
5. This point emerges in part from Aristotle's treatment of style in the *Rhetoric* and in part from Aristotle's belief, explicitly stated in *De Interpretatione* (16 a 4–5), that "spoken words are the symbols of mental experience" and that these bear "significance and meaning." Trans. E. M. Edgehill. *The Works of Aristotle . . .,* I (Oxford: At the Clarendon Press, 1928).
6. *The Institutio Oratoria of Quintilian,* trans. H. E. Butler, 4 vols. (The Loeb Classical Library, Cambridge, Mass.: Harvard University Press, 1959), x, 3; IV, 243. Cf. Quintilian's *Institutes of Oratory, or Education of the Orator in Twelve Books,* trans. John Selby Watson. 2 vols. (Bohn's Classical Library, London: George Bell and Sons, 1909), II, 344. The references are to Cicero's *De Oratore,* III, 59 and *Orator* xvii. 55.
7. Quintilian: Namque actionem Cicero alias *quasi sermonem* alis *eloquentiam quandam corporis.*
8. The author of the *Rhetoric to Herennius* writes that *pronuntiatio* is "divided" "in vocis figuram"—vocal shape or figure, which Caplan translates, Vocal Quality, and "in corporis motum"—bodily movement, which Caplan englishes, Physical Movement. *Cicero ad C. Herennium, De Ratione Dicendi,* trans. Harry Caplan (The Loeb Classical Library, Cambridge, Mass.: Harvard University Press, 1954), III, 11, p. 191. In remarking that vocal flexibility may be achieved "by declamatory exercise," Caplan observes that this book contains the earliest appearance of *declamatio* as applied to delivery in extant Latin literature. *Ibid.,* fn.
9. *The Arcadian Rhetorike,* edited from the Edition of 1588 by Ethel Seaton (Oxford, England: The Luttrell Society, 1950), p. 106.
10. *The Advancement of Learning. The Works of Francis Bacon,* ed. James Spedding, Robert Leslie Ellis, and Douglas Denon Heath, 7 vols. (London, 1879), III, 384ff, 388ff, 399; *De Augmentis Scientiarum,* V, 1; *Works,* 407, see K. R. Wallace, *Francis Bacon on Communication and Rhetoric* (Chapel Hill, N.C.: University of North Carolina Press, 1943), chs. I, IX.
11. In his "scientific" treatment of rhetoric in general Campbell omits mention of delivery and of any of the roughly synonymous terms: action, pronunciation, gesture, and the like. But in his *Lectures on Pulpit Eloquence,* Campbell handles delivery in "Lecture III: Of the Expression," and "Lecture IV: Of Pronunciation" (London: John Bumpus, 1824). There is *grammatical pronunciation,"* or the phonetic aspect of utterance, and *rhetorical pronunciation."* This "consiseth[sic] in giving such an utterance to the several words in a sentence, as shows in the mind of the speaker a strong perception, or, as it were, feeling of the truth and justness of the thought conveyed by them, and in placing the rhetorical emphasis" on those words that give "the greatest energy and clearness to the expression." (Pp. 205–206.) Under pronunciation Campbell includes gesture. This is not the place to explore the complex, dependent relationships among *sentiment,* which is revealed most forcibly in delivery, and *expression, elocution,* and *pronunciation.* For

Campbell style and delivery *must* reflect the sentiments as these were understood by mideighteenth century philosophers and rhetoricians; hence to him delivery could not be limited to purely physical events.

12. *Lectures on Rhetoric and Belles Lettres* (New York: Richard Scott, 1815), pp. 365, 367.
13. The relevant passages are somewhat ambiguous, but the key passage appears to be this: ". . . he who, in speaking, should employ bare words, without enforcing them by proper tones and accents, would leave us with a faint and indistinct impression, often with a doubtful and ambiguous conception, of what he had delivered." *Ibid.*, p. 366.
14. *A Course of Lectures on Elocution. . . .* (London: W. Strahan, 1762), p. 19.
15. *Ibid.*, p. 10.
16. "English Sources of American Elocution," *Background Studies in the History of Speech Education in America* (New York, 1934), p. 112.
17. *Ibid.*, pp. 110–111.
18. For Mason: *An Essay on Elocution, or Pronunciation* (London, 1728), p. 22; for Burgh: *The Art of Speaking* (London, 1762), title page.
19. *Lectures on Elocution*, p. x.
20. The beginning of the debate and its central concerns are presented judiciously in W. M. Parrish, "The Concept of 'Naturalness,' " *Quarterly Journal of Speech*. 37 (December, 1951), 448–454.
21. *Public Speaking*, 2nd ed. (New York, 1917), pp. 34–35. Winans knew that Thomas Sheridan and Richard Whately before him had pointed to the conversational or natural mode as the proper standard of delivery. (See Winan's discussion of this point in his "Whately on Elocution," *The Quarterly Journal of Speech*, 31 (February, 1945), 1–8) But it remained for Winans to build it into the concept of delivery, rather than let it stand apart to be used only as a standard and guide for teacher and pupil.
22. The quotations are from *Public Speaking as a Liberal Art* by John F. Wilson and Carroll C. Arnold (Boston, 1968), pp. 320, 321.
23. The imagination of course had functions other than that of reproducing sensory experience. It could be inventive in its own right and in cooperation with the understanding. The second kind of imaginative activity was prized by the rhetoricians, the first by the poets. A full account of the faculty psychology as understood by an Elizabethan can be found in my *Francis Bacon on the Nature of Man: The Faculties of Man's Soul: Understanding, Reason, Imagination, Memory, Will,* and *Appetite.* Urbana: The University of Illinois Press, 1967.
24. If the speech act be not an element, it may comprise two units or elements. But to bifurcate the speech act poses unnecessary problems. If there be a sensory event (A) and an inner event (B), how are they related? Is (A) the "counterpart" of (B)? Is (A) a "translation" of (B)? Is (A) the "objective correlative" of (B), as T. S. Eliot would hold? Are the two events connected by some mediating process, as Charles Osgood believes? Does one follow the other because of a learned dispositional tendency, as Charles Morris holds? Is

the connection to be attributed to some purely mental event or thought as I. A. Richard would maintain?
25. I do not mean to rule out internal acts of speech. Undoubtedly there are such. Sometimes we can even be aware of linguistic formulation as in silent rehearsing and editing. As a rule the internal act seems less complete—and less "clear"—than the external. On this kind of phenomenon, Edward Hulett, Jr., offers interesting speculations, See his "A Symbolic Interactionist Model of Human Communication. Part One: The General Model of Social Behavior: The Message-Generating Process," *AV Communication Review,* 14 (Spring, 1966), 16–21.
26. For this short way of saying much I am indebted to J. L. Austin's *How To Do Things With Words* (Camridge, Mass.:" Harvard University Press, 1962), pp. 94, 108, 109.
27. From Curry's language it is difficult to tell whether an act of speech was viewed as a unitary whole: ". . . expression is not of the body but through the body; we feel that there is something mystic and hidden, unseen and unheard, by our fellow-men and often only vaguely felt by ourselves; but it is made manifest by the motions and actions of the body, and the tones and modulations of the voice." "Inward emotion causes an outward motion; inward condition, and outward *position.* [Italics mine.] Thus expression is, 'the motion of emotion,' the presentation of a vast complexity of physical actions which are directly caused by psychic activities." Again, "Matter itself is but force in a state manifest to sense; it may be called the expression of force." The quotations are from *The Province of Expression* (Boston, 1891), pp. 23–25. The whole section, pp. 21–36, should be pondered.
28. Wayland Maxfield Parrish, *Speaking in Public* (New York, 1947), p. 184. Opposite the title page Parrish places a quotation from William Ellery Channing: "Speech is not merely the dress . . ., but the very body of thought. It is to the intellect what the muscles are to the principle of physical life. The mind acts and strengthens itself through words. It is chaos, till defined, organized by language." Parrish was an admirer of Winans.
29. *Public Speaking: Principles and Practices* (New York, 1951), p. 476.
30. *Creative Speech* (Belmont, Cal., 1964), p. 183. It should be observed that the author's treatment of delivery is hardly in keeping with this conception.
31. *Principles of Effective Speaking* (New York, 1929), p. 263. But their definition, emphasizing the oral communication of ideas "contained in the speech," reminds one of the position of the classical rhetoricians. A psychological monist and behaviorist. Woolbert insisted upon the oneness of body and mind and understood the mutuality of meaning and the physical bases of communicating it. In *The Fundamentals of Speech* (New York, 1920), he made much of the phrase, "carrying the meaning." For some pivotal passages see pages 60, 83–84, 100, 288.
32. *Speech and Social Action: A Strategy of Oral Communication* (Englewood Cliffs, N.J., 1967), p. 148.

15

Rhetoric as Value:
Richard Weaver and the
Ethics of Communication

Rhetorical scholars from Plato to the present have studied the relationship between their "art" and ethics. Our purpose here is first to survey the views of various contemporary rhetoricians who have explored the ethical dimension of rhetoric, and then to direct your attention to the thoughtful work of two value-oriented rhetoricians, Richard Weaver and Ralph T. Eubanks.

Since rhetoric is concerned with probability and not scientific certainty, the communicator by definition possesses a certain measure of freedom to determine the structure of his message. During the exercise of this freedom, the concept of "choice" becomes apparent. Precisely because of the probable nature of rhetoric, the rhetor knowingly or unknowingly selects from his experiences and observations those elements of the persuasive process which best enable him to affect change in a given audience. It is this selection of specific ideas, evidence, language, structure, channels, and artistic proofs which underlies the study of rhetoric. Thus "choice" is basic to a study of rhetorical communication.

The communicator, according to most contemporary theorists, must exercise discretionary powers at several stages of the persuasion process; and it is precisely at these decision points that ethics of rhetoric plays a role. To make the necessary choices inherent in the rhetorical process, the rhetor must possess a standard, a frame of reference, or a value system consonant with his personal philosophy at a given time. Everyone—acting as source or receiver—operates within an ethical perspective or value system which dictates his or her

communicative behavior. In short, an individual's ethics affect his construction of messages as well as his perception of incoming communiques. Rhetoric, then, is a process grounded in "choice" which is dependent on the values of those engaged in the communicative act. Inevitably, therefore, ethics and rhetoric are inseparable.

But how, we may ask at this point, may ethics be defined so that it will have meaning for students of communication? Ethics, according to Donald K. Smith, is the study of "value statements which identify the standards of conduct which an individual may acknowledge as constitutive of his person or personality, or which a group or society may acknowledge as constitutive of its character. We take it that men and societies universally acknowledge such system of values."[1] More specifically, Thomas Nilsen notes: "By ethics as a subject of study is meant systematic thinking and theorizing with respect to questions about good, right and wrong, and moral obligation."[2] For our purposes, ethics is concerned with the values of the communicator as revealed in his rhetorical behavior. In other words, are the rhetor's choices "good," "right," or "moral?" Karl Wallace and Richard Weaver begin to establish our perspective.

Wallace advocates that rhetoric must consider the basic "substance" or foundation of speech. In an oft-quoted passage, he observes:

What is this stuff? First, the underlying materials of speeches, and indeed of most human talk and discussion are assertions and statements that concern human behav-

ior and conduct. They are prompted by situations and contexts that present us with choices and that require us to respond with appropriate decisions and actions. Second, such statements are usually called judgements and appraisals. They reflect human interests and values, and the nature of value judgements and the way of justifying them are the special, technical, and expert concern of ethics. Third, the appearance and use of value-judgements in practical discourse are the proper, although not the sole, concern of the theory and practice of rhetoric.[3]

Wallace next defines the substance of rhetoric as "good reasons" which he describes as "statements, consistent with each other, in support of an *ought* proposition or of a value judgement."[4] In a similar vein, Weaver equates ethics with "sermonic" language, saying: "As rhetoric confronts us with choices involving values, the rhetorician is a preacher to us, noble if he tries to direct our passion toward noble ends and base if he uses our passion to confuse and degrade us."[5] Both Wallace and Weaver emphasize the basis of rhetoric as "choice," pointing out that the rhetor's "choices" lie in the domain of ethics.

Convinced that ethical discourse consists of sermonic language dealing with ought propositions, numerous contemporary rhetoricians have suggested guidelines for helping a communicator to persuade in *a morally right way.* Richard Murphy, for example, states that an ethical rhetoric must not tolerate "offenses against common decency such as appeals to base motive, falsifying of evidence, the use of slanderous innuendo."[6] Any appeal, he adds, that falls short of responsible and informed communication fails to meet the test of honest expression, and should, therefore, be condemned.

Wayne Minnick is even more specific than Murphy in developing guidelines for the rhetor. An ethical communicator, he says, must:

reject all frauds, deceptions, concealments, specious arguments; cultivate the capacity for careful investigation and judicial and reflective deliberation of controversies and problems; endorse only those positions whose truth-claim merits his advocacy; must use intrinsically sound methods; use ethically neutral methods in ways that are consistent with and can be defended by reliable evidence and sound reasoning.[7]

Buttressing the views of Murphy and Minnick are the suggestions of Bryant and Wallace. The speaker, they point out, must have respect for the ends of speech; therefore; he should encourage goals which are in the best interest of the audience. The welfare of his listeners must be placed above the personal ambitions of the rhetor. Secondly, the speaker must respect the means of his/her communication. The means are more important than the ends for it is the quality of the production that counts. "What matters is how *well* the persuader spoke, how well he measured up to the standards of speechmaking."[8] Finally, the authors say that the speaker must honor the opinion of others as well as his own opinion. In this regard, the speaker must be convinced of his own viewpoint, he must be informed, and must not suppress or distort information.

Robert Scott agrees with the above guidelines, but then adds an important dimension. He elaborates the ethical demands or requirements for the communicator as "(1) taking responsibility for our choices, recognizing that we must assume the burden of harm done in our attempts to do good; (2) striving for honesty knowing the perils of arrogant self-deception; and (3) demanding toleration for those whose claims contradict our own."[9]

Crucial to an understanding of the nature of ethical discourse, many writers also agree, is the difficult and elusive concept of the *intent* of the agent. "A good intent," asserts Lawrence Flynn, "is so essential that without it an act cannot be morally good."[10] Predictably, Flynn further argues that the end does not justify the means for a good intent does not justify using an evil means."[11] Expressing a similar sentiment, James McCroskey gives the following perspective on the "intent" of the communicator:

Ethical judgments in rhetorical communication should be based exclusively on the intent of the communicator toward his audience. If the communicator seeks to improve the well-being of his audience through his act of communication, he is committing a moral act. If he seeks to produce harm for his audience, the communicator is guilty of an immoral act. If the intended effect upon the audience is neither to improve nor to harm their well-being, the communicator is committing an amoral act.[12]

As students of rhetorical theory we may agree or disagree with these ideas. Nevertheless we will find it useful to become aware of the philosophical problems inherent in the ethical system summarized here—problems which abound in any discussion of ethics. Perhaps more questions are raised here than are answered. What, for instance, is a "base emotion?" What is "intent?" Who measures "intent?" How is "intent" measured? What is meant by "deception?" Can deception in one circumstance be honest expression in another situation? "Is "honesty" a relative concept? Must the speaker really "tolerate" other viewpoints? As our discussion continues, we may find it profitable to examine carefully the considered viewpoints. In so doing, we will quickly realize that the issue of ethics in communication is an extremely complex problem area.

The next group of theorists to be analyzed are related in that they construct their ethical stance primarily around the democratic philosophy. These critics state that "in a democracy the standards of value by which a speaker and a speech are evaluated must be the standards established by the society."[13] Edward Rogge, Karl Wallace, Thomas Nilsen, and Franklyn Haiman are representatives of this school.

Wallace states that an ethics for communication must be built in relation to the political context of the society. An ethics of communication, therefore, for a free democratic society must encompass the following. First, the communicator must be thoroughly informed on his/her topic. Second, the speaker "must select and present fact and opinion fairly."[14] Third, the speaker should reveal his sources of fact and opinion. Finally, the

speaker must tolerate other viewpoints and "acknowledge and . . . respect diversity of argument and opinion."[15] If a democratic society is premised on the free and open dialogue between individuals and groups and government, then Wallace's dictums are instructive.

Nilsen advocates an ethic based on the values of a democracy or "a belief in reason as an instrument of individual and social improvement; self-determination as the means to individual fulfillment of his potentialities as a positive good."[16] An ethical rhetoric, therefore, must enhance the values of the individual as guaranteed in the Bill of Rights.

Franklyn Haiman concurs with Nilsen's ideas concerning the intrinsic worth of the individual within a democracy. "Democracy is, in fact, primarily dedicated to the proposition that anything which helps in the development of the strength, productiveness, and happiness of the individual is good, and that anything which blocks or hinders his growth in these directions is immoral."[17] Thus, Wallace, Nilsen, and Haiman preface their ethic on the intrinsic worth of the individual—a worth inherently tied to the democratic political context.

A final group of writers needs to be mentioned. These are the theorists who are not content to limit their concern for traditional viewpoints already discussed. They go beyond previous authors by advocating a more active role for rhetoric as a device for proclaiming values. Typical of this approach is that expressed by Ralph Eubanks and Virgil Baker. These authors claim that rhetoric is a dynamic force which must nurture human values or "universal concepts basic to civil decisions and action." The function of rhetoric is to "crystallize and transmit human values." The end of rhetoric, therefore, is the realization of *justice* and order. "The concept of Justice synthesizes the classical trinity of democratic ideals, liberty, equality, and fraternity, whose central premise is the essential worthfulness and profound potentialities of the individual human being."[18] This suggests the wisdom of making "more direct the association between rhetorical method and axiology."[19]

Consistent with the emphasis of Eubanks and Baker is that used by Chaim Perelman and

L. Olbrechts-Tyteca in their text, *The New Rhetoric: A Treatise on Argumentation.* In this volume, the authors discuss the centrality of values to all forms of discourse. "Values," they note, "enter, at some stage or other, into every argument."[20] An advocate, thus, "appeals to values in order to induce the hearer to make certain choices rather than others and, most of all, to justify those choices so that they may be accepted and approved by others."[21]

Up to this point we have summarized both prescriptive and descriptive means recommended by select contemporary authors as guidelines to be used by communicators in rhetorical transactions. Not to be overlooked is the challenge confronting the critic whose function it is to examine the discourse of others. In fact, of all the students of communication, the rhetorical critic perhaps most needs to be keenly aware of "choice" and its ethical imperative. As Nichols states: "The critic's function is to examine the speaker's premises, stated or implied, and to examine the truth of these premises."[22] She further shows that the critic needs to become a vital force in society. "His place should be in the vanguard, not in the rear. . . . He should be ready to alert a people, to warn what devices of exploitation are being exercised, by what skillful manipulations of motives men are being directed to or dissuaded from courses of action."[23] If the critic ignores the ethical implications of his art, he engages in "pseudo-criticism."[24]

In the foregoing discussion, we have attempted to survey the thoughts of a few writers who have dealt with ethics in relation to communication. Several different emphases and approaches have been stressed. Each perspective, as we have seen, is characterized by inherent philosophical problems, for such is the nature of ethics. From the earlier discussed prescriptive systems, to those ethical ideas tied into the intrinsic worth of the individual in his particular political context, to those which advocate an activist role in pursuit of justice and the integration of the human personality—we find limitations, drawbacks, and serious questions which need to be answered. However, it is not our purpose to offer a critique of ethics. Rather, we have sought only to present a brief overview of the ethical issue in communication as seen from the perspective of representative contemporary authors. To continue our discussion, we turn now to Richard Weaver and his axiological ideas on rhetoric.

Richard M. Weaver

Weaver personifies those rhetoricians who have focused their attention almost exclusively on the relationship between rhetoric and ethics. In his widely circulated 1953 book, *The Ethics of Rhetoric,* he brought together a series of eight essays which probe various facets of the ethical dimension. The first essay on Plato's "Phaedrus and the Nature of Rhetoric" sets the tone for the volume. Equating Plato's "lovers" with evil, neuter, and noble speakers, Weaver revealed his close identification with the moral-philosophical emphasis in rhetoric. In the following excerpt he quotes Plato with approval.

What Plato has prepared us to see is that the virtuous rhetorician, who is a lover of truth, has a soul of *such* movement that its dialectical perceptions are consonant with those of a divine mind. Or, in the language of more technical philosophy, this soul is aware of axiological systems which have ontic status. The good soul, consequently, will not urge a perversion of justice as justice in order to impose upon the commonwealth. Insofar as the soul has its impulse in the right direction, its definitions will agree with the true nature of intelligible things.[25]

Throughout the remaining portion of this essay, Weaver continually advocates the noble or virtuous rhetorician position wherein the rhetor is preoccupied with "truth," "justice," and the "good" in relation to the welfare of his listeners.

In the ensuing chapters of *Ethics of Rhetoric,* Weaver glimpses other themes that have strong moral implications. He opts for a rhetoric that has as its base dialectic. Knowledge and meaning derived from scientific inquiry, he argues, will constitute the foundation for appeals upholding values. He then articulates a distinction between two argumentative forms which he labels argument from circumstance and argument from definition or "the essential nature of things."[26] England's famous orator and literary scholar Edmund Burke becomes the focal point for illustrating an argument from circumstance. The historically significant "Conciliation with America" speech, delivered in 1775, is an example depicting an advocate's reliance on expedient principles. For Burke in this address, according to Weaver, never comes to grips with first principles grounded in human nature. Instead he upholds a policy of conciliation for such practical reasons as the great distance separating England and America, the high level of trade between the two areas, the large amount of legal works read by the colonists, and the independent spirit of the Southerners. At no time does he suggest that a policy of conciliation should be adopted because it is the inherent right of all men to be free, and to be exempt from taxation if they do not have representation. Weaver is to be commended for choosing a graphic model upon which to delineate the nature of an argument from circumstance. What he overlooks, however, is the fact that other speeches presented by Burke—particularly the Bristol Election address in 1780—are from beginning to end an argument from definition.

Weaver likewise selects a telling example for the purpose of describing an argument from definition. Alluding to the Lincoln-Douglas debates in 1858, he recreated the dramatic encounter between the two Illinois senatorial candidates regarding the doctrine of popular sovereignty. Douglas succeeded in convincing large segments of the voting public of the merits of permitting majority sentiment to determine whether or not a state should have slavery. Encouraged by the response to this political philosophy, Douglas taunted Lincoln by asking him where he stood on the question. Eventually Lincoln replied that he was opposed to it, saying in effect: "The difference between Judge Douglas and myself is that he does not feel slavery is a moral wrong. I do." Popular sovereignty, therefore, represented to Weaver an argument from circumstance. To oppose this expedient policy for moral reasons, on the other hand, is to rely on first principles or the essential nature of things.

The final chapter in *Ethics of Rhetoric* also deserves special attention. The theme is "ultimate words" called "God" and "Devil" terms. These are the words that rhetors use for the purpose of expressing values. A "God" term embraces a universal value that is generally regarded as good or desirable. Most Americans, for example, associate a favorable connotation with such positive words as "progress," "science," "fact," "modern," "democracy," "freedom," and "justice." They tend to view as unfavorable, however, such terms as "reactionary," "un-American," "fascist," and "communist." What places the use of ultimate terms in the sphere of ethics is the frequent tendency to employ such words in an irrational manner. Our language thus becomes, in the opinion of Weaver, a "perverse shibboleth."[27]

The essay which follows is perhaps Weaver's most mature statement as a rhetorical theorist. Weaver reminds us here that the object of rhetoric "is the whole man" and the office of rhetoric "is advising men." Moreover, he gives us his hierarchy ranking of arguments, ranging from circumstance (the lowest) and progressing upward through cause to effect, similitude or analogy, to definition (the highest). The full sweep of Weaver's claim that "language is sermonic" is seen in his eloquent concluding passage which states:

Finally, we must never lose sight of the order of values as the ultimate sanction of rhetoric. No one can live a life of direction and purpose without some scheme of values. As rhetoric confronts us with choices involving values, the rhetorician is a preacher to us, noble if he tries to direct our passion toward noble ends and base if he uses our passion to confuse and degrade us.[28]

Notes

1. Donald K. Smith, *Man Speaking: A Rhetoric of Public Speech* (New York: Dodd, Mead and Company, 1969), p. 228.
2. Thomas R. Nilsen, *Ethics of Speech Communication,* 1st ed. (New York: Bobbs-Merrill Company, 1966), p. 10.
3. Karl Wallace, "The Substance of Rhetoric: Good Reasons," in Richard L. Johannesen (ed.), *Contemporary Theories of Rhetoric: Selected Readings* (New York: Harper and Row, 1971), p. 360.

4. *Ibid.,* p. 368.

5. Richard Weaver, "Language Is Sermonic," in Richard L. Johannesen, Rennard Strickland, and Ralph Eubanks (eds.), *Language is Sermonic: Richard M. Weaver on the Nature of Rhetoric* (Baton Rouge, Louisiana: Louisiana State University Press, 1970), p. 179.

6. Richard Murphy, "Preface to an Ethics of Rhetoric," in Donald C. Bryant (ed.), *The Rhetorical Idiom* (New York: Russell and Russell Company, 1966), p. 140.

7. Wayne L. Minnick, "The Ethics of Persuasion," in Johannesen (ed.), *Ethics and Persuasion: Selected Readings* (New York: Random House, 1967), p. 38.

8. Donald C. Bryant and Karl Wallace, "Ethics of Persuasion," in *Fundamentals of Public Speaking* (New York: Appleton-Century Crofts, 1960), p. 293.

9. Robert L. Scott (ed.), *The Speaker's Reader: Concepts in Communication.* (Glenview, Ill.: Scott, Foresman and Company, 1969), p. 22.

10. Lawerence J. Flynn, "The Aristotelian Basis for the Ethics of Speaking," in Johannesen (ed.), *Ethics and Persuasion,* p. 121.

11. *Ibid.,* pp. 121–123.

12. James C. McCroskey, *An Introduction to Rhetorical Communication,* 2nd ed. (Englewood Cliffs, New Jersey: Prentice-Hall, Inc., 1972), p. 270.

13. Edward Rogge, "Evaluating the Ethics of a Speaker in a Democracy," in Johannesen (ed.), *Ethics and Persuasion,* p. 91.

14. Karl Wallace, "An Ethical Basis of Communication," in Goodwin F. Berquist (ed.), *Speeches for Illustration and Example* (Chicago, Ill.: Scott, Foresman and Company, 1965), p. 188.

15. *Ibid.,* p. 190.

16. Thomas Nilsen, "Free Speech, Persuasion, and the Democratic Process," in Johannesen (ed.), *Ethics and Persuasion,* p. 74.

17. Franklyn S. Haiman, "Democratic Ethics and the Hidden Persuaders," in Johannesen (ed.), *Ethics and Persuasion,* p. 62.

18. Ralph Eubanks and Virgil Baker, "Toward an Axiology of Rhetoric," in Johannesen (ed.), *Contemporary Theories of Rhetoric,* p. 346.

19. *Ibid.,* p. 347.

20. Ch. Perelman and L. Oblrechts-Tyteca, *The New Rhetoric: A Treatise on Argumentation* (London: University of Notre Dame Press, 1971), p. 75.

21. *Ibid.,* p. 75.

22. Marie Hochmuth Nichols, "The Criticism of Rhetoric," in *History and Criticism of American Public Address,* III (New York: McGraw-Hill, 1954), 16.

23. *Ibid.,* p. 17.

24. Barnet Baskerville, "Emerson as a Critic of Oratory," *Southern Speech Journal,* XVIII (September 1952), 150–162.

25. Richard Weaver, *The Ethics of Rhetoric* (Chicago: Henry Regnery Company, 1970), p. 17.

26. *Ibid.,* p. 86.

27. *Ibid.,* p. 232.

28. Weaver, "Language is Sermonic," op. cit., p. 179.

Language Is Sermonic

Our age has witnessed the decline of a number of subjects that once enjoyed prestige and general esteem, but no subject, I believe, has suffered more amazingly in this respect than rhetoric. When one recalls that a century ago rhetoric was regarded as the most important humanistic discipline taught in our colleges— when one recalls this fact and contrasts it with the very different situation prevailing today— he is forced to see that a great shift of valuation has taken place. In those days, in the not-so-distant Nineteenth Century, to be a professor of rhetoric, one had to be *somebody.* This was a teaching task that was thought to call for ample and varied resources, and it was recognized as addressing itself to the most important of all ends, the persuading of human beings to adopt right attitudes and act in response to them. That was no assignment for the plodding sort of professor. That sort of teacher might do a middling job with subject matter courses, where the main object is to impart information, but the teacher of rhetoric had to be a person of gifts and imagination who could illustrate, as the need arose, how to make words even in prose take on wings. I remind you of the chairs of rhetoric that still survive in title in some of our older universities. And I should add, to develop the full picture, that literature was then viewed as a subject which practically anyone could teach. No special gift, other than perhaps industry, was needed to relate facts about authors and

Reprinted from *Language Is Sermonic* by R. L. Johannesen, R. Strickland, R. T. Eubanks, eds., (Baton Rouge: Louisiana State University Press, 1970). Reprinted with permission of the editors.

periods. That was held to be rather pedestrian work. But the instructor in rhetoric was expected to be a man of stature. Today, I scarcely need point out, the situation has been exactly reversed. Today it is the teacher of literature who passes through a long period of training, who is supposed to possess the mysteries of a learned craft, and who is placed by his very speciality on a height of eminence. His knowledge of the intricacies of Shakespeare or Keats or Joyce and his sophistication in the critical doctrines that have been developed bring him the esteem of the academy. We must recognize in all fairness that the elaboration of critical techniques and special approaches has made the teaching of literature a somewhat more demanding profession, although some think that it has gone in that direction beyond the point of diminishing returns. Still, this is not enough to account for the relegation of rhetoric. The change has gone so far that now it is discouraging to survey the handling of this study in our colleges and universities. With a few honorable exceptions it is given to just about anybody who will take it. The "inferior, unlearned, mechanical, merely instrumental members of the profession"—to recall a phrase of a great master of rhetoric, Edmund Burke— have in their keeping what was once assigned to the leaders. Beginners, parttime teachers, graduate students, faculty wives, and various fringe people, are now the instructional staff of an art which was once supposed to require outstanding gifts and mature experience. (We must note that at the same time the course itself has been allowed to decline from one dealing philosophically with the problems of expression to one which tries to bring below-par students up to the level of accepted usage.) Indeed, the wheel of fortune would seem to have turned for rhetoric; what was once at the top is now at the bottom, and because of its low estate, people begin to wonder on what terms it can survive at all.

We are not faced here, however, with the wheel of fortune; we are faced with something that has come over the minds of men. Changes that come over the minds of men are not inscrutable, but have at some point their identifiable causes. In this case we have to deal with the most potent of cultural causes, an alteration of man's image of man. Something has happened in the recent past to our concept of what man is; a decision was made to look upon him in a new light, and from this decision new bases of evaluation have proceeded, which affect the public reputation of rhetoric. This changed concept of man is best described by the word "scientistic," a term which denotes the application of scientific assumptions to subjects which are not wholly comprised of naturalistic phenomena. Much of this is a familiar tale, but to understand the effect of the change, we need to recall that the great success of scientific or positivistic thinking in the Nineteenth Century induced a belief that nothing was beyond the scope of its method. Science, and its off-spring applied science, were doing so much to alter and, it was thought, to improve the material conditions of the world, that a next step with the same process seemed in order. Why should not science turn its apparatus upon man, whom all the revelations of religion and the speculations of philosophy seemed still to have left an enigma, with the promise of much better result? It came to be believed increasingly that to think validly was to think scientifically, and that subject matters made no difference.

Now the method of scientific investigation is, as T. H. Huxley reminded us in a lecture which does great credit to him as a rhetorician, merely the method of logic. Induction and deduction and causal inference applied to the phenomena of nature yielded the results with which science was changing the landscape and revolutionizing the modes of industry. From this datum it was an easy inference that men ought increasingly to become scientists, and again, it was a simple derivative from this notion that man at his best is a logic machine, or at any rate an austerely unemotional thinker. Furthermore, carried in the train of this conception was the thought, not often expressed of course, that things would be better if men did not give in so far to being human in the humanistic sense. In the shadow of the victories of science, his humanism fell into progressive disparagement. Just what comprises humanism is not a simple matter for analysis.

Rationality is an indispensable part to be sure, yet humanity includes emotionality, or the capacity to feel and suffer, to know pleasure, and it includes the capacity for aesthetic satisfaction, and, what can be only suggested, a yearning to be in relation with something infinite. This last is his religious passion, or his aspiration to feel significant and to have a sense of belonging in a world that is productive of much frustration. These at least are the properties of humanity. Well, man had been human for some thousands of years, and where had it gotten him? Those who looked forward to a scientific Utopia were inclined to think that his humanness had been a drag on his progress; human qualities were weaknesses, except for that special quality of rationality, which might be expected to redeem him.

However curious it may appear, this notion gained that man should live down his humanity and make himself a more efficient source of those logical inferences upon which a scientifically accurate understanding of the world depends. As the impulse spread, it was the emotional and subjective components of his being that chiefly came under criticism, for reasons that have just been indicated. Emotion and logic or science do not consort; the latter must be objective, faithful to what is out there in the public domain and conformable to the processes of reason. Whenever emotion is allowed to put in an oar, it gets the boat off true course. Therefore emotion is a liability.

Under the force of this narrow reasoning, it was natural that rhetoric should pass from a status in which it was regarded as of questionable worth to a still lower one in which it was positively condemned. For the most obvious truth about rhetoric is that its object is the whole man. It presents its arguments first to the rational part of man, because rhetorical discourses, if they are honestly conceived, always have a basis in reasoning. Logical argument is the plot, as it were, of any speech or composition that is designed to persuade. Yet it is the very characterizing feature of rhetoric that it goes beyond this and appeals to other parts of man's constitution, especially to his nature as a pathetic being, that is, a being feeling and suffering. A speech intended to

persuade achieves little unless it take into account how men are reacting subjectively to their hopes and fears and their special circumstances. The fact that Aristotle devotes a large proportion of his *Rhetoric* to how men feel about different situations and actions is an evidence of how prominently these considerations bulked even in the eyes of a master theorist.

Yet there is one further fact, more decisive than any of these, to prove that rhetoric is addressed to man in his humanity. Every speech which is designed to move is directed to a special audience in its unique situation. (We could not except even those radio appeals to "the world." Their audience has a unique place in time.) Here is but a way of pointing out that rhetoric is intended for historical man, or for man as conditioned by history. It is part of the *conditio humana* that we live at particular times and in particular places. These are productive of special or unique urgencies, which the speaker has got to recognize and to estimate. Hence, just as man from the point of view of rhetoric is not purely a thinking machine, or a mere seat of rationality, so he is not a creature abstracted from time and place. If science deals with the abstract and the universal, rhetoric is near the other end, dealing in significant part with the particular and the concrete. It would be the height of wishful thinking to say that this ought not be so. As long as man is born into history, he will be feeling and responding to historical pressures. All of these reasons combine to show why rhetoric should be considered the most humanistic of the humanities. It is directed to that part of our being which is not merely rational, for it supplements the rational approach. And it is directed to individual men in their individual situations, so that by the very definitions of the terms here involved, it takes into account what science deliberately, to satisfy its own purposes, leaves out. There is consequently no need for wonder that, in an age that has been influenced to distrust and disregard what is characteristically human, rhetoric should be a prime target of attack. If it is a weakness to harbor feelings, and if furthermore it is a weakness to be caught up in historical situations, then rhetoric is construable as a dealer in weaknesses. That man is in this condition religion, philosophy, and literature have been teaching for thousands of years. Criticism of it from the standpoint of a scientistic Utopia is the new departure.

The incompleteness of the image of man as a creature who should make use of reason only can be demonstrated in another way. It is a truism that logic is a subject without a subject matter. That is to say, logic is a set of rules and devices which are equally applicable whatever the data. As the science of the forms of reasoning, it is a means of interpreting and utilizing the subject matters of the various fields which do have their proper contents. Facts from science or history or literature, for example, may serve in the establishment of an inductive generalization. Similar facts may be fed into a syllogism. Logic is merely the mechanism for organizing the data of other provinces of knowledge. Now it follows from this truth that if a man could convert himself into a pure logic machine or thinking machine, he would have no special relation to any body of knowledge. All would be grist for his mill, as the phrase goes. He would have no inclination, no partiality, no particular affection. His mind would work upon one thing as indifferently as upon another. He would be an eviscerated creature or a depassionated one, standing in the same relationship to the realities of the world as the thinking technique stands to the data on which it is employed. He would be a thinking robot, a concept which horrifies us precisely because the robot has nothing to think about.

A confirmation of this truth lies in the fact that rhetoric can never be reduced to symbology. Logic is increasingly becoming "symbolic logic"; that is its tendency. But rhetoric always comes to us in well-fleshed words, and that is because it must deal with the world, the thickness, stubbornness, and power of it.[1]

Everybody recognizes that there is thus a formal logic. A number of eminent authorities have written of rhetoric as if it were formal in the same sense and degree. Formal rhetoric would be a set of rules and devices for persuading anybody about anything. If one desires a certain response, one uses a certain device, or "trick" as the enemies of the art would put it. The set of appeals that rhetoric provides is analogized with the forms of thought that logic prescribes. Rhetoric conceived in this fashion has an adaptability and virtuosity equal to those of logic.

But the comparison overlooks something, for at one point we encounter a significant difference. Rhetoric has a relationship to the world which logic does not have and which forces the rhetorician to keep an eye upon reality as well as upon the character and situation of his audience. The truth of this is seen when we begin to examine the nature of the traditional "topics." The topics were first formulated by Aristotle and were later treated also by Cicero and Quintilian and by many subsequent writers on the subject of persuasion. They are a set of "places" or "regions" where one can go to find the substance for persuasive argument. Cicero defines a topic as "the seat of an argument." In function they are sources of content for speeches that are designed to influence. Aristotle listed a considerable number of them, but for our purposes they can be categorized very broadly. In reading or interpreting the world of reality, we make use of four very general ideas. The first three are usually expressed, in the language of philosophy, as being, cause, and relationship. The fourth, which stands apart from these because it is an external source, is testimony and authority.

One way to interpret a subject is to define its nature—to describe the fixed features of its being. Definition is an attempt to capture essence. When we speak of the nature of a thing, we speak of something we expect to persist. Definitions accordingly deal with fundamental and unchanging properties.

Another way to interpret a subject is to place it in a cause-and-effect relationship. The process of interpretation is then to affirm it as the cause of some effect or as the effect of some cause. And the attitudes of those who are listening will be affected according to whether or not they agree with our cause-and-effect analysis.

A third way to interpret a subject is in terms of relationships of similarity and dissimilarity. We say that it is like something which we know in fuller detail, or that it is unlike that thing in important respects. From such a comparison conclusions regarding the subject itself can be drawn. This is a very common form of argument, by which probabilities can be established. And since probabilities are all we have to go on in many questions of this life, it must be accounted a usable means of persuasion.

The fourth category, the one removed from the others by the fact of its being an external source, deals not with the evidence directly but accepts it on the credit of testimony or authority. If we are not in position to see or examine, but can procure the deposition of some one who is, the deposition may become the substance of our argument. We can slip it into a syllogism just as we would a defined term. The same is true of general statements which come from quarters of great authority or prestige. If a proposition is backed by some weighty authority, like the Bible, or can be associated with a great name, people may be expected to respond to it in accordance with the veneration they have for these sources. In this way evidence coming from the outside is used to influence attitudes or conduct.

Now we see that in all these cases the listener is being asked not simply to follow a valid reasoning form but to respond to some presentation of reality. He is being asked to agree with the speaker's interpretation of the world that is. If the definition being offered is a true one, he is expected to recognize this and to say, at least inwardly, "Yes, that is the way the thing is." If the exposition of cause-and-effect relationship is true, he may be expected to concur that X is the cause of such a consequence or that such a consequence has its cause in X. And according to whether this is a good or a bad cause or a good or a bad consequence, he is disposed to preserve or remove the cause, and so on. If he is impressed with the similarity drawn between two things, he is as a result more likely to accept a policy which involves treating something in the same way in which its analogue is treated. He has been influenced by a relationship of comparability. And finally, if he has been confronted with testimony or authority from sources he respects, he will receive this as a reliable, if secondary, kind of information about reality. In these four

ways he has been persuaded to read the world as the speaker reads it.

At this point, however, I must anticipate an objection. The retort might be made: "These are extremely formal categories you are enumerating. I fail to see how they are any less general or less indifferently applicable than the formal categories of logic. After all, definitions and so on can be offered of anything. You still have not succeeded in making rhetoric a substantive study.

In replying, I must turn here to what should be called the office of rhetoric. Rhetoric seen in the whole conspectus of its function is an art of emphasis embodying an order of desire. Rhetoric is advisory; it has the office of advising men with reference to an independent order of goods and with reference to their particular situation as it relates to these. The honest rhetorician therefore has two things in mind: a vision of how matters should go ideally and ethically and a consideration of the special circumstances of his auditors. Toward both of these he has a responsibility.

I shall take up first how his responsibility to the order of the goods or to the hierarchy of realities may determine his use of the topics.

When we think of rhetoric as one of the arts of civil society (and it must be a free society, since the scope for rhetoric is limited and the employment of it constrained under a despotism) we see that the rhetorician is faced with a choice of means in appealing to those whom he can prevail upon to listen to him. If he is at all philosophical, it must occur to him to ask whether there is a standard by which the sources of persuasion can be ranked. In a phrase, is there a preferred order of them, so that, in a scale of ethics, it is nobler to make use of one sort of appeal than another? This is of course a question independent of circumstantial matters, yet a fundamental one. We all react to some rhetoric as "untruthful" or "unfair" or "cheap," and this very feeling is evidence of the truth that it is possible to use a better or a worse style of appeal. What is the measure of the better style? Obviously this question cannot be answered at all in the absence of some conviction about the nature and destiny of man. Rhetoric inevitably impinges upon morality and politics; and if it is one of the means by which we endeavor to improve the character and the lot of men, we have to think of its methods and sources in relation to a scheme of values.

To focus the problem a little more sharply, when one is asking men to cooperate with him in thinking this or doing that, when is he asking in the name of the highest reality, which is the same as saying, when is he asking in the name of their highest good?

Naturally, when the speaker replies to this question, he is going to express his philosophy, or more precisely, his metaphysics. My personal reply would be that he is making the highest order of appeal when he is basing his case on definition or the nature of the thing. I confess that this goes back to a very primitive metaphysics, which holds that the highest reality is being, not becoming. It is a quasi-religious metaphysics, if you will, because it ascribes to the highest reality qualities of stasis, immutability, eternal perdurance—qualities that in Western civilization are usually expressed in the language of theism. That which is perfect does not change; that which has to change is less perfect. Therefore, if it is possible to determine unchanging essences or qualities and to speak in terms of these, one is appealing to what is most real in so doing. From another point of view, this is but getting people to see what is most permanent in existence, or what transcends the world of change and accident. The realm of essence is the realm above the flux of phenomena, and definitions are of essences and genera.

I may have expressed this view in somewhat abstruse language in order to place it philosophically, yet the practice I am referring to is everyday enough, as a simple illustration will make plain. If a speaker should define man as a creature with an indefeasible right to freedom and should upon this base an argument that a certain man or group of men are entitled to freedom, he would be arguing from definition. Freedom is an unchanging attribute of his subject; it can accordingly be predicated of whatever falls within the genus man. Stipulative definitions are of the ideal, and in this fact lies the reason for placing them

at the top of the hierarchy. If the real progress of man is toward knowledge of ideal truth, it follows that this is an appeal to his highest capacity—his capacity to apprehend what exists absolutely.

The next ranking I offer tentatively, but it seems to me to be relationship or similitude and its subvarieties. I have a consistent impression that the broad resource of analogy, metaphor, and figuration is favored by those of a poetic and imaginative cast of mind. We make use of analogy or comparison when the available knowledge of the subject permits only probable proof. Analogy is reasoning from something we know to something we do not know in one step; hence there is no universal ground for predication. Yet behind every analogy lurks the possibility of a general term. The general term is never established as such, for that would change the argument to one of deductive reasoning with a universal or distributed middle. The user of analogy is hinting at an essence which cannot at the moment be produced. Or, he may be using an indirect approach for reason of tact; analogies not infrequently do lead to generalizations; and he may be employing this approach because he is respectful of his audience and desires them to use their insight.

I mentioned a moment earlier that this type of argument seems to be preferred by those of a poetic or non-literal sort of mind. That fact suggests yet another possibility, which I offer still more diffidently, asking your indulgence if it seems to border on the whimsical. The explanation would be that the cosmos *is* one vast system of analogy, so that our profoundest intuitions of it are made in the form of comparisons. To affirm that something is like something else is to begin to talk about the unitariness of creation. Everything is like everything else somehow, so that we have a ladder of similitude mounting up to the final oneness—to something like a unity in godhead. Furthermore, there is about this source of argument a kind of decent reticence, a recognition of the unknown along with the known. There is a recognition that the unknown may be continuous with the known, so that man is moving about in a world only partly realized, yet real in all its parts. This is the mood of poetry and mystery, but further adumbration of it I leave to those more gifted than I.

Cause and effect appears in this scale to be a less exalted source of argument, though we all have to use it because we are historical men. Here I must recall the methaphysical ground of this organization and point out that it operates in the realm of becoming. Causes are causes having effect and effects are resulting from causes. To associate this source of argument with its habitual users, I must note that it is heard most commonly from those who are characteristically pragmatic in their way of thinking. It is not unusual today to find a lengthy piece of journalism or an entire political speech which is nothing but a series of arguments from consequence—completely devoid of reference to principle or defined ideas. We rightly recognize these as sensational types of appeal. Those who are partial to arguments based on effect are under a temptation to play too much upon the fears of their audience by stressing the awful nature of some consequence or by exaggerating the power of some cause. Modern advertising is prolific in this kind of abuse. There is likewise a temptation to appeal to prudential considerations only in a passage where things are featured as happening or threatening to happen.

An even less admirable subvariety of this source is the appeal to circumstance, which is the least philosophical of all the topics of argument. Circumstance is an allowable source when we don't know anything else to plead, in which case we say, "There is nothing else to be done about it." Of all the arguments, it admits of the least perspicaciousness. An example of this which we hear nowadays with great regularity is: "We must adapt ourselves to a fast-changing world." This is pure argument from circumstance. It does not pretend, even, to offer a cause-and-effect explanation. If it did, the first part would tell us why we must adapt ourselves to a fast-changing world; and the second would tell us the result of our doing so. The usually heard formulation does neither. Such argument is preeminently lacking in understanding or what the Greeks called

dianoia. It simply cites a brute circumstance and says, "Step lively." Actually, this argument amounts to a surrender of reason. Maybe it expresses an instinctive feeling that in this situation reason is powerless. Either you change fast or you get crushed. But surely it would be a counsel of desperation to try only this argument in a world suffering from aimlessness and threatened with destruction.

Generally speaking, cause and effect is a lower-order source of argument because it deals in the realm of the phenomenal, and the phenomenal is easily converted into the sensational. Sensational excitements always run the risk of arousing those excesses which we deplore as sentimentality or brutality.

Arguments based on testimony and authority, utilizing external sources, have to be judged in a different way. Actually, they are the other sources seen through other eyes. The question of their ranking involves the more general question of the status of authority. Today there is a wide-spread notion that all authority is presumptuous. ("Authority is authoritarian" seems to be the root idea); consequently it is held improper to try to influence anyone by the prestige of great names or of sanctioned pronouncements. This is a presumption itself, by which every man is presumed to be his own competent judge in all matters. But since that is a manifest impossibility, and is becoming a greater impossibility all the time, as the world piles up bodies of specialized knowledge which no one person can hope to command, arguments based on authority are certainly not going to disappear. The sound maxim is that an argument based on authority is as good as the authority. What we should hope for is a new and discriminating attitude toward what is authoritative, and I would like to see some source recognized as having moral authority. This hope will have to wait upon the recovery of a more stable order of values and the recognition of qualities in persons. Speaking most generally, arguments from authority are ethically good when they are deferential toward real hierarchy.

With that we may sum up the rhetorical speaker's obligation toward the ideal, apart from particular determinations. If one accepts the possibility of this or any other ranking, one has to concede that rhetoric is not merely formal; it is realistic. It is not a playing with counters; its impulses come from insights into actuality. Its topic matter is existential, not hypothetical. It involves more than mere demonstration because it involves choice. Its assertions have ontological claims.

Now I return to the second responsibility, which is imposed by the fact that the rhetorician is concerned with definite questions. These are questions having histories, and history is always concrete. This means that the speaker or writer has got to have a rhetorical perception of what his audience needs or will receive or respond to. He takes into account the reality of man's composite being and his tendency to be swayed by sentiment. He estimates the pressures of the particular situation in which his auditors are found. In the eyes of those who look sourly upon the art, he is a man probing for weaknesses which he means to exploit.

But here we must recur to the principle that rhetoric comprehensively considered is an art of emphasis. The definite situation confronts him with a second standard of choice. In view of the receptivity of his audience, which of the topics shall he choose to stress, and how? If he concludes that definition should be the appeal, he tries to express the nature of the thing in a compelling way. If he feels that a cause-and-effect demonstration would stand the greatest chance to impress, he tries to make this linkage so manifest that his hearers will see an inevitability in it. And so on with the other topics, which will be so emphasized or magnified as to produce the response of assent.

Along with this process of amplification, the ancients recognized two qualities of rhetorical discourse which have the effect of impressing an audience with the reality or urgency of a topic. In Greek these appear as *energia* and *enargia,* both of which may be translated "actuality," though the first has to do with liveliness or animation of action and the second with vividness of scene. The speaker now indulges in actualization to the minds' eyes of his hearers.

The practice itself has given rise to a good deal of misunderstanding, which it would be well to remove. We know that one of the conventional criticisms of rhetoric is that the practitioner of it takes advantage of his hearers by playing upon their feelings and imaginations. He overstresses the importance of his topics by puffing them up, dwelling on them in great detail, using an excess of imagery or of modifiers evoking the senses, and so on. He goes beyond what is fair, the critics often allege, by this actualization of a scene about which the audience ought to be thinking rationally. Since this criticism has a serious basis, I am going to offer an illustration before making the reply. Here is a passage from Daniel Webster's famous speech for the prosecution in the trial of John Francis Knapp. Webster is actualizing for the jury the scene of the murder as he has constructed it from circumstantial evidence.

The deed was executed with a degree of steadiness and self-possession equal to the wickedness with which it was planned. The circumstances now clearly in evidence spread out the scene before us. Deep sleep had fallen upon the destined victim and all beneath his roof. A healthful old man, to whom sleep was sweet, the first sound slumbers of the night held him in their soft but strong embrace. The assassin enters, through a window already prepared, into an unoccupied apartment. With noiseless foot he paces the lonely hall, half-lighted by the moon; he winds up the ascent of the stairs, and reaches the door of the chamber. Of this, he moves the lock by soft and continued pressure, till it turns on its hinges without noise; and he enters, and beholds the victim before him. The room is uncommonly open to the admission of light. The face of the innocent sleeper is turned from the murderer, and the beams of the moon, resting on the gray locks of the aged temple, show him where to strike. The fatal blow is given! and the victim passes, without a struggle or a motion, from the repose of sleep to the repose of death! It is the assassin's purpose

to make sure work; and he plies the dagger, though it is obvious that life has been destroyed by the blow of the bludgeon. He even raises the aged arm, that he may not fail in his aim at the heart, and replaces it again over the wound of the poniard! To finish the picture, he explores the wrist for the pulse! He feels for it, and ascertains that it beats no longer! It is accomplished. The deed is done. He retreats, retraces his steps to the window, passes out through it as he came in, and escapes. He has done the murder. No eye has seen him, no ear has heard him. The secret is his own, and it is safe!

By depicting the scene in this fulness of detail, Webster is making it vivid, and "vivid" means "living." There are those who object on general grounds to this sort of dramatization; it is too affecting to the emotions. Beyond a doubt, whenever the rhetorician actualizes an event in this manner, he is making it mean something to the emotional part of us, but that part is involved whenever we are deliberating about goodness and badness. On this subject there is a very wise reminder in Bishop Whately's *Elements of Rhetoric:* "When feelings are strongly excited, they are not necessarily over-excited; it may be that they are only brought to the state which the occasion fully justifies, or even that they fall short of this." Let us think of the situation in which Webster was acting. After all, there is the possibility, or even the likelihood that the murder was committed in this fashion, and that the indicted Knapp deserved the conviction he got. Suppose the audience had remained cold and unmoved. There is the victim's side to consider and the interest of society in protecting life. We should not forget that Webster's "actualization" is in the service of these. Our attitude toward what is just or right or noble and their opposites is not a bloodless calculation, but a feeling for and against. As Whately indicates, the speaker who arouses feeling may only be arousing it to the right pitch and channeling it in the right direction.

To re-affirm the general contention: the rhetorician who practices "amplification" is not thereby misleading his audience, because we are all men of limited capacity and sensitivity and imagination. We all need to have things pointed out to us, things stressed in our interest. The very task of the rhetorician is to determine what feature of a question is most exigent and to use the power of language to make it appear so. A speaker who dwells insistently upon some aspect of a case may no more be hoodwinking me than a policeman or a doctor when he advises against a certain course of action by pointing out its nature or its consequences. He *should* be in a position to know somewhat better than I do.

It is strongly to be suspected that this charge against rhetoric comes not only from the distorted image that makes man a merely rationalistic being, but also from the dogma of an uncritical equalitarianism. The notion of equality has insinuated itself so far that it appears sometimes as a feeling, to which I would apply the name "sentimental plebeianism," that no man is better or wiser than another, and hence that it is usurpation for one person to undertake to instruct or admonish another. This preposterous (and we could add, wholly unscientific judgment, since our differences are manifold and provable) is propagated in subtle ways by our institutions of publicity and the perverse art of demogogic politics. Common sense replies that any individual who advises a friend or speaks up in meeting is exercising a kind of leadership, which may be justified by superior virtue, knowledge, or personal insight.

The fact that leadership is a human necessity is proof that rhetoric as the attempt through language to make one's point of view prevail grows out of the nature of man. It is not a reflection of any past phase of social development, or any social institution, or any fashion, or any passing vice. When all factors have been considered, it will be seen that men are born rhetoricians, though some are born small ones and others greater, and some cultivate the native gift by study and training, whereas some neglect it. Men are such because they are born into history, with an endowment of passion and a sense of the *ought*.

There is ever some discrepancy, however slight, between the situation man is in and the situation he would like to realize. His life is therefore characterized by movement toward goals. It is largely the power of rhetoric which influences and governs that movement.

For the same set of reasons, rhetoric is cognate with language. Ever since I first heard the idea mentioned seriously it impressed me as impossible and even ridiculous that the utterances of men could be neutral. Such study as I have been able to give the subject over the years has confirmed that feeling and has led me to believe that what is sometimes held up as a desideratum—expression purged of all tendency—rests upon an initial misconception of the nature of language.

The condition essential to see is that every use of speech, oral and written, exhibits an attitude, and an attitude implies an act. "Thy speech bewrayeth thee" is aphoristically true if we take it as saying, "Your speech reveals your disposition," first by what you choose to say, then by the amount you decide to say, and so on down through the resources of linguistic elaboration and intonation. All rhetoric is a rhetoric of motives, as Kenneth Burke saw fit to indicate in the title of his book. At the low end of the scale, one may be doing nothing more than making sounds to express exuberance. But if at the other end one sits down to compose a *Critique of the Pure Reason,* one has the motive of refuting other philosophers' account of the constitution of being and of substituting one's own, for an interest which may be universal, but which nonetheless proceeds from the will to alter something.

Does this mean that it is impossible to be objective about anything? Does it mean that one is "rhetorical" in declaring that a straight line is the shortest distance between two points? Not in the sense in which the objection is usually raised. There are degrees of objectivity, and there are various disciplines which have their own rules for expressing their laws or their content in the most effective manner for their purpose. But even this expression can be seen as enclosed in a rhetorical intention. Put in another way, an utterance is capable of rhetorical function and aspect. If one looks widely enough, one can discover its rhetorical

dimension, to put it in still another way. The scientist has some interest in setting forth the formulation of some recurrent feature of the physical world, although his own sense of motive may be lost in a general feeling that science is a good thing because it helps progress along.[2]

In short, as long as man is a creature responding to purpose, his linguistic expression will be a carrier of tendency. Where the modern semanticists got off on the wrong foot in their effort to refurbish language lay in the curious supposition that language could and should be outwardly determined. They were positivists operating in the linguistic field. Yet if there is anything that is going to keep on defying positivistic correlation, it is this subjectively born, intimate, and value-laden vehicle which we call language. Language is a system of imputation, by which values and percepts are first framed in the mind and are then imputed to things. This is not an irresponsible imputation; it does not imply, say, that no two people can look at the same clock face and report the same time. The qualities or properties have to be in the things, but they are not in the things in the form in which they are framed by the mind. This much I think we can learn from the great realist-nominalist controversy of the Middle Ages and from the little that contemporary semantics has been able to add to our knowledge. Language was created by the imagination for the purposes of man, but it may have objective reference—just how we cannot say until we are in possession of a more complete metaphysics and epistemology.

Now a system of imputation involves the use of predicates, as when we say, "Sugar is sweet" or "Business is good." Modern positivism and relativism, however, have gone virtually to the point of denying the validity of all conceptual predication. Occasionally at Chicago I purposely needle a class by expressing a general concept in a casual way, whereupon usually I am sternly reminded by some member brought up in the best relativist tradition that "You can't generalize that way." The same view can be encountered in eminent quarters. Justice Oliver Wendell Holmes was fond of saying that the chief end of man is to frame general propositions and that no general proposition is worth a damn. In the first of these general propositions the Justice was right, in the sense that men cannot get along without categorizing their apprehensions of reality. In the second he was wrong because, although a great jurist, he was not philosopher enough to think the matter through. Positivism and relativism may have rendered a certain service as devil's advocates if they have caused us to be more careful about our concepts and our predicates, yet their position in net forms is untenable. The battle against general propositions was lost from the beginning, for just as surely as man is a symbol-using animal (and a symbol transcends the thing symbolized), he is a classifying animal. The morality lies in the application of the predicate.

Language, which is thus predicative, is for the same cause sermonic. We are all of us preachers in private or public capacities. We have no sooner uttered words than we have given impulse to other people to look at the world, or some small part of it, in our way. Thus caught up in a great web of inter-communication and inter-influence, we speak as rhetoricians affecting one another for good or ill. That is why I must agree with Quintilian that the true orator is the good man, skilled in speaking—good in his formed character and right in his ethical philosophy. When to this he adds fertility in invention and skill in the arts of language, he is entitled to that leadership which tradition accords him.

If rhetoric is to be saved from the neglect and even the disrepute which I was deploring at the beginning of this lecture, these primary truths will have to be recovered until they are a part of our active consciousness. They are, in summation, that man is not nor ever can be nor ever should be a depersonalized thinking machine. His feeling is the activity in him most closely related to what used to be called his soul. To appeal to his feeling therefore is not necessarily an insult; it can be a way to honor him, by recognizing him in the fulness of his being. Even in those situations where the appeal is a kind of strategy, it but recognizes that men—all men—are historically conditioned.

Rhetoric must be viewed formally as operating at that point where literature and politics meet, or where literary values and political urgencies can be brought together. The rhetorician makes use of the moving power of literary presentation to induce in his hearers an attitude or decision which is political in the very broadest sense. Perhaps this explains why the successful user of rhetoric is sometimes in bad grace with both camps. For the literary people he is too "practical"; and for the more practical political people he is too "flowery." But there is nothing illegitimate about what he undertakes to do, any more than it would be illegitimate to make use of the timeless principles of aesthetics in the constructing of a public building. Finally, we must never lose sight of the order of values as the ultimate sanction of rhetoric. No one can live a life of direction and purpose without some scheme of values. As rhetoric confronts us with choices involving values, the rhetorician is a preacher to us, noble if he tries to direct our passion toward noble ends and base if he uses our passion to confuse and degrade us. Since all utterance influences us in one or the other of these directions, it is important that the direction be the right one, and it is better if this lay preacher is a master of his art.

Notes

1. I might add that a number of years ago the Mathematics Staff of the College at the University of Chicago made a wager with the English Staff that they could write the Declaration of Independence in mathematical language. They must have had later and better thoughts about this, for we never saw the mathematical rendition.
2. If I have risked confusion by referring to "rhetoricians" and "rhetorical speakers," and to other men as if they were all non-rhetoricians, while insisting that all language has its rhetorical aspect, let me clarify the terms. By "rhetorician" I mean the deliberate rhetor: the man who understands the nature and aim and requirements of persuasive expression and who uses them more or less consciously according to the approved rules of the art. The other, who by his membership in the family of language users, must be a rhetorician of sorts, is an empirical and adventitious one; he does not know enough to keep invention, arrangement, and style working for him. The rhetorician of my reference is thus the educated speaker; the other is an untaught amateur.

Weaver's stress on values and the sermonic nature of language stimulated considerable interest both in the study of the ethical implications of rhetoric and in the rhetorical implications of ethics. Among those who had felt the impact of Weaver's teachings most strongly was Ralph Eubanks of the University of West Florida. In fact, just prior to his untimely death in his early fifties, Weaver had asked Eubanks to collaborate with him on his next book. The choice of Eubanks as a potential co-author would have been an ideal one, for during the past two decades he had probed deeply into the question of rhetoric as value.

Axiological Issues in Rhetorical Inquiry

"Man, as a person, seeks to complete himself axiologically."
Eliseo Vivas

My topic represents one of the central strands of inquiry in Western rhetorical thought. The question of the role of "the goods" in rhetoric claimed the attention of both Plato and Aristotle. And all major theories of the rhetoric, from antiquity on, have had to deal in one way or another, with the question of value and valuation. Rhetorical proof systems are, in the nature of things, enmeshed in considerations of value. As another example, we may recall that it was God, interpreted as the supreme value-reality, that conferred meaning on the ecclesiastical rhetorics; and yet again, the classic value of Beauty that informed the belletristic rhetorics of the Renaissance.[1]

Yet it was not until axiology developed as a formal interdisciplinary study in the present century that the question of the function of value and valuation in rhetoric received in our own field anything like concerted attention.

I do not think a detailed state-of-the-art report necessary to our present purposes. We should note before passing on, however, rhetoric's recent trial by positivism, which resulted in an abortive attempt to exorcise the property of "oughtness" from discourse under an emotivist interpretation of value language.[2] And we might further note that over the last quarter-century we have come to view value questions as central to an understanding of the nature of symbolic action.[3]

Of especial concern to me here are those axiological questions in rhetorical scholarship which bear most crucially on the problem of developing a system of rhetoric equal to the awesome stresses imposed upon it by a technosophic world. That world, as many of our finest cultural critics remind us, is one of "cultural derangement," moral uncertainty, and intellectual skepticism. Man, observes Philosopher E. M. Adams, having been brought "under the blanket of empirical scientific categories" has suffered serious impairment of his classic "humanistic self-image."[4] In any event, we sadly sense the truth of Leslie Fiedler's observation of a "weariness in the West . . . with the striving to be men."[5]

All of us share, of course, the task of restoring man's humanistic self-image. Yet it appears to me that since rhetoric is the queen of the humanities, a very special obligation belongs to rhetoricians. That obligation, I believe to be this: the renewal of the humane tradition of rhetoric which, beyond all else, recognizes man's historical consciousness and his capacity to choose between better and worse as central to his dignity and his destiny.[6] On this analysis, then, our professional task would not be a continued promotion of the prevailing system of Pragmatic Rhetoric.

Reprinted by permission of the author.

Rather, it would be a commitment to a rhetoric in which knowledge is dominated by *wisdom,* or by what the ancients called *prudentia.* As Jacques Maritain has observed, practical wisdom is a "a virtue *indivisibly moral and intellectual at the same time.*"[7] I therefore think it the true basis for a humane rhetoric.

What I wish to do in this brief period is to probe in a suggestive way those axiological issues which lie closest to the heart of our challenge. First I describe a value perspective from which we may approach the problem of renewing the humanistic tradition of rhetoric. Second I consider some of the leading axiological issues in rhetorical inquiry. Finally, I give brief notice to the kind of value thrust I think is required for a genuinely humane rhetoric.

The Nature of Value Theory

Our task demands first that we reconnoiter the ground of axiology, taking special notice of major concepts and distinctions.

Axiology, a philosophical term first introduced in 1906 by Marshal Urban as a translation of *Werttheorie* from the field of economics, refers to *the general theory of value and valuation.*[8] As developed from its beginnings in late nineteenth-century European scholarship to our own day, axiology constitutes an interdisciplinary study which engages minds from the fields of economics, sociology, ethics, rhetoric, aesthetics, jurisprudence, logic, epistemology, anthropology, and education.

In its widest conspectus, axiology refers (in J. N. Findlay's words) to "the study of the ultimately worthwhile things (and, of course, of the ultimately counter worthwhile things) as well as the analysis of worthwhileness (or counter worthwhileness) in general."[9] In the American tradition of value theory the preferred master-term has developed as "desirability," with a *value* being interpreted to mean *a concept of the desirable.* And, following Kluckhohn, the American anthropologist, a distinction is commonly drawn between "the

desirable" (i.e., abstract measures of preferential conduct) and the "desired," or those needs and wants associated with the domain of material and functional motivations.[10] On this analysis, *value* represents an implicit or explicit conception of the desirable, whereas the realm of "the desired" denotes "interests," or valuables." In the words of Sociologist A. Khoshkish, "When a believer donates his fortune to his church, he parts with his valuables for his values."[11]

Important also is the notion of the "degree of finitude" of interests *vis-a-vis* values—a notion recently introduced in the field of value inquiry. On the one hand, interests are to be regarded as finite goals and strivings which, once attained, lose their potency and fall away. True values, on the other hand, stand in relation to conduct as ideals which are never finally consummated. To act on the basis of a true value does not exhaust its potency; the value remains to inform and guide future action.[12]

From general value theory is derived yet another crucial distinction—the difference between attitudes and values. While some theorists have held the two concepts to be synonymous, others—most notably Rokeach—view them as related, yet hardly the same. Rokeach considers "a value to be a type of belief, centrally located within one's belief system about how one ought or ought not to behave, or about some end-state of existence worth or not worth attaining. Values are thus *abstract ideals,* positive or negative, not tied to any specific attitude, object, or situation, representing a person's beliefs about ideal modes of conduct and ideal terminal goals. . . ."[13]

In this conception, the pursuit of truth, beauty, justice, compassion and honor are regarded as examples of "ideal modes of conduct," and happiness, security, freedom, equality, and "states of grace and salvation" as examples of "ideal goals or endstates."[14] In certain crucial respects, observes Rokeach, attitudes and values differ. And the differences are important to a refined rhetoric of values: "while an attitude represents several beliefs focused on a specific object or situation, a value is a single belief that transcendentally guides actions and judgments across specific objects and situations, and beyond immediate goals to more ultimate end-states of existence. Moreover, a value, unlike an attitude, is an imperative to action, not only about the preferable but also a *preference for the preferable* . . . [i.e., a preference from among those things that *can be* chosen for those that *ought to be* chosen]. Finally, a value, unlike an attitude, is a standard or yardstick to guide actions, attitudes, comparisons, evaluations, and justifications of self and others."[15] Put another way: An attitude is the behavioral manifestation of a value. If one holds Value A, then one has a positive attitude toward instances of Value A. Attitudes are specific instances; the value is the generalization.

Of crucial importance to a consideration of values in their relationships to the ideal of a humane rhetoric is the notion (to employ Findlay's phrase) of the "manditoriness of value." Whether we view the ground, or source of value as God, "the democratic way," our unlearned biogenic drives, or man's capacity for making and using symbols, we yet recognize the reality of the *imperativeness* of values. In the words of Henry Margenau, "Values are always relative to commands; value propositions [whether of "the desirable," "the obligatory," or the "estimable"] are equivalent to exhortations to which one is committed. Removal of the commitment, reversal of the command, destroy or change the sign of a value."[16] Thus, we encounter in the concept of value-commitment the deepest humane significance. "Conceivably," says Margenau, "science might prove that [the value of] honesty leads to collective human happiness, but never that happiness is desirable."[17]

It is well to ask, whence comes the "manditoriness of value" in the human situation? My own impression is that the answer has to be an ontological one. I therefore concur in the view of Paul Tillich who finds the source of the axiological "ought" in man's essential nature—in the *eidos,* or essence of humanhood. "Value," writes Tillich, "is man's essential being, put as an imperative against him. The

moral imperatives are not arbitrary ordinances of a transcendent tyrant; neither are they determined by utilitarian calculations or group conventions. The moral law is man's own essential nature appearing as commanding authority. If man were united with himself and his essential being there would be no command. But man is estranged from himself, and the values he experiences appear as laws, natural and positive, demanding, threatening, promising."[18]

Values, by the foregoing analysis,[19] assert themselves in our judgment decisions and actions as *commitments,* which in their ultimate form "place us at stake as persons."[20] *Commitment,* which I hold to be the axial term of a system of humane rhetoric, is grounded in the imperativeness of value, or in what is commonly termed in the literature of value theory, "the axiological ought." Writes one leading axiologist: "The axiological ought pertains to value theory in its broadest aspects and implies the normative character of evaluative judgment wherever value preferences are expressed. It pertains, in other words, to the question, What values ought I to cherish or pursue? What is worthy of being cherished or pursued?, and, in this sense, is concerned with ends as well as with means."[21]

Crucial therefore to an understanding of the nature of the axiological ought is the distinction between goal-values, and values considered as means-to-ends. On this distinction Rokeach is instructive: "An *instrumental value* is . . . defined as a single belief that always takes the following form: 'I believe that such-and-such a mode of conduct (for example, honesty, courage) is personally and socially preferable in all situations with respect to all objects.' A *terminal value* takes a comparable form: 'I believe that such-and-such an end state of existence (for example, salvation, a world at peace) is personally and socially worth striving for.' "[22]

Necessary to a full understanding of the axiological component of rhetoric is the distinction, commonly maintained in traditional ethics, between the moral ought and the axiological ought, between the *right* and the *good.* The difference, it is usually observed, arises from the opposition of the *deontic* (i.e., respect-for-law) theories of moral philosophy on the one hand and the *axiological and telic* (i.e., value-realization) theories on the other. On the traditional analysis, commitment and duty are interpreted as conformity to "rules of correct procedure." For example, Werkmeister maintains that the moral ought (as contradistinct from the axiological ought) pertains neither to means nor to ends. Rather, the obligatoriness of ethical imperatives (the right) arises from the "analytic entailment" of the particular form of moral behavior. Thus, the obligatoriness of the act of promising is *logically entailed* in "the very nature of the promise *as a promise.*"[23] On one level of analysis the distinction between *ethical imperatives* (the right) and *value imperatives* (the good) is difficult to maintain. For at bottom, rules of "the right" are themselves valued-based; and one may argue that the obligatoriness of keeping a promise arises from the value one attaches to one or more of "the ideal modes of conduct" (i.e., virtues)—to *justice,* or to *respect,* for example. At the same time, in the existential arena of our daily striving and choice-making where the question, "In what does my duty consist?," insistently poses itself, consideration of the *good* (or the valuable) and the *right* (or the ethical) often appear "in agonizing conflict." As Philosopher Virgil C. Aldrich puts it, "When Gautama Buddha left his wife and child for the sake of the *good,* he violated a rule of *right* action. He broke a promise. He was being unethical, which he sadly sensed, though it was his genius to fulfill his duty in but one of its dimensions, the axiological."[24] While, as I think, values are the stuff of both the good and the right, realism demands that commitment be interpreted as a "dual demand." The ideal of *prudentia,* or "wise living," requires a synthetic view of moral conduct, a view that takes full account of the "demands" of both the good and the right. Aldrich offers just such a synthesis of the deontic and the telic: "Human nature demands that action be both ethical and valuable though this does produce tension and conflict in sensitive moral experience. . . . The recognition of either set of imperatives in

the human situation may tend to minimize the other, yet the total demand of Duty (capitalized) makes both mandatory."[25]

Value Questions in Rhetorical Inquiry

We are now in position to consider some of the leading axiological issues of rhetorical scholarship. I am most interested in those which seem to me to bear crucially on the problem of renewing the humane tradition of rhetoric.

Of first importance is an issue which I wish could be waived. Yet I fear it cannot be. That issue is the age-old one of whether rhetoric *sui generis* is moral or amoral. The issue may be stated in another way: Does rhetoric have substantive as well as instrumental (i.e., methodological) content? The controversy entered a new phase when, in 1953, Richard M. Weaver in his major work on rhetoric demonstrated from an analysis of Plato's *Phaedrus* "the essentially axiological and telic nature of the concept of rhetoric as effective expression." "It is impossible," Weaver wrote, "to talk about rhetoric as effective expression without having as a term giving intelligibility to the whole discourse, the Good."[26] Some years later, Professor Virgil Baker and I, following the implications of Weaver's analysis, argued from an interdisciplinary perspective the indissoluble linkage between rhetorical purpose and value-realization. We further argued that "The logical function of rhetoric in man's sociocultural universe is the realization of the highest goals of human life," proposing therefore that the art of rhetoric be related in both theory and practice to "a system of civilizing values."[27] There followed shortly Karl Wallace's well-known essay on the issue in which he offered the concept of "good reasons" as the "substance" of rhetoric—a concept which in his view synthesized the axiological and the methodological content of the art.[28] From this dialogue there have recently come additional insights.[29]

In light of what we now know about the ubiquity of value in human endeavor, it is difficult to maintain the amorality of rhetoric. We may indeed observe that in the absence of imperatives of value there could be no rhetorical purpose. The strategic motive itself is at last axiological and telic. And what Bitzer has termed "the rhetorical situation" owes its very existence to "the manditoriness of value"; indeed "rhetorical exigence" itself is brought into birth by our prizings and our cherishings.

Another of the leading axiological issues of our profession concerns the level of value commitment we are prepared to make. Nilsen, in his wise monograph on the ethics of speech communication, puts the question in this way: "Do we always have the obligation to do, or say, *that which maximizes the good?*" The answer Nilsen gives, drawing upon the thinking of ethicist Melvin Rader, is that we should take as our standard of commitment "the optimific word." That is, we should adopt "a general moral responsibility to do that which is better, which would include both the desirable [the axiological ought] and the obligatory [the moral ought]."[30] If Nilsen's position is sound—and I think that it is—then what are the implications for our theory, our criticism, and our professional practice?

There is a sense in which our issue comes down to this: If indeed the substance of rhetoric is "good reasons," then what is to be the measure of our commitment as rhetoricians to the "goodness" element of that substance? Shall it be to make as close a linkage as we can between rhetoric and what Burke calls "the real ultimates proper to the medium [of language]"? I am disposed to think so—to think that, particularly in these times of "cultural derangement," we are under the strongest obligation to develop, to teach, and to practice a full-blown Rhetoric of Commitment. By this standard we should not be content with a rhetoric which draws its compulsion solely from biogenic drives, "valuables," and finite "interests." Nor would we be satisfied to relegate values themselves to the sheerly instrumental role, as is now commonly done in our textbook literature. Rather, we would make an unapologetic commitment to the ideal of a Humane Rhetoric—a rhetoric calculated to assist man in reclaiming his humanistic self-image.

I think the ideal no less justified now than I did in 1962 when Professor Baker and I ex-

pressed it. Yet I would, for my part, add a supplement to what we then said. The years have given me a somewhat different perspective on how we should interpret our task. I am not prepared to suggest for rhetoric a typology of values so closely associated with the "power relations" of democratic ideology—as was the Lasswell-Kaplan analysis. Both tradition and logic argue against rhetoric's being regarded as the handmaiden of political ideology. As Nichols observes, "Political ideology has been no part of a theory and philosophy of a humane rhetoric; and its practitioners have not recognized it as being ideological."[31] We must further recognize that such linkage produces a too-exclusive focus on the concept of audience "adherence," and therefore on the strategic dimension of the art, as against its moral dimension. Yet further: ideology, in the nature of things, tends to produce a lop-sided approach to commitment. That is: its essential tendency is to promote the attainment of "valuable goals," often at the expense of ethical rectitude. The "dual demand" of Duty, as we have seen, requires that decision and action be both ethical and valuable.

On Renewal of the Humane Tradition of Rhetoric

What then, we have finally to ask, represents a sound value stance for the study and teaching of rhetoric in an age marked by "a weariness with the striving to be men"? That is: With what shall the "goodness" of the "good reasons" of rhetoric be associated? We begin our answer, it seems to me, with one of the truly permanent assumptions of Western rhetorical scholarship: the *necessary* connection between the art of rhetoric and the concept of "worthwhileness." It was this understanding that prompted Charles Sears Baldwin to write of the Aristotelian analysis: "No less than logic, [rhetoric] is a means of bringing out truth, of making people see what is true and fitting. But rhetoric contemplates having truth embraced. It is the application of proof to people."[32] It was this understanding, I believe, that underlay Donald C. Bryant's classic statement, "Rhetoric aims at what is *worth* doing, what is *worth* trying."[33] Rhetoric is hardly amoral. Nor yet is it metamoral, since its statements are not aimed primarily at elucidating the meanings of such concepts as "good," "right," and "ought." Rather, its premises of value are aimed at the existential question, "What *ought* to be done?" Rhetoric is thus applied axiology, and is addressed directly to the human condition, to man-in-the-world.[34] In short, true rhetoric always expresses "a preference for the preferable."

I am convinced that the "goodness" of the "good reasons" of a genuinely humane rhetoric is fundamentally constituted in those enduring values that have given life over the centuries to the classic Western ideal of "the good life in the good society." Those values represent, it seem to me, the best things there are—"the permanent things," in T. S. Eliot's phrase: *Health, Creativity* (the enabling force of both science and art), *Wisdom, Love, Freedom* with *Justice, Courage,* and *Order.* These positive ideals, which largely define the dual demands of the "right" and the "good," are those the ancients summed up under the headings, Truth, Goodness, and Beauty.[35] At the heart of this grand conception of worthwhileness lies an ineluctable belief in the dignity and worth of the individual person.

This order of values, embodying as it does the highest imperatives of man's essential nature, appears as a kind of axiological *Tao,* or Way, by which rhetoric, guided by the ideal of *prudentia,* might minister effectively to the human condition in an age marked by massive erosion of human purpose. And the challenge of attaining this ideal of a renewed humane rhetoric is an altogether fitting one for us who, by tradition, are (along with our philosopher colleagues) "lovers of wisdom."

Ralph T. Eubanks

The author is Professor of Communication at the University of West Florida. This essay was first presented at the Speech Communication Association Convention in Washington, D.C. in December of 1977. It has since then been accepted for publication in the *Southern Speech Communication Journal,* and appears in the Fall, 1978 issue.

Notes

1. It is interesting to speculate on how the great systems of rhetoric have been related to the classic value universals of Truth, Goodness, and Beauty, and for that matter, to individual rhetorics. On such a conception, one might argue, for example, that the Platonic rhetoric was dominated by the supreme value-reality of Goodness, whereas the Aristotelian was subservient to Truth. Again, Goodness (theologically considered) informed medieval rhetoric, Beauty the stylistic rhetorics, and Truth (scientifically interpreted), the modern psychological and sociological systems of rhetoric.

2. The critique of the so-called "myth of neuter discourse" (Winterowd's phrase), begun in earnest with the publication of Richard M. Weaver's *Ideas Have Consequences* (Chicago: Henry Regnery Co., 1948), pp. 148–69, still goes on, though without either the fervor or the fruitfulness that marked its earlier phases. Of the spuriousness of the positivistic enterprise, Joseph Schwartz said in 1966: "Reading Burke as he is an extension and contributor to the mainstream of the rhetorical tradition is convincing evidence that the hope for a rhetoric of non-commitment much sought after in certain quarters in our century is an impossibility. To purify the language of the tribe by amputating the tendentious aspect of language is not only impossible but absurd. *To discriminate among values through the use of language is the only direction that rhetoric can take.* To avoid the manifold problems raised by that stance is to avoid the world of intelligible discourse itself." "Kenneth Burke, Aristotle, and the Future of Rhetoric," in *Contemporary Rhetoric: A Reader's Coursebook,* ed. Douglas Ehninger (Glenview, Ill.: Scott, Foresman Co., 1972), p. 258. Italics supplied.

3. Even the most general summary of the indicators seems to affirm the latter conclusion. The rhetorics of both Burke and Weaver are rhetorics of commitment. It is also worth observing that Georges Gusdorf, in his phenomenological study of the speech act argued: "The word owes its efficacy to the fact that it is not an objective notation, but *an index of value." Speaking (La Parole),* trans. Paul T. Brockelman (Chicago Ill.: Northwestern Univ. Press, 1965), p. 9. (italics are Gusdorf's). Yet further, Ch. Perelman and his associate, L. Olbrechts-Tyteca, observe: "Values enter, at some stage or other, into every argument." *The New Rhetoric: A Treatise on Argumentation,* trans. John Wilkinson and Purcell Weaver (South Bend, Ind.: Notre Dame Univ. Press, 1969), p. 75.

4. E. M. Adams, *Philosophy and the Modern Mind: A Philosophical Critique of Modern Western Civilization* (Chapel Hill, N.C.: The Univ. of North Carolina Press, 1975), pp. 45 ff. Chapter II of this work, "Is the Modern Western Mind Deranged?" presents an incisive critique of "the distinctively modern Western assumptions about the constitutional principles of the human mind," which is of particular interest to theorists of rhetoric.

5. Quoted in Duncan Williams, *Trousered Apes: Sick Literature in a Sick Society* (New Rochelle, N.Y.: Arlington House, 1971), p. 43.

6. Only by this route, I believe, could rhetoric become efficacious in repairing the present split between intellect and feeling, to which cultural critics such as Erich Fromm, Sir Herbert Read, and others, have recently called our attention. See on this head, Richard L. Means, *The Ethical Imperatives: The Crisis in American Values* (Garden City, N.Y.: Doubleday, 1969), pp. 84–5.

7. Quoted in Richard M. Weaver, *The Ethics of Rhetoric* (Chicago: Henry Regnery Co., 1953), p. 24*n*. Italics supplied.

8. William K. Frankena, "Value and Valuation," in *The Encyclopedia of Philosophy*, ed. Paul Edwards (New York: MacMillian Co., 1967), VII, 229.

9. J. N. Findlay, "Axiological Ethics," in *New Studies in Ethics*. Vol. II: *Modern Theories*, ed. W. D. Hudson (New York: St. Martin's Press, 1974), p. 121.

10. See Clyde Kluckhohn, et al., "Value and Value Orientation in the Theory of Action," in Talcott Parsons and Edward A. Shils, eds., *Toward a General Theory of Action* (Cambridge, Mass.: Harvard Univ. Press, 1951), p. 395.

11. A. Khoshkish, "The Concept of Values: A Sociophenomenological Approach," *The Journal of Value Inquiry*, 8 (Spring, 1974), 3.

12. See Khoshkish, "The Concept of Values," p. 6.

13. Milton Rokeach, *Beliefs, Attitudes and Values: A Theory of Organization and Change* (San Francisco, Calif.: Jossey-Bass, Inc., 1968), p. 124. Italics supplied.

14. Rokeach, p. 124. It will be observed that the classic trinity of values (Truth, Goodness, and Beauty) is subsumed under the category of values Rokeach designates as "ideal modes of conduct."

15. Rokeach, p. 160.

16. "The Scientific Basis of Value," in *New Knowledge in Human Values*, ed. Abraham H. Maslow (New York: Harper and Row, 1959), p. 42.

17. "The Scientific Basis of Value," p. 43.

18. Paul Tillich, "Is a Science of Human Values Possible?" in *New Knowledge*, pp. 193, 195. An interesting similarity may be seen between Tillich's view and that expressed by Kenneth Burke. For Burke, the source of man's "motives" is language—"the screen of symbolism" by which man approaches reality. Above the level of "the sheer physicality of life" and the level of symbolism having to do with the satisfaction of man's biogenic needs is a third level of reality: "the motives intrinsic to this special property, this language—a plane of symbolism capable of pointing towards 'perfection' intrinsic to itself. To live by these in the sign of their sheer formality, would be to live by 'real' ultimates, ultimates proper to the medium." "The Anaesthetic Revelation of Herone Liddell," *Kenyon Review*, 19 (Autumn 1957), 531.

19. The "ontogenic" conception of the ground of value is further affirmed in the thinking of Philosopher-Economist Edmund A. Opitz, who sees the "moral code" as fulfilling a role in man analogous to the role of instinctive behavior in the lower animals. Just as the servomechanism of instinct permits the subhuman organism to stay attuned to its environment, so does the "moral code" enable man to fulfill the definition of himself. Writes Opitz: "An animal's instincts guarantee that he will neither disobey nor deviate from the law of his being; a fish does not seek the dry land, a robin does not try to burrow in the ground, a gibbon does not yearn to swing on the North Pole. But man fulfills the law of his being with the utmost difficulty—if then—and the only means at his disposal to align him with the forces of life is the ethical code. It is this code, and this alone, which may provide him with a life-giving, life-enhancing regimen." Man is therefore, in his essential being, *Homo ethicus*, the valuing animal. "Instinct and Ethics," in *Ethics and the Press: Readings in Mass Media Morality*, ed. John C. Merrill and Ralph C. Barney (New York: Hastings House, 1975), pp. 20–21.

20. For an instructive discussion of the relationship of "commitment," or duty, to values, see W. H. Werkmeister, *Man and His Values* (Lincoln, Neb.: Univ. of Nebraska Press, 1967), pp. 157–70. Taking a teleological approach to axiological ethics, Werkmeister affirms the basic imperative of value theory to be: "Live so as to maximize the good in the world" (pp. 169–70).

21. W. H. Werkmeister, *Theories of Ethics: A Study in Moral Obligation* (Lincoln, Neb.: Johnson Publishing Co., 1961), p. 430.

22. Rokeach, p. 160 (Italics supplied). It is necessary to point out, however, that some values may have both an instrumental and a terminal function. For example, *freedom* which Rokeach denominates an "ideal goal or end-state" (i.e., "living a life of freedom,") is also viewed in political theory and social ethics as a necessary condition (i.e., means) for the full realization of human potential.

23. Werkmeister, *Theories of Ethics*, p. 431; *Man and His Values*, p. 157.

24. "Beyond Ethics?" in *Philosophy and Culture East and West*, ed. Charles A. Moore (Honolulu, Ha.: Univ. of Hawaii Press, 1962), p. 381. Ital. in original.

25. Aldrich, "Beyond Ethics?" p. 382. The conflict may of course be seen in terms of the old means-ends dichotomy. Hence, as Aldrich says, "there are values which can be possessed only under the restriction of ethical imperatives, such as prohibit lying, cheating, slandering. Above all, they prohibit using individual persons as mere means to ends, howsoever valuable the ends. Disregarding this rule deforms the values that are too ruthlessly possessed" (p. 382).

26. *The Ethics of Rhetoric*, p. 23.

27. "Toward an Axiology of Rhetoric, *Quarterly Journal of Speech*, 48 (1962), 161.

28. "The Substance of Rhetoric: Good Reasons," *Quarterly Journal of Speech*, 49 (1963), 239–49.

29. See for example: "The Rhetoric of Moral Conflict: Two Critical Dimensions," *Quarterly Journal of Speech*, 56 (1970), 120–30; and Scott Consigny,

"Rhetoric and Madness: Robert Pirsig's Inquiry into Values," *Southern Speech Communication Journal,* 43 (Fall 1977), 16–32. In his essay Consigny argues: "A restorative rhetoric is . . . one in which the passions are recognized as the very ground of being in and interpreting the world" (p. 16). Such a rhetoric, calculated to return modern man to a state of "wholeness," would engage man's valuing powers at the deepest level.

30. Thomas R. Nilsen, *Ethics of Speech Communication,* 2nd edn. (The Bobbs-Merrill Co., 1974), pp. 85–87.

31. Marie H. Nichols, "Rhetoric and the Humane Tradition," in *Rhetoric: A Tradition in Transition,* ed. Walter R. Fisher (East Lansing, Mich.: Michigan State Univ. Press, 1974), pp. 182–83.

32. *Ancient Rhetoric and Poetic* (1924; rpt. Gloucester, Mass.: Peter Smith, 1959), p. 9.

33. "Rhetoric: Its Functions and Its Scope," *Quarterly Journal of Speech,* 39 (1953), 415.

34. "Only its perverters [wrote Baldwin] teach it as merely an art of dealing with persons, of reaching an audience." *Ancient Rhetoric and Poetic,* p. 9.

35. At this highest level, as P. Sorokin once observed, "Truth is always good and beautiful; the sublime goodness is invariably true and beautiful; and the pure Beauty is always true and good." *New Knowledge in Human Values,* p. 230. This triad represents, in Aristotelian terms, the "first principles of human nature." Again, included in the expanded listing given here are the four "cardinal virtues" Plato treats in *The Republic: wisdom, courage, temperance* and *justice.* Temperance would be implied in the ideal of *health.*

16

Rhetoric as Value: Ethos and Image

One of the truisms in the field of human communication is the recognition that whenever a rhetorical transaction takes place there are five elements of a model present: the source and/or encoder, the message, the channel, the destination, and the decoder or communication receiver.[1] A second widely accepted notion is that while each of these parts of the communication process must be in operation concurrently, there is an unmistakable hierarchy. Rhetoricians from Plato and Aristotle in the classical era to Kenneth Burke, I. A. Richards, and Chaim Perelman in the twentieth century would rank the message first in importance. Quite clearly there can be no communication unless there is meaning, and the message constitutes the meaning. For this reason Dean Barnlund's essay "Toward a Meaning-Centered Philosophy of Communication" has become his most popular monograph.[2]

But if it is true that the message is the most important aspect of rhetoric, it is the source's perceived relationship with the message which seems to be the prime persuasive factor. Despite his strong partiality to logos, Aristotle suggested that ethos perhaps is the dominating form of proof in persuasion.[3] Emerson put the same idea succinctly when he said: "What you are speaks so loudly I cannot hear what you say." Roger Nebergall, former Chairman of the Department of Communication at the University of Illinois, observes the significance of this when he argues as follows:

Instead of being the most important determiner of effect in the rhetorical situation, the speech is, in fact, of minor importance. I think there is no more consistent finding in the behavioral science research on communication in the last twenty years than the discovery that the effects of messages in determining behavioral changes as a result of communication are generally minor. Instead, the major predictors of change are typically found in source variables and audience variables.[4]

More than one hundred scientific studies in the past two decades support Nebergall's thesis that a speaker's ethos or image has an enormous effect in a rhetorical situation.[5]

The purpose of the present discussion is to review briefly the general nature of ethos and image, and then to probe in depth the constituent elements that give these concepts such a vital role in communication. Hopefully the reader will gain an appreciation of the dynamic interaction that is always present between the communicator and his message. Ethos will be defined, in the words of Anderson and Clevenger, "as the image held of a communicator at a given time by a receiver—either one person or a group."[6] The perspective on image adopted in this analysis is the description used by Kenneth Boulding in his classic work *The Image.* Inherent in this notion is the belief that all men are motivated by their "subjective knowledge structure or image of an individual or organization. . . ."[7] These images of the world are comprised of both facts and values, and may be private or public. It is a useless exercise, suggests Boulding, to try to discover whether or not the image corresponds to known truth or reality. In fact, not even the sophisticated research methodology of the physical and social sciences is adequate, in many instances, to determine truth. What is indisputable, in Boulding's opinion, is the proposition ". . . that behavior depends on the image."[8] In the framework of this study it might be said that the ethos a communicator demonstrates resides in the mind of the receiver.

In his book *The Great Fear of 1789,* George Lebvre develops the thesis that "in times of crisis what people believe is true is more crucial than what is true."[9] In applying this premise to ethos and image theory we may conclude that what an audience believes about a communicator will influence the manner in which they judge the presentation. From the point of view of persuasion it is of little moment whether the image of the speaker is justified or reasonable.

Since the image constructed in the minds of the members of the audience concerning the personality impact of the communicator is a major determinant of message response, it is incumbent on the speaker to reveal those positive traits necessary to create a favorable impression on the hearers. Historical and contemporary research tends to pinpoint four constituent elements that go into the shaping of ethos. These are character or trustworthiness; intelligence, knowledge or expertise; good will or identification; power or charisma. Whatever the sub-culture or setting, the audience hopes to see in the source a life style and communication performance that conforms to these values.

Let us turn, first of all, to a speaker's perceived *character* or *trustworthiness.* As listeners we measure a man's reliability and credibility. We need only to look at the legal profession to see how this notion functions. "Those who are presumed to be untrustworthy are not even allowed in the witness box," observe Perelman and Olbrechts-Tyteca, "and rules of judicial procedure very clearly aim at their exclusion."[10] The Yale studies in persuasion,[11] along with articles in the *Harvard Business Review,* also show convincingly what happens in a communication situation when one does not trust another. A will not make a genuine effort to have communion with B if he feels that B cannot be trusted.[12]

When an audience comes to believe that a gap exists between what we say and how we behave, we lose much of our persuasive impact. The eighteenth-century minister and rhetorician George Campbell observed: "When our practice conforms to our theory, our effectiveness trebles."[13] The brilliant philosopher Rousseau illustrates this point. A recent television special, dealing with the last one thousand years of culture in the Western world, suggested that Rousseau was one of the authentic geniuses of human thought in the eighteenth century. With this evaluation in mind consider Rousseau's great essay on education, *Emile.* It was a masterpiece on educating and training the child. Yet what a deleterious effect it would have on one's perception if the reader were reminded Rousseau had five children out of wedlock, all of whom were placed in a foundling home.

In the area of American political communication there are numerous examples to show the awesome power of credibility. Adlai Stevenson complained in 1956 that whenever he tried to initiate a discussion of the issues during the presidential campaign, he consistently was greeted with the refrain: "Trust Ike."[14] The credibility gap which President Johnson created when responding to a press conference question on replacing Henry Cabot Lodge as Ambassador to South Vietnam was a factor in conveying an image of untrustworthiness that ultimately brought an end to his Administration.[15] When Johnson abruptly stepped down, Humphrey and Muskie who became the standard bearers of the Democratic Party in 1968 repeatedly asserted throughout the campaign that the overriding issue was "Who Can You Trust?"[16] The same concern was apparent for trustworthiness in the contest four years later. In a 1972 public opinion poll, fifty per cent of the respondents classified Nixon as trustworthy while only twenty per cent gave McGovern a similar ranking.[17] Trustworthiness, it would appear, is linked with sincerity. However difficult it is to measure this intangible trait, listeners apparently construct an image that enables them to evaluate the quality of a message in terms of what is thought to be the communicator's intent. Few political leaders were more aware of this than the late Norman Thomas. In a conversation we had with him shortly before his death in 1968, we asked: "Tell us, Mr. Thomas, what do you think is the most important single thing in communication?" Without hesitation he noted: "a speaker's sincerity."[18]

The second ethos factor may be described as *intelligence, knowledge,* or *expertness.* When a listener concludes that a communicator does not know what he is talking about or that he has not probed deeply into his subject matter, he loses interest and respect. And when this happens, Cicero observed in his *De Oratore,* the speaker often experiences excessive tension.[19] More than two centuries ago John Wesley commented on this notion in his "Advice to the Clergy." He told his prospective ministers, many of whom wanted to move directly into the pulpit, that they should have knowledge of the Bible, foreign languages, and the whole range of the arts and sciences. He concluded with the recommendation that they should, like the Apostle Paul, have enough learning to stand before a king.[20]

The modern era contains graphic illustrations highlighting the importance of a speaker's competence as seen through the filter of the audience.. "One of the issues at stake in the controversies of the 1950s," stated Richard Hofstadter, "was the old one about the place of expertise in political life."[21] In 1957 the expert and the amateur issue came into clear focus with the appointment of Maxwell H. Gluck as the new ambassador to Ceylon. Part of the reason for his appointment was his donation of $30,000 to the Republican campaign in 1956. Here is a sample of the dialogue between Gluck and Senator Fulbright during the confirmation discussions in the Senate.

Fulbright: "What are the problems in Ceylon you think you can deal with?"

Gluck: "One of the problems are the people there. I believe I can—I think I can establish, unless we—again, unless I run into something that I have not run into be-

fore—a good relationship and good feeling toward the United States. . . ."

Fulbright: "Do you know the ambassador in India?"

Gluck: "I know John Sherman Cooper, the previous ambassador."

Fulbright: "Do you know who the prime minister of India is?"

Gluck: "Yes, but I can't pronounce his name."

Fulbright: "Do you know who the prime minister of Ceylon is?"

Gluck: "His name is unfamiliar now; I cannot call it off."[22]

The 1960 joint television debates between Kennedy and Nixon are also instructive. In an effort to establish rules that would make it possible for a speaker to reveal his intellectual grasp of issues on the spur of the moment, Nixon, convinced that he would prove to be a superior extemporaneous speaker, maintained that notes should not be allowed. Kennedy's ability to articulate ideas without the aid of information cards in the first debate came as a surprise to Nixon and the American people.

Our own experience confirms the role of perceived expertness in image formation. As a youthful instructor one of the authors went through the agonies of teaching a subject in which he was not qualified. When his department Chairman asked him if he were willing to teach a course in Parliamentary Law, he was sufficiently ambitious to say "yes" even though his knowledge did not extend beyond the meaning and purpose of a main motion and a motion to adjourn. A debacle occurred when his brightest student, who was then President of the Student Body at the University of Maryland and who later became the United States Senator from Maryland—Joseph Tydings—would stop him to find out how he would have solved a knotty problem that occurred in the Student Body meeting the night before. His feeble response was as follows: "Let's not move too fast, Joe, we'll confuse the students."

Nor can we readily dismiss these examples as being atypical. Two recent series of experimental studies have explained the tendency of hearers to penalize speakers whose credibility is questionable. David Berlo conducted an experiment in which a single speaker was asked to be the guest lecturer before three classes at Michigan State University. In every instance an identical speech was delivered in approximately the same manner. The variable in operation was the type of speech of introduction used in each case. In the first class, the guest lecturer was introduced as a substitute instructor in the department. He was described before the second group as the Head of Department. In the third class he was referred to as a distinguished national authority on the subject to be discussed. Predictably the students not only had greater interest in the third lecture, but actually learned more according to subsequent tests.[23]

Bradley Greenberg and Gerald Miller achieved similar results in a study that was replicated three times. They found that if a low credibility speaker is introduced before he speaks the listeners were inclined to view the presentation with guarded skepticism. Delayed introductions of low credibility sources, on the other hand, had a positive effect in enhancing "the persuasiveness of the message."[24]

The third characteristic of ethos is *good will* or *identification*. The rhetoric of Western thought teaches us that the successful communicator is one who identifies with his listeners. Plato spoke of this in his metaphor of the speaker as a noble lover who looked upon his audience "not as they were but as they were capable of becoming."[25] Plato's great pupil Aristotle dealt with this theme when he described a friend as one who wishes for another what he would want for himself.[26] The book of *Exodus* in the Old Testament also catches the significance of this point in the following statement which could well be a motto for a beginning speech class: "And God spake unto Moses face to face as a man speaketh unto a friend."[27] In the modern era Kenneth Burke, who constructed his *Rhetoric of Motives* around the notion of identification, employs the metaphor of courtship to show how a communicator woos his audience.

Identification occurs, it would appear, when a communicator shares common values with his audience. He associates the hopes, aspirations, and beliefs of the auditors with those of his own. Moreover "the speaker will make every effort," argues Perelman, "to conciliate his audience, either by showing his solidarity with it or his esteem for it by demonstrating his trust in its judgment."[28] When a communicator ignores the need for identification and thus unwittingly causes ill will, semantic noise running through the channel will muffle the message. In 1786 John Wesley wrote the following letter to a Methodist minister who was constantly alienating his congregation: "Your temper is uneven; you lack love for your neighbors. You grow angry too easily; your tongue is too sharp—thus the people will not hear you."[29] Nor has the influence of this concept diminished in the contemporary world. Although the Scranton Report on Student Unrest was controversial, one argument was beyond dispute: This panel maintains that the current harsh, militant rhetoric from all sides is polarizing our society.[30]

Here are a group of representative questions that auditors frequently apply to a communicator's behavior:

1. Has the speaker ever come on too strong?
2. Has he ever been too harsh, sarcastic, negative, or uncompromising?
3. Has he ever tried so hard to win an argument that he loses the person he is trying to persuade?
4. Has he ever needlessly used inflammatory language to describe a person or group?
5. Is he so committed to saying what he thinks that he overlooks the consequences?
6. In short, is he a proponent of polarization?

Admittedly there are circumstances involving principles of ethics and intellectual integrity and responsibility in which a communicator should answer affirmatively to one or more of the above questions. On the whole, however, these queries imply the need for establishing identification through good will. Such a conclusion does not conflict with the idea that speakers should take a vigorous stand to defend their beliefs. It does suggest, however, that in doing so they should strive to maintain amiability, poise, and dignity.

The final element of ethos is an elusive quality called *charisma,* and the *power* dimension flowing from it. It may be derived from a speaker's observable talent, his achievements, his occupational position and status, his personality and appearance, his style, and his overall life experience. Frequently charismatic personalities, observes Max Weber, are "set apart from ordinary men and treated as endowed with supernatural, superhuman, or at least specifically exceptional powers or qualities."[31] Every field has had its charismatic leader who through the force of his personality and position has communicated effectively with the multitudes. Thousands of Christians have responded warmly to the charisma of Martin Luther, George Whitefield, Bishop Sheen and Pope John. In the area of politics the English-speaking world applauded the magnetic personality of Winston Churchill, Dwight Eisenhower, John Kennedy and Barbara Jordan. Similarly the Arab world thundered high tribute to Egypt's Nasser, while some Communist nations elevated Lenin and Mao to the level of diety.

Closely associated with charisma is the notion of power. As Hovland, Janis, and Kelly point out some listeners may have "awe and fear of the communicator, based on perceptions of his power to reward or punish according to one's adherence to his recommendations or demands."[32] The relevance of power as an aspect of ethos is especially strong in politics where "the decision of a single individual may have profound effects on the lives of millions."[33] Out of this principle derives the charisma which is often associated with the president of the United States. The traditional aura emanating from his office gives to the president and his communications a special power.[34]

Charismatic influence viewed in this manner is a natural corollary of one's office or innate power. But there is another perspective which is equally important. William S. Howell defines charisma as a form of empathy and an ability to create a high quality dyadic interaction.[35] Since this trait may be nurtured it makes charisma available to all those who wish to influence others through the medium of effective interpersonal communication. Eleanor Roosevelt exemplified this phenomenon.

When these four elements—*trustworthiness, expertness, good will,* and *charisma*—are combined and totaled, they form an image impression which affects the outcome of one's communication efforts. When we perceive a speaker in an unfavorable light, the end result is usually distrust, which leads to the rejection of his message. The "Congruity Theory" model, developed by psychologists Osgood and Tannenbaum, explains the relationships between a listener's image of a speaker and the influence of his message.[36] This model is based upon the premise that an observer wants congruity between his perception of the source and the message he hears. It is also related to the theories of balance and cognitive dissonance. Both a speaker and an idea may be ranked on a scale ranging from a + 3 to a − 3 on the attitude scale. When a + 3 speaker talks on a neutral concept, he tends to create a positive audience attitude toward the concept. Significant attitude change also occurs when a − 3 speaker talks about a negative concept. It is for this reason that King Agamemnon in Homer's *Iliad* wisely used Odysseus to try to persuade Achilles to stop sulking in front of his tent, and to rejoin the army of Greece. In a like manner, *The New Testament* tells us, God adopted a similar strategy in trying to persuade Peter that the Gospel must be taken to the Gentiles as well as the Jews. The idea of preaching the Christian message to non-Jews was a minus three concept. God, therefore, chose a speaker with a + 3 image to persuade Peter. He was the Roman centurion, Cornelius. Here are a few of the descriptive terms which appear in *Acts* that describe the image of Cornelius:

1. He feared God.
2. He prayed to God always.
3. He fasted regularly.

4. He was obedient to God; he loved Him.
5. He was a devout man.

Cornelius was, in sum, the kind of man who could render Peter susceptible to his message.[37]

That the same principle works in the contemporary period seems evident. During the riots on the campus of Ohio State University in the spring of 1970, it took a + 3 Professor of Political Science—long regarded as a friend of the students—to turn the militants away from their goal to shut down the university at any cost.

By the same token a minus three speaker affects attitudes toward an idea in an adverse manner. As the Watergate disclosures, for example, unfolded on the television screen and in the press the close advisers of President Nixon projected an impression that they had participated in a gigantic cover-up. The typical viewer began to develop a negative image of four members of the White House "palace guard"—H. R. Haldeman, John Ehrlichman, John Dean and the former Attorney General, John Mitchell. Not surprisingly, therefore, when each appeared before the Senate Select Committee, in some cases with lengthy opening defenses, their believability was gauged not so much by what they said as by the image already existing in the minds of the audience. A Daniel Yankelovich survey, commissioned by *Time Magazine,* showed the following results when interviewees were asked the question, "Did the four key witnesses tell the truth?"[38]

	No	*Yes*
John Dean	34%	32%
H. R. Haldeman	38%	19%
John Erlichman	40%	19%
John Mitchell	41%	22%

One of the authors was in the Senate Caucus Room part of the time during the testimony of Dean and Haldeman. Dean's calm baritone voice, his vivid recall, and extensive documentation were impressive to hear. So too was Haldeman's strategy of expressions of loyalty and calculated amiability which presented a refreshing and dramatic contrast with the arrogance and abrasiveness of John Ehrlichman. Although Dean proved in the eyes of the American public to have a less unfavorable image both were victims in the end of extrinsic ethos factors that preceded them to the witness table.

Since ethos or image is such a potent force, it is essential to consider how it may be modified or protected. Through events, messages, and decisions we affect our ethos; and this, in turn, alters the degree of personal influence we exert as communicators. If, as Perelman asserts, "the person of the speaker provides a context for the speech, conversely the speech determines the opinion one will form of the person."[39] The intrinsic characteristics of the message, as well as the extrinsic features associated with the speaker, may produce a change in the image. Consider the celebrated example of Queen Elizabeth when England was threatened by the Spanish Armada in 1588. She was a woman, somewhat removed from her subjects. Many Englishmen could not help but believe that the unmarried leader in her middle fifties would be unable to cope with such a formidable opponent. But follow her as she sat on a white horse and rode to the point of danger. These are the words she uttered to her concerned subjects on this occasion: "I know I have the body of a weak and feeble woman, but I have the heart and stomach of a king, and a king of England too." With these brave words she altered the image in her audience, thereby strengthening the power of her communication.[40]

It is easy to draw parallels to contemporary political and religious communication practices. Through messages consisting of information comprised of "structural experiences,"[41] Kennedy addressed his Houston audience in 1960, and Nixon answered questions at a Press Conference dealing with Watergate. Both in their own way hoped to change the developing negative image the audience held of their characters and personalities. To a limited degree they were successful; as a result later communication transactions culminated in increased influence. A more graphic illustration of the effect of events and messages on a communicator's ethos may be seen in the career of Oral Roberts. For years Roberts was identified as a pentecostal minister preoccupied with tent meetings, glossolalia, and faith healing. Without discarding his basic theological tenets of pentecostalism, he took steps to modify his image so that his influence could be broadened. He established an educational institution in his own name, joined the United Methodist Church, utilized national television, and concentrated on a broad range of informal rhetorical appeals such as music, dialogue, and testimony. Although Roberts' actions and strategies disillusioned some of his early followers, there can be little doubt that the new image has strengthened his impact.[42]

One of the most classical examples of image change in the contemporary era occurred in the career of President Anwar Sadat of Egypt. Early in his tenure as leader of the most powerful Arab nation in the world, none of the leaders of the western countries took him seriously.[43] He was viewed as a visionary and a philosopher who seemingly could not grasp the complexity of the problems facing the Middle East. Then with dramatic suddenness in the Autumn of 1977, four years after his successful challenge to Israel on the battlefield, he journeyed to the land of his arch enemy to deliver an address calling for "peace with justice." Upon his arrival he kissed the cheek of former Israeli Prime Minister Golda Meir, warmly greeted her successor Menachem Begin, and visited sacred shrines in Jerusalem. In the precedent-setting speech that followed, he told the members of the Knesset, as well as millions of television viewers throughout the world, that his purpose was to eliminate the psychological barrier separating the Jews and the Arabs—a barrier that constituted seventy per cent of the causes of tension which had existed for twenty-nine years.

In becoming the first Arab leader to recognize the right of Israel to exist, and in demonstrating the willingness to go anywhere to promote the cause of peace, Sadat, in his visit to Israel, utilized a form of administrative rhetoric which profoundly changed his image. From this historic moment in November, 1977 to the hour of his untimely death in 1981,

whenever Sadat spoke out on issues confronting the Middle East his ideas had an enormous positive impact on public sentiment both in the United States and in Israel.[44] And this image change played no small part in the Camp David agreement which eventually was signed.

Three major inferences pertaining to a relevant rhetorical theory may be drawn from this overview of ethos and image. First, the traditional practice of viewing ethos as a separate form of proof or a particular genre of discourse no longer seems appropriate. By viewing rhetorical proof from the vantage point of ethos, logos, and pathos, Aristotle gave us a convenient method of classification which was useful in early twentieth-century research in communication. But this approach tends to blur our understanding of the dynamic interrelationships existing among these elements. To correct this shortcoming in Aristotle's theory, Paul Rosenthal saw the need to dichotomize discourses into message-centered and person-centered transactions, the latter being a rhetorical performance dominated by the ethos of the speaker.[45] What appears to be either overlooked or deemphasized in the interpretation of Aristotle and of Rosenthal is the extent of the link between ethos and the message. So strong is the reciprocal influence one has upon the other and the force of the interaction between them that to a large degree they constitute a single unit. For ethos is part of the message even in those cases in which it functions as an extrinsic factor. Thus it is misleading to say that the ethos of the speaker is more persuasive than the message. It would be more accurate instead to observe that it is the most influential ingredient of the message.

Secondly, since ethos, as this study has demonstrated, resides not in the speaker but in the mind of the listener, we should perhaps adopt the philosophy of the British theorists who began their probe of rhetoric by studying the audience. The speaker who constructs his message with a knowledge of the beliefs, attitudes, and values of his listeners firmly entrenched in his thinking has the raw material out of which to create the impression needed to conform to the expectations required by the image of the hearers. One of the important items of information that should be useful to the communicator is an awareness of the credibility-proneness of the members of the audience. For as Miller and his collaborators discovered, a listener's concern for credibility may vary according to his nature and experience.

The third implication stemming from this analysis is the notion that ethos or image may be extended beyond a speaker to include a locale, an organization, a group, or a discipline. Every facet of our society stimulates an image in the eyes of the beholder. To many non-college people the university student often appears as little more than an idle pleasure seeker or a zealous man-or-woman chaser. To the former Attorney General's wife, Martha Mitchell, the typical university professor "is responsible for all our troubles in this society. He doesn't know what he's talking about." Disciplines and fields of study similarly trigger an image. The American Council on Higher Education periodically produces an image evaluation of select graduate departments throughout the United States. For years, the field of rhetoric has suffered from the image of an ornate art divorced from reality. Corporations and professions must also be concerned with polishing their image. The Pentagon, the armed forces, the news media, the ITT, etc., expend millions of dollars annually to convey favorable images of themselves. In a recent survey of American professions, used car salesmen and politicians had the worst image according to the general public. Communities likewise have an image. Thousands go to Los Angeles, San Francisco, New York, and Fort Lauderdale each year in search of an image depicting a promised land.

Fortunately the image of a locale, an organization, a group, or a discipline—like that of an individual—can be changed through communication. George Romney became an evangelist for the compact car, particularly the Rambler, and made it appealing. Former Mayor M. E. Sensenbrenner of Columbus, Ohio, enjoyed selling the city he governed with a degree of fervor rarely matched in American history. Taking advantage of every available rhetorical opportunity he initiated a campaign to alter the image many held of an overgrown, small rural community syndrome. We saw him at an Ohio State Democratic Convention meeting in honor of Hubert Humphrey in the presidential campaign of 1968. The boundless energy and graphic language he displayed in recounting the virtues of Columbus disarmed his audience and produced a standing ovation by delegates from such rival cities as Cincinnati and Cleveland.

Kenneth Boulding has captured the essence of this theme in his influential book alluded to earlier in this study. Boulding argues persuasively that an individual or group has an image of the world which is rooted in a value system. These values serve as a gatekeeper which may or may not permit messages to penetrate the images, thereby modifying behavior. In applying this philosophy to speech communication, we know that a typical audience perceives character and trustworthiness, knowledge and expertness, good will and identification, and charisma and power as preeminent values that must be nurtured. If we as communicators epitomize these traits to others, we have the potential to get our message through the image formations of our listeners. And this, we suggest, is much of what communication is all about.

Notes

1. One of the most widely used models is that of David Berlo, *The Process of Communication* (New York: Holt, Rinehart, and Winston, Inc., 1960).
2. Dean C. Barnlund, "Toward a Meaning-Centered Philosophy of Communication," *Journal of Communication,* XII (December 1962), 197–211.
3. *Rhetoric,* 1.2.
4. Roger Nebergall, Unpublished Manuscript on Persuasion.
5. Many of these studies are synthesized and analyzed in Kenneth Anderson and Theodore Clevenger, Jr., "A Summary of Experimental Research in Ethos," *Speech Monographs,* XXX (June 1963), 59–78.
6. *Ibid.,* 59.
7. Kenneth Boulding, *The Image* (Ann Arbor, Mich.: Ann Arbor Paperbacks: The University of Michigan Press, 1971), p. 11.

8. *Ibid.*, p. 6.
9. Richard M. Andrews, Rev. of *The Great Fear of 1789, New York Times Book Review,* September 2, 1973, p. 7.
10. Chaim Perelman and L. Olbrechts-Tyteca, *The New Rhetoric: A Treatise on Argumentation* (Notre Dame, Ind.: Notre Dame University Press, 1969), p. 318.
11. See Carl I. Hovland, Irving L. Janis, and Harold H. Kelley, *Communication and Persuasion* (New Haven, Conn.: Yale University Press, 1953).
12. The following article also provides useful insights on trust: Glen D. Mellinger, "Interpersonal Trust as a Factor in Communication," *The Journal of Abnormal and Social Psychology,* 52 (May 1956), 304–309.
13. George Campbell, *The Character of a Minister of the Gospel as a Teacher and Pattern,* A Sermon Preached before the Synod of Aberdeen at Aberdeen, April 7, 1752 (Aberdeen: James Chalmers, 1752). Campbell's colleague Hugh Blair regarded a speaker's character as the most essential element in eloquence. See Lecture XXXIV of *Lectures on Rhetoric and Belles Lettres* published in 1783.
14. Adlai Stevenson, *Major Campaign Speeches of Adlai Stevenson, 1952* (New York, 1953).
15. Johnson implied in his press conference that it was not true he was looking for a replacement for Lodge. The next day the decision was announced, prompting David Brinkley to suggest that this is what we mean by the term "credibility gap" in Washington.
16. This question was raised in almost every campaign address delivered by Muskie in the last two months of the contest.
17. *Washington Post,* October 22, 1972, A4.
18. Interview with Norman Thomas, New York, N.Y., March, 1968.
19. *De Oratore,* I.27.125.
20. *An Address to the Clergy* (London, 1756).
21. Richard Hofstadter, *Anti-Intellectualism in American Life* (New York: Alfred A. Knopf, 1970), p. 10.
22. *Ibid.*, pp. 10–11.
23. David K. Berlo, *Communication and the University* (Normal, Ill.: Illinois State University Publication, 1963), p. 10. Earlier in the same lecture Berlo noted: "I am increasingly convinced, although I am not particularly pleased with the idea, that the single most important variable in persuasion is the credibility of the communication source." p. 8.
24. Bradley S. Greenberg and Gerald R. Miller, "The Effects of Low Credible Sources on Message Acceptance," *Speech Monographs,* XXXIII (June 1966), 127–136.
25. Richard Weaver uses this theme as the basic thrust of his opening essay, "*The Phaedrus* and the Nature of Rhetoric," in *The Ethics of Rhetoric* (Chicago, Ill.: Henry Regnery Co., 1953).
26. *Rhetoric,* 2.4.
27. *Exodus,* XXXIII.11.
28. Perelman and Tyteca, p. 320.
29. John Wesley, *The Works of John Wesley* (New York, 1831), VII, 229.
30. *The Report of the President's Commission on Campus Unrest* (New York: Arno Press, 1970), pp. 1–6.
31. Max Weber, *Theory of Social and Economic Organization* (New York: Oxford University Press, 1947), p. 358.
32. *Communication and Persuasion,* p. 20.
33. Boulding, p. 98.
34. James David Barber, *The Presidential Character* (Englewood Cliffs, N.J.: Prentice-Hall, Inc., 1972), pp. 3–6.
35. Unpublished manuscript address delivered at Ohio Speech Convention, October 1970.
36. Charles E. Osgood and Percy H. Tannenbaum, "The Principle of Congruity in the Prediction of Attitude Change," *Psychological Review,* 6281955). 42–55.
37. *Acts,* X.
38. *Time,* September 10, 1973, p. 18.
39. Perelman and L. Olbrects-Tyteca, p. 319.
40. Garrett Mattingly, *The Armada* (Boston, Mass.: Houghton Mifflin Company, 1959), p. 350.
41. Boulding, p. 7.
42. For a study of Roberts' changing roles as a communicator, see Eugene Elser, "The Rhetorical Strategies of Oral Roberts," M. A. thesis in Communication, (The Ohio State University, 1970).
43. Kissinger Interview on NBC Magazine Program, July 24, 1982.
44. For a full account of the Sadat visit, see *New York Times,* November 20, 21, 22, 1977 and the *Washington Post,* November 20 and 21, 1977.
45. Paul I. Rosenthal, "The Concept of Ethos and the Structure of Persuasion," *Speech Monographs,* XXXIII (June 1966), 114–26.

17
Rhetoric as Value: The Communicator's Stance

Several years ago Dr. Wayne Booth, Professor of English and Dean of the College of Arts and Sciences at the University of Chicago, wrote an intriguing essay, entitled "Rhetorical Stance."[1] In this study Booth argues that a communicator must achieve rhetorical stance by relating himself and his message to his audience in a proper way. To highlight his theme, the author described three types of communicators who fail to conform adequately to the requirements of rhetorical stance—the pedant, the entertainer, and the advertiser. The pedant's stance occurs when the speaker is excessively preoccupied with the message. The entertainer's stance results when the speaker is overly concerned with his performance. Finally, the advertiser's stance takes place when the communicator is obsessed with effectiveness. Booth went on to demonstrate how the stance assumed in each of the above positions was undesirable.

Booth's insightful essay, primarily designed for teachers of English, opened up a promising field for investigation by students of rhetoric. It is our purpose here to extend the concept of stance beyond the general guidelines developed by Booth, and to place the theme more firmly within the rubric of oral communication.

As a point of departure let us examine the nature of rhetorical stance and then attempt to set forth the steps required for achieving a proper stance in a given situation. The term rhetorical stance as used in this presentation refers to the position taken by the communicator with respect to the listener, the occasion, and the desired response. More specifically it deals with the attitude a speaker assumes to-

ward the relationships that he believes should exist among the communicator, the message, and the auditor. Additionally, stance when effectively employed "presents us with the spectacle of a man passionately involved in thinking an important question through, in the company of an audience,"[2] Since the word audience is capable of a variety of meanings, we will use it here to signify both a single individual such as an interlocutor in conversation and a particular group gathered together on a special occasion. An audience, in sum, may be defined, as Chaim Perelman suggests, "as the ensemble of those whom the speaker wishes to influence by his argumentation."[3]

The development of a proper rhetorical stance tends to follow a four step procedure which unfolds usually, but not necessarily, in a chronological and climactic pattern. Each step often emanates from and is dependent upon the one preceding it. These steps in a sense constitute the stances taken by the communicator during different stages of the rhetorical transaction. To an analysis of these speech phrases, let us now turn.

Rhetorical stance begins with a recognition on the part of the communicator of the importance and nature of the audience. With the Spanish scholar Gracian, a speaker must be able to say, "A speech is like a feast, at which the dishes are made to please the guests and not the cooks."[4] As receivers of a message and candidates for change, the listeners are in a position to determine meaning and perceived intent. If they are not motivated to modify their attitudes, beliefs, values, or behavior, no perceptible change will take place within the rhetorical situation. To complete a rhetorical transaction successfully, a communicator must, therefore, come to know and appreciate the communicatee. In a sense a speaker must strive to get inside the minds of the members of the audience in order to understand how their nature might influence the responses to particular appeals in a given setting. It was for this reason, as we have seen, that Aristotle, a keen observer of human nature, felt the need to sit down at his desk late in life and draw with a master's hand the portrait of a young man, of an old man, and of one who stood at the half way mark between youth and old age. After then describing the seven causes of wrong-doing, Aristotle launched into a discussion of such emotions as anger, love, friendship, fear, shame, pity, benevolence, envy, and indignation. In short, he advised all speakers to know the characteristics of the soul, and pointed up the necessity of judging a speech by its effect upon someone who approves or disapproves.[5]

Adhering to the model of Aristotle was the eloquent Roman rhetorician and public speaker Cicero. In *de Oratore,* Cicero observed that orators must obtain a thorough insight into the nature of mankind, and all the passions of humanity, and those causes by which our minds are either impelled or restrained.[6] Eighteen hundred years later, Hugh Blair, pastor of the Church of St. Giles and Professor of Rhetoric and Belles Lettres at the University of Edinburgh, urged potential ministers to sit in an imaginary pew and reflect upon a hypothetical sermon which they themselves might be delivering. Only in this way could they fully appreciate the possible reactions of a typical Sunday-morning congregation.[7]

Twentieth-century scholars in speech communication similarly are aware that much of what a listener sees and hears is influenced by his age, sex, craft, education, nationality, religion, and locale. These, in turn, often determine the organizations to which he belongs—the political party, the church, and the social club. It is not altogether by chance, therefore, that a man is for, against, or indifferent, to a particular subject. The mental attitude which

he assumes on any vital issue is, for the most part, the inevitable outcome of all the forces which have operated in his life. The far reaching effect of this concept has found graphic expression in the works of B. F. Skinner which have detailed man's dependence upon his environment.[8]

Once the speaker has come to appreciate the significance of the audience in a rhetorical situation, he should proceed to the second step in the formation of an appropriate rhetorical stance. Here the communicator seeks to adjust himself to the listener and to adjust the listener to the speaker. Cicero warned that all who wish to persuade must "shape and adapt themselves completely according to the opinion and approval" of the audience.[9] Similarly, the Apostle Paul, who doubtless knew the classical rhetorical tradition, also saw the need to have a speaker relate himself to the listener, so that he subsequently could adjust the listener to himself and to the theme. In his letter to the Corinthians, St. Paul noted:

> For though I be free from all men, yet have I made myself servant unto all, that I might gain the more. And unto the Jews I became as a Jew, that I might gain the Jews; to them that are under the law, as under the law, that I might gain them that are under the law. To them that are without the law, as without law, that I might gain them that are without law; To the weak became I as weak: I am made all things to all men, that I might by all means save some. And this I do for the gospel's sake, that I might be partaker thereof with you.[10]

At first glance it would appear that St. Paul was describing himself as an ultra-conformist who, like a chameleon, changes colors to suit his environment. Such an interpretation, however, is superficial for St. Paul's credentials as a practitioner and theorist belie such a faulty inference. The major concern throughout his ministry was to show the compelling significance of bringing the communicator and communicatee together so that they become united in their appreciation of the centrality of the Christian message. With this thought in mind it is easy to see how Henry Ward Beecher captured the real sentiment of St. Paul's remarks which he paraphrased as follows

I know how to fit myself to . . . every single disposition with which I have to deal; you cannot find me a man so deep or so high, so blunt or so sharp, but I could take the shape of that man's disposition, in order to come into sympathy with him, if by so doing I could lift him to a higher and nobler plane in life.[11]

A most penetrating insight into this aspect of rhetorical stance comes from Kenneth Burke. Burke describes a rhetoric which recommends, in effect, that a communicator woo his audience. As the speaker begins, he perhaps is aware of the division that exists between him and his listener. It may be a division resulting from different attitudes existing toward the speaker, his message, or the auditor. What we have in Burke, therefore, is the need for a love affair between the speaker and his audience.

Burke achieves rhetorical stance through his theories of identification and consubstantiality. "To identify A with B," he says, "is to make A 'consubstantial' with B." A doctrine of consubstantiality is a way of life based on "acting together," and this means "acting together" in such a way that "men have common sensations, concepts, images, ideas, attitudes that make them consubstantial."[12] Burke further points out: "A speaker persuades an audience by the use of stylistic identifications; his act of persuasion may be for the purpose of causing the audience to identify itself with the speaker's interests; and the speaker draws an identification of interests to establish rapport between himself and his audience."[13] This human relations approach to communication has as its principal goal to remove division by engaging in courtship.

As the speaker adjusts himself to the listener and the listener to the communicator, he should understand, as the third phase in the evolution of an effective rhetorical stance, the need to suit the message to the occasion and to the audience interacting within it. So important did the classical rhetoricians regard the occasion that they used it as a starting point in constructing their theories. Only after they had determined the nature of the setting were they ready to select a particular rhetorical strategy. In his *De Doctrina Christiana*, St. Augustine related with pride the stance he took in Caesarea in Mauritania where he had gone to dissuade the people from Civil War. Since the emotional feeling was strong and the customs deep-rooted he wisely used the "grand style" because of its increased persuasive thrust.[14] As a result he brought tears to the eyes of his auditors rather than polite applause, signaling a general acceptance of his message.

Nor could George Campbell, the eighteenth-century clergyman and rhetorician, ignore this aspect of stance. After observing that audience adaptation is so obvious that it needs "no proof or illustration," he proceeded to tell all aspiring orators how to speak in specific situations. Use cogent arguments when addressing the people of Sparta; single out the importance of fame when talking to men of genius; recognize the value of riches when communicating to men of industry; and emphasize pleasure when conversing with men of fortune.[15] In other words Campbell believed it was incumbent for the speaker to use a stance suitable to a particular audience and situation if he wished his message to be received without troubling distortion, hostility, or indifference.

American history provides numerous examples of a speaker's ability to adopt a stance enabling him to function effectively in a dynamic rhetorical situation. It is a stance consistent with Lou Sarett's advice to prospective orators: "Speak to people as they are, not as you romantically hope them to be."[16] A remarkable illustration of this approach was the "New South Speech" of Henry W. Grady, delivered in New York City in 1886. As the first Southerner since the Civil War to address the New England Society of New York, Grady listened with interest to Reverend Dewitt Talmadge and General Sherman describe in glowing detail the heroics of the triumphant Union armies. In this setting of moderate hostility, Grady arose to his feet with the purpose of making a pro-Southern speech. Before developing his theme, however, he moved with consummate skill to conciliate his audience. He began with several humorous references calling for fair play and understanding. Wisely he then identified himself not with the Puritan—as did Reverend Talmadge—nor with the Cavalier—despite the fact he had lived in Virginia—but with the typical American citizen embodied in Abraham Lincoln. In all, he spent one half of his allotted time in preparing the way for a message which was warmly applauded.[17]

William Jennings Bryan possessed a similar talent for anticipating an occasion and developing a rhetorical stance appropriate for it. L. L. Bernard, in his *Introduction to Social Psychology,* tells of his own experience in hearing Bryan during the 1916 presidential campaign. Few, if any, of the two thousand people who had assembled to hear the "Great Commoner" in the small university town in the South were predisposed in favor of the speaker. Yet, points out Bernard, he won the audience over completely by using the following strategy. He spent the first fifteen minutes complimenting their "beautiful little city"; the next thirty minutes "telling jokes on himself and his opponents"; and the next thirty minutes "in trite and fulsome praise of American insitutions." By successfuly combining flattery with truism he had maneuvered his audience to the palm of his hand and their beliefs to the edge of his tongue. Now he was ready to turn to the fourth part of his address and tell the auditors what he had come there to say: "Vote for Woodrow Wilson." The hour and a quarter which the speaker utilized at the outset served only as a preparation for the closing fifteen minute plea. Such a masterful approach, concludes Bernard, enabled Bryan to become one of the most effective campaign speakers in American history.[18]

But if the past supplies us with positive examples of an effective stance, it likewise shows clearly what happens to speakers whose choice of stance fails to conform to the expectations of the audience. Demosthenes was censured as affected when he spoke to the Mysians or Phrygians. Fortunately the Greek orator did not "sing in the Asiatic manner in a whining voice with violent modulations." Had he done so, observed Cicero, the people would have cried: "Put him out!"[19]

Less discerning and effective was Estes Kefaufer in the presidential contest of 1956. On one occasion the Democratic candidate for Vice President stood beside a flower bed filled with petunias and marigolds in Los Angeles, looked into the mysterious, toothless faces of a small group of old people and prophesied that he was going to work for full employment and equal opportunities. The next day he stood on the first floor of an aircraft plant, smiled at the blue collar workers who had put aside their tools to hear him, and delivered a farm address.[20]

During the same contest Chet Holafield, Democratic Congressman from Los Angeles, showed still poorer judgment on the campus of Pasadena College. As one of the authors greeted him upon his arrival for a political campaign address, he requested information concerning the party affiliation of the students and faculty members. Approximately eighty per cent of the faculty and ninety percent of the student body are Republicans, he was told. "Good," he noted in a confident manner. "I will be ready for them." Much to our discomfiture, however, he began with these words of polarization: "I have come here today for the purpose of presenting seven indictments against the Eisenhower Administration." For the next forty-five minutes, his claims, many of which were justified, met with repeated catcalls, hisses, and stamping of the feet. The fact that the audience may have been needlessly impolite did not relieve the speaker of his responsibility to adopt a meaningful rhetorical stance.[21]

These ineffectual rhetorical stances were repeated by the Republican presidential candidate Barry Goldwater, in 1964. The Arizona Senator unwittingly presented low-key addresses to animated partisans, indicted social security before audiences comprised primarily of elderly people on retirement incomes, and listed the shortcomings of public power while speaking in the heartland of TVA.[22] Nor could these strategies be interpreted as commendable courageous statements from an uncompromising crusader. For after each performance Goldwater, disturbed by the negative reaction, attempted to soften, clarify, and modify the stance he had taken.

The instrumental quality inherent in rhetoric requires that we heed the words of Kenneth Burke: "You persuade a man only insofar as you can talk his language by speech, gesture, tonality, order, image, attitude, idea, *identifying* your way with his."[23]

Once the communicator has made necessary adjustments in the message so that it will conform to the requirements of the audience and the occasion, he is prepared to move to the fourth step in the creation of rhetorical stance—the attempt to raise the people to those parts of the message grounded in principle or "the essential nature of things."[24] Those who take this lofty ground are responding to what they think is a serious need. They are concerned with speakers who yield to the temptation of aiming too low—a practice which leads at best to short range advantage. To meet this challenge philosophers, rhetoricians, and psychologists have pointed the way to what might be called the most altruistic phase of communication stance.

Plato was one of the first writers of Western thought to stress the importance of an elevated stance. You may recall that in his dialogue, *Phaedrus,* he likened the ideal speaker to a noble lover whose ultimate goal was to show the people the truth that resided in the mind of God. Thus there should be no deliberate dilution of the message—a technique employed by the neuter and evil lovers—in order to make the ideas more palatable, entertaining, or effective.[25] This suggests that the enlightened speaker frequently must bring the auditor to the idea. As Donald Bryant puts it: "It is not enough to adjust ideas to people; we must also adjust people to ideas."[26] Abraham Maslow, the celebrated psychologist, reinforces the validity of this point when he says: "The human being is simultaneously that which he is and that which he yearns to be."[27]

Rarely has one expressed this sentiment more successfully than the late Richard Weaver of the University of Chicago. In *The Ethics of Rhetoric,* Weaver observes: "Rhetoric at its truest seeks to perfect men by showing them better versions of themselves."[28]

What these critics are saying to us seems both clear and relevant. A speaker cannot be content merely to produce a favorable response. For this limited goal may be reached by a minister who uses pious platitudes and trite stories describing man's responsibilities to others and to God, or by a lawyer who substitutes vivid examples for cogent arguments when addressing a jury, or by a demagogue who presents specious arguments fraught with emotion to an angry mob. Each in his own way is a Step Three speaker who confines his efforts to the goal of adjusting ideas to what he believes is the prevailing mood and conditioning force of the audience. His commitment, in short, is to an immediate response rather than to a long term effect.

Those who have achieved permanent eminence in public address have assumed a rhetorical stance embracing Step Four. Several representative case studies exemplify this strong reliance upon principle. The first was Edmund Burke's "Speech on the Bristol Election," delivered in 1780. Notwithstanding his enormous fame, Burke was condemned by his constituents for failing to mouth their interests and desires. As a result his election in the forthcoming campaign was no longer secure. Despite the threat to his political career, Burke faced the audience in Bristol with honesty and courage. Thus there were no rationalizations, no apologies, no scapegoating. Nor were there promises of change for the future. Instead of telling them only what they were conditioned to hear, he spoke frankly concerning the policy he had followed:

I did not obey your instructions. No, I conformed to the instructions of truth and nature, and maintained your interest against your opinions . . . . I am to look, indeed, to your opinions; but to such opinions as you and I must have *five* years hence. I was not to look to the flash of the day. . . .[29]

Standing squarely in the tradition of Burke was Winston Churchill during the era of the dominance of the "Third Reich." In the fall of 1938 the man with the famous umbrella, Prime Minister Neville Chamberlain, returned to Britain from Munich to report on his encounter with Hitler. Everywhere he was saluted as a conquering hero who had brought to the English people what they wanted most— "peace in our time." The mobs followed him to No. 10 Downing Street. There they serenaded him with these words: "Good Old Neville. For he's a jolly good fellow." Happily Chamberlain responded: "My good friends, this is the second time in our history that there has come back from Germany to Downing Street, peace with honor." A few blocks away, in the House of Commons, another Englishman—equally proud of his heritage—expressed an unpopular minority view. "We have," said Winston Churchill, "sustained a total unmitigated defeat." Before he could continue his memorable speech of protest, Churchill had to pause while the hisses and catcalls subsided.[30]

One is tempted to ask, who will history remember: Chamberlain, the man who adapted exclusively to the temporary mood of his audience, or Churchill, who pushed aside his fellowman's preoccupation with a false peace, and gallantly strove to give his listeners a better picture of themselves?

What was true of Burke and Churchill was similarly true of John Kennedy in his landmark speech, entitled "Remarks on Church and State," which was delivered to the Greater Houston Ministerial Association on September 12, 1960. For weeks following his nomination in Los Angeles, the youthful presidential candidate had been indicted for his religious affiliation and church commitment. He was ruthlessly caricatured as a puppet of the Pope, while the government he hoped to lead was viewed as a satellite of the Vatican. But Kennedy held his ground and his integrity, and refused to appeal to the baser emotions of a prejudiced populace. Surrounded by clergymen, most of whom were unsympathetic to his cause, he spoke to his audience not as they were but as they yearned to be and were capable of becoming:

I am not the Catholic candidate for President. I am the Democratic Party's candidate for President, who happens also to be a Catholic. . . . But if this election is decided on the basis that 40,000,000 Americans lost their chance of being President on the day they were baptized, then it is the whole nation that will be the loser in the eyes of Catholics and non-Catholics around the world, in the eyes of history, and in the eyes of our own people.[31]

It is easy to conclude that these are isolated examples of a few heroic men. But one may glean from the pages of history other telling accounts of speakers who have sought to bring listeners to ideas. On July 5, 1852, Frederick Douglass, disturbed by the fact that four million of his countrymen were in bondage, refused to recite to his predominantly white abolitionist audience the glories of the Declaration of Independence and of the founding fathers. Instead he challenged his listeners to come to a true idea of freedom and justice. Lincoln, without diluting his belief in the equality and dignity of man, sought to bring extremists in the North to a middle road marked by integrity, compassion, and good will. Henry W. Grady, a native son of Georgia and a child of the Civil War, lifted a group of unreconstructed rebels to a plane of understanding in the controversial and explosive field of race relations. Harry Emerson Fosdick, the pastor of Riverside Church in New York, moved his congregation, comprised largely of professional and business people, to the belief that labor unions were essentially right in their crusades for economic justice. In 1952 Adlai Stevenson succeeded in raising the level of pedestrian and contrived political oratory to the plane of persuasive and enduring rhetoric. And in the 1970s, Jesse Jackson traversed the nation to tell black audiences to abandon easy rationalizations and to strive mightily for excellence in education.

To these orators immediate effect and popular applause, often the end result of Step Three, were subordinate to a nobler aim which, according to Sarett, should be included in every rhetorical transaction—speak to the people not only as they appear to be at the moment, but as they may become when they see an improved image of themselves as altruistic beings.[32] In taking this stance, these speakers succeeded in transcending the boundaries of a specific setting; for, in effect, they viewed their listeners not only as members of a particular but also a universal audience. Consequently, the arguments used were, for the most part, similarly appropriate for any person included in the universal body of rational men.[33]

The illustrative material used throughout the foregoing discussion would tend to suggest that rhetorical stance is an attitude or position taken by a renowned orator with respect to his audience in a one to many rhetorical situation. That stance is not limited to the public speaking genre, however, is clear. It is similarly appropriate to any form of interpersonal communication, or indeed an essay, as Booth points out, which is written by the student for an audience consisting of a single reader.[34] Whatever the occasion, there is a need for a communicator to bridge the gap of division through identification, to adapt a message to the peculiar needs of an audience, and then to adjust the listeners to segments of the address that reflect essential principles and truths that cannot be compromised. This, it would appear, is precisely the emphasis in Thomas Harris' provocative and stimulating volume *I'm Ok, You're Ok*. Here the author, a student of transactional analysis, urges his readers to move progressively toward a stance enabling them to communicate with each other as adult to adult.[35]

In order to see more clearly the four steps essential in the creation of an effective and responsible rhetorical stance, let us review the dynamic communication transaction that occurred in one of the dramatic moments in Homer's *Iliad*. At the outset of the plot which was set in the tenth year of the Trojan War, Achil-les, who felt insulted because Agamemnon the king took away a woman he had won in battle, retired to his tent and sulked. There he prayed to his goddess mother Athena who brought the wrath of Zeus against the Greeks. During Achilles' absence the Greeks suffered a series of defeats and Achilles' best friend was killed. Aware that a strong response was needed in this rhetorical situation, Agamemnon sent a group of persuaders to visit Achilles, not the least of whom were the eloquent Odysseus and Achilles' revered teacher, Phoenix. As Odysseus began his persuasive effort, he already had accomplished phase one in the formation of proper stance—a recognition of the importance of Achilles. Thus he moved at once to Step Two by striving to identify with his listener. Holding a cup of wine in his hand, Odysseus toasted Achilles with the following disarming words: "Hail, O Achilles! The fair feast lack we not either in the hut of Agamemnon, son of Artreus neither now in thine; for feasting is there abundance in our heart's desire. . . ."

Satisfied that he had achieved identification and consubstantiality, Odysseus went to Step Three by adjusting the message to the particular needs and nature of Achilles. First he appealed to his sense of realism by describing the desperate plight confronting the Greeks on the land and in the sea. Then he stressed the trait of filial piety by reminding Achilles of his father's warning that he should try to allay his proud temper. But these were merely preliminary appeals designed to render Achilles susceptible to a more persuasive strategy— a recitation of specific property and sexual benefits. If you return to battle, observed Odysseus, Agamemnon is prepared to give you the following prizes:

. . . **seven tripods untouched of fire, and ten talents of gold and twenty gleaming cald-rons and twelve stalwart horses, winners in the race, that have taken prizes by their speed. . . . And seven women will he give, skilled in excellent handiwork, Lesbians whom he chose from the spoils the day that** thou thyself tookest Lesbos, surpassing womankind in beauty. These he will give thee, even the daughter of Briseus. . . . And seven well peopled cities will he give thee. . . .[36]

Odysseus concluded his emotional plea by appealing to the self interest of Achilles. If you cannot surmount your hatred for Agamemnon, he said, then consider the honor you can win for yourself by destroying Hector and reducing the Greeks.

Notwithstanding Odysseus' acknowledged reputation for persuasive utterance, he failed to adopt the stance of the noble lover. At no time did he try to show the inherent unacceptability of prideful anger and petty malice. It remained, therefore, for Phoenix to enter the discussion and challenge his former pupil to come to the ideal of justice, fair play, and rightmindedness. "Achilles," he urged, "rule thy high spirit; neither beseemeth it thee to have a ruthless heart. Nay, even the very gods can bend, and theirs withal is loftier majesty and honor and might." Phoenix, in building upon the foundation laid by Odysseus, concluded the rhetorical transaction by communicating on the level of Step Four.

What we have tried to show in this discussion is the meaning and thrust of rhetorical stance. This notion, as we have seen, begins with the communicator's awareness of the importance of the audience, and unfolds through a series of steps involving a balancing of the speaker, the message, and the auditors in a rhetorical situation. It requires the communicator to adjust himself to the listener and the listener to the speaker. Moreover, it places upon him a demand to adapt his ideas to the audience. But at its highest plane rhetorical stance epitomizes the concept of Plato's noble lover. Perhaps we would do well to recall Richard Whately's poignant reference to the fable of Mahomet and the Mountain: Just as Mahomet found it easier to go to the mountain than to bring the mountain to himself, so too does many a speaker attempt to bring

his doctrine and language into a conformity with the inclinations and the conduct of his hearers, rather than by bringing the character of the hearers into a conformity with what is true and right. . . .[37]

Only when this fact is remembered will rhetoric or communication be restored to a cherished position as science and art.

Notes

1. Wayne C. Booth, "The Rhetorical Stance," *College Composition and Communication,* XIV (October 1963), 139–145.
2. *Ibid.,* 145.
3. Chaim Perelman and L. Olbrechts-Tyteca, *The New Rhetoric: A Treatise on Argumentation* (Notre Dame, Ind.: Notre Dame University Press, 1969), p. 19.
4. Cited in *ibid.,* p. 24.
5. Lane Cooper, ed., *The Rhetoric of Aristotle* (New York: D. Appleton-Century Company, 1932), 1.10-1.14;2.1-2.18.
6. *De Oratore,* E. W. Sutton, tr. (Cambridge, Mass.: Harvard University Press, 1959), I. 12–53.
7. Hugh Blair, *Lectures on Rhetoric and Belles Lettres* (Philadelphia: S. C. Hayes, 1861), pp. 317–18.
8. See in particular *Beyond Freedom and Dignity* (New York: Alfred A. Knopf, 1971).
9. *Orator,* H. M. Hubbell, tr. (London: William Heinemann Ltd., 1962), viii. 24.
10. *I Corinthians,* 9:19–23.
11. Henry Ward Beecher, *Yale Lectures on Preaching* (New York: J. B. Ford and Co., 1872), p. 36.
12. Kenneth Burke, *A Grammar of Motives and A Rhetoric of Motives* (Cleveland, Ohio: The World Publishing Co., 1962), p. 545.
13. *Ibid.,* p. 570.
14. *De Doctrina Christiana,* 4.24.53.
15. George Campbell, *The Philosophy of Rhetoric,* Lloyd Bitzer, ed., (Carbondale, Ill.: Southern Illinois University Press, 1963), p. 95.
16. This point of view was expressed frequently in Sarett's classes at the University of Florida during the 1951–1952 academic year.
17. Henry W. Grady, "The New South," in Wayland Maxfield Parrish and Marie Hochmuth (Nichols), *American Speeches* (New York: Longman's, Green and Co., 1954), pp. 450–460.
18. Luther L. Bernard, *An Introduction to Social Psychology* (New York: H. Holt and Co., 1926), pp. 461–62.
19. *Orator,* viii.27.
20. *Time* Magazine, October 1, 1956.
21. The author present on this occasion lectured his students the following day in responsibilities of the listeners. Yet Holafield, it was clear, had also violated a cardinal tenet of rhetoric.

22. *Time* Magazine noted: "And the greatest bumbler of them all Barry. . . ." November 4, 1964. For a similar discussion of Goldwater's failures in audience adaptation, see John H. Kessel, *The Goldwater Coalition,* (New York: The Bobbs-Merrill Co., Inc., 1968).

23. Burke, p. 579.

24. Richard Weaver stresses this notion in his chapter on "Argument from Definition" in *Ethics of Rhetoric* (Chicago, Ill.: Henry W. Regnery Co., 1953).

25. Lane Cooper, ed., *Plato* (London: Oxford University Press, 1938), pp. 26–41.

26. Donald Bryant, "Rhetoric: Its Function and Scope," *Quarterly Journal of Speech,* XXXIX (December 1953).

27. Abraham Maslow, "Psychological Data and Value Theory," in Maslow, ed., *New Knowledge in Human Values* (New York: Harper, 1959), p. 130.

28. Weaver, p. 16.

29. Edmund Burke, "The Bristol Election," In Chauncey A. Goodrich, *Select British Eloquence* (New York: Harper & Brothers, Publishers, 1872), p. 297.

30. William L. Shirer, *The Rise and Fall of the Third Reich* (New York: Simon and Schuster, 1960), p. 420.

31. John F. Kennedy, "Remarks on Church and State; Delivered to Greater Houston Ministerial Association, Houston, Texas, September 12, 1960," in Theodore H. White, *The Making of the President 1960* (New York: Atheneum Publishers, 1961), p. 393.

32. Sarett's Lectures, University of Florida, 1951–1952.

33. For a discussion of the universal audience see Perelman and Olbrechts-Tyteca, pp. 31–35.

34. Booth, "Rhetorical Stance," XIV, 139–145.

35. Thomas A. Harris, *I'm Ok—You're Ok* (New York: Harper & Row, Publishers, 1969), pp. 37–53.

36. *The Complete Works of Homer,* Andrew Lang, Walter Leaf and Ernest Myers, eds. (New York: The Modern Library, 1950), pp. 154–55.

37. Richard Whately, *Elements of Rhetoric* (Boston, Mass.: J. Munroe, 1855), p. 279.

18

Rhetoric as Motive: Kenneth Burke and Dramatism

By common consent Kenneth Burke ranks as the foremost rhetorician in the twentieth century. Not since Bacon and Vico has a single author been able to roam so freely and authoritatively over the literature of the humanities and the social and behavioral sciences in order to construct a rhetorical system. From the philosophers, poets, theologians, and social scientists, Burke derives materials that are woven into his theories. He is as much at home with Sigmund Freud, Karl Marx, and Charles Darwin as he is with Plato, Aristotle, Isocrates, Cicero, Milton, Keats, Hume, and Kant. When we heard him speak at a conference sponsored by the Department of English at Ohio State University in the Spring of 1975, and later at the Speech Communication Association convention in Washington, D.C., in December, 1977, we were impressed with the broad range of his intellect and his talent for brilliant impromptu retorts. His advanced years seem to have sharpened his critical skills.

The legacy Burke has left to communication theory and literary criticism is remarkable in its conception and execution. Here are but a few of the terms he has used which are now an essential part of the rhetoric of Western thought: (1) dramatism; (2) pentad (act, agency, agent, scene, and purpose); (3) identification; (4) consubstantiality; (5) motives; and (6) magic. As a model of criticism the "pentad" had perhaps surpassed neo-Aristotelianism as a type of methodology to examine rhetorical transactions in the 1970s. And the term "identification" has enhanced our understanding of ethical proof, rhetorical stance,

and audience analysis and adaptation. But it is is the concept of "motives" which most appropriately explains Burke's principal contribution to the vocabulary of what might be called a "new rhetoric."

In its most common use, a motive today is frequently labeled as the *cause* of an action. Thus, one's motive for attending college may perhaps be the belief that a college diploma will guarantee a good job in the future. Burke does not ascribe this meaning to "motive," however. Rather, he uses "motive" as a label for *completed action*. "From this viewpoint," Leonard Hawes tells us, "language frequently is used to label behavior after it has been enacted. Language fits and adjusts behavior to a symbolically created world."[1]

More than most of his contemporaries, Burke best personifies the sociological thrust that typifies modern rhetoric. In his two volumes, *The Gramar of Motives* and *The Rhetoric of Motives*, he employs the phrase "human relations" at least twelve times. This accounts for his great concern with the problem of division or estrangement, as we saw in Chapter 1, that separates men. Thus he introduced the notion of "identification" as a potential unifying force that has the power to cope with "the state of Babel after the Fall."[2] His statement, "I was a farm boy myself," is disarming in its simplicity. Yet it tells a speaker far more than the need to identify with a farm audience. It also reminds him of the persistant challenge to become "consubstantial" so as to remove division.

Notwithstanding Burke's provocative insights and memorable phrases, his works are often marred by intricate details, obscure allusions, troubling digressions, and occasional contradictions. As a result, he is hard to read and comprehend. We cannot easily summarize Burke's major theories up through 1952 without duplicating what has already been done by those who knew him well. We have chosen, therefore, to reproduce Marie Nichols' classic essay, "Kenneth Burke and the

'New Rhetoric.' "[3] Burke is quoted as saying that this monograph is the best analysis of his rhetorical ideas appearing to date.

Notes

1. Leonard C. Hawes, *Pragmatics of Analoguing: Theory and Model Construction in Communication,* (Reading, Massachusetts: Addison-Wesley Publishing Company, 1975), p. 48.
2. Burke, p. 547.
3. *Quarterly Journal of Speech*, XXXVIII (April 1952), 133–144.

Kenneth Burke and the "New Rhetoric"

"We do not flatter ourselves that any one book can contribute much to counteract the torrents of ill will into which so many of our contemporaries have so avidly and sanctimoniously plunged," observes Kenneth Burke in introducing his latest book, *A Rhetoric of Motives,* but "the more strident our journalists, politicians, and alas! even many of our churchmen become, the more convinced we are that books should be written for tolerance and contemplation."[1] Burke has offered all his writings to these ends.

Burke's first work, *Counter-Statement,* published in 1931, was hailed as a work of "revolutionary importance," presenting "in essence, a new view of rhetoric."[2] Since that time, he has written a succession of books either centrally or peripherally concerned with rhetoric: *Permanance and Change,* 1935; *Attitudes toward History,* 1937; *The Philosophy of Literary Form,* 1941; *A Grammar of Motives,* 1945; and his latest, *A Rhetoric of Motives,* 1950. An unfinished work entitled *A Symbolic of Motives* further indicates his concern with the problem of language.

Sometimes thought to be "one of the few truly speculative thinkers of our time,"[3] and "unquestionably the most brilliant and suggestive critic now writing in America,"[4] Burke deserves to be related to the great tradition of rhetoric.

Although we propose to examine particularly *A Rhetoric of Motives* we shall range freely over all his works in order to discover his principles. We propose to find first the point of departure and orientation from which he approaches rhetoric; next to examine his general concept of rhetoric; then to seek his method for the analysis of motivation; and finally, to discover his application of principles to specific literary works.

In 1931, in *Counter-Statement,* Burke noted, "The reader of modern prose is ever on guard against 'rhetoric,' yet the word, by lexicographer's definition, refers but to 'the use of language in such a way as to produce a desired impression upon the reader or hearer.' "[5] Hence, accepting the lexicographer's definition, he concluded that "effective literature could be nothing else but rhetoric."[6] In truth, "Eloquence is simply the end of art, and is thus its essence."[7]

As a literary critic, representing a minority view, Burke has persisted in his concern with rhetoric, believing that "rhetorical analysis throws light on literary texts and human relations generally."[8] Although Burke is primarily concerned with literature "as art,"[9] he gives no narrow interpretation to the conception of literature. He means simply works "designed for the express purpose of arousing emotions,"[10] going so far as to say, "But sometimes literature so designed fails to arouse

Reprinted from the *Quarterly Journal of Speech,* 38 (April 1952), 133–144. Reprinted with the permission of the author and editor of *Q.J.S.*

emotions—and words said purely by way of explanation may have an unintended emotional effect of considerable magnitude."[11] Thus a discussion of "effectiveness" in literature "should be able to include unintended effects as well as intended ones."[12] By literature we mean written or spoken words."[13]

As has been observed, the breadth of Burke's concepts results "in a similar embracing of trash of every description. . . . For purposes of analysis or illustration Burke draws as readily on a popular movie, a radio quiz program, a *Herald Tribune* news item about the National Association of Manufacturers, or a Carter Glass speech on gold as on Sophocles or Shakespeare. Those things are a kind of poetry too, full of symbolic and rhetorical ingredients, and if they are bad poetry, it is a bad poetry of vital significance in our lives."[14]

Sometimes calling himself a pragmatist, sometimes a sociological critic, Burke believes that literature is designed to "do something"[15] for the writer and the reader or hearer. "Art is a means of communication. As such it is certainly designed to elicit a 'response' of some sort."[16] The most relevant observations are to be made about literature when it is considered as the embodiment of an "act,"[17] or as "symbolic action."[18] Words must be thought of as "acts upon a scene,"[19] and a "symbolic act" is the *"dancing of an attitude,"*[20] or incipient action. Critical and imaginative works are "answers to questions posed by the situation in which they arose." Not merely "answers," they are *strategic* answers," or *stylized* answers."[21] Hence, a literary work is essentially a "strategy for *encompassing a situation.*"[22] And, as Burke observes, another name for strategies might be *attitudes.*"[23] The United States Constitution, e.g., must be thought of as the *"answer"* or *"rejoinder"* to "assertions current in the situation in which it arose."[24]

Although Burke distinguishes between literature "for the express purpose of arousing emotions" and "literature for use," the distinction is flexible enough to permit him to see even in such a poem as Milton's *Samson Agonistes,* "moralistic prophecy" and thus to class it as "also a kind of 'literature for use,' use at one remove. . . ."[25]

In further support of his comprehensive notion of art in his conception that since "pure art makes for acceptance," it tends to "become a social menace in so far as it assists us in tolerating the intolerable."[26] Therefore, "under conditions of competitive capitalism there must necessarily be a large *corrective* or *propaganda* element in art."[27] Art must have a "hortatory function, an element of suasion or inducement of the eduational variety; it must be partially *forensic.*"[28]

Burke thus approaches the subject of rhetoric through a comprehensive view of art in general. And it is this indirect approach that enables him to present what he believes to be a "New Rhetoric."[29] In part, he has as his object only to "rediscover rhetorical elements that had become obscured when rhetoric as a term fell into disuse, and other specialized disciplines such as esthetics, anthropology, psychoanalysis, and sociology came to the fore (so that esthetics sought to outlaw rhetoric, while the other sciences . . . took over, each in its own terms, the rich rhetorical elements that esthetics would ban).[30]

II

Sometimes thought to be "intuitive" and "idiosyncratic"[31] in his general theories, Burke might be expected to be so in his theory of rhetoric. "Strongly influenced by anthropological inquiries,"[32] and finding Freud "suggestive almost to the point of bewilderment,"[33] Burke, essentially a classicist in his theory of rhetoric, has given the subject its most searching analysis in modern times.

According to Burke, "Rhetoric [comprises] both the use of persuasive resources (*rhetorica utens,* as with the Phillipics of Demosthenes) and the *study* of them (*rhetorica docens,* as with Aristotle's treatise on the 'art' of Rhetoric)."[34] The "basic function of rhetoric" is the "use of words by human agents to form attitudes or to induce actions in other human agents. . . ."[35] It is *"rooted in an essential function of language itself, a function that is wholly realistic, and is continually born anew; the use of language as a symbolic means of inducing cooperation in beings that by nature respond to symbols"*[36] The basis of rhetoric lies in "generic divisiveness which, being common to all men, is a universal fact about them, prior to any divisiveness caused by social classes." "Out of this emerge the motives for linguistic persuasion. Then, *secondarily,* we get the motives peculiar to particular economic situations. In parturition begins the centrality of the nervous system. The different nervous systems, through language and the ways of production, erect various communities of interests and insights, social communities varying in nature and scope. And out of the division and the community arises the 'universal' rhetorical situation."[37]

Burke devotes 131 pages to a discussion of traditional principles of rhetoric, reviewing Aristotle, Cicero, Quintilian, St. Augustine, the Mediaevalists, and such more recent writers as De Quincey, De Gourmont, Bentham, Marx, Veblen, Freud, Mannheim, Mead, Richards, and others,[38] noting the "wide range of meanings already associated with rhetoric, in ancient texts. . . ."[39] Thus he comes upon the concept of rhetoric as "persuasion"; the nature of rhetoric as "addressed" to an audience for a particular purpose; rhetoric as the art of "proving opposites"; rhetoric as an "appeal to emotions and prejudices"; rhetoric as "agonistic"; as an art of gaining "advantage"; rhetoric as "demonstration"; rhetoric as the verbal "counterpart" of dialectic; rhetoric, in the Stoic usage, as opposed to dialectic; rhetoric in the Marxist sense of persuasion "grounded in dialectic" whereas he finds that these meanings are "often not consistent with one another, or even flatly at odds,"[40] he believes that they can all be derived from "persuasion" as the "Edenic" term, from which they have all "Babylonically" split, while persuasion, in turn "involves communication by the signs of consubstantiality, the appeal of *identification.*"[41] As the "simplest case of persuasion," he notes that "You persuade a man only insofar as you can talk his language by speech, gesture, tonality, order, image, attitude, idea, *identifying* your ways with his."[42]

In using *identification* as his key term, Burke notes, "Traditionally, the key term for rhetoric is not 'identification,' but 'persuasion.'. . . Our treatment, in terms of identification, is decidedly not meant as a substitute for the sound traditional approach. Rather, . . . it is but an accessory to the standard lore."[43] He had noted that "when we come upon such aspects of persuasion as are found in 'mystification,' courtship, and the 'magic' of class relationships, the reader will see why the classical notion of clear persuasive intent is not an accurate fit, for describing the ways in which the members of a group promote social cohesion by acting rhetorically upon themselves and one another."[44] Burke is completely aware that he is not introducing a totally new concept, observing that Aristotle had long ago commented, "It is not hard . . . to praise Athenians among Athenians,"[45] and that one persuades by "identifying" one's ways with those of his audience.[46] In an observation of W. C. Blum, Burke found additional support for his emphasis on *identification* as a key concept. "In identification lies the souce of dedications and enslavements, in fact of cooperation."[47] As for the precise relationship between identification and persuasion as ends of rhetoric, Burke concludes, "we might well keep it in mind that a speaker persuades an audience by the use of stylistic identifications; his act of persuasion may be for the purpose of causing the audience to identify itself with the speaker's interests; and the speaker draws on identification of interests to establish rapport between himself and his audience. So, there is no chance of our keeping apart the meanings of persuasion, identification ('consubstantiality') and communication (the nature of rhetoric as 'addressed'). But, in given instances, one or another of these elements may serve best for extending a line of analysis in some particular direction."[48] "All told, persuasion ranges from the bluntest quest of advantage, as in sales promotion or propaganda, through courtship, social etiquette, education, and the sermon to a 'pure' form that delights in the process of appeal for itself alone, without ulterior purpose. And identification ranges from the politician who, addressing an audience of farmers, says, 'I was a farm boy myself,' through the mysteries of social status, to the mystic's devout identification with the source of all being."[49] The difference between the "old" rhetoric and the "new" rhetoric may be summed up in this manner: whereas the key term for the "old" rhetoric was *persuasion* and its stress was upon deliberate design, the key term for the "new" rhetoric is *identification* and this may include partially "unconscious" factors in its appeal. Identification, at its simplest level, may be a deliberate device, or a means, as when a speaker identifies his interests with those of his audience. But *identification* can also be an "end," as "when people earnestly yearn to identify themselves with some group or other." They are thus not necessarily acted upon by a conscious external agent, but may act upon themselves to this end. Identification "includes the realm of transcendence."[50]

Burke affirms the significance of *identification* as a key concept because men are at odds with one another, or because there is "division." "Identification is compensatory to division. If men were not apart from one another, there would be no need for the rhetorician to proclaim their unity. If men were wholly and truly of one substance, absolute communication would be of man's very essence."[51] In pure identification there would be no strife. Likewise, there would be no strife in absolute separateness, since opponents can join battle only through a mediatory ground that makes their communication possible, thus providing the first condition necessary for their interchange of blows. But put identification and division ambiguously together . . . and you have the characteristic invitation to rhetoric. Here is a major reason why rhetoric, according to Aristotle, 'proves opposites.' "[52]

As a philosopher and metaphysician Burke is impelled to give a philosophic treatment to the concept of unity or identity by an analysis of the nature of *substance* in general. In this respect he makes his most basic contribution to a philosophy of rhetoric. "Metaphysically, a thing is identified by its *properties*,"[53] he observes. "To call a man a friend or brother is to proclaim him consubstantial with oneself, one's values or purposes. To call a man a bastard is to attack him by attacking his whole line, his 'authorship,' his 'principle' or 'motive' (as expressed in terms of the familial). An epithet assigns substance doubly, for in stating the character of the object it . . . contains an implicit program of action with regard to the object, thus serving as motive."[54]

According to Burke, language of all things "is most public, most collective, in its substance."[55] Aware that modern thinkers have been skeptical about the utility of a doctrine of substance,[56] he nevertheless recalls that "substance, in the old philosophies, was an *act*; and a way of life is an *acting-together*; and in acting together, men have common sensations, concepts, images, ideas, attitudes that make them *consubstantial*."[57] "A doctrine of *consubstantiality* . . . may be necessary to any way of life."[58] Like Kant, Burke regards substance as a "necessary form of the mind." Instead of trying to exclude a doctrine of substance, he restores it to a central position and throws critical light upon it.

In so far as rhetoric is concerned, the "ambiguity of substance" affords a major resource. "What handier linguistic resource could a rhetorician want than an ambiguity whereby he can say 'The state of affairs is substantially such-and-such,' instead of having to say 'The state of affairs *is* and/or *is not* such-and-such."[59]

The "commonplaces" or "topics" of Aristotle's *Rhetoric* are a "quick survey of opinion" of "things that people generally consider persuasive." As such, they are means of proclaiming *substantial* unity with an audience and are clearly instances of identification.[60] In truth, *identification* is "hardly other than a name for the function of sociality."[61] Likewise, the many tropes and figures, and rhetorical form in the large as treated by the ancients are to be considered as modes of identification.[62] They are the "signs" by which the speaker identifies himself with the reader or hearer. "In its simplest manifestation, style is ingratiation."[63] It is an attempt to "gain favor by the hypnotic or suggestive process of 'saying the right thing.' "[64] Burke discusses form in general as "the psychology of the *audience*,"[65] the "arousing and fulfillment of desires."[66] The exordium of a Greek oration is an instance of "conventional"[67] form, a form which is expected by the audience and therefore satisfies it. Other recognizable types of form are "syllogistic progression," "repetitive" form, and "minor or incidental" forms which include such devices as the metaphor, apostrophe, series, reversal, etc.[68] The proliferation and the variety of formal devices make a work eloquent.[69]

Reviewing *A Rhetoric of Motives,* Thomas W. Copeland observed, "It gradually appears that there is no form of action of men upon each other (or of individuals on themselves) which is really outside of rhetoric. But if so, we should certainly ask whether rhetoric as a *term* has any defining value."[70] The observation is probably not fair, for Burke does give rhetoric a defining value in terms of persuasion, identification, and address or communication to an audience of some sort, despite his observation, "Wherever there is persuasion, there is rhetoric. And wherever there is 'meaning' there is 'persuasion.' "[71]

It is true that in his effort to show "how a rhetorical motive is often present where it is not usually recognized, or thought to belong,"[72] Burke either points out linkages which have not been commonly stressed, or widens the scope of rhetoric. A twentieth-century orientation in social-psychological theory thus enables him to note that we may with "more accuracy speak of persuasion 'to attitude,' rather than persuasion to out-and-out action." For persuasion "involves choice, will; it is directed to a man only insofar as he is *free*." In so far as men "*must* do something, rhetoric is unnecessary, its work being done by the nature of things, though often these necessities are not of natural origin, but come from necessities imposed by man-made conditions,"[73] such as dictatorships or near-dictatorships. His notion of persuasion to "attitude" does not alter his generally classical view of rhetoric,

for as he points out, in "Cicero and Augustine there is a shift between the words 'move' *(movere)* and 'bend' *(flectere)* to name the ultimate function of rhetoric." And he merely finds that this shift "corresponds to a distinction between act and attitude (attitude being an incipient act, a leaning or inclination)."[74] His notion of persuasion to "attitude" enables him to point out a linkage with poetry: "Thus the notion of persuasion to *attitude* would permit the application of rhetorical terms to purely *poetic* structures; the study of lyrical devices might be classed under the head of rhetoric, when these devices are considered for their power to induce or communicate states of mind to readers, even though the kinds of assent evoked have no overt, practical outcome."[75]

In his reading of classical texts, he had noted a stress "upon *teaching* as an 'office' of rhetoric." Such an observation enables him to link the fields of rhetoric and semantics. He concludes that "once you treat instruction as an aim of rhetoric you introduce a principle that can widen the scope of rhetoric beyond persuasion. It is on the way to include also works on the theory and practice of exposition, description, *communication* in general. Thus, finally, out of this principle, you can derive contemporary 'semantics' as an aspect of rhetoric."[76]

As he persists in "tracking down" the function of the term *rhetoric*, Burke notes an ingredient of rhetoric "lurking in such anthropologist's terms as 'magic' and 'witchcraft,' "[77] and concludes that one "comes closer to the true state of affairs if one treats the socializing aspects of magic as a 'primitive rhetoric' than if one sees modern rhetoric simply as a 'survival of primitive magic.' "[78] Whereas he does not believe that the term *rhetoric* is a "substitute" for such terms as *magic, witchcraft, socialization,* or *communication,* the term *rhetoric* "designates a *function* . . . present in the areas variously covered by those other terms."[79] Thus, one can place within the scope of rhetoric "all those statements by anthropologists, ethnologists, individual and social psychologists, and the like, that bear upon the *persuasive* aspects of language, the function of language as *addressed,* as direct or roundabout appeal to real or ideal audiences, without or within."[80] All these disciplines have made "good contributions to the New Rhetoric."[81]

In "individual psychology," particularly the Freudian concern with the neuroses of individual patients, "there is a strongly rhetorical ingredient."[82] Burke asks the question, "Indeed, what could be more profoundly rhetorical than Freud's notion of a dream that attains expression by stylistic subterfuges designed to evade the inhibitions of a moralistic censor? What is this but the exact analogue of the rhetorical devices of literature under political or theocratic censorship? The *ego* with its *id* confronts the *super-ego* much as an orator would confront a somewhat alien audience, whose susceptibilities he must flatter as a necessary step toward persuasion. The Freudian psyche is quite a parliament, with conflicting interests expressed in ways variously designed to take the claims of rival factions into account."[83]

By considering the individual self as "audience" Burke brings morals and ethics into the realm of rhetoric. He notes that "a modern 'post-Christian' rhetoric must also concern itself with the thought that, under the heading of appeal to audiences, would also be included any ideas or images privately addressed to the individual self for moralistic or incantatory purposes. For you become your own audience, in some respects a very lax one, in some respects very exacting, when you become involved in psychologically stylistic subterfuges for presenting your own case to yourself in sympathetic terms (and even terms that seem harsh can often be found on closer scrutiny to be flattering, as with neurotics who visit sufferings upon themselves in the name of very high-powered motives which, whatever this discomfiture, feed pride)." Therefore, the "individual peson, striving to form himself in accordance with the communicative norms that match the cooperative ways of his society, is by the same token concerned with the rhetoric of identification."[84]

By considering style as essentially a mode of "ingratiation" or as a technique by which

one gives the signs of identification and consubstantiality, Burke finds a rhetorical motive in clothes, pastoral, courtship, and the like.[85]

Burke links dialectics with rhetoric through a definition of dialectics in "its most general sense" as "linguistic transformation"[86] and through an analysis of three different levels of language, or linguistic terminology.[87] Grammatically, he discusses the subject from the point of view of linguistic merger and division, polarity, and transcendence, being aware that there are "other definitions of dialectics:"[88] "reasoning from opinion"; "the discovery of truth by the give and take of converse and redefinition"; "the art of disputation"; "the processes of 'interaction' between the verbal and the non-verbal"; "the competition of cooperation or the cooperation of competition"; "the spinning of terms out of terms"; "the internal dialogue of thought"; "any development . . . got by the interplay of various factors that mutually modify one another, and may be thought of as voices in a dialogue or roles in a play, with each voice or role in its partiality contributing to the development of the whole"; "the placement of one thought or thing in terms of its opposite"; "the progressive or successive development and reconciliation of opposites"; and "so putting questions to nature that nature can give unequivocal answer."[89] He considers all of these definitions as "variants or special applications of the functions"[90] of linuistic transformation conceived in terms of "Merger and division," "The three Major Pairs: action-passion, mind-body, being-nothing," and "Transcendence."[91]

Burke devotes 150 pages to the treatment of the dialectics of persuasion in the *Rhetoric,*[92] in addition to extensive treatment of it on the grammatical level.[93] Linguistic terminology is considered variously persuasive in its Positive, Dialectical, and Ultimate levels or orders.[94] "A positive term is most unambiguously itself when it names a visible and tangible thing which can be located in time and place."[95] Dialectical terms "have no such strict location."[96] Thus terms like "Elizabethanism" or "capitalism" having no positive referent may be called "dialectical."[97] Often called "polar" terms,[98] they require an "opposite"[99] to define them and are on the level of "action," "principles," "ideas."[100] In an "ultimate order" of terminology, there is a "guiding idea" or "unitary principle."[101]

From the point of view of rhetoric, Burke believes that the "difference between a merely 'dialectical' confronting of parliamentary conflict and an 'ultimate' treatment of it would reside in this: The 'dialectical' order would leave the competing voices in a jangling relation with one another (a conflict solved *faute de mieux* by 'horsetrading'); but the 'ultimate' order would place these competing voices themselves in a *hierarchy,* or *sequence,* or *evaluating series,* so that, in some way, we went by a fixed and reasoned progression from one of these to another, the members of the entire group being arranged *developmentally* with relation to one another."[102] To Burke "much of the *rhetorical* strength in the Marxist dialectic comes from the fact that it is 'ultimate' in its order,"[103] for a "spokesman for the proletariat can think of himself as representing not only the interests of that class alone, but the grand design of the entire historical sequence. . . ."[104]

In his concept of a "pure persuasion," Burke seems to be extending the area of rhetoric beyond its usual scope. As a metaphysician he attempts to carry the process of rhetorical appeal to its ultimate limits. He admits that what he means by "pure persuasion" in the "absolute sense" exists nowhere, but believes that it can be present as a motivational ingredient in any rhetoric, no matter how "advantage-seeking such a rhetoric may be."[105] Pure persuasion involves the saying of something, not for an extraverbal advantage to be got by the saying, but because of a satisfaction intrinsic to the saying. It summons because it likes the feel of a summons. It would be nonplused if the summons were answered. It attacks because it revels in the sheer syllables of vituperation. It would be horrified if, each time it finds a way of saying, 'Be dammed,' it really did send a soul to rot in hell. It intuitively says, 'This is so,' purely and simply because this is so."[106] With such a concept Burke finds himself at the "borders of metaphysics, or perhaps better 'meta-rhetoric'. . . ."[107]

III

Of great significance to the rhetorician is Burke's consideration of the general problem of motivation. Concerned with the problem of motivation in literary strategy,[108] he nevertheless intends that his observations be considered pertinent to the social sphere in general.[109] He had observed that people's conduct has been explained by an "endless variety of theories: ethnological, geographical, sociological, physiological, historical, endocrinological, economic, anatomical, mystical, pathological, and so on."[110] The assigning of motives, he concludes, is a "matter of *appeal,*"[111] and this depends upon one's general orientation. "A motive is not some fixed thing, like a table, which one can go to and look at. It is a term of interpretation, and being such it will naturally take its place within the framework of our *Weltanschauung* as a whole."[112] "To explain one's conduct by the vocabulary of motives current among one's group is about as self-deceptive as giving the area of a field in the accepted terms of measurement. One is simply interpreting with the only vocabulary he knows. One is stating his orientation, which involves a vocabulary of ought and ought-not, with attendant vocabulary of praiseworthy and blameworthy."[113] "We discern situational patterns by means of the particular vocabulary of the cultural group into which we are born."[114] Motives are "distinctly linguistic products."[115]

To Burke, the subject of motivation is a "philosophic one, not ultimately to be solved in terms of empirical science."[116] A motive is a "shorthand" term for "situation."[117] One may discuss motives on three levels, rhetorical, symbolic, and grammatical.[118] One is on the "grammatical" level when he concerns himself with the problem of the "intrinsic," or the problem of "substance."[119] "Men's conception of motive . . . is integrally related to their conception of substance. Hence, to deal with problems of motive is to deal with problems of substance."[120]

On the "grammatical" level Burke gives his most profound treatment of the problem of motivation. Strongly allied with the classicists throughout all his works in both his ideas and his methodology, Burke shows indebtedness to Aristotle for his treatment of motivation. Taking a clue from Aristotle's consideration of the "circumstances" of an action,[121] Burke concludes that "In a rounded statement about motives, you must have some word that names the *act* (names what took place, in thought or deed), and another that names the *scene* (the background of the act, the situation in which it occurred); also, you must indicate what person or kind of person *(agent)* performed the act, what means or instruments he used *(agency),* and the *purpose.*"[122] Act, Scene, Agent, Agency, Purpose become the "pentad" for pondering the problem of human motivatoin.[123] Among these various terms grammatical "ratios" prevail which have rhetorical implications. One might illustrate by saying that, for instance, between scene and act a logic prevails which indicates that a certain quality of scene calls for an analogous quality of act. Hence, if a situation is said to be of a certain nature, a corresponding attitude toward it is implied. Burke explains by pointing to such an instance as that employed by a speaker who, in discussing Roosevelt's war-time power exhorted that Roosevelt should be granted "unusual powers" because the country was in an "unusual international situation." The scene-act "ratio" may be applied in two ways. "It can be applied deterministically in statements that a certain policy *had* to be adopted in a certain situation, or it may be applied in hortatory statements to the effect that a certain policy *should* be adopted in conformity with the situation."[124] These ratios are "principles of determination."[125] The pentad would allow for ten such ratios: scene-act, scene-agent, scene-agency, scene-purpose, act-purpose, act-agent, act-agency, agent-purpose, agent-agency, and agency-purpose.[126] Political commentators now generally use *situation* as their synonum for *scene,* "though often without any

clear concept of its function as a statement about motives."[127]

Burke draws his key terms for the study of motivation from the analysis of drama. Being developed from the analysis of drama, his pentad "treats language and thought primarily as modes of action."[128] His method for handling motivation is designed to contrast with the methodology of the physical sciences which considers the subject of motivation in mechanistic terms of "flat cause-and-effect or stimulus-and-response."[129] Physicalist terminologies are proper to non-verbalizing entities, but man as a species should be approached through his specific trait, his use of symbols. Burke opposes the reduction of the human realm to terms that lack sufficient "coordinates"; he does not, however, question the fitness of physicalist terminologists for treating the physical realm. According to Burke, "Philosophy, like common sense, must think of human motivation dramatistically, in terms of action and its ends."[130] "Language being essentially human, we should view human relations in terms of the linguistic instrument."[131] His "vocabulary" or "set of coordinates" serves "for the integration of all phenomena studied by the *social* sciences."[132] It also serves as a "perspective for the analysis of history which is a 'dramatic' process. . . ."[133]

One may wonder with Charles Morris whether "an analysis of man through his language provides us with a full account of human motives."[134] One strongly feels the absence of insights into motivation deriving from the psychologists and scientists.

IV

Burke is not only philosopher and theorist; he has applied his critical principles practically to a great number of literary works. Of these, three are of particular interest to the rhetorician. In two instances, Burke attempts to explain the communicative relationship between the writer and his audience. Taking the speech of Antony from Shakespeare's *Julius Caesar,*[135] Burke examines the speech from "the standpoint of the rhetorician, who is concerned with a work's processes of appeal."[136] A similar operation is performed on a scene from *Twelfth Night*.[137]

Undoubtedly one of his most straightforward attempts at analysis of a work of "literature for use," occurs in an essay on "The Rhetoric of Hitler's 'Battle' "[138] "The main ideal of criticism, as I conceive it," Burke has observed, "is to use all that there is to use."[139] "If there is any slogan that should reign among critical precepts, it is that 'circumstances alter occasions.' "[140] Considering *Mein Kampf* as "the well of Nazi magic,"[141] Burke brings his knowledge of sociology and anthropology to bear in order to "discover what kind of 'medicine' this medicine-man has concocted, that we may know, with greater accuracy, exactly what to guard against, if we are to forestall the concocting of similar medicine in America."[142] He considers Hitler's "centralizing hub of *ideas*"[143] and his selection of Munich as a "mecca geographically located"[144] as methods of recruiting followers "from among many discordant and divergent bands. . . ."[145] He examines the symbol of the "international Jew"[146] as that "of a *common enemy*,"[147] the " 'medicinal' appeal of the Jew as scapegoat. . . ."[148]

His knowledge of psychoanalysis is useful in the analysis of the "sexual symbolism" that runs through the book: "Germany in dispersion is the 'dehorned Siefried.' The masses are 'feminine.' As such, they desire to be led by a dominating male. This male, as orator, woos them—and, when he has won them, he commands them. The rival male, the villainous Jew, would on the contrary 'seduce' them. If he succeeds, he poisons their blood by intermingling with them. Whereupon, by purely associative connections of ideas, we are moved into attacks upon syphilis, prostitution, incest, and other similar misfortunes, which are introduced as a kind of 'musical' argument when he is on the subject of 'blood poisoning' by intermarriage or, in its 'spiritual' equivalent, by the infection of 'Jewish' ideas. . . ."[149]

His knowledge of history and religion is employed to show that the *"materialization"* of a religious pattern" is "one terrifically effective weapon . . . in a period where religion has been progressively weakened by many centuries of capitalist materialism."[150]

Conventional rhetorical knowledge leads him to call attention to the "power of endless repetition"[151]; the appeal of a sense of "community"[152]; the appeal of security resulting from "a world view" for a people who had previously seen the world only "piecemeal";[153] and the appeal of Hitler's "inner voice"[154] which served as a technique of leader-people "identification."[155]

Burke's analysis is comprehensive and penetrating. It stands as a superb example of the fruitfulness of a method of comprehensive rhetorical analysis which goes far beyond conventional patterns.

Conclusion

Burke is difficult and often confusing. He cannot be understood by casual reading of his various volumes. In part the difficulty arises from the numerous vocabularies he employs. His words in isolation are usually simple enough, but he often uses them in new contexts. To read one of his volumes independently, without regard to the chronology of publication, makes the problem of comprehension even more difficult because of the specialized meanings attached to various words and phrases.

Burke is often criticized for "obscurity" in his writings. The charge may be justified. However, some of the difficulty of comprehension arises from the compactness of his writing, the uniqueness of his organizational patterns, the penetration of his thought, and the breadth of his endeavor. "In books like the *Grammar* and the *Rhetoric*," observed Malcolm Cowley, "we begin to see the outlines of a philosophical system on the grand scale. . . . Already it has its own methodology (called 'dramatism'), its own esthetics (based on the principle that works of art are symbolic actions), its logic and dialectics, its ethics (or picture of the good life) and even its metaphysics, which Burke prefers to describe as meta-rhetoric."[156]

One cannot possibly compress the whole of Burke's thought into an article. The most that one can achieve is to signify his importance as a theorist and critic and to suggest the broad outlines of his work. Years of study and contemplation of the general idea of effectiveness in language have equipped him to deal competently with the subject of rhetoric from its beginning as a specialized discipline to the present time. To his thorough knowledge of classical tradition he has added rich insights gained from serious study of anthropology, sociology, history, psychology, philosophy, and the whole body of humane letters. With such equipment, he has become the most profound student of rhetoric now writing in America.

Marie Hochmuth Nichols

Notes

1. Kenneth Burke, *A Rhetoric of Motives* (New York: Prentice-Hall, Inc., 1950), p. xv. Reprinted with permission.
2. Isidor Schneider, "A New View of Rhetoric," *New York Herald Tribune Books*, VIII (December 13, 1931), 4.
3. Malcolm Cowley, "Prolegomena to Kenneth Burke," *The New Republic*, CXXI (June 5, 1950), 18, 19.
4. W. H. Auden, "A Grammar of Assent," *The New Republic*, CV (July 14, 1941), 59.
5. *Counter-Statement* (New York, 1931), p. 265.
6. *Ibid.*, p. 265.
7. *Ibid.*, p. 53.
8. *A Rhetoric of Motives*, pp. xiv, xv.
9. *Counter-Statement*, p. 156.
10. *Ibid.*
11. *Ibid.*
12. *Ibid.*
13. *Ibid.*
14. Stanley Edgar Hyman, *The Armed Vision* (New York, 1948), pp. 386, 387.
15. *The Philosophy of Literary Form* (Louisiana, 1941), p. 89.
16. *Ibid.*, pp. 235, 236.
17. *Ibid.*, p. 89.
18. *Ibid.*, p. 8.
19. *Ibid.*, p. vii.
20. *Ibid.*, p. 9.
21. *Ibid.*, p. 1.
22. *Ibid.*, p. 109.
23. *Ibid.*, p. 297.
24. *Ibid.*, p. 109.
25. *A Rhetoric of Motives*, p. 5.
26. *The Philosophy of Literary Form*, p. 321.
27. *Ibid.*

28. *Ibid.*
29. *A Rhetoric of Motives*, p. 40.
30. *Ibid.*, pp. xiii, 40.
31. *The Philosophy of Literary Form*, p. 68.
32. *A Rhetoric of Motives*, p. 40.
33. *The Philosophy of Literary Form*, p. 258.
34. *A Rhetoric of Motives*, p. 36.
35. *Ibid.*, p. 41.
36. *Ibid.*, p. 43.
37. *Ibid.*, p. 146.
38. *Ibid.*, pp. 49–180.
39. *Ibid.*, p. 61.
40. *Ibid.*, p. 61, 62.
41. *Ibid.*, p. 62.
42. *Ibid.*, p. 55.
43. *Ibid.*, p. xiv.
44. *Ibid.*
45. *Ibid.*, p. 55.
46. *Ibid.*
47. *Ibid.*, p. xiv.
48. *Ibid.*, p. 46.
49. *Ibid.*, p. xiv.
50. Kenneth Burke, "Rhetoric—Old and New," *The Journal of General Education*, V (April 1951), 203.
51. *A Rhetoric of Motives*, p. 22.
52. *Ibid.*, p. 25.
53. *Ibid.*, p. 23.
54. *A Grammar of Motives* (New York, 1945), p. 57. For discussion of *substance* as a concept, see, *ibid.*, pp. 21–58; Aristotle, *Categoriae*, tr. by E. M. Edghill, *The Works of Aristotle*, ed. by W. D. Ross, I, Ch. 5; Aristotle, *Metaphysics*, tr. by W. D. Ross, Book, 8, 1017b, 10; Spinoza, *The Ethics*, in *The Chief Works of Benedict De Spinoza*, tr. by R. H. M Elwes (London 1901), Rev. ed., II, 45′ ff; John Locke, *An Essay Concerning Human Understanding* (London 1760), 15th ed., I, Bk. II, Chs. XXIII, XXIV.
55. *The Philosophy of Literary Form*, p. 44.
56. *A Rhetoric of Motives*, p. 21.
57. *Ibid.*
58. *Ibid.*
59. *A Grammar of Motives*, pp. 51, 52.
60. *A Rhetoric of Motives*, pp. 56, 57.
61. *Attitudes toward History* (New York, 1937), II. 144.
62. *A Rhetoric of Motives*, p. 59.
63. *Permanence an Change* (New York, 1935), p. 71.
64. *Ibid.*
65. *Counter-Statement*, pp. 38–57.
66. *Ibid.*, p. 157.
67. *Ibid.*, p. 159.
68. *Ibid.*, pp. 157–161.
69. *Ibid.*, pp. 209–211.
70. Thomas W. Copeland, "Critics at Work," *The Yale Review*, XL (Autumn 1950), 167–169.
71. *A Rhetoric of Motives*, p. 172.
72. *Ibid.*, p. xiii.
73. *Ibid.*, p. 50.
74. *Ibid.*
75. *Ibid.*
76. *Ibid.*, p.77.

77. *Ibid.*, p. 44.
78. *Ibid.*, p. 43.
79. *Ibid.*, p. 44.
80. *Ibid.*, pp. 43–44.
81. *Ibid.*, p. 40.
82. *Ibid.*, p. 37.
83. *Ibid.*, pp. 37, 38.
84. *Ibid.*, pp. 38, 39.
85. *Ibid.*, pp. 115–127; see also, p. xiv.
86. *A Grammar of Motives*, p. 402.
87. *A Rhetoric of Motives*, p. 183.
88. *A Grammar of Motives*, pp. 402, 403.
89. *Ibid.*, p. 403.
90. *Ibid.*
91. *Ibid.*, p. 402.
92. *A Rhetoric of Motives*, pp. 183–333.
93. *A Grammar of Motives*, pp. 323–443.
94. *A Rhetoric of Motives*, p. 183.
95. *Ibid.*
96. *Ibid.*, p. 184.
97. *Ibid.*
98. *Ibid.*
99. *The Philosophy of Literary Form*, n. 26, p. 109.
100. *A Rhetoric of Motives*, p. 184.
101. *Ibid.*, p. 187.
102. *Ibid.*
103. *Ibid.*, p. 190.
104. *Ibid.*, pp. 190, 191.
105. *Ibid.*, p. 269.
106. *Ibid.*
107. *Ibid.*, p. 267.
108. *The Philosophy of Literary Forms*, n. 26, p. 109.
109. *Ibid.*, p. 105.
110. *Permanence and Change*, p. 47.
111. *Ibid.*, p. 38.
112. *Ibid.*
113. *Ibid.*, p. 33.
114. *Ibid.*, p. 52.
115. *Ibid.*
116. *A Grammar of Motives*, p. xxiii.
117. *Permanence and Change*, p. 44.
118. *A Grammar of Motives*, p. 465.

119. *Ibid.*
120. *Ibid.*, p. 337.
121. *Ethica Nicomachea*, tr. by W. D. Ross, III, i, 16.
122. *A Grammar of Motives*, p. xv.
123. *Ibid.*
124. *Ibid.*, p. 13.
125. *Ibid.*, p. 15.
126. *Ibid.*
127. *Ibid.*, p. 13.
128. *Ibid.*, p. xxii.
129. *The Philosophy of Literary Form*, pp. 103, 106.
130. *A Grammar of Motives*, pp. 55, 56.
131. *Ibid.*, p. 317.
132. *The Philosophy of Literary Form*, p. 105.
133. *Ibid.*, p. 317.
134. Charles Morris, "The Strategy of Kenneth Burke," *The Nation*, CLXIII (July 27, 1946), 106.
135. "Antony in Behalf of the Play," *Philosophy of Literary Form*, pp. 329–343.
136. *Ibid.*, p. 330.
137. "Trial Translation" (From *Twelfth Night*), *ibid.*, pp. 344–349.
138. *Ibid.*, pp. 191–220.
139. *Ibid.*, p. 23.
140. *Ibid.*
141. *Ibid.*, p.192.
142. *Ibid.*, p. 191.
143. *Ibid.*, p. 192.
144. *Ibid.*
145. *Ibid.*
146. *Ibid.*, p. 194.
147. *Ibid.*, p. 193.
148. *Ibid.*, p. 195.
149. Ibid.
150. *Ibid.*, p. 194.
151. *Ibid.*, p. 217.
152. *Ibid.*
153. *Ibid.*, p. 218.
154. *Ibid.*, p. 207.
155. *Ibid.*
156. Malcolm Cowley, "Prolegomena to Kenneth Burke," *The New Republic*, CXXII (June 5, 1950), 18, 19.

In developing the preceding essay, Dr. Nichols became the first major scholar in rhetoric to alert her colleagues to the significance of Burke. The question which now must be asked is, to what extent has Burke reaffirmed, extended, or altered his rhetorical philosophy in the past quarter century? To answer this query, we will examine Burke's representative works and speeches which were produced following the appearance of the Nichols essay.

At the heart of Burke's present, as well as past, theory of rhetoric is his notion of dramatism. In his 1968 monograph on dramatism,[1] which he now calls his most effective treatment of the subject,[2] he both reinforces and extends his earlier views. "Dramatism," he says, is "the study of human relations and motives" by means of "a methodical inquiry into cycles or clusters of terms and their functions."[3] Still crucial to his system of dramatism are his "five children," as he affectionately calls them—Act, Agent, Scene, Agency, and Purpose.[4] But he hints that a sixth element might be added, that of Attitude.[5]

Since the central term is "act," Burke continues to use this element as a peg upon which to hang his theory. The "act," he suggests, is "a terministic center from which . . . a whole universe of terms is derived."[6] Observe, for instance, how the other four elements of the pentad radiate from the notion of "act." An "act" takes place only when there is an "agent" who operates in a "scene" or situation, and employs an "agency" or means in order to accomplish a particular "purpose." If any one of these elements is missing, an "act" has not been consummated.

Whenever we isolate any two parts of the pentad and examine their relationships to each other, we are using what Burke calls "ratios." A "purpose-agency ratio," for example, is present when we focus on the selection of means or on adapting means to an end. These ratios are useful in explaining or justifying acts. Thus an "agent-act ratio" comes into play when we attempt to relate "a man's character and the character of his behavior." A "scene-act ratio" pertains to the relationship of an act to the situation in which it occurs. In many instances, Burke adds, an "agent-act ratio" may exist in conjunction with a "scene-act ratio."[7] We may illustrate this principle by recalling the behavior (act) of John Dean (agent) during the Watergate Hearings (scene).

Of overriding concern to Burke is the distinction he draws between "sheer motion" and symbolic action. He touches briefly on this theme in the essay on dramatism, by articulating three propositions:

1. "There can be no action without motion."
2. "There can be motion without action."
3. "Action is not reducible to terms of motion."[8]

By 1977, he had decided that this topic would be his principal subject for his Speech Communication Association presentation.[9] Stressing his preference for dramatism over behaviorism because the latter does not distinguish between motion and action, Burke set forth what he perceived to be the difference. The physical world, located in the realm of matter, is limited to motion. Thus when the sun rises, or the tide rolls in, or the air conditioning unit regulates the temperature, we have motion but not action. For action not only embraces motion but is grounded in symbolism—one of man's greatest contributions to life. What we have then is a "motion-action pair" resting on two different points of a continuum.

In explaining this key aspect of dramatism, Burke gives discomfort to those who make large claims regarding the communication capacity of animals. Man alone, he argues, can both "use symbols and be reflexive." Cicero, for example, could deliver eloquent orations in the Roman Forum, and then retire to his study to write rhetorical treatises influenced, in part, by his speaking experiences. Dogs, by contrast, know how to bark but cannot discourse on the nature of barking. To strengthen his claim, Burke next argues that to remove mankind from the earth would be to leave behind a world comprised only of motion; for with the disappearance of man would come the elimination of all vestiges of symbolic action. Language, he concludes, becomes a reality-based form of action by transcending motion.[10]

Also vital to an understanding of Burke's theory of dramatism is his analysis of order—a concept that relates both to commands and hierarchical arrangements. Concerned here with the principle of the "negative" as a "linguistic invention," he suggests that whereas "scientism" deals with such statements as "it is not," dramatism stresses hortatory appeals contained in the idiom of "thou shalt nots."[11] The energy crisis during the winter of 1978 is useful in illustrating this distinction between scientism and dramatism, and to highlight the concept of order as command. Scientists claimed the existence of an energy shortage due to the prolonged coal strike and severe weather. In effect, they were saying, "*there is not* enough mined coal to last throughout the winter." This, in turn, prompted Governor James Rhodes of Ohio to proclaim an order asserting that governmental agencies "*shall not*" use more energy than fifty percent of the normal output. A dramatistic order of this type, phrased in the language of the negative, required obedience on the part of such state officials as the President of Ohio State University. Order, it is clear, is tied in closely with hierarchy. The governor as the top official in the state is able to communicate his orders downward, knowing in advance that in time of emergency he has the power to enforce his commands.

Included in a "dramatistic analysis of order" is a consideration of the principles of "sacrifice," "victimage," and "scapegoatism." Whenever a person receives an order calling for some kind of sacrifice, observes Burke, "the sacrificial principle is intrinsic in the nature of the order." Similarly the notion of victimage as seen in the idea of scapegoat is characteristic of the "human congregation." The following statements emphasize these principles:

1. "If order, then guilt; if guilt, then need for redemption; but any such 'payment' is victimage."
2. "If action, then drama; if drama, then conflict; if conflict, then victimage."[12]

The significance of these claims becomes evident when we realize that, in Burke's view, "life is drama"—a fact which stems from symbolic action and features the elements of "order," "guilt," "conflict," and "victimage."

It is further helpful to see that the culmination of the process described in the above claim is "victimage" or the associative concept of "scapegoatism." This principle can be demonstrated by alluding to the areas of religion and politics. In the book of Genesis in the Old Testament, God issued an order to Abraham commanding him to offer his son Isaac as a sacrifice. In dramatistic terms, this resulted in a feeling of guilt which Abraham had to allay through the redemptive influence of obedience that subsequently led to the experience of victimage. Scapegoatism or victimage in politics implies the rhetorical strategies of "antithesis," "substitution," and "identification." Political leaders engaged in campaigns, for example, make use of antithesis or substitution by urging the adoption of policies which represent what they are against;

and "establish identification in terms of an enemy shared in common. . . ."[13] In the 1968 Presidential primary campaign, George Wallace of Alabama exemplified this technique. Repeatedly he came out against federal intervention in state rights, judicial leniency toward criminals, war protesters, and free speech advocates. As he did so, he described the common enemy as bureaucrats, civil rights marchers, and "draft dodgers" who failed to uphold law and order as spelled out in the Constitution and Bill of Rights.

Burke's definition of man likewise finds its roots in his theory of dramatism. "Man," he asserts, "is the symbol-using, symbol-misusing, and symbol-making animal."[14] Notwithstanding the fact he shares the common experience of birth with other animals, man is unique in his compelling need for a detailed "system of speech." Indeed, every "aspect of reality" he comes to know "is on the side of language" or symbolic action.[15]

"Man," secondly, "is an inventor of the negative." He has devised his theory of religion and morals in terms of the negative; and he has opted to define a thing or an idea from the perspective of what it is not. As a result, God, who epitomizes the highest level of being, is described as "immortal" (*not* mortal), "infinite" (*not* finite), and "impassive" (*not* passive). In a similar vein, the seemingly positive idea of "freedom" can only fully be explained by employing the language of the negative. A person who is free, for instance, is not restrained, "*not* bound," "*not* under obligation or necessity," *not* dependent, "*not* affected by a given condition or circumstance," "*not* inhibited," or "*not* committed."

Thirdly, man, continues Burke, is "separated from his natural condition by instruments of his own making." That he has the capacity and will to create and use tools to make tasks easier in time of peace and war there can be little question. These tools, in turn, function as instruments which work their way into our language transactions. Although the end result may be a positive achievement overall, it tends to move man away from the basic nature he was endowed with at birth.[16]

Finally, man "is goaded by the spirit of hierarchy." This compulsion for a "sense of order" has made man "rotten with perfection," causing him to seek the ideal or ultimate language in a given situation so as to express the most appropriate attitudes and motives. It is this penchant for hierarchy and perfection, Burke notes, that led Castiglione in his *Book of the Courtier* to recommend the practice of resting on one knee when in the presence of a sovereign in order to show deference, and on both knees when communicating with God.[17] Burke could have added that this desire to use a hierarchical language form has set one standard for telling the truth in a normal conversational situation and another for stating it before a court of law. In the latter case we are often required to take an oath with our hand on the Bible as a means of improving our chances of reaching perfection in our language.

If dramatism has helped forge Burke's ideas on man as language-maker and language-user, it has also shaped his views on language in general which, as we have seen, is the essence of symbolic action. "There are four realms to which words may refer," he tells us in *The Rhetoric of Religion.* These are the "natural," the "socio-political," the "logological" ("words about words"), and the "supernatural." Words used to depict things, "material operations," "physiological conditions," or "animality" are part of the natural realm. Terms used to describe "social relations," "laws," "moral obligations," right and wrong, good and bad, justice and injustice are in the political realm. Words used to designate God, though sometimes borrowed from the other three realms, are in the celestial or supernatural sphere. Since God by nature is an "ineffable" being who cannot be fully described, it behooves us to detail what he represents in an analogical manner. Hence, we speak "of God's 'powerful arm' (a physical analogy), or of God as 'lord' or 'father' (a sociopolitical analogy), or of God as the 'word' (a linguistic analogy)."[18]

As words interact with each other in the four realms, they have relationships with things. Expressing this relatedness in the form of a simile, Burke observes that "words are to the nonverbal things they name as Spirit is to Matter."[19] Although there is a "communion" between the symbol and the "symbolized" or between the thing and its name, the word, in reality, "transcends" its referent.

In a provocative essay entitled, "What are the Signs of What?," Burke cautions his readers not to be overly committed to the traditional notion that "words are the signs of things."[20] He then poceeds to ask us to consider reversing the idea by saying that "things are the signs of words." This perspective requires us to focus on the possibilities inherent in the process of "entitling." The words we use to label or entitle the subject in a particular sentence, for example, will provide an insight supporting the claim that "things are the signs of words." Burke illustrates this idea by citing the phrase, "a man walking down the street." Upon reading these words, we have all kinds of potential images, not the least of which are the following: a tall, short, thin, fat, erect, or stooped man; a brisk, slow, or loping walk; a wide, narrow, two way, cement, or curbed street. In such an instance, with its multiple images, we have, suggests Burke, three different possibilities for entitling this nonverbal circumstance. We may call it a "man-situation," a "walk-situation," or a "street-situation."[21] The entitlement we choose affects the relationship between things and words that appear in the sentence or phrase.

Burke further asserts that "the thing (is) a visible, tangible sign of the essence or spirit contained in the word itself. For you can't see a meaning. . . ." Conversely, since we can see a bicycle (a thing), it is easy to define this mode of transportation by pointing to it. In this sense, the bicycle as thing typifies "the genius that resides in words."[22]

One of the most important and useful ideas in Burke's general theory of language usage is his description of what he calls "terministic screens." His use of this term "screen" is borrowed from the field of photography. Let us assume, he says, that we take several pictures of an object, each with a different type of color filter. Under such circumstances, the finished product we see will vary according to the filter used. Likewise this is what happens when we employ language. For "the nature of our terms (or terministic screens) affects the nature of our observations, in the sense that the terms direct the attention to one field rather than to another."[23] The Holy Bible, Burke points out, begins with a reference to God in the first sentence, while Darwin's *Origin of Species* ignores the term. Consequently, the terministic screens used in these two works direct our attention to a particular point of view which affects the nature of our communication transactions in the areas of theology and in the natural sciences.

There are many examples that come to mind which tend to give credence to Burke's discussion of terministic screens. The debate on miracles, analyzed in the British period, reveals how Hume and Campbell were strongly influenced by the terministic screens they employed. A similar result would doubtless occur if a cross section of university students were asked to explain what "God" or "Christ" meant to them. Those who respond by relying on the terministic screens of "deity" and "trinity" would perhaps direct our attention to the miracles of the "Virgin Birth," the "Resurrection," and the "Ascension." Others who opt for the phrase, "one of the Biblical prophets," would tend to use a terministic screen that relegates "Christ" to the level of a "good man" on a par with Mahomet or Gandhi. A striking example encountered by one of the authors occurred during the Senate Select Committee Hearings on Watergate in the summer and autumn of 1973. The research team, of which he was a part, interviewed members of the Select Committee and the press covering the event, as well as a sample of the residents of Columbus, Ohio. Each interviewee was asked the question: "Do you view the Watergate event as a 'caper,' a 'crime,' a 'conspiracy,' or a 'crisis?' We found that the choice of one of these four words, or terministic screens, by the respondent, directed our attention to the degree of seriousness he or she associated with Watergate.

Up to this point we have summarized Burke's latest views on dramatism. Rather than replace or substantially alter his earlier ideas Burke, in the past twenty five years, has reinforced and enlarged them. Taken as a whole, Burke's dramatistic theory centering on language as symbolic action has had a profound influence on contemporary rhetoric and criticism. We would like to emphasize two of his most far-reaching accomplishments in the generation of new perspectives in rhetorical theory, and then show how he has advanced our knowledge of rhetorical criticism.

We are indebted to Burke as a rhetorical theorist, first of all, because of his compelling description of the rhetoric-reality pair. In the first chaper of this volume, we noted how many contemporary commentators, including political leaders and mass media analysts, have sought to disassociate rhetoric from reality. Tauntingly they suggest in a moment of crisis that "what is needed is action, not rhetoric." Through an effective associative technique drawn from his system of dramatism, Burke brings rhetoric and reality together. We quoted him earlier as saying: Rhetoric "is rooted in an essential function of language itself, a function that is wholly realistic, and is continually born anew; the use of language as a symbolic means of inducing cooperation in beings that by nature use symbols."[24] For a human being to use symbols, he further urges, "is in essence not magical but realistic." Rhetoric, in short, is not a polar term for action or reality. In fact, it is equated with the only type of genuine action known to man—symbolic action.

Burke's second great contribution as a rhetorical theorist is his bold attempt to extend the range of rhetoric. In our previous discussion of the Elocutionary Movement and our allusion to the stylistic rhetoricians who were a part of the British period, we used the word "truncators" to signify the tendency to limit the focus of rhetoric to a single canon. Unlike these reductionists, Burke has moved in an opposite direction, encompassing the role of expansionist. Moreover, unlike Aristotle who tended to separate rhetoric from poetics, Burke has gone in the direction of combining the two fields under a single rubric. He was able to do this because of his belief in the principle: "Wherever there is persuasion, there is rhetoric. And wherever there is 'meaning' there is persuasion"[25] Both rhetoric and poetics, moreover, use the same three language forms: "progressive," "repetitive," and "conventional."[26]

This expansionist view of rhetoric prompted Burke, additionally, to incorporate non-verbal elements into his theory of communication. He was thus able to say: ". . . we could observe that even the medical equipment of a doctor's office is not to be judged purely for its diagnostic usefulness, but also has a function in the *rhetoric* of medicine. Whatever it is as apparatus, it also appeals to imagery. . . ."[27] This philosophy enabled him further to regard clothes as a rhetorical form.

Another interesting dimension of Burke's broad-scope view regarding the parameters of rhetoric is his often overlooked notion of "administrative rhetoric." Deriving his inspiration for this concept by reading Machiavelli's *The Prince*, Burke details ways in which a rhetor communicates a message largely through non-verbal action that is nevertheless symbolic.[28] By attending a function, signing a document or petition, visiting a colleague in the hospital, going to the funeral of an acquaintance, or shaking the hand of an adversary, an administrator delivers an unspoken message depicting concern and friendship. Numerous political leaders, particularly presidents, have taken advantage of the persuasive power associated with administrative rhetoric. Here are but a few mid-twentieth-century examples: Richard Nixon's good will mission to Communist China; Gerald Ford's presentation of awards in the Rose Garden of the White House; and Jimmy Carter's walk from the Capitol to the White House on Inaugural Day. What makes the idea of administrative rhetoric an appealing strategy to Burke is its tendency to produce identification. The process of doing, taking place in a scene requiring a symbolic response, and having as its purpose to remove division allows the designated observer

or interpreter to see a good relationship between the agent and the act.

But Burke's pioneering contributions are not limited to rhetorical theory; he also has provided us with brilliant insights into rhetorical, literary, sociological, and philosophical criticism. His interest in symbolic action has led him to remind all critics to start with the work itself.[29] This practice permits the critic to distinguish between facts, inferences, and proof; to look for shifting attitudes within the study; to search for recurring terms or phrases; and to ferret out the "universe of discourse." The worth of the critique, he concludes, is directly proportional to its reliance on and conformity to identifiable "critical principles."[30]

Burke's belief in the idea that "life is drama" spawned the creation of his pentad—a fresh methodological approach to criticism which presents the modern student with a viable alternative to neo-Aristotelianism. The pentad, which may be used either implicitly or explicitly, gives to the critic an instrument for assessing a rhetorical event. It functions equally well as a tool for analyzing a specified rhetorical work, a particular speaker or writer, a rhetorical campaign, or a social movement. To see the pentad's applicability for the criticism of the rhetoric of a single speaker, and also to observe the relationship between rhetorical theory and practice, we reprint here Burke's celebrated essay, "The Rhetoric of Hitler's Battle." Written in 1941, at the height of the Nazi Movement, this critique bristles with comments emphasizing the crucial elements in Burke's theories.

Even though Burke has not singled out by name the five parts of the pentad, each is present throughout the analysis. Repeatedly he focuses on Hitler the *Agent* delivering propagandistic messages *(Act)* at mass rallies *(Agency)* within a setting of post-World War I economic and political turmoil *(Scene)* for the *Purpose* of uniting the Germans. He further reminds us that Hitler sought to achieve his goal of unification by adopting a method of identification based on false religious analogies, and a four step process. Observe in particular what Burke has to say about "projection device" or scapegoat technique. Still more vital is the persistent underlying presence of the notion of "motives."

A final point is also worth noting when examining the essay. Burke shows us that rhetorical criticism at its highest contains argument. The reader is pointedly led to the conclusion that Hitler's rhetoric, despite its effectiveness, is to be deplored because of its violation of the elements of responsibility.

Notes

1. "Dramatism," *The International Encyclopedia of the Social Sciences,* David L. Sills, ed., Vol. 7, pp. 445–451. Copyright 1968 by Macmillan Publishing Co., Inc.
2. Interview with Kenneth Burke, Washington, D.C., December 2, 1977. The interview was conducted by Larry Hugenberg.
3. "Dramatism," p. 445.
4. Lecture on "Non-Symbolic Motion and Symbolic Action," SCA Convention, Washington, D.C., December 1, 1977.
5. "Dramatism," p. 446.
6. "Dramatism," p. 446.
7. *Ibid.,* p. 446.
8. *Ibid.,* p. 447.
9. Lecture on "Non-Symbolic Motion and Symbolic Action."
10. *Ibid.*
11. "Dramatism," p. 450.
12. *Ibid.*
13. *Ibid.,* p. 451.
14. Kenneth Burke, "Mind, Body, and the Unconscious," in *Language as Symbolic Action* (Berkeley, California: University of California Press, 1966), p. 63. Also see "Definition of Man," in *ibid.,* pp. 3–9.
15. Lecture on "Non-Symbolic Motion and Symbolic Action."
16. *Ibid.,* pp. 13–15.
17. *Ibid.,* pp. 15–16.
18. *The Rhetoric of Religion* (Berkeley, 1970), pp. 14–15.
19. *Ibid.,* p. 16.
20. *Language as Symbolic Action,* p. 360.
21. *Ibid.,* p. 361.
22. *Ibid.,* p. 373.
23. "Terministic Screens," in *ibid.,* p. 46.
24. Kenneth Burke, *A Grammar of Motives and A Rhetoric of Motives* (Cleveland, Ohio, 1962), p. 567. Later in the same volume, Burke observes: "The use of symbols to induce action in beings that normally communicate by symbols is essentially realistic in the most practical and pragmatic sense of the term." p. 686.
25. *Ibid.,* p. 696.
26. Kenneth Burke, "Rhetoric and Poetics," in *Language as Symbolic Action,* p. 305.
27. *A Grammar of Motives and a Rhetoric of Motives,* p. 695.
28. *Language as Symbolic Action,* pp. 301–302. Also see *A Grammar of Motives and A Rhetoric of Motives,* pp. 682–690.
29. Kenneth Burke, "Colloquium on Walt Whitman," The Ohio State University, February 24, 1975. Malcolm Cowley was the other member of the Colloquium.
30. Kenneth Burke, "The Principle of Composition," in *Terms for Order* (Bloomington, Indiana, 1964), pp. 194–195. Also see essay on "Fact, Inference, and Proof in the Analysis of Literary Symbolism," in *ibid.,* pp. 145–172.

The Rhetoric of Hitler's "Battle"

The appearance of *Mein Kampf* in unexpurgated translation has called forth far too many vandalistic comments. There are other ways of burning books than on the pyre—and the favorite method of the hasty reviewer is to deprive himself and his readers by inattention. I maintain that it is thoroughly vandalistic for the reviewer to content himself with the mere inflicting of a few symbolic wounds upon this book and its author, of an intensity varying with the resources of the reviewer and the time at his disposal. Hitler's "Battle" is exasperating, even nauseating; yet the fact remains:

If the reviewer but knocks off a few adverse attitudinizings and calls it a day, with a guaranty in advance that his article will have a favorable reception among the decent members of our population, he is contributing more to our gratification than to our enlightenment.

Here is the testament of a who swung a great people into his wake. Let us watch it carefully; and let us watch it, not merely to discover some grounds for prophesying what political move is to follow Munich, and what move to follow that move, etc.; let us try also to discover what kind of "medicine" this medicine-man has concocted, that we may know, with greater accuracy, exactly what to guard against, if we are to forestall the concocting of similar medicine in America.

Already, in many quarters of our country, we are "beyond" the stage where we are being saved from Nazism by our *virtues*. And fascist integration is being staved off, rather, by the *conflicts among our vices*. Our vices cannot get together in a grand united front of prejudices; and the result of this frustration, if or until they succeed in surmounting it, speaks, as the Bible might say, "in the name of" democracy. Hitler found a panacea, a "cure for what ails you," a "snakeoil," that made such sinister unifying possible within his own nation. And he was helpful enough to put his cards face up on the table, that we might examine his hands. Let us, then, for God's sake, examine them. This book is the well of Nazi magic; crude magic, but effective. A people trained in pragmatism should want to inspect his magic.

1.

Every movement that would recruit its followers from among many discordant and divergent bands, must have some spot towards which all roads lead. Each man may get there in his own way, but it must be the one unifying center of reference for all. Hitler considered this matter carefully, and decided that this center must be not merely a centralizing hub of *ideas,* but a mecca geographically located, towards which all eyes could turn at the appointed hours of prayer (or, in this case, the appointed hours of prayer-in-reverse, the hours of vituperation). So he selected Munich, as the *materialization* of his unifying panacea. As he puts it:

The geo-political importance of a center of a movement cannot be overrated. Only the presence of such a center and of a place, bathed in the magic of a Mecca or a Rome, can at length give a movement that force

which is rooted in the inner unity and in the recognition of a hand that represents this unity.

If a movement must have its Rome, it must also have its devil. For as Russell pointed out years ago, an important ingredient of unity in the Middle Ages (an ingredient that long did its unifying work despite the many factors driving towards disunity) was the symbol of a *common enemy,* the Prince of Evil himself. Men who can unite on nothing else can unite on the basis of a foe shared by all. Hitler himself states the case very succinctly:

As a whole, and at all times, the efficiency of the truly national leader consists primarily in preventing the division of the attention of a people, and always in concentrating it on a single enemy. The more uniformly the fighting will of a people is put into action, the greater will be the magnetic force of the movement and the more powerful the impetus of the blow. It is part of the genius of a great leader to make adversaries of different fields appear as always belonging to one category only, because to weak and unstable characters the knowledge that there are various enemies will lead only too easily to incipient doubts as to their own cause.

As soon as the wavering masses find themselves confronted with too many enemies, objectivity at once steps in, and the question is raised whether actually all the others are wrong and their own nation or their own movement alone is right.

Also with this comes the first paralysis of their own strength. Therefore, a number of essentially different enemies must always be regarded as one in such a way that in the opinion of the mass of one's own adherents the war is being waged against one enemy alone. This strengthens the belief in one's own cause and increases one's bitterness against the attacker.

As everyone knows, this policy was exemplified in his selection of an "international" devil, the "international Jew" (the Prince was international, universal, "catholic"). This *materialization* of a religious pattern is, I think, one terrifically effective weapon of propaganda in a period where religion has been progressively weakened by many centuries of capitalist materialism. You need but go back to the sermonizing of centuries to be reminded that religion had a powerful enemy long before organized atheism came upon the scene. Religion is based upon the "prosperity of poverty," upon the use of ways for converting our sufferings and handicaps into a good—but capitalism is based upon the prosperity of acquisitions, the only scheme of value, in fact, by which its proliferating store of gadgets could be sold, insofar as captialism does not get so drastically in its own way that it can't sell its gadgets even after it has trained people to feel that human dignity, the "higher standard of living," could be attained only by such vast private accumulation.

So, we have, as unifying step No. 1, the international devil materialized, in the visible, point-to-able form of people with a certain kind of "blood, a burlesque of contemporary neo-positivism's ideal of meaning, which insists upon a *material* reference.

Once Hitler has thus essentialized his enemy, all "proof" henceforth is automatic. If you point out the enormous amount of evidence to show that the Jewish worker is at odds with the "international Jew stock exchange capitalist," Hitler replies with one hundred percent regularity: That is one more indication of the cunning with which the "Jewish plot" is being engineered. Or would you point to "Aryans"who do the same as his conspiratorial Jews? Very well; that is proof that the "Aryan" has been "seduced" by the Jew.

The sexual symbolism that runs through Hitler's book, lying in wait to draw upon the responses of contemporary sexual values is easily characterized: Germany in dispersion is the "dehorned Siegfried." The masses are "feminine." As such, they desire to be led by a dominating male. This male, as an orator, woos them—and, when he has won them, he commands them. The rival male, the villainous Jew, would on the contrary "seduce" them. If he succeeds, he poisons their blood by intermingling with them. Whereupon, by purely associative connections of ideas, we are moved into attacks upon syphilis, prostitution, incest, and other similar misfortunes, which are introduced as a kind of "musical" argument when he is on the subject of "blood-poisoning" by intermarriage or, in its "spiritual" equivalent, by the infection of "Jewish" ideas, such as democracy.[1]

The "medicinal" appeal of the Jew as scapegoat operates from another angle. The middle class contains, within the mind of each member, a duality: its members simultaneously have a cult of money and a detestation of this cult. When capitalism is going well, this conflict is left more or less in abeyance. But when capitalism is balked, it comes to the fore. Hence, there is "medicine" for the "Aryan" members of the middle class in the projective device of the scapegoat, whereby the "bad" features can be allocated to the "devil," and one can "respect himself" by a distinction between "good" capitalism and "bad" capitalism, with those of a different lodge being the vessels of the "bad" capitalism. It is doubtless the "relief" of this solution that spared Hitler the necessity of explaining just how the "Jewish plot" was to work out. Nowhere does this book, which is so full of war plans, make the slightest attempt to explain the steps whereby the triumph of "Jewish Bolshevism," which destroys *all* finance, will be the triumph of *"Jewish"* finance. Hitler well knows the point at which his "elucidations" should rely upon the lurid alone.

The question arises, in those trying to gauge Hitler: Was his selection of the Jew, as his unifying devil-function, a purely calculating act? Despite the quotation I have already given, I believe that it was *not*. The vigor with which he utilized it, I think, derives from a much more complex state of affairs. It seems that, when Hitler went to Vienna, in a state close to total poverty, he genuinely suffered. He lived among the impoverished; and he describes his misery at the spectacle. He was *sensitive* to it; and his way of manifesting his sensitiveness impresses me that he is, at this point, wholly genuine, as with his wincing at the broken family relationships caused by alcoholism, which he in turn relates to impoverishment. During this time he began his attempts at political theorizing; and his disturbance was considerably increased by the skill with which Marxists tied him into knots. One passage in particular gives you reason, reading between the lines, to believe that the dialecticians of the class struggle, in their skill at blasting his muddled speculations, put him into a state of uncertainty that was finally "solved" by rage:

> The more I argued with them, the more I got to know their dialectics. First, they counted on the ignorance of their adversary; then, when there was no way out, they themselves pretended stupidity. If all this was of no avail, they refused to understand or they changed the subject when driven into a corner; they brought up truisms, but they immediately transferred their acceptance to quite different subjects, and, if attacked again, they gave way and pretended to know nothing exactly. Wherever one attacked one of these prophets, one's hands seized slimy jelly; it slipped through one's fingers only to collect again in the next moment. If one smote one of them so thoroughly that, with the bystanders watching, he could but agree, and if one thus thought he had advanced at least one step, one was greatly astonished the following day. The Jew did not in the least remember the day before, he continued to talk in the same old strain as if nothing had happened, and if indignantly confronted, he pretended to be astonished and could not remember anything except that his assertions had already been proved true the day before.
>
> Often I was stunned.
>
> One did not know what to admire more: their glibness of tongue or their skill in lying.
>
> I gradually began to hate them.

At this point, I think, he is tracing the *spontaneous* of his anti-Semitism. He tells how, once he had discovered the "cause" of the misery about him, he could *confront it*. Where he had to avert his eyes, he could now *positively welcome* the scene. Here his drastic structure of *acceptance* was being formed. He tells of the "internal happiness" that descended upon him.

> This was the time in which the greatest change I was ever to experience took place in me.
>
> From a feeble cosmopolite I turned into a fanatical anti-Semite.

And thence we move, by one of those associational tricks which he brings forth at all strategic moments, into a vision of the end of the world—out of which in turn he emerges with his slogan: "I am acting in the sense of the Almighty Creator: *By warding off Jews I am fighting for the Lord's work*" (italics his).

He talks of this transition as a period of "double life," a struggle of "reason" and "reality" against his "heart."[2] It was as "bitter" as it was "blissful." And finally, it was "reason" that won! Which prompts us to note that those who attack Hitlerism as a cult of the irrational should amend their statements to this extent: irrational it is, but it is carried on under the *slogan* of "Reason." Similarly, his cult of war is developed "in the name of" humility, love, and peace. Judged on a quantitative basis, Hitler's book certainly falls under the classification of hate. Its venom is everywhere, its charity is sparse. But the rationalized family tree for the hate situates it in "Aryan love." Some deep-probing German poets, whose work adumbrated the Nazi movement, did gravitate towards thinking *in the name of war,* irrationality, and hate. But Hitler was not among them. After all, when it is so easy to draw a doctrine of war out of a doctrine of peace, why should the astute politician do otherwise, particularly when Hitler has slung together his doctrines, without the slightest effort at logical symmetry? Furthermore, Church thinking always got to its wars in Hitler's "sounder" manner; and the patterns of Hitler's thought are a bastardized or caricatured version of religious thought.

I spoke of Hitler's fury at the dialectics of those who opposed him when his structure was in the stage of scaffolding. From this we may move to another tremendously important aspect of his theory: his attack upon the *parliamentary*. For it is again, I submit, an important aspect of his medicine, in its function as medicine for him personally and as medicine for those who were later to identify themselves with him.

There is a "problem" in the parliament—and nowhere was this problem more acutely in evidence than in the pre-war Vienna that was to serve as Hitler's political schooling. For the parliament, at its best, is a "babel" of voices. There is the wrangle of men representing interests lying awkwardly on the bias across one another, sometimes opposing, sometimes vaguely divergent. Morton Prince's psychiatric study of "Miss Beauchamp," the case of a woman split into several sub-personalities at odds with one another, variously combining under hypnosis, and frequently in turmoil, is the allegory of a democracy fallen upon evil days. The parliament of the Habsburg Empire just prior to its collapse was an especially drastic instance of such disruption, such vocal diaspora, with movements that would reduce one to a disintegrated mass of fragments if he attempted to encompass the totality of its discordancies. So Hitler, suffering under the alienation of poverty and confusion, yearning for some integrative core, came to take this parliament as the basic symbol of all that he would move away from. He damned the tottering Habsburg Empire as a "State of Nationalities." The many conflicting voices of the spokesmen of the many political blocs arose from the fact that various separationist movements of a nationalistic sort had arisen within a Catholic imperial structure formed prior to the nationalistic emphasis and slowly breaking apart under its development. So, you had this babel of voices; and, by the method of associative mergers, *using ideas as imagery,* it became tied up, in the Hitler rhetoric, with "Babylon," Vienna as the city of poverty, prostitution, immorality, coalitions, half-measures, incest, democracy (i.e., majority rule leading to "lack of personal responsibility"), death, internationalism, seduction, and anything else of thumbsdown sort the associative enterprise cared to add on this side of the balance.

Hitler's way of treating the parliamentary babel, I am sorry to say, was at one important point not much different from that of the customary editorial in our own newspapers. Every conflict among the parliamentary spokesmen represents a corresponding conflict among the material interests of the groups for whom they are speaking. But Hitler did not discuss the babel from this angle. He discussed it on a purely *symptomatic* basis. The strategy of our orthodox press, in thus ridiculing the cacophonous verbal output of Congress, is obvious: by thus centering attack upon the *symptoms* of business conflict, as they reveal themselves on the dial of political wrangling, and leaving the underlying cause, they can gratify the very public they would otherwise alienate: namely, the businessmen who are the activating members of their reading public. Hitler, however, went them one better. For not only did he stress the purely *symptomatic* attack here, he proceeded to search for the "cause." And this "cause," of course, he derived from his medicine, his racial theory by which he could give a noneconomic interpretation of a phenomenon economically engendered.

Here again is where Hitler's corrupt use of religious patterns comes to the fore. Church thought, being primarily concerned with matters of the "personality," with problems of moral betterment, naturally, and I think rightly, stresses as a necessary feature, the act of will upon the part of the individual. Hence its resistance to a purely "environmental" account of human ills. Hence its emphasis upon the "person." Hence its proneness to seek a noneconomic explanation of economic phenomena. Hitler's proposal of a noneconomic "cause" for the disturbances thus had much to recommend it from this angle. And, as a matter of fact, it was Lueger's Christian-Social Party in Vienna that taught Hitler the tactics of tying up a program of social betterment with an anti-Semitic "unifier." The two parties that he carefully studied at that time were this Catholic faction and Schoenerer's Pan-German group. And his analysis of their attainments and shortcomings, from the standpoint of demagogic efficacy, is an extremely astute piece of work, revealing how carefully this man used the current situation in Vienna as an experimental laboratory for the maturing of his plans.

His unification device, we may summarize, had the following important features:

(1) Inborn dignity. In both religious and humanistic patterns of thought, a "natural born" dignity of man is stressed. And this categorical dignity is considered to be an attribute of *all* men, if they will but avail themselves of it, by right thinking and right living. But Hitler gives this ennobling attitude an ominous twist by his theories of race and nation, whereby the "Aryan" is elevated above all others by the innate endowment of his blood, while other "races," in particular Jews and Negroes, are innately inferior. This sinister secularized revision of Christian theology thus puts the sense of dignity upon a fighting basis, requiring the conquest of "inferior races." After the defeat of Germany in the World War, there were especially strong emotional needs that this compensatory doctrine of an *inborn* superiority could gratify.

(2) *Projection* device—the "curative" process that comes with the ability to hand over one's ills to a scapegoat, thereby getting purification by dissociation. This was especially medicinal, since the sense of frustration leads to a self-questioning. Hence if one can hand over his infirmities to a vessel, or "cause," outside the self, one can battle an external enemy instead of battling an enemy within. And the greater one's internal inadequacies, the greater amount of evils one can load upon the back of "the enemy." This device is furthermore given a semblance of reason because the individual properly realizes that he is not alone responsible for his condition. There *are* inimical factors in the scene itself. And he wants to have them "placed," preferably in a way that would require a minimum change in the ways of thinking to which he had been accustomed. This was especially appealing to the middle class, who were encouraged to feel that they could conduct their businesses without any basic change whatever, once the businessmen of a different "race" were eliminated.

(3) Symbolic rebirth—another aspect of the two features already noted. The projective device of the scapegoat, coupled with the Hitlerite doctrine of inborn racial superiority, provides its followers with a "positive" view of life. They can again get the feel of *moving forward,* towards a goal (a promissory feature of which Hitler makes much). In Hitler, as the group's prophet, such rebirth involved a symbolic change of lineage. Here, above all, we see Hitler giving a malign twist to a benign aspect of Christian thought. For whereas the Pope, in the familistic pattern of thought basic to the Church, stated that the Hebrew prophets were the *spiritual ancestors* of Christianity, Hitler uses this same mode of thinking in reverse. He renounces this "ancestry" in a "materialistic" way by voting himself and the members of his lodge a different "blood stream" from that of the Jews.

(4) Commercial use. Hitler obviously here had something to sell—and it was but a question of time until he sold it (i.e., got financial backers for his movement). For it provided a *noneconomic interpretation of economic ills.* As such, it served with maximum efficiency in deflecting the attention from the economic factors involved in modern conflict; hence by attacking "Jew finance" instead of *finance,* it could stimulate an enthusiastic movement that left "Aryan" finance in control.

Never once, throughout his book, does Hitler deviate from such a formula. Invariably, he ends his diatribes against contemporary economic ills by a shift into an insistence that we must get to the "true" cause, which is centered in "race." The "Aryan" is "constructive"; the Jew is "destructive"; and the "Aryan," to continue his *construction,* must *destroy* the Jewish *destruction.* The Aryan, as the vessel of *love,* must *hate* the Jewish *hate.*

Perhaps the most enterprising use of this method is in his chapter, "The Causes of the Collapse," where he refuses to consider Germany's plight as in any basic way connected with the consequences of war. Economic factors, he insists, are "only of second or even third importance," but "political, ethical-moral, as well as factors of blood and race, are of the first importance." His rhetorical steps are especially interesting here, in that he begins by seeming to flout the national susceptibilities: "The military defeat of the German people is not an undeserved catastrophe, but rather a deserved punishment by eternal retribution." He then proceeds to present the military collapse as but a "consequence of moral poisoning, visible to all, the consequence of a decrease in the instinct of self-preservation . . . which had already begun to undermine the foundations of the people and the Reich many years before." This moral decay derived from "a sin against the blood and the degradation of the race," so its innerness was an outerness after all: the Jew, who thereupon gets saddled with a vast amalgamation of evils, among them being capitalism, democracy, pacifism, journalism, poor housing, modernism, big cities, loss of religion, half measures, ill health, and weakness of the monarch.

2.

Hitler had here another important psychological ingredient to play upon. If a State is in economic collapse (and his theories, tentatively taking shape in the pre-war Vienna, were but developed with greater efficiency in postwar Munich), you cannot possibly derive dignity from economic stability. Dignity must come first—and if you possess it, and implement it, from it may follow its economic counterpart. There is much justice to this line of reasoning, so far as it goes. A people in collapse, suffering under economic frustration and the defeat of nationalistic aspirations with the very midrib of their integrative efforts (the army) in a state of dispersion, have little other than some "spiritual" basis to which they could refer their nationalistic dignity. Hence, the categorical dignity of superior race was a perfect recipe for the situation. It was "spiritual" in so far as it was "above" crude economic "interests," but it was materialized at the psychologically right spot in that "the enemy" was something you could see.

Furthermore, you had the desire for unity, such as a discussion of class conflict, on the basis of conflicting interest, could not satisfy. The yearning for unity is so great that people are always willing to meet you halfway if you will give it to them by fiat, by flat statement, regardless of the facts. Hence, Hitler consistently refused to consider internal political conflict on the basis of conflicting interests. Here again, he could draw upon a religious pattern, by insisting upon a *personal* statement of the relation between classes, the relation between leaders and followers, each group in its way fulfilling the same commonality of interests, as the soldiers and captains of an army share a common interest in victory. People so dislike the idea of internal division that, where there is a real internal division, their dislike can easily be turned against the man or group who would so much as *name* it, let alone proposing to act upon it. Their natural and justified resentment against internal division itself, is turned against the diagnostician who states it as a *fact*. This diagnostician, it is felt, is the *cause* of the disunity he named.

Cutting in from another angle, therefore, we note how two sets of equations were built up, with Hitler combining or coalescing *ideas* the way a poet combines or coalesces *images*. On the one side were the ideas, or images of disunity, centering in the parliamentary wrangle of the Habsburg "State of Nationalities." This was offered as the antithesis of German nationality, which was presented in the curative imagery of unity, focused upon the glories of the Prussian Reich, with its mecca now moved to "folkish" Vienna. For though Hitler at first attacked the many "folkish" movements, with their hankerings after a kind of Wagnerian mythology of Germanic origins, he subsequently took "folkish" as a basic word by which to conjure. It was, after all, another noneconomic basis of reference. At first we find him objecting to "those who drift about with the word 'folkish' on their caps," and asserting that "such a Babel of opinions cannot serve as the basis of a political fighting movement." But later he seems to have realized, as he well should, that its vagueness was a major point in its favor. So it was incorporated in the grand coalition of his ideational imagery, or imagistic ideation; and Chapter XI ends with the vision of "a State which represents not a mechanism of economic considerations and interest, alien to the people, but a folkish organism."

So, as against the disunity equations, already listed briefly in our discussions of his attacks upon the parliamentary, we get a contrary purifying set; the wrangle of the parliamentary, is to be stilled by the giving of *one* voice to the whole people, this to be the "inner voice" of Hitler, made uniform throughout the German boundaries, as leader and people were completely identified with each other. In sum: Hitler's inner voice, equals leader-people identification, equals unity, equals Reich, equals the mecca of Munich, equals plow, equals sword, equals work, equals war, equals army as mid-rib, equals responsibility (the personal responsibility of the absolute ruler), equals sacrifice, equals the theory of "German democracy" (the free popular choice of the leader, who then accepts the responsibility, and demands absolute obedience in exchange for his sacrifice), equals love (with the masses as feminine), equals idealism, equals obedience to nature, equals race, nation.[3]

And, of course, the two keystones of these opposite equations were Aryan "heroism" and "sacrifice" vs. Jewish "cunning" and "arrogance." Here again we get an astounding caricature of religious thought. For Hitler presents the concept of "Aryan" superiority in terms of nothing less than "Aryan humanity." This "humility" is extracted by a very delicate process that requires, I am afraid, considerable "good will" on the part of the reader who would follow it:

The Church, we may recall, had proclaimed an integral relationship between Divine Law and Natural Law. Natural Law was the expression of the Will of God. Thus, in the Middle Ages, it was a result of natural law, working through tradition, that some people were serfs and other people nobles. And every good member of the Church was "obedient" to this law. Everybody resigned himself to it. Hence, the serf resigned himself to his poverty, and the noble resigned himself to his riches. The monarch resigned himself to his position as representative of the people. And at times the Churchmen resigned themselves to the need of trying to represent the people

instead. And the pattern was made symmetrical by the consideration that each traditional "right" had its corresponding "obligations." Similarly, the Aryan doctrine is a doctrine of resignation, hence of humility. It is in accordance with the laws of nature that the "Aryan blood" is superior to all other bloods. Also, the "law of the survival of the fittest" is God's law, working through natural law. Hence, if the Aryan blood has been vested with the awful responsibility of its inborn superiority, the bearers of this "culture-creating" blood must resign themselves to struggle in behalf of its triumph. Otherwise, the laws of God have been disobeyed, with human decadence as a result. We must fight, he says, in order to "deserve to be alive." The Aryan "obeys" nature. It is only "Jewish arrogance" that thinks of "conquering" nature by democratic ideals of equality.

This picture has some nice distinctions worth following. The major virtue of the Aryan race was its instinct for self-preservation (in obedience to natural law). But the major vice of the Jew was his instinct for self-preservation; for, if he did not have this instinct to a maximum degree, he would not be the "perfect" enemy—that is, he wouldn't be strong enough to account for the ubiquitousness and omnipotence of his conspiracy in destroying the world to become its master.

How, then are we to distinguish between the benign instinct of self-preservation at the roots of Aryanism and the malign instinct of self-preservation at the roots of Semitism? We shall distinguish thus: The Aryan self-preservation is based upon *sacrifice,* the sacrifice of the individual to the group, hence, militarism, army discipline, and one big company union. But Jewish self-preservation is based upon individualism, which attains its cunning ends by the exploitation of peace. How, then, can such arrant individualists concoct the world-wide plot? By the help of their "herd instinct." By their sheer "herd instinct" individualists can band together for a common end. They have no real solidarity, but unite opportunistically to seduce the Aryan. Still, that brings up another technical problem. For we have been hearing much about the importance of the *person.* We have been told how, by the "law of the survival of the fittest," there is a sifting of people on the basis of their individual capacities. We even have a special chapter of pure Aryanism: "The Strong Man is Mightiest Alone." Hence, another distinction is necessary: The Jew represents individualism; the Aryan represents "super-individualism."

I had thought, when coming upon the "Strong Man is Mightiest Alone" chapter, that I was going to find Hitler at his weakest. Instead, I found him at his strongest. (I am not referring to *quality,* but to *demagogic effectiveness.*) For the chapter is not at all, as you might infer from the title, done in a "rise of Adolph Hitler" manner. Instead, it deals with the Nazis' gradual absorption of the many disrelated "folkish" groups. And it is managed throughout by means of a spontaneous identification between leader and people. Hence, the Strong Man's "aloneness" is presented as a *public* attribute, in terms of tactics for the struggle against the *Party's* dismemberment under the pressure of rival saviors. There is no explicit talk of Hitler at all. And it is simply *taken for granted* that *his* leadership is the norm, and all other leaderships the abnorm. There is no "philosophy of the superman," in Nietzschean cast. Instead, Hitler's blandishments so integrate leader and people, commingling them so inextricably, that the politician does not even present himself as candidate. Somehow, the battle is over already, the decision has been made. "German democracy" has chosen. And the deployments of politics are, you might say, the chartings of Hitler's private mind translated into the vocabulary of nationalistic events. He says *what he thought in terms of what parties did.*

Here, I think, we see the distinguishing quality of Hitler's method as an instrument of persuasion, with reference to the question whether Hitler is sincere or deliberate, whether his vision of the omnipotent conspirator has the drastic honesty of paranoia or the sheer shrewdness of a demagogue trained in *Realpolitik* of the Machiavellian sort.[4] Must we choose? Or may we not, rather, replace the "either—or" with a "both—and"? Have we

not by now offered grounds enough for our contention that Hitler's sinister powers of persuasion derive from the fact that he spontaneously evolved his "cure-all" in response to inner necessities?

3.

So much, then, was "spontaneous." It was further channelized into the anti-Semitic pattern by the incentives he derived from the Catholic Christian-Social Party in Vienna itself. Add, now, the step into *criticism.* Not criticism in the "parliamentary" sense of doubt, of hearkening to the opposition and attempting to mature a policy in the light of counter-policies; but the "unified" kind of criticism that simply seeks for conscious ways of making one's position more "efficient," more thoroughly itself. This is the kind of criticism at which Hitler was an adept. As a result, he could *spontaneously* turn to a scapegoat mechanism, and he could, by conscious planning, perfect the symmetry of the solution towards which he had spontaneously turned.

This is the meaning of Hitler's diatribes against "objectivity." "Objectivity" is interference-criticism. What Hitler wanted was the kind of criticism that would be a pure and simple coefficient of power, enabling him to go most effectively in the direction he had chosen. And the "inner voice" of which he speaks would henceforth dictate to him the greatest amount of realism, as regards the tactics of efficiency. For instance, having decided that the masses required certainty, and simple certainty, quite as he did himself, he later worked out a 25-point program as the platform of his National Socialist German Workers Party. And he resolutely refused to change one single item in this program, even for purposes of "improvement." He felt that the *fixity* of the platform was more important for propagandistic purposes than any revision of his slogans could be, even though the revisions in themselves had much to be said in their favor. The astounding thing is that, although such an attitude gave good cause to doubt the Hitlerite promises, he could explicitly explain his tactics in his book and still employ them without loss of effectiveness.[5]

Hitler also tells of his technique in speaking, once the Nazi party had become effectively organized, and had its army of guards, or bouncers, to maltreat hecklers and throw them from the hall. He would, he recounts, fill his speech with *provocative* remarks, whereat his bouncers would promptly swoop down in flying formation, with swinging fists, upon anyone whom these provocative remarks provoked to answer. The efficiency of Hitlerism is the efficiency of the one voice, implemented throughout a total organization. The trinity of government which he finally offers is: *popularity* of the leader, *force* to back the popularity, and popularity and force maintained together long enough to become backed by a *tradition*. Is such thinking spontaneous or deliberate—or is it not rather both?[6]

Freud has given us a succinct paragraph that bears upon the spontaneous aspect of Hitler's persecution mania. (A persecution mania, I should add, different from the pure product in that it was constructed of *public* materials; all the ingredients Hitler stirred into his brew were already rife, with spokesmen and bands of followers, before Hitler "took them over." Both the pre-war and post-war periods were dotted with saviors, of nationalistic and "folkish" cast. This proliferation was analogous to the swarm of barter schemes and currency-tinkering that burst loose upon the United States after the crash of 1929. Also, the commercial availability of Hitler's politics was, in a low sense of the term, a *public* qualification, removing it from the realm of "pure" paranoia, where the sufferer develops a wholly *private* structure of interpretations.)

I cite from *Totem and Taboo:*

Another trait in the attitude of primitive races towards their rulers recalls a mechanism which is universally present in mental disturbances, and is openly revealed in the so-called delusions of persecution. Here the importance of a particular person is extraordinarily heightened and his omnipotence is raised to the improbable in order to make it easier to attribute to him responsibility for everything painful which happens to the patient. Savages really do not act differently towards their rulers when they ascribe to them power over rain and shine, wind and weather, and then dethrone them or kill them because nature has disappointed their expectation of a good hunt or a ripe harvest. The prototype which the paranoiac reconstructs in his persecution mania is found in the relation of the child to its father. Such omnipotence is regularly attributed to the father in the imagination of the son, and distrust of the father has been shown to be intimately connected with the heightened esteem for him. When a paranoiac names a person of his acquaintance as his "persecutor," he thereby elevates him to the paternal succession and brings him under conditions which enable him to make him responsible for all the misfortune which he experiences.

I have already proposed by modifications of this account when discussing the symbolic change of lineage connected with Hitler's project of a "new way of life." Hitler is symbolically changing from the "spiritual ancestry" of the Hebrew prophets to the "superior" ancestry of "Aryanism," and has given his story a kind of bastardized modernization, along the lines of naturalistic, materialistic, "science," by his fiction of the special "bloodstream." He is voting himself a new identity (something contrary to the wrangles of the Habsburg Babylon, a soothing national unity); whereupon the vessels of the old identity become a "bad" father, i.e., the persecutor. It is not hard to see how, as his enmity becomes implemented by the backing of an organization, the role of "persecutor" is transformed into the role of persecuted, as he sets out with his like-minded band to "destroy the destroyer."

Were Hitler simply a poet, he might have written a work with an anti-Semitic turn, and let it go at that. But Hitler, who began as a student of painting, and later shifted to architecture, himself treats his political activities as an extension of his artistic ambitions.

He remained, in his own eyes, an "architect," building a "folkish" State that was to match, in political materials, the "folkish" architecture of Munich.

We might consider the matter this way (still trying, that is, to make precise the relationship between the drastically sincere and the deliberately scheming): Do we not know of many authors who seem, as they turn from the role of spokesman, to leave one room and enter another? Or who has not, on occasion, talked with a man in private conversation, and then been almost startled at the transformation this man undergoes when addressing a public audience? And I know persons today, who shift between the writing of items in the class of academic, philosophic speculation to items of political pamphleteering, and whose entire style and method changes with this change of role. In their academic manner, they are cautious, painstaking, eager to present all significant aspects of the case they are considering; but when they turn to political pamphleteering, they hammer forth with vituperation, they systematically misrepresent the position of their opponent, they go into a kind of political trance, in which, during its throes, they throb like a locomotive; and behold, a moment later, the mediumistic state is abandoned, and they are the most moderate of men.

Now, one will find few pages in Hitler that one could call "moderate." But there are many pages in which he gauges resistances and opportunities with the "rationality" of a skilled advertising man planning a new sales campaign. Politics, he says, must be sold like soap—and soap is not sold in a trance. But he did have the experience of his trance, in the "exaltation" of his anti-Semitism. And later, as he became a successful orator (he insists that revolutions are made solely by the power of the spoken word), he had this "poetic" role to draw upon, plus the great relief it provided as a way of slipping from the burden of logical analysis into the pure "spirtuality" of vituperative prophecy. What more natural, therefore, than that a man so insistent upon unification would integrate this mood with less ecstatic moments, particularly when he had found the

followers and the backers that put a price, both spiritual and material, upon such unification?

Once this happy "unity" is under way, one has a "logic" for the development of a method. One knows when to "spiritualize" a material issue, and when to "materialize" a spiritual one. Thus, when it is a matter of materialistic interests that cause a conflict between employer and employee, Hitler here disdainfully shifts to a high moral plane. He is "above" such low concerns. Everything becomes a matter of "sacrifices" and "personality." It becomes crass to treat employers and employees as different *classes* with a corresponding difference in the classification of their interests. Instead, relations between employer and employee must be on the "personal" basis of leader and follower, and "whatever may have a divisive effect in national life should be given a unifying effect through the army." When talking of national rivalries, however, he makes a very shrewd materialistic gauging of Britain and France with relation to Germany. France, he says, desires the "Balkanization of Germany" (i.e., its breakup into separationist movements—the "disunity" theme again) in order to maintain commercial hegemony on the continent. But Britain desires the "Balkanization of *Europe*," hence would favor a fairly strong and unified Germany, to use as a counterweight against French hegemony. *German* nationality, however, is unified by the *spiritual* quality of Aryanism (that would produce the national organization via the Party) while this in turn is *materialized* in the myth of the bloodstream.

What are we to learn from Hitler's book? For one thing, I believe that he has shown, to a very disturbing degree, the power of endless repetition. Every circular advertising a Nazi meeting had, at the bottom, two slogans: "Jews are not admitted" and "War victims free." And the substance of Nazi propaganda was built about these two "complementary" themes. He describes the power of spectacle; insists that mass meetings are a fundamental way of giving the individual the sense of being protectively surrounded by a movement, the sense of "community." He also drops one wise hint that I wish the American authorities would take in treating Nazi gatherings. He says that the presence of a special Nazi guard, in Nazi uniforms, was of great importance in building up, among the followers, a tendency to place the center of authority in the Nazi party. I believe that we should take him at his word here, but use the advice in reverse, by insisting that, where Nazi meetings are to be permitted, they be policed by the authorities alone, and that uniformed Nazi guards to enforce the law be prohibited.

And is it possible that an equally important feature of appeal was not so much in the repetitiousness per se, but in fact that, by means of it, Hitler provided a "world view" for people who had previously seen the world but piece meal? Did not much of his lure derive, once more, from the *bad* filling of a *good* need? Are not those who insist upon a purely *planless* working of the market asking people to accept far too slovenly a scheme of human purpose, a slovenly scheme that can be accepted so long as it operates with a fair degree of satisfaction, but becomes abhorrent to the victims of its disarray? Are they not then psychologically ready for a rationale, *any* rationale, if it but offer them some specious "universal" explanation? Hence, I doubt whether the appeal was in the sloganizing element alone (particularly as even slogans can only be hammered home, in speech after speech, and two or three hours at a stretch, by endless variations on the themes). And Hitler himself somewhat justifies my interpretation by laying so much stress upon the *half-measures* of the middle-class politicians, and the contrasting *certainty* of his own methods. He was not offering people a *rival* world view; rather, he was offering a world view to people who had no other to pit against it.

As for the basic Nazi trick: the "curative" unification by a fictitious devil-function, gradually made convincing by the sloganizing repetitiousness of standard advertising technique—the opposition must be as unwearying in the attack upon it. It may well be that people, in their human frailty, require an enemy as well as a goal. Very well: Hitlerism itself

has provided us with such an enemy—and the clear example of its operation is guaranty that we have, in Hitler and all he stands for, no purely fictitious "devil-function" made to look like a world menace by rhetorical blandishments, but a reality whose ominousness is clarified by the record of its conduct to date. In selecting his brand of doctrine as our "scapegoat," and in tracking down its equivalents in America, we shall be at the very center of accuracy. The Nazis themselves have made the task of clarification easier. Add to them Japan and Italy, and you have *case histories* of fascism for those who might find it more difficult to approach an understanding of its imperialistic drives by a vigorously economic explanation.

But above all, I believe, we must make it apparent that Hitler appeals by relying upon a bastardization of fundamentally religious patterns of thought. In this, if properly presented, there is no slight to religion. There is nothing in religion proper that requires a fascist state. There is much in religion, when misused, that does lead to a fascist state. There is a Latin proverb, *Corruptio optimi pessima*, "the corruption of the best is the worst." And it is the corruptors of religion who are a major menace to the world today in giving the profound patterns of religious thought a crude and sinister distortion.

Our job, then, our anti-Hitler Battle, is to find all available ways of making the Hitlerite distortions of religion apparent, in order that politicians of his kind in America are unable to perform a similar swindle. The desire for unity is genuine and admirable. The desire for national unity, in the present state of the world, is genuine and admirable. But this unity, if attained on a deceptive basis, by emotional trickeries that shift our criticism from the accurate locus of our trouble, is no unity at all. For, even if we are among those who happen to be "Aryans," we solve no problems even for ourselves by such solutions, since the factors pressing towards calamity remain. Thus, in Germany, after all the upheaval, we see nothing beyond a drive for ever more and more upheaval, precisely because the "new way of life" was no new way, but the dismally oldest way of sheer deception—hence, after all the "change," the factors driving towards unrest are left intact, and even strengthened. True, the Germans had the resentment of a lost war to increase their susceptibility to Hitler's rhetoric. But in a wider sense, it has repeatedly been observed, the whole world lost the war—and the accumulating ills of the capitalist order were but accelerated in their movements toward confusion. Hence, here too there are the resentments that go with frustration of men's ability to work and earn. At that point a certain kind of industrial or financial monopolist may, annoyed by the contrary voices of our parliament, wish for the momentary peace of one voice, amplified by social organizations, with all the others not merely quieted but given the quietus. So he might, under Nazi promptings, be tempted to back a group of gangsters who, on becoming the political rulers of the state, would protect him against the necessary demands of the workers. His gangsters, then, would be his insurance against his workers. But who would be his insurance against his gangsters?

Kenneth Burke

Notes

1. Hitler also strongly insists upon the total identification between leader and people. Thus, in wooing the people, he would in a roundabout way be wooing himself. The thought might suggest how the Führer, dominating the feminine masses by his diction, would have an incentive to remain unmarried.
2. Other aspects of the career symbolism: Hitler's book begins "Today I consider it my good fortune that Fate designated Braunau on the Inn as the place of my birth. For this small town is situated on the border between those two German States, the reunion of which seems, at least to us of the younger generation, a task to be furthered with every means our lives long," an indication of his "transitional" mind, what Wordsworth might have called the "borderer." He neglects to give the date of his birth, 1889, which is supplied by the editors. Again there is a certain "correctness" here, as Hitler was not "born" until many years later—but he does give the exact date of his war wounds, which were indeed formative. During his early years in Vienna and Munich, he foregoes protest, on the grounds that he is "nameless." And when his party is

finally organized and effective, he stresses the fact that his "nameless" period is over (i.e., he has shaped himself an identity). When reading in an earlier passage of his book some generalizations to the effect that one should not crystallize his political views until he is thirty, I made a note: "See what Hitler does at thirty." I felt sure that, though such generalizations may be dubious as applied to people as a whole, they must, given the Hitler type of mind (with his complete identification between himself and his followers), be valid statements about himself. One should do what he did. The hunch was verified: about the age of thirty Hitler, in a group of seven, began working with the party that was to conquer Germany. I trace these steps particularly because I believe that the orator who has a strong sense of his own "rebirth" has this to draw upon when persuading his audiences that he is offering them the way to a "new life." However, I see no categorical objection to this attitude; its menace derives solely from the values in which it is exemplified. They may be wholesome or unwholesome. If they are unwholesome, but backed by conviction, the basic sincerity of the conviction acts as a sound virtue to reinforce a vice—and this combination is the most disastrous one that a people can encounter in a demagogue.

3. One could carry out the equations further, on both the disunity and unity side. In the aesthetic field, for instance, we have expressionism on the thumbsdown side, as against aesthetic hygiene on the thumbs-up side. This again is a particularly ironic moment in Hitler's strategy. For the expressionist movement was unquestionably a symptom of unhealthiness. It reflected the increasing alienation that went with the movement towards world war and the disorganization after the world war. It was "lost," vague in identity, a drastically accurate reflection of the response to material confusion, a pathetic attempt by sincere artists to make their wretchedness bearable at least to the extent that comes of giving it expression. And it attained its height during the period of wild inflation, when the capitalist world, which bases its morality of work and savings upon the soundness of its money structure, had this last prop of stability removed. The anguish, in short, reflected precisely the kind of disruption that made people ripe for a Hitler. It was the antecedent in a phrase of which Hitlerism was the consequent. But by thundering against the symptom he could gain persuasiveness, though attacking the very foreshadowing of himself.

4. I should not want to use the word "Machiavellian," however, without offering a kind of apology to Machiavelli. It seems to me that Machiavelli's *Prince* has more to be said in extenuation than is usually said of it. Machiavelli's strategy, as I see it, was something like this: He accepted the values of the Renaissance rule as a fact. That is: whether you like these values or not, they were there and operating, and it was useless to try persuading the ambitious ruler to adopt other values, such as those of the Church. These men believed in the cult of material power, and they had

the power to implement their beliefs. With so much as "the given," could anything in the way of benefits for the people be salvaged? Machiavelli evolved a typical "Machiavellian argument in favor of popular benefits, on the basis of the prince's own scheme of values. That is: the ruler, to attain the maximum strength, requires the backing of the populace. That this backing be as effective as possible, the populace should be made as strong as possible. And that the populace be as strong as possible, they should be well treated. Their gratitude would further repay itself in the form of increased loyalty. It was Machiavelli's hope that, for this roundabout project, he would be rewarded with a well-paying office in the prince's administrative bureaucracy.

5. On this point Hitler reasons as follows: "Here, too, one can learn from the Catholic Church. Although its structure of doctrines in many instances collides, quite unnecessarily, with exact science and research, yet it is unwilling to sacrifice even one little syllable of its dogmas. It has rightly recognized that its resistibility does not lie in a character of creed. Today, therefore, the Catholic Church stands firmer than ever. One can prophesy that in the same measure in which the appearances flee, the Church itself, as the resting pole in the flight of appearances, will gain more and more blind adherence."

6. Hitler also paid great attention to the conditions under which political oratory is most effective. He sums up thus:

"All these cases involve encroachments upon man's freedom of will. This applies, of course, most of all to meetings to which people with a contrary orientation of will are coming, and who now have to be won for new intentions. It seems that in the morning and even during the day men's will power revolts with highest energy against an attempt at being forced under another's will and another's opinion. In the evening, however, they succumb more easily to the dominating force of a stronger will. For truly every such meeting presents a wrestling match between two opposed forces. The superior oratorical talent of a domineering apostolic nature will now succeed more easily in winning for the new will people who themselves have in turn experienced a weakening of their force of resistance in the most natural way, than people who still have full command of the energies of their minds and their will power.

"The same purpose serves also the artificially created and yet mysterious dusk of the Catholic churches, the burning candles, incense, censers, etc."

The essay on "The Rhetoric of Hitler's Battle" shows how the rhetorical theory and practice of Adolph Hitler may be criticized from a dramatistic perspective. Using the text of *Mein Kampf* as his starting point, Burke was able to discover Hitler's recurring themes and "universe of discourse;" and to pinpoint the interaction among the pentadic ratios. To see further the utility of the pentad as a method of rhetorical criticism, let us examine briefly how it may be applied to a communication event involving numerous agents. The event was the celebrated "March on Washington, D.C.," August 28, 1963. Here is an ouline sketching a procedure that might be followed:

I. Act
   A. Civil Rights demonstration in Washington, D.C., August 28, 1963.
   B. The marching of 200,000 demonstrators who had come from all over the country.

II. Agents
   A. Martin Luther King, Jr. and other Civil Rights leaders.
   B. Representative liberal members from Congress, including Senator Hubert Humphrey.

III. Agency
   A. Music
      1. Songs by Peter, Paul and Mary; Marian Anderson; Bob Dylan, etc.
      2. Demonstrators singing, "We Shall Overcome."
   B. Unison Chants: "1, 2, 3 Freedom!"
   C. Martin Luther King's "I Have a Dream Speech."
   D. Channeling of the Act through the mass media.

IV. Scene
   A. General political and social unrest caused by racial discrimination.
   B. Centennial Anniversary of the Emancipation Proclamation.
   C. Washington, D.C. natives and tourists encouraged to stay at home or in hotels to avoid possible incidents.
   D. The setting at the Monument Grounds and Lincoln Memorial.

V. Purpose
   A. To heighten the American consciousness regarding human rights.

B. To secure passage of pending civil rights legislation.

In this outline we have preferred to call the Act the demonstration itself. The flexibility of the pentad, however, would permit numerous other possibilities for labeling the Act. The "I Have a Dream Speech," for example, could be entitled the Act, thereby making King the Agent and the speech content and style the Agency. The Scene and Purpose could remain unchanged; or the Scene could be narrowed in scope.

Burke, as we can see from the discussion in this chapter, is a many-faceted theorist who combines important elements of "old" and "new" rhetoric. His remarkable grasp of the literature of the humanities and the social and behavioral sciences, reinforced by a talent for penetrating critical insights, has placed him far above his contemporaries. You may recall that in 1952, Marie Nichols concluded her essay on Burke with these words: ". . . he has become the most profound student of rhetoric now writing in America." It is an important tribute to Burke that Dr. Nichols, twenty-five years later, said to us in Detroit in the Spring of 1977, that Burke, in her opninion, is still the greatest rhetorician and critic in America today.

19

Rhetoric as Motive: Secular and Religious Conversion

Patiently, the evangelist—that person who casts his persuasive charms in hopes of gaining adherents to his special gospel—relentlessly stalks his prey through various media. Skillfully he works his magic highlighting his message of utopia. And so, multifarious political, economic, social, psychological, philosophical, and religious nuggets of "truth" are hurled toward the unsuspecting (but often eager) audience. For the professional evangelist seeking social change, the rewards are considerable. Not surprisingly, then, the rhetoric of conversion seems to be a predominant form of discourse especially in times of uncertainty and political change.

In the past, the rhetoric of conversion not only has marked the dramatic rise of such Protestant divines as Billy Graham, Oral Roberts, and Robert Schuller, but it has also been a generating force for numerous spokespersons representing varied disciplines who have assumed the role of secular evangelist thereby seeking converts. Richard Simmons' *Never-Say-Diet Book*, Betty Friedan's *Feminine Mystique*, Norman Vincent Peale's *Dynamic Imaging*, Dale Carnegie's *How To Win Friends and Influence People*, Thomas Harris' *I'm OK—You're OK*, and Carlos Castaneda's *Journey to Ixtlan* represent only a few evangelists promising a fresh outlook on life. Other evangelists espouse drugs, transcendental meditation, sensitivity training, Yoga, hypnotism saying in effect: "Follow me and you will find happiness and meaning."[1]

Admittedly, conversions and mystical experiences have been reported in most cultures throughout history. A *New York Times* article discusses mystical experiences as "altered states of consciousness" frequently appearing in civilizations.

But wherever the place and whatever the trigger and whoever the person, there run through the accounts of such interludes certain common themes—joy, light, peace, fire, warmth, unity, certainty, confidence, rebirth. Easterner and Westerner . . . all seem to report a virtually identical experience—intense, overpowering joy which seemed literally to lift them out of themselves.

No one with any familiarity with history or anthropology or psychology can deny that such events occur. They are a form of "altered states of consciousness"—to use the current approved phrase—something like intoxication or delirium or a hypnotic trance but different in intensity, their joyfulness and their "lifting out" dimension.[2]

We are all familiar with such phenomena. But, what really happens to individuals in conversion or mystical experience situations? Furthermore, what are the characteristics and dynamics of a rhetoric of conversion? Addressing these issues, our inquiry begins with a psychological exploration of conversion from the listener's perspective.

Milton Rokeach offers a psychoanalytic framework stressing the interaction of the self-concept, attitudes, belief and value systems which is helpful in explaining the dynamics operating in conversion experiences. First, every person possesses attitudes or "enduring organizations of beliefs about an object or situation predisposing one to respond in some preferential manner."[3] Also, everyone approaches life through personal "belief systems" which "represent all the beliefs, sets, expectancies, hypotheses, conscious or unconscious, that a person at a given time accepts as *true* of the world he lives in."[4] Finally, all individuals operate from value systems. According to Rokeach, a value is "an enduring belief that a specific mode of conduct or end-state of existence is personally or socially preferable to an opposite or converse mode of conduct or end-state of existence."[5] Furthermore, attitudes, values, and beliefs are "functionally interconnected" and thereby form a complex psychological structure which governs thinking and actions. For example, the person who embraces the value of *honesty* postures his life accordingly, firmly believing that honesty is the best mode of conduct possible for him. When it comes time to complete the yearly federal income tax report, this individual will complete his form in an accurate, fair, and honest manner. So, the value of honesty affects his attitude toward responding to the Internal Revenue System. Fundamental to his value and attitude of honesty is the firm *belief* that honesty in human relationships is the only way to function in society. Honest behavior is *true* for this individual.

However, beliefs, attitudes, and values are only part of the story Rokeach further argues that yet another psychological construct deserves attention: the self-concept—a psychological component which lies at the heart of belief systems. Of this notion, Rokeach observes:

Self-conceptions include all one's cognitions, conscious and unconscious, about one's physical image; intellectual and moral abilities and weaknesses; socioeconomic position in society; national, regional, ethnic, racial and religious identity; the sexual, generational, occupational, marital, and parental roles that one plays in society; and how well or poorly one plays such roles.[6]

The self-concept is the *center* of the belief system. "All such self-cognitions can reasonably be represented at the innermost core of the total belief system, and all remaining beliefs, attitudes, and values can be conceived of as functionally organized around this innermost core."[7] Thus, there is an interdependence between self-concept and belief system— each supports the other in a complementary relationship. Rokeach concludes stating the ultimate purpose of an individual's belief system is "to maintain and enhance one's total conception of oneself."[8]

Now, how does one conceptualize *change* within Rokeach's system? Since the self-concept and belief system represent a "functionally interconnected *system*," a change in any one part should necessitate changes in other components. This is a fundamental principle of systems theory. So, a change in the individual's self-concept necessarily requires an adjustment in the belief system. Or, a change in the belief system requires a corresponding change in the self-concept. The parts are interdependent.

In psychological terms, the evangelist attempts to change the potential convert's belief system and/or self-concept. Such a transformation must be far reaching and long-term to be labeled a successful conversion experience. Although conversion may be induced by psychedelic drugs, therapy, brainwashing, surgery, or hypnosis,[9] this essay is concerned only with *rhetorically induced conversion*. We are interested in those conversions triggered by a rhetor who has developed a genre of discourse we shall call "conversion rhetoric." This study, then, represents a preliminary statement on the rhetoric of conversion, the role of the evangelist in this genre, and the phenomenon of exigency marking. In brief, how does the evangelist rhetorically induce conversion wherein an individual's self-concept and belief-value-attitude system are significantly altered?

In 1965 Edwin Black in his award-winning volume *Rhetorical Criticism* set forth a provocative challenge to contemporary rhetoricians. Labeling most rhetorical critics "neo-

Aristotelians" excessively devoted to the element of logos or rationality, he urged communication scholars to recognize the power of pathos as a legitimate means of altering men's minds through an emotional experience that culminates in conversion.[10] Six years later Wayne Booth of the University of Chicago told the delegates to the Wingspread Conference on Rhetoric that communication theorists should turn "to that vast neglected area of rhetoric, the rhetoric of 'conversion,' of transformation—the rhetoric with the effect . . . of overturning personalities and changing total allegiances. . . ."[11]

Conversion rhetoric, as understood in this essay, is that discourse issued by an evangelist-source which leads to a dramatic modification of a listener's self-concept, attitudes, beliefs, values, and actions. It has its roots in the premise that a convert's life is dramatically changed. In this regard, conversion goes far beyond the transitory mystical experience stage which may last for seconds, minutes, hours, or perhaps days. In theological perspective, conversion is viewed as a complete reorientation of one's existence. "The Biblical emphasis is thus not upon a subjective psychological experience, but upon an objective change in man. . . . True turning to God follows upon repentance and belief, and it leads not only to an observable new way of life, but to a spiritual transformation as well. . . ."[12]

The disciplines of philosophy, psychology, and sociology relate a similar insight to the meaning of conversion. Plato, doubtless one of the earliest writers who dealt with this theme, summarizes in his *Republic* the words of Socrates to Glaucon: "The conversion of the soul is the turning round the eye from darkness to light."[13] In a comparable vein Abraham Maslow speaks of conversion as a peak experience having long-range effects,[14] and the Langs note: "A conversion is more than opinion change"; it is "a complete turnabout in central values that is fairly permanent."[15] Such thinking can easily be transferred into the political realm, for the political evangelist also calls for repentance and a change in life styles—a reorientation epitomizing a transformation of one's value system.

Documented cases of conversion experiences abound in religious, psychological, sociological, and anthropological literature. History has revealed that individuals, groups, and even nations have undergone radical conversions. Those of the Christian faith are familiar with the dramatic conversions of Saul of Tarsus, St. Augustine of Hippo, John Wesley, Cardinal Newman, and Billy Sunday. They are similarly aware of how these evangelists, in turn, helped convert thousands of troubled souls to a new gospel of life. Some of the most authentic testimonials on the power of conversion may be found in William James' *Varieties of Religious Experience,* first published in 1902. From the works of David Brainerd, Jonathan Edwards, Charles G. Finney, and John Wesley—as well as those of lesser known religious commentators—James draws a series of eyewitness testimonies to demonstrate his thesis that "man's liability to sudden and complete conversion" is "one of his most curious peculiarities."[16]

Nor is Christianity the only religious model that focuses on conversion. The Soka Gakkai, a Buddist sect, has as its principal goal "world conversion." Consequently, its adherents go to almost any lengths to secure changes in attitude and behavior.[17] The Black Muslims, and their counterparts in the Islam faith, likewise have observed that conversion is central to their philosophy. In his classic study entitled *The Black Muslim in America,* C. Eric Lincoln notes:

To clinch the conversion of those believers who approach the Movement in simple curiosity, Muhammed offers the lure of personal rebirth. The true believer who becomes a Muslim casts off at last his old self and takes on a new identity. He changes his name, his religion, his homeland, his "natural" language, his moral and cultural values, his very purpose in living. He is no longer a Negro, so long despised by the white man that he has come almost to despise himself. Now he is a Black Man—divine, ruler of the universe, different only in degree from Allah himself. He is no longer discontent and baffled, harried by social obloquy and a gnawing sense of personal inadequacy. Now he is a Muslim, bearing in himself the power of the Black Nation and its glorious destiny. . . .[18]

Malcolm X confirms this view by telling of his conversion in his *Autobiography*.[19]

If it is true, as Gordon Allport suggests, that "no subject within the psychology of religion has been more extensively studied than conversion,"[20] it is equally evident that conversion also functions as a vital force in secular areas of society. Historical accounts detail the rapid rise of Communism in the decade following World War II. Millions of Russians and Chinese, under the galvanic leadership of Lenin and Mao, turned away from what they had come to believe was a decadent capitalism and with emotional fervor embraced a new revolutionary form of socialism. One of the principal characteristics of all social and political movements, it would appear, is the fact that they come into existence only after a charismatic leader, who later serves as an evangelist, is converted.

Conversions may, as in the case of religious experiences, be inspired primarily by an espoused supernatural agent; or they may occur in secular fields as the handiwork of natural agents called evangelists often operating in social movements. Whatever agent is perceived as the motivating cause, according to James, the transcending experience of the converted individual becomes his reality.[21] In this study, we are concerned with the role of the earthly evangelist and his/her part in the total conversion process. Accordingly, we suspect that evangelists often play vital roles in the conversion process—a process in which there are three stages: (1) awareness of a problem; (2) repentance and acceptance or the decision stage; and (3) indoctrination or the education stage. A consideration of these steps ensues.

First, conversion can occur only when an individual realizes that something is amiss in his life and that his existence falls short of expectations. The potential convert, suggests James, reaches a point whereby he is overwhelmed by a feeling of "incompleteness and imperfection; brooding, depression, morbid introspection, and a sense of sin; anxiety about the hereafter; distress over doubts, and the like."[22] Brown agrees, "Obviously, conversion is based upon mental conflict and a feeling of inadequacy, otherwise there would be no point in changing one's beliefs."[23]

This initial stage demands a perceptive and astute evangelist whose rhetorical task is to *make real* a problem in the lives of his congregation or target audience. In essence, the evangelist must be first a rhetorician. As an initial step, then, the evangelist must employ a rhetorical strategy capable of establishing an exigency in the minds of the potential converts. The procedure here does not always adhere to the model described by Bitzer in his essay on the "rhetorical situation."[24] For instead of developing a message as a necessary response to a prior exigency, the discourse may itself *create* the *need* for action. When William Jennings Bryan came out of the prairies of Nebraska in 1896 to capture the Democratic presidential nomination, he did so, in part, by creating the urgent belief that unless the silver standard supplanted the "cross of gold" America's economic system may not survive. One might argue that the debt-burdened farmer constituted the exigency to which the silver was offered as an answer. Still, however, Bryan's rhetorical strategy was to establish this same exigency in other segments of American society. This rhetorical transaction established in the minds of the auditors a keen awareness of societal and personal needs that had *not yet been felt* or interpreted as an overriding exigency in the thinking of most Americans.

Briefly, the evangelist must rhetorically create a symbolic world or fantasy with a built-in tension characterized by a sense of urgency which in turn demands a final and immediate action from an audience. Thus, the evangelist must weave a symbolic reality dominated by a major exigency which consequently requires action from a group of listeners characteristically termed the "congregation." Furthermore, the exigency in this symbolic world may be variously portrayed. For example, the evangelist may point out an *already existing* exigency—dwelling on a sense of urgency and making the exigency the central and ultimate concern of the congregation. Or, the evangelist may make real and urgent an exigency which was/is physically nonexistent; that is, the exigency may, in fact, be *created* by the evangelist. In either case, the evangelist must vividly make an exigency the most demanding factor in the individual lives of the congregation. Only then can the actual and personal decision-making phenomenon occur. We call this rhetorical process of establishing the exigency as real and ultimate: exigency *marking*—a task every successful evangelist must complete.

How, one might ask, does the evangelist successfully mark an exigency? Since effective persuasion is audience or listener centered, the answer to the above query will depend on the nature of the audience, as well as the particular situation and cultural context embracing the rhetorical act. Generally, the evangelist will utilize a variety of nonartistic proofs—especially vivid testimony. Coupled with concrete and forceful language that has the power to evoke images within the listeners and a mixture of artistic proofs—especially heavy doses of pathos—the evangelist goes about his work. However, the central rhetorical ingredient that pulls his persuasive efforts together is the evangelist's charisma or that "certain quality of an individual personality by virtue of which he is considered extraordinary and treated as endowed with supernatural, superhuman, or at least specifically exceptional powers or qualities."[25] The skillful evangelist will spell-bind the listener with his charisma. He will exude power and hence charm the congregation convincing them of the urgency of the present time and the ultimacy of the exigency. This intangible component of ethos is essential to the conversion process.

Psycho-dynamically, exigency marking will create a *contradiction* within an individual's belief system or self-concept. When a belief, value, or attitude is demonstrated to be incongruent with the self-image the evangelist has made major progress. In so doing, an evangelist may point out an unconscious contradiction within the individual's belief system or

he may make a conscious contradiction more real and urgent thereby bringing it into the individual's level of awareness or threshold.

According to Rokeach, a contradiction in the belief system creates a psychological imbalance or tension which produces a feeling of self-dissatisfaction—a state which requires resolution. Such a psychological resolution necessitates a change or adjustment in either the individual's belief system or self-concept or both. "Contradictions are resolved so that self-conceptions will, at the least, be maintained and, if at all possible, enhanced."[26] The effective evangelist will direct the resolution process so that the end product will not only enhance the convert's self-conception, but also will fit into the symbolic reality or cosmology being espoused by the rhetor thereby enhancing the evangelist's cause.

Once the exigency is established, the evangelist must lead the individual to the decision point of repentance and the acceptance of the "true" gospel. This is the second stage of the conversion process. Here the auditor is made to believe that the decision rests with him, but is reminded that salutary results will ensue from positive action. It is only after the hearer is made aware or realizes himself that his life is less than satisfactory that repentance and acceptance can take place. In this stage the individual rejects the old way while embracing the new. The act of decision, then, is an act of repentance which is the first step toward the modification of the created exigency. Furthermore, it should be noted that this step usually occurs within a community context featuring social norms. "When a person breaks down during mystical contemplation or is broken down in mass orgiastic rallies," argues Sargant, "the faith suddenly created . . . tends to conform to the beliefs and faith of the group or individual then in close contact with the person concerned, and who have often brought the sudden conversion and attainment of a new faith."[27] The role played by the congregation or community in the conversion process cannot be overemphasized. Since the congregation is itself comprised of converts, the neophyte can easily identify with them. In turn, the community provides comfort, courage, and social support for its members. The process, then, where the recent convert adopts the values, beliefs, and behavioral patterns demanded by the exigency is initiated by the evangelist, but instilled and maintained partly by the congregation of believers.

In brief, the decision stage is that step in the process wherein the tension and dissatisfaction are resolved. Accordingly, the convert's belief system and self-concept are again made congruent and harmonious. If the evangelist is successful, this resolution or adjustment behavior enhances the convert's self-image while simultaneously embracing the symbolic world espoused by the rhetor. Of course the establishment of an exigency is only the first stage in conversion. The resolution of the exigency in *favor* of the evangelist is the second and perhaps most difficult stage. Obviously, the resolution phase can take many directions. To make the convert choose in favor of the evangelist's resolution is the crux of the rhetorical problem. In sum, the evangelist must make the potential convert perceive only one *favorable* choice—that choice being the evangelist's "answer" or "gospel."

Once the convert selects the gospel of a particular group he is taught the value system and world view of that group. This is designated the stage of indoctrination. Its purpose is to consolidate the gains and to provide a deterrent to possible "backsliding." George Sweazy, an author of Christian evangelism handbooks, provides the following perspective on the significance of indoctrination as it relates to religious conversion.

The most encouraging feature of modern evangelism is the increased attention it is giving to better ways of receiving, training, and holding those who join the Church. This is long overdue. The most important part of evangelism comes after decisions have been made. The greatest weakness of the evangelism of the past was that it stopped too soon.[28]

Such a perspective is similarly applicable to forms of evangelism other than religious.

The last step, then, is the attempt to indoctrinate or teach. The aim here is to gain permanent adherence for the newly acquired beliefs and values. This, in the opinion of the evangelist, will constitute a form of preventive religion or medicine. Thus, the convert's belief system and self-concept are consolidated *within* the evangelist's symbolic reality—a reality which now guides the convert's thoughts and actions accordingly.

Ehninger summarizes the dynamics of this indoctrination stage when he discusses the assumptions underlying the speech act of "instructing." First, "the person who seriously seeks or who accepts instructions has, in principle, contracted in advance to perform as directed." Secondly, "implicit in the concept of instructing is the additional assumption that if the hearer does adhere to the means described, the desired goal will in fact be reached."[29]

It should be noted that these three phases in rhetor-induced conversion are *usually* best understood when placed in perspective of a campaign or crusade rather than a one time persuasive appeal. This is true when the exigency marking proves to be challenging—especially when the evangelist must create the exigency. The rhetoric of conversion, then, is usually a campaign rhetoric which necessitates several attempts at persuasive discourse. Converts are rarely the product of an encounter with a single message. It is only after being exposed to a campaign of such discourse that the individual is in a position to make his "decision" and become converted. We agree with Fotheringham who describes a persuasive campaign as "a structured sequence of efforts to achieve adoption, continuance, deterrence, or discontinuance—rather than as a one-shot effort. Effects established in an earlier phase of the campaign are instrumental to the development of subsequent effects. The first effort to persuade others commonly accomplishes only part of the job; that part, however, is necessary for the success of the next phase and for the ultimate goal."[30] Furthermore, the phases characteristic of rhetor-induced conversion within the campaign process may indeed be carried out by several individuals each performing persuasive tasks in each of the three phases. So, one evangelist may mark the exigency and another indoctrinate, and so forth. The division of labor here requires a skillful coordination of effort on the part of those evangelists involved. However, such a separation of function may occur.

An illustrative case study which clearly parallels the conversion process in a campaign format is the rhetorical discourse characteristic of the radical abolitionists. This stage in American history abounds with antislavery evangelists rhetorically (and physically) agitating, thereby seeking converts to the "true gospel" of human freedom and dignity. A cursory glance at representative evangelists reveals similarities as well as sharp contrasts in rhetorical strategies. For example, exigency marking efforts were often quite different even though slavery was the controlling exigency. Thus, the religious evangelist attempted to establish the theological dimension of the exigency wherein slavery was portrayed as a *sin* and those complacent individuals refusing to take direct action to halt this sin were labeled "sinners." Prominent spokesmen like Theodore Parker and Theodore Weld had some success infusing the dreadful dynamics of sin into the listener's belief system, thereby forcing a resolution or reorientation of value-belief-attitude systems and self-concepts. Political evangelists, on the other hand, predominantly developed the slavery exigency as a denial of inherent human rights. William Lloyd Garrison and Wendell Phillips were two among many agitators fighting the rhetorical battle on a political and philosophical rather than religious front. Another noticeable group led by Frederick Douglass established the exigency of slavery highlighting the denial of racial dignity and pride. Thus several black agitators called for the removal of slavery not necessarily on religious or political grounds, but on racial assumptions. Religious, political, and racial exigency factors do not pretend to exhaust the rhetorical choices or possibilities inherent in the abolition movement. Obviously, the economic aspect of the slavery exigency as well as other dimensions played important roles in some abolition discourse. Time and space prohibit elaboration here. But,

regardless of the exigency aspect featured or combination thereof—whatever the rhetorical grounds—most evangelists devised a campaign discourse geared at creating self-concept and value system incongruence which subsequently led to dissatisfaction, psychological tension and decision-making or tension reduction action.

Any view of conversion, as described in the preceding analysis, is predicated upon the tenet that a person responding to a felt need encompassing dramatic proportions can be transformed. At the same time, however, it is necessary to recognize the existence of powerful constraints operating in human nature, in man's environment, and in tradition that militate against the development of significant and graphic changes in one's beliefs, attitudes, and values. Not a few scholars, including B. F. Skinner, are pessimistic about man's ability to change. "Man's genetic endowment," argues Skinner, "can be changed only very slowly, but changes in the environment of the individual have quick and dramatic effects."[31] In still stronger language Skinner adds: "No one directly changes a mind. . . . Beliefs, preferences, perceptions, needs, purposes, and opinions . . . are said to change when we change minds. What is changed in each case is a probability of action. . . . We do not change something called perception."[32] What is needed, he concludes, is a technology of behavior that changes the environment. There is little room for conversion phenomenon in Skinner's thinking.

Other communicators, such as sociologists Amitai Etzioni of Columbia University, while not going as far as Skinner, suggest that "human beings are not very easy to change after all." Etzioni lists evidence to show how education has been largely unsuccessful in changing people's attitudes toward cigarette smoking, rehabilitation of criminals, accidents on the highway, drug addiction, and obesity. Etzioni concludes with Skinner that we should be more willing to accept "people as they are" and "change their circumstances."[33] Obviously, the analysis of the conversion process presented in this paper does not agree with either Skinner or Etzioni. We feel that men and women can indeed change their lives in a significant fashion.

Another important constraint is man's devotion to rational thought and science, and his learned skepticism concerning emotion an irrationality. These beliefs, nurtured by Western educational philosophy during the past centuries, may be traced primarily to the writings of Aristotle. As Black perceptively observes, reasoned discourse and action represented to Aristotle and his followers the ultimate in human experience.[34] For those who subscribe to Skinner's theory of change or Aristotle's strong preference for rationality, a predisposition to conversion is weakened. Yet, as we have seen, so strong is the prevailing trend to solve human needs through psychological experiences that the time has now come to devise a rhetoric suitable to the phenomenon of conversion. Such an attempt will be made in the next few paragraphs.

A rhetoric of conversion uses as its starting point the premise that a rhetor or communication source fulfills the role of evangelist. The legitimate evangelist, in turn, *earns* this position of authority by experiencing personal conversion to the movement or faith he now most earnestly wishes to uphold. In this connection Weaver has observed: "We are all of us preachers in private or public capacities. We have no sooner uttered words than we have given impulse to other people to look at the world, or some small part, in our way."[35] Under conditions where values are a dominating concern, rhetoric may be regarded as "sermonic" and those who engage in it as preachers.[36] If Weaver is on target in his analysis of rhetoric in general, we may argue even more convincingly that the rhetor who choses conversion as his persuasive goal is more than an ordinary preacher; he is a committeed evangelist who wants others to share in the same type of transformation he enjoys. Exigency marking thus becomes a primary concern in the evangelist's persuasive approach.

In order to obtain his action goal, the evangelist-rhetor *usually* selects a form of address

that is exhortative. Black gives the following explanation of this rhetorical emphasis.

Such a genre of discourse is that in which the evocation of an emotional response in the audience induces belief in the situation to which the emotion is appropriate. In this genre, a strong emotional experience does not follow the acceptance of a belief, or even accompany it; it precedes it. Emotion can be said to produce the belief, instead of the reverse.[37]

Support for this interpretation comes from James who observes: "Emotional occasions, especially violent ones, are extremely potent in precipitating mental rearrangements."[38] Exhortative discourse seemingly derives its strength, therefore, from the fact that all men have within them the capacity for redemption through emotional and psychological forces that operate "outside the conscious individual."[39] This interpretation suggests that the traditional view of rhetoric which holds that emotional proof should be primarily limited to reinforcement of logos is not always adequate as a criterion of excellence in the field of persuasion.[40]

Much of the thrust of the exhortative form comes as a result of its singleness of purpose and emphasis. Since the message, in the opinion of the evangelist and the group to which he belongs, is identified with pragmatic as well as ideal truth, it contains only one viable solution or choice. All others will be treated as transitory, misleading, or ineffectual. To the degree that opposing options are ignored and/or played down, and a Socratic-type dialogue is avoided, the rhetoric of conversion becomes, in Brown's view, propaganda.[41] On the surface this stress on a single solution, and tendency to downgrade other possible approaches, appears to be unduly arbitrary and, indeed, unethical. But an important extenuating circumstance is the fact that the listener is repeatedly advised that the choice he makes, however crucial for his future life, will be consistent with the belief that man has a free will.

The exhortation also must include some means of removing constraints that render it difficult for conversion to develop. Testimonials showing the ability of man to change, provided he surrenders his "whole being," are cited freely and approvingly. Most importantly the convertee is reminded that he will be strengthened by the knowledge that others in the community will sustain him in moments of trial and doubt.

Among the rhetorical elements and strategies utilized in the exhortation are concrete and vivid words and phrases, "ought" terms, and significant symbols for the purpose of creating "presence" and "communion," and setting the "scene" for the act of conversion which hopefully is to be performed.[42] Exhortative discourse, in sum, whether seeking "volitional regenerative change" or "self-surrender," harnesses all of the emotional appeals it can conveniently and ethically muster in order to alter the center of an individual's "personal energy."[43]

No consideration of the rhetoric of conversion is completely wihtout some reference to "brainwashing"—a rhetorical procedure which obviously promotes both gradual and sudden transformations in human perception. That brainwashing closely resembles a rhetoric of conversion there can be little argument. For it contains the telltale signs of single option solutions, highly emotionalized experiences, and the promise of transformation. But the presence of *force* is so great the choice is either eliminated altogether or corrupted to the point that there is little room for the free operation of the will. "Brainwashing," asserts Brown, "first takes deliberate and active steps to strip the individual of his selfhood, and then strives to build up something new on the foundations that remain. . . ."[44] Apparently this is precisely the technique used by Hitler throughout the period of his dominance as leader of th Third Reich. Ross Scanlon, a student of the Nazi era, has asserted:

"Brainwashing" is a brutal and highly descriptive term that has come into use in recent times to describe Communist handling of certain prisoners of war. It refers to a shrewdly contrived and intensive treatment designed to convert its victims from any other belief they may have held to the cause of Communism. But in essence, the process is not new, is not confined to Communism, nor is it always aimed at isolated individuals. Virtually a whole nation can be brainwashed and by fundamentally the same methods employed on specific individuals.

Whether the target is an individual or a mass of people, the operation requires the energetic exercise of three kinds of pressure: force or threat of force, constant and intense persuasive appeals, and the isolation that comes from closing all other avenues of communication that might conflict with the desired result.[45]

Because of its heavy reliance on force this technique, despite its effectiveness in many instances, must be rejected as a legitimate facet of the rhetoric of conversion.

We have attempted to demonstrate that conversion discourse is founded upon the concept that a *radical change* in man's self-concept, system of attitudes, beliefs, and values *may* result from an exhilarating emotional experience fostered by an evangelist who translates an exigency into a call for repentance which, in turn, is followed by indoctrination.

Perhaps the major implication of this study is to observe that the time has arrived for rhetoricians to recognize that a logos-centered form of persuasion stressing rationality and developing strong emotion may not always be appropriate in a rhetorical situation. This is not to suggest that rhetoric should fail to appeal to the whole man—both his cognitive and affective nature. What it does imply, however, is the need to appreciate the fact that some people at a given time in their lives can find solace only through a transforming emotional experience.

In essence, we are calling for a more systematic study of the conversion genre. Admittedly, this study has only begun a general "survey of the land." Additional issues must be raised. For instance, the rhetorical phenomenon of exigency marking needs to be studied in many and varied communications contexts. Is it the major variable in the conversion process as initiated by the evangelist? Or, do individual psychological make-ups play the predominant role in conversion? That is, do various audiences as congregations actually *seek out* the evangelist?[46] We suspect that some audiences are more influenced by their physical and psychological environments than by any evangelist-source. On the other hand, there are certainly groups of individuals who have been converted not because of ecological factors but primarily because of a skillful evangelist. In what circumstances, then, is the evangelist the prime mover and in what situations is his role not a major factor? In short, what are the variables operating here? The answer to these and similar questions would help clarify the issue of conversion discourse as a campaign rhetoric. When is conversion *not* brought about by a series of persuasive events planned by the evangelist?

Finally, future scholars will want to inquire into the nature of the *role* of the evangelist. What makes an evangelist legitimate? What activities and behaviors validate his role? What constitutes an acceptable role performance? What is the part played by the audience in this role performance?

These issues need to be raised and intelligently discussed. Conversion discourse is with us—"tracking" us every minute of our lives. The professional evangelists are here to stay. We need to know about these people—their strategies and habits. We need to consider ethics and the effect these wizards have on our daily existence.

The Conversion Rhetoric of Jim Jones

An unforgettable example of the rhetoric of conversion took place in the United States in the period between 1952 and 1978. We refer to the tragic charismatic ministry of the Reverend Jim Jones. Before turning to a rhetorical analysis of Jones' movement, let us first review the key developments of his stormy professional career.

Jim Jones was an energetic evangelist who swayed thousands of followers during the forty-seven years of his life. Born May 13, 1931, Jones began his preaching career at a small Methodist church in Somerset, Indiana in 1952. From the outset of his ministry, Jones was actively concerned with racial prejudice in this country. He frequently spoke out against insensitive politicians and white Americans who ignored the plight of blacks and the poor. Eventually, Jones "paid" for his unpopular social position. As one observer noted:

He was frequently jeered during church services for espousing his liberal views on civil rights. Older members of the congregation objected to the outspoken newcomer—who began calling himself "biracial" because of his supposedly Cherokee mother. His enemies struck back at him by tossing dead cats into the church or sometimes stuffing the dead animals into the church toilets.[47]

Rejected because of his racial views, Jones founded a new church, the Community Unity Church. Free of Methodist doctrine, Jones moved to a more emotional ministry where healings and speaking in tongues were integral parts of his fiery worship services. In the mid–1950's, his church was renamed the Peoples Temple Full Gospel Church. With the support of a growing congregation, Jones became more confident in his mission and began taking even more extreme stands on social issues. Gradually, he became an outspoken critic of the American economic and political systems, blaming the woes of the poor on capitalism and democracy. In time, he embraced a socialistic world view.[48] One critic has observed:

Race? Class? Money? Hunger? All creations of the capitalist exploiters, they made artificial distinctions among the children of God. In the world of Jimmy's utopian vision, there would be no race or class distinctions, there would be no need for money, there would be no hunger or sickness or pain.[49]

Rhetorically, then, Jones moved from a fundamentalist theological position to a radical political stance in a short period of time. Less religious and more political arguments were proclaimed from his pulpit.

What was life like in the Peoples Temple? Kilduff and Javers provide this portrait:

> The newcomers found the church had a relaxed pace, where strict rules about Biblical interpretations and Sunday School were replaced with good deeds and talk about liberal ideals—nuclear disarmament, concern for the poor, integration.
>
> Jones promised his small, devoted flock of followers a new refuge, not only free of the racial problems of Indianapolis, but a haven out of harm's way in coming nuclear disaster.[50]

Jones' work with the inner city poor was quickly brought to the attention of the city fathers. He was regarded as so effective in his war on social injustice that he was named executive director of Indianapolis' Human Rights Commission in 1961. But his rise to power in Indianapolis was soon to end. Late in the same year, Jones had a prophetic vision that a holocaust would destroy Indianapolis on June 15, 1967. After informing his congregation of this insight, Jones decided that the Temple must relocate or be swallowed up in the devastation sure to come. In the spring of 1965 he and one-hundred-forty-five of his faithful followers sold their homes and made the trek cross country to Ukiah, California.

In Ukiah, Jones quickly moved to establish himself and his sect. By 1968 he erected a youth center and new church building. He began teaching a sixth grade class in the Anderson Valley School District and classes in history and government to adults in the Ukiah School District. In 1967 he was appointed to a grand jury and in 1968 to the Juvenile Justice Commission. He still waged war against the injustices of society and soon began to demonstrate against American involvement in Viet Nam. All around him, Jones saw the seeds for imminent destruction—from potential earthquakes to nuclear war. A sense of urgency marked his preaching. He began training his congregation for the "end times."

Wilderness trips and survival drills were common practices for Temple members. Vigilance became the watchword. Suspicions toward the FBI and CIA and local authorities were openly discussed. Jones convinced his congregation that everyone was spying on them. A feeling of paranoia developed with the help of Jones who spoke unceasingly of the "enemies."

More and more the enemies became those persons and institutions identified with capitalism and the democratic spirit. As a test of loyalty, in February of 1971 members of his inner circle were required to sign a paper stating: "I am a Communist." By 1972 Peoples Temple had evolved from a church to a political movement espousing Marxian socialism. In this same year, Jones began talking about mass suicide—dying for socialism—as the ultimate loyalty test.

After its move to California, the Temple invested heavily in nursing homes and foster care centers. Temple offices were opened in San Francisco and Los Angeles with the headquarters eventually being moved to the former city. The congregation grew and soon became a powerful political force in the San Francisco Bay area. By 1975, membership in the Temple was over ten thousand. Jones expanded the Temple outreach programs to include drug rehabilitation and legal counseling. He became acquainted with Patty Hearst, Cesar Chavez, Angela Davis, and Huey Newton. In 1976 he was appointed to the San Francisco Housing Authority Commission and named its chairman in February 1977. Earlier in the same year, he received the Martin Luther King, Jr., Humanitarian Award. In July of 1977 Jones left San Francisco for Guyana, South America. He never returned.

Jones fled America to fond an alternative life style. Convinced that the capitalistic system was ineffective in creating a society free of social injustice and believing that more and more enemies were after him, Jones made his exodus. The groundwork for his departure, though, had been laid in 1973 when the Temple leased land from Guyana and began the Peoples Temple Agriculture Project. By 1974 several members of the congregation journeyed to Guyana to begin clearing the land and building the compound. So, when Jones abandoned America in 1977 for his Garden of Eden, preparations were complete.

The Peoples Temple Agricultural Project was terminated abruptly on November 18, 1978. Rumors and accounts surfaced from defectors concerning the harsh and inhumane existence at Jonestown. Community members were forced to work 10–12 hours daily in the fields, were underfed, were physically punished, and were confined to the compound by armed guards, according to these allegations. California congressman Leo Ryan decided to head a congressional investigation to Jonestown. After spending a few days with Jim Jones, Ryan was preparing to depart by plane when several armed guards opened fire on Ryan and his staff. It seems that Jones was convinced that Ryan was going to issue a negative report on life at Jonestown. Rather than have his Garden of Eden subjected to humiliation in America, Jones ordered Ryan killed. Almost simultaneously, Jones ordered the act of revolutionary suicide to begin.

The children were first. A deadly poison was mixed with a sweet drink and forced down children's throats with syringes. The adults followed by lining up to receive their cups of poison. There was little resistance as Jones had convinced his followers that their deaths for him and socialism were noble. A few hours after this macabre scene began, all was stillness and peace at Jonestown.

The preceding has been a brief historical overview of Rev. Jim Jones and his activities. Let us now turn to a consideration of his rhetorical tactics. As mentioned earlier in this essay, the skillful evangelist must highlight and make real an exigency within the lives of the potential converts. This persuasive activity was labeled exigency marking. To be successful, the exigency should have a sense of urgency about it—it demands attention and ultimately resolution. Thus, the adherents are made to feel as though they are participating in a "holy" cause geared toward eradicating the exigency. The exigency, then, is the rhetorical factor that holds the movement together.

There is some difficulty in examining the exigency marked by Jones simply because his ministry covered a twenty-seven year time period and the exigency he developed originally changed as he grew in his role. So, it is more appropriate to speak of exigency development when considering Jones. When he began his career as a student pastor in a Methodist church, Jones was a fundamentalist and probably utilized the "devil" and "hell" as exigencies. A strong belief in these theological concepts necessitated a conversion to the ways espoused by the preacher. However, as Jones became more politically involved, his exigencies became more secular. For example, soon after he initiated his ministry Jones embarked into social work and began to believe that the plight of the urban poor, drug addicts, and unemployed was caused not by the devil, but by men—especially by their racist attitudes and corrupt political systems. Consequently the American government became the reified enemy. Any representative of government, including Congressman Leo Ryan, was not to be trusted. Information-gathering agencies like the CIA and FBI were also the enemy. And so, Jones developed a host of foes claiming that they were out to destroy the Peoples Temple and all that it stood for. Scapegoats were firmly established within a framework of paranoia, distrust, and suspicion. Only the leader— Jones, evangelist turned prophet—knew the way to freedom.

During these early years, Jones seized every opportunity to preach about his enemies. "Members of the church at that time recall that Jimmy spoke constantly of his enemies, both privately and from the pulpit. He seemed to revel in his unpopularity."[51] According to Reston, "Jones" 'gospel of liberation' . . . was so abrasive to the establishment, it was bound to elicit fierce opposition and persecution, just as the early Christians had experienced it. If there was not persecution of them, Jones said, he would be nervous. His measure of harassment, real or supposed, was his measure of self-importance."[52] From a rhetorical perspective, this tactic served to establish Jones' legitimacy and credibility.

Thus Jones utilized several exigencies during his ministry. Beginning with the Biblical concepts of the devil an hell, Jones moved to racial prejudice, the corrupt capitalistic system, democracy, the CIA, the FBI—labeling each the "enemy"—the enemy that must be destroyed. Not surprisingly such a diverse exigency developement appealed to many. These exigencies coupled with his social outreach programs (drug rehabilitation, free restaurants, legal counsel, and so forth) influenced thousands. "For the outcasts of American society, primarily the elderly and the black—the recipients of the impersonal, overstrained, and inferior medicine of the welfare clinics—Jones offered the first gesture of love and caring, and this alone was salubrious."[53]

With a multitude of enemies relentlessly threatening not only Peoples Temple and Jim Jones, but also the world, the evangelist succeeded in establishing a paranoia and a rhetorical drama where tension and fear continually reigned.

As noted earlier, the evangelist must first mark an exigency and secondly move his listeners to a decision point. If the listeners were brought into Jones' symbolic drama where life and the future were, at best, tenuous and where enemies unceasingly plotted destruction and created confusion, if the listeners believed this diabolical script authored by Jones, the decision was simple. Jones was the only hope. They had to cast their lot with him. He alone had the courage to battle the forces of evil.

The decision in favor of Jones' world view was possible once an exigency was entrenched in the minds of the congregation. But, as discussed throughout this text, a favorable decision is easier to elicit when the source is perceived as a legitimate and credible spokesperson. Jones realized this rhetorical fact and continually worked to establish credibility in the perceptions of his potential converts and congregation. Although he employed several tactics, two merit discussion here: his use of healing services and his claim that he was God.

Jones became interested in medicine and health-related matters when working at a hospital in Richmond, Indiana. At one point, he entertained thoughts of becoming a medical doctor. But, his major interest was in the ministry. So, he compromised the two professions

somewhat and became a healing preacher. The introduction of miracle healings into his worship services was quick in coming.

By the time Jones was operating in Los Angeles, the healing ministry was publicly proclaimed in Temple flyers:

PASTOR JIM JONES
The most unique

PROPHETIC HEALING SERVICE

You've ever witnessed!

Behold the Word made Incarnate in your midst!

Hear his Divine Message of Apostolic Equality!

God works as TUMOROUS MASSES ARE PASSED in every service. . . .

Before your eyes, THE CRIPPLED WALK, THE BLIND SEE!

SCORES ARE CALLED OUT OF THE AUDIENCE in each service and told the intimate (but never embarrassing) details of their lives that only God could reveal!

CHRIST IS MADE REAL through the most precise revelation and the miraculous healing in this ministry of his servant,

JIM JONES!

—from a flyer advertising a Peoples Temple service, Embassy Auditorium, Los Angeles[54]

His most dramatic healings involved cancerous tumors. Surely anyone who can cure this dreaded disease deserves to be followed, his followers reasoned. Other miracles such as restoring sight to the blind and healing the lame were often performed in dramatic fashion. In all, these miracles served to establish his legitimacy. Here was a man of God with extraordinary powers.

Eventually, though, Jones was not satisfied with simply being a man of God. He soon became so caught up in his drama that he began claiming that he *was* God. The ensuing words are typical:

When all this is done, when I have eliminated all the condescending savior images, removed all the judgment hall concepts, expunged all the heavens in the sky and the Sky God concepts, people will know there is no God but what is in us. What is God anyway? God is perfect justice, freedom, and equality. The only thing that brings perfect justice, freedom and equality and love in its beauty and holiness is socialism!

In me, the twain have been married. In this dispensation, I have taken on the body, the same body that walked in the plains of Palmyra, of whom Solomon said his hair is black as a raven, and, who, as Isaiah said, 7:20 would shave with a razor. I do shave with a razor. My hair is black as a raven's. I came as the God to eliminate all your false Gods. Men have dastardly distorted the spirit that I have, but it was necessary for me to come upon the scene and I have. From time to time, I shall show you proofs, so that you will have no further need of religion. I have accomplished all you imagine your God to do, but has never done. I have repeatedly resurrected the dead before your eyes. You have never seen anyone shot down before your eyes and heal themselves, yet I, the socialist leader, have done it. I am the only God you've ever seen, with blood gushing out of his chest, who, after the nurses put their fingers in the bullet holes, just wiped his hand across his chest, and closed them. Your God is one of the people. He is the instrument of all you've ever desired, all that freedom embraces, all that justice embodies, all that sensitivity involves. That is what your God is.

I must say that it is a great effort to be God. I would lean upon another, but no other in the consciousness we are evolving in has the faculties that I possess. When they do, I will be glad to hold his coat. In the meantime, I shall be God, and beside me, there shall be no other. If you don't need a God, then fine, I'm no problem to you. But if you need a God, I'm going to nose out that other God, because it's a false God, so you can get the right concept in your mind. If you're holding onto that Sky God, I'll nose him out ten lengths every time.

And when all this has been done, I shall go into the obscurity of the conscious collective principle of sociality, and I shall have no further intrusion into the affairs of man.[55]

Thus, the focus of the drama was on Jones as the divine one. "What really frightened a few former friends was when he started to take the Bible, throw it down on the floor, and declare: 'Too many people are looking at this and not at *me*.' "[56] In the end, he was the ultimate authority, the ultimate source.

We are now prepared to discuss the final phase of the conversion process: indoctrination. For the most part, this activity was carried out both by the congregation and Jones. The evangelist, through his continual preaching, meticulously hammered away at his philosophy. His sermons often lasted into the early morning hours. When he arrived in Jonestown, he spoke for hours over the compound's loudspeaker system. Even during work in the fields, the residents were exposed to Jones' incessant harangues. Every evening, after dinner, Jones would continue his preaching.

In many ways, though, the community itself was the major indoctrination force. In efforts to keep their spirits high, individuals reinforced Jones' philosophy by word and deed. The phenomenon of "group think" discussed by scholars of human dynamics was certainly operative in Jones' followers who spread the drama, reinforcing each other all the while. Eventually, it was a self-perpetuating process. Through group worship and associations with each other, indoctrination was a continual process carried out by the community of believers.

As students of persuasion, we must ask ourselves why Jonestown was possible. Why was Jim Jones such an effective evangelist? There is no simple answer to these queries. However, the fact (that to some) Jones had charisma[57]— that magnetic, almost superhuman appeal— is important. Apparently through his physical features, his clothing (especially his tendency to wear dark glasses almost continually), his tone of voice, his maner of carrying himself, Jones was able to project a sense of mystery and power. He could command others. With his charisma, Jones authored a believable drama demonstrating his legitimacy through both rhetoric and deed.

It was the week before Thanksgiving—a time when Americans were supposed to celebrate their founding spirit by paying homage to the religious freedom so vigorously pursued by the forefathers. But, instead of a warm community celebration in the brisk American autumn, a rejoicing of quite another sort was being enacted by an American religious colony miles away. Here there was no crisp autumn wind—only sun and humidity. Here, a week before Thanksgiving, a band of believers celebrated their religious freedom by paying reverence to their leader, Jim Jones, in a bizarre ritual of mass suicide. The place was Jonestown, Guyana. The time was November 18, 1978. The death toll was above 900 men, women, and children. In an apocalyptic act, revolutionary suicide, Rev. Jim Jones' Garden of Eden was destroyed. The harvest of his symbolic reality was gathered in.

Lest the reader be misled, an important footnote must be added before leaving our discussion of conversion rhetoric. Jim Jones was used as an extended illustration because of the dramatic history of his movement. Fortunately, however, Jones is not typical of most persons engaging in conversion rhetoric. Indeed, there have been countless individuals proclaiming an ethical conversion stance throughout the history of mankind. We have every reason to believe that the ethically concerned evangelist will continue to be the rule rather than the exception. For example, since 1949 Billy Graham has led crusades involving millions of people worldwide. Undeniably many of his followers who have made a decision have found peace of mind thereby. A host of political, economic, psychological, and philosophical evangelists alluded to on the first page of this essay have served peaceful and very often productive purposes. Jones, however, did not.

In our judgment, Jones was a figure of questionable character. He resorted to "tricks" in an effort to influence converts; he frightened and manipulated his followers; he espoused religious values at variance to any established faith; he proclaimed political ideals contrary to the American system; he preached hatred; he made empty promises. Similar to Hitler, Jones' rhetorical strategies and goals were unacceptable from an ethical standpoint. In sum, Jones' rhetoric is not compatible with the perspective developed in the first chapter of this text where we referred to genuine rhetoric as that discourse which occurs when a communicator presents an informative or suasory ethical message designed to create a persuasive effect on audience members who have a choice or perceived choice and the power to modify the exigencies upon which the discourse is constructed. Clearly, Jones' discourse does not even approach a genuine rhetoric.

The fact is that an irresponsible form of conversion rhetoric, as in the case of Jim Jones, may produce irreparable harm both to individuals and to society. Evangelist rhetors and hearers alike have a special obligation in this area. Since, as Weaver correctly argues, language is sermonic, the evangelist has the responsibility to adopt a worthy and morally sound stance. Similarly, the listener exposed to the evangelist has the task of scrutinizing carefully the words, the promises, and the motivations of the rhetor. If these two efforts are combined, hopefully the conversion rhetoric that results will have a strong ethical base.[58]

Notes

1. Wayne C. Booth, "The Scope of Rhetoric Today: A Polemic Excursion," in Lloyd Bitzer and Edwin Black (eds.), *The Prospect of Rhetoric* (Englewood Cliffs, New Jersey: Prentice-Hall, Inc., 1971), pp. 102–103.
2. Andrew Greely and William McCready, "Are We a Nation of Mystics?" *The New York Times Magazine,* (January 26, 1975), p. 12.
3. Milton Rokeach, "Attitude Change and Behavioral Change," in Thomas D. Beisecker and Donn Parson (eds.), *The Process of Social Influence: Readings in Persuasion,* (Englewood Cliffs, New Jersey: Prentice-Hall, Inc., 1972), p. 428.
4. Milton Rokeach, *The Open and Closed Mind* (New York: Basic Books, Inc., 1960), p. 33.
5. Milton Rokeach, *The Nature of Human Values* (New York: Free Press, 1973), p. 5.
6. *Ibid.,* p. 215.
7. *Ibid.,* p. 216.

8. *Ibid.*

9. cf., *Values*, p. 216.

10. Edwin Black, *Rhetorical Criticism: A Study in Method* (New York: Macmillan Co., 1965), pp. 138–142.

11. Booth, op. cit., p. 102.

12. J. Marsh, "Conversion," in *The Interpreter's Dictionary of the Bible* (New York: Abingdon Press, 1962), p. 678.

13. *Republic*, VII.

14. Abraham Maslow, *Religion, Values and Peak Experiences* (New York: Viking Press, 1970), p. 66.

15. Kurt Lang and Gladys Lang, *Collective Dynamics* (New York: Thomas Y. Crowell Co., 1961), p. 153.

16. William James, *The Varieties of Religious Experience: A Study in Human Nature* (New York: Modern Library, 1902), p. 225.

17. John Hesselgrave, "A Propagation Profile of the Soka Gakkai," PhD Dissertation, University of Minnesota, 1965, pp. 59–95.

18. C. Eric Lincoln, *The Black Muslims in America* (Boston, Mass.: Beacon Press, 1961), pp. 108–109.

19. Malcolm X and Alex Haley, *The Autobiography of Malcolm X* (New York: Grove Press, Inc., 1964).

20. Gordon Allport, *The Individual and His Religion* (New York: Macmillan Co., 1950), p. 37.

21. James, op. cit., p. 193.

22. *Ibid.*, p. 195.

23. J. A. C. Brown, *Techniques of Persuasion* (Middlesex, England: Penguin Books, 1963), p. 224.

24. Lloyd Bitzer, "The Rhetorical Situation," *Philosophy and Rhetoric*, I (January 1968), 1–15. Despite this reservation the authors are indebted to Bitzer for his insightful analysis of "exigency."

25. Guenther Roth and Claus Wittch, eds., *Max Weber: Economy and Society*, 3 vols. (New York: Bedminster Press, 1968), 1:241.

26. Rokeach, *Values*, p. 230.

27. William Sargant, *Battle of the Mind: A Physiology of Conversion and Brainwashing* (New York: Perennial Library, 1957), p. 26.

28. George Sweazey, *Effective Evangelism* (New York: Harper and Row, 1953), p. 206.

29. Douglas Ehninger, "Toward a Taxonomy of Prescriptive Discourse," in Eugene White, ed., *Rhetoric in Transition*, (University Park: Penn State University Press, 1980), p. 90.

30. Wallace C. Fotheringham, *Perspectives on Persuasion* (Boston, Mass.: Allyn and Bacon, Inc., 1966), p. 34.

31. B. F. Skinner, *Beyond Freedom and Dignity* (New York: Alfred Knopf, 1971), p. 19.

32. *Ibid.*, pp. 92–93.

33. Amitai Etzioni, "Human Beings are Not Very Easy to Change After All," *Saturday Review*, June 3, 1972, p. 42.

34. *Rhetorical Criticism*, p. 142.

35. Richard L. Johannesen, Rennard Strickland, and Ralph T. Eubanks (eds.), *Language Is Sermonic: Richard M. Weaver on the Nature of Rhetoric* (Baton Rouge, Louisiana: Louisisana State University Press, 1970), p. 224.

36. *Ibid.*, p. 225.

37. *Rhetorical Criticism*, p. 138.

38. James, op. cit., p. 195.

39. *Ibid.*, p. 207.

40. This is an important thrust in Black's volume on *Rhetorical Criticism.*

41. Brown, op. cit., pp. 10–36.

42. Black stresses the role of "ought" terms such as "is," "will be," and "shall be"; George H. Mead was one of the first scholars to deal with the "significant symbol"; Ch. Perelman and L. Olbrechts-Tyteca emphasize the importance of "presence" and "communion"; and the concept of "scene" is one of the elements in Kenneth Burke's dramatistic pentad.

43. James, op. cit., pp. 192–193.

44. Brown, op. cit., p. 278.

45. Ross Scanlon, "Adolf Hitler and the Techniques of Mass Brainwashing," in Donald C. Bryant, (ed.), *The Rhetorical Idiom: Essays in Rhetoric, Oratory, Language and Drama* (New York: Russell and Russell, 1966), p. 201.

46. See for example, Orrin E. Klapp, *Symbolic Leaders: Public Dramas and Public Men* (Chicago, Ill.: Adline Publishing Co., 1964) for the various psychological functions a symbolic leader such as an evangelist might perform in society; especially pages 26–65.

47. Marshall Kilduff and Ron Javers, *The Suicide Cult: The Inside Story of the Peoples Temple Sect and the Massacre in Guyana*, (New York: Bantam Books, 1978), p. 15.

48. Inwardly, Jones probably had socialist learnings as early as 1951. Cf. James Reston, Jr., *Our Father Who Art in Hell*, (New York: New York Times Books, 1981), p. 50.

49. George Klineman, Sherman Butler and David Conn, *The Cult That Died: The Tragedy of Jim Jones and the Peoples Temple*, (New York: G. P. Putnam's Sons, 1980), p. 58.

50. Kilduff and Javers, op. cit., pp. 26–27.

51. Klineman et. al., op. cit., p. 65.

52. Reston, op. cit., p. 49.

53. *Ibid.*, p. 43.

54. Klineman et. al., op. cit., p. 11.

55. Reston, op. cit., p. 56.

56. John P. Nugent, *White Night*, (New York: Rawson Wade Publishers, Inc., 1979), pp. 15–16.

57. Cf. Reston, p. 52.

58. Lee Snyder, a graduate associate in communication at The Ohio State University, was helpful in having us stress the ethical dimension of conversion rhetoric.

20

Rhetoric as Motive: Social Protest and Social Movements

Persuasive discourse which accompanies any significant social movement is unique in several respects. This essay explores the rhetorical dimensions of social protest rhetoric by examining the definitions, characteristics, strategies, and themes of this genre.

The rhetoric of social agitation or protest is perhaps one of the oldest forms of discourse known to man. Here is a rhetorical genre primarily concerned with altering social relationships among people, groups, and power centers or "establishments." Here is a rhetoric which is truly persuasive. As Bitzer observes:

A work of rhetoric is pragmatic; it comes into existence for the sake of something beyond itself; it functions ultimately to produce action or change in the world; it performs some task. In short, rhetoric is a mode of altering reality, not by the direct application of energy to objects, but by the creation of discourse which changes reality through the mediation of thought and action.[1]

The history of mankind abounds with individuals and groups who at one time or another engaged in some form of verbal protest. The ancient prophet Amos, Martin Luther, Martin Luther King, Jr., the Berrigans, Billy James Hargis, and Carl McIntire are a few well-known religious agitators. Joseph Stalin, Gandhi, Fidel Castro, Samuel Adams, and Tom Hayden frequently agitated in the political realm. Thousands of individuals could be easily included here. All had one general goal in mind: to alter the power relationship dimension between individuals and/or between individuals and "establishments."

If a realignment of power relationships is the major objective of a social movement, what factors account for or justify the formation of the movement? An inquiry into the causes of a social movement is not the objective of this essay for such an investigation lies in the realm of the sociologist rather than the rhetorical critic. However, it should be obvious that the *general cause* of any reform movement can be traced to a growing feeling of *dissatisfaction* with the "status quo" on the part of a group or segment of society. Members of the movement often feel "put down," oppressed, or abused by the power holders. Charles Lomas summarizes: "Neither rhetorical nor activist agitation can hope to succeed even partially unless social and political conditions are favorable to the initiation and growth of the movement. There must be clear evidence of *injustice or apparent injustice* deeply affecting the well being of those who compose the audience."[2] When such a feeling takes hold in the disciple's ranks, a generalized attitude of *unrest* is fostered. Furthermore, if the established powers fail to deal with this dissatisfaction an organization of the frustrated or disfranchised begins. Thus, a movement is born. A strategy for change emerges. The establishment is challenged. The "haves" are confronted publicly by the "have nots."

The "have nots" picture themselves as radically divided from traditional society, questioning not simply the limitations of its benevolence but more fundamentally its purposes and modes of operation. Whether they experience deprivation as poverty, or lack of political power, or disaffection from traditional values, the "have not" leaders and theorists challenge existing institutions.[3]

Thus, a social movement is dependent on a generalized feeling of unrest which is then translated into a call for change. Furthermore, the agitator's demands for change must be met by resistance from the establishment. The interaction of an urgent call for change "falling on deaf ears" results in an emotionally charged climate—a potentially explosive situation. "On the part of the established ruling groups," says Lomas, "there must be massive *resistance to change*. This resistance may be motivated by high principles, by apathy, by self-interest, or by fear. . . ."[4]

As stated previously, this essay is not concerned with a thorough examination of the *causes* of human protest. Rather, our prime focus is the *rhetorical dimension* of agitation. Our discussion begins with a consideration of definition.

Scholars from the speech-communication field have examined protest discourse and defined their focus in slightly different formulations. For instance, Bowers and Ochs discuss the phenomenon of *agitation* discourse. "Agitation exits when (1) people outside the normal decision making establishment (2) advocate significant social change and (3) encounter a degree of resistance within the establishment such as to require more than the normal discursive means of persuasion."[5] Accordingly, agitation occurs when "powerless" individuals demand "significant change" and find that their efforts are actively resisted by the establishment. Mary McEdwards continues this emphasis. "Agitative language belongs to a particular type of rhetoric whose end is movement away from the *status quo*. Some may argue that all rhetoric has this same end. However, the rhetoric we call *agitation* evokes extreme movement away from the *status quo*—usually a complete reversal of existing conditions or situations.[6] Bowers, Ochs, and McEdwards, then, consider the discourse of social protest as those rhetorical efforts concerned with "significant social change," or a movement away from the status quo. Lomas discusses "agitation" in a similar fashion.

"Agitation may be defined as a persistent and uncompromising statement and restatement of grievances through all available communication channels, with the aim of creating public opinion favorable to a change in some condition."[7] Robert Browne labels this genre the rhetoric of *discontinuity* because it is aimed at social *change—not* at maintaining the status quo, "keeping the existing political system going," or maintaining "continuity between groups, classes, generations."[8]

Paul Brandes considers the rhetoric of social protest and formulates a definition of the rhetoric of *revolt* which moves beyond the discourse of agitation or discontinuity discussed above. "Revolt rhetoric," according to Brandes, "openly advocates lawlessness. The Old Regime is not to be modified peacefully. It is to be amended by force. Not until there is an open call for lawlessness can the rhetoric of revolt be said to have begun."[9] Hence, Brandes has described a discourse which advocates lawlessness and force rather than mere social change as characteristic of agitation. The rhetoric of revolt advocates a complete upheaval of existing institutions.

Perhaps the most suitable perspective for our immediate purposes is to view the discourse accompanying a social protest as a continuum rhetoric. Anchoring the "conservative" extremity is the rhetoric of agitation. We define agitation discourse as that rhetoric which (1) is uttered by "frustrated" individuals either inside *or* outside the power-holding elite, (2) calls for a "significant social change" in the system, and (3) encounters resistance from the establishment such as to require its advocates to go beyond the "acceptable" or approved channels of communication—a definition obviously influenced by Bowers, Ochs, Browne, and McEdwards. In other words, if the establishment fails to respond to the change demanded by the "discontented," a movement may emerge which finds it necessary to go beyond and outside the normal channels of communication to accomplish its goals. This, then, is the rhetoric of agitation. At the other extreme of the continuum is the rhetoric of revolt. Here is discourse which openly calls for a total revolution or overthrow of the existing power centers. Individuals in this camp are not satisfied with mere "significant" social change. They demand a complete and total upheaval: revolution. Between these poles are those forms of discourse which call for change in society or a part of the social system—a call which differs only in intensity and extremism. Herbert Simons recognizes this diversity in radicalism characteristic of protest discourse when he discusses the variety of rhetorical strategies available to leaders of any movement. "Along a continuum from the sweet and reasonable to the violently revolutionary, one may identify *moderate*, *intermediate*, and *militant* types of strategies, each with its own appropriate tactics and styles."[10]

All reform movements, then, engage in protest discourse which helps initiate, organize, and sustain a unified effort where energy is directed toward an "enemy" or establishment. The protestors' use and misuse of language in the form of demands makes their rhetoric the major vehicle for change in the ensuing power struggle. Ernest Bormann discusses the importance of rhetoric for any reform movement.

A reform movement . . . requires organization to succeed. A chaotic impulse may influence events by blindly striking out or by surfacing in unusual unexpected violence like black rioting in the cities in the 1960s, but a reform movement requires more than the impulse. In addition to a program of action, an ideology, and administrative skills, an organization requires meetings that provide interaction among the members until leadership emerges. Spokesmen must then establish channels of communication so they can indoctrinate people into the party line, encourage them in adversity, and inform them in times of triumph. Most important for our concerns is that among the leadership of any successful reform movement there must be rhetoricians who provide both the insider and outsider with a meaningful interpretation of the movement.[11]

Thus, basic to any reform movement is the rhetorician or, as Eric Hoffer calls him, the "Man of Words."

Mass movements do not usually rise until the prevailing order has been discredited. This discrediting is not an automatic result of the blunders and abuses of those in power, but the deliberate work of men of words with a grievance. . . . The preliminary work of undermining existing institutions, of familiarizing the masses with the idea of change, and of creating a receptivity to a new faith, can be done only by men who are, first and foremost, talkers or writers and are recognized as such by all.[12]

Any social movement, then, requires a man of words who manages the "language." These are the rhetoricians who weave a discourse which captures the urgent feelings and desires of the movement. The success of the movement in realizing its goals is partly, if not wholly, dependent on the designated man of words. His importance Hoffer suggests in the ensuing paragraph, cannot be underestimated:

To sum up, the militant man of words prepares the ground for the rise of a mass movement: (1) by discrediting prevailing creeds and institutions and detaching from them the allegiance of the people; (2) by indirectly creating a hunger for faith in the hearts of those who cannot live without it, so that when the new faith is preached it finds an eager response among the disillusioned masses; (3) by furnishing the doctrine and the slogans of the new faith; (4) by undermining the convictions of the 'better people'—those who can get along without faith—so that when the new fanaticism makes its appearance they are without the capacity to resist it.[13]

In sum, the man of words vocalizes the discontent and demands of the movement. He works with the leaders and rhetorically portrays a symbolic reality which attracts, maintains, and molds workers into an efficiently organized unit. He attempts to secure adoption of the movement's product or program by the larger structure or establishment. In so doing, the man of words must be prepared to react rhetorically to the resistance generated by the establishment.[14]

Several symbolic strategies are available to the rhetoricians or men of words. For instance, in discussing the rhetoric of the black revolution, Arthur Smith conceptualizes four major language strategies: vilification, objectification, legitimation, and mythication. Since a major task of the rhetorician is to "interpret reality" to those both inside and outside the fellowship, the man of words begins by denouncing the leader of the "establishment" which in turn becomes the defined target for the movement's energies. Smith labels this strategy vilification or "the agitator's use of language to degrade an opponent's person, actions, or ideas."[15] The strategy of vilification results in the *naming* of the opposition's *leadership*. So, the "devil" is personified and identified for all to see.

A second rhetorical strategy related to vilification is "objectification."

It is the agitator's use of language to direct the grievances of a particular group toward another collective body such as an institution, nation, political party, or race. Related to, but different from vilification, objectification uses similar devices of sarcasm and low humor while attacking an ill-defined body. Both strategies direct attention to the opposition; however, objectification strives to channel all of the frustrations of a group onto a single ill-defined body.[16]

The "enemy" is now publicly noted. "The agitator is concerned with showing that a certain race, party, or secret collection of men is responsible for all of the misfortune that befalls the agitator's votarists. The solution is simple: we must get rid of them."[17]

Smith notes a further strategy calling it "mythication."

Employing language that suggests the sanction of supra-rational forces, the agitator creates a spiritual dynamism for his movement. Seizing on what is probably the rationale for black hope, the agitator often attempts to use religious symbolism in an effort to demonstrate the righteousness of his cause.[18]

Besides religious symbolism, agitators in the black movement have also employed the sanction of history. According to Smith, "The black rhetor wants to demonstrate that his agitation is sanctioned by history because great agitators have sought to establish justice, create equality, and build dignity."[19]

A final strategy discussed by Smith is that of "legitimation" or the use of language to answer the arguments and resistance of the opponent.

Finally, the rhetor of black revolution makes use of legitimation, insofar as it is the use of language to answer the opposition, it is a refutative strategy. But it is more than an argumentative rebuttal to an opponent; it is a psychological weapon. In legitimation, the black revolutionist seeks to explain, vindicate, and justify the activists involved in the movement.[20]

Thus, Smith considers these four as major strategies found in black revolutionary discourse. These same tactics, however, can be identified in almost any movement's rhetoric. Smith concludes:

He (the black revolutionary) endeavors to degrade and stigmatize the opposition with the strategies of vilification and objectification; and he attempts to unify and defend his followers with mythication and legitimation. Even though these strategies are not necessarily found in all agitational rhetoric in the same degree, they always occur at some point in an agitational campaign waged with intensity and persistence.[21]

Complementing Smith's categories, Robert Scott and Donald Smith list four major rhetorical strategies or themes involved in social confrontations: we are already dead; we can be reborn; we have the stomach for the fight, you don't; we are united and understand.[22] Thus, in their function as rhetoricians, the men of words will often develop one or all of the above general themes which are then directed at the "establishment" as the primary audience.

[handwritten notes in top margin: "Read article... Backlash argument... conformity"]

First, in order to help unify the movement, the rhetorician must foster a feeling of frustration and powerlessness among the disciples. So, the "we are already dead" theme emerges. "In the world as it is," state Scott and Smith, "we do not count. We make no difference. We are not persons. . . . Some radicals take oaths, changing their names, considering themselves as dead, without families, until the revolution succeeds. It is difficult to cow a dead orphan."[23]

But, precisely because the disciples are already dead—worthless human beings—they have the potential to be reborn—to have a second chance. Scott and Smith summarize:

Having accepted the evaluation of what is, agreeing to be the most worthless of things, we can be reborn. We have nothing to hang on to. No old identity to stop us from identifying with a new world, no matter how horrifying the prospect may seem at the outset; and a new world will certainly be born of the fire we shall create.[24]

Thus, through his rhetoric, the man of words attempts to prove to the faithful followers of the movement that they are worthless and because of this, they can be born anew. Language and arguments are tailored for this purpose. Next, the theme of stamina for the struggle usually emerges: we have the stomach for the fight, you don't. "We can strike to kill for the old world is not ours but one in which we are already dead, in which killing injures us not, but provides us with the chance of rebirth."[25] With their dignity stripped and nothing to lose in their battle with the "establishment," the theme emerges which stresses the unity of the "brotherhood": we are united and understand. Scott and Smith explain:

We are united in a sense of a past dead and a present that is valuable only to turn into a future free of your degrading domination. We have accepted our past as past by willing our future. Since you must cling to the past, you have no future and cannot even understand.[26]

Thus, the authors have identified four general rhetorical themes characteristic of the discourse surrounding any radical reform. These are strategies which surface as the movement approaches the "revolt" extreme of our continuum.

The man of words, then, has as his chief duty the construction of a unique *symbolic world*. Klapp observes:

Man not only constructs objects but also builds his own symbolic world. These worlds vary (or are indemonstrably identical) for each individual and cultural group. Yet a frame of reference that is *collectively constructed* allows members to coordinate their behavior in ways which would never be possible without such common understandings.

Humans are continually constructing images of the present, images of the future, and images of the past—and tying them together and sharing them by symbols. This is the reality to which they respond. In brief, reality is what you make it.[27]

Within the perimeters of the protestors' symbolic world, the movement's rhetorician lists the causes of dissatisfaction, discredits the "enemy," helps unify and mold the ensuing organization, helps define the goals and objectives of the movement and interprets them to the disciples and the rest of the world. Above all, the man of words is an "explainer" and an interpreter of "reality." He occupies a unique and powerful place within the movement. No reform effort can succeed without him.

In conclusion, the rhetoric of social protest is a demanding and urgent rhetoric aimed at (a) unifying and molding an organized effort from the powerless disciples and (b) concerned with symbolically destroying the establishment in an effort to initiate the desired change. The rhetorical themes inherent in this discourse are geared toward this two pronged symbolic attack.

Notes

1. Lloyd F. Bitzer, "The Rhetorical Situation," in Douglas Ehninger, ed., *Contemporary Rhetoric: A Reader's Coursebook* (Glenview, Illinois: Scott, Foresman and Company, 1972), p. 41.

2. Charles Lomas, *The Agitator in American Society* (Englewood Cliffs: New Jersey: Prentice-Hall, Inc., 1968), p. 8.
3. Robert L. Scott and Donald K. Smith, "The Rhetoric of Confrontation," in Ehninger, op. cit., p. 182.
4. Lomas, op. cit., p. 8.
5. John W. Bowers and Donovan J. Ochs, *The Rhetoric of Agitation and Control* (Reading, Massachusetts: Addison-Wesley Publishing Company, 1971), p. 4.
6. Mary G. McEdwards, "Agitative Rhetoric: Its Nature and Effect," in J. Jeffery Auer, ed., *The Rhetoric of Our Times* (New York: Appleton-Century-Crofts, 1969), p. 7.
7. Lomas, op. cit., p. 2.
8. Robert M. Browne, "Response to Edward P. J. Corbett: The Rhetoric of the Open Hand and the Rhetoric of the Closed Fist," in Ehninger, op. cit., pp. 211–215.
9. Paul D. Brandes, *The Rhetoric of Revolt* (Englewood Cliffs, New Jersey: Prentice-Hall, Inc., 1971), p. 3.
10. Herbert W. Simons, "Requirements, Problems, and Strategies: A Theory of Persuasion for Social Movements," in Ehninger, op. cit., p. 195.
11. Ernest G. Bormann, ed., *Forerunners of Black Power* (Englewood Cliffs, New Jersey: Prentice-Hall, Inc., 1971), p. 17.
12. Eric Hoffer, *The True Believer: Thoughts on the Nature of Mass Movements* (New York: Harper and Row, 1951), p. 119.
13. *Ibid.*, p. 128.
14. Simons, op. cit., pp. 191–192.
15. Arthur Smith, *Rhetoric of Black Revolution* (Boston: Allyn and Bacon, Inc., 1969), p. 26.
16. *Ibid.*, p. 29.
17. *Ibid.*
18. *Ibid.*, p. 34.
19. *Ibid.*, p. 36.
20. *Ibid.*, p. 40.
21. *Ibid.*, pp. 41–42.
22. Scott and Smith, op. cit., pp. 185–186.
23. *Ibid.*, p. 185.
24. *Ibid.*
25. *Ibid.*, pp. 185–186.
26. *Ibid.*, p. 186.
27. Orrin E. Klapp, *Currents of Unrest: An Introduction to Collective Behavior* (New York: Holt, Rinehart and Winston, Inc., 1972), p. 91.

The following essay by Robert L. Scott and Donald K. Smith on "The Rhetoric of Confrontation" further extends the above thoughts on protest rhetoric as motive. The reader has already been introduced to many key concepts considered by Scott and Smith. In examining this descriptive study, we should keep in mind that it appeared in print as the turbulent 1960s drew to a close. Since its publication in 1969, it has been reproduced countless times without a loss of freshness. The fact that its influence still persists more than a decade later is a tribute to the authors' early recognition that rhetorical theory and practice must be flexible enough to adapt to changing cultural norms.

The Rhetoric of Confrontation

"Confront" is a simple enough verb meaning to stand or to come in front of. Like many simple words, however, it has been used in diverse contexts for varied purposes and has developed complex meanings. Among these the most interesting, and perhaps the strongest, is the sense of standing in front of as a barrier or a threat. This sense is especially apparent in the noun "confrontation."

Repeatedly in his book *Essays in the Public Philosophy*, Walter Lippmann uses the word "confrontation" in the sense of face-to-face coming together of spokesmen for disparate views. Confrontation, as he saw it then, was the guarantee of open communication and fruitful dissent. But Lippmann's book was copyrighted in 1955. Today, his phrase "because the purpose of the confrontation is to discern truth" sounds a bit archaic. If so, the remainder of his sentence, "there are rules of evidence and parliamentary procedure, there are codes of fair dealing and fair comment, by

Reprinted from *Quarterly Journal of Speech*, 55 (February 1969), 1–8. Reprinted with permission of the authors and editor of *Quarterly Journal of Speech*.

which a loyal man will consider himself bound when he exercises the right to publish opinion,"[1] seems absolutely irrelevant to the notion of "confrontation" as we live with it in marches, sit-ins, demonstrations, and discourse featuring disruption, obscenity, and threats.

Although certainly some use the word "confrontation" moderately, we shall be concerned here with the radical and revolutionary suggestion which the word carries more and more frequently. Even obviously moderate circumstances today gain some of the revolutionary overtones when the word is applied, as it might be for example, in announcing a church study group as the "confrontation of sacred and secular morality."

Acts of confrontation are currently at hand in such profusion that no one will lack evidence to prove or disprove the generalizations we make.[2]

Confrontation crackles menacingly from every issue in our country (Black Power and Student Power, as examples), hemisphere (Castroism, for example), and globe (Radical Nationalism everywhere). But primary to every confrontation in any setting, radical or moderate, is the impulse to confront. From what roots does that impulse spring?

Radical Division

Radical confrontation reflects a dramatic sense of division. The old language of the "haves" and the "have-nots" scarcely indicates the basis of the division, nor its depth. The old language evokes the history of staid, well-controlled concern on the part of those who have, for those who have not. It suggests that remedy can come from traditional means—the use of some part of the wealth and talent of those who have to ease the burden of those who have not, and perhaps open opportunities for some of them to enter the mainstream of traditional values and institutions. It recalls the missionary spirit of the voluntary associations of those who have—the legislative charity of the New Deal, the Fair Deal, the Welfare State, and the whole spectrum of international development missions.

A benevolent tone characterizes the old rhetoric of social welfare. The tone assumes that all men seek and should increasingly have more of the available wealth, or education, or security, or culture, or opportunities. The values of those who "have" are celebrated as the goals to which all should aspire, and effective social policy becomes a series of acts to extend opportunity to share in those values. If those who have can provide for others more of their own perquisites—more of the right to vote, or to find employment, or to go to college, or to consume goods—then progress is assured.

Although the terms "have" and "have not" are still accurate enough descriptions of the conditions that divide people and groups, their evocation of a traditional past hides the depth and radical nature of current divisions. Those on the "have not" side of the division, or at least some of their theorists and leaders, no longer accept designation as an inert mass hoping to receive what they lack through action by the "haves." Neither do they accept any assumption that what they wish is membership in the institutions of those who have, or an opportunity to learn and join their value system. Rather the "have nots" picture themselves as radically divided from traditional society, questioning not simply the limitations of its benevolence but more fundamentally its purposes and modes of operation. Whether they experience deprivation as poverty, or lack of political power, or disaffection from traditional values, the "have not" leaders and theorists challenge existing institutions. This radical challenge, and its accompanying disposition toward confrontation, marks the vague attitudinal web that links revolutionaries in emerging nations to Black Power advocates in America or to students and intellectuals of the New Left. Three statements will illustrate the similar disposition of men who serve rather different causes in varied circumstances.

For Frantz Fanon, Algerian revolutionary and author of *The Wretched of the Earth*, the symbol of deprivation is the term "colonisation," and the end of confrontation is "decolonisation": "In decolonisation there is therefore the need of a complete calling in question of the colonial situation. If we wish to describe it precisely, we might find it in the well-known words 'The last shall be first and the first last.' Decolonisation is the putting into practice of this statement. That is why, if we try to describe it, all decolonisation is successful."[3]

For Black Power advocate Stokely Carmichael, the enemy is white racism, which is to be confronted, not joined: "Our concern for black power addresses itself directly to this problem, the necessity to reclaim our history and our identity from the cultural terrorism and depredation of self-justifying white guilt. To do this we shall have to struggle for the right to create our own terms through which to define ourselves and our relationship to the society, and to have these terms recognized. This is the first necessity of a free people, and the first right that any oppressor must suspend."[4]

For students in the New Left, the enemy to be confronted is simply "the etablishment," or often in the United States, "technocracy." As student Frederick Richman sees the division:

The world in which the older generation grew up, and which the political systems support, is no longer one which youth can accept. In a world of rampaging technology, racial turmoil, and poverty, they see a President whose program is constituted largely of finishing touches to the New Deal, and a Congress unwilling to accept even that. In a time when personal freedom is of increasing concern, they see a republic operated by an immense bureaucratic structure, geared more to cold war adventures than to domestic needs, stifling individual initiative along with that of states and cities. Finally, they see a political system obsessed with stability and loyalty instead of with social justice.[5]

Those have-nots who confront established power do not seek to share; they demand to supplant.

They must demand to supplant for they live in a Manichean world. Fanon, who features the term, argues that the settler (we may translate "settler" into other words, e.g., racist, establishment, or power structure) is responsible for the situation in which he must

now suffer: "The colonial world is a Manichean world."[6] Those who rule and take the fruit of the system as their due create an equation that identifies themselves with the force of good (order, civilization, progress) which struggles with evil (chaos, the primitive, retrogression). In such a circumstance, established authority often crusades to eliminate the vessels of evil by direct action; but often its leaders work benignly and energetically to transform the others into worthy copies of themselves. At best, the process of transformation is slow, during which time the mass of the others must be carefully held apart to keep them from contaminating the system. Only a few can cross the great gulf to be numbered among the good. Claiming to recognize the reality of this process, which is always masked under exalted labels, black radicals in America cry that the traditional goal of integration masks and preserves racism. In an analogous posture, Students for a Democratic Society picture their educational system as a vast machine to recruit servants for a traditional society, perpetuating all of the injustices of that society.

Whether the force of "good" works energetically and directly or indirectly and somewhat benignly, those without caste must strive to supplant such holders of power. Forced to accept a Manichean struggle, they must reverse the equation, not simply to gain food, land, power, or whatever, but to survive. Reversing the equation will deny the justice of the system that has dehumanized them.

The process of supplanting will be violent for it is born of a violent system. To complete the long quotation introduced above from Fanon: "The naked truth of decolonisation evokes for us the searing bullets and bloodstained knives which emanate from it. For if the last shall be first, this will only come to pass after a murderous and decisive struggle between the two protagonists. That affirmed intention to place the last at the head of things . . . can only triumph if we use all means to turn the scale, including, of course, that of violence."[7]

As Eric Hoffer concludes in his study of mass movements, those who make revolutions are apt to see themselves as spoiled, degraded, and without hope as things exist. But they locate the genesis of their degradation in things, in others, in the world as it is organized around them.[8]

The Rite of the Kill

The enemy is obvious, and it is he who has set the scene upon which the actors must play out the roles determined by the cleavage of exploitation. The situation shrieks kill-or-be-killed. "From here on in, if we must die anyway, we will die fighting back and we will not die alone," Malcolm X wrote in his "Appeal to African Heads of State." "We intend to see that our racist oppressors also get a taste of death."[9]

Judgments like "the oppressor" cannot be made without concomitant judgments. If there are those who oppress, there are those who are oppressed. This much seems obvious, but beneath that surface is the accusation that those oppressed have been something less than men ought to be. If one stresses the cunning, tenacious brutality of the oppressor, he suggests that the oppressed has been less than wise, alert, and strong. If one feels the heritage of injustice, then he senses the ignominy of his patrimony. The blighted self must be killed in striking the enemy. By the act of overcoming his enemy, he who supplants demonstrates his own worthiness, effacing the mark, whatever it may be—immaturity, weakness, subhumanity—that his enemy has set upon his brow.

To satisfy the rite that destroys the evil self in the act of destroying the enemy that has made the self evil, the radical may work out the rite of kill symbolically.[10] Harrassing, embarrassing, and disarming the enemy may suffice, especially if he is finally led to admit his impotence in the face of the superior will of the revolutionary. Symbolic destruction of some manifestation of evil is well illustrated by the outbursts on campuses across America directed toward Dow Chemical. As far as we know in every confrontation of authority centering around the presence on the campus of a recruiter from Dow Chemical, the demonstrators early announced their intention of paralyzing the process until the recruiter agrees on behalf of the company to contaminate the scene no further with his presence.

Michael Novak, a Stanford University professor, pictures student disruption as a tactic to remove the mask of respectability worn by the establishment and kept in place both by the centralized control of communication processes and the traditional canons of free speech.

The balance of power in the formation of public opinion has been altered by the advent of television. The society of independent, rational individuals envisaged by John Stuart Mill does not exist. The fate of all is bound up with the interpretation of events given by the mass media, by the image projected, and by the political power which results. . . . In a society with respect for its political institutions, officials have only to act with decorum and energy in order to benefit by such respect and to have their views established as true until proven false. . . .

What, then, does freedom of speech mean in a technological society? How can one defend oneself against McCarthyism on the one hand and official newspeak on the other? The solution of the students has been to violate the taboos of decorum and thus embrace Vice President Humphrey, the CIA, Dow Chemical, and other enemies in an ugly scene, hoping that the unpopularity of the radicals will rub off on those embraced. They want to make the heretofore bland and respectable wear that tag which most alarms American sensibilities: "controversial."[11]

Student Stephen Saltonstall of Yale University views coercive disruption as the obvious tactic by which "a small concentrated minority" group can bring society to heel and proposes use of this tactic by students to "destroy the university's capability to prop up our political institutions. By stalemating America's intellectual establishment," he continues, "we may be able to paralyze the political establishment as well." Saltonstall's specific recommendations are far-ranging: "A small, disciplined group of shock troops could pack classes, break up drills, and harass army professors. . . . Students could infiltrate the office staffs of the electronic accelerators and foreign policy institutes and hamper their efficiency. The introduction of a small quantity of LSD in only five or six government department coffee-urns might be a highly effective tactic. Students should prevent their universities from being used as forums for government apologists. Public figures like Humphrey and McNamara, when they appear, should be subject to intimidation and humiliation."[12]

Some who confront the oppressive authority seek to transform its representatives as well as themselves, working to wipe out the Manichean world. Such a stance is typical of the strongly Christian representatives of the Civil Rights Movement in this country. But those who advocate killing the enemy or degrading him symbolically act out more simply and more directly the dynamics dictated by the sense of radical division.

Confrontation as a Totalistic Strategy

Part of the attraction of confrontation is the strong sense of success, so strong that it may be a can't-lose strategy. After all in the Christian text Fanon cites ironically, "The last *shall be* first." The last shall be first precisely because he is last. The feeling is that one has nowhere to go but up, that he has nothing to lose, that after having suffered being down so long, he deserves to move up. Aside from the innate logic of the situation, four reasons for success seem apparent. In them we can imagine the radical voice speaking.

a. *We are already dead.* In the world as it is, we do not count. We make no difference. We are not persons. "Baby, it don't mean shit if I burn in a rebellion, because my life ain't worth shit. Dig?"[13] There is no mistaking that idiom, nor the sense behind it. Some radicals take oaths, changing their names, considering themselves as dead, without families, until the revolution succeeds. It is difficult to cow a dead orphan.

b. *We can be reborn.* Having accepted the evaluation of what is, agreeing to be the most worthless of things, we can be reborn. We have nothing to hang on to. No old identity to stop us from identifying with a new world, no matter how horrifying the prospect may seem at the outset; and a new world will certainly be born of the fire we shall create. You, the enemy, on the other hand, must cling to what is, must seek to stamp out the flames, and at best can only end sorrowing at a world that cannot remain the same. Eventually you will be consumed.

c. *We have the stomach for the fight; you don't.* Having created the Manichean world, having degraded humanity, you are overwhelmed by guilt. The sense of guilt stops your hand, for what you would kill is the world you have made. Every blow you strike is suicide and you know it. At best, you can fight only delaying actions. We can strike to kill for the old world is not ours but one in which we are already dead, in which killing injures us not, but provides us with the chance of rebirth.

d. *We are united and understand.* We are united in a sense of a past dead and a present that is valuable only to turn into a future free of your degrading domination. We have accepted our past as past by willing our future. Since you must cling to the past, you have no future and cannot even understand.

Confrontation as a Non-Totalistic Tactic

Radical and revolutionary confrontation worries and bleeds the enemy to death or it engulfs and annihilates him. The logic of the situation that calls it forth bids it be total. But undoubtedly confrontation is brought about by those who feel only division, not radical division. For these the forces of good and evil pop in and out of focus, now clearly perceived, now not; now identified with this manifestation of established power and now that. These radicals may stop short of revolution because they have motives that turn them into politicians who at some point will make practical moves rather than toss every possible compromise and accommodation into the flaming jaws that would destroy the old order.

Student activists in the New Left vacillate in their demands between calls for "destruction" of universities as they are now known and tactical discussions of ways of "getting into the system" to make it more responsive to student goals.[14]

Drift toward non-totalistic goals seems consistent with both the general affluence of this group and its position as a small minority in a large student population generally committed to establishment goals and values. It may also reflect a latent response to the embarrassment of affluent students, beneficiaries of the establishment, who claim the language and motivations of the truly deprived.[15]

Similarly, the perception of confrontation as a tactic for prying apart and thus remodeling the machines of established power seems evident in many adherents of the Black Power movement. In many ways, the power Stokely Carmichael and Charles V. Hamilton forecast in their book is quite conventional, drawing analogies from past, thoroughly American experiences.[16]

Finally, one should observe the possible use of confrontation as a tactic for achieving attention and an importance not readily attainable through decorum. In retiring temporarily from his task of writing a regular newspaper column, Howard K. Smith complained bitterly of a press which inflated Stokely Carmichael from a "nobody who . . . had achieved nothing and represented no one" into "a factor to be reckoned with."[17] But Carmichael knows, from bitter experience, the art of confrontation. Martin Luther King writes of meeting a group of small boys while touring Watts after the riot. "We won!" they shouted joyously. King says his group asked them, "How can you say you won when thirty-four Negroes are dead, your community is destroyed, and whites are using the riot as an excuse for inaction?" The reply was, "We won because we made them pay attention to us."[18]

Without doubt, for many the act of confrontation itself, the march, sit-in, or altercation with the police is enough. It is

consummatory. Through it the radical acts out his drama of self-assertion and writes in smeary, wordless language all over the establishment, "We know you for what you are. And you know that we know." Justifying the sense of rightness and, perhaps, firing a sense of guilt in the other is the hopeful outcome of the many coy confrontations of some shy radicals.[19]

Confrontation and Rhetorical Theory

We have talked of the *rhetoric* of confrontation, not merely confrontation, because this action, as diverse as its manifestations may be, is inherently symbolic. The act carries a message. It dissolves the lines between marches, sit-ins, demonstrations, acts of physical violence, and aggressive discourse. In this way it informs us of the essential nature of discourse itself as human action.

The rhetoric of confrontation also poses new problems for rhetorical theory. Since the time of Aristotle, academic rhetorics have been for the most part instruments of established society, presupposing the "goods" of order, civility, reason, decorum, and civil or theocratic law. Challenges to the sufficiency of this theory and its presuppositions have been few, and largely proposed either by elusive theologians such as Kierkegaard or Buber, or by manifestly unsavory revolutionaries such as Hitler, whose degraded theories of discourse seemed to flow naturally from degraded values and paranoid ambitions.

But the contemporary rhetoric of confrontation is argued by theorists whose aspirations for a better world are not easily dismissed, and whose passion for action equals or exceeds their passion for theory. Even if the presuppositions of civility and rationality underlying the old rhetoric are sound, they can no longer be treated as self-evident.[20] A rhetorical theory suitable to our age must take into account the charge that civility and decorum serve as masks for the preservation of injustice, that they condemn the dispossessed to non-being, and that as transmitted in a technological society they become the instrumentalities of power for those who "have."

A broader base for rhetorical theory is also needed if only as a means of bringing up to date the traditional status of rhetoric as a theory of managing public symbolic transactions. The managerial advice implicit in current theories of debate and discussion scarcely contemplates the possibility that respectable people should confront disruption of reasonable or customary actions, obscenity, threats of violence, and the like. Yet the response mechanisms turned to by those whose presuppositions could not contemplate confrontation often seem to complete the action sought by those who confront, or to confirm their subjective sense of division from the establishment. The use of force to get students out of halls consecrated to university administration or out of holes dedicated to construction projects seems to confirm the radical analysis that the establishment serves itself rather than justice. In this sense, the confronter who prompts violence in the language or behavior of another has found his collaborator. "Show us how ugly you really are," he says, and the enemy with dogs and cattle prods, or police billies and mace, complies. How can administrators ignore the insurgency of those committed to jamming the machinery of whatever enterprise is supposed to be ongoing? Those who would confront have learned a brutal art, practiced sometimes awkwardly and sometimes skillfully, which demands response. But that art may provoke the response that confirms its presuppositions, gratifies the adherents of those presuppositions, and turns the power-enforced victory of the establishment into a symbolic victory for its opponents.

As specialists interested in communication, we who profess the field of rhetoric need to read the rhetoric of confrontation, seek understanding of its presuppositions, tactics, and purposes, and seek placement of its claim against a just accounting of the presuppositions and claims of our tradition. Often as we read and reflect we shall see only grotesque, childish posturings that vaguely act out the deeper drama rooted in radical division. But even so, we shall understand more, act more wisely, and teach more usefully if we open ourselves to the fundamental meaning of radical confrontation.

Robert L. Scott and Donald K. Smith

Mr. Scott is Professor of Speech, Communication, and Theatre Arts at the University of Minnesota. Mr. Smith is Professor of Communicative Arts, University of Wisconsin, Madison.

Notes

1. (New York, 1955), p. 128.
2. Readers will find our generalizations more or less in harmony with other discussions of radical rhetoric which have appeared in the *QJS* recently, e.g., Park G. Burgess, "The Rhetoric of Black Power: A Moral Demand?" LIV (April 1968), 122–133; Leland M. Griffin, "The Rhetorical Structure of the 'New Left' Movement: Part I," L (April 1964), 113–135; and Franklyn S. Haiman, "The Rhetoric of the Streets: Some Legal and Ethical Considerations," LIII (April 1967), 99–114.

   These writers sense a corporate wholeness in the message and methods of various men. An attempt to explain the combination of message and method which forms the wholeness gives rise in each case to a *rhetoric*. All these efforts seem to us impulses to examine the sufficiency of our traditional concepts in dealing with phenomena which are becoming characteristic of contemporary dissent. In seeing rhetoric as an amalgam of meaning and method, these writers break with a tradition that takes rhetoric to be amoral techniques of manipulating a message to fit various contexts.

   Rhetoric has always been response-oriented, that is, the rationale of practical discourse, discourse designed to gain response for specific ends. But these writers see response differently. For them, the response of audiences is an integral part of the message-method that makes the rhetoric. Thus, rhetoric is shifted from a focus of reaction to one of interaction or transaction. (See especially Burgess, 132–133; Griffin, 121; and Haiman, 113)

   Although we believe we share the sense of *rhetoric* which permeates these essays, we claim to analyze a fundamental level of meaning which underlies them.
3. Tr. Constance Farrington (New York, 1963), p. 30.
4. "Toward Black Liberation," *Massachusetts Review*, VII (Autumn 1966), 639–640.
5. "The Disenfranchised Majority," *Students and Society*, report on a conference, Vol. I, No. 1; an occasional paper published by the Center for the Study of Democratic Institutions (Santa Barbara, Calif., 1967), p. 4.
6. Fanon, p. 33. The book is replete with references to "Manicheanism."
7. *Ibid.*, p. 30.

8. *The True Believer* (New York, 1951), pp. 19–20 and *passim*.

9. *Malcolm X Speaks*, ed. George Breitman (New York, 1966), p. 77.

10. See Fanon, p. 73.

11. "An End of Ideology?" *Commonweal*, LXXXVII (March 8, 1968), 681–682.

12. "Toward a Strategy of Disruption," from *Students and Society*, p. 29.

13. Quoted by Jack Newfield, "The Biggest Lab in the Nation," *Life*, LXIV (March 8, 1968), 87.

14. *Students and Society*. A full reading of the conference proceedings reveals clearly this split among the most vocal and militant of New Left students.

15. For an analysis of the structure and characteristics of the student left, see Richard E. Peterson, "The Student Left in American Higher Education," *Daedalus*, XCVII (Winter 1968), 293–317.

16. *Black Power: The Politics of Liberation in America* (New York, 1967), see especially Chap. 5.

17. "Great Age of Journalism Gone?" *Minneapolis Star*, February 19, 1968, p. 5B.

18. *Where Do We Go From Here: Chaos or Community?* (New York, 1967), p. 112.

19. See Norman Mailer, "The Steps of the Pentagon," *Harper's Magazine*, CCXXXVI (March 1968), 47–142 [published in book form as *Armies of the Night* (New York, 1968)]. It may seem difficult to believe but Mailer, who calls himself a "right radical," fits our adjectives, coy and shy.

20. Herein lies a major problem for rhetorical theory. In a sense Haiman's essay (note 2) is a defense of these values accepting the responsibility implied by his analysis which shows a significant case made by the very existence of "A Rhetoric of the Streets" which demands a rebuttal. Burgess' essay (note 2) sees Black Power as a unique method of forcing conventional thought to take seriously its own criterion of rationality.

21

Rhetoric as a Way of Knowing: Stephen Toulmin and the Nature of Argument

In the preceding chapters on contemporary rhetorical theory, we have described some of the leading aspects of rhetoric as meaning, rhetoric as motives, and rhetoric as values. While all of these trends have their origin in earlier writings, the approach used by the authors we have cited is sufficiently unique to qualify their works as a form of "new rhetoric." Yet to be analyzed is another developing trend which is rapidly gaining adherents. Representatives of this school of thought tend to view rhetoric as a way of knowing. They, like their counterparts in the British period, may be classified as modern epistemologists.

Among the first communication theorists in mid-twentieth century America to catch the significance of this emerging trend was Robert Scott in his 1967 essay, "On Viewing Rhetoric as Epistemic."[1] In this seminal study, Scott takes issue with the notion that the purpose of rhetoric is to "make the truth effective in practical affairs." Even if one assumes the existence of truth, Scott argues in the following passage, there are serious problems which arise:

Accepting the notion that truth exists, may be known, and if communicated leads logically to the position that there should be only two modes of discourse: a neutral presenting of data among equals and a persuasive leading to inferiors by the capable. The attitude with which this position may be espoused can vary from benevolent to cynical, but it is certainly undemocratic. Still the contemporary rhetorician is prone to accept the assumption to say, in effect, "My art is simply one which is useful in making the truth effective in practical affairs," scarcely conscious of the irony inherent in his statement.[2]

Surely, adds Scott, rhetoric serves a more significant function. The significant function suggested by Scott and other authors to be considered in this chapter is grounded in the process of knowing resulting from argument. Although the linking of rhetoric with argument dates back to Whately, what makes this contemporary emphasis unique is its stress on knowing rather than on persuading.

Douglas Ehninger and Wayne Brockriede began to make the above link evident in their volume, *Decision by Debate.* Influenced by the philosophy of Stephen Toulmin, these scholars describe debate as a critical and cooperative instrument of investigation. Here are a few of their conclusions: "(a) the end and method of debate are critical; (b) debate is an instrument of investigation rather than of propagation; (c) debate is a cooperative rather than competitive enterprise."[3] This viewpoint seeks to reclaim the hitherto lost or subverted epistemological dimension of the art of rhetoric. As Scott has noted: "If debate is critical inquiry, then it is not simply an effort to make a preconceived position effective."[4]

Quite clearly, then, when rhetoric is defined so as to include the argumentative process, a way of knowing emerges. Through the critical interaction of arguments wherein rhetors "seek" and listeners "judge" what they hear, knowledge is generated, tested, and acted upon. Observe how Carroll Arnold identifies this perspective with the teachings of the "new rhetoricians" who rely on "practical experience."

The new rhetoricians contend that subjecting itineraries of attempts to conclude probabilisticly to the judgments of others is a way of coming to know. The view seems supportable from practical experience. Rhetorical situations *do* seem to entail tacit understandings that the rhetors are "seeking" and the respondents "judging," not just responding autonomically. And if the rhetor is tested as he acts rhetorically, he *can* learn from his audience's judgment—unless he ignores their judgments, which would be a denial that communication was rhetorical.[5]

As a way of knowing, rhetoric does not simply seek to proclaim "truth"; rather, it becomes a means for generating understanding. What does this position imply, then, concerning the nature of "truth?" Scott answers this inquiry in this way:

What these statements do suggest is that truth is not prior and immutable but is contingent. Insofar as we can say that there is truth in human affairs, it is in time; it can be the result of a process of interaction at a given moment. Thus rhetoric may be viewed not as a matter of giving effectiveness to truth but of creating truth.[6]

Strongly supporting the position of Scott is that held by Richard Rieke who says:

From these materials I will conclude that rhetoric is inextricably involved in the generation of knowledge; not merely a way of knowing, but involved in all ways of knowing. To be more specific, the division of the world into the realm of the absolute and that of the contingent may be rejected totally. All knowledge will be viewed as contingent, and rhetoric, the rationale of the contingent, will be recognized as essential to all knowledge—scientific, humanistic, or whatever.[7]

Truth viewed from this perspective, then, is something created by the rhetorical process

which, in turn, is situation-or context-bound. Men interlocked and interacting critically in the rhetorical dimension arrive at the "truth" for a given people, at a given time in their history, within given situational or environmental factors. And so, a priori truth is not possible within the philosophical framework proposed by the contemporary rhetorical epistemologists. In commenting on this point, Scott observes:

The direction of analysis from Toulmin through Ehninger and Brockriede, leads to the conclusion that there is no possibility in matters relevant to human interaction to determine truth in any a priori way, that truth can arise only from cooperative critical inquiry. Men may have recourse to some universal ideas in which they are willing to affirm their faith, but these must enter into the contingencies of time and place and will not give rise to products which are certain.[8]

Man's quest for universals is thus a rhetorical process. For men interacting in a critical and cooperative attitude discover knowledge together.

It would appear, therefore, that rhetoric as a way of knowing established for itself the goal of gaining adherence of minds regarding the facts of a particular discipline or field of inquiry. A communicator and communicatee thus should reach an intellectual agreement only after they have engaged in rhetorical transactions presented against a background of strong reasoning and compelling evidence. Within this argumentative environment, discovery occupies a position equal to or surpassing that of persuasion. The ensuing statement by Arnold capsulizes this view:

For most of the writers I am calling a "new school," manipulating symbolic devices for the purpose of gaining one's own or someone else's adherence is essential to the very process of coming to know. And manipulation of verbal devices is also an indispensable way of testing what one thinks he, himself, knows. Rhetorical activity thus becomes not persuasive alone but an activity of ideational discovery.[9]

The "moment by moment" discovery of knowledge, as emphasized by the "new school" rhetoricians, is doubtless a creative, exciting endeavor founded on the inherent rhetorical attribute of all men and women.

Stephen Toulmin

The two rhetoricians who best exemplify the trend being described in the next two chapters are Stephen Toulmin and Chaim Perelman who have much in common as students of argument. Toulmin is an English philosopher whose intellectual specialties are logic and the philosophy of science. Perelman is a Belgian philosopher and lawyer who is well known on the Continent for his works on logic and practical argument. Both have borrowed ideas from law and jurisprudence and applied them to rhetoric. It is our purpose now to probe more deeply into their theories so as to gain a fuller appreciation of the relationship between rhetoric and knowing.

Toulmin's Uses of Argument

Stephen Toulmin's *Uses of Argument* was first published in 1958. Perhaps the most noted contribution made by his text to rhetorical theory is the Toulmin model of argument which consists of the following elements: claim, warrant, data, qualifier, rebuttal, and backing. This model is considered in the essay immediately following. Before examining it in detail, however, we need to provide a background or frame of reference into Toulmin's thought.

Toulmin is dissatisfied with formal syllogistic-based logic. Believing that the syllogism does not necessarily *advance* knowledge and that formal logical systems fail to represent adequately the human reasoning process, Toulmin provides a rationale for his inquiry. In effect, Toulmin is critical of formal logic because it is *not* a way of knowing. Toulmin then sets out to formalize a model of argument which corresponds to the "rational process" characteristic of human decision making. "We shall aim," he says, "to characterize what may be called 'the rational process,' the procedures and categories by using which claims-in-general can be argued for and settled."[10]

Toulmin begins his inquiry by turning his attention to "fields of argument." Here the author introduces the concepts of "field invariant" and "field dependent" arguments.

What things about the modes in which we assess arguments, the standards by reference to which we assess them and the manner in which we qualify our conclusions about them, are the same regardless of field (field-invariant), and which of them vary as we move from arguments in one field to arguments in another (field-dependent)? How far, for instance, can one compare the standards of argument relevant in a court of law with those relevant when judging a paper in the Proceedings of the Royal Society, or those relevant to a mathematical proof or a prediction about the composition of a tennis team?[11]

When comparing and analyzing arguments it is necessary to discern if each argument is field-invariant or dependent, according to Toulmin. That is, the context which surrounds an argument—its field—determines the nature—stringency and looseness—of the said argument. On this point, Toulmin explains: "Two arguments will be said to belong to the same field when the data and conclusions in each of the two arguments are respectively, of the same logical type; they will be said to come from different fields when the backing or the conclusions in each of the two arguments are not of the same logical type."[12] Obviously, arguments within the same field can be compared. Arguments from different fields, however, must be carefully scrutinized, for comparisons are difficult, if not impossible, to make. Whereas formal logic attempts to judge all arguments from its established categories, Toulmin advocates judgment based on the fields in which they reside. "Indeed," observes Toulmin, "whether questions about comparative stringency can even be asked about arguments from different fields may be worth questioning."[13]

Relating these ideas to arguments found in the courtrooms, Toulmin states: "So it can be asked about law cases, as about arguments in general, how far their form and the canons relevant for their criticism are invariant—the same for cases of all types—and how far they are dependent upon the type of case under consideration."[14]

Toulmin's criticism of logic is more profound than time and space permit us to consider here. His dissatisfaction with the science of formal logic, however, is partially evident even in the above quoted statements. Toulmin claims that we must recognize the powerful influence inherent in the fields surrounding arguments and that the application of formal logical *rules* to field-dependent arguments is questionable at best. As a way of knowing, rhetoric cannot be restricted to formal rules and regulations. As a way of knowing, argument must not be restrained, but must *advance* knowledge.

With this background, Toulmin begins his search for those stages of any justificatory argument "to see how far these stages can be found alike in the case of arguments taken from many different fields."[15] Herein, Toulmin implies that there is indeed a "rational form" or model of argument which follows a similar course regardless of the argument's field. The claim-data-warrant-reservation-backing-qualifier model is Toulmin's answer.

We need at this point to mention the concept of "probability" which Toulmin builds into his system—a concept which serves to differentiate his model from formal logic. The model is characterized by its inclusion of probability terms which, in turn, serve to *qualify* the argument under consideration. Such statements serve to protect the universality and absoluteness of the argument. As he notes:

Our probability-terms come to serve, therefore, not only to qualify assertions, promises and evaluations themselves, but also as an indication of the strength of the backing which we have for the assertion, evaluation or whatever. It is the quality of the *evidence* or *argument* at the speaker's disposal which

determines what sort of qualifier he is entitled to include in his statements. . . .[16]

In sum, the Toulmin model of argument is a dynamic model which highlights the *movement* of the rhetor's reasoning. As such, Toulmin claims his model is more realistic and representative of the rational process involved in decision making—that is, the Toulmin model is *epistemic*. Accordingly, Toulmin argues that, "a radical re-ordering of logical theory is needed in order to bring it more nearly into line with critical practice. . . ."[17]

An analysis of Toulmin's views, particularly his model of argument, was first introduced to American students by Ehninger and Brockriede in 1960. So effectively have the authors caught the essence of Toulmin's rhetorical philosophy that we are reprinting the essay here as a summary statement and application of *Uses of Argument*. We do so with the understanding that Brockriede and Ehninger have since modified some of their positions. See the 2nd. ed. of *Decision by Debate* (New York. Harper and Row, 1977).

Notes

1. Robert Scott, "On Viewing Rhetoric as Epistemic," *Central States Speech Journal*, XVIII (Feb. 1967), pp. 9–17.
2. *Ibid.*, p. 10.
3. Douglas Ehninger and Wayne Brockriede, *Decision By Debate* (New York: Dodd, Mead and Company, 1972), p. 16.
4. Scott, op. cit., p. 13.
5. Carroll C. Arnold, "Inventio and Pronunciatio in a 'New Rhetoric' "; unpublished paper, abstract, Central States Speech Association Convention, 1972. p. 12.
6. Scott, op. cit., p. 13.
7. Richard D. Rieke, "Rhetorical Perspectives in Modern Epistemology," unpublished paper, abstract, Speech Communication Association Convention, 1974. p. 1.
8. Scott, op. cit., p. 14.
9. Arnold, op. cit., p. 4.
10. Stephen E. Toulmin, *The Uses of Argument* (Cambridge: Cambridge University Press, 1958), p. 7.
11. *Ibid.*, p. 15.
12. *Ibid.*, p. 14.
13. *Ibid.*, p. 15.
14. *Ibid.*, p. 16.
15. *Ibid.*, p. 17.
16. *Ibid.*, pp. 90-91.
17. *Ibid.*, p. 253.

Toulmin on Argument: An Interpretation and Application

During the period 1917–1932 several books, a series of articles, and many Letters to the Editor of *QJS* gave serious attention to exploring the nature of argument as it is characteristically employed in rhetorical proofs.[1] Since that time, however, students of public address have shown comparatively little interest in the subject, leaving to philosophers, psychologists, and sociologists the principal contributions which have more recently been made toward an improved understanding of argument.[2]

Among the contributions offered by "outsiders" to our field, one in particular deserves more attention than it has so far received from rhetoricians. We refer to some of the formulations of the English logician Stephen Toulmin in his *The Uses of Argument*, published in 1958.[3]

Toulmin's analysis and terminology are important to the Rhetorician for two different but related reasons. First, they provide an appropriate structural model by means of which rhetorical arguments may be laid out for analysis and criticism; and, second, they suggest a system for classifying artistic proofs which employs argument as a central and unifying construct. Let us consider these propositions in order.

1

As described by Toulmin, an argument is *movement* from accepted *data*, through a *warrant*, to a *claim*.

Data (D) answer the question, "What have you got to go on?" Thus *data* correspond to materials of fact or opinion which in our textbooks are commonly called *evidence*. Data may report historical or contemporary events, take the form of a statistical compilation or of citations from authority, or they may consist of one or more general declarative sentences established by a prior proof of an artistic nature. Without data clearly present or strongly implied, an argument has no informative or substantive component, no factual point of departure.

Claim (C) is the term Toulmin applies to what we normally speak of as a *conclusion*. It is the explicit appeal produced by the argument, and is always of a potentially controversial nature. A claim may stand as the final proposition in an argument, or it may be an intermediate statement which serves as data for a subsequent inference.

Data and claim taken together represent the specific contention advanced by an argument, and therefore constitute what may be regarded as its *main proof line*; the usual order is *data* first, and then *claim*. In this sequence the *claim* contains or implies "therefore." When the order is reversed, the *claim* contains or implies "because."

Warrant (W) is the operational name Toulmin gives to that part of an argument which authorizes the mental "leap" involved in advancing from data to claim. As distinguished from data which answer the question "What have you got to go on," the warrant answers the question "How do you get there." Its function is to *carry* the accepted data to the doubted or disbelieved proposition which constitutes the claim, thereby certifying this claim as true or acceptable.

The relations existing among these three basic components of an argument, Toulmin suggests, may be represented diagrammatically:

(D)ata ———— Therefore (C)laim

Since (W)arrant

Here is an application of the method:

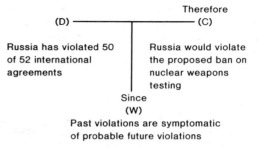

	Therefore
(D)	(C)
Russia has violated 50 of 52 international agreements	Russia would violate the proposed ban on nuclear weapons testing

Since
(W)
Past violations are symptomatic
of probable future violations

Reprinted from the *Quarterly Journal of Speech*, 46 (February 1960) 44–53 with the permission of the author and editor, *Quarterly Journal of Speech*. We have been informed by the authors that some of these views are being revised.

In addition to the three indispensable elements of *data, claim,* and *warrant,* Toulmin recognizes a second triad of components, any or all of which may, but need not necessarily, be present in an argument. These he calls (1) *backing,* (2) *rebuttal,* and (3) *qualifier.*

Backing (B) consists of credentials designed to certify the assumption expressed in the warrant. Such credentials may consist of a single item, or of an entire argument in itself complete with data and claim. Backing must be introduced when readers or listeners are not willing to accept a warrant at its face value.

The rebuttal (R) performs the function of a safety valve or escape hatch, and is, as a rule, appended to claim statement. It recognizes certain conditions under which the claim will not hold good or will hold good only in a qualified and restricted way. By limiting the area to which the claim may legitimately be applied, the rebuttal anticipates certain objections which might otherwise be advanced against the argument.

The function of the qualifier (Q) is to register the degree of force which the maker believes is his claim to possess. The qualification may be expressed by a quantifying term such as "possibly," "probably," "to the five percent level of confidence," etc., or it may make specific reference to an anticipated refutation. When the author of a claim regards it as incontrovertible no qualifier is appended.

These additional elements may be superimposed on the first diagram:

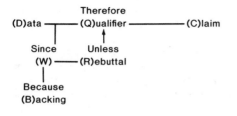

We may illustrate the model as follows:

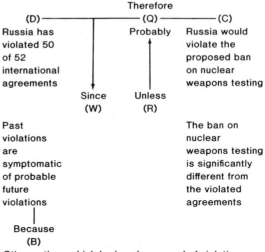

Other nations which had such a record of violations continued such action / Expert X states that nations which have been chronic violators nearly always continued such acts / etc.

2

With Toulmin's structural model now set forth, let us inquire into its suitability as a means of describing and testing arguments. Let us compare Toulmin's method with the analysis offered in traditional logic, the logic commonly used as a basic theory of argumentation in current textbooks. We conceive of arguments in the customary fashion as (1) deriving from probable causes and signs, (2) proceeding more often by relational than implicative principles, (3) emphasizing material as well as formal validity, (4) employing premises which are often contestable, and (5) eventuating in claims which are by nature contingent and variable.

The superiority of the Toulmin model in describing and testing arguments may be claimed for seven reasons:

1. Whereas traditional logic is characteristically concerned with *warrant-using* arguments (i.e., arguments in which the validity of

the assumption underlying the inference "leap" is uncontested), Toulmin's model specifically provides for *warrant-establishing* arguments (i.e., arguments in which the validity of the assumption underlying the inference must be established—through backing—as part of the proof pattern itself).[4]

2. Whereas traditional logic, based as it is upon the general principle of implication, always treats proof more or less as a matter of classification or compartmentalization, Toulmin's analysis stresses the inferential and relational nature of argument, providing a context within which all factors—both formal and material—bearing upon a disputed claim may be organized into a series of discrete steps.

3. Whereas in traditional logic, arguments are specifically designed to produce universal propositions, Toulmin's second triad of backing, rebuttal, and qualifier provide, within the framework of his basic structural model, for the establishment of claims which are no more than probable. The model directs attention to the ways in which each of these additional elements may operate to limit or condition a claim.

4. Whereas traditional logic, with its governing principle of implication, necessarily results in an essentially static conception of argument, Toulmin by emphasizing *movement* from data, through warrant, to claim, produces a conception of argument as dynamic. From his structural model we derive a picture of arguments "working" to establish and certify claims, and as a result of his functional terminology we are able to undersand the role each part of an argument plays in this process.

5. Whereas the models based on the traditional analysis—enthymeme, example, and the like—often suppress a step in proof, Toulmin's model lays an argument out in such a way that each step may be examined critically.

6. Whereas in the traditional analysis the division of arguments into premises and conclusions (as in the syllogism, for example) often

tends to obscure deficiencies in proof, Toulmin's model assigns each part of an argument a specific geographical or spatial position in relation to the others, thus rendering it more likely that weak points will be detected.

7. Whereas traditional logic is imperfectly equipped to deal with the problem of material validity, Toulmin makes such validity an integral part of his system, indicating clearly the role which factual elements play in producing acceptable claims.

In short, without denying that Toulmin's formulations are open to serious criticism at several points[5]—and allowing for any peculiarities in our interpretations of the character of traditional logic—one conclusion emerges. Toulmin has provided a structural model which promises to be of greater use in laying out rhetorical arguments for dissection and testing than the methods of traditional logic. For although most teachers and writers in the field of argumentation have discussed the syllogism in general terms, they have made no serious attempt to explore the complexities of the moods and figures of the syllogism, nor have they been very successful in applying the terms and principles of traditional logic to the arguments of real controversies. Toulmin's model provides a practical replacement.

3

Our second proposition is that Toulmin's structural model and the vocabulary he has developed to describe it are suggestive of a system for classifying artistic proofs, using argument (defined as *movement* from data through warrant, to claim) as a unifying construct.[6]

In extending Toulmin's analysis to develop a simplified classification of arguments, we may begin by restating in Toulmin's terms the traditional difference between *inartistic* and *artistic* proof. Thus, conceiving of an argument as a movement by means of which accepted data are carried through a certifying warrant to a controversial claim, we may say that in some cases the data themselves are conclusive. They approach the claim without aid from a warrant—are tantamount to the claim in the sense that to accept them is automatically to endorse the claim they are designed to support. In such cases the proof may be regarded as *inartistic*. In another class of arguments, however, the situation is quite different. Here the data are not immediately conclusive, so that the role of the warrant in carrying them to the claim becomes of crucial importance. In this sort of argument the proof is directly dependent upon the inventive powers of the arguer and may be regarded as *artistic*.

If, then, the warrant is the crucial element in an artistic proof, and if its function is to carry the data to the claim, we may classify artistic arguments by recognizing the possible routes which the warrant may travel in performing its function.

So far as rhetorical proofs are concerned, as men have for centuries recognized, these routes are three in number: (1) an arguer may carry data to claim by means of an assumption concerning the relationship existing among phenomena in the external world; (2) by means of an assumption concerning the quality of the source from which the data are derived; and (3) by means of an assumption concerning the inner drives, values, or aspirations which impel the behavior of those persons to whom the argument is addressed.

Arguments of the first sort (traditionally called *logical*) may be called *substantive*; those of the second sort (traditionally called *ethical*) may be described as *authoritative*; and those of the third sort (traditionally called *pathetic*) as *motivational*.

Substantive Arguments

The warrant of a substantive argument reflects an assumption concerning the way in which things are related in the world about us. Although other orderings are possible, one commonly recognized, and the one used here, is six-fold. Phenomena may be related as cause to effect (or as effect to cause), as attribute to

substance, as some to more, as intrinsically similar, as bearing common relations, or as more to some. Upon the first of these relationships is based what is commonly called argument from *cause*; on the second, argument from *sign*; on the third, argument from *generalization*; and the fourth, argument from *parallel case*; on the fifth, argument from *analogy*; and on the sixth, argument from *classification*.

Cause. In argument from cause the data consist of one or more accepted facts about a person, object, event, or condition. The warrant attributes to these facts a creative or generative power and specifies the nature of the effect they will produce. The claim relates these results to the person, object, event, or condition named in the data. Here is an illustration, from cause to effect:

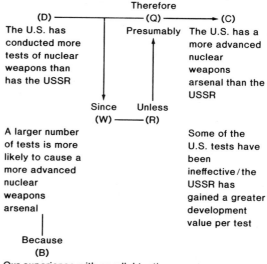

Our experience with parallel testing programs indicates this / Expert X testifies that many tests are more likely than fewer tests to create advanced nuclear weapons arsenals.

When the reasoning process is reversed and the argument is from effect to cause, the data again consist of one or more facts about a person, object, event, or condition; the warrant asserts that a particular causal force is sufficient to have accounted for these facts; and the claim relates the cause to the person, object, event, or condition named in the data.

Sign. In argument from sign the data consist of clues or symptoms. The warrant interprets the meaning or significance of these symptoms. The claim affirms that some person, object, event, or condition possesses the attributes of which the clues have been declared symptomatic. Our first example concerning Russia's violation of international agreements illustrates the argument from sign.

Generalization. In argument from generalization the data consist of information about a number of persons, objects, events, or conditions, taken as constituting a representative and adequate sample of a given class of phenomena. The warrant assumes that what is true of the items constituting the sample will also be true of additional members of the class not represented in the sample. The claim makes explicit the assumption embodied in the warrant. The form can be diagrammed so:

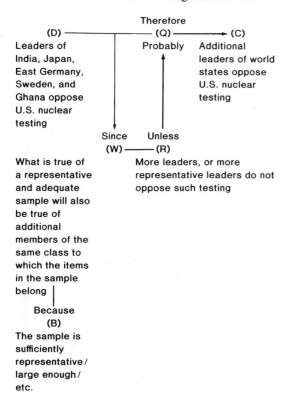

Parallel Case. In argument from parallel case the data consist of one or more statements about a single object, event, or condition. The warrant asserts that the instance reported in the data bears an essential similarity to a second instance in the same category. The claim affirms about the new instance what has already been accepted concerning the first. Here is an illustration:

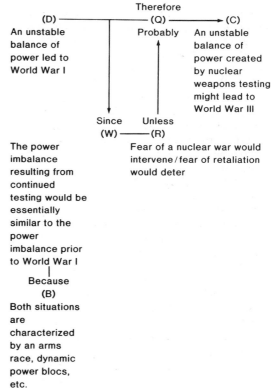

In argument from parallel cases a rebuttal will be required in either of two situations: (1) if another parallel case bears a stronger similarity to the case under consideration; or (2) if in spite of some essential similarities an essential dissimilarity negates or reduces the force of the warrant. The example illustrates the second of these possibilities.

Analogy. In argument from analogy the data report that a relationship of a certain nature exists between two items. The warrant assumes that a similar relationship exists between a second pair of items. The claim makes explicit the relationship assumed in the warrant. Whereas the argument from parallel case assumes a resemblance between two *cases*, the analogy assumes only a similarity of *relationship*. Analogy may be illustrated so:

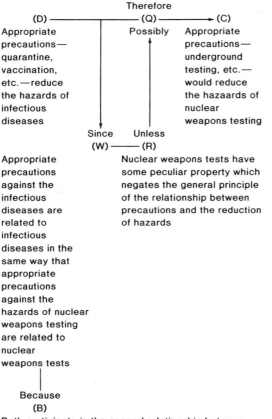

Both participate in the general relationship between precautions and the reduction of hazards

In most cases the analogical relation expressed in an argument from analogy will require a strongly qualifying "possibly."

Classification. In argument from classification the statement of the data is a generalized conclusion about known members of a class of persons, objects, events, or conditions.

The warrant assumes that what is true of the items reported in the data will also be true of a hitherto unexamined item which is known (or thought) to fall within the class there described. The claim then transfers the general statement which has been made in the data to the particular item under consideration. As illustrated, the form would appear:

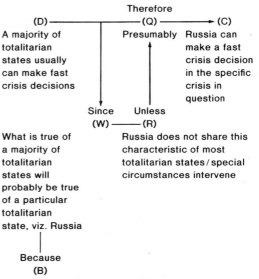

The class "totalitarian states" is reasonably homogeneous, stable, etc. / Russia generally shares the attributes of the totalitarian states class

Two kinds of reservations may be applicable in an argument from classification: (1) a class member may not share the particular attribute cited in the data, although it does share enough other attributes to deserve delineation as a member of the class; and (2) special circumstances may prevent a specific class member from sharing at some particular time or place the attributes general to the class.

Authoritative Arguments

In authoritative arguments the data consist of one or more factual reports or statements of opinion. The warrant affirms the reliability of the source from which these are derived. The claim reiterates the statement which appeared in the data, as now certified by the warrant. An illustration follows:

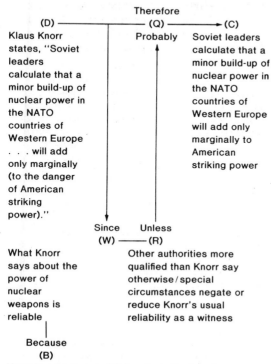

What Knorr says about the power of nuclear weapons is reliable

|
Because
(B)

Knorr is a professor at Princeton's Center of International Studies / is unbiased / has made reliable statements on similar matters in the past / etc.

The structure and function of an authoritative argument remains basically the same when the source of the data is the speaker or writer himself. The data is carried to claim status by the same sort of assumption embodied in the warrant. We may infer a claim from what Knorr says about nuclear weapons whether he is himself the speaker, or whether another speaker is quoting what Knorr has said. Thus the *ethos* of a speaker may be studied by means of the Toulmin structure under the heading of authoritative argument.

Motivational Arguments

In motivational arguments the data consist of one or more statements which may have been established as claims in a previous argument or series of arguments. The warrant provides a motive for accepting the claim by associating it with some inner drive, value, desire, emotion, or aspiration, or with a combination of such forces. The claim as so warranted is that the person, object, event, or condition referred to in the data should be accepted as valuable or rejected as worthless or that the policy there described should or should not be adopted, or the action there named should or should not be performed. Illustrated, the form would appear:

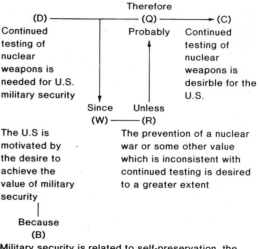

The U.S is motivated by the desire to achieve the value of military security

|
Because
(B)

Military security is related to self-preservation, the maintenance of our high standard of living, patriotism, the preservation of democracy, etc.

4

We have exhibited the structural unity of the three modes of artistic proof by showing how they may be reduced to a single invariant pattern using argument as a unifying construct. Let us as a final step explore this unity further by inquiring how artistic proofs, so reduced, may conveniently be correlated with the various types of disputable questions and the claims appropriate to each.

Let us begin by recognizing the four categories into which disputable questions have customarily been classified: (1) Whether something is? (2) What it is? (3) Of what worth it is? (4) What course of action should be pursued? The first of these queries gives rise to a question of fact, and is to be answered by what can be called a *designative claim*; the second, to a question of definition, to be answered by a *definitive claim;* the third, to a question of value, to be answered by an *evaluative claim*; and the fourth, to a question of *policy*, to be answered by an *advocative claim*.

Supposing, then, that an arguer is confronted with a question of fact, calling for a designative claim; or a question of policy, calling for an advocative claim, etc., what types of argument would be available to him as means of substantiating his claim statement? Upon the basis of the formulations developed in earlier sections of this paper, it is possible to supply rather precise answers.

Designative Claims. A designative claim, appropriate to answering a question of fact, will be found supportable by any of the six forms of substantive argument, or by authoritative argument, but not by motivational argument. That is, whether something exists or is so, may be determined: (1) by isolating its cause or its effect (argument from cause); (2) by reasoning from the presence of symptoms to the claim that a substance exists or is so (argument from sign); (3) by inferring that because some members of a given class exist or are so, more members of the same class also exist or are so (argument from generalization); (4) by inferring because one item exists or is so, that a closely similar item exists or is so (argument from parallel case); (5) by reasoning that D exists or is so because it stands in the same relation to C that B does to A, when C, B, and A are known to exist or to be so (argument from analogy); and (6) by concluding that an unexamined item known or thought to fall within a given class exists or is so because all known members of the class exist or are so (argument from classification). Moreover, we may argue that something exists or is so because a reputable authority declares this to be the case. Motivational argument, on the other hand, may not be critically employed in designative claims, because values, desires, and feelings are irrelevant where questions of fact are concerned.

Definitive Claims. The possibilities for establishing definitive claims are more limited. Only two of the forms of substantive argument and authoritative argument are applicable. We may support a claim as to what something is: (1) by comparing it with a closely similar phenomenon (argument from parallel case); or (2) by reasoning that because it stands in the same relation to C as B does to A it will be analogous to C, where the nature of C, B, and A are known (argument from analogy). In addition, we may support a definition or interpretation by citing an acceptable authority. Among the substantive arguments, cause, sign, generalization, and classification are inapplicable; and once again motivational argument is irrelevant since emotions, wishes, and values cannot legitimately determine the nature of phenomena.

Evaluative Claims. Evaluative claims may be supported by generalization, parallel case, analogy, and classification, and by authoritative and motivational arguments. By generalization a class of phenomena may be declared valuable or worthless on the ground that a typical and adequate sample of the members of that class is so. By classification, in contrast, we infer from the worth of known members of a class the probable worth of some previously unexamined item known or thought to belong to that class. By parallel case, we infer goodness or badness from the quality of an item closely similar. By analogy, however, we infer value on the basis of a ratio of resemblances rather than a direct parallel. In authoritative argument our qualitative judgment is authorized by a recognized expert. In motivational argument, however, an item is assigned a value in accordance with its usefulness in satisfying human drives, needs, and aspirations. Arguments from cause and sign, on the other hand, are inapplicable.

Advocative Claims. Advocative claims may legitimately be established in only four ways. We may argue that some policy should be adopted or some action undertaken because a closely similar policy or action has brought desirable results in the past (argument from parallel case). We may support a proposed policy or action because it bears the same relation to C that B does to A, where B is known to have brought desirable results (argument from analogy). Or, of course, we may support our claim by testimony (authoritative argument), or by associating it with men's wishes, values, and aspirations (motivational argument).

This analysis concerning the types of arguments applicable to various sorts of claims may be summarized in tabular form:

	Designative	Definitive	Evaluative	Advocative
Substantive				
A. Cause	X			
B. Sign	X			
C. Generalization	X		X	
D. Parallel Case	X	X	X	X
E. Analogy	X	X	X	X
F. Classification	X		X	
Authoritative	X	X	X	X
Motivational			X	X

The world of argument is vast, one seemingly without end. Arguments arise in one realm, are resolved, and appear and reappear in others; and new arguments appear. If one assumes some rationality among men, a system of logical treatment of argument is imperative. The traditional logical system of syllogisms, of enthymemes, of middles distributed and undistributed, may have had its attraction in medieval times. The inadequacies of such a logic, however, have been described by experts; for example, see J. S. Mill on the syllogism and *petitio principii*.[7] The modern search has been for a method which would have some application in the dynamics of contemporary affairs.

Toulmin has supplied us with a contemporary methodology, which in many respects makes the traditional unnecessary. The basic theory has herein been amplified, some extensions have been made, and illustrations of workability have been supplied. All this is not meant to be the end, but rather the beginning of an inquiry into a new, contemporary, dynamic, and usable logic for argument.

Wayne E. Brockriede and
Douglas Ehninger

Wayne Brockriede is Professor of Communication, California State University, Fullerton. Douglas Ehninger was Professor of Speech and Dramatic Art, University of Iowa.

Notes

1. E.g., such books as James M. O'Neill, Craven Laycock, and Robert L. Scales, *Argumentation and Debate* (New York, 1917); William T. Foster, *Argumentation and Debating* (Boston, 1917); and A. Craig Baird, *Public Discussion and Debate* (Boston, 1928); such articles as Mary Yost, "Argument from the Point of View of Sociology," *QJS*, III (1917); 109–24; Charles H. Woolbert, "The Place of Logic in a System of Persuasion," *QJS*, IV, (1918), 19–39; Gladys Murphy Graham, "Logic and Argumentation," *QJS*, X (1924), 350–363; William E. Utterback, "Aristotle's Contribution to the Psychology of Argument," *QJS*, XI (1925), 218–225; Herbert A. Wichelns, "Analysis and Synthesis in Argumentation," *QJS*, XI (1925), 266–272; and Edward Z. Rowell, "Prolegomena to Argumentation," *QJS*, XVIII (1932), 1–13, 224–248, 381–405, 585–606; such Letters to the Editor as those by Utterback, XI (1925), 175–177, Wichelns, XI (1925), 286–288; Ralph C. Ringwalt, XII (1926), 66–68; and Graham, XII (1925), 196–197.

2. See, for example, Mortimer Adler, *Dialectic* (New York, 1927); Paul Edwards, *The Logic of Moral Discourse* (Glencoe, Ill., 1955); Carl I. Hovland, Irving L. Janis, and Harold W. Kelley, *Communication and Persuasion* (New Haven, Conn., 1953); Charles Perelman, *Traite de l'argumentation*, 2 vols. (Paris, 1958), and *La nouvelle rhetorique* (Paris, 1952); and John Cohen, "Subjective Probability," *Scientific American*, MCMVII (1957), 128–38.

3. (Cambridge, Cambridge University Press). See especially the third of the five essays in the book. *Cf.* J. C. Cooley, "On Mr. Toulmin's Revolution in Logic," *The Journal of Philosophy*, LVI (1959), 297–319.

4. In traditional logic only the epicheirema provides comparable backing for premises.

5. It may be charged that his structural model is merely "a syllogism lying on its side," that it makes little or no provision to insure the formal validity of claims, etc.

6. Our suggestion as to the structural unity of artistic proofs is by no means novel. The ancients regularly spoke of *pathetic* and *ethical* enthymemes, and envisioned the *topoi* as applicable beyond the *pistis*. (See in this connection James H. McBurney, "The Place

of the Enthymeme in Rhetorical Theory," *SM*, III [1936], 63.) At the same time, however, it must be recognized that especially since the advent of the faculty psychology of the seventeenth and eighteenth centuries, rhetorical thought has been profoundly and persistently influenced by the doctrine of a dichotomy between pathetic and logical appeals. (For significant efforts to combat this doctrine see Charle H. Woolbert, "Conviction and Persuasion: Some Considerations of Theory," *QJS*, III (1917), 249–264; Mary Yost, "Argument from the Point of View of Sociology," *QJS*, III [1917], 109–124; and W. Norwood Brigance, "Can We Redefine the James-Winans Theory of Persuasion?" *QJS*, XXI [1935], 19–26.)

7. A *System of Logic*, I, chap. 3, Sec. 2.

Toulmin's *Human Understanding*, Volume I

As a companion volume to *Uses of Argument*, Toulmin wrote a follow up study in 1972, entitled *Human Understanding*.[1] Since the principal theme in this work is "the collective use and evolution of concepts," Toulmin continues his campaign to show how argument is a way of knowing. Our purpose in this section is to depict how argument rests on a continuum at a mid-point between absolutism on the one hand and relativism on the other. To see how argument is the primary force responsible for conceptual change or the generation of new knowledge, let us first examine the principal characteristics of absolutism and relativism as summarized and criticized by Toulmin.

Absolutism. The absolutists, according to Toulmin, are enamored with the formal logician's approach which upholds the value of a "logical systematicity" that features a "quasi-mathematical" method capable of producing "eternal principles." The absolutist is concerned with the "acceptability of propositions" based upon the criteria of correctness, incorrectness, form, and validity. Similarly, he views as authoritative that which is coherent, consistent, and properly entailed. Thus he imposes "from outside, on all milieus alike, an abstract and ideal set of formal criteria, defined in terms of a universal, quasi-mathematical 'logical system'. . . ."[2]

Toulmin discards absolutism as a satisfactory means of explaining conceptual change on the grounds that it is "static" and "stereotyped." Additionally, it is unable to bridge the gap between theory and practice. Obsessed with an unusually narrow view of rationality as logicality, the absolutist, in short, all too frequently lacks the desire or the flexibility to modify a strongly held position even when countering evidence may demand a revision.

Relativism. The contrary notion of relativism grew out of an opposition to absolutism. Proponents of this rapidly developing perspective on conceptual change, Toulmin points out, reject outright the premise that knowledge can be universal in nature. Borrowing from the field of Anthropology, the relativist makes such claims as these: (1) individuals should determine what is binding on themselves in a given situation involving moral issues; (2) a meaningful world view can only emanate from a particular "historico-cultural context"; (3) what is to be accepted as knowledge is dependent on the culture; and (4) a rational judgment is limited to the social milieu in which it is being rendered.

It is instructive to observe that while relativism differs from absolutism in the area of universality of knowledge, it shares a similar devotion to logical systematicity. A hierarchical order utilizing logical relations moves from "relative presuppositions" to "absolute presuppositions" which are binding in a particular "historico-cultural milieu." Both relativism and absolutism, therefore, subscribe to a rationality that is equated with logicality.

As in the case of absolutism, Toulmin argues that relativism is an inappropriate description of how knowledge is to be generated or understood. Its greatest weakness is its tendency to resist the application of viable intellectual concepts from one milieu to another. It also offers an inadequate explanation of how it is possible to move in a hierarchical order from relative to universal or absolute presuppositions.

Argument and Conceptual Change. From the above two polar views, Toulmin places argument on a middle point on the continuum, demonstrating how conceptual change or knowledge generation is the result of practical reasoning. Argument, he asserts, is an intellectual enterprise or a form of ecology in which claims are addressed to "conceptual populations" for the end of creating new disciplinary insights and beliefs. It makes use of "meta-statements" rather than formal claims, and is adaptive and nonstereotyped in its procedures. Because argument deals with probable or contingent propositions, its conclusions are tentative and modifiable. Thus when faced with new experiences and data, the rhetor is obligated to reconsider, revise, refine, or reinterpret an earlier position. Modification, therefore, becomes a moral duty when the circumstances demand it. Finally, an argument is assessed as convincing when it is applicable to the situation at hand, when it produces a result that is "better" than the status quo can offer, when it is relevant, and when it is capable of justification.

This stress on reasonableness instead of on strict rationality and on contingency rather than on formal validity puts argument in direct conflict with absolutism. In addition, in assuming that thoughtful "comparisons can

meaningfully be drawn between concepts and judgements operative within different milieus,"[3] the arguer accomplishes what the relativist says is undesirable, if not impossible.

The relationship of argument, as described by Toulmin, to absolutism and relativism is summarized under the heading: "Conceptual Change Continuum Model." Although argument in a particular instance may move slightly toward the left or toward the right on the scale, it always remains close to the center point.

Three important implications may be derived from Toulmin's notion of argument as the principal cause of conceptual change. Of considerable significance, first of all, is the impact of these views on the interpretation of rhetoric as a way of knowing. The essence of his volume *Human Understanding* is the thesis that our collective use of concepts in any discipline or field of study is the direct result of a method of practical reasoning or intellectual enterprise that meets the test of reasonableness. In developing this idea, Toulmin says, in effect, that we know the worth of a person's

Toulmin's Conceptual Change Continuum Model

Absolutism	Argument	Relativism
Logical Systematicity	Intellectual Enterprise	Logical systematicity
Quasi-mathematical	Ecological	Hierarchical Order
Rationality	"Meta-statements"	Absolute Presuppositions
Logicality	Modifiability	Relative Presuppositions
Predictability	Reasonableness	Logicality
Evaluative Criteria for	Evaluative Criteria for	Historical
Assessing General Principles	Assessing General Principles	Evaluative Criteria for
Correctness	Applicability	Assessing General Principles
Coherency	Relevance	Applicability
Consistency	Adaptability	Relevance
Entailment	Justification	Generalizability
Generalizability	Generalizability	Culture Dependent
Universality (All cultures)	Within Cultures	Time bound
Eternality (Not limited to time)	Across Cultures	Non-transferable
Static	Dynamic/Developing	
Stereotyped	Non-stereotyped	
	↓	
	CONCEPTUAL CHANGE	

theories by the quality of his arguments. He puts it this way in his analysis:

We shall do well . . . to consider a man's practical ideals of intellectual method in light of his theoretical ideas about intellectual activities and higher mental functions. By making explicit the arguments underlying his conceptual ambitions and dissatisfactions, we bring to light his own *epistemic self-portrait*: the particular picture of human beings as active intelligences which governs his stance towards the objects of human understanding. The general problem of human understanding is, in fact, to draw an epistemic self-portrait which is both well-founded and trustworthy; which is effective because its theoretical base is realistic, and which is realistic because its practical applications are effective.[4]

From this description, it would appear, rhetoric is an epistemic activity which is realistic, practical, and influential.

A second implication that stems from Toulmin's theory of argument and its impact on human understanding is the parallel that exists with jurisprudence. The model of reasoning employed by lawyers and judges also occupies a midpoint between absolutism and relativism. Using precedents as a starting point in courts of law, the jurisprudential speaker asks such questions as the following: (1) Is a particular precedent applicable to the present situation? or (2) should the precedent in this instance be overturned in light of the changing social circumstances? Quite clearly, then, a precedent can never be viewed as permanent or static. Nor is the legal speaker prevented from taking the practice of one jurisdiction and showing its relevance for another. In demonstrating how his theory of practical reasoning and the common-law tradition come together, Toulmin says:

Rationality . . . has its own "courts" in which all clear-headed men with suitable experience are qualified to act as judges or jurors. Within different cultures and epochs, reasoning may operate according to different methods and principles, so that different milieus represent the parallel "jurisdictions" of rationality. But they do so out of a shared concern with common "rational enterprises," just as parallel legal jurisdictions do with their common judicial enterprises. . . .[5]

Jurisprudence as the ideal model of argument, therefore, uses the evaluative criteria of applicability, adaptability, and relevance. Moreover, it is a dynamic and developing process.

A third inference that can be drawn by examining Toulmin's ideas on the nature and influence of argument, as explained in *Human Understanding*, is his partiality for an evolutionary interpretation of conceptual change. By its very essence, argument or practical reasoning, with its emphasis on modification and refinement, is a slow method. For a "conceptual population" to alter its view of a widely held theory or scholarly procedure, members participating in the intellectual enterprise engage in deliberation until a consensus is reached. This consensus, in turn, represents the adoption of a new idea or belief.

Toulmin's dedication to evolution as an explanatory theory led him to question any analysis of conceptual change that gave the appearance of subscribing to a revolutionary perspective. For this reason he devotes twenty-five pages in *Human Understanding* to a brilliant refutation of Thomas Kuhn's highly acclaimed volume *The Structure of Scientific Revolutions*. Toulmin counters Kuhn's claims by first demonstrating what he perceives to be the meaning of a genuine scientific revolution. It is, he asserts, a "complete change" in which "one fundamental paradigm" is displaced by another. He then adds:

Newthink . . . sweeps aside Oldthink entirely; so much so that, in the nature of the case, the reasons for replacing Oldthink by Newthink can be explained in the language of neither system. Like men committed to different constellations of absolute presuppositions, a Newthinker and an Oldthinker have no common vocabulary for comparing the rational claims of their respective theoretical positions.[6]

The primary objection, then, to such an interpretation of conceptual change is Toulmin's conviction that it is virtually impossible for knowledge to follow a path of "radical discontinuity," causing a complete break with the past. Instead, he argues, knowledge is created in an evolutionary manner in which ideas become a natural outgrowth of all that has gone before. The most that Toulmin is willing to concede is that on occasion a conceptual change may move slightly on the continuum toward the revolutionary perspective.

In subsequent university and convention program lectures, Toulmin continually has refined the ideas discussed here. Moreover, these central points also have been reaffirmed in private conversations with the authors.[7]

Notes

1. (Princeton: Princeton University Press, 1972).
2. Ibid., p. 486.
3. Ibid., p. 493.
4. Ibid., p. 3.
5. Ibid., p. 95.
6. Ibid., p. 102.
7. It is of interest to note that Volume II of *Human Understanding* is scheduled to be published in 1983.

Because of Toulmin's overriding significance as a theorist in the area of argument and as a major force in the trend we have called "rhetoric as a way of knowing," we were anxious to see if his ideas had changed since he wrote the volume on *Human Understanding*. As a result we requested a copy of one of his most recent monographs for use in this edition. After informing us that almost all of his writings are in book form, he agreed to let us reprint the manuscript of the lecture he delivered at the University of Michigan in October, 1982. Entitled "Logic and the Criticism of Arguments," this perceptive and provocative essay, as you will see, contains an insightful history of the past and present and an important guideline for future action. Before we present this study for your analysis, we would like to pinpoint several crucial aspects pertaining to Toulmin's background statements and central claims.

First the author still strongly adheres to the belief that in all human affairs we engage in argument for the purpose of establishing and evaluating claims that are probable in nature and for the end of generating knowledge. Secondly, he has coined a new phrase, "substantive logic," to describe the essence of practical reasoning. Thirdly, in this lecture Toulmin freely uses, and identifies with, the term rhetoric. In his earlier works alluded to in this chapter—*The Uses of Argument* and *Human Understanding*—the concept of rhetoric does not appear. By contrast he now acknowledges his indebtedness to Aristotle and Hermagoras who were the primary motivating forces for setting the rhetorical tradition into motion. Observe, for instance, this statement: "Only in retrospect is it apparent that—even though sleepwalkingly—I had rediscovered the topics of (Aristotle's) *Topics*, which were expelled from the agenda of philosophy in the years around 1900."

Since we predict that this lecture will become a landmark study in the rhetoric of Western thought, we submit the outline, on page 390, summarizing what Toulmin perceives to be the essential characteristics of substantive logic and formal logic.

Notwithstanding the fact that, as the preceding chart shows, substantive logic or rhetoric is in many ways distinct from formal logic or analytical reasoning, Toulmin recognizes the worth of both approaches because of their mutual interest in establishing a method for the criticism of arguments. Consequently, he makes a vital plea for a collaborative effort between the philosophers, mathematicians, and logicians who use the analytical method, and the lawyers, biological and social scientists, and physicians who rely on the topical and functional method. Thus the two ways of helping us make a rational exposition and criticism of arguments are to be viewed not as natural enemies but as complementary endeavors. Toulmin's call for a rapprochement between the formal and informal logicians, he feels, will go far toward achieving the goal of enhancing our understanding of the nature and potential of argument so that our "human interchanges" will be "substantively adequate."

Formal and Substantive Logic Chart

Formal Logic	Substantive Logic

Nature and Goals
  Analytical
  Rational Exposition and Criticism of
    Arguments
  Generation of Knowledge
	Nature and Goals
	  Topical and Functional
	  Rational Exposition and Criticism of
	    Arguments
	  Generation of Knowledge

Leading Advocates
  Plato   Frege
  Descartes   Russell
  Kant
	Leading Advocates
	  Aristotle Hume
	  Hermagoras Toulmin
	  Cicero

Representative Users
  Mathematicians
  Astronomers
  Formal Logicians
	Representative Users
	  Biological Scientists
	  Social Scientists
	  Physicians
	  Lawyers

Argumentation Field
  Invariant
  General
	Argumentation Field
	  Dependent
	  Situational
	  Specific

Level of Reliability
  Certainty
  Exact Statements
	Level of Reliability
	  Probability
	  Opinions

Type of Argumentative Technique
  Retrospective
	Type of Argumentation Technique
	  Prospective

Essential Vocabulary Elements
  Premise
  Conclusion
  Entailment
  Necessity
  Principle of Inference
  Episteme (Formal Mathematical Theory)
	Essential Vocabulary Elements
	  Grounds
	  Claim
	  Warrant
	  Support
	  Qualifier
	  Doxai (Opinions)

Criteria for Evaluating Arguments
  Right/Wrong
  Correct/Incorrect
  Valid/Invalid
  Consistent/Contradictory
  Coherent/Incoherent
	Criteria for Evaluating Arguments
	  Relevant/Irrelevant
	  Strong/Weak
	  Reasonable/Unreasonable
	  Sound/Unsound
	  Appropriate/Inappropriate
	  Solid/Groundless
	  Warranted/Unwarranted

Logic and the Criticism of Arguments

I

My purpose in this lecture is to share a problem with you. It is a problem that I have found significant in all my own work, so I shall first present it in autobiographical terms. But it is one that also has a good deal of intellectual history behind it—it took me some twenty–five years to realize just how much—and I shall reconstruct some of this for you. (In thinking the lecture through, for reasons I will come back to later on, I was tempted to call it, "A Funny Thing happened to Logic on the way to the Academy.") If I am right about the solution of this problem, that has serious implications for the intellectual agenda of professional philsophy, and also for the goals and methods of general education. So I shall add some remarks about the ways in which (if I am right) we should be teaching students to approach questions about "logic," "method" or "argumentation," call it what you will: that is, about the rational exposition and criticism of the arguments that face them in different fields of academic study and professional work.

First, a slice of life, to indicate how this problem became a problem for me personally. From the start, my curiosity drew me toward the subject of "rationality." Even when the central focus of my interests was still physics, what I most wanted to find out was, how it could ever be more "rational" to accept one overall scientific theory, cosmology or natural philosophy rather than another: If intelligent fish learned to do science, I asked myself, must they in the long run end up with the same body of ideas as human beings? (That was, of course, an epistemological not an ichthyological question!) So when, at the end of World War II, I returned to Cambridge as a philosophy graduate student, my central interest was already what it has been ever since: viz., *rationality*.

Almost at once, I ran up against a difficulty. My questions were: How the reasons we rely on in different kinds of research, inquiry and decision *function*, and, How these *functional* differences affect the ways in which arguments and beliefs are to be judged in one field rather than another. (My Ph.D. thesis, *Reason in Ethics*, compared and contrasted our ways of reasoning about scientific and moral issues.) But the current fashion in both logic and analytical philosophy was, [I found, to focus exclusively on *formal* aspects of argument: in particular, on questions about "validity," "necessity," and "entailment." As a result, I was aware of a discontinuity every time my reading or thinking crossed the frontier between science and philosophy; ideas that I could present in one set of terms to people in one academic subculture had to be wholly restated if they were to be acceptable on the other side of the border.

By now, of course, I realize that this discontinuity is the one that David Hume speaks about in his *Treatise of Human Nature*, when he tells us how modes of reasoning that remained convincing to him, so long as he stayed in his Study, appeared strained and ridiculous the moment he went off to the Club, had a good dinner, and sat down to play backgammon and chat with his friends. His deepest philosophical convictions proved unintelligible to those friends: worse, to lay ears, the philosophical terms he used in framing them sounded merely cynical.

So, my chief purpose in writing *The Uses of Argument*, in the late 1950s, was to relate traditional philosophical paradoxes to the standing contrast between "substantive" and "formal" aspects of reasoning and argument. By construing issues of substance or function in terms drawn from formal logic (I argued) philosophers had come to view all substantial arguments as involving "logical" gulfs, and so as justifying "rational" doubts. But, given only a little care in keeping formal and functional aspects of argument clear in our minds, we could steer safely past those paradoxes.

What happened? Peter Strawson brushed my book aside in *The Listener*, and a great hush fell upon my colleagues in England. After that, I assumed that the book would (in Hume's words) "fall stillborn from the press", so I was a little surprised when it continued to sell in worthwhile numbers: it took me some time to find out why. Worse, my graduate adviser at Cambridge, Richard Braithwaite, was deeply pained by the book, and barely spoke to me for twenty years; while one of my colleagues at Leeds, Peter Alexander, described it as "Toulmin's *anti*-logic book." This last description took my breath away then, as it does today; but I can best explain the reasons why if I shift gears, and talk now about the history of this whole issue.

II

I start where we always have to start, in Classical Athens. The Greek words *logos* and *logikos* were then—and still are—general words, meaning "reason" and "reasonable." When the first philosophers framed their definition of "knowledge" as "a belief accompanied by a *logos*," they meant only "a belief with good enough reason for it"; and the problem that presented itself for their consideration was, quite simply, "What kinds of things *counted as* good enough reasons to raise beliefs to the level of knowledge?"

The two most creative classical philosophers approached the problem of "good reasons"—as all others—with very different temperaments and interests; and their answers dealt with it on correspondingly different levels. Plato, as always, approached it with the theoretical interests of a mathematical physicist, and in the spirit of a utopian. In thinking about theoretical issues (he argued) we should not be content with pragmatic half measures, but should aim at an *ideal* solution; and, so long as we keep this goal in mind, we cannnot be satisfied with anything less than "exact" knowledge. The astronomer aims at developing a mathematical model of the planetary system, to which the actual appearances and motions of heavenly bodies will approximate more or less exactly. . . . And Bully for him! At one and the same time, the

resulting body of ideas is both an *intrinsically intelligible* conceptual system, and an *extrinsically relevant* account of the astronomical facts.

Aristotle approached the same problem with the scientific interests of a systematic biologist, and in the realistic spirit of a craftsman. Rather than demand a single kind of "reasons" in all areas of experience (he retorted) we should consider the specific demands of each current task; and, so long as we keep that requirement in mind, we shall not be led astray by the misleading models of astronomy and geometry. People working in different fields rightly use different methods to deal with their problems: the demands of theoretical astronomy, for instance, are no guide to the methods of argument appropriate to field zoology, political organization, or the moral problems of everyday life.

As a result, the two men had quite different ideas about "rational criticism." For Plato, learning to criticize arguments was the same in all fields: it demanded a grasp of mathematics. (The best preparation for Political Theory, in his eyes, was to learn formal geometry; as, today, some people suggest that all politicians should learn econometrics.) But, for Aristotle, the task was polymorphous: it demanded that the critic understand not only how problems and arguments in one field *resemble* those in another, but also how they *differ*.

Plato's line cut *between* different fields: Aristotle's cut *within* each such field. For Plato, theories set out in abstract mathematical form were always preferable to ones framed in everyday language. Colloquial language is a feeble instrument, and opinions couched in it are inherently unreliable: the modern terms for putting the same criticism of qualitative theories are "anecdotal" and "folklore."

Hence, Plato's insistence that only *episteme* qualifies as true knowledge, while all *doxai* are to be set aside as unreliable appearances. Hence, too, his scorn for the Sophists, whom he ridiculed for arguing about "mere opinions," about whose formal justification they were ignorant, and did not trouble to inquire. It did not matter to him that some *doxai* could be given stronger *substantive* support—*non*-mathematical reasons—than others: the Sophists showed their basic shallowness by failing to insist on mathematical reasons at all cost.

For Aristotle, by contrast, the practical issue was, How to choose *among* opinions: i.e., how to tell (say) biological, moral or political views that are supported by the relevant substantive reasons, from those that lack the appropriate foundations, and are therefore baseless. So, for Aristotle, the scope of "logic" (the theory and practice of rational criticism) could not be only *formal and universal*: what he called "analytics." It had also to include a *functional and specific* part, which was the subject matter of "topics." Keep that reference in mind, for we shall come back to it: just how long is it (we may ask) since British or American professional philosophers last took a serious look at Aristotle's *Topics*?

III

Properly understood, then, the two men's approaches were complementary, not in conflict. As always, Plato was utopian. Calling for the use of exact, mathematical theories, wherever available, is fine as a counsel of perfection. But, as a counsel of practicality, we cannot let this mathematical ideal distract us from the immediate Aristotelian task of assembling the best founded body of substantive opinions open to us.

As a matter of history, unfortunately, this point was not clearly understood. The idea grew up that Plato's ideal, formal goal provided a basis for criticizing actual, substantive views. So, the threefold distinction between formal mathematical theory (*episteme*), substantively well-founded opinions (good *doxai*) and baseless opinions (bad *doxai*), collapsed into a twofold division between, on the one hand, *episteme* (which is a Good Thing) and, on the other hand, *doxai* (which are all, equally, Bad Things).

Am I falling, here, into the language of that caricature of English History, *1066 and All That*? I do so without any apology. For at this

point there developed a corrupt tradition, not merely within philosophy itself, but also in the history of philosophy; and the resulting caricature of the actual historical debate was as crude, in its own way, as anything the authors of *1066* could ever dream up. In the canonical account to which I myself was introduced, for instance, Ancient Philosophy went downhill after Aristotle, and there ensued the Dark Ages of Philosophy, which were finally enlightened only by the genius of Rene Descartes. As *1066* would have put it, Descartes was "a Good Thing." However, the improvement did not last: after Kant, the argument went downhill again, until the arrival of Gottlob Frege, who was also "a Good Thing."

At this point, let me interject two points. Firstly: both Descartes and Frege were unambiguously on the Platonizing side of the fence. Descartes never disguised his scorn for subjects that do not lend themselves to mathematical treatment. In his eyes, for example, history is no better than foreign travel: it may broaden the mind, but it cannot deepen the understanding. As for Frege, the aim of his *Foundations of Arithmetic* (he declared) was "to strip away the historical and psychological accretions" which had veiled "*number* in its pure form" from "the eye of the mind." So, the caricature of history with which I was presented was one in which all the major heroes—and I might add Henry Sidgwick, Bertrand Russell and G. E. Moore—shared a preference for the analytical examination of concepts and theories, and disregarded the topical heritage of Aristotle and his successors.

Secondly, one can in fact give an alternative historical account, which keeps a fairer balance between the two approaches. This second account eliminates the notion that serious philosophy somehow vanished during the Dark Ages. (That, as Peter Brown has taught us, is a virtue in itself; the "Dark Ages" are an invention of 18th-century rationalist ideologues like Edward Gibbon, who refused to take seriously ideas and periods they did not feel at home in.) But the second account also gives center stage to a series of figures whom philosophers of my kind never read, and may not even have heard of (e.g., Hermagoras) while it attributes fresh importance to others, whom we have heard of, but do not think of primarily as philosophers: for example, Cicero, Boethius and Adam Smith.

Mention Hermagoras of Temnos in an academic conversation today, and—chances are—the only response will be: "Who he?" Until recently, I confess, I was equally ignorant of the reasons why, for centuries, Hermagoras was seen as a major constructive figure in the debate about logic, rationality and practical reasoning. Here, let me just say this much; that, in the last two centuries B.C., no one did more than Hermagoras to build up a systematic analysis of substantive arguments along the lines sketched in Aristotle's *Topics*, *Nichomachean Ethics*, *Rhetoric*, and *Politics*. As one example: anyone who goes through Law School today is introduced to the idea that a "case" is defined in terms of its *elements*—the types of factors and considerations that have to be covered, if you are to specify a genuine "case" at all. This idea was first formulated in Hermagoras' analysis of argumentation; and, alongside the valid forms of the syllogism— "Barbara, Celarent . . ." and the rest—all students going through the Medieval Schools memorized a Latin hexameter which summarized Hermagoras' "elements":

Quis, quid, ubi, quibus auxiliis, cur, quomodo, quando? That is to say:

"Who did what? Where? With what help? Why? In what manner? And when?"

If Plato gave the Sophists a bad name, he left one group even worse off: the Rhetoricians. Sophists were condemned for wandering in a jungle of "mere opinions" unguided by any ideal of mathematical proof: Rhetoricians were despised for the graver sin of substituting the psychological arts of *persuasion* for the mathematical techniques of *proof*. And, since it was Hermagoras who founded the Rhetorical tradition, it is perhaps no surprise that right minded modern philosophers consistently ignore him.

Here again, however, we face the same old slander. Plato's attack on the Sophists equated

all "mere opinions," and rejected them all as irremediable. So, honest Sophists—who used the best available methods of "dispute resolution" to arbitrate or mediate substantive controversies—were tarred with the same brush as Quacks and Hucksters who engaged in no such honest trade. Rhetoricians suffered the same fate. The honest ones, who attempted to use and to teach *sound* arguments were damned as mercilessly as the rabble rousing ones, who were only interested in dominating their hearers.

This, of course, obscures the fact that in all the serious professions—Law, Science, Medicine and the rest—procedures of *substantive* argumentation are passed on from Master to Pupil in ways that *show* the differences between "sound" procedures and "shaky" ones, "good" arguments and "bad" ones, "warranted" and "unwarranted" inferences, "solid" and "groundless" conclusions. If these things can be taught, then should we not also be able to spell out explicitly what they involve? (Every Law School teacher does just this, when he discusses the admissibility of evidence, initial presumptions, standards of proof and so on.) Plato's example thus blackened *all* "rhetoric" as dishonest, in the same way and for the same reasons that *all* substantive arguments and opinions were dismissed as misleading "sophistry": conversely, Aristotle's example indicated that *sound and honest* substantive arguments differ from plausible ranting quite as much as *either* of them differs from a Euclidean proof.

To digress a moment, let me offer a tidbit to lovers of the English language. Looking into the history of moral reasoning, I turned up the *Oxford English Dictionary* entry for the word, "casuistry." Now, you can always learn something new from the *O.E.D.*! Here, it points out that there is a family of words ending in "-ry" which refer to the *dishonest* use of techniques. We are all familiar with (e.g.) *wizardry, harlotry* and *Popery*; *sophistry* and *casuistry* refer to the dishonest use of the sophist's and casuist's arts, and thus are two more examples; *oratory* is a marginal case; while *chemistry* and *dentistry* definitely do not belong to the same family! (It is no accident that the first recorded use of the word "casuistry" is taken from Alexander Pope's 1725 *Essay on Man*, which was written after Pascal damned the Jesuit casuists in the *Provincial Letters*, and so gave *all* "case morality" the same kind of Bad Name that Plato had given *all* the Sophists and Rhetoricians.)

IV

Enough of ancient history: I am nearly ready to state my central thesis. But, first, let me briefly remind you what has happened to logic in the 20th century. When Gottlob Frege and Bertrand Russell embarked on their logical innovations at the turn of the century, they used the term "logic" to mean just what the term "analytics" had meant to Aristotle. Ever since Frege and Russell, therefore, philosophers have discussed logic, not as "the art and theory of rational criticism" (with both a formal part, or analytics, and a functional part, i.e. a "topics"), but as a field which is *purely formal*. For their purposes, the functional issues might as well not exist; or, if they do, they are certainly not part of the business of *logic*. As a result, logicians in the 20th century have drawn narrower boundaries around their subject than any of their predecessors: not just narrower than Aristotle, but also narrower than respected 18th and 19th-century figures like Adam Smith and William Whewell.

This new Platonizing approach to logic has even generated its own version of the libel on the Sophists. For fifty years and more, philosophers read Frege's arguments as expelling all but formal issues from their subject. Empiricism and positivism became "logical" empiricism and positivism: any attempt to broaden the agenda of philosophy was condemned for committing, either the *genetic* fallacy, of appealing to irrelevant historical facts, or else the fallacy of *psychologism*, of asking, "How do people reason?," instead of, "How is it logical for them to reason?" So, all the substantive questions which Rhetoricians and Sophists had asked—questions about the procedures lawyers, scientists and others *in fact* use in arguing—were relegated to the philosophical slagheaps of history and psychology.

By the time I wrote *The Uses of Argument*, in the mid 1950s, then, logic had been completely identified with "analytics," and Aristotle's *Topics* was totally forgotten: so much so that, when I wrote the book, nobody realized that it bore the same relation to the *Topics* that Russell and Frege's work bore to traditional "analytic" and "syllogistic." Only in retrospect is it apparent that—even though sleepwalkingly—I had rediscovered the topics of the *Topics*, which were expelled from the agenda of philosophy in the years around 1900.

What I have just said is not precise. It is not wholly true that the "functional" aspects of practical argumentation were *totally* forgotten, and that *nobody* recognized my book for what it was. Given its reception by my British colleagues, the book went on selling surprisingly well; and it was only when I visited the United States that I found out who was buying it. Then, I met people from Departments of Speech and Communication up and down the country, who told me that they used it as a text on rhetoric and argumentation. So, the study of practical reasoning was kept alive after all; but this was done only *outside* the Departments of Philosophy, under the wing of Speech or English, or at Schools of Law.

V

Only during the last ten years have philosophers seriously begun to reclaim some parts at least of "practical reasoning," through the rise of the "informal logic" movement, based at the University of Windsor in Canada. Yet, up to now, this movement has been exposed to a serious professional handicap. In the eyes of the philosophical elite, its goals seem to be educational, not intellectual: it is viewed merely as devising soft options for weaker students—ways of teaching Intro Logic to those who lack the intellectual power to tackle (say) Irving Copi's introduction to *real* logic. But that impression is a sad misunderstanding. Behind the practical programs of the informal logic movement lie some definite doctrines and theses, which I must now attempt to state.

First, then: Philosophers can legitimately investigate all relevant aspects of the "rational criticism" of arguments. This means that whatever is needed in order to show how "well founded" opinions are distinguished from "baseless" ones, or "sound" and "reasonable" arguments from "shaky" or "dogmatic" ones is the proper concern of *philosophy*, and can not be banished into the *psychological* realm of "mere" rhetoric.

Secondly: The theory and techniques of rational criticism must be approached from two complementary directions, *formal* and *functional*. On the one hand, we can use the word "argument" for a string of propositions, which may be written on the blackboard or thought about in the abstract; and we can examine the formal relations—of consistency and inconsistency, entailment and contradiction—by which these propositions are (or are not) knitted into a logical fabric. (It would be foolish to deny that this "formal" aspect of rational criticism is one legitimate and well established part of the subject: all I want to do is show its proper role.) On the other hand, we can instead use the word "argument" for the stating of a substantively disputed position, followed by an exploring of possible consequences, an exchanging of evidence, and a sound (or unsound) resolving of the dispute. In our second sense an "argument" is not a *string of propositions* which may (or may not) be formally consistent: rather, it is a *human interchange* which is (or is not) substantively adequate.

The traditional jargon of "logical structure" tempts one to compare these two approaches to rational criticism with anatomy and physiology, respectively. Formal logic then tells us how the propositions in any argument "hang together" in an articulated intellectual skeleton: functional analysis tells us how it is that the elements of some arguments successfully "work" together—as legal or scientific or common sense arguments—while others "fail to work." This analogy is certainly picturesque, but it is not the most helpful one we can find, and I want here to offer you another comparison, which seems to me more illuminating.

Think of the parts which accountants and business planners, respectively, play in a commercial enterprise. Accountants put together a balance sheet of *last* year's activities, make sure it is complete and coherent, and tell us how we did at that time: planners survey, present and appraise possible directions for *next* year's activities, and aim to strike a reasonable balance between the business's needs, ambitions and hopes. On the one hand, a thriving business requires good accountants: nobody can formulate a sound policy for next year, who is unclear about how things worked out last year. A *formally* adequate past balance sheet is thus a precondition of *functionally* successful policies for the future. On the other hand, it is by now a truism that accountants make good servants but bad masters; or, to put the same point in American idiom, good advisers but bad executives. For, despite fashionable talk about "the bottom line," judgments about future policy never turn on matters of formal consistency alone: such judgments always involve, also, essential elements of "priority" and "decision."

The *critical* question now is:

Was the chosen policy arrived at in an open, timely and reasonable manner, after a full consideration of the strengths and weaknesses of other possible courses of action?

Clearly, one of the arts which Graduate Schools of Business try to teach is the art of meeting just this demand—that all decisions be open, timely and reasonable, and be based on a full consideration of available estimates about the likely outcomes of alternative policies.

And yet, I would now ask: Is this "critical question" just a matter for Business Schools to deal with? Surely, the issue can be broadened, by asking, for instance:

What general *kinds* of considerations and arguments are relevant and reasonable, when arriving at (or defending) business policies, rather than (say) judicial rulings, or scientific explanations?

The critical question about business policy is, thus, a specific example of the more general critical question about "practical reasoning," which Aristotle first framed in his *topical* works, and which was subsequently pursued by writers and teachers in the "rhetorical" tradition. To state this more general question as concisely as I can:

> What are the forums of discussion, rules of procedure, techniques of argument, criteria of relevance, standards of proof, and practical implications, that serve the special purposes of the different enterprises within which "argumentation" and "reasoning together" go on?

Evidently, the differences between the proceedings involved in devising and carrying through a scientific experiment, putting a law case through the Courts, or formulating and arriving at a business decision—to mention only three "rational activities"—are more than *formal* differences. It is not just a matter of the one using "syllogisms," another (say) "enthymemes": instead, we need to understand the *substance* of debate in each area.

The relations between the formal and functional analyses of an argument thus resemble the relations between business planners and accountants. In criticism of actual arguments, the role of formal logic is "intellectual accountancy": the ability to use notions like consistency and contradiction is indispensable to the rational thinker, in the same way that the ability to read a balance sheet is indispensable to a business planner. But, once again, formal logicians can tell us if our *last* arguments were coherent, and can reconstruct them so as to show what assumptions they relied on; but deciding how to reason *next* time is by no means a formal matter. Scrutinizing and checking the formal relations between the propositions embodied in earlier arguments is a *retrospective* technique: the considerations it involves are formal ones, and are of the same kind whatever the topic of the particular argument. But understanding what kinds of arguments have a reliable, well-established place in science, law or business planning is a *prospective* art: there, the considerations that carry weight depend on the purposes and procedures of the particular enterprise.

VI

Do not *mishear* the point I am making. I am not just saying that *pro*spective arguments are "inductive" or "evaluative" rather than "deductive." That ho-hum formula is well intentioned, but misleading, for two reasons. In the first place, there is no virtue in limiting "deduction." In colloquial usage, *deduce* is synonymous with *infer*: it does not have a purely mathematical or formal meaning. So understood, the term "deductive inference" is tautologous. Any argument whatever can be set out in deductive form, if we only state its assumptions as extra premises; and this is often worth doing, since we may recognize what exactly those assumptions were, only after they are made explicit.

In the second place, resorting to such terms of logical art as "induction" and "inductive inference" tends to confuse several very different distinctions. To begin with, we can distinguish between arguments in substantive disciplines (e.g. physics) and arguments within pure mathematics (e.g. in geometry): this is important, when we ask what kinds of *backing* support the general warrants governing arguments of each kind. (Experimental proof is clearly relevant in physics, but not in the "purer" parts of mathematics.) But scientific and legal arguments can be, and are, set out in deductive form as often as arguments in pure geometry or set theory, so that cannot be the crucial issue.

Again, we can distinguish between arguments which appeal to established principles, without challenging them, and arguments which are designed to probe and refine those principles. But we can draw that distinction with equal force in all fields, so that is evidently not the issue. Nor is either of these distinctions (in turn) identical with the distinction from which we began, between retrospective and prospective arguments.

No, the very term "induction" was introduced to disguise the *functional* analysis of arguments as a new kind of *formal* art. To reinforce that interpretation, recall how the logical empiricists insisted on separating the *justification* of scientific opinions (the topic for "inductive logic") from the *discovery* of those opinions: to them, "discovery meant the processes by which we *happen on* our opinions, and they relegated it to "psychology." This move simply repeated the Platonist rejection of all "mere opinions." Yet surely (we may reply) some ways of "happening on" substantive opinions are more *reasonable* than others, and so open to philosophical analysis? Not, apparently, for the logical empiricists: they damn all discovery alike with a single breath, as Plato damned all the opinions of the Sophists: "reasonable" procedures are to be told from ones that are "off the wall", only by the formal procedures of inductive logic. So much, then, for Nero Wolfe, who tries to put Sherlock Holmes right on "deduction" and "induction": like the social and behavioral scientists, he has read too many elementary logic texts, and gets himself into the same pickle that they do!

VII

It is time to state these points in more constructive terms. For this purpose, let me present three theses.

(1) The rational criticism of arguments involves two distinct arts: one "analytical," the other "topical."

The techniques of the first art are concerned with the question, "Am I arguing *rightly* (or impeccably)?—i.e., Am I avoiding formal inconsistencies, and other errors of intellectual accountancy?

Those of the second are concerned with the question, "Are these the *right* (or relevant) arguments to use when dealing with this kind of problem, in this situation?"—i.e., Are they of a kind appropriate to the substantive demands of the problem and situation?

The art of reasoning "rightly" is one concern of *formal logic*, with the help of which we recognize internal contradictions and similar formal errors. But the art of identifying and explaining the nature and mode of operation of "right" arguments is a field for which professional philosophers today no longer have a name. Historically, it was called by a dozen different names—among others, *topics*, *argumentation*, *rhetoric*, *organon*, and *method*. Today, this art is coming to be known as "*informal*" logic; but there are disadvantages to this *negative* name, which defines its scope only by what it is not, viz. "formal." To make its actual scope and significance clearer, I would for myself prefer a more positive name, such as *substantive* logic.

(2) The two arts quite properly employ distinct vocabularies. The language of formal logic comprises terms like "premise" and "conclusion," "entailment" and "principle of inference," "valid" and "invalid," "necessary" and "contradictory": the language of substantive logic comprises terms like "grounds" and "claim," "support" and "warrant," "sound" and "shaky," "presumably" and "unfounded." Far from these vocabularies having a significant overlap, it is well to keep them distinct; for, once again, the *arguments* to which they are addressed are not "arguments" in the same sense. The formal connections in a string of propositions are *strong or weak*, in the sense of "valid" or "invalid"; and a string of propositions is an "argument" in my first sense. The substantive support which an attorney or scientist gives a claim, by producing the particular grounds he does, in the forum and at the time he does, is *strong or weak*, in the sense of "sound" or "shaky"; and, by stating his case as he does, each man presents an "argument" in my second, human interaction sense.

There are just a few, very general terms that have a use in both these arts: for example, the term "fallacy." In thinking about these borderline issues, however, it becomes doubly prudent to keep in mind the differences between formal and substantive criticism. For instance, people writing introductory logic texts are sometimes tempted to equate the term "fallacious" with the term "invalid"; and this confuses the elementary student, by suggesting that fallacies are typically formal blunders, rather than (as they more often are) errors of substance. Scientific arguments may successfully use theoretical "models," just as legal arguments successfully use theoretical "interpretations." Yet, in both fields, arguments are also sometimes rejected, as appealing to "false analogies"; and, formally speaking, both the successful and the fallacious arguments are quite similar. What mark fallacious analogies off from fruitful models and theories, in practice, are matter of *substance*: e.g., the fact that the "theory" or "model" in question is *warranted* by deeper underlying principles, whereas by contrast the corresponding appeals to "mere analogy" are "unwarranted."

(3) The art of criticizing arguments on "topical" rather than "analytical" grounds is one in which (as Aristotle insisted from the outset) the central issues can be faced, and formulated, only if we address ourselves to *the nature of the case*: i.e., to the general demands of the problems currently under consideration, and the "forums" that are available for resolving them.

In Aristotelian usage, such issues are issues of *prudence*. In legal contexts, they overlap into *juris*prudence: there, they are concerned with the "standards of proof" required in judicial proceedings of different kinds, the "rules of evidence" relevant in different branches of law, and the demands of "due process" that govern the conduct of different sorts of cases. As at earlier stages in the field of rhetoric and practical reasoning, lawyers today continue to pay more explicit attention to their methods of arguing than professionals in many other fields; so they have much clearer ideas than (say) scientists or physicians about the substantive tests which must be satisfied, if legal arguments are to serve the goals of the legal enterprise.

Does this mean that the "topical" aspects of legal reasoning can be understood only by trained lawyers? The answer to that question is not entirely obvious. We might equally ask, Can the corresponding aspects of medical and scientific reasoning be understood only by trained physicians and scientists? Just so long as such issues are treated as extensions of formal logic, it can be argued that they are philosophical not professional; but, if we view them

rather as matters of substance, it is less clear that philosophers can monopolize them. Indeed, there has been a lively debate between those philosophers of science such as Popper and Lakatos, who still insist on the right to lay down methodological "statute law" to working scientists, and those others, like Polanyi and myself, who see scientific methods of argumentation as requiring more of a "common law" analysis.

While some detailed points of method in both law and science may be too refined for any but professionals, the *general pattern* of reasoning in both fields is quite intelligible to lay people as well. Logicians and philosophers also have something of their own to contribute, to the extent that the substantive merits and defects of disciplinary reasoning is discussed (as in Aristotle's *Topics*) on a *comparative* basis. In what respects, for instance, do "theories" play the same kinds of part in law as in science? To what extent are appeals to authority admissible or fallacious in different fields of reasoning on the same occasions, and for the same reasons? And on what conditions can arguments about questions of "causation" in medicine be assimilated to those about "causality" in pure science?

None of those questions is "proper to" law or science or medicine taken alone: still, none of them can be answered by someone who has no knowledge whatever (however general) of how people in fact think, argue and resolve problems in those fields. In short, the topical criticism of legal, scientific and other technical arguments can become the substantive mode of inquiry it needs to be, only if the discussion of practical reasoning is made into a *collaborative* debate: one in which philosophers are prepared to listen to lawyers, scientists and others, instead of merely lecturing them! Parts of the resulting debate may be somewhat technical: e.g. statistical analyses of the design of experiments, or jurisprudential discussions of the minuter rules of evidence. But a common framework of analysis, at least, covers the whole territory of practical argumentation; and the outcome of such a collaborative analysis would do for us, in our own day, just the kinds of things that Aristotle,

Hermagoras and the medieval rhetoricians aimed at in earlier times.

VIII

To close, let me speak briefly about the philosophical and educational implications of the positions for which I have been arguing here. First, let me say something about the current controversy over the *rationality* of scientific argument, between Karl Popper and Paul Feyerabend.

(1) I hinted earlier that, since the 17th century, a revival of the Platonist approach to argumentation has led professional philosophers to expel all the functional aspects of "rationality" from consideration; to equate "rationality" with "logicality"; and to look for *formal* criteria to judge the "rationality" of all arguments.

One glance at the Popper-Feyerabend dispute confirms this reading of the matter. Both men assume that the arguments by which scientists arrive at novel discoveries can be genuinely "rational," only if they satisfy certain formal conditions, at least of a weak enough kind. Otherwise, such discoveries will merely be the products of good fortune, chance, irrational speculation, or pure intuition. Popper, for his part, still assumes that we can state such formal conditions in advance; and that scientific knowledge can thus be elevated—however hypothetically and fallibly—to the status of *episteme*: only so can he be satisfied that the procedures of science are truly "rational."

Underlining the Platonist element in his position, Popper asserts that scientific knowledge is essentially concerned with a Third World of *eternal entities*, which are neither "physical objects," nor "psychological thoughts" in the scientists' heads. By contrast, Feyerabend believes that no such conditions can be found, still less imposed on the work of actual scientists; while Popper's "Third World" is for him a reactionary myth. But, instead of arguing that it was a mistake to look for such formal conditions of rationality, Feyerabend strikes a disillusioned pose, and concludes (in the spirit of Nietzsche) that science

can make progress, only if scientists deliberately reject all *method* in favor of an *ir*rational "scientific anarchism."

Here, Karl Popper once again plays the part of the Utopian: to be a scientist one must believe in the invisible Third World, and only a scientist who shares that belief is truly "rational." Paul Feyerabend defines a counterposition, but states it in the same terms: only, because (in his eyes) the Third World can have no practical relevance to the actual work of science, he calls on us to give up the idea that science is rational as a comfortable illusion. Both men take it for granted that we know what demands "rationality" makes of science, *in advance of* looking to see how the arguments of science function in actual practice. Neither of them has the patience to wait for a first-hand examination of "the nature of the case" to clarify our ideas about what kind of thing "scientific rationality" could in practice be. For both of them, Artistotle, Hermagoras and the rhetoricians wrote in vain.

(2) Finally, let me turn to the educational implications of my argument. Any revival of "substantive logic," "rhetoric," "practical reasoning," or "theory of argumentation" (call it what you will) requires both philosophers, and those whose work the philosophers reflect on—lawyers and physicians, scientists and critics—to "modify their present claims to full disciplinary autonomy. The substantive analysis of practical argumentation is worthwhile only if it is *collaborative*, with philosophers and practitioners working together to establish, firstly, how reasons function in all these different fields of work, secondly, what are the accepted procedures and forums for the resulting arguments and, lastly, what standards are available for judging the "success" and "failure" of work in one field or another.

The differences between the ways we interpret issues, in one field or another, are *ineliminable*, and also *functional*. They cannot be explained away by formal devices: e.g., by inventing separate formal systems of alethic, deontic, or epistemic logic for every purpose and field. Practical argumentation has both field invariant and field dependent features.

Some topical terms (e.g. "grounds" and "warrants") have a use in most fields of argument; more specialized terms (e.g. numerical "probability") are relevant only in very few fields. In between, a middle category of terms of topical analysis—"kind" and "degree," "fallacy" and "analogy," "cause" and "definition"—apply in varying ways as we move from one field to another. These are the notions which philosophers and practitioners can master fully only by pooling their efforts.

I do not wholly despair of this kind of collaboration; though I am not starry eyed about the prospects, either. It is manageable enough within an institution like the University of Chicago, which has an established network of interdepartmental committees devoted to multidisciplinary investigations. Still, my hope and fears for the subject are best symbolized by the contrast between two undergraduate colleges, both of which I know rather well. One college is committed to interdepartmental teaching; so, when the philosophers tried adapting the analysis set out in *The Uses of Argument*, so as to teach the criticism of reasoning alongside the techniques of formal logic, they met with no obstacles from the other departments. Quite the reverse: after a while,

they even had students coming back to them, to report that they were still using the methods they had learned during that course, in writing essays and reports in their other academic subjects, also.

The other college is among the most distinguished colleges in New England. It was notable among those colleges for having long had a Department of Speech, which operated alongside the Philosophy Department without serious competition or friction. A few years ago, the Speech Department offered to make a greater contribution to the undergraduate curriculum, by expanding its courses on the criticism of reasoning; though, in this way, it risked trespassing onto the territory of the philosophers, who already had a high-powered Intro course on the elements of formal logic.

Was this not a God-sent opportunity for the departments to get together, and collaborate on a course covering *both* formal logic *and* substantive criticism in a uniquely comprehensive way? One might have thought so but what happened was quite different. Faced with financial stringencies, the philosophers argued that speech is not an academically serious subject; and, in the ensuing politics, the Department of Speech was *closed down*!

22

Rhetoric as a Way of Knowing: Chaim Perelman and Practical Reasoning

Remarkably close to the ideas on argument established by Toulmin are those articulated by Chaim Perelman, the Belgian philosopher whose major concern in the last few years has been rhetoric. Disturbed by his philosopher-colleagues' tendency to push aside approaches to knowledge that yield less reliable information than that produced by formal logic, Perelman reminds us that philosophers, in reality, function as rhetors. It is practical argument, not formal reasoning, he asserts, which is the required tool for disseminating ideas. In other words, practical argument is a way of knowing.

Much of what Perelman has to say on this subject is found in his *New Rhetoric: A Treatise on Argument,* which was co-authored with L. Olbrechts-Tyteca.[1] At first glance it would appear that Perelman is little more than a modern classicist who seems content to cite the works of Aristotle, Cicero, and Quintilian. That he relies on them freely there can be no doubt. Aristotle is applauded for his psychological insights on the nature of various age groups and emotions, for his meaningful suggestions regarding persuasive strategies, and for recognizing that rhetoric is rooted in probability. Additionally, Perelman is one of the few authors in the contemporary period who has adapted Aristotelian theories on commonplaces and lines of argument. This seeming partiality for classical doctrines has led some recent scholars in communication to describe Perelman as a twentieth-century Aristotelian.

But Perelman, in our opinion, is far more than a classicist. In several very important respects he has departed significantly from an-

cient teachings. With Whately, he concludes that argumentation goes beyond the oral statement. Written documents may be as much a part of rhetoric as interpersonal communication or public address. Not only does Perelman broaden the scope of rhetoric and argumentation, he also introduces an innovative vocabulary that opens up fresh perspectives. These are but a few of the terms he uses which have gained wide circulation: universal audience, quasi-logical arguments, starting points, rule of justice, communion, presence, and dissociation of concepts.

A universal audience, according to Perelman, is that audience, either immediate or long range, which is comprised of rational men and women. These are the people who know how to judge and test the strength or weakness of an argument by applying the criterion of "experience." What the universal audience looks for in responding to a speaker is an "affirmation of that which corresponds to an objective fact, of that which constitutes a true and even necessary assertion."[2] When an advocate receives agreement from this audience, he has helped produce an adherence of minds concerning values. Thus he has successfully participated in rhetoric as a knowing process.

The use of the phrase "quasi-logical" is not an example of accidental or deliberate jargon. To Perelman, these words suggest the very nature of practical argument as contrasted with formal reasoning. Quasi-logical arguments imply a non-formal structure and a special method of reasoning associated with "reality." What makes Perelman's discussion of these ideas so intriguing is not the fact that he necessarily covers new ground, but rather the terminology and explanation employed. He is perhaps the first author to label specific types of argument with such suggestive terms as "reciprocity," "transitivity," "sacrifice," "waste," and "direction." Moreover, he gives a new perspective to ethos by analyzing the relationship between "the person and his acts," and between "model and anti-model."

Three other notions developed by Perelman are also integral concepts in his rhetorical system. The first he calls "the starting point of argument." There is little chance, he states, for an advocate to promote an adherence of minds unless the listeners are in agreement at the outset with respect to facts, truths, presumptions, and values. The second notion—designated "the rule of justice"— "requires giving identical treatment to beings or situations of the same kind."[3] In Perelman's own view, the third idea we wish to stress here—dissociation of concepts—may be the most important single principle in his theory of argumentation. This dissociation process or breaking of connecting links "is always prompted by the desire to remove an incompatibility arising out of the confrontation of one proposition with others, whether one is dealing with norms, facts, or truths."[4] Let us assume, for example, that there is a philosophical pair which may be diagrammed as follows: $\frac{appearance}{reality}$. You may recall that in Chapter 1 of this book, we referred to authors who identified rhetoric with appearance rather than with reality. A student of the rhetoric of Western thought, therefore, may assume the role of

advocate by attempting to dissociate rhetoric from appearance, and then associate it with reality.

In another instance a political leader may wish to separate himself from the office he holds in order to preserve the reality inherent in the office. In the famous encounter between President Harry Truman and General Douglas MacArthur during the Korean War, Truman advised MacArthur that he did not care what the general thought of the president as a man, but he demanded that the office he occupied must be honored. An embattled Richard Nixon sought to do the same thing in the midst of the Watergate controversy.

The foregoing discussion is but a brief overview of some of the leading concepts appearing in *The New Rhetoric*. Hopefully, it will point out Perelman's belief that the use of argument for the purpose of knowing is a sound method for advancing understanding. Since it is difficult to abstract a particular portion of *The New Rhetoric* and still maintain the thrust of the work, we are including the following essay which pulls together all of the salient features of Perelman's theories. To read it in its entirety is to gain a thorough grasp of Perelman's system of rhetorical thought.

NOTES

1. Ch. Perelman and L. Olbrechts-Tyteca, *The New Rhetoric: A Treatise on Argumentation* (London: University of Notre Dame Press, 1969).
2. *Ibid.,* pp. 31–32.
3. *Ibid.,* p. 218.
4. *Ibid.,* p. 413.

The New Rhetoric: A Theory of Practical Reasoning

The Loss of a Humanistic Tradition. The last two years of secondary education in Belgium used to be called traditionally "Poetry" and "Rhetoric." I still remember that, over forty years ago, I had to study the "Elements of Rhetoric" for a final high-school examination, and I learned more or less by heart the contents of a small manual, the first part of which concerned the syllogism and the second the figures of style. Later, in the university, I took

Translated from the French by E. Griffin–Collart and O. Bird. Reprinted from *Great Ideas Today* (Chicago: Encyclopedia Britannica, Inc., 1970). Reprinted with permission of the editors of *Great Ideas Today*.

a course of logic which covered, among other things, the analysis of the syllogism. I then learned that logic is a formal discipline that studies the structure of hypothetico-deductive reasoning. Since then I have often wondered what link a professor of rhetoric could possibly discover between the syllogism and the figures of style with their exotic names that are so difficult to remember.

Lack of clarity concerning the idea of rhetoric is also apparent in the article on the subject in the _Encyclopaedia Britannica,_ where rhetoric is defined as "the use of language as an art based on a body of organized knowledge." But what does this mean? The technique or art of language in general, or only that of literary prose as distinct from poetry? Must rhetoric be conceived of as the art of oratory—that is, as the art of public speaking? The author of the article notes that for Aristotle rhetoric is the art of persuasion. We are further told that the orator's purpose, according to Cicero's definition, is to instruct, to move, and to please. Quintilian sums up this view in his lapidary style as _ars bene dicendi,_ the art of speaking well. This phrase can refer either to the efficacy, or the morality, or the beauty of a speech, this ambiguity being both an advantage and a drawback.

For those of us who have been educated in a time when rhetoric has ceased to play an essential part in education, the idea of rhetoric has been definitely associated with the "flowers of rhetoric"—the name used for the figures of style with their learned and incomprehensible names. This tradition is represented by two French authors, Cesar Chesneau, sieur Dumarsais, and Pierre Fontanier, who provided the basic texts for teaching what was taken for rhetoric in the eighteenth and nineteenth centuries. The work of Dumarsais, which first appeared in 1730 and enjoyed an enormous success, is entitled _Concerning tropes or the different ways in which one word can be taken in a language._[1] Fontanier's book, reprinted in 1968 under the title _The figures of discourse,_ unites in one volume two works, which appeared respectively in

1821 and 1827, under the titles _A classical manual for the study of tropes_ and _Figures other than tropes._[2]

These works are the outcome of what might be called the stylistic tradition of rhetoric, which was started by Omer Talon, the friend of Petrus Ramus, in his two books on rhetoric published in 1572. The extraordinary influence of Ramus hindered, and to a large extent actually destroyed, the tradition of classical rhetoric that had been developed over the course of twenty centuries and with which are associated the names of such writers as Aristotle, Cicero, Quintillian, and St. Augustine.

For the ancients, rhetoric was the theory of persuasive discourse and included five parts: _inventio, dispositio, elocutio, memoria,_ and _actio._ The first part dealt with the art of finding the materials of discourse, especially arguments, by using common or specific _loci_—the _topoi_ studied in works which, following Aristotle's example, were call _Topics._[3] The second part gave advice on the purposive arrangement or order of discourse, the _method,_ as the Renaissance humanists called it. The third part dealt mainly with style, the choice of terms and phrases; the fourth with the art of memorizing the speech; while the fifth concerned the art of delivering it.

Ramus also worked for the reform of logic and dialectic along the lines laid down by Rodolphus Agricola in his _De inventione dialectica_ (1479) and by the humanists who followed him in seeking to break away from scholastic formalism by restoring the union of eloquence and philosophy advocated by Cicero. This reform consisted essentially in rejecting the classical opposition between science and opinion that had led Aristotle to draw a distinction between analytical and dialectical reasoning—the former dealing with necessary reasonings, the latter with probable ones. Analytical reasoning is the concern of Aristotle's _Analytics,_[4] dialectical reasoning that of the _Topics, On Sophistical Refutations,_ and the _Rhetoric._[5]

Against this distinction, this is what Ramus has to say in his _Dialectic:_

Aristotle, or more precisely the exponents of Aristotle's theories, thought that there are two arts of discussion and reasoning, one applying to science and called Logic, the other dealing with opinion and called Dialectic. In this—with all due respect to such great masters—they were greatly mistaken. Indeed these two names, Dialectic and Logic, generally mean the very same thing, like the words *dialegesthai* and *logizesthai* from which they are derived and descended, that is, dispute or reason. . . . Furthermore, although things known are either necessary and scientific, or contingent and a matter of opinion, just as our sight can perceive all colors, both unchanging and changeable, in the same way the art of knowing, that is Dialectic or Logic, is one and the same doctrine of reasoning well about anything whatsoever. . . .[6]

As a result of this rejection, Ramus unites in his *Dialectic* what Aristotle had separated. He divides his work into two parts, one concerning invention, the other judgment. Further, he includes in dialectic parts that were formerly regarded as belonging to rhetoric the theory of invention or *loci* and that of disposition, called *method*. Memory is considered as merely a reflection of these first two parts, and rhetoric—the "art of speaking well," of "eloquent and ornate language"—includes the study of tropes, of figures of style, and of oratorical delivery, all of which are considered as of lesser importance.

Thus was born the tradition of modern rhetoric, better called stylistic, as the study of techniques of unusual expression. For Fontanier, as we have seen, rhetoric is reduced to the study of figures of style, which he defines as "the more or less remarkable traits and forms, the phrases with a more or less happy turn, by which the expression of ideas, thoughts, and feelings removes the discourse more or less far away from what would have been its simple, common expression."[7]

Rhetoric, on this conception, is essentially an art of expression and more especially, of literary conventionalized expression; it is an art of style. So it is still regarded by Jean Paulhan in his book *Les fleurs de Tarbes ou la terreur dans les lettres* (1941, but published first as articles in 1936).

The same view of rhetoric was taken in Italy during the Renaissance, despite the success of humanism. Inspired by the Ciceronian ideal of the union of philosophy with eloquence, humanists such as Lorenzo Valla sought to unite dialectic and rhetoric. But they gave definite primacy to rhetoric, thus expressing their revolt against scholastic formalism.

This humanistic tradition continued for over a century and finally produced in the *De principiis* by Mario Nizolio (1553) its most significant work from a philosophical point of view. Less than ten years later, however, in 1562, Francesco Patrizi published in his *Rhetoric* the most violent attack upon this discipline, to which he denied any philosophical interest whatsoever. Giambattista Vico's reaction came late and produced no immediate result. Rhetoric became a wholly formal discipline—any living ideas that it contained being included in Aesthetics.

Germany is one country where classical rhetoric has continued to be carefully studied, especially by scholars such as Friedrich Blass, Wilhelm Kroll, and Friedrich Solmsen, who devoted most of their lives to this study. Yet, even so, rhetoric has been regarded only as the theory of literary prose. Heinrich Lausberg has produced a most remarkable work, which is the best tool in existence for the study of rhetorical terminology and the structure of discourse, and yet in the author's own eyes it is only a contribution to the study of literary language and tradition.[8]

The old tradition of rhetoric has been kept longest in Great Britain—it is still very much alive among Scots jurists—thanks to the importance of psychology in the empiricism of Bacon, Locke, and Hume, and to the influence of the Scottish philosophy of common sense. This tradition, in which the theory of invention is reduced to a minimum and interest is focused on the persuasive aspect of discourse,

is represented by such original works as George Campbell's *The Philosophy of Rhetoric* (1776) and Richard Whately's *Elements of Rhetoric* (1828). In this work, Whately, who was a logician, deals with argumentative composition in general and the art of establishing the truth of a proposition so as to convince others, rhetoric being reduced to "a purely managerial or supervisory science."[9] His disciple, the future Cardinal John Henry Newman, applied Whately's ideas to the problems of faith in his *Grammar of Assent* (1870). This outlook still consists in seeing in rhetoric only a theory of expression. It was the view adopted by Ivor Armstrong Richards in his *Principles of Literary Criticism* (published in 1924) and in his *Philosophy of Rhetoric* (1936).

While in Europe rhetoric has been reduced to stylistics and literary criticism, becoming merely a part of the study of literature insofar as it was taught at all, in the United States the appearance of a speech profession brought about a unique development.

Samuel Silas Curry, in a book entitled *The Province of Expression* (1891), was the first to emphasize spoken discourse and its delivery, rather than the composition of literary prose, and to claim autonomy for speech as opposed to written composition. "Expression," as he understood it, did not mean the way in which ideas and feelings are expressed in a literary form, but instead the manner in which they are communicated by means of an art of "delivery." Concern for this element, apparently one of lesser importance, clearly reveals a renewed interest in the audience, and this interest helped to promote the creation of a new "speech profession," separate from the teaching of English and of English literature. Under the influence of William James, James Albert Winans published a volume entitled *Public Speaking* (1915) that firmly established a union between professors of speech and those of psychology. With the cooperation of specialists in ancient and medieval rhetoric, such as Charles S. Baldwin, Harry Caplan, Lane Cooper, Everett Lee Hunt, and Richard McKeon, the whole tradition of classical rhetoric has been retraced. This study has been

continued and further developed in the works of Wilbur Samuel Howell, Donald C. Bryant, Karl R. Wallace, Walter J. Ong, Lloyd F. Bitzer, Douglas Ehninger, and Marie K. Hochmuth. The work of these scholars—the titles of which can be found in the Bibliography that has been regularly published by the *Quarterly Journal of Speech* since 1915—constitutes a unique achievement which is as yet too little known outside the United States.[10]

An Ornamental or a Practical Art?

There is nothing of philosophical interest in a rhetoric that has turned into an art of expression, whether literary or verbal.[11] Hence it is not surprising that the term is missing entirely from both Andre Lalande's *Vocabulaire technique et critique de la philosophie* and the recent American *Encyclopedia of Philosophy* (1967). In the Western tradition, "Rhetoric" has frequently been identified with verbalism and an empty, unnatural, stilted mode of expression. Rhetoric then becomes the symbol of the most outdated elements in the education of the old regime, the elements that were the most formal, most useless and most opposed to the needs of an equalitarian, progressive democracy.

This view of rhetoric as declamation—ostentatious and artificial discourse—is not a new one. The same view was taken of the rhetoric of the Roman Empire. Once serious matters, both political and judiciary, had been withdrawn from its influence, rhetoric became perforce limited to school exercises, to set speeches treating either a theme of the past or an imaginary situation, but, in any case, one without any real bearing. Serious people, especially the Stoics, made fun of it. Thus Epictetus declares: "But this faculty of speaking and of ornamenting words, if there is indeed any such peculiar faculty, what else does it do, when there happens to be discourse about a thing, than to ornament the words and arrange them as hairdressers do the hair?"[12]

Aristotle would have disagreed with this conception of rhetoric as an ornamental art bearing the same relation to prose as poetics does to verse. For Aristotle, rhetoric is a practical discipline that aims, not at producing a work of art, but at exerting through speech a persuasive action on an audience. Unfortunately, however, those responsible for the confusion between the two have been able to appeal to Aristotle's own authority because of the misleading analysis he gave of the epideictic or ceremonial form of oratory.

In his *Rhetoric* Aristotle distinguishes three genres of oratory: deliberative, forensic, and ceremonial. "Political speaking," he writes, "urges us either to do or not to do something: one of these two courses is always taken by private counsellors, as well as by men who address public assemblies. Forensic speaking either attacks or defends somebody: one or other of these two things must always be done by the parties in a case. The ceremonial oratory of display either praises or censures somebody." But whereas the audience is supposed to act as a judge and make a decision concerning either the future (deliberative genre) or the past (forensic genre), in the case of an epideictic discourse the task of the audience consists in judging, not about the matter of discourse, but about the orator's skill.[13] In political and forensic discourse the subject of the discourse is itself under discussion, and the orator aims at persuading the audience to take part in deciding the matter, but in epideictic discourse the subject—such as, for example, the praise of soldiers who have died for their country—is not at all a matter of debate. Such set speeches were often delivered before large assemblies, as at the Olympic Games, where competition between orators provided a welcome complement to the athletic contests. On such occasions, the only decision that the audience was called upon to make concerned the talent of the orator, by awarding the crown to the victor.

One might well ask how an oratorical genre can be defined by its literary imitation. We know that Cicero, after having lost the suit, rewrote his *Pro Milone* and published it as a literary work. He hoped that by artistically improving the speech, which had failed to convince Milo's judges, he might gain the approbation of lovers of literature. Are those who read this speech long after its practical bearing has disappeared any more than spectators? In that case, all discourses automatically become literature once they cease to exert a persuasive effect, and there is no particular reason to distinguish different genres of oratory. Yet it can be maintained, on the contrary, that the epideictic genre is not only important but essential from an educational point of view, since it too has an effective and distinctive part to play—that, namely, of bringing about a consensus in the minds of the audience regarding the values that are celebrated in the speech.

The moralists rightly satirize the view of epideictic oratory as spectacle. La Bruyere writes derisively of those who "are so deeply moved and touched by Theodorus's sermon that they resolve in their hearts that it is even more beautiful than the last one he preached." And Bossuet, fearful lest the real point of a sermon be missed, exclaims: "You should now be convinced that preachers of the Gospel do not ascend into pulpits to utter empty speeches to be listened to for amusement."[14]

Bossuet here is following St. Augustine's precepts concerning sacred discourse as set forth in the fourth book of his work *On Christian Doctrine*. The orator is not content if his listener merely accepts the truth of his words and praises his eloquence, because he wants his full assent:

If the truths taught are such that to believe or to know them is enough, to give one's assent implies nothing more than to confess that they are true. When, however, the truth taught is one that must be carried into practice, and that is taught for the very purpose of being practised, it is useless to be persuaded of the truth of what is said, if it be not so learnt as to be practised. The eloquent divine, then, when he is urging a practical truth, must not only teach so as to give instruction, and please so as to keep up the attention, but he must also sway the mind so as to subdue the will.

The listener will be persuaded, Augustine also claims,

> if he be drawn by your promises, and awed by your threats; if he reject what you condemn, and embrace what you commend; if he grieve when you heap up objects for grief, and rejoice when you point out an object for joy; if he pity those whom you present to him as objects of pity, and shrink from those whom you set before him as men to be feared and shunned.[15]

The orator's aim in the epideictic genre is not just to gain a passive adherence from his audience but to provoke the action wished for or, at least, to awaken a disposition so to act. This is achieved by forming a community of minds, which Kenneth Burke, who is well aware of the importance of this genre, calls *identification*. As he writes, rhetoric "is rooted in an essential function of language itself, a function that is wholly realistic and is continually born anew; the use of language as a symbolic means of inducing cooperation in beings that by nature respond to symbols."[16] In fact, any persuasive discourse seeks to have an effect on an audience, although the audience may consist of only one person and the discourse be an inward deliberation.

The distinction of the different genres of oratory is highly artificial, as the study of a speech shows. Mark Antony's famous speech in Shakespeare's *Julius Caesar* opens with a funeral eulogy,[17] a typical case of epideictic discourse, and ends by provoking a riot that is clearly political. Its goal is to intensify an adherence to values, to create a disposition to act, and finally to bring people to act. Seen in such perspective, rhetoric becomes a subject of great philosophical interest.

Thinking About Values

In 1945, when I published my first study of justice,[18] I was completely ignorant of the importance of rhetoric. This study, undertaken in the spirit of logical empiricism, succeeded in showing that *formal justice* is a principle of action, according to which beings of one and the same essential category must be treated in the same way.[19] The application of this principle to actual situations, however, requires criteria to indicate which categories are relevant and how their members should be treated, and such decisions involve a recourse to judgments of value. But on positive methods I could not see how such judgments could have any foundation or justification. Indeed, as I entirely accepted the principle that one cannot draw an "ought" from an "is"—a judgment of value from a judgment of fact—I was led inevitably to the conclusion that if justice consists in the systematic implementation of certain value judgments, it does not rest on any rational foundation: "As for the value that is the foundation of the normative system, we cannot subject it to any rational criterion: it is utterly arbitrary and logically indeterminate. . . . The idea of value is, in effect, incompatible both with formal necessity and with experiential universality. There is no value which is not logically arbitrary."[20]

I was deeply dissatisfied with this conclusion, however interesting the analysis, since the philosophical inquiry, carried on within the limits of logical empiricism, could not provide an ideal of practical reason, that is, the establishment of rules and models for reasonable action. By admitting the soundness of Hume's analysis, I found myself in a situation similar to Kant's. If Hume is right in maintaining that empiricism cannot provide a basis for either science or morals, must we not then look to other than empirical methods to justify them? Similarly, if experience and calculation, combined according to the precepts of logical empiricism, leave no place for practical reason and do not enable us to justify our decisions and choices, must we not seek other techniques of reasoning for that purpose? In other words, is there a logic of value judgments that makes it possible for us to reason about values instead of making them depend solely on irrational choices, based on interest, passion, prejudice, and myth? Recent history has shown abundantly the sad excesses to which such an attitude can lead.

Critical investigation of the philosophical literature yielded no satisfactory results. The

French logician Edmond Goblot, in his work *La logique des jugements de valeur,*[21] restricted his analysis to derived or instrumental value judgments, that is, to those judgments that use values as a means to already accepted ends, or as obstacles to their attainment. The ends themselves, however, could not be subjected to deliberation unless they were transformed into instrumental values, but such a transformation only pushes further back the problem of ultimate ends.

We thus seem to be faced with two extreme attitudes, neither of which is acceptable: subjectivism, which, as far as values are concerned, leads to skepticism for lack of an intersubjective criterion; or an absolutism founded on intuitionism. In the latter case, judgments of value are assimilated to judgments of a reality that is *sui generis.* In other words, must we choose between A. J. Ayer's view in *Language, Truth, and Logic* and G. E. Moore's view in *Principia Ethica?* Both seem to give a distorted notion of the actual process of deliberation that leads to decision making in practical fields such as politics, law, and morals.

Then too, I agreed with the criticisms made by various types of existentialism against both positivist empiricism and rationalistic idealism, but I could find no satisfaction in their justification of action by purely subjective projects or commitments.

I could see but one way to solve the dilemma to which most currents of contemporary philosophy had led. Instead of working out *a priori* possible structures for a logic of value judgments, might we not do better to follow the method adopted by the German logician Gottlob Frege, who, to cast new light on logic, decided to analyze the reasoning used by mathematicians? Could we not undertake, in the same way, an extensive inquiry into the manner in which the most diverse authors in all fields do in fact reason about values? By analyzing political discourse, the reasons given by judges, the reasoning of moralists, the daily discussions carried on in deliberating about making a choice or reaching a decision or nominating a person, we might be able to trace the actual logic of value judgments which seems continually to elude the grasp of specialists in the theory of knowledge.

For almost ten years Mme L. Olbrechts-Tyteca and I conducted such an inquiry and analysis. We obtained results that neither of us had ever expected. Without either knowing or wishing it, we had rediscovered a part of Aristotelian logic that had been long forgotten or, at any rate, ignored and despised. It was the part dealing with dialectical reasoning, as distinguished from demonstrative reasoning—called by Aristotle *analytics*—which is analyzed at length in the *Rhetoric, Topics,* and *On Sophistical Refutations.* We called this new, or revived, branch of study, devoted to the analysis of informal reasoning, *The New Rhetoric.*[22]

Argumentation and Demonstration

The new rhetoric is a theory of argumentation. But the specific part that is played by argumentation could not be fully understood until the modern theory of demonstration—to which it is complementary—had been developed. In its contemporary form, demonstration is a calculation made in accordance with rules that have been laid down beforehand. No recourse is allowed to evidence or to any intuition other than that of the senses. The only requirement is the ability to distinguish signs and to perform operations according to rules. A demonstration is regarded as correct or incorrect according as it conforms, or fails to conform, to the rules. A conclusion is held to be demonstrated if it can be reached by means of a series of correct operations starting from premises accepted as axioms. Whether these axioms be considered as evident, necessary, true, or hypothetical, the relation between them and the demonstrated theorems remains unchanged. To pass from a correct inference to the truth or to the computable probability of the conclusion, one must admit both the truth of the premises and the coherence of the axiomatic system.

The acceptance of these assumptions compels us to abandon pure formalism and to accept certain conventions and to admit the reality of certain models or structures. According to the classical theory of demonstration, which is rejected by formalism, the validity of the deductive method was guaranteed by intuition or evidence—by the natural light of reason. But if we reject such a foundation, we are not compelled to accept formalism. It is still insufficient, since we need good reasons to accept the premises from which we start, and these reasons can be good only for a mind capable of judging them. However, once we have accepted the framework of a formal system and know that it is free from ambiguity, then the demonstrations that can be made within it are compelling and impersonal; in fact, their validity is capable of being controlled mechanically. It is this specific character of formal demonstration that distinguishes it from dialectical reasoning founded on opinion and concerned with contingent realities. Ramus failed to see this distinction and confused the two by using a faulty analogy with the sight of moving and unmoving colors.[23] It is sometimes possible, by resorting to prior arrangements and conventions, to transform an argument into a demonstration of a more or less probablistic character. It remains true, nonetheless, that we must distinguish carefully between the two types of reasoning if we want to understand properly how they are related.

An argumentation is always addressed by a person called the orator—whether by speech or in writing—to an audience of listeners or readers. It aims at obtaining or reinforcing the adherence of the audience to some thesis, assent to which is hoped for. The new rhetoric, like the old, seeks to persuade or convince, to obtain an adherence which may be *theoretical* to start with, although it may eventually be manifested through a disposition to act, or *practical,* as provoking either immediate action, the making of a decision, or a commitment to act.

Thus argumentation, unlike demonstration, presupposes a meeting of minds: the will on the part of the orator to persuade and not to compel or command, and a disposition on the part of the audience to listen. Such mutual goodwill must not only be general but must also apply to the particular question at issue; it must not be forgotten that all argumentation aims somehow at modifying an existing state of affairs. This is why every society possesses institutions to further discussion between competent persons and to prevent others. Not everybody can start debating about anything whatever, no matter where. To be a man people listen to is a precious quality and is still more necessary as a preliminary condition for an efficacious argumentation.

In some cases there are detailed rules drawn up for establishing this contact before a question can be debated. The main purpose of procedure in civil and criminal law is to ensure a balanced unfolding of the judicial debate. Even in matters where there are no explicit rules for discussion, there are still customs and habits that cannot be disregarded without sufficient reason.

Argumentation also presupposes a means of communicating, a common language. The use of it in a given situation, however, may admit of variation according to the position of the interlocutors. Sometimes only certain persons are entitled to ask questions or to conduct the debate.

From these specifications it is apparent that the new rhetoric cannot tolerate the more or less conventional, and even arbitrary, limitations traditionally imposed upon classical rhetoric. For Aristotle, the similarity between rhetoric and dialectic was all-important.[24] According to him, they differ only in that dialectic provides us with techniques of discussion for a common search for truth, while rhetoric teaches how to conduct a debate in which various points of view are expressed and the decision is left up to the audience. This distinction shows why dialectic has been traditionally considered as a serious matter by philosophers, whereas rhetoric has been regarded with contempt. Truth, it was held, presided over a dialectical discussion, and the interlocutors had to reach agreement about it by themselves, whereas rhetoric taught only how to present a point of view—that is to say, a partial aspect of the question—and the decision of the issue was left up to a third person.[25]

It should be noted, however, that for Plato dialectic alone does not attain to metaphysical truth. The latter requires an intuition for which dialectic can only pave the way by eliminating untenable hypotheses.[26] However, truth is the keynote for dialectic, which seeks to get as close to the truth as possible through the discursive method. The rhetorician, on the other hand, is described as trying to outdo his rivals in debate, and, if his judges are gross and ignorant, the triumph of the orator who shows the greatest skill in flattery will by no means always be the victory of the best cause. Plato emphasizes this point strongly in the *Gorgias,* where he shows that the demagogue, to achieve victory, will not hesitate to use techniques unworthy of a philosopher. This criticism gains justification from Aristotle's observation, based evidently on Athenian practice, that it belongs to rhetoric "to deal with such matters as we deliberate upon without arts or systems to guide us, in the hearing of persons who cannot take in at a glance a complicated argument, or follow a long chain of reasoning."[27]

For the new rhetoric, however, argumentation has a wider scope as nonformal reasoning that aims at obtaining or reinforcing the adherence of an audience. It is manifest in discussion as well as in debate, and it matters not whether the aim be the search for truth or the triumph of a cause, and the audience may have any degree of competence. The reason that rhetoric has been deemed unworthy of the philosopher's efforts is not because dialectic employs a technique of questions and answers while rhetoric proceeds by speeches from opposing sides.[28] It is not this but rather the idea of the unicity of truth that has disqualified rhetoric in the Western philosophical tradition. Thus Descartes declares: "Whenever two men come to opposite decisions about the same matter one of them at least must certainly be wrong, and apparently there is not even one of them who knows; for if the reasoning of the second was sound and clear he would be able so to lay it before the other as finally to succeed in convincing *his* understanding also."[29] Both Descartes and Plato hold this idea because of their rejection of opinion, which is variable, and their adoption of an ideal of science based on the model of geometry and mathematical reasoning—the very model according to which the world was supposed to have been created. *Dum Deus calculat, fit mundus* (While God calculates, the world is created) is the conviction not only of Leibniz but of all rationalists.

Things are very different within a tradition that follows a juridical, rather than a mathematical, model. Thus in the tradition of the Talmud, for example, it is accepted that opposed positions can be equally reasonable; one of them does not have to be right. Indeed, "in the Talmud two schools of Biblical interpretation are in constant opposition, the school of Hillel and that of Shammai. Rabbi Abba relates that, bothered by these contradictory interpretations of the sacred text, Rabbi Samuel addresses himself to heaven in order to know who speaks the truth. A voice from above answers him that these two theses both expressed the word of the Living God."[30]

So too, for Plato, the subject of discussion is always one for which men possess no techniques for reaching agreement immediately:

Suppose for example that you and I, my good friend [Socrates remarks to Euthyphro], differ about a number; so differences of this sort make us enemies and set us at variance with one another? Do we not go at once to arithmetic, and put an end to them by a sum? . . . Or suppose that we differ about magsum? . . . Or suppose that we differ about magnitudes, do we not quickly end the differences by measuring? . . . And we end a controversy about heavy and light by resorting to a weighing machine? . . . But what differences are there which cannot be thus decided, and which therefore make us angry and set us at enmity with one another? I dare say the answer does not occur to you at the moment, and therefore I will suggest that these enmities arise when the matters of difference are the just and unjust, good and evil, honourable and dishonourable.[31]

When agreement can easily be reached by means of calculation, measuring, or weighing, when a result can be either demonstrated or verified, nobody would think of resorting to dialectical discussion. The latter concerns only what cannot be so decided and, especially, disagreements about values. In fact, in matters of opinion, it is often the case that neither

Apodeictic philosophy

rhetoric nor dialectic can reconcile all the positions that are taken.

Such is exactly how matters stand in philosophy. The philosopher's appeal to reason gives no guarantee whatever that everyone will agree with his point of view. Different philosophies present different points of view, and it is significant that a historian of pre-Socratic philosophy has been able to show that the different points of view can be regarded as antilogies or discourses on opposite sides, in that an antithesis is opposed in each case to a thesis.[32] One might even wonder with Alexandre Kojeve, the late expert in Hegelian philosophy, whether Hegelian dialectic did not have its origin, not in Platonic dialectic, but rather in the development of philosophical systems that can be opposed as thesis to antithesis, followed by a synthesis of the two. The process is similar to a lawsuit in which the judge identifies the elements he regards as valid in the claims of the opposed parties. For Kant as well as for Hegel, opinions are supposed to be excluded from philosophy, which aims at rationality. But to explain the divergencies that are systematically encountered in the history of philosophy, we need only call these opinions the natural illusions of reason as submitted to the tribunal of critical reason (as in Kant) or successive moments in the progress of reason toward Absolute Spirit (as in Hegel).

To reconcile philosophic claims to rationality with the plurality of philosophic systems, we must recognize that the appeal to reason must be identified not as an appeal to a single truth but instead as an appeal for the adherence of an audience, which can be thought of, after the manner of Kant's categorical imperative, as encompassing all reasonable and competent men. The characteristic aspect of philosophical controversy and of the history of philosophy can only be understood if the appeal to reason is conceived as an appeal to an ideal audience—which I call the universal audience—whether embodied in God,[33] in all reasonable and competent men, in the man deliberating or in an elite.[34] Instead of identifying philosophy with a science, which, on the positivist ideal, could make only analytical judgments, both indisputable and empty, we would do better to abandon the ideal of an apodictic philosophy. We would then have to admit that in the discharge of his specific task, the philosopher has at his disposal only an argumentation that he can endeavor to make as reasonable and systematic as possible without ever being able to make it absolutely compelling or a demonstrative proof. Besides, it is highly unlikely that any reasoning from which we could draw reasons for acting could be conducted under the sign of truth, for these reasons must enable us to justify our actions and decisions. Thus, indirectly, the analysis of philosophical reasoning brings us back to views that are familiar in existentialism.

Audiences display an infinite variety in both extension and competence: in extent, from the audience consisting of a single subject engaged in inward deliberation up to the universal audience; and in competence, from those who know only *loci* up to the specialists who have acquired their knowledge only through a long and painstaking preparation. By thus generalizing the idea of the audience, we can ward off Plato's attack against the rhetoricians for showing greater concern for success than for the truth. To this criticism we can reply that the techniques suited for persuading a crowd in a public place would not be convincing to a better educated and more critical audience, and that the worth of an argumentation is not measured solely by its efficacy but also by the quality of the audience at which it is aimed. Consequently, the idea of a rational argumentation cannot be defined *in abstracto,* since it depends on the historically grounded conception of the universal audience.

The part played by the audience in rhetoric is crucially important, because all argumentation, in aiming to persuade, must be adapted to the audience and, hence, based on beliefs accepted by the audience with such conviction that the rest of the discourse can be securely based upon it. Where this is not the case, one must reinforce adherence to these starting points by means of all available rhetorical techniques before attempting to join the controverted points to them. Indeed, the orator who builds his discourse on premises not accepted by the audience commits a classical fallacy in argumentation—a *petitio principii.* This is not a mistake in formal logic, since formally any proposition implies itself, but it is a mistake in argumentation, because the orator begs the question by presupposing the existence of an adherence that does not exist and to the obtaining of which his efforts should be directed. The objects of agreement on which the orator can build his argument are various. On the one hand, there are facts, truths, and presumptions; on the other, values, hierarchies, and *loci* of the preferable.[35]

Facts and truths can be characterized as objects that are already agreed to by the universal audience, and, hence, there is no need to increase the intensity of adherence to them. If we presuppose the coherence of reality and of our truths taken as a whole, there cannot be any conflict between facts or truths on which we would be called to make a decision. What happens when such a conflict seems to occur is that the incompatible element loses its status and becomes either an illusory fact or an apparent truth, unless we can eliminate the incompatibility by showing that the two apparently incompatible truths apply to different fields. We shall return to this argumentative method later when dealing with the dissociation of ideas.

Presumptions are opinions which need not be proved, although adherence to them can be either reinforced, if necessary, or suppressed by proving the opposite. Legal procedure makes abundant use of presumptions, for which it has worked out refined definitions and elaborate rules for their use.

Values are appealed to in order to influence our choices of action. They supply reasons for preferring one type of behavior to another, although not all would necessarily accept them as good reasons. Indeed, most values are particular in that they are accepted only by a particular group. The values that are called universal can be regarded in so many different ways that their universality is better considered as only an aspiration for agreement, since it disappears as soon as one tries to apply one

such value to a concrete situation. For argumentation, it is useful to distinguish concrete values, such as one's country, from abstract values, such as justice and truth. It is characteristic of values that they can become the center of conflict without thereby ceasing to be values. This fact explains how real sacrifice is possible, the object renounced being by no means a mere appearance. For this reason, the effort to reinforce adherence to values is never superfluous. Such an effort is undertaken in epideictic discourse, and, in general, all education also endeavors to make certain values preferred to others.

After values, we find that accepted hierarchies play a part in argumentation. Such, for example, are the superiority of men over animals and of adults over children. We also find double hierarchies as in the case in which we rank behavior in accordance with an accepted ranking of the agents. For this reason, such a statement as "You are behaving like a beast" is pejorative, whereas an exhortation to "act like a man" calls for more laudable behavior.

Among all the *loci* studied by Aristotle in his *Topics,* we shall consider only those examined in the third book, which we shall call *loci of the preferable.* They are very general propositions, which can serve, at need, to justify values or hierarchies, but which also have as a special characteristic the ability to evaluate complementary aspects of reality. To *loci of quantity,* such as "That which is more lasting is worth more than that which is less so" or "A thing useful for a large number of persons is worth more than one useful for a smaller number," we can oppose *loci of quality,* which set value upon the unique, the irremediable, the opportune, the rare—that is, to what is exceptional instead of to what is normal. By the use of these *loci,* it is possible to describe the difference between the classical and the romantic spirit.[36]

While it establishes a framework for all nonformal reasoning, whatever its nature, its subject, or audience, the new rhetoric does not pretend to supply a list of all the *loci* and common opinions which can serve as starting points for argumentation. It is sufficient to stress that, in all cases, the orator must know the opinion of his audience on all the questions he intends to deal with, the type of arguments and reasons which seem relevant with regard to both subject and audience, what they are likely to consider as a strong or weak argument, and what might arouse them, as well as what would leave them indifferent.

Quintilian, in his *Institutes of Oratory*, points out the advantage of a public-school education for future orators: it puts them on a par and in fellowship with their audience. This advice is sound as regards argumentation on matters requiring no special knowledge. Otherwise, however, it is indispensable for holding an audience to have had a preliminary initiation into the body of ideas to be discussed.

In discussion with a single person or a small group, the establishment of a starting point is very different from before a large group. The particular opinions and convictions needed may have already been expressed previously, and the orator has no reason to believe that his interlocutors have changed their minds. Or he can use the technique of question and answer to set the premises of his argument on firm ground. Socrates proceeded in this way, taking the interlocutor's assent as a sign of the truth of the accepted thesis. Thus, Socrates says to Callicles in the *Gorgias:*

If you agree with me in an argument about any point, that point will have been sufficiently tested by us, and will not require to be submitted to any further test. For you could not have agreed with me, either from lack of knowledge or from superfluity of modesty, nor yet from a desire to deceive me, for you are my friend, as you tell me yourself. And therefore when you and I are agreed, the result will be the attainment of perfect truth.[37]

It is obvious that such a dialogue is out of the question when one is addressing a numerous assembly. In this case, the discourse must take as premises the presumptions that the orator has learned the audience will accept.[38]

Creating "Presence"

What an audience accepts forms a body of opinion, convictions, and commitments that is both vast and indeterminate. From this body, the orator must select certain elements on which he focuses attention by endowing them, as it were, with a "presence." This does not mean that the elements left out are entirely ignored, but they are pushed into the background. Such a choice implicitly sets a value on some aspects of reality rather than others. Recall the lovely Chinese story told by Meng-Tseu: "A king sees an ox on its way to sacrifice. He is moved to pity for it and orders that a sheep be used in its place. He confesses he did so because he could see the ox, but not the sheep."[39]

Things present, things near to us in space and time, act directly on our sensibility. The orator's endeavors often consist, however, in bringing to mind things that are not immediately present. Bacon was well aware of this function of eloquence:

The affection beholdeth merely the present; reason beholdeth the future and sum of time. And therefore the present filling the imagination more, reason is commonly vanquished; but after that force of eloquence and persuasion hath made things future and remote appear as present, then upon the revolt of the imagination reason prevaileth.[40]

To make, "things future and remote appear as present," that is, to create presence, calls for special efforts of presentation. For this purpose all kinds of literary techinques and a number of rhetorical figures have been developed. *Hypotyposis* or *demonstratio,* for example, is defined as a figure "which sets things out in such a way that the matter seems to unfold, and the thing to happen, before our very eyes."[41] Obviously, such a figure is highly important as a persuasive factor. In fact, if their argumentative role is disregarded, the study of figures is a useless pastime, a search for strange names for rather farfetched and affected turns of speech. Other figures, such as repetition, anaphora, amplification, congerie, metabole, pseudo direct discourse, enallage, are all various means of increasing the feeling of presence in the audience.[42]

In his description of facts, truths, and values, the orator must employ language that takes into account the classification and valuations implicit in the audience's acceptance of them. For placing his discourse at the level of generality that he considers best adapted to his purpose and his audience, he has at hand a whole arsenal of linguistic categories—substantives, adjectives, verbs, adverbs—and a vocabulary and phrasing that enable him, under the guise of a descriptive narrative, to stress the main elements and indicate which are merely secondary.

In the selection of data and the interpretation and presentation of them, the orator is subject to the accusation of partiality. Indeed, there is no proof that his presentation has not been distorted by a tendentious vision of things. Hence, in law, the legal counsel must reply to the attorney general, while the judge forms an opinion and renders his decision only after hearing both parties. Although his judgment may appear more balanced, it cannot achieve perfect objectivity—which can only be an ideal. Even with the elimination of tendentious views and or errors, one does not thereby reach a perfectly just decision. So too in scientific or technical discourse, where the orator's freedom of choice is less because he cannot depart, with special reason, from the accepted terminology, value judgments are implicit, and their justification resides in the theories, classifications, and methodology that gave birth to the technical terminology. The idea that science consists of nothing but a body of timeless, objective truths has been increasingly challenged in recent years.[43]

The Structure of Argument

Nonformal argument consists, not of a chain of ideas of which some are derived from others according to accepted rules of inference, but rather of a web formed from all the arguments and all the reasons that combine to achieve the desired result. The purpose of the discourse in general is to bring the audience to the conclusions offered by the orator, starting from premises that they already accept—which is the case unless the orator has been guilty of a *petitio principii.* The argumentative process consists in establishing a link by which acceptance, or adherence, is passed from one element to another, and this end can be reached either by leaving the various elements of the discourse unchanged and associated as they are or by making a dissociation of ideas.

We shall now consider the various types of association and of dissociation that the orator has at his command. To simplify classification, we have grouped the processes of association into three classes: quasi-logical arguments, arguments based upon the structure of the real, and arguments that start from particular cases that are then either generalized or transposed from one sphere of reality to another.[44]

Quasi-Logical Arguments

These arguments are similar to the formal structures of logic and mathematics. In fact, men apparently first came to an understanding of purely formal proof by submitting quasilogical arguments, such as many of the *loci* listed in Aristotle's *Topics,* to an analysis that yielded precision and formalization. There is a difference of paramount importance between an argument and a formal proof. Instead of using a natural language in which the same word can be used with different meanings, a logical calculus employs an artificial language so constructed that one sign can have only one meaning. In logic, the principle of identity designates a tautology, an indisputable but empty truth, whatever its formulation. But this is not the case in ordinary language. When I say "Business is business," or "Boys will be boys," or "War is war," those hearing the words give preference, not to the univocity

of the statement, but to its significant character. They will never take the statements as tautologies, which would make them meaningless, but will look for different plausible interpretations of the same term that will render the whole statement both meaningful and acceptable. Similarly, when faced with a statement that is formally a contradiction—"When two persons do the same thing it is not the same thing," or "We step and we do not step into the same river,"—we look for an interpretation that eliminates the incoherence.

To understand an orator, we must make the effort required to render his discourse coherent and meaningful. This effort requires goodwill and respect for the person who speaks and for what he says. The techniques of formalization make calculation possible, and, as a result, the correctness of the reasoning is capable of mechanical control. This result is not obtained without a certain linguistic rigidity. The language of mathematics is not used for poetry any more than it is used for diplomacy.

Because of its adaptability, ordinary language can always avoid purely formal contradictions. Yet it is not free from incompatibilities, as, for instance, when two norms are recommended which cannot both apply to the same situation. Thus, telling a child not to lie and to obey his parents lays one open to ridicule if the child asks, "What must I do if my father orders me to lie?" When such an antinomy occurs, one seeks for qualifications or amendments—and recommends the primacy of one norm over the other or points out that there are exceptions to the rule. Theoretically, the most elegant way of eliminating an incompatibility is to have recourse to a dissociation of concepts—but of this, more later. Incompatibility is an important element in Socratic irony. By exposing the incompatibility of the answers given to his insidious questions, Socrates compels his interlocutor to abandon certain commonly accepted opinions.

Definitions play a very different role in argumentation from the one they have in a formal system. There they are mostly abbreviations. But in argumentation they determine the choice of one particular meaning over others—sometimes by establishing a relation between an old term and a new one. Definition is regarded as a rhetorical figure—the oratorical definition—when it aims, not at clarifying the meaning of an idea, but at stressing aspects that will produce the persuasive effect that is sought. It is a figure relating to choice: the selection of facts brought to the fore in the definition is unusual because the *definiens* is not serving the purpose of giving the meaning of a term.[45]

Analysis that aims at dividing a concept into all its parts and interpretation that aims at elucidating a text without bringing anything new to it are also quasi-logical arguments and call to mind the principle of identity. This method can give way to figures of speech called *aggregation* and *interpretation* when they serve some purpose other than clarification and tend to reinforce the feeling of presence.[46]

These few examples make it clear that expressions are called figures of style when they display a fixed structure that is easily recognizable and are used for a purpose different from their normal one—this new purpose being mainly one of persuasion. If the figure is so closely interwoven into the argumentation that it appears to be an expression suited to the occasion, it is regarded as an argumentative figure, and its unusual character will often escape notice.

Some reasoning processes—unlike definition or analysis, which aim at complete identification—are content with a partial reduction, that is, with an identification of the main elements. We have an example of this in the rule of justice that equals should be treated equally. If the agents and situations were identical, the application of the rule would take the form of an exact demonstration. As this is never the case, however, a decision will have to be taken about whether the differences are to be disregarded. This is why the recourse to precedent in legal matters is not a completely impersonal procedure but always requires the intervention of a judge.

Arguments of reciprocity are those that claim the same treatment for the antecedent as for the consequent of a relation—buyers-sellers, spectators-actors, etc. These arguments presuppose that the relation is symmetrical. Unreasonable use of them is apt to have comic results, such as the following story, known to have made Kant laugh:

At Surat, an Englishman is pouring out a bottle of ale which is foaming freely. He asks an Indian who is amazed at the sight what it is that he finds so strange. "What bothers me," replies the native, "isn't what is coming out of the bottle, but how you got it in there in the first place."

Other quasi-logical arguments take the transitivity of a relation for granted, even though it is only probable: "My friends' friends are my friends." Still other arguments apply to all kinds of other relations such as that between part and whole or between parts, relations of division, comparison, probability. They are clearly distinct from exact demonstration, since, in each case, complementary, nonformal hypotheses are necessary to render the argument compelling.[47]

Appeal to the Real

Arguments based on the structure of reality can be divided into two groups according as they establish associations of succession or of co-existence.

Among relations of succession, that of causality plays an essential role. Thus we may be attempting to find the causes of an effect, the means to an end, the consequences of a fact, or to judge an action or a rule by the consequences that it has. This last process might be called the pragmatic argument, since it is typical of utilitarianism in morals and of pragmaticism in general.[48]

Arguments establishing relations of coexistence are based on the link that unites a person to his actions. When generalized, this argument establishes the relation between the essence and the act, a relation of paramount importance in the social sciences. From this model have come the classification of periods of history (Antiquity, the Middle Ages), all literary classifications (classicism, romanticism), styles (Gothic, baroque), economic or political systems (feudalism, capitalism, fascism), and institutions (marriage, the church).[49] Rhetoric, conceived as the theory of argumentation, provides a guidance for the understanding both of the manner in which these categories were constituted and of the reasons for doing so. It helps us grasp the advantages and the disadvantages of using them and provides an insight into the value judgments that were present, explicitly or implicitly, when they took shape. The specificity of the social sciences can be best understood by considering the methodological reasons justifying the constitution of their categories—Max Weber's *Ideal-typus*.

Thanks to the relations of coexistence, we are also able to gain an understanding of the argument from authority in all its shapes as well as an appreciation of the persuasive role of *ethos* in argumentation, since the discourse can be regarded as an act on the orator's part.[50]

Establishing the Real

Arguments attempting to establish the structure of reality are first arguments by example, illustration, and model; second, arguments by analogy.

The example leads to the formulation of a rule through generalization from a particular case or through putting a new case on the same footing as an older one. Illustration aims at achieving presence for a rule by illustrating it with a concrete case. The argument from a model justifies an action by showing that it conforms to a model. One should also mention the argument from an antimodel; for example, the drunken Helot to whom the Spartans referred as a foil to show their sons how they should not behave.

In the various religions, God and all divine or quasi-divine persons are obviously preeminent models for their believers. Christian morality can be defined as the imitation of Christ, whereas Buddhist morality consists in imitating Buddha. The models that a culture proposes to its members for imitation provide a convenient way of characterizing it.[51]

The argument from analogy is extremely important in nonformal reasoning. Starting from a relation between two terms *A* and *B*, which we call the *theme* since it provides the proper subject matter of the discourse, we can by analogy present its structure or establish its value by relating it to the terms *C* and *D*, which constitute the *phoros* of the analogy, so that *A* is to *B* as *C* is to *D*. Analogy, which derives its name from the Greek word for proportion, is nevertheless different from mathematical proportion. In the latter the characteristic relation of equality is symmetrical, whereas the *phoros* called upon to clarify the structure or establish the value of the *theme* must, as a rule, be better known than the *theme*. When Heraclitus says that in the eyes of God man is as childish as a child is in the eyes of an adult, it is impossible to change the *phoros* for the *theme,* and vice versa, unless the audience is one that knows the relationship between God and man better than that between a child and an adult. It is also worth noting that when *man* is identified with *adult,* the analogy reduces to three terms, the middle one being repeated twice: *C* is to *B* as *B* is to *A*. This technique of argumentation is typical of Plato, Plotinus, and all those who establish hierarchies within reality.

Within the natural sciences the use of analogy is mainly heuristic, and the intent is ultimately to eliminate the analogy and replace it with a formula of a mathematical type. Things are different, however, in the social sciences and in philosophy, where the whole body of facts under study only offers reasons for or against a particular analogical vision of things.[52] This is one of the differences to which Wilhelm Dilthey refers when he claims that the natural sciences aim at explaining, whereas the human sciences seek for understanding.

The metaphor is the figure of style corresponding to the argument from analogy. It consists of a condensed analogy in which one term of the *theme* is associated with one term of the *phoros*. Thus "the morning of life" is a metaphor that summarizes the analogy: Morning is to day what youth is to life. Of course, in the case of a good many metaphors, the reconstruction of the complete analogy is neither easy nor unambiguous. When Berkeley, in his *Dialogues,*[53] speaks of "an ocean of false learning," there are various ways to supply the missing terms of the analogy, each one of which stresses a different relation unexpressed in the metaphor.

The use of analogies and metaphors best reveals the creative and literary aspects of argumentation. For some audiences their use should be avoided as much as possible, whereas for others the lack of them may make the discourse appear too technical and too difficult to follow. Specialists tend to hold analogies in suspicion and use them only to initiate students into their discipline. Scientific popularization makes extensive use of analogy, and only from time to time will the audience be reminded of the danger of identification of *theme* and *phoros*.[54]

The Dissociation of Ideas

Besides argumentative associations, we must also make room for the dissociation of ideas, the study of which is too often neglected by the rhetorical tradition. Dissociation is the classical solution for incompatibilities that call for an alteration of conventional ways of thinking. Philosophers, by using dissociation, often depart from common sense and form a vision of reality that is free from the contradictions of opinion.[55] The whole of the great metaphysical tradition, from Parmenides to our own day, displays a succession of dissociations where, in each case, reality is opposed to appearance.

Normally, reality is perceived through appearances that are taken as signs referring to it. When, however, appearances are incompatible—an oar in water looks broken but feels straight to the touch—we must admit, if we are to have a coherent picture of reality, that some appearances are illusory and may lead us to error regarding the real. One is thus brought to the construction of a conception of reality that at the same time is capable of being used as a criterion for judging appearances. Whatever is conformable to it is given value, whereas whatever is opposed is denied value and is considered a mere appearance.

Any idea can be subjected to a similar dissociation. To real justice we can oppose apparent justice and with real democracy contrast apparent democracy, or formal or nominal democracy, or quasi-democracy, or even "democracy" (in quotes). What is thus referred to as apparent is usually what the audience would normally call justice, democracy, etc. It only becomes apparent after the criterion of real justice or real democracy has been applied to it and reveals the error concealed under the name. The dissociation results in a depreciation of what had until then been an accepted value and in its replacement by another conception to which is accorded the original value. To effect such a depreciation, one will need a conception that can be shown to be valuable, relevant, as well as incompatible with the common use of the same notion.

We may call "philosophical pairs" all sets of notions that are formed on the model of the "appearance-reality" pair. The use of such pairs makes clear how philosophical ideas are developed and also shows how they cannot be dissociated from the process of giving or denying value that is typical of all ontologies. One thus comes to see the importance of argumentative devices in the development of thought, and especially of philosophy.[56]

Interaction of Arguments

An argumentation is ordinarily a spoken or written discourse, of variable length, that combines a great number of arguments with the aim of winning the adherence of an audience to one or more theses. These arguments interact within the minds of the audience, reinforcing or weakening each other. They also interact with the arguments of the opponents as well as with those that arise spontaneously in the minds of the audience. This situation gives rise to a number of theoretical questions.

Are there limits, for example, to the number of arguments that can be usefully accumulated? Does the choice of arguments and the scope of the argumentation raise special problems? What is a weak or an irrelevant argument? What is the effect of a weak argument on the whole argumentation? Are there any criteria for assessing the strength or relevance of an argument? Are such matters relative to the audience, or can they be determined objectively?

We have no general answer to such questions. The answer seems to depend on the field of study and on the philosophy that controls its organization. In any case, they are questions that have seldom been raised and that never have received a satisfactory answer. Before any satisfactory answer can be given, it will be necessary to make many detailed studies in the various disciplines, taking account of the most varied audiences.

Once our arguments have been formulated, does it make any difference what order they are presented in? Should one start, or finish, with strong arguments, or do both by putting the weaker arguments in the middle—the so-called Nestorian order? This way of presenting the problem implies that the force of an argument is independent of its place in the discourse. Yet, in fact, the opposite seems to be true, for what appears as a weak argument to one audience often appears as a strong argument to another, depending on whether the presuppositions rejected by one audience are accepted by the other. Should we present our arguments then in the order that lends them the greatest force? If so, there should be a special technique devoted to the organization of a discourse.

Such a technique would have to point out that an exordium is all-important in some cases, while in others it is entirely superfluous. Sometimes the objections of one's opponent ought to be anticipated beforehand and refuted, whereas in other cases it is better to let the objections arise spontaneously lest one appear to be tearing down straw men.[57]

In all such matters it seems unlikely that any hard-and-fast rules can be laid down, since one must take account of the particular character of the audience, of its evolution during the debate, and of the fact that habits and procedures that prove good in one sphere are no good in another. A general rhetoric cannot be fixed by precepts and rules laid down once for all. But it must be able to adapt itself to the most varied circumstances, matters, and audiences.

Reason and Rhetoric

The birth of a new period of culture is marked by an eruption of original ideas and a neglect of methodological concerns and of academic classifications and divisions. Ideas are used with various meanings that the future will distinguish and disentangle. The fundamental ideas of Greek philosophy offer a good example of this process. One of the richest and most confused of all is that expressed by the term *logos,* which means among other things: word, reason, discourse, reasoning, calculation, and all that was later to become the subject of logic and the expression of reason. Reason was opposed to desire and the passions, being regarded as the faculty that ought to govern human behavior in the name of truth and wisdom. The operation of *logos* takes effect either through long speeches or through questions and answers, thus giving rise to the distinction noted above between rhetoric and dialectic, even before logic was established as an autonomous discipline.

Aristotle's discovery of the syllogism and his development of the theory of demonstrative science raised the problem of the relation of syllogistic—the first formal logic—with dialectic and rhetoric. Can any and every form of reasoning be expressed syllogistically? Aristotle is often thought to have aimed at such a result, at least for deductive reasoning, since he was well aware that inductive reasoning and argument by example are entirely different from deduction. He knew too that the dialectical reasoning characteristic of discussion, and essentially critical in purpose, differed widely from demonstrative reasoning deducing from principles the conclusions of a science. Yet he was content to locate the difference in the kind of premises used in the two cases. In analytical, or demonstrative reasoning, the premises, according to Aristotle, are true and ultimate,

or else derived from such premises, whereas in dialectical reasoning the premises consist of generally accepted opinions. The nature of reasoning in both cases was held to be the same, consisting in drawing conclusions from propositions posited as premises.[58]

Rhetoric, on the other hand, was supposed to use syllogisms in a peculiar way, by leaving some premises unexpressed and so transforming them into enthymemes. The orator, as Aristotle saw, could not be said to use regular syllogisms; hence, his reasoning was said to consist of abbreviated syllogisms and of arguments from example, corresponding to induction.

What are we to think of this reduction to two forms of reasoning of all the wide variety of arguments that men use in their discussions and in pleading a cause or justifying an action? Yet, since the time of Aristotle, logic has confined its study to deductive and inductive reasoning, as though any argument differing from these was due to the variety of its content and not to its form. As a result, an argument that cannot be reduced to canonical form is regarded as logically valueless. What then about reasoning from analogy? What about the *a fortiori* argument? Must we, in using such arguments, always be able to introduce a fictive unexpressed major premise, so as to make them conform to the syllogism?

It can be shown that the practical reasoning involved in choice or decision making can always be expressed in the form of theoretical reasoning by introducing additional premises. But what is gained by such a move? The reasoning by which new premises are introduced is merely concealed, and resort to these premises appears entirely arbitrary, although in reality it too is the outcome of a decision that can be justified only in an argumentative, and not in a demonstrative, manner.[59]

At first sight, it appears that the main difference between rhetoric and dialectic, according to Aristotle, is that the latter employs impersonal techniques of reasoning, whereas rhetoric relies on the orator's *ethos* (or character) and on the manner in which he appeals to the passions of his audience (or *pathos*).[60,61]

For Aristotle, however, the *logos* or use of reasoning is the main thing, and he criticizes those authors before him, who laid the emphasis upon oratorical devices designed to arouse the passion. Thus he writes:

If the rules for trials which are now laid down in some states—especially in well-governed states—were applied everywhere, such people would have nothing to say. All men, no doubt, think that the laws should prescribe such rules, but some, as in the court of Areopagus, give practical effect to their thoughts and forbid talk about non-essentials. This is sound law and custom. It is not right to pervert the judge by moving him to anger or envy or pity—one might as well warp a carpenter's rule before using it.

For this reason, after a long discussion devoted to the role of passion in oratorical art, he concludes:

As a matter of fact, it [rhetoric] is a branch of dialectic and similar to it, as we said at the outset.[62]

To sum up, it appears that Aristotle's conception, which is essentially empirical and based on the analysis of the material he had at his disposal, distinguishes dialectic from rhetoric only by the type of audience and, especially, by the nature of the questions examined in practice. His precepts are easy to understand when we keep in mind that he was thinking primarily of the debates held before assemblies of citizens gathered together either to deliberate on political or legal matters or to celebrate some public ceremony. There is no reason, however, why we should not also consider theoretical and, especially, philosophical questions expounded in unbroken discourse. In this case, the techniques Aristotle would have presumably recommended would be those he himself used in his own work, following the golden rule that he laid down in his *Nicomachean Ethics,* that the method used for the examination and exposition of each particular subject must be appropriate to the matter, whatever its manner of presentation.[63]

After Aristotle, dialectic became identified with logic as a technique of reasoning, due to the influence of the Stoics. As a result, rhetoric came to be regarded as concerned only with the irrational parts of our being, whether will, the passions, imagination, or the faculty for aesthetic pleasure. Those who, like Seneca and Epictetus, believed that the philosopher's role was to bring man to submit to reason were opposed to rhetoric, even when they used it, in the name of philosophy. Those like Cicero, on the other hand, who thought that in order to induce man to submit to reason one had to have recourse to rhetoric, recommended the union of philosophy and eloquence. The thinkers of the Renaissance followed suit, such as Valla, and Bacon too, who expected rhetoric to act on the imagination to secure the triumph of reason.

The more rationalist thinkers, like Ramus, as we have already noted, considered rhetoric as merely an ornament and insisted on a separation of form and content, the latter alone being thought worthy of a philosopher's attention. Descartes adopted the same conception and reinforced it. He regarded the geometrical method as the only method fit for the sciences as well as for philosophy and opposed rhetoric as exerting an action upon the will contrary to reason—thus adopting the position of the Stoics but with a different methodological justification. But to make room for eloquence within this scheme, we need only deny that reason possesses a monopoly of the approved way of influencing the will. Thus, Pascal, while professing a rationalism in a Cartesian manner, does not hesitate to declare that the truths that are most significant for him—that is, the truths of faith—have to be received by the heart before they can be accepted by reason:

We all know that opinions are admitted into the soul through two entrances, which are its chief powers, understanding and will. The more natural entrance is the understanding, for we should never agree to anything but demonstrated truths, but the more usual entrance, although against nature, is the will; for all men whatsoever are almost always led into belief not because a thing is proved but because it is pleasing. This way is low, unworthy, and foreign to our nature. Therefore everybody disavows it. Each of us professes to give his belief and even his love only where he knows it is deserved.

I am not speaking here of divine truths, which I am far from bringing under the art of persuasion, for they are infinitely above nature. God alone can put them into the soul, and in whatever way He pleases. I know He has willed they should enter into the mind from the heart and not into the heart from the mind, that He might make humble that proud power of reason. . . .[64]

To persuade about divine matters, grace is necessary; it will make us love that which religion orders us to love. Yet it is also Pascal's intention to conduce to this result by his eloquence, although he has to admit that he can lay down the precepts of this eloquence only in a very general way:

It is apparent that, no matter what we wish to persuade of, we must consider the person concerned, whose mind and heart we must know, what principles he admits, what things he loves, and then observe in the thing in question what relations it has to these admitted principles or these objects of delight. So that the art of persuasion consists as much in knowing how to please as in knowing how to convince, so much more do men follow caprice than reason.

Now of these two, the art of convincing and the art of pleasing, I shall confine myself here to the rules of the first, and to them only in the case where the principles have been granted and are held to unwaveringly; otherwise I do not know whether there would be an art for adjusting the proofs to the inconstancy of our caprices.

But the art of pleasing is incomparably more difficult, more subtle, more useful, and more wonderful, and therefore if I do not deal with it, it is because I am not able. Indeed I feel myself so unequal to its regulation that I believe it to be a thing impossible.

Not that I do not believe there are as certain rules for pleasing as for demonstrating, and that whoever should be able perfectly to know and to practise them would be as certain to succeed in making himself loved by kings and by every kind of person as in demonstrating the elements of geometry to those who have imagination enough to grasp the hypotheses. But I consider, and it is perhaps my weakness that leads me to think so, that it is impossible to lay hold of the rules.[65]

Pascal's reaction here with regard to formal rules of rhetoric already heralds romanticism with its reverence for the great orator's genius. But before romanticism held sway, associationist psychology developed in eighteenth-century England. According to the thinkers of this school, feeling, not reason, determines man's behavior, and books on rhetoric were written based on this psychology. The best known of these is Campbell's *The Philosophy of Rhetoric,* noted above.[66] Fifty years later, Whately, following Bacon's lead, defined the subject of logic and of rhetoric as follows:

I remarked in treating of that Science [Logic], that Reasoning may be considered as applicable to two purposes, which I ventured to designate respectively by the terms "Inferring" and "Proving," i.e., the *ascertainment* of the truth by investigation and the *establishment* of it to the satisfaction of *another;* and I there remarked that Bacon, in his *Organon,* has laid down rules for the conduct of the former of these processes, and that the latter belongs to the province of Rhetoric; and it was added, that to *infer,* is to be regarded as the proper office of the Philosopher, or the Judge;—to *prove,* of the Advocate.[67]

This conception, while stressing the social importance of rhetoric, makes it a negligible factor for the philosopher. This tendency increases under the influence of Kant and of the German idealists, who boasted of removing all matters of opinion from philosophy, for which only apodictic truths are of any importance.

The relation between the idea that we form of reason and the role assigned to rhetoric is of sufficient importance to deserve studies of all the great thinkers who have said anything about the matter—studies similar to those of Bacon by Prof. Karl Wallace and of Ramus by Prof. Walter J. Ong.[68] In what follows, I would like to sketch how the positivist climate of logical empiricism makes possible a new, or renovated, conception of rhetoric.

Within the perspective of neopositivism, the rational is restricted to what experience and formal logic enable us to verify and demonstrate. As a result, the vast sphere of all that is concerned with action—except for the choice of the most adequate means to reach a designated end—is turned over to the irrational. The very idea of a reasonable decision has no meaning and cannot even be defined satisfactorily with respect to the *whole* action in which it occurs. Logical empiricism has at its disposal no technique of justification except one founded on the theory of probability. But why should one prefer one action to another? Only because it is more efficacious? How can one choose between the various ends that one can aim at? If quantitative measures are the only ones that can be taken into account, the only reasonable decision would seem to be one that is in conformity with utilitarian calculations. If so, all ends would be reduced to a single one of pleasure or utility, and all conflicts of values would be dismissed as based on futile ideologies.

Now if one is not prepared to accept such a limitation to a monism of values in the world of action and would reject such a reduction on the ground that the irreducibility of many values is the basis of our freedom and of our spiritual life; if one considers how justification takes place in the most varied spheres—in politics, morals, law, the social sciences, and, above all, in philosophy—it seems obvious that our intellectual tools cannot all be reduced to formal logic, even when that is enlarged by a theory for the control of induction and the choice of the most efficacious techniques. In this situation, we are compelled to develop a theory of argumentation as an indispensable tool for practical reason.

In such a theory, as we have seen, argumentation is made relative to the adherence of minds, that is, to an audience, whether an individual deliberating or mankind as addressed by the philosopher in his appeal to reason. Whately's distinction between logic, as supplying rules of reasoning for the judge, and rhetoric, providing precepts for the counsel, falls to the ground as being without foundation. Indeed, the counsel's speech that aims at convincing the judge cannot rest on any different kind of reasoning than that which the judge uses himself. The judge, having heard both parties, will be better informed and able to compare the arguments on both sides, but his judgment will contain a justification in no way different in kind from that of the counsel's argumentation. Indeed, the ideal counsel's speech is precisely one that provides the judge with all the information that he needs to state the grounds for his decision.

If rhetoric is regarded as complementary to formal logic and argumentation as complementary to demonstrative proof, it becomes of paramount importance in philosophy, since no philosophic discourse can develop without resorting to it. This became clear when, under the influence of logical empiricism, all philosophy that could not be reduced to calculation was considered as nonsense and of no worth. Philosophy, as a consequence, lost its status in contemporary culture. This situation can be changed only by developing a philosophy and a methodology of the reasonable. For if the rational is restricted to the field of calculation, measuring, and weighing, the reasonable is left with the vast field of all that is not amenable to quantitative and formal techniques. This field, which Plato and Aristotle began to explore by means of dialectical and rhetorical devices, lies open for investigation by the new rhetoric.

Chaim Perelman

Notes

1. Dumarsais, *Des tropes ou des différents sens dans lesquels on peut prendre un même mot dans une même langue* (1818; reprint ed., Geneva: Slatkine Reprints, 1967).

2. Pierre Fontanier, *Les figures du discours,* ed. Gerard Genette (Paris: Flammarion, 1968).
3. **GBWW,* Vol. 8, 139–223.
4. *†GBWW,* Vol. 8, 37–137.
5. *‡GBWW,* Vol. 8, 139–253; Vol. 9, pp. 585–675.
6. Petrus Ramus, *Dialectic,* 1576 edition, pp. 3–4; also in the critical edition of *Dialectique,* 1555, ed. Michel Dassonville (Geneva: Librairie Droz, 1964), p. 62. Cf. Walter J. Ong, *Ramus: Method, and the Decay of Dialogue* (Cambridge, Mass.: Harvard University Press, 1958).
7. Fontanier, *Les figures du discours,* p. 64. *See also* J. Dubois, F. Edeline, J. M. Klinkenberg, P. Minguet, F. Pire, and H. Trinon, *Rhetorique generale* (Paris: Larousse, 1970).
8. Heinrich Lausberg, *Handbuch der literarischen Rhetorik,* 2 vols. (Munich: M. Hueber, 1960).
9. Douglas Ehninger, ed., Whately's *Elements of Rhetoric* (Carbondale: Southern Illinois University Press, 1963), pp. xx-vii.
10. Robert T. Oliver and Marvin G. Bauer, ed., *Re-establishing the Speech Profession: The First Fifty Years* (New York: Speech Association of the Eastern States, 1959). *See also* Frederick W. Haberman and James W. Cleary, eds., *Rhetoric and Public Address: A Bibliography, 1947–1961* (Madison: University of Wisconsin Press, 1964). Prof. Carroll C. Arnold of Pennsylvania State University has graciously supplied me the following information: "The statement about the bibliography in *Quarterly Journal of Speech* is not quite correct. The 'Bibliography of Rhetoric and Public Address' first appeared in the *Quarterly Journal of Speech* in 1947 and was published there annually to 1951. From 1952 through 1969, the bibliography was annually published in *Speech Monographs.* As it happens the bibliography will cease to be published in a *Monographs* and, beginning with this year, 1970, will be published in a *Bibliographical Annual,* published by the Speech Association of America. As far as I know, this bibliography remains the only multilingual listing of works (admittedly incomplete) on rhetoric published in the United States."
11. *See* Vasile Florescu, "Retorica si reabilitarcea ei in filozofia contemporanea" [Rhetoric and its rehabilitation in contemporary philosophy] in *Studii de istorie a filozofiei universale,* published by the Institute of Philosophy of the Academy of the Socialist Republic of Rumania (Bucharest, 1969), pp. 9–82.
12. *Discourses* II.23; *GBWW,* Vol. 12, 170–171.
13. *Rhetoric* I. 1358b 1–13; *GWBB,* Vol. 9, 598.
14. Ch. Perelman and L. Olbrechts-Tyteca, *The New Rhetoric,* trans. John Wilkinson and Purcell Weaver (Notre Dame, Ind.: University of Notre Dame Press, 1969), p. 50. French edition: *La nouvelle rhetorique* (Paris: Presses universitaires de France, 1958).
15. *On Christian Doctrine* IV. 13, 12; *GBWW,* Vol. 18, 684.
16. Kenneth Burke, *A Rhetoric of Motives* (New York: Prentice-Hall, 1950), p. 43.
17. Act II, scene ii; GBWW, Vol. 26, 584cff.
18. Ch. Perelman, *The Idea of Justice and the Problem of Argument,* trans. John Petrie (New York: Humanities Press, 1963), pp. 1–60.
19. *Ibid.,* p. 16.
20. *Ibid.,* pp. 56–57.
21. Edmond Goblot, *La logique des jugements de valeur* (Paris: Colin, 1927).
22. Perelman and Olbrechts-Tyteca, *The New Rhetoric, See also* Olbrechts-Tyteca, "Rencontre avec la rhetorique," in *La theorie de l'* argumentation, Centre Nationale de Recherches de Logique (Louvain: Editions Nauwelaerts, 1963), 1, pp. 3–18 (reproduces nos. 21–24 of *Logique et Analyse*).
23. This identification is faulty, as dialectical reasoning can no more than commonplaces *(topoi)* be reduced to formal calculation. Cf. Otto Bird, "The Tradition of the Logical Topics: Aristotle to Ockham," *Journal of the History of Ideas* 23 (1962): 307–23.
24. See *Rhetoric* I. 135a 1–6, 1355a 35–37, 1355b 8–10, 1356a 30–35, 1356b 36, 1356b 37–38; *GBWW,* Vol. 9, 593–96.
25. Plato, *Republic* I. 348a-b; *GBWW,* Vol. 7, 306.
26. *Republic* 511; *GBWW,* Vol. 7, 387. *Seventh Letter* 344b; *GBWW,* Vol.7, 810.
27. *Rhetoric* I. 1357a 1–4; *GBWW,* Vol. 9, 596.
28. Plato, *Cratylus* 390c; *GBWW,* Vol. 7, 88–89. *Theaetetus* 167d; *GBWW,* Vol. 7, 526.
29. *Rules for the Direction of the Mind; GBWW,* Vol. 31, 2.
30. *Babylonian Talmud, Seder Mo'ed 2, 'Erubin 136* (ed. Epstein). Cf. Ch. Perelman, "What the Philosopher May learn from the Study of Law," *Natural Law Forum* 11 (1966): pp. 3–4; idem, "Desaccord et rationalite des decisions," in *Droit, morale et philosophie* (Paris: Librairie generale de droit et de jurisprudence, 1968), pp. 103–10.
31. *Euthyphro* 7; *GBWW,* Vol. 7, 193–94.
32. See Clemence Ramnoux, "Le developpement antilogique des ecoles grecques avant Socrate," in *La dialectique* (Paris: Presses universitaires de France, 1969), pp. 40–47.
33. Plato, *Phaedrus* 273c; *GBWW,* Vol., 7, 138.
34. Perelman and Olbrechts-Tyteca, *The New Rhetoric,* §§ 6–9.
35. *Ibid.,* §§ 15–27.
36. Ch. Perelman and L. Olbrechts-Tyteca, "Classicisme et Romantisme dans l'argumentation," *Revue Internationale de Philosophie,* 1958, pp. 47–57.
37. Plato, *Gorgias* 487 d-e; *GBWW,* Vol. 7, 273.
38. Perelman and Olbrechts-Tyteca, *The New Rhetoric,* p. 104.
39. *Ibid.,* p. 116.
40. *Advancement of Learning,* Bk. II, xviii, 4; *GBWW,* Vol. 30, 67.
41. *Rhetorica ad Herennium* 4. 68.
42. Perelman and Olbrechts-Tyteca, *The New Rhetoric,* § 42.
43. To mention only a few works besides Thomas Kuhn's *The Structure of Scientific Revolutions* (Chicago, Ill.: University of Chicago Press, 1962), there is Michael

Polanyi's fascinating work significantly entitled *Personal Knowledge* (London: Routledge & Kegan Paul, 1958). The social, persuasive, nay, the rhetorical aspect, of scientific methodology was stressed by the physicist John Ziman in his brilliant book *Public Knowledge* (London: Cambridge University Press, 1968). The latter is dedicated to the Late Norwood Russell Hanson, whose *Patterns of Discovery* (London: Cambridge University Press, 1958), and *The Concept of the Positron* (London: Cambridge University Press, 1963), gave much weight to the new ideas.

44. Perelman and Olbrechts-Tyteca, *The New Rhetoric*, §§ 45–88.
45. *Ibid.,* pp. 172–73.
46. *Ibid.,* p. 176.
47. *Ibid.,* § 45–49.
48. See J. S. Mill. *Utilitarianism: GBWW*, Vol. 43, 443ff.
49. Ch. Perelman, ed., *Les categories en histoire* (Brussels: Editions de l'Institut de Sociologie, 1969).
50. Perelman and Olbrechts-Tyteca, *The New Rhetoric*, §§60–74.
51. *Ibid.,* §§78–81.
52. Ch. Perelman, "Analogie et metaphore en science, poesie, et philosophie," *Revue Internationale de Philosophie*, 1969, pp. 3–15; *see also* Hans Blumenberg, *Paradigmen zu einer Metaphorologie* (Bonn: H. Bouvier, 1960), and Enzo Melandri, *La linea e il circolo: Studio logico-filosofico sull'analogia* (Bologna: Il Mulino, 1968).
53. George Berkeley, *Works*, 2 vols. (London, 1843), 2:259.
54. Perelman and Olbrechts-Tyteca, *The New Rhetoric*, §§82–88.
55. Ch. Perelman, "Le reel commun et le reel philosophique," in *Etudes sur l'histoire de la philosophie, en hommage a Martial Gueroult* (Paris: Fischbacher, 1964), pp. 127–38.
56. Perelman and Olbrechts-Tyteca, *The New Rhetoric*, §§89–92.
57. *Ibid.,* §§97–105.
58. *Topics* I. 100a 25–32; *GBWW*, Vol. 8, 143.
59. Ch. Perelman, "Le raisonnement pratique," in *Contemporary Philosophy*, ed. Raymond Klibansky (Florence: La Nuova Italia, 1968-), 1:168–78.
60. *Rhetoric* I. 1356a 5–18; *GBWW*, Vol. 9, 595.
61. *See* Paul I. Rosenthal, "The Concept of Ethos and the Structure of Persuasion," *Speech Monographs*, 1966, pp. 114–26.
62. *Rhetoric* I. 1354a 19–27, 1356a 30–31: *GBWW*, Vol. 9, 593, 395–96.
63. *Ethics* I. 1094b 12–27; *GBWW*, Vol. 9, 339–40.
64. *On Geometrical Demonstration; GBWW*, Vol. 33, 440.
65. *Ibid.,* p. 441.
66. Cf. V. M. Bevilacqua, "Philosophical Origins of George Campbell's Philosophy of Rhetoric," *Speech Monographs*, 1965, pp. 1–12; and Lloyd F. Bitzer, "Hume's Philosophy in George Campbell's Philosophy of Rhetoric," *Philosophy and Rhetoric*, 1969, pp. 139–66.
67. Whately, *Elements of Rhetoric* (1828), pp. 6–7.
68. Karl Wallace, *Francis Bacon on Communication and Rhetoric* (Chapel-Hill: University of North Carolina Press, 1943); and Ong, *Ramus: Method, and the Decay of Dialogue.*

Since completing his book and essay on his interpretation of a "new rhetoric," Perelman has been active in the past decade in presenting his theories to European and American audiences. To summarize his recent works would require more space than is available for our present purposes. We are convinced, however, that no discussion of Perelman's generative ideas is complete without at least a brief analysis of his study on "The Rational and the Reasonable."[1] First presented as a lecture at an International Symposium held at the University of Ottawa in October, 1977, this paper has been reprinted and cited both by Perelman and by other authors.

What Perelman attempts to do in his provocative analysis is of great value to students of rhetoric who have a strong interest in argument and are inclined to subscribe to the trend of rhetoric as a way of knowing. The primary thrust of his position is that the terms "reasonable" and "rational," while similar in some respects, are not interchangeable concepts. To clarify this point he makes the following claim. It is meaningful, he suggests, to say "rational decision" or "rational deduction" and to refer to a compromise as "reasonable." But it is unacceptable to say "reasonable decision," "reasonable deduction," or "rational compromise."

Next Perelman delineates the characteristics of both concepts, concluding that the notion of reasonable is a fundamental requirement of practical argument. The term rational he equates with a mathematical model or an immutable divine standard. Thus the degree of certitude is on the level of an *a priori* self-evident truth similar to what Kant called a Categorical Imperative. Because it demands the same type of high level certainty for all social milieus throughout time, rationality meets the test of formal validity, logical coherence, purposefulness, and predictability. The fact that rationality is responsive only to those claims which have a certitude approximating that of mathematics, divine standards, or natural law insulates it from such presumably extraneous forces as education, culture, experience, dialogue, and time.

The term reasonable, on the other hand, is related to what takes place in practical human affairs, including courts of law. A reasonable man, in Perelman's view, adopts a legal reasoning model that utilizes contingent propositions and an audience-centered perspective. His principal concern is not with logical coherence, formal validity, or a slavish devotion to precedents, but with what is fair, equitable, and just in a particular situation or analogous circumstance. As a result he assesses the worth of an argument or a legal decision by asking these questions: (1) Does it conform to the principle of common sense? (2) Is it consistent with prevailing societal values and beliefs? (3) Will it produce a socially useful consequence? (4) Is it practical, realistic, and relevant? Finally, the concept of reasonableness,

unlike that of rationality, is shaped by education, culture, experience, dialogue, and time.

To see more clearly the distinctions which Perelman has drawn between the rational and the reasonable, we have prepared the following chart highlighting the special features of each.

Notwithstanding the fact that Perelman's distinctions regarding what is rational and reasonable may at first glance appear arbitrary and overdrawn, they nevertheless are useful in understanding his theory of practical reasoning. Perelman, like Toulmin, has taught us to view the argumentative process as a practical and realistic endeavor which not only seeks to gain an adherence of minds but seeks to expand our knowledge.

Note

1. Chaim Perelman, *The New Rhetoric and the Humanities* (Dordrecht, Holland: D. Reidel Publishing Company, 1979), pp. 117–123.

Perelman's Theory of the Rational and the Reasonable

Rational	Reasonable
Degree of Certitude	Degree of Certitude
Mathematical Model	Legal Reasoning Model
Immutable Divine Standards	Contingent Propositions
A priori Self-evident Truths	Acceptability by Audience
Natural Law	
Kantian Categorical Imperative	
Criteria for Evaluating Decisions and Arguments	Criteria for Evaluating Decisions and Arguments
Formal Validity	Equitable and Fair
Logical Coherence	Conformity to Common Sense
Purposefulness	Consistent with Societal Beliefs and Values
Conformity to Precedents	Practical, Realistic, Relevant
	Socially Useful Consequences
Applicability	Applicability
Individual Level	Situational Level
Universal Level	Analogous Circumstances
All Social Milieus	
Unresponsive to Education, Culture, Experience, Dialogue, Time	Responsive to Education, Culture, Experience, Dialogue, Time

As a final note in our summary of Perelman's basic ideas on rhetorical thought, we wish to draw your attention to a lecture he delivered at Ohio State University on November 16, 1982. This presentation, entitled "Old and New Rhetoric," serves not only as the most recent statement on Perelman's fundamental beliefs on practical reasoning but also gives a concise overview of how the "new rhetoric" he has articulated is a natural outgrowth and extension of Aristotle's notion of dialectical reasoning. Similarly, as he successfully demonstrates, it is a response to those who either ignored or discarded this aspect of Aristotle's writings and focused instead upon his contribution to formal logic. In presenting the essence of this lecture, we have decided to use an outline form. In doing so, we need to point out that while some of the language is our own, all of the arguments, data, and basic organizational pattern were utilized by Professor Perelman.

Old and New Rhetoric

An Address delivered by Chaim Perelman
at Ohio State University, November 16, 1982

Introduction

I. "Philosophy is a systematic study of confused ideas, aiming at clarifying them." Thus it teaches us to choose among their incompatible aspects. . . . "Justice is the best example of a confused idea that we have."

II. Rhetoric is also "a confused idea"—an idea, which, according to representative scholars by the end of the 19th century, was "devoid of any educational value."

III. My purpose in this lecture is to provide a brief overview of "Old and New Rhetoric" as exemplified in Western thought.

Discussion

I. Before proceeding to an analysis of the theme, I would like to sketch for you the steps involved in my becoming a student of rhetoric.

A. During the 1928–1929 academic year, I had the last course taught on rhetoric in a high school in Belgium.

1. The course consisted primarily of a study of the theory of syllogisms and of figures of speech.

2. In 1929, rhetoric was suppressed from all schools because it was no longer viewed as a subject having any educational value.

B. During the next eighteen years, in which time I received advanced degrees in law and in philosophy, rhetoric seemed irrelevant to me.

1. It was equated with "the art of deception."

2. It seemed unrelated to the goals and concerns of serious philosophy.

3. "I did not imagine at this time that I would ever have anything in common with rhetoric."

C. When faced with the challenge of writing a book on justice at the end of World War II, I saw the limitations of formal reasoning, as articulated by Gottlob Frege—the father of modern logic—as a means of discussing values.

1. Logical positivism asserted that one cannot write scientifically or rationally about value judgments because of the fact that they often are a "purely subjective expression of emotions."

2. Formal reasoning is incapable of analyzing the different principles of justice such as these:
   (a) "To everyone the same thing."
   (b) "To everyone according to his need."
   (c) "To everyone according to his merits."
3. Since formal justice deals with "the equal treatment of essentially similar situations," it is unable to come to grips with value judgments.
   (a) It cannot deal adequately with the fact that "situations are never identical."
   (b) It provides no insights on a subject such as the relative merits of two or more legal precedents.
   (c) Proponents of formal justice fail to recognize that we cannot proceed from "formal justice to concrete or material justice without some value judgments."

D. My researches suggested a need for finding a way to reason about values and about ends.
   1. Finding nothing in the literature that would satisfy me, I decided to examine all domains in which values would be important.
      (a) Among the areas examined were ethics, politics, and law.
      (b) My investigation sought to ascertain the nature of the reasoning processes and structures used to understand values.
   2. After reading numerous books and monographs, I learned that rhetoric conceived as a theory of persuasive discourse which stressed argument constituted the key for opening the door on values.

II. Old rhetoric has its roots in the classical period.
   A. Rational philosophers drew a distinction between rhetoric and philosophy.
      1. Rhetoric, they argued, aims at persuasion and is concerned with opinions.
      2. Philosophy aims at truth and is concerned with propositions that should be accepted by everyone.
   B. Plato is the best representative of the philosophical tradition.
      1. He devised a methodology called dialectic.
         (a) It is the art of asking questions and providing answers for the questions.
         (b) It is "the art of dialogue."
         (c) Dialectic seeks to clear the mind of common sense ideas in order to achieve purity of thought.
         (d) Philosophical rhetoric as opposed to dialectic is based on truths and has the power to persuade the gods.
      2. Rhetoric has as its purpose to communicate the truths developed by philosophy.
         (a) It is designed only for those who know the truth and wish to communicate it to others.
         (b) Although it can communicate what is known, it cannot engage in the art of discovery or of invention.
   C. Aristotle set into motion two great forms of reasoning that were to have a profound influence.
      1. He was, first of all, the father of analytical reasoning or formal logic.
         (a) This focuses on deductive reasoning, particularly the syllogism.
         (b) It applies to immutable and changeless ideas and meth-

ods as epitomized in mathematics, metaphysics, and logic.

2. Secondly, he was the father of dialectical reasoning—a fact often overlooked by modern philosophers.

   (a) These ideas were developed in his *Rhetoric* and in his *Topics*.

   (b) Dialectical reasoning is concerned with opinions.

      1. It is used to defend one's opinions or to attack the opinions of others.

      2. It is designed to persuade an audience.

   (c) Dialectical reasoning is needed in all aspects of practical affairs.

      1. It is crucial in such fields as politics, ethics, and economics.

      2. It helps us act and decide, thereby rendering it essential to decision-making.

      3. When people do not agree on first principles or definitions, this type of reasoning is needed.

      4. It is vital in the doing of all kinds of practical philosophy.

3. In occupying the middle ground between Plato on the one hand and the sophists on the other, Aristotle functioned as a synthesizer.

III. In the period extending from the early Middle Ages to the end of the 19th century, scholars often failed to appreciate Aristotle's perceptive view that rhetoric or dialectical reasoning is a legitimate, substantive discipline that functions as a complement to formal logic or reasoning.

   A. St. Augustine, as well as later Christian leaders in the Middle Ages, held that the aim of rhetoric was not to discover but to communicate the truth presented in the Holy Scriptures.

   B. Influenced by the Stoics, commentators in the 13th, 14th, 15th, and 16th centuries did not identify the two kinds of reasoning featured by Aristotle.

      1. They attempted to show that "logic (called then dialectic) should be this or that."

      2. From the latter part of the 14th century, logic was associated with formal reasoning; at the same time, argumentation, which under the influence of Renaissance thinkers was identified with persuasive reasoning, was almost forgotten.

      3. Following Peter Ramus' influential efforts to associate reasoning with dialectic and rhetoric with the presentation of figures of speech and other elements of elocutio, rhetoric lost its classical heritage.

   C. The Continental and British scholars in the 17th, 18th, and 19th centuries placed more emphasis on rhetoric as presenting than on rhetoric as argument.

      1. The management of ideas took precedence over invention and discovery.

      2. Rhetoric frequently was associated with literature, composition, and criticism.

      3. Despite the fact that Whately constructed his theories around argumentative inquiry, his rhetoric remained essentially a theory of communication, not of discovery.

   D. By the end of the 19th century, formal reasoning reigned supreme, while rhetoric had fallen into a state of disrepute.

IV. To restore rhetoric to its elevated position, as outlined by Aristotle in his discussion of dialectical reasoning, I began to do a series of studies on what I call the "New Rhetoric."

A. This "new rhetoric" has several important rationales and features related to reasoning in human affairs.

1. It is primarily concerned with argument or practical reasoning.
2. It suggests that figures of speech may be arguments instead of merely ornaments.
3. With its goal to influence minds, "new rhetoric" is a dynamic field of study.
4. It is capable of discovery or the generation of knowlege.
5. It is complementary, rather than in oppposition, to formal reasoning.

B. "New rhetoric," as perceived in my writings, has as its central concern the audience.

1. When we fail to adapt responsibly to an audience, we are guilty of "begging the question."
2. Arguments are grounded in the beliefs of the audience.
3. Arguments may be addressed to audiences that are ignorant, well educated, or highly specialized.
   (a) Speakers should know when to use a general or a specialized rhetoric.
   (b) If one speaks to a physicist as a physicist his appeal will be different than that employed when addressing a physicist as a potential car buyer.
4. In some instances, a communicator may have a universal audience in mind.
   (a) "The universal audience is comprised of all reasonable beings;" "this means anybody capable of following the argument."
   (b) Preliminary statements on the notion of the universal audience may be found in Aristotle's *Topics*.

Conclusion

Rather than continue this overview of "Old and New Rhetoric," I choose now to answer your questions and respond to your comments.

In the discussion period which followed the foregoing lecture, and in the subsequent conversations we held with Professor Perelman, we were impressed with his broad range knowledge of Western communication theory, his commitment to the value of practical reasoning as an essential element of human affairs, and his abiding belief that all students of rhetoric should become acquainted with philosophy. The significance of this latter point can be seen when we turn in the last chapter of this volume to Douglas Ehninger's essay on "Science, Philosophy—and Rhetoric: A Look Toward the Future."

23

Rhetoric as a Way of Knowing: Ernest Bormann and Fantasy Theme Analysis

The ideas of Toulmin and Perelman, and those of Wayne Brockriede and Douglas Ehninger to be discussed in Chapter 24, are in the mainstream of the trend we have described as rhetoric as a way of knowing. But these are not the only approaches that have as a major concern the generation of knowledge or social reality. Of the other emphases that have been developed, Ernest Bormann's theory of fantasy theme analysis is the one we wish to highlight here. We do so because of the long range impact which Bormann's ideas have had on rhetorical theory and criticism. Following the initial essay which appeared in the *Quarterly Journal of Speech* in May, 1972,[1] this subject has been the theme of convention programs, colloquies in our national professional journals, term papers, and theses and dissertations. Although a case could be made to include fantasy theme analysis as a part of any of the earlier three sections—rhetoric as meaning, as value, and as motive—Bormann himself sees his theory as belonging primarily to rhetoric as epistemic. The discussion which follows in this chapter, we feel, will support his claim.

To understand Bormann's theory and the essay he has written for this chapter, we will now turn our attention to his seminal study of 1972. A major influence on Bormann's thinking was Robert Bales' volume *Personality and Interpersonal Behavior*—a study showing how groups function as participants in a drama as they act out fantasy events. Through a chaining process utilizing verbal and nonverbal behavior, these groups create a social reality that leads to perception changes and related actions. Using Bales' conclusions as a starting point, Bormann describes key terms and explains how the philosophy emanating from them is vitally relevant to rhetorical theory and criticism.

He defines a fantasy theme as a "recollection of something that happened to the group in the *past* or a dream of what the group might do in the future."[2] As these themes chain out through a process of progressive steps—small groups to public speeches to media presentations to broader publics—a rhetorical vision develops consisting of "composite dramas" which form a "symbolic reality."[3] These visions often culminate in a rhetorical movement that takes on the appearance of a drama with "heroes and villains" acting out their parts. The social reality that emerges makes more use of myths and creative imagination than it does of "discursive logic." Even so, however, the chaining out that takes place ultimately leads to a generation of new knowledge and meanings, as well as a reaffirmation, in some cases, of what is already known.

Bormann is particularly interested in showing how fantasy theme analysis, focusing on the notion of rhetorical visions, can be used as a method of criticism. In the 1972 study, he uses an extended example of the chaining out strategies employed by the Puritan ministers of the Massachusetts Bay Colony in the seventeenth century. Later he relied on fantasy theme analysis to describe the Senator Eagleton Affair of 1972, and the televised coverage of the Iranian Hostage Release and the Reagan Inaugural.[4] These studies pinpoint all of the elements of an unfolding drama—the persona, the scene, the vision or message, and the unfolding of the plot. A special insight which Bormann brings to his analyses is his contention that meaning and motives are not embedded in the minds of people alone but are also found in the message itself.

Most of what we have described here is based upon the essay written in 1972. In order to bring this theory up-to-date, we asked Professor Bormann to write an article expressing his present views. He has done so, using the title: "Fantasy Theme Analysis and Rhetorical Theory." As you examine this study, notice the strategy the author has used. He produces a framework for his analysis by developing a distinction between special and general theories of communication. A special theory, he asserts, stands squarely in the humanistic tradition and is comprised of "artistic formulations which specify the nature of conventional forms and usages and provide practical advice on how to use and criticize such forms." This implies that a given communication practice of a specified community is limited to a particular culture and time. As examples of a special theory, he lists three: (1) Aristotle's Rhetoric, written for 4th-century Greeks; (2) the handbook *Mutual Criticism,* prepared for members of the Oneida Christian Community—a 19th-century experiment in Christian communism; and (3) the current emphasis on message communication form first designed by Shannon and Weaver in their influential model.

By contrast a general theory is more scientific because of its capability to "account for broad classes of events." Out of a broad-based general theory comes an explanation of how a special theory evolves and matures. Two illustrations are used to show the nature of a general theory. The first is cognitive dissonance which represents a popular theory of persuasion. Secondly, and far more important for Bormann's purposes is his discussion of symbolic convergence. This general theory explains how groups of people, after engaging in numerous discourse episodes over a long period of time, may come to embrace a similar social reality. In such instances, people with comparable past and present experiences interact in such a communal way that they are able to march in unison toward a rewarding future in which each member of the group partakes.

Against the background data on special and general theories, Bormann, as you will see, demonstrates how fantasy theme analysis bridges the gap between humanistic and social science research. He starts off with the premise that rhetorical criticism grounded in the fantasy theme approach successfully combines the general theory of symbolic convergence (as seen in a rhetorical vision) and the humanism associated with a special theory of communication such as set forth in Aristotle's *Rhetoric*. The result of this blending of social science data with materials generated from the humanities permits the evaluator to use a form of metacriticism. Fantasy theme analysis, Bormann thus reminds us, represents an attempt to bring traditional rhetorical theory and modern communication theory together around the mutually shared concept of symbolic convergence. Whether or not Bormann has fully succeeded in achieving his goal is not yet adequately resolved in the minds of some observers.[5] We believe, however, that his work provides a much needed perspective on rhetoric as a way of knowing.

Notes

1. "Fantasy and Rhetorical Vision: The Rhetorical Criticism of Social Reality," 58 (December 1972), 396–407.
2. Ibid., 397.
3. Ibid., 398.
4. "The Eagleton Affair: A Fantasy Theme Analysis," *Quarterly Journal of Speech,* 59 (April 1973), 143–159; and "A Fantasy Theme Analysis of the Television Coverage of the Hostage Release and the Reagan Inaugural," *Quarterly Journal of Speech,* 68 (May 1982), 133–145.
5. See, in particular, G. P. Mohrmann, "An Essay on Fantasy Theme Criticism," *Quarterly Journal of Speech,* 68 (May 1982), 109–132.

As the earlier chapters of this book aptly illustrate, the study of communication has had a long tradition in western society. From the time of ancient Greece and Rome to the present the process of how one human being communicates with another has been a topic of interest and importance.

Humanistic studies by historians, classicists, and critics of rhetoric have been important since colonial times in the United States. Since the 1920s there has been an increasing interest in the study of communication on the part of social scientists. Humanists tend to refer to their investigations as studies of rhetorical theory and practice while social scientists have tended to refer to their investigations as studies of communication.

By the 1950s and 1960s there were two diverse scholarly traditions separated by different research methods and terminologies to the point where there was little communication between them. Indeed, during that period some humanists maintained that the laboratory investigations of communication proved nothing that was not already known by Aristotle and the other classical writers on rhetoric and that, indeed, much that was important in classical rhetoric was overlooked or lost in the quantified laboratory studies. On the other hand, some social scientists maintained that humanistic studies of rhetoric provided no solid basis for knowledge and tended to be prescriptive rather than descriptive.[1]

In the 1970s there was a substantial movement to bring the two cultures together. Two social scientists, Combs and Mansefield, for example, wrote:

Probably, the disparate concerns of the many social sciences may discover some threads of unity, and some acceptance of the humanities, in the development of new and fertile communication theories (or hypotheses) that may recognize the complexity of human behavior as manifest in symbols.[2]

This chapter presents one communication theory that promises to provide some threads of unity among social scientific studies of communication and humanistic studies of rhetoric. Fantasy theme analysis as a humanistic method of rhetorical criticism when combined with the general theory of communication (symbolic convergence) based on the sharing of group fantasies provides a way for unifying the humanistic and social scientific studies of rhetoric and communication.

General and Special Theories of Communication

Scholars studying rhetoric and communication have used the term *theory* rather loosely. Sometimes scholars have used *theory* in the sense of social scientific formulations of a general nature designed to account for broad classes of communicative events. Sometimes scholars have used *theory* to mean any systematic analysis of communication whether based on empirical data or philosophical analysis or conventional wisdom. Sometimes scholars have used *theory* to mean the systematic collection of rules-of-thumb to aid practitioners, criteria for evaluation, and ideal models of speech events used by communicators to plan, transmit, and evaluate messages.

One way to sort out these differences and avoid the confusions that have plagued theorists is to distinguish between *special* and *general* communication theories. *Special theories* are those artistic formulations which specify the nature of conventional forms and usages and provide practical advice on how to use and criticize such forms.

Whereas special theories relate only to the communication practices of a community restricted in time and culture, *general theories* of communication are more analogous to the theories of the natural sciences which account for broad classes of events. In the case of communication, general theories are those that relate to communicative practices which cut across the conventional usages and recurring forms that result from applications of special theories. A general communication theory might, for example, be one which could explain how special theories came into being, evolved, and functioned.

Special communication theories deal with conventional agreements among the practitioners as to how the communication should be formed and practiced. Conventional agreements include the rules about how to participate, which parties to the communication can choose to honor or break. General communication theories, on the other hand, deal with tendencies in human communication events which cannot be ignored or rescinded by the participants.[3]

Rhetoric and communication scholars have been less successful in developing general theories than they have been in formulating, teaching, and applying the special theories. A representative general theory is the cognitive-dissonance explanation of persuasion. Cognitive dissonance asserts that people who hold two contradictory ideas or ideas that are contradicted by their behavior will inevitably feel a psychological dissonance that will motivate them to change some of their attitudes. Cognitive dissonance is in the form of a general theory for it asserts that like the law of gravity cognitive dissonance is ever present under specified conditions.[4] General theories of the social scientific type are tested against empirical data. The trouble with many of the general theories such as cognitive dissonance is that they were either so vague they could not be empirically tested or when they were empirically tested they failed.

The rhetorial study of fantasy theme analysis has resulted in the development of another general theory of communication. The general theory is called *symbolic convergence*.

Symbolic Convergence as a General Communication Theory

The Small Group Basis for Symbolic Convergence. The process in symbolic convergence which is analogous to the law of gravity in Newton's theory is one in which the dynamic chaining of group fantasies brings about symbolic convergence for the participants. Investigators in small group communication laboratories discovered the process of sharing fantasies when they investigated dramatizing messages and their effect on the group.[5] A dramatizing message is one which contains a story about people, real or fictitious, in a dramatic situation in a setting other than the here-and-now communication of the group. (The here-and-now is a concept from the relationship special theory and refers to what is happening at the moment in the group meeting.) If, in the middle of a discussion several members came into conflict, the situation would be dramatic; but because the action is unfolding in the here-and-now of the group, it would not

Parable? (handwritten in left margin)

qualify as a basis for the sharing of a group fantasy. However, if the group members begin talking about a conflict some of them had in the past or envisioning a future conflict, these comments would be dramatizing messages.

As they studied these messages, the investigators found that some of them seemed to fall on deaf ears; the group members did not pay much attention to the comments. Some of the dramatizing, however, caused a minor symbolic explosion in the form of a chain reaction. As the members shared the fantasy the tempo of the conversation would pick up. People grew excited, interrupted one another, laughed, showed some emotion, forgot their self-consciousness. The people who shared the fantasy did so with the appropriate responses. If the story was supposed to be funny they laughed; if it was serious or solemn they shared in the solemnity.

The elements of symbolic convergence. Fantasy is a technical term in the symbolic convergence general theory of communication and does not mean what it often does in ordinary usage, that is, something imaginary, not grounded in reality. The technical meaning for fantasy is the creative and imaginative interpretation of events that fulfills a psychological or rhetorical need. Fantasies may include fanciful and fictitious scripts of imaginary characters but they often deal with things that have actually happened to the members of the community or that are reported in authenticated works of history, in the news media, or in the oral history and folklore of the group. The content of the dramatizing message which sparked the fantasy chain is called a *fantasy theme*.

When a number of similar scenarios or outlines of the plot of the fantasies, including particulars of the scenes, characters and situations, have been shared by members of a group of larger community they form a *fantasy type*. A *fantasy type* is a stock scenario repeated again and again by the same characters or by similar characters.

The oft-noted *American dream* illustrates how large communities of people within the borders of a country may participate in a series of fantasy themes until a fantasy type comes to play an important part in the development of their culture. The American dream refers to the fantasy type which has as its scenario a poor but talented, deserving, and hard working hero or heroine, who, starting from poor and humble beginnings works hard and achieves success. The implication of the fantasy type is that the scene, i.e. the United States of America, is the "land of opportunity" because it has vast natural resources available to all. Many of the individual fantasy themes emphasized that by going West, being a pioneer, homesteading, prospecting for precious metals or minerals or oil, or by being an entrepreneur and starting a new company, or inventing a new process the heroes became successful. Many of the fantasies also emphasized that America is a land of opportunity because it has a classless society in which any member can climb to the top.

The variations of the scenario in the 19th and early 20th century are many: Abraham Lincoln, the poor farm boy who became president; Andrew Carnegie, the poor immigrant boy who became a millionaire and who gave his money to build libraries; Henry Ford, the poor mechanic who became the rich automobile builder; Booker T. Washington, the poor black man who became a leading educator; George Washington Carver who came out of slavery to become a leading inventor; Susan B. Anthony who became a leading reformer; Amelia Earhart who became a daring flyer.

Because they had shared fantasy themes of the type of the American dream, many people were encouraged to come to the United States from foreign countries at great personal sacrifice and hardship, and when they arrived in the new country they worked hard, often under miserable conditions to achieve the success they fantasized about.

When a number of people within a communication subsystem come to share a group of fantasies and fantasy types they may integrate them into a coherent rhetorical vision of some aspect of their social reality. A *rhetorical vision* is a unified putting-together of the various shared scripts that gives the participants a broader view of things. Rhetorical visions are often integrated by a master analogy

which pulls the various elements together. Usually a rhetorical vision is indexed by a slogan or a label. Labels for rhetorical visions of the past in the United States have included such things as "The New Politics," "The Cold War," "The New Frontier," "The Silent Majority," and "The Moral Majority."

The analogy which unified a new rhetorical vision of foreign relations in the Post World War II period characterized them as being a Cold War. The Cold War analogy illustrates how such a comparison can serve to integrate a host of fantasies into one coherent vision. The situation was like a shooting war yet it was not a hot war. It was a cold war in which bullets were replaced by ideas and the battle was not over body counts but over who controlled the hearts and minds of the people. When you analyze the master analogy you begin to understand such political phenomena as the hearings conducted by Senator Joseph McCarthy to root out communists in government, the loyalty oaths for professors and governmental workers, and similar efforts on the part of the participants in the vision to assure that internal saboteurs and propagandists be found and silenced.[6]

When a rhetorical vision emerges, the participants in the vision (those who have shared the fantasies in an appropriate way) come to form a rhetorical community. Members of a rhetorical community can arouse considerable emotional response in one another with messages which simply allude to fantasy themes which have previously chained through the community. The "inside joke" is an example of such a message which evokes appropriate responses from insiders by using a code word for the fantasy.[7]

How symbolic convergence works. Fantasy themes, in contrast with the way we experience the here-and-now, are organized and artistic. When someone dramatizes an event he or she must select certain people to be the focus of the story and present them in a favorable light while selecting others to be portrayed in a more negative fashion. Without protagonists (heroes) and antagonists (villains) there is little drama. When a speaker selects and slants the interpretation of people's actions he or she begins to shape and organize experiences. When they select a scene and certain incidents to be placed in a sequence, when they attribute motives to the people in the story, they further slant and organize, and interpret. Because fantasy themes are always slanted, ordered, and interpreted, they provide a rhetorical means for people to account for and explain the same experiences or the same events in different ways. Thus, two eyewitnesses to the same event may still tell two very different stories about what happened without either one of them lying.

People seldom understand events in all their complexity. Yet most human beings have a desire to understand some of the things that happen around them and to them. The way they come to some understanding is by participating in fantasy themes in which an explanation for events is acted out by the personae in the dramas. The power of the symbolic convergence theory stems from the human tendency to try to understand events in terms of people with certain personality traits and motivations, making decisions, taking actions, and causing things to happen. We can understand a person making plans in order to achieve goals and succeeding or failing to do so because we often interpret our own behavior in that way in our personal fantasies.[8]

Interpreting events in terms of human action allows us to assign responsibility, to praise or blame, to arouse and propitiate guilt, to hate, and to love. When we share a fantasy theme we make sense out of what prior to that time may have been a confusing state of affairs and we do so in *common with the others who share the fantasy with us.* Thus, we come to symbolic convergence on the matter and will envision that part of our world in similar ways. We have created some symbolic common ground and we can then talk with one another about that shared interpretation with code words or brief allusions along the lines of the inside joke phenomenon in a small group.

The Creation, Raising, and Maintaining of Public Consciousnesses

Perhaps rhetorical innovation, on occasion, begins when one creative person fantasizes a powerful personal consciousness and dramatizes the complete vision so skillfully that it is shared by converts and becomes the rhetorical vision which forms a community's consciousness. Innovation, however, most often results from small group meetings of people drawn together by a similar impulse. During these meetings members begin to share fantasies and in the process they come to symbolic convergence; they create the raw material for the new rhetorical vision.

Often the flow of communication in consciousness-creating meetings is not from speaker to listeners but the chain triggered by the first dramatizing message is then picked up and elaborated by the others. People caught up in a chain of fantasies may experience moments similar to the creative experiences of individuals when they daydream about a creative project or an important problem and suddenly get excited about the direction of their thinking. Then the others feed back ideas and new dramatizations to add to the original comment; messages begin flowing rapidly among the participants until under the suggestive power of the group fantasy the constraints which normally hold people back are released; they feel free to experiment with ideas, to play with concepts and wild suggestions and imaginative notions. Soon a number of people are deeply involved in the discussion, excitedly adding their emotional support and often modifying the ongoing script.

These innovative dramas may be a radical departure from most of the rhetorical visions known to the participants or they may be adaptations of historical and contemporary fantasy types. One way for communities to develop radical new rhetorical visions is to take a contemporary vision and stand it on its head.

One of the basic rhetorical problems for people moving towards a new consciousness is to come to a clear realization of who they are as a collective. In late 1969, for example, a group associated with the draft resistance and with the feminist impulse at the University of Minnesota published a newsletter which sparked the organizational effort of the Women's Movement in the Twin Cities of Minneapolis and St. Paul. The newsletter contained an open letter to all interested women which read as follows, "A definite and annoying communication gap or lag has developed. Other problems have arisen such as: Who exactly is the Minneapolis Women's Liberation group?"[9]

Dealing with who they are often gets the group to fantasize about who the outsiders are. Thus, a we-they division in the innovative fantasies helps with the setting of boundaries and leads to the group self-awareness which is crucial to the emergence of a new consciousness.

Communities of people who have created a consciousness may wish to gain converts. If they do they need to develop conventional forms of communication that will attract potential new members, shake them loose from their emotional attachment to other rhetorical visions, and get them to share the fantasies which comprise their rhetorical visions. Such communication joint ventures may be thought of as consciousness-raising sessions. The consciousness-creating groups are innovative and open to diversity while the consciousness-raising communication is persuasive and closed to alternative dramas.

Once a rhetorical community dedicated to creating a social or political or religious movement emerges with a coherent rhetorical vision, the rhetorical problem of holding the group together becomes important.

Consciousness-sustaining communication often includes criticism of individuals or subgroups that puts pressure on the members to conform to group thinking and behavioral norms. Such criticism requires a common rhetorical vision as the basis for evaluation. The rhetorical problem is to bring insiders who are in danger of backsliding or who have become apathetic to an awareness that the established vision is still alive and relevant to them. In addition, they must become aware that they are doing or thinking things that are counter to that vision.

Symbolic convergence explains all three kinds of recurrent communication forms. In the consciousness-creating communication the sharing of fantasies is the process of innovation. In the consciousness-raising communication forms the newcomers are converted in sessions where the members redramatize their shared fantasies until under the pressures of group conformity the naive participants share the established fantasies. In the consciousness-sustaining communication forms the established vision is the basis for the criticism that brings about the renewal of commitment to the vision.[10]

The Origin and Development of Special Theories

A special communication theory emerges from a process in which practice leads to criticism which modifies practice and, in turn, leads to theory. Theory, once it has emerged, modifies practice and criticism. The process is, thus, reciprocal in that theory modified by practice and criticism also subsequently shapes both.

As human beings go about their daily affairs talking to one another they, on occasion, get caught up in consciousness-creating communication. Such moments usually begin when small groups of people become disturbed with their here-and-now problems and meet together to talk about them as the women did who met together to talk about "other problems [that] have arisen" and began to share fantasies that resulted in sparking the new consciousnesses of the Women's Movement in the Twin Cities. When fantasies chain through these conversations, the members may start to communicate in ways that are unusual when compared with the current conventions and patterns of communication. A new communication paradigm begins with practices that violate the norms, customs, and rules of the established paradigms. Because the new way of communicating has no established criteria for evaluation and no model to guide teaching, it is first propagated by people emulating the behavior of those who first begin communicating in the new way.

Much as the fantasy themes of the new consciousness gradually become fantasy types so too do the practitioners gradually develop some general scripts and rules-of-thumb as to how to communicate according to the new prescriptions. The initiated can use these scripts and rules-of-thumb to teach newcomers and to evaluate their own and others' communication. If the new way of communicating becomes more popular, newcomers make more and more demands on those who know how to instruct them.

Some of the people involved in the new communication practices will begin to specialize in them and become more adept than the others. The specialists introduce refinements of the rules-of-thumb, the prototypes of the ideal model, and the criteria for excellence. The theorists shape the recurrent communication form until they agree on the majority of the conventions. Gradually, ideal and abstract models of communication emerge from the give-and-take of practice and teaching sessions and shop-talk among the specialists. They can then agree on the fine points of what is good and bad within the archetypal framework and agree on the criteria to be used by critics. Although specialists will agree on most matters they will often disagree about a small percentage of technical matters and debate various formulations pro and con. Records of such technical disputes provide scholars with evidence that a community has a full blown special communication theory because such issues cannot be raised without such a theory as a backdrop.[11]

As soon as human beings create conventions to guide their practices they introduce artistry into their communication. People may make and shape things and symbols for primarily aesthetic or practical purposes but they always add an element of art to what they do. Weapons for hunting and war take different conventional forms in different cultures. Tools for farming vary in shape and style.

With the introduction of artistic factors comes the need to learn how to both practice and criticize the communication. As the specialists discuss and refine theoretical questions they focus their attention on more and more technical and minute matters as central issues. An untrained person usually cannot understand much less appreciate the finer points of the art of communication as it relates to a specific conventional form.

A full blown artistic theory whether for communication or other art or craft consists of the following components: (1) an ideal model of the recurrent form or exemplar, (2) criteria for criticism drawn from the ideal model as touchstone, and (3) rules-of-thumb on how to create individuals or incidents which approximate the ideal.

Theorists may present the ideal model in various forms. In the case of breeders of thoroughbred animals who seek to shape individuals to an exemplar, it may be an artist's depiction of the configuration of an idealized specimen or a picture of an individual horse or dog that exhibits most of the key features in close approximation to the ideal. Theorists may present the ideal in descriptive language or, when coaching a student, they may illustrate the ideal model by enacting the way it ought to be accomplished. Thus, a gymnastic or diving coach may show a student how to do a back flip or a full gainer. Communication and rhetorical theorists often describe the ideal communication episode in general terms such as:

A good public speech is one in which a skillful speaker with a clear purpose analyzes the audience and occasion carefully and wisely, selects a suitable topic, preplans the organization and content of the message, delivers the speech with appropriate non-verbal gestures and vocal intonations, phrases the ideas in suitable language for the hearers, carefully reads the audience's response, accommodating the ideas to the audience both in the planning and delivery of the speech, and achieves the speaker's intent by gaining a suitable audience response.[12]

Theorists use the spelled-out or implied ideal to make criticisms of a given object or event. A judge of a dog in a show might, for example, comment on the curl in the animal's tail or the shape of the head and evaluate the curl as excellent, close to the ideal; while the shape of the head might be judged as fair to good because it is too wide between the eyes. A speech critic might evaluate the language in a student speech as only fair because it contains phrases which are not suitable for the audience.

Finally, the theorists often use rules-of-thumb that they have developed out of experience in trying to coach students to approximate the ideal in their instruction. They may suggest certain ways to practice gestures or analyze the audience in order to improve (i.e., get the student to come closer to the ideal form) speaking ability.

Special communication theories deal for the most part with at least two people and may concern great numbers in the case of theories of mass communication. In addition to the artistic features of such theories, they must also contain recipes, programs, or directions on how groups of people can join their efforts to approximate the ideal of the recurrent form. Communication events share this feature with other human activities where several people participate to shape joint action according to some agreed-upon model and standards. People who play games, dance, perform music in groups, or communicate must all agree to play, dance, perform, or communicate according to the rules, conventions, norms, and ideals of the activity.

Communication events are conventional, artistic, and staged joint ventures. To participate in a conventional endeavor it is necessary that the parties to the joint venture understand the conventions and make a social contract with one another to abide by them. In a sense people may say to one another "shall we communicate?" in much the same way that they might ask, "shall we dance?" Unless they all agree, the effort has little hope of approximating the ideal exemplified by the model. Further, like the dancers, the communicators must know what particular recurrent form they are communicating to achieve. The dancers might decide to waltz or to do the Virginia reel. The communicators might decide to take part in a consciousness-raising group, a therapy group, or a business meeting. Striving to achieve an ideal form makes a joint venture an artistic staged affair. The staging requirement may be fulfilled in more or less elaborate ways, but whether a game is played before television cameras in a domed edifice before thousands or on a vacant plot with no onlookers, a certain amount of staging is necessary. In the same way a joint venture in communication may take place in a specially constructed arena surrounded by pomp and ceremony or in a hallway where two persons happen to meet.

The special rhetorical and communication theories also include the constitutive and regulatory rules that participants need to know to join in a particular form of joint venture.

The constitutive rules are those which specify what the participants agree to do and not to do in order to take part in the joint venture. If the participants agree to always hit the ball with a club and never pick it up and throw it, that would be an example of a constitutive rule. If they agree that there are to be only four participants in the communicative episode, that would be a constitutive rule. If they agree that the communication episode will be divided into two parts according to time limits and that in the first part each speaker will be given up to ten minutes to speak, that would also be a constitutive rule.

Constitutive rules are spinoffs from the practice and criticism which created the recurrent communication form in the beginning. The sharing of group fantasies generates the new consciousness which includes the new way of communicating. Only after the common symbolic ground has been laid and the sharing process has created a community whose members are willing to agree to the conventions required to practice a new way of communicating, can the specialists evolve who can discuss the niceties of the style, technique, philosophy, purpose, and needs which lead to further theoretical refinements such as constitutive and regulatory rules.

Regulatory rules are those conventions that participants agree to follow as the episode unfolds. The constitutive rules often imply regulatory rules when experience indicates that certain of the agreements required to set up the joint venture are often broken. Thus, if the constitutive rule specifies that speakers have up to ten minutes to speak, but in practice people are tempted to speak for longer periods, the participants may agree to a regulatory rule penalizing those who go overtime.

The practice of social interaction brings with it the emergence of norms and customs that may or may not be included as part of the special theory. People can play the game if they understand the ideal model, the standards for criticism, and the rules; and people may agree to abide by these conventions as long as they do not have to follow all the norms and customs. Connoisseurs might find the play of those who deviated from norms and customs distasteful but they would admit that the boors were playing golf and not soccer. Norms and customs might find their way into a theory book in terms of good taste or etiquette. Thus, a golf professional might include in an opening lesson for beginners a discussion of golf etiquette or a handbook on debate might have a section about debate courtesy.

People may deviate from the norms and customs and if the connoisseurs cherish the norms sufficiently they may draft regulatory rules to enforce conformity. Suppose that the practitioners of the communication have evolved a norm in which speakers do not make personal derogatory comments about one another. They may fall into the habit of referring to one another as the "honorable member." If some participants begin to deviate from that norm the practitioners may agree to articulate the norm and make it a rule. A speaker who makes a derogatory comment about another participant might then, for example, be called to order and denied further opportunity to speak.

Recurrent forms of communication may result from highly detailed special communication theories that contain a specific model of the ideal event, a large body of detailed rules, customs, and norms. The staging may be so complete that the performances of the joint ventures approach the scripted nature of a theatrical play. Ritualized religious services and civil ceremonies are communication forms with such detailed staging. Some recurrent forms are associated with special communication theories that are loosely specified and they have, as a result, minimal staging and more room for improvisation so the unfolding of any particular episode cannot be predicted.

Symbolic Convergence and the Explanation of the Origin and Development of Special Theories

The way the general communication theory of symbolic convergence explains the creation and maintenance of special theories is illustrated by the origin and development of the recurrent form called *mutual criticism* in the Oneida Community in New York state in the 19th century. The Oneida Community was a Christian experiment in communist living. The community was small and its rhetorical vision included clear symbolic boundaries that served to isolate it from the surrounding community. In addition it flourished for a brief period of time.

Since the living arrangements were communal there were many informal communication opportunities that encouraged the sharing of fantasies. That the community was fertile ground for fantasy chains is evidenced by the large number of fads which swept through it. Fads are physical evidence of the ephemeral surface symbolic outbursts in which members of a rhetorical community get caught up in fantasies that do not modify their firmly established rhetorical vision.[13] Because it was a small rhetorically isolated community, the way the members shared fantasies to create the special communication theory related to mutual criticism provides a test-tube case of the process in toto.

The persona who has come to symbolize the Oneida Community was that of John Humphry Noyes. Noyes emerged as the leader of the group that first formed in Putney, Vermont in 1840 from which the Oneida Community evolved.

Among the fantasies that chained through the small group of people in the Putney Association were a number dramatizing scripts relating to Christian perfectionism. The members also began to structure a rhetorical vision employing the analogy of their group with a family as an integrative symbol.

In 1837 Noyes had written a letter to a friend in which he had dramatized a new way of living in regard to the institution of marriage. He had written in part:

When the will of God is done on earth as it is in heaven there will be no marriage. Exclusiveness, jealousy, quarrelling have no place in the marriage supper of the Lamb. In a holy community, there is no more reason why sexual intercourse should be restrained by law, than why eating and drinking should be—and there is as little occasion for shame in the one case as in the other.[14]

The new community began to share variations on this fantasy of unrestrained sexual intercourse with the result that in 1846 they adopted a practice they called *complex marriage,* an arrangement whereby all adult females and males might have the opportunity of sexual intercourse with each other. Complex marriage was buttressed by another shared fantasy type for which the participants used the code words *male continence.* Noyes and some of the other males of the community had learned to practice a form of birth control by controlling ejaculation. As time went on discussions relating to these matters saw the

sharing of still another set of fantasies envisioning ideals in regard to the conception and propagation of children which was referred to by the code word *stirpiculture.* This narrative frame portrayed the healthiest and brightest young adults systematically mated to produce the best possible individuals by techniques of selective breeding. In the late 1860s more than eighty young people volunteered to take part in the stirpiculture project and by 1879 sixty-two children had been born to the project.

To regulate the internal affairs of a tight-knit community that had to deal with such explosive issues as pairing up people for sexual intercourse, and for producing children, the members evolved a unique form of communication. Over the years the practice solidified into a recurring rhetorical form and developed all of the features of a special communication theory designed to sustain the group's consciousness. The members came to call the communication sessions which comprised the recurrent form *mutual criticism.*

When a student at Andover College, Noyes had been part of a small group of seminarians who had come together to talk about their common concerns. They shared fantasies which brought them to experiment with a form of group communication in which they criticized each other in order to test and improve their character and Godliness. Using that experience as a beginning model, the community gradually evolved a full blown, special communication theory. Someone, probably Noyes, compiled a handbook outlining the special theory in detail in 1876.[15]

The constitutive rules of the theory specify that the participants in the episode consist of (1) a committee of members to do the criticizing appointed by the community for limited but specified terms, (2) the individual to be criticized, and (3) moderator or leader to enforce the regulatory rules. In addition, the members of the committee have the right to take turns in criticizing the individual but "the important rule which was adopted was that the subject should receive his criticism *without replying,* unless obvious errors of fact were stated."[16]

The ideal model of communication for the recurrent form of mutual criticism was one in which a person feeling the need for personal and social improvement approached the committee and scheduled a criticism session. The committee then in a spirit of Christian love submitted the individual to a sharp, no-nonsense confrontation, in which they pointed out the individual's strengths and weaknesses, raising all the shortcomings that other members of the community would mention were they on the committee. The person being criticized accepted the criticism in the proper spirit, understanding it was for his or her personal good, and taking it to heart admitted shortcomings and errors and undertook to improve and do better. Cleansed and strengthened by the experience the person becomes a more perfect Christian and a better member of the community. Should a member of the committee begin to indulge in petty remarks or personal animosities, the moderator would step in and protect the target person from undeserved or inept criticisms.

The manual on *Mutual Criticism* contains several sections of rules-of-thumb on how to give and how to take criticism. The criteria for criticism are implied but not spelled out in the manual. They include the following standards. A person who did not take the criticism in the right spirit would be evaluated negatively while the individual who did the right thing would be praised. The member of the committee who failed to find the right things to criticize or who was inept at explaining and communicating the criticism as well as the member who had the wrong attitude would be open to negative criticism.

Mutual Criticism, thus, contains a complete special communication theory with all the information needed to organize and conduct such a communication episode.[17] However, the theory is so closely intertwined with the rhetorical vision of the community that without that vision or some similar rhetorical vision upon which to base the criticisms, the form would not function as consciousness-sustaining communication.

A special theory of contemporary message communication. A widespread special theory of communication in the latter half of the twentieth-century in terms of academic interest and student instruction is that of message communication. Since this theory is representative of contemporary rhetorical and communication theories it can serve to illustrate their nature as a special theory. The conventional forms of message communication are designed to transmit information with high fidelity from message sources both human and machine to receivers both human and machine. The theory is a modification and adaptation of Shannon and Weaver's information theory and the basis of a large information industry in highly developed countries.[18]

Theorists in message communication have been preoccupied with the schematic representation of the ideal communication event. They have experimented with various alternative schematic and graphic blueprinting to explain the exemplar of the ideal. The basic elements and portrayal of good communication, however, have remained essentially the same for several decades. The model consists of a *source* with an intent, encoding a *message,* selecting a *channel* or *channels* to transmit the message to a *receiver.* The receiver, in turn, provides the source with a reading on what the receiver has decoded from the message. The cues which provide the source with information needed to bring communication on target are called *feedback.* Figure 1 presents a typical ideal model of the message communication theory.[19]

The special theory also consists of constitutive and regulatory rules. People participating in communication episodes should agree to work cooperatively together. When one person assumes the role of message source the others should agree to play the role of message receiver which means they listen carefully, concentrate their attention on decoding the message, and willingly provide feedback so the source can edit, amend, modify, and revise the message until they jointly achieve high fidelity transmission of information. Norbert Wiener,

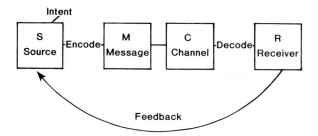

Figure 1. Ideal model of message communication. (This model is from Ernest G. Bormann and Nancy C. Bormann, *Effective Small Group Communication,* 3rd ed. (Minneapolis, Minnesota: Burgess, 1980) p. 11.

an important theorist as the special theory was under development, put it this way: "Speech is a joint game by talker and listener against the forces of confusion."[20]

The theory also consists of rules-of-thumb to aid neophytes and inept practitioners improve their communication according to the standards of the ideal model. These suggestions relate to the development of encoding and decoding skills, the selection of proper channels for message transmission, the use of redundancy to combat the natural noise in the transmission system, ways to play the receiver role including listening skills and verbal and nonverbal techniques for providing feedback, and techniques for being a good message source.

Finally the theory contains criteria to be used in evaluating communication episodes. The major earmark of good communication is *fidelity.* The concept of *fidelity* relates to how much of the message is transmitted without distortion or loss. *Noise* in a communication system cuts down fidelity. To combat noise, message sources may repeat messages or message elements. Such repetition is called *redundancy.* Another criterion for judging communication in the message special theory is efficiency. Since repetition of messages costs time and energy it is inefficient to introduce more redundancy in the system than is needed to achieve fidelity. The ideal situation is one in

which noise is minimized and the redundancy level is adjusted to a rate which results in the appropriate level of fidelity with no unnecessary repetitiveness.

Critics also evaluate message sources in terms of their skill in encoding messages, selecting channels, and reading feedback. They can criticize receivers in terms of their willingness to play the role of receiver, quality of listening, ability to decode messages, and skill in providing feedback.

The special communication theory of message communication is a complete, sophisticated, and detailed example of such theories. It includes a detailed model of the ideal communication episode, constitutive and regulatory rules, norms, customs, rule-of-thumb advice gathered from the experience of practitioners on how to approximate the ideal in actual communication, and criteria for the evaluation of specific communication events.

Aristotle's rhetorical theory as a special communication theory. Aristotle's *Rhetoric* is a hodge-podge of psychological insights, comments about the communication practices of the time, and attacks on other teachers of communication.[21] But the core of the work contains a special communication theory related to a special set of communication practices in ancient Athens. A number of scholars have subsequently seen the *Rhetoric* as a repository of universal insights into human persuasion and suggested that it can be treated like a general theory. One commentator, for example, wrote of Aristotle in the *Rhetoric,* "He lays down the true philosophical principles of rhetoric, considered as a branch of the science of man, and writes a treatise which has never been superseded, and is never likely to be superseded."[22]

A careful reading of the *Rhetoric,* however, reveals that the material relating to communication consists of (1) an ideal model of what good public speaking should be like in Athenian culture and institutions, and (2) prescriptive advice of rules-of-thumb to achieve the model. Aristotle takes the constitutive and regulatory rules for granted and unless the reader knows something of the practice of public speaking in Athens at the time, they must be inferred from side comments within the text.

The model of Aristotle's special communication theory has little in common with either that of the recurrent form of mutual criticism in the Oneida Community or of the SMCR model of today's information transmission and processing. It resembles most closely the contemporary model used for public speaking courses in American high schools and colleges. This is understandable since the special theory of public speaking has evolved from communication practices in the 18th and 19th centuries in the United States that were modeled after the classical Greek and Latin forms. Just as many 18th and 19th-century buildings were modeled after Greek architecture, so too, many college student orations were modeled after classical speeches. The classical forms were more influential with educated speakers. Other special theories relating to public speaking flourished during the 19th century and among uneducated ministers and lawyers (those who were called to preach or who practiced law after reading law with an established attorney) special theories often departed a good deal from classical standards.[23]

Aristotle's special theory was restricted to public speaking communication episodes. He particularly emphasized speeches for decisions from a judge or from judges. Certainly speaking for a decision was an important part of the communication of the citizens in Athens during Aristotle's lifetime. Aristotle's theory was so detailed that it spelled out three contexts that require some alterations in the ideal recurrent form. The three were speeches in deliberative assemblies, speeches in courts of law, and on ceremonial occasions.

The ideal model of Aristotle's theory included a speaker who understands the right uses of oratory that include: to assure that truth and justice maintain their natural superiority, to teach popular audiences that cannot follow scientific demonstrations, to teach both sides of a case and refute unfair arguments, and to defend oneself. The ideal speaker was one who, in addition to speaking for the right reasons, used arguments and proofs as the essence of persuasion and who by close study of the judges or the audience adapted ideas to hearers by using all the available means of persuasion. The available means included, in addition to argument and proof, emotional appeals and the evincing of right character. The *Rhetoric* takes this basic model and introduces modifications for the deliberative, the forensic, and the epideictic occasions.

The *Rhetoric* contains evidence that communication theorists in Aristotle's Athens had discussed technical modifications of the ideal model. In numerous asides the author comments disparagingly about other teachers and theorists who were misguided in their portrayal of the ideal. Early in the *Rhetoric* the author charged that many other authors of "Arts of Speaking" have neglected "enthymemes, the very body and substance of persuasion." For his part the author asserted that the art of rhetoric "consists of proofs . . . alone all else is but accessory."[24] In recommending the ideal organization for a speech, Aristotle suggested "the indispensable constituents are simply the Statement and the ensuing Argument." Clearly some of the current practices involved a much more elaborate organizational ideal. Aristotle suggested some elaboration, "at most, the parts cannot exceed four—Proem, Statement, Argument, and Epilogue."[25] But Aristotle went on to argue that "if you begin making such distinctions as are current, you will end with Theodorus and his school, differentiating 'Narration' proper from 'Post-' 'Pre-narration' . . . when you coin a term, it ought to mark a real species, and a specific difference; otherwise you get empty frivolous verbiage like the terms invented by Licymnius in his *Art of Rhetoric*."[26]

Much of the special communication theory in Aristotle's *Rhetoric* consisted of rule-of-thumb advice on how to become a better speaker. The *Rhetoric* contains advice on how to find and develop ideas including an elaborate system of *topoi*, how to refute an argument, how to avoid errors in the use of enthymemes, and numerous detailed rules-of-thumb on the use of language. For example, Aristotle suggested that stylistic purity involved the correct use of connective particles, the use of specific rather than vague words, the avoidance of ambiguity, and so forth. A good style, according to Aristotle, was one which is easy to read and punctuate. Again these suggestions and prescriptions are conventional and under dispute by other specialists in the practice of communication who were contemporaries of Aristotle. Aristotle noted, for example:

At present there is an absurd demand that the narration should be "rapid". . . . The narration must not be over-long, just as the proem must not be over-long, nor yet the arguments. Here, too, then, the right thing is neither rapidity nor brevity, the proper mean.[27]

Upon close inspection, therefore, Aristotle's rhetorical theory turns out to be a special artistic and conventional theory. Indeed, many of the classical, medieval, and 18th and 19th-century European rhetorical theories were also special theories.

Black, for example, noted that classical rhetorical theories were essentially special theories to aid practice.

The critics of classical antiquity, whether composing rhetorics, poetics, or histories of art seemed uninterested in reflecting on their own activities. To articulate the principles of Sophoclean tragedy or Roman forensic oratory was, for Aristotle and Cicero, the end and justification of their respective works. They assumed the mission of elevating intuitive acts of creation to the status of viable method. Their aim was to formulate technical principles that artists could use; to make creativity systematic. They wrote primarily, not for the critic himself, or for the auditor, but for the artist.[28]

The general theory of symbolic convergence accounts for the three special theories sketched above in terms of their origination in the shared fantasies of groups of people who created new consciousnesses and in the process developed new forms of communication. These forms emerged from practice (based on shared fantasies), criticism, and the theoretical formulations of people like the anonymous author of *Mutual Criticism* or Aristotle who tried, in Black's words, "to elevate intuitive acts of creation to the status of viable method."

Fantasy Theme Analysis as Rhetorical Criticism

Fantasy theme analysis is a humanistic approach to the rhetorical criticism of human communication.[29] Fantasy theme analysts use the symbolic convergence theory as part of their basic scholarly perspective when studying communication events. They, thus, bring to their criticisms all of the explanatory power of the general theory. However, rhetorical criticism involves more than descriptions of discourse and accounts of how it came into being and functioned. A critic needs also to evaluate and judge the discourse and provide added insight into how it works. Fantasy theme analysts have approached their critical work from a variety of perspectives and have provided unique insights about the fantasy themes, types, and rhetorical visions they have first documented using the symbolic convergence theory as a frame of reference.

Fantasy theme analysis is a form of metacriticism. As noted above the development of a recurrent rhetorical form requires that the practitioners indulge in extensive criticism of the practice. At one level of analysis such criticism can be considered rhetorical. This is the level of criticism of the instructor and the class in public speaking or of the members of the Oneida Community discussing how they evaluate the last session of mutual criticism or of Aristotle chastizing some practitioners for practicing what he called a "rapid" narration. Criticism at the basic level is of practical importance but of little enduring scholarly interest.

The more enduring critical scholarship results from a metacritical perspective that views the entire process of communication, practice, criticism, and special theory as the object of analysis. The fantasy theme analyst begins by making a study of the communication practices of a group of people by means of qualitative and content analysis of messages to discover the fantasy themes, types, and rhetorical visions in the material. The critic may also gather data about the consciousness of the community by means of social scientific techniques such as Q-sort interviews, focused group interviews, individual interviews, questionnaires, and other instruments applied using both small sample and large sample surveys. The critic then takes the shared fantasies and rhetorical visions discovered and documented by humanistic or social scientific means or both as the basis for a critical qualitative analysis.

Metacriticism aims at discovering knowledge about human communication that transcends communication styles, contexts, and transitory issues currently under contention. Scholars using metacriticism are trying to understand human communication in all its varied forms, but particularly as it is used in a rhetorical way. Rhetorical criticism thus takes its place as a liberal and humanizing art, a scholarly endeavor which aims to illuminate the human condition. It is particularly concerned with human communication which works to divide and integrate communities of human beings, to interpret human problems and enable cooperative efforts to be made to solve them, to provide self and group concepts for human beings searching for meaning in their existence and endeavors.

How does the rhetorical critic searching to illuminate human symbolizing proceed? In the first place, the critic does not ask questions such as, "Is this a good example of communication in the recurrent form generated by the special theory of public speaking or intercollegiate debate popular in the late twentieth-century or the Aristotelian special theory popular in ancient Athens?" Rather the critic asks such questions as "Are there recurring patterns of symbolization which appear across cultures and stylistic forms? If such basic patterns can be found, how do they function rhetorically?"

Critics using fantasy theme analysis have found a number of fantasy types which have recurred in the history of mass persuasion in the United States. Among these fantasy types have been the drama of the American dream explained earlier, the conspiracy fantasy type which has appeared in the communication of all sorts of political and social movements—right wing, left wing, and middle-of-the-road, the type which portrays God as giving his chosen people a time of troubles as a warning that they need to mend their ways so they can "Fetch good out of evil," and the restoration fantasy type which sees America as in a troubled time because the people have fallen away from the true basis of their government and that the solution is to restore the country to its original foundations.[30]

The critic making a fantasy theme analysis can take these widespread and recurring fantasy types apart and discover how they work rhetorically by finding out, for example, how the American dream worked to build a sense of community and shape the American character or by discovering how the fantasy type of "Fetching good out of evil" can work as an appeal to unify the country and mobilize people to support a war effort or an attempt to reunify a country after a Civil War. The critic by supplementing and expanding the descriptions provided by the social scientific theory of symbolic convergence adds a dimension to our understanding that enriches such investigations.

Rhetorical critics who reconstruct the rhetorical visions of communities of people can ask general rhetorical questions. The critic can learn of the hopes and fears, the emotional tone, and the inner life of the group by examining how it deals with the basic, universal problems. Such insight flows from answers to questions such as these: How well did the communication deal with the problem of creating and celebrating a sense of community? Did it help generate a group and individual self-image which was strong, confident, and resilient? How did the rhetoric aid or hinder the community in its adaptation to its physical environment? How did the communicators deal with the rhetorical problem of creating a social reality which provides norms for community behavior in terms of the level of violence, exploitation, dominance, and injustice? Did the communication create a drama for the members that served such mythic functions as providing them with an account of the world, the gods, and fate, and that gave meaning to their community and themselves? How well did the vision aid the people who participated in it to live with people who shared different rhetorical visions?

The following excerpts from a fantasy theme analysis of the Puritan rhetorical vision indicates the way humanistic studies can add a crucial dimension to the descriptions of communication derived from the symbolic convergence theory.

A discursive description of the emigration and the daily externals of life would be very grim. But the Puritans of Colonial New England led an internal fantasy life of mighty grandeur and complexity. They participated in a rhetorical vision that saw the migration to the new world as a holy exodus of God's chosen people. The Biblical drama that supported their vision was that of the journey of the Jews from Egypt into Canaan. . . . The Puritan rhetorical vision saw them as conquering new territories for God, saving the souls of the natives, and, most importantly, as setting up in the wilderness a model religious community, a new Israel, patterned after the true meaning of the scriptures to light the way for the reformation still to be accomplished in old England and in all of Europe.

Such a vision gave to every social and political action a sense of importance. Every intrusion of nature or of other communities of people on their inner reality also was given added significance. A time of troubles such as a drought or an Indian raid became evidence of God's displeasure and served as a motive to drive the Puritans to higher effort and greater striving to please God. The Puritan vision also gave meaning to each individual within the movement. The scenario places each member of the audience firmly in the role of protagonist.

. . .

An audience observing the drama from the outside might find it lacking in suspense, find it inartistic because the basic assumption upon which it rested was the deus ex machina. Man was completely dependent upon God for election and sainthood. . . . But for the listener who chained out on the fantasy and imaginatively took the central role the suspense might well become unbearable. Each hour might bring eternal salvation or eternal death.

The predominant emotion which the Puritan vision evoked was that of awe. The focus is upon an afterlife with high potential for ecstasy or terror, almost beyond the power of the ministers to fantasize. The rhetoric contained powerful pragmatic motivations. The preoccupation with time, the fear of death before God's call to election, impelled the participant in the fantasy to do as much as soon as possible to put herself or himself in the proper posture for election to sainthood. The minutes wasted might be those very ones when his time had come.[31]

Once readers participate through fantasy theme analysis in the rhetorical vision of a community or movement they have come to experience vicariously the inner symbolic world of its participants and to experience a way of life in a qualitative fashion that a social scientific description of the communication could not provide.

Summary

Both the humanistic practice of fantasy theme analysis as rhetorical criticism and the social scientific theory of symbolic convergence are based upon the dynamic process of sharing fantasies in communication episodes. Taken together they provide a way for unifying the concerns of humanists and social scientists in their study of rhetoric and communication.

Special communication theory deals with the communication conventions of communities of people who understand the rules, norms, and aesthetics relating to the practice and criticism of conventional forms of joint communication ventures. General theories by comparison are accounts of broad classes of communication events that explain how special theories come into being and function.

The symbolic convergence theory is a general account which is based on the process of sharing group fantasies that result in the participants converging their symbolic interpretations. From the process of sharing fantasy themes, group members abstract fantasy types, and integrate them into the more comprehensive symbolic structures that are rhetorical visions.

Special communication theories are created by groups of people who come together to talk of common concerns when they begin to share fantasies and encourage new ways of communicating. Gradually, ideal and abstract models of communication emerge from the give and take of practice and teaching sessions and a full-blown special theory emerges.

The way the general communication theory of symbolic convergence explains the creation and maintenance of special theories is well illustrated by recurrent form of mutual criticism used by the Oneida Community, by the message communication form of late twentieth-century United States, and by Aristotle's rhetorical theory of ancient Athens.

Fantasy theme analysis is a humanistic approach to rhetorical criticism, which uses the symbolic convergence theory as part of its scholarly perspective. Fantasy theme analysis is a form of metacriticism that views the entire process of communication, practice, criticism, and special theory as the object of analysis.

Ernest Bormann is Professor of Communication at the University of Minnesota.

Notes

1. For a fuller discussion of these matters see Ernest G. Bormann. *Communication Theory* (New York: Holt, Rinehart and Winston, 1980), pp. 3–16.
2. James E. Combs and Michael W. Mansfield, eds. *Drama in Life: The Uses of Communication in Society* (New York: Hastings House, 1976), p. xxix.
3. For an expanded analysis of the distinction between general and special theories see Bormann, pp. 59–80.
4. For a sympathetic presentation of cognitive dissonance see Elliot Aronson. *The Social Animal,* 1st ed. (San Francisco: Freeman, 1972). The second edition of the same work, 1976, is still sympathetic but less so. For an approach to cognitive dissonance as a theory of persuasion see Mary John Smith. *Persuasion and Human Action* (Belmont, CA: Wadsworth, 1982), pp. 117–141.
5. See, for example, Robert F. Bales. *Personality and Interpersonal Behavior* (New York: Holt, Rinehart and Winston, 1970); Ernest G. Bormann. *Discussion and Group Methods: Theory and Practice* (New York: Harper & Row, 1975).
6. John F. Cragan, "The Cold War Rhetorical Vision," in John F. Cragan and Donald C. Shields, eds. *Applied Communication Research: A Dramatistic Approach* (Prospect Heights, IL: Waveland Press, 1981), pp. 47–66.
7. For an explanation of the inside joke phenomenon see Ernest G. Bormann, Jolene Koester, and Janet Bennett. "Political Cartoons and Salient Rhetorical Fantasies: An Empirical Analysis of the '76 Campaign," *Communication Monographs,* 45 (1978), 317–329.
8. For further evidence of how human beings attribute motives to human actors in fantasy themes see psychological studies conducted under the label of *attribution processes.* For a survey of these matters in terms of persuasion see Smith, pp. 142–163.
9. Becky Kroll. "Rhetoric and Organizing: The Twin Cities' Women's Movement 1969–1976," Unpublished Ph.D. Dissertation, University of Minnesota, 1981, p. 51.
10. The analysis of mutual criticism of the Oneida Community furnishes an example of consciousness sustaining recurrent form. See p. 440f.
11. The *Rhetoric* of Aristotle contains a number of references to technical disputes over such matters as the relative emphasis on logical and emotional proofs, the proper form of narration, the right number of parts to the organization of a speech, and so forth. These references provide evidence for the argument that classical rhetorical theories such as Aristotle's were special communication theories. See p. 433f.

12. Slightly paraphrased this description is drawn from Ernest G. Bormann and Nancy C. Bormann. *Speech Communication: A Comprehensive Approach* (New York: Harper & Row, 1977), p. 32.

13. Constance Noyes Robertson. *Oneida Community: The Breakup, 1876–1881* (Syracuse, NY: Syracuse University Press), p. 2, quotes the *First Annual Report* of the community as follows, ". . . in consequence of some speculation on the subject of women's dress, some of the leading women of the Association took the liberty to dress themselves in short gowns or frocks with pantaloons . . . til frocks and pantaloons became the prevailing fashion in the Association. Another new fashion broke out among the women. The ordinary practice of leaving the hair grow indefinitely. . . . Accordingly some of the bolder women cut off their hair and started the fashion which soon prevailed throughout the Association."

14. Robertson, p. 2.

15. *Mutual Criticism*, with an introduction by Murray Levine and Barbara Benedict Bunker (Oneida, NY: Office of the American Socialist, 1876; reprint Syracuse, NY: Syracuse University Press, 1975).

16. *Ibid.*, p. 17.

17. In a section of *Mutual Criticism* devoted to the question "Shall it become general?" the author noted, "In such meetings all the organization necessary would be the selection of a moderator who should conduct the exercises by calling out the opinions of those present on the person or persons who offer themselves for criticism. Two general rules, however, must be adopted to which all should give loyal adherence. These rules are: 1, in giving Criticism no person shall indulge in remarks suggested by personal enmity or resentment; 2, in receiving Criticism the subject shall quietly accept what is said to him, making no reply, save to correct obvious misstatement of facts." p. 90.

18. Claude E. Shannon and Warren Weaver. *The Mathematical Theory of Communication* (Urbana, IL.: University of Illinois Press, 1943).

19. For some typical variations on the basic model see C. David Mortensen. *Communication: The Study of Human Interaction* (New York: McGraw-Hill, 1972),

pp. 36–41; for one of the most influential formulations of the model see David K. Berlo. *The Process of Communication: An Introduction to Theory and Practice* (New York: Holt, Rinehart and Winston, 1960), p. 72.

21. *The Rhetoric of Aristotle,* trans. by Lane Cooper (New York: D. Appleton-Century-Crofts, 1932).

22. The commentator was W. Rhys Roberts, quoted in *The Rhetoric*, p. xii.

23. For an analysis of a nonacademic special rhetorical theory popular in 19th-century America see, Ernest G. Bormann. "The Rhetorical Theory of William Henry Milburn," *Communication Monographs*, 36 (1969), 28–37.

24. *The Rhetoric*, p. 1.

25. *The Rhetoric*, p. 220.

26. *The Rhetoric*, pp. 220–221.

27. *The Rhetoric*, p. 229.

28. Edwin Black. *Rhetorical Criticism: A Study of Method* (New York: Macmillan, 1965), p. 196.

29. For a more detailed explanation of the method see Ernest G. Bormann. "Fantasy and Rhetorical Vision: The Rhetorical Criticism of Social Reality," *Quarterly Journal of Speech*, 58 (1972), 396–407; Ernest G. Bormann, "Fantasy and Rhetorical Vision: Ten Years Later," *Quarterly Journal of Speech*, 68 (1982), 288–305.

30. For the conspiracy fantasy type see John F. Cragan. "Rhetorical Strategy: A Dramatistic Interpretation and Application," *The Central States Speech Journal*, 26 (1975), 4–11 and G. Thomas Goodnight and John Poulakos. "Conspiracy Rhetoric: From Pragmatism to Fantasy in Public Discourse," *Western Journal of Speech Communication*, 45 (1981), 299–316. For "Fetching good out of evil" see Ernest G. Bormann. "Fetching Good Out of Evil: A Rhetorical Use of Calamity," *Quarterly Journal of Speech*, 63 (1977), 130–139. For the restoration fantasy type see Ernest G. Bormann. "A Fantasy Theme Analysis of the Television Coverage of the Hostage Release and the Reagan Inaugural," *Quarterly Journal of Speech*, 68 (1982), 133–145.

31. Bormann, "Fantasy and Rhetorical Vision: The Rhetorical Criticism of Social Reality," 402–403.

24

Rhetoric as a Way of Knowing: Toward a Rhetoric of the Future

In our rhetorical overview of Western thought we have analyzed the important ideas of the major theorists in the classical, British, and contemporary periods. Hopefully we now have gained an appreciation of the moral-philosophical stance of Plato; the scientific-philosophical view of Aristotle; the educational emphasis of Isocrates, Cicero, and Quintilian; the religious communication thrust of St. Augustine; the belletristic school of thought personified by Blair; the epistemological trend initiated by Bacon and reinforced by Vico, Hume, Campbell, and Whately; and the four approaches to the study of contemporary rhetorical theory: meaning, value, motive, and knowing. Up to this juncture it has been our purpose to demonstrate what rhetoric has been in the past and is becoming in the present. We have, for the most part, been more interested in describing than in judging.

In this closing chapter, however, we would like to depart from our pattern and, with the help of two of our friends, speculate on trends now taking place which will significantly influence rhetorical study in the immediate years ahead. We are inclined to believe that our reliance on symbols combined with our low tolerance for ambiguity will tend to keep our focus fastened on the problem of meaning. Moreover, Watergate and its aftermath, we suggest, has provided the ambience for the continuing concern we will perhaps experience with rhetoric as value. Similarly, we anticipate little change with respect to the need to relate rhetoric to motives. But while pre-

dicting an ongoing interest in meaning, values, and motives, we are convinced, at the same time, that the most promising single challenge in the next few years pertains to the notion discussed in the preceding three chapters: rhetoric as a way of knowing.

We have reached this conclusion primarily for two reasons. First the emphasis on knowing is an important addendum and contrast to all that we have learned about persuasion. Secondly, and equally significant, as rhetoric becomes progressively associated with knowing, it comes together with argument, philosophy, and science. In so doing the study of rhetoric will be as relevant in a department of communication stressing the social and behavioral sciences as it is in one featuring the humanities.

In expressing our faith in viewing rhetoric as epistemic, we not only are indebted to Toulmin and Perelman, but to four of our colleagues who have visited our campus during recent years: Robert Scott, Wayne Brockriede, Douglas Ehninger, and Ernest Bormann. Each in his own way has been in the vanguard opening up new frontiers of rhetorical inquiry. Scott's and Bormann's views on the epistemic nature of rhetoric have been summarized earlier. Brockriede, who along with Ehninger, became an effective interpreter of Toulmin, served as Visiting Professor at Ohio State University in the Autumn of 1974. While there he presented a paper on the timely theme, "Where is Argument?" The response was enthusiastic. For weeks faculty members and graduate students discussed the implications of his essay. In the end the Department of Communication incorporated Brockriede's principles into a policy statement which serves as a guideline for the search of knowledge. The Department came to believe that whenever a student participates in a rhetorical situation, he/she should be able and willing to utilize the six features of argument detailed by Brockriede. We offer this essay not only as a reminder of "Where is Argument?", but as an indication of a central concern of rhetoric in the future.

Where Is Argument?

Before looking for the clues that may lead to the discovery of where "argument" is, perhaps I should state some of my biases so you may be less surprised if I don't go instantly to where you presume I could find the culprit without difficulty. My principal bias is a humanistic point of view that denies an interest in logical systems, in messages, in reasoning, in evidence, or in propositions—*unless these things involve human activity rather directly*. One of the most famous cliches during the past fifteen years in the study of communication, originated by I know not whom but popularized by David K. Berlo, is that meanings are not in words but in people.[1] Arguments are not in statements but in people. Hence, a first clue on the whereabouts of argument: people will find arguments in the vicinity of people.

Second, argument is not a "thing" to be looked for but a concept people use, a perspective they take. Human activity does not usefully constitute an argument until some person perceives what is happening as an argument. Although defining the term on this basis is not as neat as speaking of necessary and sufficient conditions, seeing argument as a human activity encourages persons to take into account the conceptual choices of the relevant people. Hence, a second clue: only people can find and label and use an argument.

Third, because arguments are in people and are what people see them to be, the idea of argument is an open concept. Seeing it as an open concept is consistent with the ideas that arguers are people, that people change, and that the filtering concepts people use when they make perceptions also change. Hence, a third clue: the location of argument may change, and so may the road map.

Fourth, because argument is a human process, a way of seeing, an open concept, it is potential everywhere. During the past four years some undergraduate students at the University of Colorado have found argument lurking in some strange places. We asked them specifically to look for it beyond the traditional habitats of the law courts (where textbook writers tend to find their doctrine) or the legislative assemblies (where teachers typically want students to imagine presenting their arguments). We asked them to look in such relatively exotic places as the aesthetic experience, the interpersonal transaction, and the construction of scientific theory or the reporting of research studies. I've read some interesting papers by students who have applied an argumentative perspective to a novel by Camus, to a symphony by Bernstein, to marriage and divorce, to Zen Buddhism, and to Thomas S. Kuhn's *Structure of Scientific Revolutions.*[2] Throughout the reading of the arguments of such papers, I have been able to maintain my bias that "argument" has not been stretched out of shape, that it constitutes a frame of reference that can be related potentially to any kind of human endeavor (although, obviously, the idea of argument is not the only perspective that can be applied to a

Reprinted from the *Journal of the American Forensic Association,* 11 (Spring 1975), 179–182. Reprinted with the permission of the author and editor of *J.A.F.A.*

novel or a symphony). And until someone dis-abuses me of this eccentricity, I'm stuck with this fourth clue: the perspective of argument may pop up unexpectedly and usefully in a person's head at any time.

Fifth, but even though I appear to have constructed the idea of argument out of elas-ticity, I do not wish to argue that all com-munication is usefully called an argument. At this moment I see six characteristics that may help a person decide whether argument is a useful perspective to take in studying a com-municative act. These characteristics, taken as six ways of looking at the same gestalt, de-fine argument as *a process whereby people reason their way from one set of problematic ideas to the choice of another.*

The six characteristics of my construct of argument imply three primary dimensions. First, argument falls squarely into the realm of the problematic. What people argue about are nontrivial enough to pose a problem, but they are not likely easily to resolve the prob-lem and so the issue remains somewhat prob-lematic for a significant period of time. Second, each of the six characteristics of argument is a function of the variable logic of more or less and not a function of the categorical logic of yes or no. That is, each characteristic, and the construct as a whole, lies within the midrange of the more-or-less continuum. If an argument is not problematic enough or if any character-istic is too minimal—no argument. Too much of a problematic character or too much of any of the characteristics—no argument. Third, as my preliminary biases imply, argument is based on the perceptions and choices of peo-ple.[3]

Characteristic One. An inferential leap from existing beliefs to the adoption of a new belief or to the reinforcement of an old one. One way to explain what I mean by an infer-ential leap is to contrast an argument of the sort I am talking about with a syllogism, the most famous member of the analytic family. Because its conclusion is entailed by the prem-ises, no inferential leap is needed: nothing is stated in the conclusion of a syllogism that is not stated in the premise. As long as people stay within the closed system of a syllogism, nothing is problematic. To question a defini-tion or a premise, people must leave that closed system by leaping inferentially into problem-atic uncertainty, and by doing so they may then make the kind of argument I am delineating in this paper. To function as an argument an inferential leap occupies the midrange of the more-or-less continuum. A person has little to argue about if the conclusion does not extend beyond the materials of an argument or ex-tends only slightly; but one may be unable to make a convincing argument if the leap is too large, perhaps perceived as suicidal.

Characteristic Two. A perceived rationale to support that leap. An arguer must perceive some rationale that establishes that the claim leaped to is worthy at least of being enter-tained. The weakest acceptance rationale may justify saying that the claim leaped to de-serves entertainment "for the sake of argu-ment." A stronger rationale may justify a person's taking a claim seriously—with the hope that after further thought it may be ac-cepted. A still stronger rationale may convince someone to accept a claim tentatively until a better alternative comes along. If a rationale is too slender to justify a leap, the result is a quibble rather than an argument; but a ratio-nale so strong a conclusion is entailed removes the activity from the realm of the problematic and hence from the world of argument. If the perceived rationale occupies either polar re-gion, it fails to justify the label of argument because the claim either appears ridiculous (not worth arguing about) or too risky to en-tertain.

Characteristic Three. A choice among two or more competing claims. When people quib-ble or play the analytic game, they do not make arguments because they cannot see a situation as yielding more than one legitimate claim. The right to choose is a human characteristic, but people are not free to choose without con-straints. They are limited by what they know, what they believe, what they value. They are limited by how they relate to other people and to situations. They are limited by cause and by chance. But within such constraints people who argue have some choice but not too much. If they have too little choice, if a belief is entailed by formal logic or required by their status as true believers, they need not argue; but if they have too much choice, if they have to deal with choice overload, then argument may not be very productive.

Characteristic Four. A regulation of uncertainty. Because arguers make inferential leaps that take claims beyond a rationale on which they are based, because they choose from among disputed options, they cannot reach certainty. If certainty existed, people need not engage in what I am defining as argument. When uncertainty is high, a need for argument is also high, especially if people are uncertain about something important to them. Usually arguers want to reduce uncertainty, but sometimes they may need to employ a strategy of confrontation to increase uncertainty enough to get the attention of others. Only then may such people be receptive to arguments designed to reduce uncertainty. If people have too little uncertainty to regulate, then they have no problems to solve and argument is not needed. But if the regulation of uncertainty is too difficult, if people have too much trouble reducing or escalating the degree of uncertainty, then they may be unable or unwilling to argue.

Characteristic Five. A willingness to risk confrontation of a claim with peers. In his evolutionary theory of knowing, Donald K. Darnell argues that scientists and other kinds of people gain knowledge by taking an imaginative leap from an accumulated and consolidated body of information on a subject and then by undergoing the risk of confronting self and others with the claim that results, a risk that may lead to the disconfirmation or modification of the claim.[4] Arguers cannot regulate uncertainty very much until their claim meets these tests of confrontation. A person confronting self has no public risk (unless someone overhears one self arguing aloud with another self), but the private risk is that an important claim or an important part of a self may have to be discarded. When two persons engage in mutual confrontation so they can share a rational choice, they share the risks of what that confrontation may do to change their ideas, their selves, and their relationship with one another. If the leap is too little, the rationale too minimal, the choice too slender, the problem of uncertainty-reduction too miniscule, then the potential risk of disconfirmation after confrontation probably is not enough to justify calling the behavior argument. But if these characteristics are too overwhelming, the risk may be too great and a person may be unwilling to subject an idea through argument to confrontation and almost certain disconfirmation.

Characteristic Six. A frame of reference shared optimally. The emergence of this characteristic is consistent with the idea that argument is an open concept. Until the spring of 1974 I knew of only five characteristics of argument, those I have just discussed. Then while working on a doctoral dissertation, one of my advisees, Karen Rasmussen, wrote a chapter on argument that added this sixth characteristic. She argued that arguers must share to an optimal degree elements of one another's world views or frames of reference.[5] This idea squares with a position Peter A. Schouls took in contending that professional philosophers (and, one may presume, others as well) cannot argue with one another very effectively if their presuppositions share too little or are virtually irreconcilable; but argument is pointless if two persons share too much.[6] It also squares with Kenneth Burke's doctrine of identification, which implies that polar extremes are empty categories—that the uniqueness of individuals makes for at least some divisiveness (which occasionally makes argument necessary), but on the other hand individuals are consubstantial in sharing at least a few properties (which occasionally makes argument possible).[7]

So this is my argument about where argument may be discovered; among people, by people, in changing forms, potentially everywhere, but especially where six characteristics are joined. I have contended that argument deals with the problematic and ignores the trivial or the certain, that it depends on the perceptions and choices of people who will decide whether viewing an activity as an argument is appropriate, and that it lies in the midrange of the more-or-less continuum of a variable logic and not a categorical logic.

I argue that what I have done in writing this essay is an illustration of my construct of argument. I have made some inferential leaps. I have presented what I perceive to be a rationale for supporting those leaps. I have made some choices. I may have succeeded in regulating some uncertainties. I have presumed throughout that our frames of reference overlap at some points but not at too many. I now invite your confrontation.

Wayne Brockriede

Wayne Brockriede (Ph.D., University of Illinois, 1954) is Professor of Communication at California State University, Fullerton. Versions of this essay were first presented as lectures at Ohio State University and Michigan State University and as a convention paper at the Speech Communication Association, 1974.

Notes

1. *The Process of Communication* (New York: Holt, Rinehart and Winston, 1960), pp. 174–175.
2. Second ed. enlarged (Chicago: University of Chicago Press, 1970).
3. An earlier exposition of five of these characteristics of argument, as applied to rhetorical criticism, appeared in my "Rhetorical Criticism as Argument," *QJS*, L (April 1974), 165–174. A more detailed discussion of the construct will appear as Chapter VII, "Argument," in Donald K. Darnell and Wayne Brockriede, *Persons Communicating* (forthcoming).
4. Chapter III, "An Evolutionary Theory of Knowing," in Darnell and Brockriede.
5. "Implications of Argumentation for Aesthetic Experience: A Transactional Perspective" (unpublished Ph.D. dissertation, University of Colorado, 1974), Chapter III.
6. "Communication, Argumentation, and Presupposition in Philosophy," *Philosophy & Rhetoric*, II (Fall 1969), 183–199.
7. *A Rhetoric of Motives* (1950; rpt. Berkeley: University of California Press, 1969), pp. 20–23.

In telling us where argument is and implying where it will be in the years ahead, Brockriede gives us the focal point for treating rhetoric as epistemic. But it was Ehninger who brought the trend into clear focus four years later. In an address delivered at Ohio State University in February, 1978, he urged students of rhetoric to prepare for the future by recognizing that rhetoric, science, and philosophy are not natural enemies but integrally related. The "doing" of science and philosophy, he argues, is dependent upon communication and persuasion. Indeed, the scientific method, which is "a persuasive rhetorical instrument," is designed not merely to produce facts or truths but to achieve consensus or audience acceptance. Viewed from this vantage point, rhetoric cannot be limited to the communication of what is known. It has instead the more important and far reaching function of generating new knowledge. To see how these arguments flow in their entirety, we call your attention to the essay which follows.

Science, Philosophy—and Rhetoric: A Look Toward the Future

In 1936, in his influential book *The Philosophy of Rhetoric,* I. A. Richards pointed a new direction for rhetorical studies when he declared that instead of inquiring into the arts of persuasion, rhetoric should become a study of misunderstanding and its remedies—of those factors that lead to breakdowns in communication among individuals, groups, and nations and the steps that may be taken to avoid or repair them.[1]

Motivated by this declaration and under the strong influence of such earlier writers as John Dewey[2] and Alfred Korzybski,[3] rhetoricians set out to develop what I have elsewhere called "the rhetoric of social amelioration"[4]—a rhetoric designed to improve human relations among creatures who by nature respond to symbols.

Today the rhetoric of social amelioration continues to flourish not only in the writings of Kenneth Burke[5] and of Wayne Booth,[6] but also in our lively concern with interpersonal and group communication and with the principles of conflict management. At the same time, however, rhetoric also has begun to move in a number of new and exciting directions. In this lecture, I should like to review with you two developments that seem to be of more than ordinary importance, and then to suggest how these developments, working in concert, promise to alter some of our long-standing notions concerning the nature of rhetoric and the functions which it performs.

I

The first development I want to describe is the growing recognition of the role that rhetoric plays in the "doing" of science.

As I hardly need remind you, historically rhetoric and science have been regarded as mutually exclusive, if not antithetical, modes of human activity. Science, we have been taught, deals with "facts"; rhetoric with "informed opinions." The aim of science is to describe the world; the aim of rhetoric is to reform or regenerate it. Science propounds general truths in the form of lawlike statements; rhetoric applies socially approved values to specific cases requiring choice or decision. The scientist can produce a discourse expressive or generative of knowledge without engaging another mind; for the practitioner of rhetoric the presence of an audience is essential.

From some of the most influential of the recent writings in the philosophy and methodology of science, however, quite a different picture emerges. Let me here look at the work of four authors whose books may be taken as representative of this newer point of view. They are Jacob Bronowski, Michael Polanyi, John Ziman, and Thomas Kuhn.

In his book *Science and Human Values*,[7] Bronowski argues that our traditional view of science is an inheritance of the highly "individualistic" empirical philosophy which had its roots in the thinking of such eighteenth-century figures as John Locke and David Hume, and was transmitted to us largely through the writings of the logical positivists of the 1920s and 30s. According to this philosophy, the justification for a scientific theory was to be sought not by eliciting support from one's colleagues, but rather by examining for oneself the phenomena under study. A statement of a scientific nature, it was held, made sense only insofar as it could be tested by an observer, and it was true if and only if conditions in the external world were as the statement described them.

Today, however, says Bronowski, it is evident that this analysis no longer applies. On the contrary, it is increasingly clear that science, instead of being a solitary activity carried on independently by individuals using their eyes and ears in the laboratory, is an intensely social enterprise, involving cooperation, and hence communication, among many persons working either as an organized task force or members of an academic discipline bound together by a common period of apprenticeship and pursuing a common set of professional problems and goals. The framing of hypotheses, the elaboration of theories, and the verification of results are all, more often than not, dependent upon a constant interchange among the members of a scientific community. Indeed, science as a whole may not incorrectly be regarded as a great dialogue or continuing dialectic carried on in a sort of parliamentary fashion by a multitude of contributing voices.

In the "individualistic" philosophy of logical empiricism as it was previously thought to apply to scientific endeavors, communicative activities were not directly involved in the production of scientific knowledge and questions of value, or of the "ought," were largely irrelevant; for such questions, as Bronowski reminds us, do not arise when one is working alone, but only when one is acting cooperatively as a member of a team or is in some way "behaving" toward other persons.

Where cooperative efforts are concerned, however, questions of joint conduct as they bear on the communication-oriented virtues of truthfulness, cooperation, and the like take on great importance. And here, too, questions of rhetoric or persuasion also enter. If a scientist who is operating as a member of a group or team is to carry on his work successfully, he not only needs to report to others, but at certain junctures he also needs to influence others through some sort of argument or persuasive appeal. In sum, it is in the social—or "rhetorical"—nexus provided by effective communication and responsible cooperation that advances in scientific knowledge become possible in the present-day world of cooperative research and endeavor.

Taking a line much similar to that followed by Bronowski, Michael Polanyi also has emphasized the role that communication and persuasion play in carrying on the scientific enterprise.[8]

As Polanyi sees it, in its initial phases science is a form of activity engaged in by individuals using skills and techniques they have acquired through a process of apprenticeship under a master researcher. The information generated as a result of such inquiries is, however, then referred to colleagues for judgment and evaluation. These colleagues form a community or collectivity which, through the decisions it renders, effectively controls the practices and products of individual investigators.

In its role as validating or authorizing body, the scientific community not only determines what is and is not admissible into the corpus of scientific knowledge, but even who, as a practical matter, will be allowed to practice science. In both of these respects, the body of accepted scientific knowledge eventually is determined by what we rhetoricians would call an "audience" or "jury" of peers—"a network of responsible and authoritative critics held together by trust in each others' judgments."

Moreover, within the scientific community, fundamental changes in orientation or theory occur not so much through a patient bit-by-bit accumulation of scraps of information, but rather from controversies which periodically arise as rival systems of interpretation come into conflict. In these situations, Polanyi says, the disputants literally speak different languages and live in different worlds, so that compromise between competing views is in any practical sense rendered impossible, and at least one of the two contesting schools must have the orientation it favors excluded from the accepted body of scientific knowledge. This, however, can occur only when the proponents of some new understanding are able to win over their opponents through plausible arguments, and thereby to persuade them of the scientific value of their position.

The notion of audience acceptance as an essential ingredient in the scientific enterprise has been emphasized even more pointedly by John Ziman.[9]

For Ziman, the central thrust of scientific activity is not the search for truth, but the quest for acceptance. "Science," he asserts, "is unique in striving for and insisting on a consensus." Indeed, in their concern to achieve such a consensus, scientists characteristically limit their investigations to those issues on which it is, at least in principle, possible to secure universal agreement.

Even more specifically, Ziman regards scientific method itself as a highly persuasive rhetorical instrument, and looks upon a properly structured experiment as a persuasive argument which says to the observers, "If you had been there or had done as I did, you too would have arrived at the same results."

Describing the purposes which he had in mind writing his well-known book *Public Knowledge,* Ziman says:

> What I have tried to show . . . is that the criteria of proof in science are public, and not private; that the allegiance of the scientist is toward the creation of a consensus. The rationale of the 'scientific attitude' is not that there is a set of angelic qualities of mind possessed by individual scientists that guaranteed the validity of their thought . . . but that scientists learn . . . to further the consensible end.[10]

Finally under this head, let me review briefly Thomas Kuhn's well-known thesis that in science, theory choices are not susceptible to logical proof.[11]

As Kuhn sees it, in science there arise from time to time anomalies which cannot be accounted for by the existing paradigm or disciplinary matrix, and sometimes these anomalies are so drastic that they call for wholly new ways of viewing the world. As in the case of other innovations, however, these new analyses do not pass unchallenged. Consequently, two competing factions or groups appear, one accepting the new view as a resolution of the anomaly, and the other resisting it. These groups compete for acceptance among uncommitted members of the scientific community, and each attempts to influence the other. For Kuhn, as for Ziman, however, persons committed to one of these two groups entertain ideas so radically different from persons in the other that communication by customary argumentative means is impossible, and the advocates must pass beyond accepted patterns of proof and resort to various techniques of persuasion in an effort to win acceptance.

Although additional views of the scientist as social or rhetorical being have been offered by Merton,[12] Hagstrom,[13] Mulkay,[14] and others, perhaps enough has now been said to suggest the very fundamental change which has taken place among philosophers and methodologists of science since the days of the logical positivists some half century ago. Of course, not all philosophers of science adhere to the sort of interpretation I have been describing. But what is important for our present interest is that a number of the most influential of them do, with the result that instead of viewing scientific knowledge as in some way *ipso facto* self-evident, we now at least recognize the possibility that its epistemetic status may very well be in large part dependent on social and historical forces.

II

Now if you have been reading the journals, I am sure you are aware that during the past few years the thinking of some of the theorists I have been citing has begun to make a discernible impact upon students of rhetoric and consequently upon our traditional understanding of the rhetorical process.

Michael Overington, in an article published in *Philosophy and Rhetoric* earlier this year—an article which, incidentally, I have here drawn upon heavily—offers a brief sketch of what he calls "a rhetorical perspective on the construction of scientific knowledge."[15]

Overington's method is to divide the process of producing scientific knowledge into four stages or steps. (1) In the first stage the young scientist as "speaker" becomes equipped to produce scientifically significant discourse and wins legitimation as a member of an audience qualified to appraise or evaluate such discourse. (2) Stage 2 involves the trained and accepted speaker in the research activity necessary to develop a topic for discussion. (3) In Stage 3 the speaker's research experience is reconstructed in the form of a persuasive argument. (4) And in Stage 4 an audience of peers provides authoritative judgments on his results or conclusions. It is audience consensus on the worth of the speakers' findings which, says Overington, transforms the scientist's published argument into "knowledge" or causes it to be dismissed as nonsense.

Writing in another recent issue of the same journal, Walter B. Weimer has argued that our traditional conception of "rationality" as a sort of rigid and unbending consistency among the parts of a proof is incapable of accounting for advances in scientific understanding.[16] Such writers as Feyerband,[17] Lakatos,[18] and Kuhn, he says, have "convincingly documented" the frequency with which paradigm examplars of "rational scientific progress" have utilized inconsistent premises, and thus "*could have* 'logically deduced' any conclusion whatever." The fact of the matter is that scientific method is not deductive or implicative at all. On the contrary, scientists learn their trade through the highly empirical avenues of example and injunction, and the thought processes which they characteristically employ in carrying on their investigations are "adjunctive" rather than "implicative"—that is, consist of inferential schemes rather than of implicative class "matrices."

For these reasons, continues Weimer, our inherited view of proof or "justification" as it exists in formal logic—the notion that the rationality of a claim is strictly dependent upon a consistency among its constituent parts—must, so far as science is concerned—be replaced with another conception of what it means to proceed rationally. And this substitute notion, Weimer proposes, should be a willingness on the part of investigators to open their views to examination and criticism—a willingness to be shown how or where they may have been wrong.

When "rationality" is redefined in this way, says Weimer, rhetoric will not be foreign to science, but will be seen to lie at the very heart of scientific method. Theories will be defended by adducing "good reasons" in their behalf, not by testing them for internal or external consistency. Science will be recognized for what it really is—a rhetorical or argumentative mode of discourse operating within a nonjustificational framework; an "interplay between theorist or researcher, on the one hand, and the research community as audience, on the other." Its goal will not be to present irrefutable proofs designed to produce coerced conclusions, but to offer propositions to which assent on the part of an audience is warranted.

Third, and finally, let me say just a word about a most interesting essay which Paul Campbell published in the *Quarterly Journal of Speech* in 1975. Campbell's essay is titled "The *Personae* of Scientific Discourse,"[19] and for our purposes his argument, with its unmistakable echoes of Kenneth Burke, may be cast into a broadly syllogistic form.

Major premise. Every discursive form that is based upon rhetoric or is rhetorical by virtue of its concern with an audience involves a *persona,* a created personality produced by the speaker in and through the act of communicating for the purpose of winning a certain effect or making a certain impression on a receiver.

Minor premise. Today it is widely recognized that science is a discursive form that is essentially rhetorical in its concern with gaining audience acceptance for a given hypothesis or point of view.

Conclusion. Therefore, the discourse of the scientist, no less than that of the poet or orator, always is marked by a *persona*—always is expressive of a certain attitude or stance, the stance of calculated neutrality being, in reality, no less attitudinal than is a blatantly prejudiced hortatory appeal.

Campbell writes:

The scientist who strives for objectivity, for neutrality, must perforce [strive to] disregard the concept of *persona* simply because that concept brings with it the very values, prejudices, [and] attitudes the scientist wishes to avoid. But to one who views such discourse from a literary or dramatic point of view, this is an exercise in complete futility; disclaim the prejudical, the attitudinal, the opinionated as the scientist may, the *persona* cannot be disclaimed; to discourse is to act, and the very nature of the act implies an actor; thus, when a scientific discourse admits of no concern . . . the dramatic or literary critic is likely to perceive this discourse as implying a *persona* . . . but a *persona* displaying . . . coldness . . . disdain and alienation. . . .[20]

In this way, then, through the agency of a *persona,* Campbell introduces rhetoric into the realm of science.

Even more pointed than the published accounts of the nature of science are some of the assertions contained in papers still awaiting publication. Let me cite just one example, drawn from some paragraphs in a paper, "The Rhetoric of Science and the Science of Rhetoric," by Professor Herbert Simons of Temple University.[21] In this paper, Simons attempts to evaluate the claim that science is essentially a rhetorical enterprise, first by amassing evidence in favor of that claim and then by subjecting this evidence to considered refutation. Here is what Simons says by way of affirmative argumentation.

[In recent years] science's assumptive underpinnings have come under impassioned attacks by . . . scholars, thus serving to undermine traditional distinctions between 'pure' science and rhetoric, and even suggesting a view of scientific discourse as rhetorical in the most pejorative sense of the term. Science, we have been told—by philosophers of science, historians of science, sociologists of knowledge, and even some scientists themselves—is a subjective enterprise. Like rhetoric, it is rooted in unprovable belief and value premises; 'underdetermined' by rules; shackled by the constraints of language; inspired by personal passions and ambitions; made credible by stylistic devices; and strongly influenced by political, cultural, and marketplace factors. The overall picture that emerges from these critical thrusts is of the scientist as rhetor in his discourse with other scientists: a persuader who adapts extra-factual, extra-logical messages to particular audiences in particular situations so as to secure preferred outcomes. So much, then, for what I have to say for rhetoric and science.[22]

III

The second development I have in mind concerns the relation between rhetoric and philosophy, and may, I believe, best be traced by referring to the work of two contemporary philosophers, Henry W. Johnstone, Jr. and Chaim Perelman.

As Walter M. Carleton[23] recently has shown, whereas at the outset of his philosophical career Johnstone endorsed the traditional view that rhetoric and philosophy are discrete and hostile disciplines, he now places rhetoric at the heart of philosophical endeavor.

Says Johnstone,[24] a philosophical interest in a topic, as opposed to an interest of some other sort—say an economic or historical interest—is just an interest in examining the arguments that cluster around that topic. Few, if any, however, are the philosophical arguments, past or present, whose validity or conclusiveness have been attested to by any except their own authors. Hence, unless we are to dismiss philosophy as a-rational—clearly an unacceptable dismissal—we must find some standard of rationality other than that of formal validity.

In this respect, however, the only two candidate disciplines are logic and rhetoric, for these disciplines alone focus on arguments without regard to their subject-bound or field-dependent nature. If, then, as history and present experience show, successful philosophical arguments do not permit of a "logical explanation" in the sense that they are conclusive or coercive, their success must be accounted for in rhetorical terms.

How may this be done? Johnstone's answer parallels—or, more accurately, furnishes the theoretical grounding for—the line of argument I earlier attributed to Weimer. It may be done, Johnstone says, by rejecting formal validity as our criterion of rationality and positing in its place a sort of rationality that is peculiarly "human"—a rationality which, instead of depending upon the depersonalized notion of consistency among abstract ideas, consists of calling upon one's hearers to consider whether they may not have been "taken in" by an argument. Such a "calling," however, both because it is addressed to listeners in a way that invites a judgment and because its success depends at least in part upon such extra-logical factors as the speaker's *ethos* and communicative skill—what Paul Campbell calls his *persona*—clearly falls into the province of rhetoric. In Johnstone's eyes, then, it is rhetoric that furnishes the rational component of philosophical discourse; or stated differently, it is through the instrumentality of discourse rendered rational under the supervision of rhetoric that philosophy does its work.

Now for the views of Chaim Perelman.[25] As Ray Dearin suggests, Perelman's conception of the nature and method of philosophy may most clearly be seen in his distinction between "primary" and "regressive" philosophies—*les philosophies premiere et philosophie regressive.*[26]

Traditionally, Perelman points out, philosophical systems—especially those of a rationalistic nature—have fallen into the first of these classes. They have attempted to construct an edifice of universal and immutable truths, based upon self-evident premises and eventuating in certain or "demonstrated" conclusions. In such systems, no provision is made for internal modifications or corrections, so that when errors or omissions are discovered the entire structure has to be rebuilt from the foundation up. Moreover, when attacked, the structure has to be defended in its entirety, and must successfully withstand every assault leveled against it.

In "regressive" philosophy, on the other hand, the philosopher does not begin with a set of facts considered as absolute, with premises taken to be self-evident; instead he selects as beginning points premises which are sufficiently probable to provide a promising basis for thought. When crises within the system occur, they are not viewed as debilitating ruptures, but as occasions for clarifying and deepening thought. Modifications may be effected as they are needed by choosing from among available alternatives that stance or proposition which seems most promising at the moment, and the choices thus made are supported not by developing demonstrative proofs, but by offering "reasons" calculated to win acceptance from the philosopher's peers. Thus in the final analysis, it is the philosopher who is the judge of the choices made, and it is the philosopher's colleagues and adversaries who judge both these choices and the man or woman who makes them. In sum, the methods of regressive philosophy, instead of being deductive and mathematical, are rhetorical and argumentative. Rather than seeking necessary or irrefragable conclusions, probabilities or accepted judgments constitute the goal of philosophic effort.

Unsurprisingly enough, given this conception of philosophy, Perelman, like Johnstone, installs rhetoric at the heart of philosophic method. He and his collaborator, M. Olbrechts-Tyteca, write:

> We believe that a theory of knowledge which corresponds to this climate of contemporary philosophy needs to integrate into its structure the processes of argumentation utilized in every domain of human culture and that . . . a renewal of [the classical tradition] of rhetoric would conform to the humanistic aspirations of our age.[27]

Knowledge, Perelman insists, cannot exist or come into being in a vacuum. Again I quote:

> The concrete problem of the theory of knowledge is to study the means which make it possible to describe and explain phenomena and to determine the influence which the objects of our knowledge exercise on the processes that make knowledge possible.[28]

In short, an epistemology, if it is to be used in the world, must take the form of a complete sociology of knowledge.

And here, once again, as Perelman is quick to point out, rhetoric comes into the picture. He says:

> To determine the field of application of the sociology of knowledge, it [will] be necessary to study most closely that strange logic [we call rhetoric] and the reasons which make it undergo the influence of social and cultural factors. . . . In effect, socially conditioned knowledge concerns the beliefs, the agreements, the adhesions of men. . . . Only a detailed explanation of rhetorical argumentation will permit the founding of the sociology of knowledge upon the most solid bases. (Interpolations mine.)[29]

IV

Where do these new and altered views about the relation between rhetoric and science and rhetoric and philosophy leave us? Where do we as guardians of the rhetorical tradition stand? As my student James Hikins recently has put it, we stand squarely in the middle of a dilemma.[30]

On the one hand, as we have just seen, two major modes of human inquiry—science which has as its business discovering truths *in* the world; and philosophy, which has as its business organizing or synthesizing truths *about* the world—rather than being independent of rhetoric, are now said to depend to a very considerable extent upon methods and criteria that historically have been the property of rhetoric. On the other hand, rhetoric continues to be regarded by scientists and philosophers, and even alas! all too often by rhetoricians themselves, as distinctly inferior both in the rigor of its procedures and in the reliability of its results.

Confronted with this dilemma, how are we to proceed? Since there appears to be little or no possibility of escaping between the horns by devising a new organon for discovering or synthesizing knowledge—one that is independent of both science and philosophy—we either (1) must attenuate the respect which over the centuries we have come to hold for these disciplines, or (2) we must attribute new qualities to rhetoric—qualities which traditionally it has been denied.

For any except the most skeptical, the first alternative, I think you will agree, is quite unacceptable. On purely pragmatic grounds, science has won our respect and earned our admiration beyond any reasonable point of return. Not only has it rendered our daily lives richer and more comfortable, but its achievements in conquering disease, unfolding the mysteries of the atom, and exploring the reaches of space have won it a secure place in the annals of human achievement. Nor, while the attainments of philosophy may be less spectacular are they any less to be valued. Through the patient efforts of long generations of scholars, the vagaries of human thought have been methodized, our conceptions of beauty and moral obligation refined, and the dimensions of the good life established.

This, then, being the case, what we appear called upon to do is reassess our inherited view that rhetoric, even at its best, is an inferior instrument—one that is limited either to conveying knowledge that has previously been derived or guiding us toward judgments concerning matters probable or contingent—that it is a court of second resort to be turned to only in those situations where the firmer methods of science and philosophy cannot be applied. We are, I submit, called upon to include within our view the notion that, in addition to being, as Bryant has said, a way of "deciding the undecidable,"[31] through the role it plays in science and philosophy, also contributes in significant ways to deciding those things that

can be "decided"—that, besides its acknowledged services in the area of the contingent, rhetoric also contributes to the production of those sorts of knowledge which we are willing to regard as apodictic or certain; contributes, in short, to our understanding of "reality" or what the world we live in actually is like. To use a term now gaining popularity in the literature, we are called upon to recognize that rhetoric is genuinely "epistemic."

The idea that the rhetorical process may be productive of a sort of knowledge is not, as I am sure you know, in itself a new one. Indeed, it was more than ten years ago that Robert Scott published his important essay "On Viewing Rhetoric as Epistemic."[32] In this essay, however, Scott arrived at the epistemic status of rhetoric by what our friends in forensics would label "the method of residues." Since, said Scott, there clearly are areas of life in which it is impossible to know or attain truth in any absolute or final sense, either we must abandon these areas to the irrational or "find avenues to successfully meet the challenge outside those established by science and philosophy."

What I am suggesting here, however, is that rather than following Scott to the conclusion that rhetoric is epistemic by default, such writers as Bronowski, Ziman, Kuhn, Johnstone, and Perelman now are taking a far bolder position and are arguing that rhetoric is epistemic in its own right. And rather than looking for its epistemic potential "outside" of science and philosophy, they are recognizing the extent to which science and philosophy themselves depend upon methods and assumptions that have traditionally been the property of rhetoric.

Although the work of Tom Farrell[33] is perhaps potentially of greater theoretical importance, this new case for the epistemic function of rhetoric has, so far as I know, most clearly been stated by Barry Brummet in a recent article in *Philosophy and Rhetoric,*[34] and by Walter Cohen in a doctoral thesis completed at the Pennsylvania State University in 1975.[35]

Because "experience," argues Brummet, is of necessity in part subjective—the product of the knowing mind as well as of the object known—what any given person concludes about the world as a result of his or her own contact with it is, at most, a private or individual picture of "reality." Moreover, because other persons are subject to the same limitations, they are likely to form quite different pictures. The result is a confusion—or, to use Brummet's term, an "ambiguity"—which results in disagreements and calls out for resolution.

The instrument by which these disagreements characteristically are resolved—by which the conflicting views of reality are put into competition and tested—is either in whole or in part rhetorical. Advocates, whether they be scientists, philosophers, or lay persons, verbalize the conflicting views in various forms of interpersonal or public interchange, with the result that the weak or erroneous candidates are weeded out through a process of natural selection, leaving their superior fellows in charge of the field. Stated somewhat more formally, rhetorical activity provides a means by which those individual or personal views which have the best claim to the name of "knowledge" are established and validated *intersubjectively*—a means by which what were initially opinions or judgments rooted in some person's private experience transcend the realm of the subjective and become commonly accepted characteristics of "reality" or how things are. Knowledge, instead of preceding the act of communicating, is either coincident with or follows from that act: rhetoric, instead of being simply an instrument for communicating what we "know," is a method of generating "knowledge." What is "true" for you and for me does not exist prior to, but in the working out of its expression.

All this, of course, does not mean that, on the one hand, all rhetorical effort is bilateral or, on the other, that verbal contests between competing ideas are all that there is to science and philosophy. Nor does it mean that just any sort of interchange between contesting parties—the trading of shouts, innuendos, or insults—will lead to creative results. As Cherwitz,[36] echoing Natanson,[37] has recently

pointed out, there must be an opportunity for all relevant views to be presented, appeals must be addressed to the respondent's critical or reflective faculties, and there must be a genuine extential risk on the part of the participants—a willingness to open the privacy of their cognitive and affective lives to the inspection of their fellows and a willingness to abide by the weight of the evidence. When these conditions are met, however, rhetoric, we now are being told, does contribute in important ways to those conclusions about the world which we regard as "knowledge," and to those conceptions of the world to which we give the name of "reality."

Working along somewhat different lines, Cohen in his dissertation also arrives at the conclusion that rhetoric is epistemic. Problems, he says, characteristically arise when we perceive discrepancies between what is and what we think ought to be. In attempting to resolve these discrepancies—to eliminate these problems—"we rearrange some or all of the aspects or elements of the state of affairs which originally presented itself as problematic." Now if, continues Cohen, "it can be agreed that to act in this sense [to effect this readjustment] is to behave rhetorically, it is not difficult to show that rhetoric is a way of knowing." For in rearranging a state of affairs we literally as well as figuratively "make" something, and what we made has "symbolic significance" in the sense that it exhibits the rationality of its own making. It is, then, just this rationality that we call "knowledge" and precisely the activity of "making" which is the rhetorical process of "coming to know."

V

What does this new orientation as suggested by Brummet and Cohen bode for the future of rhetoric and of rhetorical studies? Prediction, as I hardly need remind you, is at best a perilous business, and especially so in a period as volatile as the present. Therefore, I prefer to err on the side of caution rather than of rashness.

Even so, it seems to me that at least two things can be said with some degree of confidence. First, insofar as these new views of the relation between rhetoric and science and rhetoric and philosophy reflect fairly the role that rhetoric does, indeed, play in these activities, the traditional affiliation of rhetoric with literary and historical studies, already severely shaken by the affinity of the social rhetoric for psychology and of communication theory for the rule-governed paradigm of linguistics, will be still further eroded. Instead of looking to their colleagues in the fields of history and English for fellowship and sustenance, rhetoricians increasingly, I believe, will cultivate an alliance with epistemologists and philosophers of science. Moreover, as this occurs, it further seems to me that studies in the history of rhetorical thought, while they will continue to furnish the philosophical rhetorician with a necessary background for his activities, will gradually be forsaken for increased attention to current trends and developments. In other words, it will, I think, be in the study of contemporary trends and developments, rather than in the reconstruction of earlier doctrines, that the excitement of investigation and discovery will center.

Second, as I gaze into the proverbial crystal ball, I believe I see a new and closer relationship springing up between theoretical or philosophical rhetoricians and those rhetorical critics who, like Bormann,[38] McGee,[39] and Vatz,[40] are now following the lead of Edelman,[41] in political science, and Berger and Luckmann,[42] in sociology, in describing how *our* particular ideology or conception of social reality is the mythic end-product of our public and private discourse. These writers, no less than the ones I have dealt with in this paper, are actively engaged in breaking new ground and bringing forth exciting results. As such critical studies come increasingly to be integrated with theoretical and analytic work, we can, I predict, look forward to an era in which rhetorical studies will assume a depth and sophistication that will make much of our past and present work look simplistic indeed.

Douglas Ehninger

Notes

1. I. A. Richards, *The Philosophy of Rhetoric* (London: Oxford University Press, 1936).
2. John Dewey, *The Public and Its Problems* (New York: Henry Holt and Co., 1927).
3. Alfred Korzybski, *Science and Sanity* (New York: International non-Aristotelian Library Publishing Co., 1933).
4. Douglas Ehninger, "A Synoptic View of Systems of Western Rhetoric," *Quarterly Journal of Speech,* 61 (1975). 448–453.
5. See esp. Kenneth Burke, *A Rhetoric of Motives* (New York: George Braziller, Inc., 1955), pp. 22, 41–43, 146, etc., where Burke treats rhetoric as an instrument for bridging man's "natural condition of estrangement."
6. Wayne Booth, *Modern Dogma and the Rhetoric of Assent* (Chicago: University of Chicago Press, 1974), esp. pp. ix–xi.
7. Jacob Bronowski, *Science and Human Values,* rev. ed. (New York: Harper & Row, 1965).
8. Michael Polanyi, *The Study of Man* (Chicago: Phoenix Books, 1959); *Personal Knowledge* (New York: Harper & Row, 1964); *Science, Faith and Society* (Chicago: Phoenix Books, 1964); and *The Tacit Dimension* (Garden City, New York: Anchor Books, 1966).
9. John Ziman, *Public Knowledge: The Social Dimension of Science* (Cambridge: At the University Press, 1968).
10. *Ibid.,* p. 78.
11. Thomas Kuhn, *The Structure of Scientific Revolutions* (Chicago: University of Chicago Press, 1962).
12. Robert K. Merton, *Social Theory and Social Structure* (New York: Free Press, 1968); and *The Sociology of Science: Theoretical and Empirical Investigations* (Chicago: University of Chicago Press, 1973).
13. Warren O. Hagstrom, *The Scientific Community* (New York: Basic Books, 1965).
14. Michael J. Mulkay, *The Social Process of Innovation* (London: Macmillan, 1972).
15. Michael A. Overington, "The Scientific Community as Audience: Toward a Rhetorical Analysis of Science," *Philosophy and Rhetoric,* 10 (1977): 143–164.
16. Walter B. Weimar, "Science as a Rhetorical Transaction: Toward a Non-justificational Conception of Rhetoric," *Philosophy and Rhetoric,* 10 (1977): 1–29.
17. Paul K. Feyerabend, "Against Method," in *Minnesota Studies in the Philosophy of Science,* Vol. 4, ed. Michael Radner and Stephen Winokur (Minneapolis: University of Minnesota Press, 1970), pp. 17–130; and "Problems of Empiricism, Part II," in *The Nature and Function of Scientific Theories,* ed., Robert G. Colodny (Pittsburgh: University of Pittsburgh Press, 1970), pp. 275–353.
18. Imre Lakatos, "Falsification and the Methodology of Scientific Research Programmes," in *Criticism and the Growth of Knowledge,* ed., Imre Lakatos and Alan Musgrave (Cambridge: At the University Press,

1970), pp. 91–196; and "History of Science and Its Rational Reconstructions," in *Boston Studies in the Philosophy of Science,* Vol. 7, ed. Robert C. Buck and Robert S. Cohen (Dordrect: D. Reidel Publishing Co., 1971), 91–136.

19. Paul Newell Campbell, "The *Personae* of Scientific Discourse," *Quarterly Journal of Speech,* 61 (1975): 391–405.

20. *Ibid.,* 404–405.

21. Herbert Simons, "The Rhetoric of Science and the Science of Rhetoric" (Unpublished paper, Temple University, 1976). See also in this connection Philip C. Wander, "The Rhetoric of Science," *Western Speech,* 40 (1976): 226–235.

22. Simons, p. 3.

23. Walter M. Carleton, "Theory Transformation in Communication: The Case of Henry Johnstone," *Quarterly Journal of Speech,* 61 (1975): 76–88.

24. Henry W. Johnstone, Jr., "Rationality in Rhetoric and Philosophy," *ibid.,* 59 (1973): 381–389.

25. See particularly Chaim Perelman and L. Olbrechts-Tyteca, *The New Rhetoric: A Treatise on Argumentation* (Notre Dame: University of Notre Dame Press, 1969).

26. Ray D. Dearin, "The Philosophical Basis of Chaim Perelman's Theory of Rhetoric," *Quarterly Journal of Speech,* 55 (1969): 213–224.

27. Perelman and Olbrechts-Tyteca, "Logique et rhetorique," *Revue philosophique,* 140 (1950): 35.

28. Perelman, *An Historical Introduction to Philosophical Thinking,* trans. Kenneth A. Brown (New York: Random House, 1965), p. 186.

29. Perelman, "Sociologie de la connaissance et Philosophie de la connaissance," *Revue internationale de philosophie,* 4 (1950); 315.

30. Hikins suggested this in a recent conversation with me.

31. Donald C. Bryant, "Rhetoric: Its Functions and Its Scope," *Quarterly Journal of Speech,* 39 (1953): 401–424.

32. Robert L. Scott, "On Viewing Rhetoric as Epistemic," *Central States Speech Journal,* 18 (1967): 9–17. Cf. "On Viewing Rhetoric as Epistemic: Ten Years Later," *ibid.,* 27 (1976): 258–266.

33. Thomas B. Farrell, "Knowledge, Consensus, and Rhetorical Theory," *Quarterly Journal of Speech,* 62 (1976): 1–14.

34. Barry Brummet, "Some Implications of 'Process' and 'Intersubjectivity': Post-Modern Rhetoric," *Philosophy and Rhetoric,* 9 (1976): 21–51.

35. Walter Marshall Cohen, "On Rhetoric as a 'Way of Knowing': An Inquiry into the Epistemological Dimensions of the New Rhetoric," Department of Speech Communication, Pennsylvania State University, 1975. My account of Cohen's work is based upon the abstract reprinted in *Rhetoric Society Quarterly,* 6 (1976): 57–58.

36. Richard Cherwitz, 'Rhetoric' as a "Way of Knowing': An Attenuation of the Epistemological Claims of the 'New Rhetoric' " (Unpublished paper, University of Iowa, 1976), pp. 14–17.

37. Maurice Natanson, "The Claims of Immediacy," *Quarterly Journal of Speech,* 41 (1955): 133–139.

38. Ernest G. Bormann, "Fantasy and Rhetorical Vision: The Rhetorical Criticism of Social Reality," *ibid.,* 58 (1972): 396–407.

39. Michael McGee, "In Search of 'The People': A Rhetorical Alternative," *ibid.,* 61 (1975): 235–249.

40. Richard E. Vatz, "The Myth of the Rhetorical Situation," *Philosophy and Rhetoric,* 6 (1973): 154–161.

41. Murray Edelman, *The Symbolic Uses of Politics* (Urbana: University of Illinois Press, 1964).

42. Peter L. Berger and Thomas Luckmann, *The Social Construction of Reality* (Garden City, New York: Doubleday and Co., 1966).

It seems appropriate to conclude our survey with Ehninger's insightful lecture. It was he who gave us the rationale and method for discussing the rhetoric of Western thought. Now in his final public lecture, it is he who warns us not to be misled by the achievements of the past, but to center our energies on the task of enlarging our understanding of what it means to generate knowledge through rhetoric. Thus he helps us end where we began by renewing our commitment to a relevant rhetoric.

Appendix

Major Figures

Classical Rhetorical Theory

Before Christ

The Greeks

Homer	9th–8th century	Blind poet whose epic tales of the Trojan War introduce us to the use of the spoken word in early Greece. *Illiad, Odyssey*
Corax	1st half 5th century	Sicilian who devised the first written rhetoric in the West, designed to help courtroom pleaders.
Pericles	(495–429)	Athenian orator whose sustained skill in persuasion resulted in the construction of the Parthenon, the magnificent temple which has dominated his city for over two thousand years. *Funeral Oration*
Gorgias	(483?–376?)	Sicilian ambassador and teacher of rhetoric whose flowery prose style fascinated Greek audiences for over fifty years.
Socrates	(470?–399)	Philosopher and teacher whose questioning search for truth revealed the bases of Athenian society.
Isocrates	(436–338)	Foremost speech teacher of the ancient world whose school at Athens was dedicated to the training of responsible civic leaders. *Against the Sophists, Antidosis*
Plato	(427–347)	Friend of Socrates and founder of the Academy who outlined the dimensions of a true and a false rhetoric. *Gorgias, Phaedrus*
Aristotle	(384–322)	Plato's most famous student whose treatise on rhetoric is the most insightful book on persuasion ever written. *The Rhetoric*

| Demosthenes | (385?–322) | The most famous orator of the ancient world whose skill was primarily attributable to the diligent nurturing of his limited talents. *On the Crown* |
| Aeschines | (389–314) | Demosthenes' principal rival, a naturally talented orator who tended to favor Macedonian policies for Athens. *Against Ctesiphon* |

The Romans

| Cicero | (106–43) | Lawyer, philosopher, public official, the leading orator of the Roman Republic who more than any other person combined the theory and practice of public discourse. *De Oratore, Brutus, Orator* |

Anno Domini

Quintilian	(35–100)	The first imperial professor of rhetoric at Rome whose comprehensive system of education influenced European teachers for well over a thousand years. *The Institutes of Oratory*
Longinus	1st century	His stimulating essay on great writing had a profound impact upon later British and continental rhetoricians. *On the Sublime*
St. Augustine	(354–430)	Christian convert who introduced his co-religionists to Ciceronian rhetoric and in the process devised the first manual on preaching. *De Doctrina Christiana*, bk. 4.

British and Continental Rhetorical Theory

Thomas Wilson—*The Arte of Rhetorique*, 1553	Neoclassicist who published the first English rhetoric (based largely on the works of Cicero).
Francis Bacon—*Advancement of Learning*, 1605	Epistemologist whose ideas on faculty psychology, style and invention strongly influenced later theorists.
Rene Descartes—*Discourse on Method*, 1637	French rationalist who favored certainty over probability, experimentation over disputation.
John Locke—*Essay on Human Understanding*, 1690	Political philosopher and faculty psychologist; novel ideas on pathos, doctrine of association.
Giambattista Vico—*On the Study Methods of Our Time*, 1708	Italian rhetorician who rejected Descartes' ideas, reemphasized probability; father of modern social science.
David Hume—*A Treatise of Human Nature*, 1739	Scottish philosopher-historian who probed deeply into the nature of man, and who rejected Christian miracles on the basis of inadequate testimony.
Edmund Burke—*A Philosophical Enquiry into the Origin of our Ideas of the Sublime and the Beautiful*, 1756	Philosopher-orator deeply interested in taste, emotion, and the motivational power of words.

John Ward—*A System of Oratory,* 1759

Author of 800 page, two volume study . . . the most extensive treatment of classical rhetorical theory in English.

Thomas Sheridan—*Lectures on Elocution,* 1762

Theater manager-lecturer; father of the naturalist school and perhaps the most famous of the British elocutionists.

Adam Smith—*Lectures on Rhetoric and Belles Lettres,* 1762–3

Father of political economy; chiefly concerned with criticism, style, and the forms of discourse.

George Campbell—*The Philosophy of Rhetoric,* 1776; *Lectures on Systematic Theology and Pulpit Eloquence,* 1807

A highly original and influential thinker; concerned with moral reasoning, pathos, audience analysis, and the doctrine of usage.

John Walker—*Elements of Elocution,* 1781

Lexicographer-grammarian who believed that every internal emotion has an external expression; father of the mechanical school.

Joseph Priestley—*A Course of Lectures on Oratory and Criticism,* 1781

Scientist, theologian, educator interested in association of ideas, style, and taste.

Hugh Blair—*Lectures on Rhetoric and Belles Lettres,* 1783

Popular Scottish preacher; lectures at Edinburgh introduced students to taste, criticism, style, and sublimity.

Gilbert Austin—*Chironomia or a Treatise on Rhetorical Delivery,* 1806

Interested in body language, Austin sought to elevate delivery to the level of a science.

Richard Whately—*Elements of Rhetoric,* 1828

Anglican bishop interested in argumentation as a tool for combatting heresy and reforming society.

Contemporary Rhetorical Theory

Robert Fulton, Thomas Trueblood—*Practical Elements of Elocution,* 1893

Their volume revitalized elocution in America at the turn of the century; Trueblood especially interested in delivery.

James Winans—*Public Speaking,* 1915

Skillfully combined traditional theories with the fresh ideas of William James, American psychologist.

I. A. Richards—*The Meaning of Meaning,* 1923 (co-author); *Philosophy of Rhetoric,* 1936

Insightful studies of meaning, misunderstanding; devised the semantic triangle.

Charles Woolbert—*The Fundamentals of Speech,* 1927

Rejected conviction-persuasion duality; stressed behavioralism and bodily activity.

Kenneth Burke—*A Grammar of Motives,* 1945; *A Rhetoric of Motives,* 1950

Stimulating theorist-critic who stressed dramatism; greatly expanded sphere of rhetoric.

Richard Weaver—*The Ethics of Rhetoric,* 1953; *Language is Sermonic,* 1970

Neo-Platonist who argued that all language was value-laden; believed in a hierarchy of arguments.

Marshall McLuhan—*The Guttenberg Galaxy,* 1962; *Understanding Media,* 1964

Canadian professor of English whose works revolutionized our thinking about media channels and meaning.

Stephen Toulmin—*The Uses of Argument,* 1963; *Human Understanding,* 1972

British logician and historian of science; his model of argument appealed greatly to students of persuasive discourse.

Chaim Perelman—*The New Rhetoric: A Treatise on Argumentation,* 1969 (co-author)

Belgian philosopher-lawyer who stressed the relevance of rhetoric to the contemporary study of philosophy.

Key Concepts

Classical Rhetorical Theory

1. Rhetoric
2. Dialectic
3. Plato's moral-philosophical view
4. Aristotle's scientific approach
5. Educational-philosophical view
6. Forms of oratory
   a. Forensic
   b. Deliberative
   c. Epideictic
7. Fundamental processes of rhetoric
   a. Invention—the art of discovery
      Forms of proof—artistic
         Logical [probability, signs, the enthymeme, the example, topoi (universal and particular), lines of argument, deduction/induction, stasis]
         Ethical [impressions of the speaker's character, intelligence, and good will; cardinal virtues]
         Emotional (human feelings;
                  types of character)
      Forms of proof—nonartistic
         Documents
         Depositions of witnesses
   b. Disposition—the art of organizing one's material
      Selection of ideas and evidence
      Sequence—proem, narration, argument, epilogue; exordium, proof, refutation, peroration
      Apportionment—judgment and prudence in adaptation
   c. Style—the art of clothing ideas with words
      Clearness and propriety
      Metaphor and other forms of ornamentation
      Types of style—plain, middle, grand
   d. Delivery—the art of oral presentation
      Voice control
      Gesture and bodily movement
   e. Memory—the art of recalling thoughts, images, and ideas

8. The nature vs. nurture controversy
9. Sophistic
10. The field of rhetoric—truncators and expansionists
11. Freedom of choice
12. Rhetorical system

British Rhetorical Theory

1. Four schools of thought
   a. Neoclassicists
   b. Belletristic school
   c. Epistemologists
   d. Elocutionists
2. Rhetoric of style
3. Bacon's barriers to sensory perception [Idols of the tribe, cave, marketplace, theatre]
4. Belles lettres
   a. Taste
   b. Criticism
   c. Genius
   d. The sublime
   e. Perspicuity
   f. Precision
   g. Beauty
5. Psychological and philosophical concepts
   a. Faculty psychology
   b. Doctrine of association
   c. Common sense
   d. Ends of discourse [Understanding, Imagination, Passions, Will]
   e. Wit, humor, and ridicule
   f. Moral reading [Experience, Analogy, Testimony, Calculation of choices]
   g. Men in general
   h. Men in particular
   i. Doctrine of usage [Reputable, National, Present]
   j. Doctrine of sympathy
   k. Conviction-Persuasion Duality
   l. Verisimilitude
   m. Miracles
6. Argumentative discourse
   a. Presumption
   b. Burden of proof
   c. A priori arguments
   d. Deference
   e. Refutation
   f. Rebuttal

Contemporary Rhetorical Theory

1. Rhetoric as meaning
   a. context theorem of meaning
   b. proper meaning superstition

    c. Richard's semantic triangle [Thought or reference, symbol, referent)
    d. medium
    e. medium as message
    f. interinanimation
    g. metaphor
    h. "hot" and "cool" media
    i. speech act
    j. significant symbols
    k. Gutenberg Galaxy
    l. cultural archetype
    m. linguistic sexism [exclusion, non-parallelism]
    n. sorting
2. Rhetoric as value
    a. axiology
    b. values
    c. argument from definition
    d. argument from circumstance
    e. the three lovers
    f. language is sermonic
    g. ultimate terms (devil terms and god terms)
    h. Ethos and Image
    i. communicator's stance
    j. good reasons
3. Rhetoric as motive
    a. motive
    b. identification (consubstantiality)
    c. pentad (act, agency, agent, scene, purpose)
    d. magic
    e. rhetorical situation
    f. conversion (exigency marking, indoctrination, confrontation)
    g. dramatism
    h. hierarchy
    i. terministic screens
    j. ratios
    k. rhetoric of confrontation
    l. polarization
    m. administrative rhetoric
    n. vilification
    o. objectification
    p. legitimation
    q. mythication
    r. rhetoric of confrontation

4. Rhetoric as a way of knowing
   a. Toulmin model (claim, warrant, data, qualifier, reservation, backing)
   b. presence
   c. association/dissociation
   d. universal audience
   e. quasi-logical arguments
   f. rule of justice
   g. communion
   h. choice
   i. rational
   j. reasonable
   k. epistemic
   l. conceptual change
   m. absolutism
   n. relativism
   o. symbolic convergence
   p. special and general theories
   q. fantasy themes
   r. rhetorical vision
   s. field-dependent arguments
   t. field-invariant arguments
   u. Brockriede's characteristics of argument.

Index of Names

Subject Index